9th (Service) Battalion
The Sherwood Foresters
(Nott's and Derby Regiment)

Fred Greaves, friends, French children and dog – somewhere in France

Fred Greaves at Buckingham Palace

9th (Service) Battalion The Sherwood Foresters (Nott's and Derby Regiment)

A tribute to the men who served in
World War One 1914-1919

We will remember them

John Stephen Morse

TOMMIES GUIDES

To my Granddaughter Aimee,
the light of my life

Tommies Guides
Menin House
13 Hunloke Avenue
Eastbourne
East Sussex
BN22 8UL

http://www.tommiesguides.co.uk

First published by Tommies Guides in 2007
2nd Edition 2008

ISBN 978 0 95556 981 4

Printed and bound by CPI Antony Rowe, Eastbourne
Typeset by Graham Hales, Derby
Cover design by Tommies Guides

Contents

The foundation of the 9th (Service) Battalion The Sherwood Foresters (Nott's and Derby Regiment).

ARMY ORDER 324. 1914

Augmentation of the Army – With reference to Army Order II of 6th August 1914 (as amended by Army Order III of 7th August 1914) introducing special terms of enlistment into the regular army, His Majesty the King has been graciously pleased to approve of the addition to the Army of six divisions and Army Troops.

The composition and nomenclature of the new units and formations will be as shown in Appendix A. The establishment of each unit will follow War Establishments (Part I) 1914.

The new battalions will be raised as additional battalions of the regiments of Infantry of the Line, and will be given numbers following consecutively on the existing battalions of their regiments. They will be further distinguished by the word "Service" after their number...

So was born, the 9th (Service) Battalion The Sherwood Foresters (Notts and Derby Regiment)

YOUR KING AND COUNTRY NEED YOU.

Will you answer your Country's Call? Each day is fraught with the gravest possibilities, and at this very moment the Empire is on the brink of the greatest war in the history of the world.

In this crisis your Country calls on all her young unmarried men to rally round the Flag and enlist in the ranks of her army.

If every patriotic young man answers her call, England and her Empire will emerge stronger and more united than ever.

If you are unmarried and between 18 and 30 years old will you answer your Country's Call? and go to the nearest Recruiter—whose address you can get at any Post Office, and

JOIN THE ARMY

Derby Telegraph 5th August 1914

AY, AUGUST 27, 1914.

MILITARY MOVEMENTS IN DERBY.

LAST OF THE FIFTH SHERWOOD FORESTERS LEAVE TO-DAY.

THE NINTH BATTALION NEARING COMPLETION.

We understand that the 9th Battalion the Sherwood Foresters, newly raised in accordance with Lord Kitchener's request, numbers now nearly 1,200. They have been mobilised at the Normanton Barracks, and their equipment is now rapidly nearing completion. They are of course a bit crowded at the Barracks, and in order to relieve the pressure up there those companies that were first enrolled and have received their equipment have been moved into Derby, and are billeted at the Temperance Hall. As others are ready, other billets will be found for them, and it is anticipated that a good many will be found at the Drill Hall shortly.

When the 5th Battalion moved off to Luton a short time ago they were 150 or so under strength, but recruits came in rapidly, and the number was quickly made up. The Drill Hall was established as their depot, and Major W. Reginald H. Whiston, who left the battalion several years ago, rejoined in the capacity of adjutant and commander of the depot. Since then most of the recruits have received their necessary equipment and clothing together with their preliminary drills, and most of them have already joined the battalion. There were a few over a dozen left, and as their arrangements are now all completed they will leave to-day for Harpenden in Herts., and then the 5th Battalion will be at full strength. This will leave the Drill Hall available for the other troops and decrease the pressure at Normanton.

Derby Telegraph 27th August 1914

203485 Corporal Fred Ashmore and friends

Private ARTHUR POULTNEY,
of Matlock, who is with

13256 Pte A Poultney.
Killed in Action, Gallipoli
21 August 1915

John Armstrong. Killed in Action September 1916

Reg Ecclestone (top right) and friends
November 1916

Major George Henry Gater, DSO and Bar

Lieut E P Basden

Capt T P Black
Killed August 1915

2/Lieut H P Carey
Killed August 1915

The three photographs above are taken from 'M Company, Staff College, February 1915

Chapter One

FROM FORMATION TO LEAVING FOR GALLIPOLI

THE BATTALION was formed at Derby on 24 August 1914 as part of K 1 (Kitcheners first 100,000 volunteers) it moved to Grantham as part of 33rd Brigade, 11th Division. The 9th Sherwood Foresters would remain with this Brigade and Division for the duration of the war. The first hundred recruits came from the Derby Depot of the Regiment on 9 August 1914, which by coincidence was the date in 1915 of the Battalions first major battle on Gallipoli in which 112 all ranks would be killed in action. This amounted to one tenth of the battalion, which had arrived a few weeks before.

The 11th (Northern) Division came into being under Army Order No 324 issued on 21st August 1914, which authorized the formation of six new Divisions of K1. It was formed from volunteers and came under War Office jurisdiction. The whole Division was based at Belton Park, near Grantham, Lincolnshire and its first commander was Major-General Hammersley with 33rd Brigade commanded by Brigadier-General R.P. Maxwell. Initially it had no equipment or arms of any kind. By the end of the Great War, the Division had had eight different commanding officers.

The following is taken from, A Record of the Battles and Engagements of the British Armies in France and Flanders, 1914-1918 by Captain E A James, published in 1924

The main movements of the 9th Battalion

In April 1915 it was in the Frensham area (near Farnham, Hampshire) and was deemed ready for active service. The Division was ordered to reinforce the beleaguered garrison on Gallipoli.

On 1st July 1915 they embarked from Liverpool for Mudros. The Division Landed at Alexandria and then went on to Mudros.

By 20th to 31st July they were in Helles. On 7 August 1915 they landed at Sulva Bay, Gallipoli. On 21st December 1915 it was withdrawn from Gallipoli and went to Imbros. By February 1916 it was in Egypt.

In July 1916 to France and landed at Marseilles. The Division spent the remainder of the war on the Western Front.

The Division took part in the following battles

- The Battle of Flers-Courcelette (sixth phase of the Battle of the Somme)
- Operations on the Ancre.
- The Battle of Messines – June 1917 3rd Ypres –
- The Battle of Langemarck (second phase)
- The Battle of Polygon Wood (fourth phase)
- The Battle of Broodseinde (fifth phase) – Battle plans in later chapter.
- The Battle of Poelcappelle (sixth phase)
- The Battle of the Scarpe (first phase of the Second Battles of Arras)
- The Battle of Drocourt-Queant (second phase of Second Battles of Arras)
- The Battle of the Canal du Nord (third phase of the Battles of the Hindenburg Line.)
- The Battle of Cambrai 1918 (sixth phase of the Hindenburg Line)
- The Pursuit to the Selle.
- The Battle of the Sambre
- The Passage of the Grand Honelle.

11 November 1918 33rd Brigade, 11th Division was in Belgium south of Mons.

On 28 June 1919, the Division was disbanded. It had more than 32,000 casualties during the war.

The Division was made up of 3 Brigades, the 32nd, 33rd and 34th. The 9th (Service) Battalion

Sherwood Foresters were part of 33rd Brigade. The Battalion joined in August 1914.

The other Battalions created were:
6th (Service) Bn The Lincolnshire Regiment, which joined in August1914
6th (Service) Bn The Border Regiment, which joined in August 1914, (It was disbanded in February 1918 at Mazingarbe)
7th (Service) Bn South Staffordshire Regiment, which joined in August 1914.

In an effort to better understand the 9th (Service) Battalion The Sherwood Foresters, a basic knowledge of their birth and place in the British Army hierarchy may be of help.

Outwardly the 9th (Service) Battalion Sherwood Foresters was just another body of men who proudly served in their local Regiment. That Regiment, latterly known as The Sherwood Foresters but to the majority of the men as the Notts & Derby Regiment had a long and illustrious military history. As part of the British Army it was no different in make up than the regular or territorial force Battalions. The 9th Battalion like all others had at its head a Lt Colonel and comprised 4 Companies plus Headquarters, being part of a Brigade, which had four Battalions and part of a Division, which had 3 Brigades. In the Great War though, this was where the similarities ended and in effect the British Army was actually made up of 4 separate and distinct armies – the final one being the conscripts of the latter years but the other three volunteers to a man.

In 1914 the Sherwood Foresters had two regular Battalions – 1st and 2nd, backed by a 3rd (reserve) and 4th (extra reserve). The two regular battalions were very well trained, tough troops who had served all over the Empire. These troops were a match for any other army at the time in skill and discipline and every man was a volunteer.

On the outbreak of war the 1st Bn was doing a tour of duty in India and was stationed in Bombay. The 2nd meanwhile was based in Sheffield ready for any call to action from anywhere it might come. The 3rd and 4th Reserves were based in Derby and in times of war would take in men to supply the two main fighting units. Of course when war came, it was like no other ever fought and the reserve battalions could never process and train the amount of men needed. The men of the 1st and 2nd Battalions would bear the brunt of the fighting on the Western Front until such time as, firstly the Territorial Force men and latterly the 'New Army' (Officially Service Battalions) were readied for the fight. This period would see the Regular Army decimated by early 1915 with over 90% casualties. Training the Territorial Force would not take a great deal of time but there was a problem. It was actually a force for home defence and men had to 'opt in' to serve abroad and of course the majority did. These Saturday afternoon soldiers had at least had some training and many were ex-soldiers who may have fought in the Boer War.

This was a force that could be quickly equipped, sent overseas and become the 2nd line (or second army) in the fighting. These men would quickly adapt to Army life and the rigours of what by now was trench warfare.

The 9th Bn Sherwood Foresters would be the third line or part of the third British Army to enter the line. These volunteers knew nothing of Army life and would take a lot of training in the mysterious ways of army life. The small matter of weapons and uniforms for these men would also cause many problems in the following months. Many men trained in their own clothes for many months, never seeing a real weapon. This would take time and when eventually they were ready to engage in battle, both the regulars and the Territorial Force would be shadows of their former selves.

The 9th Bn when formed in August 1914 at Derby was known by a number of names. Kitchener's and New Army being widely used but their official designation was 'service' Battalion. The Battalion would in effect remain in existence for the duration of the war. Thereafter its men would be demobbed back to Civvy Street and the Battalion would cease to exist, (Until WW2 that is). In effect it was part of K1, which had been raised after Kitchener called for 100,000 men to volunteer for King & Country. Eventually other Sherwood Forester 'service' Battalions would become part of K2, K3, K4, and K5 as men rushed to volunteer before the war ended.

His battalion defined the world of the new army soldier. Consisting of around 977 men of all Ranks, 30 officers and commanded by a Lieutenant Colonel, the men were minute parts of a large and complex war machine. Although during the winter of 1917-18 a large-scale reshuffle took place, the only effect on the 9th was to see one of the battalions they had served with since 1914 leave 33rd Brigade as they were reduced from 4 to 3 Battalions each.

When the call did go out, the men of Nottinghamshire and Derbyshire flocked to the colours and from these men the 9th Battalion was formed. It has to be remembered that the vast majority thought that the war would be soon over. The opportunity to get in the army, get to France, beat the Germans quickly and return home the hero appealed to many.

The exhilaration and anticipation these men felt can only be imagined as they saw, not only the chance of some excitement and a change for their dreary humdrum lives, but also to do heroic deeds for their country. No doubt getting away from the dreary lives was the main driving force though as these miners, agricultural workers, hosiery workers and the like grasped at the opportunity to get some excitement. It also has to be said that this was a different time and in fact almost a different planet. It is virtually impossible for someone in the late 20th Century or early 21st to comprehend just what these men were doing.

Love of King and Country, wanting to serve and also put their lives on the line in the belief that a great wrong needed righting was normal in 1914. One only has to read the war poetry of the time to see what service to country meant to these men. Admittedly the poetry changed as the war grew to its ghastly climax but in 1914 and 1915 national fervour was the order of the day. Workmates, friends and family members joined up together and later many would die together.

Frederick Ashmore and his friends left their homes in Tibshelf and went by train to Chesterfield as soon as war was declared. They presented themselves at the Drill hall on Ashgate Road and enlisted in the Sherwood Foresters. They were sent to a tented camp at Markeaton Park, Derby and the 9th Battalion. Frederick would go to Gallipoli with the Battalion and he saw it thus, *'the heat in the day was exhausting followed by cold nights. Snipers on both sides took their toll. The Turkish soldiers were well-trained and disciplined.'* He also recalled *'the bodies laying in no man's land, swelling and smelling terribly in the heat. The land was arid and covered in prickly pear and scrub with little or no cover. Water was also in short supply'*Frederick had severe impetigo and was evacuated via Malta to England. He would serve with the 2nd and 1/5th Battalions in France and Belgium and survive the war.

It was soon obvious that the amount of men enlisting would cause massive logistical problems. One Battalion such as the 9th had approx 1000 officers and men who needed food, accommodation, uniforms, weapons, transport plus all the mundane everyday items to function normally.

The 9th Battalion was luckier than some as when they eventually arrived at their training camp at Belton Park near Grantham Linc's, (The seat of Earl Brownlow), the basics were in place for them. They had a tented encampment, which would suffice until the winter at least, a large enough area to train properly and a good firing range. As each Company was organized and, as far as possible, equipped, it was sent to join the Headquarters at Belton.

As the photos show, photographs for the family at home showing the new soldier in his uniform were popular.

Drummer B Parker left

Drummer B Parker – Standing third from left.

Reg Ecclestone (Left standing) and Pals

Fred Ashmore
Grantham October 1914

The Battalions first C.O. was Major, temporary Lieutenant Colonel, R.A.S. Sadler, and his brief was to turn this set of individuals into a cohesive fighting force. With him were Lieut F.F. Loyd, as Adjutant, Lieut Booker as battalion Quartermaster and the RSM was Sergeant-Major Randall. This would be no mean task and the basic squad and platoon drills were practiced over and over again. The men would drill from dawn to dusk until such time as it became second nature to move in unison.

Col A E Scothern began his service with the 9th Battalion as a Lieutenant and served until he was wounded at Gallipoli on 9th August 1915. He would return to serve with the Battalion in 1916 before taking command of the 6th Battalion The Border Regiment. In 1918 he would take command of the 9th Battalion and lead it until in 1919 it was disbanded. He wrote a potted history of the Battalion which is used throughout the history. At this time he noted " *The men were keen, there was a splendid range (rifle) quite near, ample ground for training, and life went into full swing.*"

Drill was used to meld the men into a disciplined force and the men were pushed hard slowly turning them into soldiers.

An average day would consist of –

Reveille – 5.30 am – Cup of tea or coffee.
Exercise- 6.30 am – Doubling (Running) walking and brisk exercise.
Breakfast – 8 am.
Squad drill – 9.30 am – 12.30 pm.
Lunch
Drill – 2 –4 pm.

This could be followed by fatigues or working parties and of course the kit had to be cleaned.
Last Post – 9.30 pm.
Lights out – 10 pm.

Weapons drill, bayonet practice, route marches, drill, kit cleaning day after day after day would have no doubt been a culture shock to many of the men.

The top priority when trying to turn this large crowd of untrained and undisciplined men into a cohesive fighting unit was to pick good NCOs. The Non-Commissioned officers had been the British Army's backbone for hundreds of years. In the beginning there was a great reliance on the few old soldiers available. Sgt-Major Randall was given the better-educated men from each company and tasked with turning them into NCOs. This he did and it was noted that he *'turned out as fine a body of NCOs as one could wish to see'* (battalion notes). The battalion was quickly up to strength on the NCO front. The battalion notes also pointed out – *'the men who joined the battalion were the pick of the county, and the work of knocking them into shape was made a real pleasure to those responsible by the extraordinary keenness of all ranks'*

New officers would have relied on NCOs who had served before, possibly regulars wounded and returned to train the new army men. Other NCOs and officers with experience would have been drafted in, usually over age men who might well have fought in the Boer War and some even earlier. The main thing they had was experience and despite this war being unlike any other, they could turn the men into soldiers. One such man was Walter Milward aged 40 years and an ex-regular. Walter joined up in 1893 and served with the Yorkshire Light Infantry seeing action in the Boer War. He received the Queen's South African Medal with four clasps and the King's Medal with clasps, South Africa 1901 and 1902. He was put on the Army Reserve list in 1902 with the reserve lasting until 1909. On the outbreak of war Walter enlisted and was sent to the 9th Battalion and was given the rank of Platoon Sergeant in "B" Company, taking on the job of Drill Instructor. Walter had home leave after a month and the family also had the opportunity to visit him at Belton. The family were introduced to other N.C.O.'s and their families. Chief among these were the Pickford's of Leek, David Pickford being a brother Sergeant of Walter's Company and a great friend. David like Walter would die with the Battalion. Walter mentioned at around this time that the Battalion was away for a week, marching around North Nottinghamshire on a 'Recruiting Drive'. Walter's next leave in November 1914 saw him as a Colour Sergeant. He also got Christmas leave where he met up with two other 9th Battalion Sergeants – Bob Sewell and Alf Sage.

Once the Battalion moved south leave was not so easy to obtain but Walter was an old soldier and knew the ropes. Walter was by now a Company Sergeant Major of "B" Company and he was still able to get leave. His final embarkation leave came in the middle of June 1915.

The details of Walter's death later in 1915 are documented later.

Officers were also in short supply but they gradually made their appearance after short courses at the O.T.C. (Officer Training Centre) or Cadet establishments which had been set up for this purpose. Once with the battalion, their military education continued under the guidance of the company commanders.

For K1 the men would have been between the ages of 19 to 30 years and supposedly fully fit, although this was not always the case. Later the age range would grow and medicals become less difficult for a man to pass. Gentlemen wanting a commission in the new army could usually get one with ease and all he had to do was find a C.O. willing to take him on. In effect they were as green as the troops they led.

Quite often it would take months before men were issued with uniforms. The issue of the Khaki uniform was an important rite of passage for these 'New Army' men, as can be seen from the photos as they stand proudly in their uniforms. It also has to be remembered that in this pre welfare state era many men had probably never had new clothes or a decent pair of boots in their lives. Neither had they been given free health care.

Not every man who volunteered was wanted and the C.O. Lt-Col Sadler requested the removal of six men in September 1914.

"I have the honour to request that the authority may be given for the discharge of the under mentioned men on account of misconduct, in accordance with Para 392 (111) (c) K.R.

No. 12636 Pte E. Haxby – also Drunkenness.
No. 12635 Pte A. O'Malley
For breaking of Camp, deficiency of kit, travelling on the railway without a ticket (twice) once to Hitchin, and once to Kings Cross, London.
No. 12758.Pte Pell. G. Also Drunkenness.
No. 12707. Pte. Brassington. G. Also Drunkenness.
No. 12624. Pte. Rooksby. F.
For breaking out of Camp, Disorderly conduct in Ropnley and Absence.
No. 13387. Pte Boothwaite W.
for absence. Drunkenness Insolence to a N.C.O. and not complying with orders.

Signed. R. Sadler.
Lieut. Colonel.
Commanding 9th S Sherwood Foresters.

The above men are all of an undesirable class.

The 9th Battalions first major parade took place in October 1914 when Lord Kitchener himself inspected them and no doubt the men saw themselves as soldiers at last. It could be said that of more interest to the men at around that time was the erection of more suitable accommodation. As autumn turned to winter wooden huts, which would be a much preferable place to reside, replaced the Bell tents.

The rumour mill as in any large body of men was rife and some were to say the least wildly fanciful but others bearing some resemblance to the truth. In particular the real or imagined fear of an invasion by the German hordes was an ever present one and on several occasions the men in the battalion expected to find themselves on the East coast ready to repel this invasion. None of the rumours of imminent invasion became a reality but on several occasions the Battalion found itself under orders to move at short notice. The more likely destination was probably France and Flanders as the British army fought itself and the Germans to a standstill during 1st Ypres, in October 1914. It was touch and go for the British Army regulars and Territorial Force men but eventually the front settled down to trench warfare for the winter. The last place on earth the Battalion would have expected to find itself in 1915 would have been Gallipoli but that would be their destination in the near future. As the organization of the Battalion continued so did that of the higher echelons with the 9th becoming part of 33rd Infantry Brigade, 11th Division.

As 1915 began the battalion training continued and slowly they became a cohesive fighting unit, ready for anything, or so they thought. All that could be done to prepare the men had been done and they were ready for battle. In early April the 11th Division moved south to the Godalming, Surrey area and the battalion would be at Frensham Camp near Farnham, which was a regular Army barracks.

On 3rd April 1915, before the Battalion moved south, the Mayor of Nottingham Alderman J.H. Gregg and the Corporation invited them to march through the city. It would seem from all accounts that the occasion was a joy for all who took part and all who watched. Proud family members lined the route to pick out their man as he marched past. The whole city was given the opportunity to see their new battalion marching past. Col Scothern again noted:

> *"Sherwood Foresters marched via Nottingham by invitation of the Lord Mayor and Corporation of the City. The strict march discipline and fine bearing of the men caused much admiration, and they were enthusiastically received as guests of the town, the officers being entertained to dinner at the Exchange Hall. The battalion was billeted all over the city and by all accounts the greatest freedom was allowed to all ranks. Apparently though, their discipline stood the test well, with not one man missing on parade the next morning. Although no doubt many sported very sore heads.*
>
> *The battalion stayed in Bingham for the night and then marched to Grantham in a snow storm".*

The local newspapers were of course full of this significant event and I have added one such report in full to show just how important this milestone was to all those involved.

April 1915 – Nottingham Newspaper noted:

> *"Enthusiastic send-off – Sherwood Foresters leave Nottingham. Arrival at Bingham. The brief sojourn in Nottingham of the 9th Battalion, Sherwood Foresters was terminated yesterday when the men, the majority of whom are natives of the city, (well of Nottinghamshire and Derbyshire as least) left for Bingham, whence they will march to Belton Park today. As the time approached for the soldier guests to start their journey the thoroughfares it was known they would traverse became more crowded with people eager to catch a final glimpse of the men and at the Market place, where the battalion paraded, thousands of spectators were assembled. The glorious weather added the final touch to a picturesque scene. To fittingly mark the city's appreciation of the visit there were assembled the chief citizens, including the Mayor and Mayoress (Ald. J.H. and Mrs. Gregg), the Sheriff (Councillor J. G. Small), Mrs. Small, Ald. Sir John McCraith, Ald. Sir John Turney, Ald. J Ball, Ald. J Houston, Councillors H.G. Ford, H. Spray, G.V. Hutton, Mr. J.D. Player, Mr. W.J. Board (the Town Clerk) and Mr. S. Hartshorn.*
>
> *The Mayor, thanking Col. Bosanquet for the visit of the battalion, complimented the gallant officer on the character and soldierly bearing of the men who all bore the prime mark of efficiency. His Worship wished them every success wherever they might be called to go by the War Office and hoped the providence would guide and guard them in any conflict in which they might engage, so they might return and revisit the city whose inhabitants would be glad to welcome them again.*
>
> *He was confident that the men would keep up the best traditions of the British Army which had proved most gallant in the field and that they would do their duty with credit to themselves and to the honour and glory of the Army.*
>
> *Colonel Bosanquet, responding, said the men had thoroughly enjoyed their stay in the city and appreciated very highly the hospitality they had received and the entertainment provided for them. He especially desired to mention the gratitude they felt for the Sheriffs gift of cigars and cigarettes.*
>
> *As the battalion marched from the Market Place they were heartily cheered and all along*

the route to the city boundary their appearance was the signal for similar outbursts.

The battalion arrived at Bingham, after several halts shortly before two o'clock and upon being dismissed immediately proceeded to the various schools secured for their accommodation. There the majority of them were compelled to remain through the afternoon, for a heavy snowstorm descended and lasted several hours. In the evening a concert was arranged by the inhabitants of the village and the soldiers were entertained by a capital programme of music."

The battalion proceeded to Grantham (Belton) the following day and collected together all of their kit. On 5th April 1915 the Division marched from Grantham en route to Whitley and Frensham. It must have been a thrilling sight as a whole division marched past. They camped the first night at Melton Mowbray and the following night at Birstall before arriving at Lutterworth on the third day, and were no doubt relieved to entrain there for the trip south and Farnham. Once at Frensham Camp the Battalion was to be given more training as the Division prepared for its move overseas. The Division camped at Whitley with the exception of 33rd Infantry Brigade, including the 9th Battalion who camped at Frensham. The men undertook more specialized training including field exercises with the other units that made up the Division. The men learned bombing (hand grenade) techniques, machine gunning, wiring, formation attacks and the like in preparation for their forthcoming move. The training was not only specialist but also very strenuous with long marches. Usually the men would live out in bivouacs during the week and return to camp on Fridays.

During this period and only two weeks before the Battalion moved, Private E Calton died. His death certificate shows that he died of pneumonia after spending three weeks in hospital.

22511 Private Calton was the husband of Mrs. N Calton of 8, High Street, Clay Cross, Chesterfield, Derbyshire and he is buried at Aldershot Military Cemetery, grave AF. 1891. – Died 14 June 1915.

Early in June 1915 the Battalion as part of 11th Division was on parade and inspected by H.M. The King. The whole of the Division being inspected by The King must have been a marvellous sight and no doubt the men of the 9th Battalion felt great pride.

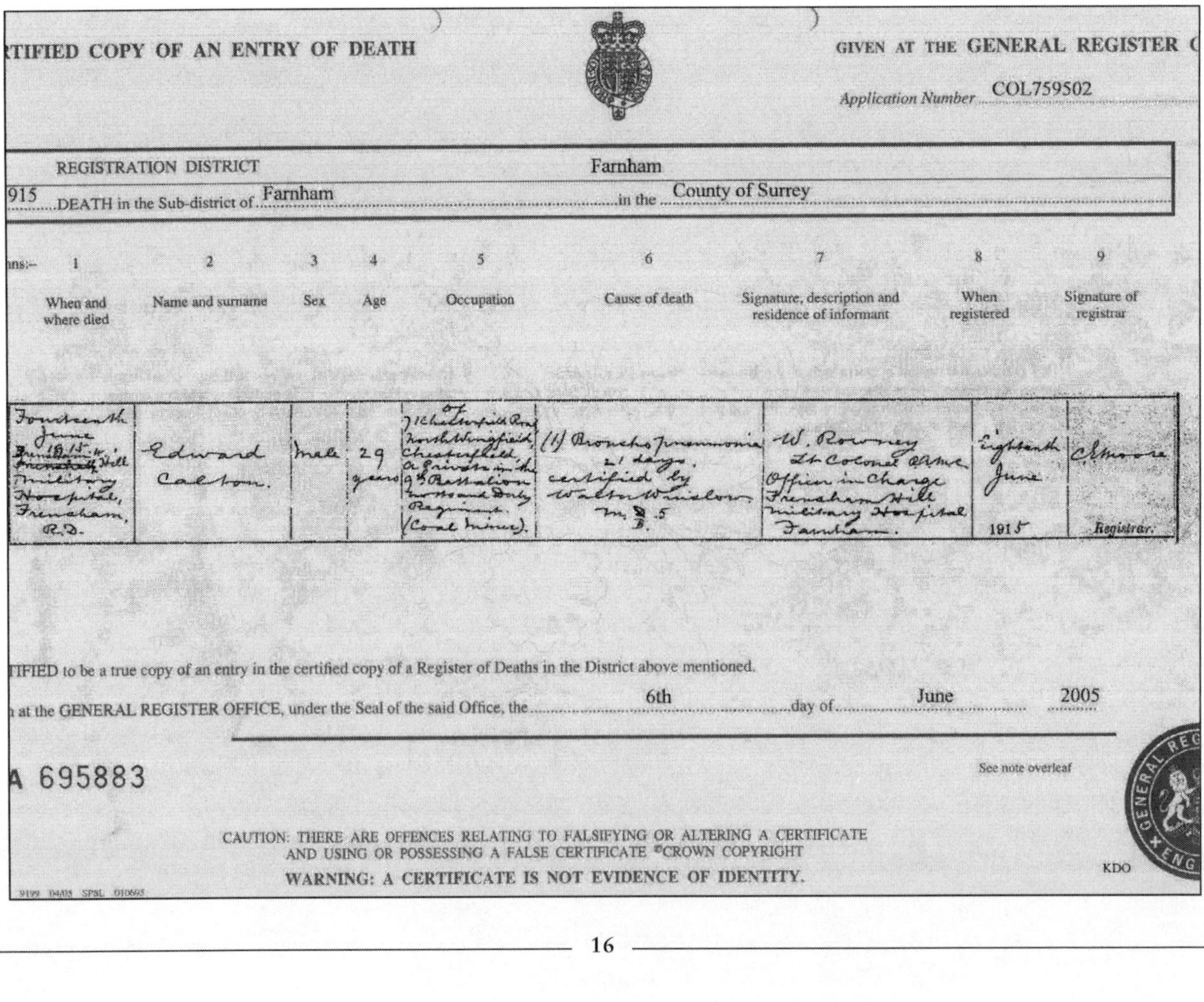

RTIFIED COPY OF AN ENTRY OF DEATH — GIVEN AT THE GENERAL REGISTER O

Application Number COL759502

REGISTRATION DISTRICT Farnham

915 DEATH in the Sub-district of Farnham in the County of Surrey

When and where died	Name and surname	Sex	Age	Occupation	Cause of death	Signature, description and residence of informant	When registered	Signature of registrar
Fourteenth June 1915 Frensham Hill Military Hospital, Frensham, R.D.	Edward Calton	Male	29 years	of 71 Chesterfield Road North Wingfield Chesterfield, a Private in the 9th Battalion Notts and Derby Regiment (Coal Miner)	(1) Broncho pneumonia 21 days, certified by Walter Winslow	W. Rowney Lt Colonel RAMC Officer in Charge Frensham Hill Military Hospital Farnham.	Eighteenth June 1915	C Moore Registrar

TIFIED to be a true copy of an entry in the certified copy of a Register of Deaths in the District above mentioned.

at the GENERAL REGISTER OFFICE, under the Seal of the said Office, the 6th day of June 2005

A 695883

See note overleaf

CAUTION: THERE ARE OFFENCES RELATING TO FALSIFYING OR ALTERING A CERTIFICATE AND USING OR POSSESSING A FALSE CERTIFICATE ©CROWN COPYRIGHT

WARNING: A CERTIFICATE IS NOT EVIDENCE OF IDENTITY.

KDO

The men of the Battalion were as ready as they would ever be for the trials ahead. Within two months they would travel thousands of miles to what for most may have seemed like another planet. Their numbers would also have been greatly diminished as they joined the great struggle at Gallipoli.

On Tuesday the 29th June orders were received for embarkation for Foreign Service. The battalion would have known that they were going east as khaki drill and Foreign Service helmets would be issued. If of course enough of the said items could be issued. The battalions first CO Lt-Col Sadler would not lead his men into battle. He had received wounds in the South African war (Boer War) and the effects of these put paid to his service in the First World War. He had been a part of the battalion's creation and had given it a splendid start to its career.

Lt-Col Bosanquet would lead the Battalion into its first battle.

Its four companies were commanded by -:
A Company – Lieut J G Blackburne
B Company – Lieut R D Squires
C Company – Capt G R Fielding
D Company – Capt A S Murray.

After ten months of training and preparation the 9th Battalion would be going to war. No doubt many of the men thought they would serve in France and, by 1916, many wished they had. Instead they were destined to fight in a theatre of war that would gain an infamous reputation – Gallipoli.

Chapter Two

GALLIPOLI

Roll of Honour

Lt.Col L A Bosanquet, C.O, 9th Sherwood Foresters, killed in action 25th September 1915 (Lionel Arthur) He was actually killed on 21st August 1915 although the official notification was 25th September. He is Commemorated Helles Memorial, Turkey, panel 150-152. Lt-Col L A Bosanquet, commanding the 9th Sherwood Foresters, had seen active service in the Tirah Campaign, and had the medal with two clasps. (Tirah N.W. Frontier/Afridis 1897-1898. The Sherwood Foresters gained Battle honours in this campaign. He was probably a Subaltern in his first campaign). A note in The Sherwood Foresters Regimental Annual 1922 states – The present Duke of Atholl, then Lord Tullibardine, found the body of Col. Bosanquet some time after the attack of August 21st, and in a letter on the subject wrote thus: – "He was lying a few yards in front of his men, who were in perfect alignment with never a back turned, a few yards from the Turkish trenches."

The same Annual gives details of the officers who landed at Suvla Bay on August 6th with the 9th (Service) Battalion The Sherwood Foresters and also their fate.

Lt.-Col. L. A. Bosanquet	– Wounded August 9th; killed August 21st
Major J.G. Blackburne	– Killed August 21st
Major A.S. Murray	– Wounded August 9th
Capt. R.D. Squires	– Killed August 9th.
Capt. H.L.B. Mills	– Wounded August 9th.
Capt. C.D Randall	– Killed August 9th.
Capt. T.B. Black	– Killed August 9th.
Lieut. E.D. Basden	– Wounded August 9th.
Lieut. S.H. Piper	– Wounded August 9th.
Lieut. W.C. Mayo	– Killed August 9th.
Lieut. A.G. Wills	– Killed August 9th.
Lieut. J.F.M. Hind	– Wounded August 9th.
Lieut. A.E. Scothern	– Wounded August 9th
Lieut. H.P. Carey	– Killed August 9th.
2nd Lieut. R.J. Nicholls	– Wounded August 9th
2nd Lieut. W. West	– Killed August 9th.
(This officer had been wounded previously while with the Battalion at Cape Helles)	
2nd Lieut. E.T. Alpass	– Killed August 21st.
2nd Lieut. C.E. Scott	– Wounded August 9th.
2nd Lieut. F.C. Brown	– Killed August 9th.
2nd Lieut. E.H. Marsh	– Wounded.
2nd Lieut. J.C. Harrison	– Wounded August 10th.
Capt. & Adjt. F.F. Loyd	– Wounded August 10th.
Lieut. & Qmr. A. Ewin	– Killed August 11th.

Never let anyone say that the 9th Battalions officers did not give their all.

Background to the Gallipoli Campaign.

Just why an untried, untested New Army Division was sent to Gallipoli is open to question, a question that may never be answered but one that would haunt British Military history for many years to come. The 11th (Northern) Division was one of Kitcheners first New Army Divisions. Volunteers flocked to the colours at the outbreak of war, keen to get some action before the War was over, for, as everyone knew, it would not last many months.

The Division came into existence under Army Order No. 324 on 21st August 1914. This order authorized the formation of six new divisions. Initially, without arms of any kind and with no military training, it would obviously take some time to turn these men into soldiers.

It would seem though that by late spring in 1915 the 11th Division was deemed ready for active service. One would have thought that a spell in or near the front lines on the Western front would have given the men the experience of war without exposing them to its full horrors. An opportunity to learn their trade without suffering the massive casualties that would occur in Gallipoli should surely have been taken.

The "Easterners" in the Government held the upper hand and Churchill's 'Great Adventure' in Gallipoli needed more cannon fodder. They advocated a large scale military diversion from the Western front believing that Germany and the Central Powers could be attacked on their strategic flanks with better success. Notable Easterners where Winston Churchill, Lloyd George and Bonar Law, whilst Haig and Robertson believed that the only way to defeat Germany was on the Western front.

It was therefore decided that the Division would reinforce the beleaguered garrison on Gallipoli. On the 30th June 1915 the Battalion entrained at Farnham for the journey to Liverpool, arriving at 07-30 hrs the next morning. The majority of the Division sailed from Avonmouth on the Mauretania, but the 33rd Brigade would embark on their journey at Liverpool. On 1 July 1915 the 9thBn SF as part of 33rd Brigade, sailed from Liverpool on H.M. Transport 'Empress of Britain' and according to all officer reports the voyage was uneventful, although the men in their cramped quarters on board may not have agreed. The ship sailed via Malta, arriving on 8th July, where she stayed for one day before sailing to Alexandria where she arrived on 12th. The voyage to Alexandria had been without incident and the ship stayed for three days whilst the transport was unshipped and reshipped. The men were no doubt overjoyed to be given route marches around Alexandria during this stop. Most of the officers were though given time to enjoy the pleasures of the port. Then the ship headed for Lemnos arriving on 16th and finally Mudros on the 18th. Mudros was the base for the troops fighting on Gallipoli. Col Scothern noted in his diary:

> *'The trip was enjoyable although the men were rather overcrowded and the greatest fatality of all, the supply of liquid refreshment ran out. Nevertheless time passed pleasantly in the hot sunshine, a rumoured chase by a submarine being the only disturbing factor'.*

One wonders if the overcrowded men felt the cruise as enjoyable as no doubt Col Scothern did. The men had gone from a temperate English climate to the heat of Lemnos and, considering that most of them had probably never left their home county before, one can only imagine how they felt. Troop ships were not pleasant forms of transport and no doubt many men suffered on the way to Egypt. It would be thought that a period of acclimatization would have been needed before these inexperienced and untried troops were thrown into battle. Less than a week was not ideal preparation for these men who would be attacking a strongly defended beach with little or no artillery support. Great store was put in the barrage put down by the Navy but these shells are not as effective as normal artillery, the trajectory being totally different.

There would have been no time to practice the forthcoming attack and the men would be reliant on their officers and NCOs leading the way. If anything happened to these men, then the other ranks would have little idea of what to do.

For the 33rd Brigade though even a week of minimal training would not be had. Once at Mudros, the battalion did not land but were transhipped first into a smaller vessel the El Kahirah and then into lighters. On the 19th July, Brigade Headquarters and the 6th Battalion Lincolnshire Regiment, under the command of Lt-Col. Phelps, embarked on the S.S. Osmanieh and the S.S. El Kahira for the Gallipoli Peninsula. On the 20th July the 7th Battalion South Staffordshire Regiment and the 9th Battalion Sherwood Foresters accompanied by one company of the 6th Battalion Border Regiment embarked on the same two vessels for the Peninsula, the Sherwood Foresters being on the El Kahira. They arrived off the Peninsula at approx 8 pm, transhipping on to trawlers for the landing on V Beach at Cape Helles. This was the location of the landings of 25th April when the 29th Division performed heroics and lost heavily. The S.S. River Clyde used then as a landing craft was now the landing stage for trawlers carrying the new troops. The 33rd brigade would be going straight into action at Cape Helles, attached to the Royal Naval Division. The Turks who could see just about everything that moved gave the Battalion a warm reception by opening up a heavy artillery barrage on the landing place. This forced the trawlers to stand away from the landing stage until the Turks slackened their barrage. During the barrage a large store of Verey lights was hit and the sky was illuminated with various coloured lights. Apparently some thought this a picturesque sight but no doubt unseasoned troops on their first landing, thought otherwise. The Battalion eventually got ashore at 2-30 am. They moved to bivouacs at the Drake Battalion, Royal Naval Division Camp rest camp. The term 'rest camp' on Gallipoli was somewhat of a misnomer as everywhere was under constant fire. These rest areas were though quieter than the front line and men could at least relax and get some sleep. The Battalion was given a nights sleep at Drake Camp before their next move on the following afternoon. At 3.30 pm on 21st July the Battalion moved forward to the reserve trenches – the Eski Line. Whilst this line was obviously safer than the front line trenches, nevertheless the men got a taste of bullets and shells flying overhead. They could get used to the daily routine of both sides, which included an artillery bombardment in the morning and evening. Once the heat of the day cooled the snipers also became active.

At 2.30pm on 23rd July they relieved the Drake and Hawke battalions in the firing line. The Battalion would now learn quickly the basics of trench life. Keeping your head down and being constantly on alert would give you the best opportunity of leaving the trenches in one piece. Front line trench occupation was not just a case of sitting and waiting though. A myriad of work had to be undertaken – the front line and communications trenches had to be improved constantly. After the various battles, many bodies still lay unburied and old sweats would probably have left them as such. These new men still had some semblance of humanity in them though and thought it right to bury as many bodies as possible.

The next day saw the first battalion death in action as a sniper killed Major Fielding. He was walking down a communication trench in the early hours of Saturday 24th when the sniper hit him. Major G. R Fielding aged 33 years son of the Rev G H Fielding and husband of Evelyn Fielding of Switzerland was killed in action on 24 July 1915 and is buried at Skew Bridge Cemetery, Gallipoli, and grave II.D.3. He would be one of the few men of the 9th Bn SF to have an identified grave. The Derby Daily Telegraph dated 5th August 1915 gave the Battalions casualties 'At the Dardanelles' as, killed – major G.R. Fielding, and wounded 2/Lt West. 2/Lt West would return to the battalion later and was killed on 7th August 1915. The first Other Rank would also die that day. Private Daniel Barfield, known to be buried in Redoubt Cemetery, Helles and special memorial A. 94 notes this fact. Private Barfield was a reservist living at Dean terrace, Langley Mill prior to the war. His army career had begun when he was aged 18 years and had been long and varied. In 1897/8 he was on the Indian frontier and saw action there. He served in South Africa during the Boer War. He had medals for both these campaigns.

He is commemorated on the Langley Mill memorial and was the first soldier from there to die in World War 1. The RSM (Regimental Sergeant Major) wrote to his widow saying:

> *"You have one thing to look back upon, your husband was killed doing his duty for his King, his Country, and the dear ones he left at home. I had known him for 23 years as we were recruits together, and always found him a brave soldier"*

6076 Pte Daniel Barfield, killed in action 24th July 1915.

Both men died holding the line in the area of Gully Ravine, with the village of Krithia to their left. From Krithia the Turks could enfilade the Battalions trench and it is to the credit of the Battalion that their casualties were so low. Before they had arrived on Cape Helles, the advance was effectively over and the line remained unchanged until the evacuation in January 1916. Again Col Scothern tells of the battalions landing and realities of war:

'There was very little opposition, but the grim reality of war was brought home to everyone by the first casualties. The weather was very hot and there was a great plague of flies. The food was not very varied, water was a great difficulty, being hard to obtain, and before long dysentery was very prevalent'

The Battalion records give details of how the next few days where spent. Time in the trenches was given over to improving positions, opening new communication trenches and burying " masses of dead bodies". One has to wonder why the battalion was here, with a new landing only days away, what possible benefit the men could have got from being sent to Helles. Giving the men a taste of warfare can be the only possible explanation, although the burying of 'masses of dead' could have done little for moral of these untested troops. They were no doubt under the impression that their job would be to sweep the Turks from Gallipoli but instead they found themselves in very overcrowded trenches and the Turks giving them a warm welcome. After a couple of days of Turkish fire and constant alarms, the men settled to their life in the trenches. Again Col Scothern noted:

'One day news came that in Mesopotamia the Turks were reported in full flight towards Baghdad and to celebrate the occasion a feu du joie was fired. In consequence, the Turks opposite took alarm and became very nasty for a time.'

After 10 days at Helles, the brigade was ordered back to 11th Division and Imbros. The Battalion were relieved by French troops at 3-15am on Sunday 1st August and marched back to the rest camp. At 10.30pm that evening they re-embarked on the S.S. Osmanieh and sailed to Imbros where they arrived the following morning. The Battalion was though, commended in Sir Ian Hamilton's Orders.

The battalion then spent the time before the Suvla Bay, practising for the landing and recovering from Helles. Men could bathe and relax, although many suffered from the effects of dysentery and the simplest of tasks became difficult.

The Plan

In its simplest form the plan of attack for the Suvla Bay landings was to land 22,000 men on a number of beaches against light Turkish opposition, then march the men four miles inland and occupy the foothills that sat in a semicircle beyond the Salt Lake. These included Chocolate Hill, Scimitar Hill and the Ismail Oglu Tepe. From this position IX Corps that included 11th Division, to which the 9thBn Sherwood Foresters were part, would link with the Anzacs and attack Sari Bair (made up of Chunuk Bair, Hill O and Koja Chemen Tepe). Surprise and speed were essential and if the plan succeeded the British would control the narrows, which in turn would allow warships to pass into the Sea of Marmara.

What is obvious from the plan above is that the man in charge had to be a decisive character that could make the difficult decisions quickly. It will be seen that the choice General Stopford was neither of these.

The Landing

The 11th (Northern) Division of which 9th Battalion Sherwood Foresters were a part, extended from near Kuchuk Anafarta Ova and Sulajik, through the Chocolate Hill and Green Hill to about Hetman Char. The Divisions vital point was Hill 100 (Ismail

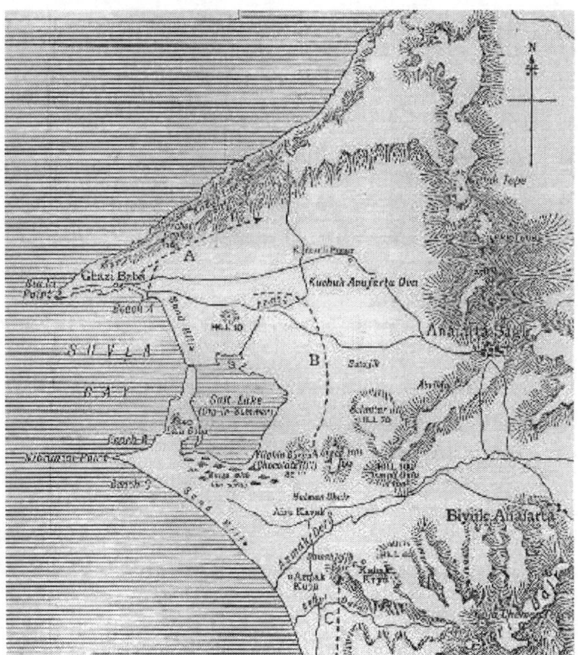

A facsimile of a contemporary map of Suvla bay

Oglu Tepe), which guarded the gap leading up to the village of Biyuk Anafarta.

The landing at Suvia Bay took place on the night of 6/7th August 1915 the men being landed from lighters. What these miners and farm workers thought as they landed on Gallipoli is difficult to imagine. The oppressive heat, the constant shelling, the flies, the appalling living conditions, the lack of water must have made many long for the Midlands and Home. Many, if not all, of the men would have been relishing the thought of going into action at last after many months of training. This was at last a chance to have a go at the enemy and to show what the Division could do. They may have had reservations had they known the fate of previous Divisions who had been on Gallipoli since April 25th. One such Division, the 29th, was the last regular army division sent into battle and had been decimated at Gallipoli. Its numbers had been replaced two or three times and few men who landed on 25th April lived to tell the tale. If a regular Division could lose so many men killed and wounded, how would a volunteer Division get on? The tragic answer would come over the following few days as the men tried and failed to take their objectives.

The attack was part of a three pronged offensive and phase one was on Friday 6th with an attack by the Anzac troops on the Lone Pine Trenches. The Anzacs took this formidable entrenchment although much heavy fighting would follow during the following days.

The main attack was at Anzac, which began on the night of 6/7th August and again would see heavy fighting over the following days. The first task of 9th Army Corps after landing was to take and hold Zilghin Burnu, (Chocolate Hill) and the Ismail Oglu Hills beyond it, together with the foothills on the north and east of Suvla Bay.

The landing itself was seen as a triumph of organization. Then again it should have been as Suvla Bay was perfect for a landing. It was a long, wide curved bay of sandy beaches and beyond it the low plains leading to the hills. The one possible problem was a large salt lake just inland but during the summer this would have caused little concern. It was also expected that as the Turks did not expect an attack, his trenches would be lightly guarded.

There was though a good reason for the Turks' light defence of this sector. The Sari Bair Ridge was virtually impassable with its dense scrub, razor edged spurs and deep gorges. The only way through was by way of single goat tracks and how the Top Brass expected these untried troops to accomplish their task is difficult to fathom. Regular troops with years of training behind them and used to the rigours of Army life may just have pulled it off given the right conditions, good artillery and luck. Men fresh from England, not yet acclimatized to the heat and many suffering from diarrhoea had little or no chance of succeeding. Amazingly the day before the landing many of the men had been given cholera inoculations. Anyone who has had this inoculation will know that for a couple of days you have a stiff and sore arm.

Adding to the men's problems was the choice of Corps Commander. It is not my intention to lay blame at any one person because many people failed in the Gallipoli campaign. It is obvious though that the choice of Corps commander was, to say the least, a strange one. An attack such as the one on Suvla Bay needed a strong commander with front line experience and used to commanding at all levels. Sadly such a man could not be found and the Corps got instead General Stopford, who although blessed with over forty years of Army experience and bedecked with honours, had never once led men into battle. He was a stalwart administrator and Staff Officer and had vast experience in this sphere. General Stopford it would seem was the most unlikely of front line commanders for this battle. Neither did he instil any confidence in his untried troops. The phrase 'blind leading the blind' comes immediately to mind when looking at IX Corps prior to the battle.

One of General Stopford's major worries, apart from his sprained knee, was the lack of artillery as attacks in France had shown that Howitzers were needed to aid the infantry. Despite this knowledge, the infantry were expected to go forward and secure areas from which the artillery would work. In the meantime the navy would lay down a barrage, despite it being known that naval gunfire was not as effective because of the trajectory of the shells.

General Stopford had good reason to worry and he, at least, seemed to have less faith in the untried New Army troops than Sir Ian Hamilton. For the attack to succeed these 'green' troops would have to land in the dark and secure a bridgehead, then advance to take the first vital positions. All against an enemy that it was thought was only about five battalions strong but who once dawn came, could see the whole of the plain and the bay. Whatever the real figures of Turkish troops ranged against them, the new army men had to gain the heights before Turkish reinforcements arrived.

From the start though it was obvious that Stopford doubted that the attack would succeed.

He told Sir Ian Hamilton via a staff officer the following:

> *"Tell Sir Ian Hamilton that I am going to do my best and that I hope to be successful. But he must realize that if the enemy proves to be holding a strong line of continuous entrenchments I shall be unable to dislodge him until more guns are landed"*

This would seem to be a man making excuses for a plan that he knew would fail. With hindsight a more robust General may have called the landing off but unfortunately for the 9th Sherwood Foresters and 11th Division they did not have such a man. The 11th Division were given the honour of landing first, although one wonders how many at the time saw it as an 'honour'

The 11th Division where paraded at 5.00pm on 6th August and embarked on the lighters which had been specially constructed for landing parties, and destroyers. Each destroyer towed two lighters, and each was detailed to a certain beach at Sulva Bay. It was not realized that the bay had shoals and some of the lighters landed on these.This left the men some way from the beach and they had to wade through water which at times was 4 to 5 feet deep. This had to be accomplished whilst carrying rifles, full packs and two days rations.

At around 9-30 pm on the evening of 6th August the first troops of the main force landed at Suvla Bay and by 10 pm four battalions had made it ashore with more on the way. During this stage of the operation only one naval rating was a casualty and that from one shot fired from the shore. As soon as it was dark the landing took place. The Battalion notes stated:

> *'Everything worked splendidly, and the discipline and training exhibited by all ranks reflected the greatest credit on themselves and those who had trained them. I have never seen better work carried out by any troops'.*

The Battalion took up their positions from a point on the south western bank of Salt Lake to the sea immediately after landing at Suvla Bay. They with the 7th Bn South Staffordshire Regiment were under the direct command of G.O.C. (General Officer Commanding) 11th Division and once they had achieved their first objective they waited for the order to press on. That order failed to materialize and any chance of taking the Turks by surprise and thereby cutting off the enemy at Helles was gone.

The troops of 11th Division came ashore at A, B, and C, beaches. The 32nd and 33rd brigades at 'B' and 'C' whilst the 34th brigade landed at 'A' beach. Only the 34th brigade encountered any serious opposition during the landing.

The 9th West Yorkshire Regiment and 6th Yorkshire Regiment of 32nd brigade advanced and took the main Turkish Garrison at Lala Baba but at a high cost. The commander of the Yorkshires (Green Howards) was killed whilst leading his men to the summit of Lala Baba.

It is here that accounts vary with some saying that the advanced stopped at this point whilst others with justification say that the 32nd were pushed towards Hill 10 in support of 34th Brigade that was in difficulties. It also seems that at times the troops suffered from what at the time was termed 'misdirected fire' and today would be termed ' friendly fire'. Whatever the real reason, it was obvious that the attack was grinding to a halt. It would seem that the lack of any real leadership on the spot led to even more confusion. As it grew lighter and the Turks began to shell 32nd and 34th brigades they seemed to have no one who could grasp the situation and take command of the

Troops relaxing on the beach after the landing at Suvla Bay and obviously there is no urgency in moving inland.

situation. From all reports it is obvious that officers and men in the Battalion expected to land and then attack but no orders came through to this effect.

It wasn't that the New Army men lacked courage, far from it, but unlike regular troops, they needed to be led and told what to do. When their officers and S.N.C.O.'s became casualties they lost momentum with disastrous results. These new untried troops fought in tropical heat, through unknown territory with full packs and little water. By morning they were parched with thirst and exhausted. They had been shelled throughout the 7th and counterattacked on a number of occasions. Even so the majority of them hung on in grim determination. Despite the urgency of the situation at the front, the beachhead seemed to be a place of peace. The bay was full of ships and by 9-30am on the 7th they had landed many more troops but there they stayed. There seemed to be a total lack of orders for a move forward. No one seemed to have any idea of what was or should be happening. Troops mingled as the Turks shelled the area and men from various regiments hung around in groups waiting for orders. Those orders never came and so the men stayed put. A young volunteer of the New Army had few, if any, ideas on the workings of the Army and without being told what to do, he did nothing. Whilst these men waited, others suffered on the front line. Sadly their Commander General Stopford knew little more than the lowest private. For some unfathomable reason he had stayed on board the destroyer Jonquil and for what good he did, he might well have stayed on Lemnos. Despite the fact that he had no idea of how the battle was going, his message to Sir Ian Hamilton was that the troops had landed but had not got far from the beach. One can only imagine the feelings of Sir Ian, as by then the troops should have been in possession of the Anafarta Hills.

The 7th was a day of frustration and suffering for the troops and by evening they were all parched with thirst and totally exhausted. These young volunteers who had never been in battle before could go no further. The preparations for providing enough water for the troops were totally inadequate and men continued to suffer and become even more disorganized. In an attempt to get more water to the front it was decided to stop the off-loading of horses, which were needed to move artillery and instead disembark the mules, which could move water. Again urgently needed artillery would have to wait whilst water was got to the men.

The 10th Division came ashore on 7th and with the 11th Division the attack, if it could be called that, was continued on Biyuk Anafarta, Yilghin Burnu and by the 13th Division on Damakjelik Bair. Despite time being of the essence, the attacks lacked vigour and were put in with no serious intent by any of the Divisions. Finally the 9th Battalion received orders to remain where they were and to dig in. Considering that the initial orders had been to move forward rapidly at daybreak this confused and irritated both officers and men of the Battalion. In fact it was mentioned in the Battalion notes

" *....All ranks were feeling so 'bucked' that I feel sure if the order for a general advance had been given we would have gone across to Maidos with little difficulty*".

The notes also state:
"The battalion had managed to get ashore without casualties" and it was also noted *"there had been few throughout the Division"*.

The 11th Manchesters of 34th Infantry Brigade would no doubt disagree with the last point. They had indeed a number of casualties as they struggled ashore under heavy rifle fire from Lala Baba and shrapnel from artillery inland. The Battalion had also received casualties as the records show. By the evening of 7th, many hundreds of men, parched with thirst, had dropped out of the ranks. Some had even pierced the hose carrying the water from the beach to tanks inland; such was the men's desperation to get water.

Yet the diary of L/Col Scothern paints a different picture for the men of 9thBn SF who were in Divisional reserve along with the 7th South Staffordshire Regt. He says:

> *'Orders had been received to dig in from Salt lake to 'C' Beach and this work was completed before morning, the scrub on the right being covered by Machine Gun Section. Patrols were sent out and gained touch with the Australians without difficulty, only being worried by odd snipers'*

It was obvious therefore those men near the beach and in reserve were having a fairly pleasant time whilst those in the front line suffered. Col Scothern's most telling piece comes next and adds weight to the argument that General Stopford had little idea of a) what was happening and b) how the landing and attack should have been executed.

Scothern states:

> *'The conditions were very pleasant, the weather being all that could be desired, and*

above all no flies. We were able to move about 'on top' and there was in addition glorious sea bathing'. Firing could be heard in the distance, but what was happening no one knew'.

Was this a beach holiday or a struggle to carry out the job in hand? As many New Army men died, others relaxed on a pleasant beach. Although Drummer Bertrand Parker of the 9th Battalion seems to disagree with Col Scothern and stated that:

'We were under shellfire directly we got on the beach and shells were falling all around us. It seemed marvellous that we were not all wiped out when we got into the open'

Drummer Parker was wounded and moved to a hospital in Alexandria.

A letter home was printed in his local Cromford Derbyshire newspaper and he tells of a week on a hospital ship before reaching Alexandria and a tented hospital close to the sea. It would seem that his wounds from bullets through the shoulder were quite serious but he survived the war. Drummer Parker was the son of Frank Parker of North Street Cromford. Bertrand was a well-known local cricketer and assistant scoutmaster. Prior to the war he worked at Lea Hosiery Mills.

All of these untried troops were unused to the hardships which faced them – the heat, lack of water, a determined enemy and little or no orders. Turkish reinforcements were on the way and the situation could only get worse. The British troops had a couple of hours at most to advance and get the job done before Turkish reinforcements arrived. With the situation the way it was, this would not happen. All the advantages were with the Turkish troops and the Divisional Commander realized that his men could not go on.

Sir Ian Hamilton was of the opinion that the troops could and should go on, but eventually he let the Divisional Commanders talk him into spending the 8th reorganizing and getting more artillery ashore. General Stopford had for some reason decided that the mere fact that his troops had got ashore was some kind of success and once rested they would take all in front of them. How General Stopford had come to think this is impossible to work out. The whole point of the landing was to sweep the Turks from the Hills and in doing so aid the Anzacs in their attacks. With dead Australians lying thick on the ground around Anzac Cove, it is hard to share General Stopfords reasoning. With Australians and British suffering and dying in the front lines why were reserves sitting in trenches at Sulva Bay?

Throughout the day the troops stayed put and reorganized and rested whilst others bathed around the shoreline of Suvla Bay. Colonel Sir Maurice Hankey sent a message to Sir Ian Hamilton which no doubt sent a shiver through the latter's body.

"Just been ashore, where I found all quiet. No rifle fire, no artillery fire, and apparently no Turks. IX Corps resting. Feel confident that golden opportunities are being lost and look upon the situation as serious".

No doubt beneath the surface Col Hankey was seething as he saw the inactivity before him. Many of the bathers would soon pay for their Commanders lack of drive in the days to come. As Col Scothern also mentioned in his diary the area of the beachhead was at the time a pleasant place to relax. The Battalion moved forward during the night of 7/8th to Hill 50 ready for the attack of the 9th August.

On the 8th August the Battalion carried out a half-hearted attack but the 13th Division on the Brigade's right and the Anzacs to the 13ths right were heavily engaged. Throughout this period, there seems to have been no clear orders from above on what the exact aims of this attack were. On the one hand, the orders were explicit – get ashore and move rapidly inland to overrun the Turks before they could re-enforce. On the other, some Brigades sat doing nothing whilst others were heavily engaged. In extreme cases one unit would actually hinder another. For instance the New Zealanders in the Anzac Division had reached the summit of Chunuk Bair. The Turks held one side of the summit and the New Zealanders the other, until that is the British artillery shelled the New Zealanders off the summit. It has been reported that the New Zealand Battalion was decimated and only a few survivors returned.

On 9th August 1915, with the renewed attack, the 9th SF and many others would pay a high price for the incompetence of senior officers. Battalion officers were, it must be said, in complete contrast to their seniors. By the end of the second attack on 21st August, the 9th Bn had one unwounded officer Lieut. Carr the Medical Officer. The Roll of Honour for all the other officers are given at the beginning of this chapter.

The tired, thirsty, disorganized and it could be argued ill-led men, after losing the element of surprise, would attack again. They would be joined by reserves including the 9th SF who had spent a couple of days 'relaxing' on the beach and even more reserves shipped in from Imbros.Once again it was a battle of might have been as the attack began but this time the Turks were ready and waiting.

At 4.45am on 9th August the Battalion received their orders to move forward, the formation for movement being two long lines some 200 to 300 yards apart – 'A' and 'B' Companies formed the front Line with 'C' and 'D' Companies in the rear. The Machine Gun Section was extended between these two lines.

At first 33rd Brigade, of which 9th SF were a part, made good progress. The 9 SF advanced about 1000 yards before encountering heavy fire and suffering many casualties. The battalion was attacking towards Hetman Char to the right of Hill 100 (Ismail Oglu Tepe). The Battalions exact advance was through the gap between Damakjelik Bair and Yilghin Burnu (Chocolate Hill).

The ground was covered in the scrubby undergrowth, with occasional patches of formerly cultivated land and two orchards. The rough and narrow goat tracks ran in all directions and funnelled troops into them with what would be disastrous results. The battalion kept up the forward movement with a series of sectional rushes (Sections moving forward whilst covering fire given by others actions).

Maps showing the area of Battalion advance on 9th August

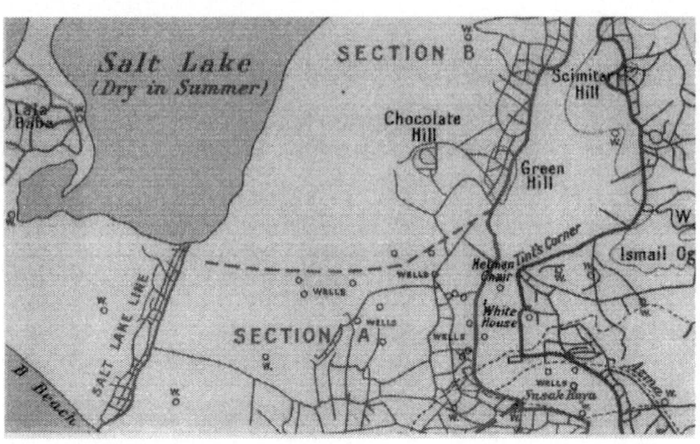

Chocolate Hill and area

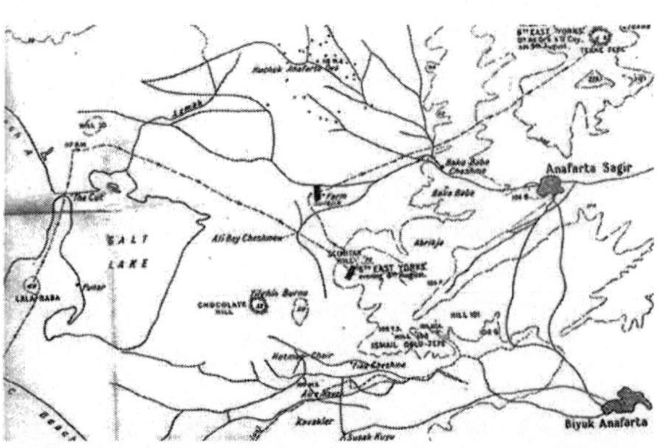

Salt Lake and beyond

The 9th advanced with 'B' and 'C' Companies in front with 'A' Company in support and 'D' Company as Battalion reserve. 'B Company led by Capt. R.D. Squires and C Company led by Capt. C.D Randall moved forward with Lieut. Piper on the right of B Company and 2nd Lieut. Allpass on the left of C knew the points upon which the flanks of the line of defence of the Battalion were to rest'. 'A' Company led by Capt. G.F. Chambers in support then moved forward to complete the occupation of the position. D Company as per the operational orders remained in battalion reserve.

Eventually though, all along the Brigade front, the advance began to stall. The 9th SF advance stalled on the right and in the centre near an orchard close to Hetman Char, although by 8am a satisfactory line of defence had been taken up but at a cost of 8 officers and 150 other ranks killed or wounded. The enemy used the scrub well and lay hidden within it putting down withering fire on the Battalion. The two sister battalions of 9th SF, 6thBn Border Regt and 6thBn Lincolns Regt were on the flanks and their steadiness and gallantry helped steady a difficult situation. In fact Capt Hansen of the 6th Lincolns won a VC for his efforts that day. He won it on Green Hill, near Hill 70. The Hill had twice been captured but the intense heat from the scrub fires made it untenable. Some wounded had been left on the hill and Capt Hansen led a party of men over the open ground to rescue the wounded men. Two men of the 6th Border Regt won DCM's on the same day.

Returning to the 9th SF and their line of defence – The 9th SF however had fared badly after being held near Hetman Char and progress was seen to be impossible. By 8 am the majority of the battalions officers had become casualties (5 were dead), but despite this the line was held until around 3 pm. The Turks then counter-attacked and forced a gap between 'A' and 'B' Companies managing to enfilade from the right flank of the battalion and hoping to envelop them. These two Companies had by this time only two 2nd Lieutenants leading them. Seeing this, the C.O. Col Bosanquet came forward leading a support attack of signallers, runners, servants and any other men he could muster and succeeding in driving the Turks back.

He then ordered a withdrawal of some four hundred yards to a more tenable position and it was here that he received a wound in the wrist. Major Blackburn then took command of the battalion, whilst the C.O. returned to the beach and the CCS. As the day ended and stock was taken, the full cost of the battle became known; it was obvious that the 9thbn SF had been hard hit.

Only two officers remained fit for active duty and 7 officers were dead, 11 wounded and 1 missing. The strength of the other ranks had been reduced to about 300 men.

At about 5pm in the evening the 1/1st Herefordshire Regt reinforced them. The 1/1st Herefords though only came up in half Battalion strength and they cited heavy shelling being the reason for leaving the rest of their men in the Salt Lake trenches. When darkness fell the Herefords took over the right of the line and the remnants of the two companies holding it were then formed into a reserve. At midnight the Herefords were withdrawn in readiness for an attack the following morning. The remnant reserve therefore moved again into the right of the line under command of the adjutant Capt. F.F. Loyd. It would seem that the enemy had no knowledge of how weak the positions held actually were, the gap between the Battalions right flank and the left flank of 13th Division held by the South Wales Borderers being upwards of a mile. Whilst there was some sporadic fighting during that night no concentrated attack was forthcoming from the Turks. It is doubtful if the positions could have been defended had such an attack took place. The men were also lacking food and water as supplies could not be got to them. The remnants of the Battalion in 92A fire trenches were finally relieved on the night of the 12th by the 11th Manchester's and returned to the beach area for a rest period.

This first real taste of battle did not bode well for the battalion and there was much hard fighting yet to do. That said, the men who remained would certainly have learned much about the art of war and would be better soldiers for their experience, from later officer casualty lists, it was also obvious that the officers had learned many lessons. The main one being that you cannot lead men if you are dead. No doubt the gung ho attitude of a few days previously had gone forever.

The list of men killed and mentioned on the Helles memorial bears testimony to the horrors of this battle. In particular one family would always remember the 9th August 1915, the date they lost two sons to the war. A/Cpl Albert Cottrell, service number 12452, aged 20 years and L/Sgt Harry Cottrell service number 12454, were listed as killed in action on 9th August 1915 and are both commemorated on the Helles Memorial. Sons of a regular soldier, Albert was born in Dublin and Harry at Devonport and from records of the 1st Battalion The Sherwood Foresters movements, it would seem that their father served with them. Early in 1890 the 1st battalion had its married quarters in Raglan Barracks Devonport. In May 1894 the battalion once again left for a tour of duty in Ireland and 1895 Albert was born.

The amount of casualties suffered would see another change in the 9thBn Sherwood Foresters and that was in its make up. On its formation the men had mostly been drawn from Nottinghamshire and Derbyshire of mining or agricultural stock. The new drafts that would come to the battalion after Gallipoli would come from many counties but they would show the same pride in 'their Regiment, The Notts and Derby'.

On 10th August another attack was envisaged and would take place on the 11th, but the Division needed rest and it was decided to use them only as a reserve. They did take part in a supporting action on the left flank but this did little except raise the toll of casualties, one of these being Lt the Honourable Arthur Ewin, the Battalions quartermaster, who was killed. The Commonwealth War Graves Commission have his date of death as between 7th-11th August 1915 but Col Scothern in his diary states the 11th as date of death. The Adjutant was also wounded in this action.

The battalion when relieved on 12th withdrew to the beach for a short rest and they were joined by reinforcements from Imbros. In keeping with Army practice a nucleus of the battalion had been kept in reserve at Imbros but, owing to the losses, these men rejoined their comrades at Suvla Bay much earlier than envisaged. One wonders what these reinforcements thought as they looked on the remnants of the battalion. No doubt also the survivors of the past days reflected that only days earlier they had relaxed and bathed on this very beach. In these few days many comrades had been lost and the full reality of war had dawned on these men. It would not be one of glory but one of pain and death as Gallipoli turned into yet more trench warfare.

The men were put to work digging trenches for the reserve line and shelters for the horses. They also made preparations for their return to the battle, no doubt with some trepidation. It has to be remembered that the Turkish troops could see most of the movements on the beach from their positions on the hills. During this stay on the Suvla Bay beach the battalion were ordered to Chocolate Hill on 18th to relieve the 6th York and Lancaster Regt in the forward trenches and on 20th were relieved and withdrawn back to the beach. The CO, Col Bosanquet rejoined the battalion despite his wound not being fully healed.

It was more as a forlorn hope than as a decisive thrust forward that Sir Ian Hamilton renewed the attack on August 21st. After reinforcing the northern wing with the 2nd Mounted Division, brought in from Egypt and who were organized as dismounted troops and the 29th Division from the southern area, the attacking troops were ready. It is interesting to note that the 29th Division had attacked at Helles on the first day of Gallipoli, 25th April 1915, and few of the regular soldiers who landed on that day survived. 53rd and 54th Territorial Divisions were tasked to hold the enemy.

The main difficulty as the top brass saw it was that the area of concentration prior to the attack was open and shallow. In fact the only cover afforded the men was Lala Baba Hill some 200 yards from the sea, and Chocolate Hill (Yilghin Burnu) half a mile from the Turkish Front. The ground between these two points was a flat plain and exposed to the view and fire of the enemy.

The almost impossible task of storming the Turkish positions was given to 29th and 11th Divisions. The night before the battle, 20th August, the 29th Division was ranged along the line from Hill 70 (Scimitar Hill) to Hill 112, the 87th Brigade on the left and the 86th on the right, with the South Wales Borderers in the centre connecting the two Brigades. The 88th Brigade being held in reserve.

The 11th Division was to attack on the right of the 29th Division and occupied the front trenches on the right of Chocolate Hill.

The attack was to begin at 3 pm on 21st August and the time was chosen for good reason. The setting sun would blind the Turkish gunners and the Turkish trenches would be shown clearly in the evening light. The weather though conspired against the British as a strange mist crept up and enveloped Suvla Bay and the plain. During the afternoon the enemy trenches could hardly be seen and it would have been logical to postpone the attack. The majority of days were fine and this mist an unusual occurrence, so a delay of 24 hours would not have been a problem. Even the Commander in Chief wanted a postponement but for some unfathomable reason the go ahead was given.

Prior to the advance, the 9th SF were formed up behind Lala Baba and, with only 7 officers able to take part, the omens were not good for the battalion.

Ismail Oglu Tepe was a hill forming the southwest corner of the Anafarta Sagar Spur and this was the 11th Divisions objective. The hill rose 350 feet from the plain and it was covered in dense holly oak scrub which was almost impenetrable and broke up attacks, forcing troops to move in single file along goat tracks between the bushes.

The comparatively small number of artillery pieces landed up to the date of the battle was another weakness as the men had to storm the enemy trenches from the plain. Again naval artillery was used as a back up but the targeting and trajectory as previously stated was inadequate for the job in hand. The bombardment was limited to a narrow front of one mile and it was hoped the men would be able to take the enemy trenches and the impetus of their charge would take them to the top of the hill. Again Col Scothern stated in his diary:

'After a slight bombardment, an advance was made across the open, south of Salt Lake towards Hetman Char in artillery formation'

The slight bombardment was from 2-30pm to 3pm and although heavy, it was far from accurate or effective. The idea was to neutralize the enemy trenches but lack of direction failed to do this. Adding to the fire were 24 Machine Guns positioned on Yilghin Burnu, which could bring down fire on the enemy trenches.

34th Brigade of 11th Division launched the infantry attack on the right of the line and it had immediate success as the enemy trenches between Hetman Char and Aire Kavak were taken with few casualties. Unfortunately 32nd Brigade lost direction in its advance on the left of Hetman Char and the communication trench connecting it with the southwest corner of the Ismail Oglu Tepe spur. This caused a failure of the 29th Divisions attack and was a disaster. The 32nd brigade who had moved northeast instead of east attempted with great bravery, to take the communication trench from that direction, but it could not succeed in rectifying its original error. The capture of the communication trench was a vital part of the plan and therefore 33rd brigade including the 9th SF were sent up and ordered to take it at all costs. It has to be remembered that the 9thBn SF had already suffered grievous losses on 9th August and were a remnant of a battalion on 21/22 August. Col Scothern in his diary seemed less than sure of the outcome but worryingly unsure of exactly where they should be attacking. He says:

'The orders as far as can be ascertained, were to half left form on passing the original trenches dug near the orchard in the vicinity of Hetman Char'

It is not surprising that they repeated the same mistake as 32nd brigade and part of the Brigade marched northeast and the other southeast to Susak

Kuyu. Despite heroic efforts and many casualties the attack was yet another failure. With the Brigade machine gun section protecting the right flank, the 9th SF made some progress but the advance was again held up. On the 22nd they withdrew to the reserve trenches and the Battalion could take stock of the previous two weeks.

The Commander in Chief, Sir Ian Hamilton gave the 9thBn a special mention for their gallant bearing that day. He said in a supplementary dispatch dated 27th March 1916:

> *"Constantly maintaining stout hearts and a soldiery spirit in despite of heavy losses they had suffered when carrying out their costly duty of closing the big gap between the left of the Anzac troops and Chocolate Hill from August 8th – 14th. On August 21st this same battalion, together with the 6th Border regiment, displayed, in the words of the commander in chief, " a vigorous initiative combined with very steady discipline throughout the attack".*

Lieutenant-Colonel L. A. Bosanquet

9th Sherwood Foresters. He served at Tirah, and was in the action of Dargai and at the capture of the Sampagha and Arhanga Passes. He also served in the Bazar Valley obtained the medal with two clasps

Lieutenant-Colonel Bosanquet

To prevent even more loss of life the following morning, under cover of darkness, the troops were pulled back to their original line.

The 9thBn Sherwood Foresters lost their CO, Col Bosanquet who had not even recovered from his early wound before being killed in this battle. He has no known grave and is commemorated on the Helles Memorial with his date of death given as 22 August 1915. Major Blackburne was another officer killed in action and by the end of the day the 9th Bn had only two unwounded officers left. Major Blackburne is buried at Green Hill Cemetery not far from were he fell aged 42 years. He is one of the few identified men in the cemetery and his grave is I.C.2.

Also lost that day was 2nd/Lt E T Alpass who is also remembered on the Helles Memorial. Amongst the other ranks killed that day and commemorated on the Helles Memorial are Private George Dakin, Private Arthur Barlow aged 29 years, son of Mr and Mrs. G H Barlow of Staveley, Chesterfield Derby's and Private John S Brooke, aged 27 years, son of Mr.

BOSANQUET, LIONEL ARTHUR, of Cleddon Hall, co. Monmouth, Lieut.-Col., 9th Battn. The Sherwood Foresters (Notts. and Derby Regt.), eldest s. of the late Arthur Bosanquet, of Cleddon Hall, J.P., I.C.S., Judge, Bombay Presidency, by his wife, Matilda, dau. of Col. Andrew Crawford, and grandson of Augustus Henry Bosanquet, of Ossidge, Southgate, H.E.I.C.S.; *b.* Southgate, co. Herts., 29 Jan. 1862; educ. Mr. Rose's private school, Ramsgate, and Harrow; and the Royal Military College, Sandhurst; gazetted Lieut. to the Sherwood Foresters, 10 March, 1883, and promoted Capt. 8 May 1892, and Major 9 May, 1903. He served in the Tirah Campaign 1897-8, took part in the operations in the Bazar Valley (25-30 Dec. 1897), the action at Dargai, and in the capture of the Sampagha and Arhanga Passes, receiving the medal with two clasps; and retired in 1911. On the outbreak of war he rejoined and was given command of the 9th (Service) Battn. of his regt., 26 Oct., 1914. He went out to the Dardanelles and was in action from the 23 July to 22 Aug. 1915. He was wounded on 9 Aug. but rejoined in a week and was killed in action 22 Aug. 1915. Col. Bosanquet was killed (believed by machine guns) in Dead Man's Gully, while leading his battn. To quote from a General's letter, whose brigade found and buried his body: " He must have done well, for he was close up to the enemy, ahead of most of his men, who were stretched out behind him, never a one with his back turned, and all in perfect alignment." He was mentioned in Sir Ian Hamilton's Despatch of 11 Dec. 1915 [and published in the Supplement to the London Gazette dated 28 Jan. 1916], for gallant and distinguished service in the field. Col. Bosanquet *m.* at Crockham Hill, Kent, 31 Aug. 1892, Alice Emily (7, Springfield Place, Bath), 2nd dau. of the Rev. John Erskine Campbell-Colquhoun, of Killermont and Garscaddon, co. Dumbarton, M.A., J.P., D.L., formerly Vicar of Southwold and Crockham Hill, and grand-daughter of the late John Campbell-Colquhoun, of Killermont and Garscaddon, by his wife, the Hon. Henrietta Maria, née Powys, dau. of Thomas, 2nd Lord Lilford, and had issue: Cicely Alice Colquhoun, *b* 25 Nov. 1893; and Eveline Louise Emmeline, *b* 11 Jan. 1899.

Lionel A. Bosanquet.

The Sphere 20th November 1915

and Mrs. Brooke of 8 Upton Drive, Sherwood, Notts who also left a young widow Rose Mary.

Col Scothern put in his diary:

> *'...the casualties were again heavy. Only two officers were left, Lt-Col Bosanquet and Major Blackburn both being killed.'*

Lieutenant-Colonel Bosanquet is mentioned in the De Ruvigny Roll of Honour

The battalion was relieved on the night of the 22nd August and went to No 1 beach where a much-needed reorganization of the brigade took place. The 33rd brigade was formed into two composite battalions and the Sherwood Foresters found themselves combined with the 7th South Staffordshire battalion, the 6th Lincolns and the 6th Borders forming the other composite Battalion. The Brigade had been in the Sulva Bay area for two weeks and already the four Battalions had become two. The Sherwoods/South Staffs Battalion being commanded by Capt Duck. This in itself shows the amount of losses sustained in this period. Not only were they down to two fully functioning battalions but the C.O. was not a Lt-Colonel but a Captain.

Col Scothern listed casualties for this period as -:

Officers – killed 12 and wounded 17. Other Ranks – killed 143 and wounded 321.

An Infantry battalions' average establishment was about 1,000 all ranks, so it can be seen just how high the 9th SF Bn casualties had been in these two weeks, close to 50 % of the battalion killed or wounded in two battles. Even the 10% of the first reserve left at Mudros had been brought over after the battle of 9th August which meant that the Battalion had no men

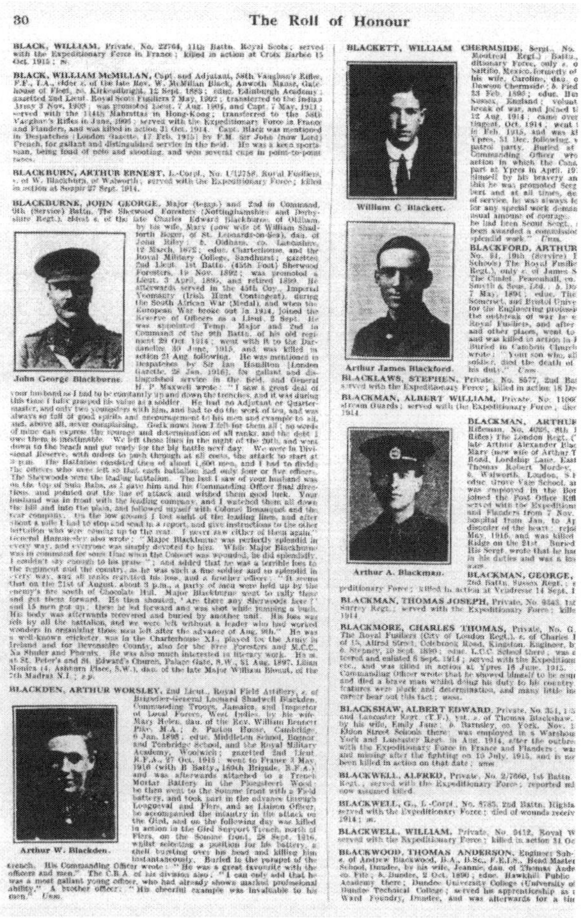
30 The Roll of Honour

John George Blackburne.

William C. Blackett.

Arthur James Blackford.

Arthur A. Blackman.

Arthur W. Blackden.

Major Blackburne is also mentioned in De Ruvigny

to call on as reserves. The men who did survive would though be battle hardened troops after the steepest of learning curves and the casualty figures would be lower throughout the rest of the war.

After the attacks of August it was slowly dawning on even the most ardent 'easterner' that the hoped for breakthrough would not happen. Slowly the ranks were thinned for other theatres of the war. The men survived, for that is what it had become, a battle for survival, on one pint of water and one tin of bully beef a day. The tinned bully beef turned to a soggy mushy mess in the heat and was more a drink than a food. Even the strongest of men succumbed to dysentery, cholera, heat stroke and various stomach ailments with very few escaping without contracting some disease or other. The official figures for the period 25 May to 30 October 1915 showed that of the 127,000 casualties, some 90,000 were through illness.

The composite battalion of 9th Sherwood's and 7th South Staffordshire moved up to positions on the eastern slope of Karakol Dagh on 27th August and began tours of duty in the front line around the area of Jephson's Post. They spent September and October in this area, firstly in the sector south of Jephson's Post and then just North, where the Battalion supplied many working parties. They alternated between the rest camp at West Beach and front line tours of duty. The tours were as follows – 27th August – 12 September – front line, 12th to 20th rest camp. Reinforcements including 23097 Private John Bateman arrived on 14th September. On 21st September the temporary amalgamation with the 7th South Staffordshire came to an end and the 9th were a battalion in their own right once again. The term in reserve at the rest camp is actually somewhat misleading as the battalion would provide working parties each night in the various trenches, particularly for the 9th around the Rotten Row area.

Col Scothern again gives mention to the battalions work during the month of September in the Jephson's Post area:

> *'Here they provided working parties for work on Green Lane, suffering considerable casualties in the process. It was exciting and dangerous work both here and in the Essex Ravine sector where a good deal of wiring was done. The work also included the building of grouse butts, and joining them up with sandbag walls'*

It is interesting to note how 'normal' Col Scothern seems to have found this period as he devotes one paragraph to the two months and terms it 'holding the line'.

October like September saw tours of duty in the front line followed by periods in reserve, which would see more trench digging. Men arrived as reinforcements on Sunday 10th October, one of these was 23175 Private John Newbold and he kept a diary. The reinforcements left Sunderland at 9 pm on Monday 13th September arriving at Devonport at 12 pm on 14th. The transport ship Aeneas sailed at 9 am on 15th arriving at Gibraltar at 9.30pm on 19th. They arrived at Malta on 23rd at 8 am leaving the following day at 5 pm. On Monday 27th the ship arrived at Mudros on Lemnos and the men would remain until 10th October. An attempt was made to sail for Gallipoli on 9th October but after four or five miles the ship returned owing to the rough seas. At 6 am on 10th, the men marched to the coast leaving Mudros on the S.S. Osmanieh at 1.30 pm. The ship arrived in Suvla Bay at midnight and then the men had a three-hour march up hills with full pack, rifle and 120 rounds of SAA. All the time the Turkish snipers were very busy. John would remain until 26th November when he reported sick with septic soles and was sent to Malta and hospital arriving on 3rd December. His diary entries for the period Monday 11th October to 15th November –

Monday 11th Trench digging from 11 pm to 4 am.
Tuesday 12th Bathing parade 11 am. On guard in Ducks Nest from 6.30pm to 6.20 pm (13th) 24 hours
Wednesday 13th ————
Thursday 14th. Digging from 11 pm to 4 am (the 15th)
Friday 15th ————
Saturday 16th On Guard Green Nullah 11pm to 11pm on the 17th. Bread jam and water for meals.
*Sunday 17th and Monday 18th – (*nothing mentioned*)*
Tuesday 19 Road repairing, Bathing parade 2.30.
Wednesday 20. Timber carrying, Groceries etc.
Thursday 21 Digging 11 to 2. 5 to 8. Tea 8.30. Had to gather sticks to boil water (quite dark) Turks busy sniping.
Friday 22 Digging 8 am to 3. Trenches 8 to 10 pm.
Saturday 23 Rifle inspection 10.30.
Sunday 24. Making dugouts.
Monday 25. Making dugouts 8 to 11 am. Bathing parade 12pm Dinner (stew) 1pm. 1.30 to 5 pm carrying provisions.
Tuesday 26 Making dugouts 7.30 am to 5 pm (Dinner one slice of bread and jam)
Wednesday 27th Rifle exercises, water carrying. Digging 6 to 10 pm. No time for tea.
Thursday 28 Rifle exercises 7.45 to 8.45 Digging 6 to 10 pm.
Friday 29- 25 hours guard (no tea)
Saturday 30 Making dugouts 7.30
Sunday 31st Removed to A Beach.
Monday Nov 1.to Thursday 4th – Digging 2 pm to 5pm
Friday 5th Drill 9 to 10. Bomb throwing. (Also on 6th)
Sunday 7th Bomb throwing. Feet inspection.
Monday 8th to 15th – In trenches.
Nov 26. Reported sick with septic soles. Sent to hospital by doctor. Terrible storm in Gallipoli. Left Suvla Bay on the hospital boat Rewa. Arrived Malta Dec 3rd.

After recovering John would be transferred and serve in the Loyal North Lancs Regiment.

More men joined the battalion on 25th October including 15298 Private Harry Goodall and 25003 Private Thomas Harris.

8890 Corporal Edward Wood also joined the Battalion. He had served as a regular from 1903 to 1906 and as a reservist since then. On the outbreak of war he was recalled and went to France with the 2nd battalion. At some point in1915 he returned to England and on 19th August was in "K" Company, 3rd Reserve Battalion. The next entry in his pay book shows September 12th at Mudros West followed by 29th October – Gallipoli. Edward was with the Battalion in Egypt and remembered visiting the Pyramids and also bathing in the Nile. Edward spent some time as a Company Clerk during 1917. From 22 December 1917 until 5 January 1918 he was on leave in England. He was transferred to the Army Reserve on 4th March 1919.

23175 Private John Newbold

The men would no doubt have been heartened to know that decisions in October would see their suffering come to an end but not for two more agonizing months. Sir Charles Monro replaced Sir Ian Hamilton and he quickly realized that the troops had to be withdrawn.

At the beginning of November the battalion went for seven days rest and into Corps reserve. It has to

8890 Corporal Edward Wood

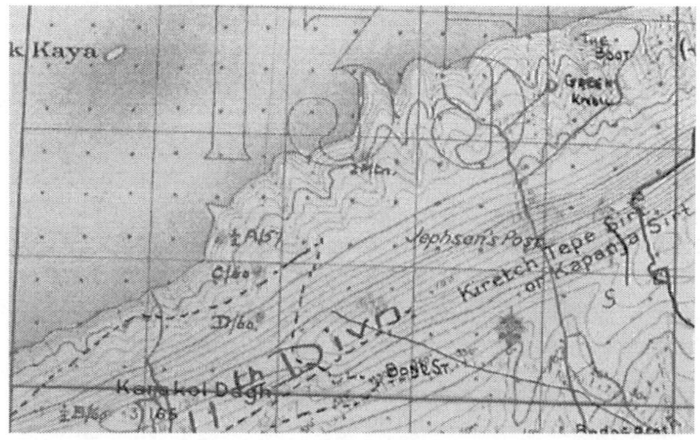

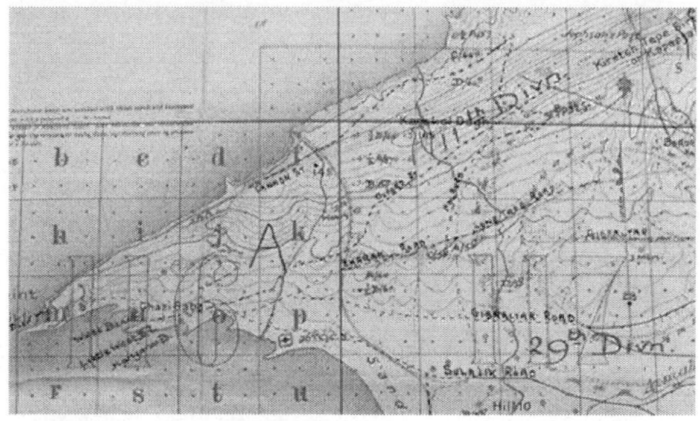

11th Division 15th November 1915 – the 9th Battalion was located around Jephson's Post

be remembered that, although in reserve, they did not leave the Sulva area and as one wag mentioned when talking of 'rest' on Gallipoli – ' As a shell burst nearby, he was asked, why is it called a rest camp. He replied – the front line get most of the shells and bullets and we get the rest' – How true this was.

The Battalion moved to the forward area on 11th November and were in the Lone Tree Gully sector of the line. This area was Leather Lane, near Oxford Circus, Oxford Street behind Jephson's Post. This was the sector that the Brigade would hold until the evacuation. Once again they enjoyed the pleasures of digging communication trenches near Jephson's Post before going into the firing line at Jephson's post itself. The battalion being relieved by their sister Battalion the 6th Lincolnshire's on 24th November, but not going into reserve but to a line on the slopes leading from Karakol Dagh to Salt Lake. This would be a significant move and in the following days cause the battalion more casualties.

On 26th November 1915 the area was again affected by 'unusual weather' and this time gales and thunderstorms would cause havoc. Trenches filled with water and those on the slopes became white water rapids as they swept all before them, equipment, kit and men. The men who had suffered from heat, flies, dysentery, lack of food and water must have wondered what they had done to deserve this torrent. To compound matters, the torrential rain was followed by a hard frost and a blizzard. Many men suffered from exposure and at least 200 died during this period. Col Scothern continues with what he calls:

> *'...the only noteworthy incident of November' '...the great gale on the 27th. The battalion was in support at the time. A heavy S.W. gale brought a thunderstorm accompanied by torrents of rain, which lasted for 24 hours. The trenches were flooded, and the men were carried off their feet by the force of water. All the dugouts were flooded, and there was not a dry corner in the whole battalion area. Battalion H.Q., which had a roof made of beaten out biscuit tins covered with earth, leaked like a sieve, and a spring developed in the side of it. Notwithstanding, the battalion was much more fortunate than those in the line'. He continues to describe the snow that followed and the casualties ' Later, the wind changed to north, and snow descended in whirling blizzards for nearly two days and nights. The surface of the pools and trenches froze to thick ice, and many men were frost*

bitten. Some could not be accounted for until a search had been made at the Field Ambulance and casualty Clearing Station on the Beach. The sight there almost defied description. The whole area was covered with stretchers, on which lay men so enfeebled that they could not move to perform the ordinary duties of nature. Some men were even lying on the ground. Few can realize the suffering entailed.'

The only ray of hope was that in two weeks the men would be at last rid of Gallipoli for good. Private Newbold would take no further part though as a foot infection curtailed his stay on Gallipoli. Young James Walters was in the same draft as Newbold and he would survive until 1916.

Major Gater took command of the Battalion in mid November and life until the evacuation went on as normal or as normal as it could be on Gallipoli. The trench routine and the digging of reserve defences combined with the erection of strong bands of wire and mining operations along the whole front. The forthcoming evacuations only chance of success was in duping the Turks into believing that everything was normal. As the battalion waited for their evacuation the trench tours of duty continued. On 1st December they moved to Lone Tree Gully in reserve and on 8th relieved the 7th South Staffordshire's in the firing line and on 9th found themselves in the Grouse Butts, which they had helped construct in September. Finally on the 18th/19th December the evacuation began the battalion left the trenches and embarked for Imbros. Col Scothern saw it thus *'Sunday December 19th was abnormally quiet and depressing'.*

Only depleted Battalions were holding the line and there were no troops in support or reserve. If the Turks had got wind of the planned withdrawal then there would be little hope for the remaining troops. The Turks did shell the area during the morning but, despite fears of an attack being imminent, nothing happened.

Col. Scothern again noted in his diary:

"In the evening a message came through saying that a Turkish prisoner just captured had stated that the noises on the beach had alarmed the Turks, who thought they signified preparations for a new attack".

No doubt the few remaining men left holding the front line felt the same alarm as the Turkish shelling commenced.

At about 8 pm on the evening of 19th, the Battalion HQ and the remainder of the 9th Bn, less some 70 men, left the line and on reaching the third line defences, waited for orders. A message was received that all had gone well and the remaining 70 men vacated the frontline trenches at 12.15 am on 20th. Before leaving the front line they destroyed or damaged any remaining stores. The automatic rifle firing system was also set in motion, which would keep the Turks in their trenches and stop any enemy probing.

The feelings of those last 70 Sherwood Foresters can only be imagined, for death or capture would have been certain had the Turks suspected anything at all. Amazingly the Battalion's withdrawal went unnoticed by the Turks and also without any problems. A weary but relieved Battalion finally vacated the hell which was Gallipoli and arrived safely at Imbros. The Battalions withdrawal had also been without one casualty, which in itself was amazing.

At Imbros the battalion could relax, despite the occasional attentions of the Turkish Air Force that is. The men of the Battalion spent a pleasant few weeks and enjoyed a 'peaceful' Christmas and New Year. After their trials and tribulations since the end of July, few expected to see Christmas or 1916, let alone enjoy the festive season.

Col Scothern again noted:

"The stay at Imbros was pleasant. Many parcels arrived for the men and on Boxing night around a bonfire an impromptu concert was arranged which was enjoyed vastly by all present. The time was spent in training and sports..."

Depleted battalions were left holding the line and by 9th January 1916, Suvla Bay, Cape Helles and Anzac were empty but many of their comrades would remain forever.

The allied troops would leave behind some 25,000 men, many of whom are commemorated on the Helles Memorial. The 9thBn Sherwood Foresters have their share of names on this memorial and they would return a much different Battalion than the one that sailed from Liverpool on 1st July 1915. The men from Nottinghamshire and Derbyshire who had volunteered from August 1914 had done their counties and its Regiment proud. The Battalion would have a total of 716 fatalities of all ranks during the war, whilst in Gallipoli 221 all ranks were killed in action, died of wounds or illness. This means that of the total fatalities during World War 1 suffered by the Battalion, some 29% were during the

Gallipoli campaign. Taking the average of two wounded for every man killed, the Battalions casualties for this period would be about 400 wounded to add to the deaths.

So ended the year 1915 for the 9th Battalion Sherwood Foresters. Not a man knew what lay ahead but they did know that it would not be pleasant. Before the next New Year many more of their comrades would lie under some foreign soil.

The Newspapers at home would soon be telling the tale of this epic Battle and listing the casualties. The dreaded telegrams would be delivered to over 200 families of the 9th Battalion's men. The men wounded would send their letters home to a relieved family. The men who survived unscathed would spend months in Egypt, recovering from their ordeal. Newspaper reports, cards and photos – these deserve to be printed in full to show the feeling of the time. The first article gives a first hand account of the fighting on the 9th August and the cost in men.

The Derby Daily Telegraph, Tuesday August 31st 1915

"Derby Soldier's Experiences in Gallipoli
Lay wounded on Battlefield four days.
Maimed but Cheerful

Further corroborations on the terrible fighting which has taken place in Gallipoli is furnished by Lance-corporal A. C. Heath, of the 9th Sherwoods, in a letter received from him this (Tuesday) morning by his parents, Mr. and Mrs. Arthur Heath, of Statham street, Derby. The writer enlisted as soon as war broke out last year, and was one of first to volunteer at Dalbury Lees, where he was a pupil on a farm. He went out from Liverpool on July 1st with the 9th Sherwoods and after stopping at Alexandria three days, landed at Gallipoli where his regiment was destined to suffer many casualties. His parents were naturally anxious, as they had no news concerning him for some time, but they have now had a letter describing the wounds he received and his experiences when lying wounded and helpless on the battlefield for four days. Although maimed for life however, this young man of 22 treats the matter with remarkable pluck, and this should help lessen his parents' grief. Writing to his mother from on board the hospital ship Salta on August 15, Lance-corporal Heath says: -

Just a few lines to let you know I have at last got wounded. I am not half wounded, either. I had a bullet right through my right knee, and I also had an explosive bullet right through my left leg, which shattered it to bits. This happened just a week ago. It wasn't until last Thursday that I was found, and then I lay all that while with nothing to eat or drink. I can't get much on this P.C. (Postcard), but will write as soon as I am settled down in hospital. We should reach Malta tonight. All men got very seriously wounded will stay there, the others going on to Southampton. I will write from there when I know my address. There are a few things I should like. When we left the Gallipoli Peninsula there were over 800 wounded officers and men, but over 30 have died since then. Tell everybody that I can't write, as I have not got a scrap of paper till I get to hospital. It's just like being at home on here. The nurses and doctors are very nice, and nothing is too much trouble for the orderlies. My two doctors say I shall be at least three months before fit for anything.

In a letter written to his mother from E Ward of the Royal Naval Hospital at Malta on August 22nd, Lance-corporal Heath says:

It's not very nice having to be on my back all this while, and to lie here and write this miserable letter. I told you on the postcard that I got severely wounded on the Monday, August 9th, and was four days before anybody dare go and find me. Fancy me all that while without anything to eat or drink! The Turks kept having a shot at me as I lay there, but, thank goodness, they didn't wound me any more. A very near shave I had when a bullet just entered my tunic (Khaki drill), but it turned out again, that was plump in the middle of my back. I have cut the piece of cloth out to send you so that you can keep it as a souvenir. I guess I do look pretty; I have not had a shave for over a fortnight. I shall be leaving this hospital soon for England, then you can send me what I want. Whilst I lay in hospital here my leg started to bleed like a tap. The doctor said I should have bled to death in ten minutes had I not have told them soon enough. Through this I had to undergo an operation to have my arteries nipped and fastened. I was under chloroform about one and three-quarter hours. The day after I had to go under another operation to have my leg taken off. It is only off for about four or six inches below the knee, so when it gets properly healed up I shall be able to have something fastened on it, and nobody will know that I am short of anything. It has been very painful since it was taken off, and I have been put on milk diet. I haven't had a crumb of anything to eat for three days. My temperature was 102 when I was admitted to hospital. It has been lower, but has got to 102 again now. I haven't time to write more now, as it is time for letters to be in. Remember me to every-body.

A brave young man indeed.

Mansfield & North Notts Advertiser 17 September 1915

The Gallant Sherwoods.

"The Duke of Portland (Welbeck Abbey) has received a letter from an officer of the 9th Service Battalion, The Sherwood Foresters, noting the fact that it was on the 9th August, 1914, that the first hundred recruits for that battalion were obtained at the Derby Depot, and that it was on the anniversary of that day that the men of the battalion were severely and seriously engaged on important duty in the Dardanelles.

'I do not know,' the officer writes, ' how much I may say about the show we made, but I can say that the job carried out by the battalion would not have been an easy job for a brigade. The battalion did it, and was holding on 48 hours after the time I was hit. Our losses were very heavy, as you will no doubt have heard, especially in officers. All ranks were perfectly splendid, and I think I may say that Nottinghamshire and Derbyshire will have no need to be ashamed of anything they hear of the battalion collectively or individually.'

It will, as the Duke of Portland remarks, interest the inhabitants of Nottinghamshire and Derbyshire to be reminded of this anniversary and to have this testimony of one who was in the action. ' I am sure,' adds his Grace, ' we shall feel proud of the services rendered by the men of the two counties".

One of the men killed on 9th August 1915 was William Johnson son of William and Annie of Kings Mead Lodge Wantage Berks. Prior to the war he was a gardener on the Duke of Portland's estate at Welbeck Abbey.

Below the 9th Bn Sherwood Foresters report is another as follows –

First Eakring Soldier to fall

"On Friday last the sad news reached the village of Eakring of the death of Private H. Rowland at the Dardanelles. This promising young soldier is the first of Eakring's sons to lay down his life for King and country during the present war, and much sympathy is felt with his parents who have two other sons taking their part in the struggle against German aggression. The organist played the ' Dead March', at the evening service at the Parish Church, and several of the congregation were moved to tears."

Private H Rowland died of wounds at sea on 22 August 1915 and is buried at East Mudros Military Cemetery.

PRIVATE JOHN DRING.

Private John Dring, of the 9th Sherwood Foresters, has been wounded during the fighting in the Gallipoli Peninsula, where the 9th have sustained heavy losses. He joined last October, when he was a miner at Crown Farm Colliery, and his home is at 3, Bull-yard, Westgate, Mansfield. Since he was wounded in the foot, he has been taken ill with dysentery and is now in hospital at Malta. Although very weak, he was getting on satisfactorily when the last letter arrived from him.

John Dring – News article Friday 8 October 1915. ***The Mansfield and North Notts Advertiser.***

Casualty lists were printed daily in all of the newspapers.

The casualty list reveals and emphasizes the severity of the fighting on the Gallipoli Peninsula in which the 9th. Batt. Sherwood Foresters have taken a strenuous and fearless part. Monday's list contained the names of 52 killed, 80 wounded and 9 missing. The high percentage of the killed as compared with the total demonstrates the unexampled fierceness of this grim struggle which is being waged there. The list brings sad news to many local homes, for it will be remembered that the battalion, which was raised in August and September, is composed mainly of men from Nottinghamshire."

It was only after starting my research that I found that John Dring was in fact a member of the family.

The bad news in the newspapers continued into October as more casualty lists were printed.

The Mansfield and Notts Advertiser of 15th October 1915 had the following :-

Sherwood's Losses
Heavy Casualties during recent fighting
"A considerable number of casualties among the Sherwood Foresters have been issued for publication during the week. They include the following: –

Killed – 9th Battalion – Dardanelles
Pte J Bowler 13322, Pte. S W Hodgkiss 21279. Pte. G. Hudson 17824, Pte G. Luntley 12615.
Died Of Wounds
Pte. R C. Britland 12779, Pte, A Howitt 12998.
Wounded and Missing –
Private A.E. Turton, 13934.
Wounded –
C.G.M.S, J Whitworth, 9645.
L/Cpls D. Barber, 13039. W. Broomhead, 12783. J A Reeds, 12744.
Privates, Allesbrook, 12578. H Booth, 12849. H Brocklehurst, 12824. N Butler, 17812.
H Cameron, 17817. D Hobson, 13395. G Muran, 13107. J Taylor, 12687. A Thorp, 18095.

There is also an article on the same page –
Tenth Huthwaite Victim
"A memorial service was held at Huthwaite church on Sunday night to Private Jos' Bowler 13322, 9th Sherwoods, who was recently killed in action. He was 22 years of age, and lived at 85, Blackwell Road, Huthwaite, and became the tenth Huthwaite man to be killed in the war. The Rev. F. N. Beswick conducted the service, which was of a very impressive character. The Union Jack flew at half-mast on the church tower, and on the conclusion of the service the Dead March from 'Saul' was played"

Private Joseph Bowler was killed on 6th September 1915 and is buried at Azmak Military Cemetery, Sulva – grave I F 8

Drummer Bertrand Parker wrote home from Hospital in Alexandria. Not all is readable but it is worth including.

"... resting favourably, but I cannot. I shall remain here some time. ......The bullets passed through some.. the shoulder and they have strapped it tightly. We had a week on the hospital ship before we were taken to Alexandria. This place is not bad but it is terribly hot as you will expect but we are close down by the sea in a canvas hospital so we do not feel the heat as much as you would think. I have received no letters since I left England, (although his Mother had sent many letters and parcels).

The Doctor seemed to think mine was a serious case. We were under shellfire directly we got on the beach and shells were falling all around us. It seemed marvellous that we were not all wiped out when we got into the open. I had a .... in the trenches. This writing is not so bad for one arm."

On the Friday August 13th edition of The Derby Daily Telegraph, Bert Parker was mentioned.

Cromford Comrades Wounded
"News has reached Cromford that two local comrades had been wounded, one in France and the other at the Dardanelles.

They are Private John Gould and Private Bert Parker, the first being reported wounded in the head, not seriously, in France. No further details are yet to hand of the second man. Private Parker was Assistant Scoutmaster of the Cromford Boy Scouts, and Private Gould a member of the troop. Both wounded soldiers worked at the Lea Hosiery Mill prior to the war".

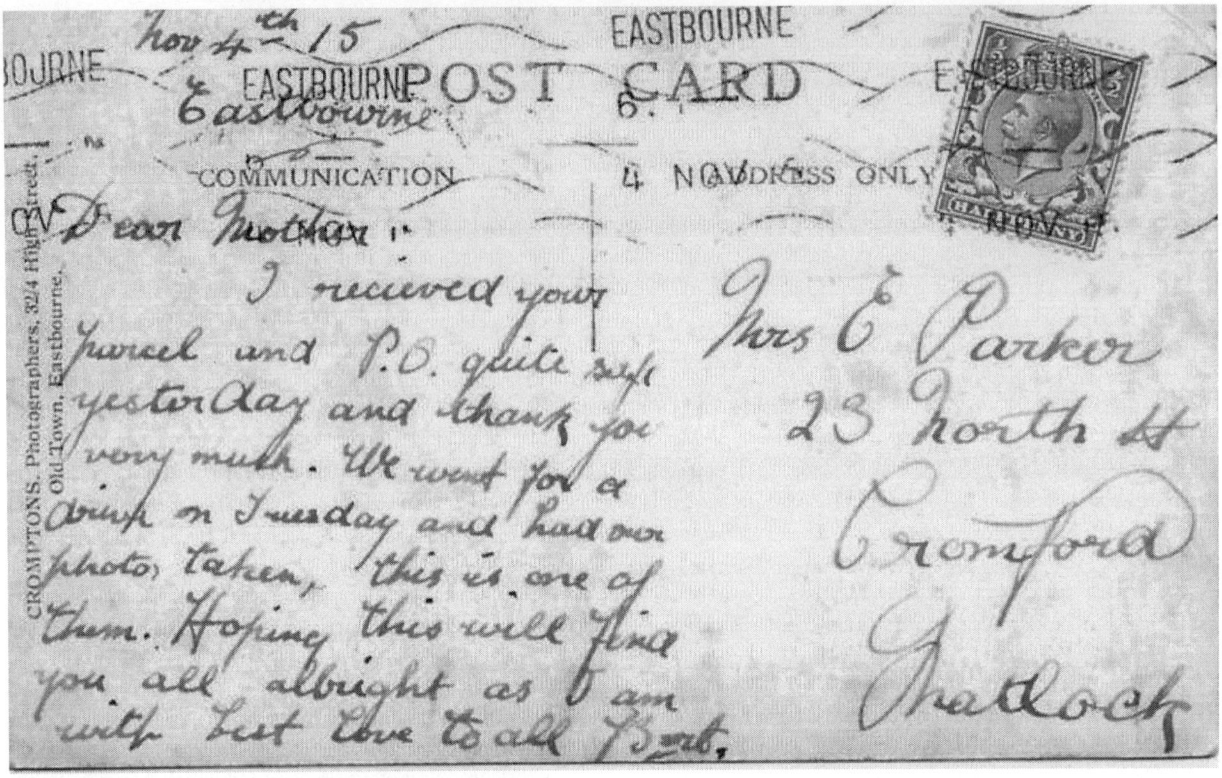

POST CARD

COMMUNICATION

ADDRESS ONLY

CROMPTONS, Photographers, 32/4 High Street, Old Town, Eastbourne.

Nov 4th 15
Eastbourne

Dear Mother
I recieved your parcel and P.O. quite safe yesterday and thank you very much. We went for a drive on Tuesday and had our photo taken, this is one of them. Hoping this will find you all alright as I am with best love to all Bert

Mrs E Parker
23 North St
Cromford
Matlock

Drummer Parkers Card to his Mother

Bertrand Parker and Friend continue on their road to recovery.

The *Derby Daily Telegraph* dated Monday August 23rd 1915 mentioned officers wounded:

Lieut Colonel L A Bosanquet, 9th Sherwoods
Lieut J F M Hind, 9th Sherwoods

By the time this newspaper hit the streets the C.O. Lieut Colonel Bosanquet was already dead, being killed on 22 August. Lieut Hind would be killed on the Somme, 27 September 1916.

The *Derby Daily Telegraph* dated 27th August 1915 listed men wounded:

All of the men mentioned, being Privates in the 9th Battalion.

E, Cheetham, 22556. A. Fox, 18093. L. Grindle, 9535. A.H. Hardwidge, 6074.

W.G. Mitchell, 12837. W.H. Randall, 13167. W. Spurr, 13247. E. Townsend, 21411.

C.A. Turner, 13364. W.H. Vernon, 12890. J. Wells, 13195.

Towns and Villages throughout Nottinghamshire and Derbyshire would be grieving. The Mansfield, Nott's War Memorial shows that the following men of that town were killed during the Gallipoli campaign:

William Ainsworth – 9 August 1915.
Levi Thomas Grice – 30 December 1915 (Died of Wounds in Malta)

Drummer Parker with fellow convalesces – 4th November 1915 after returning to England

William Charles Hazelwood – 23 November 1915.
John William Lenton – 9 August 1915.
Tom Wilcockson – 9 August 1915.
Arthur Willies – 24 September 1915.

Roll of Honour for the 9th Battalion

The majority of the men have no known grave.
Of those men killed in action, Died of wounds or illness -:
14 are buried in Azmak Cemetery, Suvla Bay.
4 are buried in Hill 10 Cemetery, Suvla.
6 are buried in Green Hill Cemetery, Suvla.
1 is buried at Lala Baba Cemetery, Suvla.
3 are buried at Lancashire Landing Cemetery, Helles.
2 are buried at Redoubt Cemetery, Helles.
1 is buried at Skew Bridge Cemetery, Helles.
7 are buried at Alexandria (Chatby) Military and War Memorial Cemetery.
5 are buried at East Mudros Military Cemetery.
10 are buried at Pieta Military Cemetery, Malta.
1 is buried at Portianos Military Cemetery, Lemnos
166 are commemorated on the Helles Memorial.

Surname	Forename	Number	Rank		Date	Grave/Memorial
Buxton	Ernest	22628	Private	d o w	04/10,1915	Alexandria (Chatby) mil
Chatterton	Arthur Francis	12986	Private	d o w	25/09,1915	Alexandria (Chatby) mil
Deary	Joseph	13249	Private	d o w	27/11,1915	Alexandria (Chatby) mil
Ford	George Henry	12502	Private	d o w	25/08,1915	Alexandria (Chatby) mil
Mills	Job	13272	Private	d o w	14/09,1915	Alexandria (Chatby) mil
Taylor	George	13066	Private	died	12/08,1915	Alexandria (Chatby) mil
Webster	Arthur	18090	Private	d o w	29/08,1915	Alexandria (Chatby) mil
Stocks	Joseph Henry	13155	Private	k in a	13/11,1915	Azmak Cem Suvla
Kitchen	Frederick	22003	Private	k in a	14/11,1915	Azmak Cem Sulva
Street	Samuel	17004	A/Cpl	k in a	29/11,1915	Azmak Cem Suvla
Paull	Frederick Major		2/Lt	k in a	27/11,1915	Azmak Cem Suvla
Palmer	Samuel J	22290	Private	k in a	27/11,1915	Azmak Cem Suvla
Heywood	Frank	20307	Private	k in a	29/11,1915	Azmak Cem Suvla
Jarvis	John	22968	Private	k in a	13/11,1915	Azmak Cem Suvla
Hopkinson	John Thomas	13512	Private	died	17/11,1915	Azmak Cem Suvla
Griffiths	Stanley	17012	Private	k in a	16/12,1915	Azmak Cem Suvla

Lowe	Charles	12678	Private	k in a	29/08,1915	Azmak Cem Suvla
Goddard	William	20320	Private	d o w	05/10,1915	Azmak Cem Suvla
Bowler	Joseph	13322	Private	k in a	06/09,1915	Azmak Cem Suvla
Hodgkiss	Frederick W	21279	Private	k in a	06/09,1915	Azmak Cem Suvla
Sheldon	William	5061	Private	k in a	19/11,1915	Azmak Cem Suvla
Black	Robert	6480	Private	died at sea	16/10,1915	East Mudros Mil Cem
Dickin	George Henry	22022	Private	died at sea	04/12,1915	East Mudros Mil Cem
Patterson	William Arthur	13396	Private	d o w	09/10,1915	East Mudros Mil Cem
Rowland	John H	12572	Private	d o w at sea	22/08,1915	East Mudros Mil Cem
Towey	James	18000	Private	died	14/08,1915	East Mudros Mil Cem
Thorpe	Edgar Wilkes	22961	Private	k in a	15/10,1915	Green Hill Cemetery
Malkin	Walter	6107	Drummer	k in a	09/08,1915	Green Hill Cemetery
Mitchell	Joseph	8421	Corporal	k in a	09/08,1915	Green Hill Cemetery
Wortley	Frank	18113	Private	k in a	09/08,1915	Green Hill Cemetery
Blackburne	John George		Major	k in a	22/08,1915	Green Hill Cemetery
West	William		2/Lt	k in a	07/08,1915	Green Hill Cemetery
Ainsworth	William	13406	Private	k in a	09/08,1915	Helles Memorial
Allpass	Esmond Theodore		2/Lt	k in a	21/08,1915	Helles Memorial
Ambridge	George William	12879	L/Cpl	k in a	09/08,1915	Helles Memorial
Annison	Richard W	6102	CSM	k in a	09/08,1915	Helles Memorial
Arthurs	Henry	12494	Private	k in a	09/08,1915	Helles Memorial
Bacon	James	22029	Private	d o w	05/12,1915	Helles Memorial
Bancroft	Frederick	3952	Cpl	k in a	09/08,1915	Helles Memorial
Barber	Joseph	12793	L/Cpl	k in a	09/08,1915	Helles Memorial
Barlow	Arthur H	12411	Private	k in a	21/08,1915	Helles Memorial
Beard	Fred	13300	Private	k in a	09/08,1915	Helles Memorial
Birks	Thomas	13376	Private	k in a	09/08,1915	Helles Memorial
Black	Thomas Porteous		Captain	k in a	09/08,1915	Helles Memorial
Blythe	George	12525	Private	k in a	09/08,1915	Helles Memorial
Boilstone	Horace	12768	Private	k in a	14/10,1915	Helles Memorial
Bosanquet	Lionel Arthur		Lt-Col	k in a	22/08,1915	Helles Memorial
Bradbury	Edward	6464	Corporal	k in a	09/08,1915	Helles Memorial
Brooke	John Stanley	20321	Private	k in a	21/08,1915	Helles Memorial
Brown	Frederick Charles		2/Lt	k in a	07/08,1915	Helles Memorial
Bugg	Arthur James	27853	Private	k in a	09/08,1915	Helles Memorial
Burgess	Fred	12532	Private	k in a	09/08,1915	Helles Memorial
Burgess	Robert Clark	23152	L/Cpl	k in a	02/10,1915	Helles Memorial
Burton	Henry Cecil	18069	Private	k in a	09/08,1915	Helles Memorial
Calvert	Maurice	12560	Private	k in a	09/08,1915	Helles Memorial
Camm	Harry	12347	L/Cpl	k in a	09/08,1915	Helles Memorial
Card	Arthur S	12545	L/Cpl	k in a	09/08,1915	Helles Memorial
Carey	Henry Pattison		Lt.	k in a	7-11/08,1915	Helles Memorial
Cartwright	Joseph	22508	Private	k in a	10/08,1915	Helles Memorial
Carver	Walter CS	17011	Private	k in a	10/08,1915	Helles Memorial
Casburn	Edward	13054	A/Sgt	k in a	27/08,1915	Helles Memorial
Checkley	Herbert	13276	Private	k in a	09/08,1915	Helles Memorial
Clark	John J H	21264	Private	k in a	09/08,1915	Helles Memorial
Clarke	John Percy	13160	Private	k in a	09/08,1915	Helles Memorial
Cooper	Richard	17928	Private	d o w at sea	03/12.1915	Helles Memorial
Cottrell	Albert	12452	Corporal	k in a	09/08,1915	Helles Memorial
Cottrell	Henry (Harry)	12454	L/Sgt	k in a	09/08,1915	Helles Memorial
Croysdill	Norman	12552	Private	k in a	09/08,1915	Helles Memorial
Daft	George	3919	Private	k in a	09/08,1915	Helles Memorial

Dakin	George	21275	'Private	k in a	21/08,1915	Helles Memorial
Dallison	John William	17924	Private	k in a	09/08,1915	Helles Memorial
Dawn	John	17948	L/Cpl	k in a	09/08,1915	Helles Memorial
Dawson	John James	13019	L/Sgt	k in a	09/08,1915	Helles Memorial
Elliott	Hiram	13199	Private	k in a	09/08,1915	Helles Memorial
Evans	William L	12799	Private	k in a	09/08,1915	Helles Memorial
Everett	John	12588	Private	k in a	09/08,1915	Helles Memorial
Ewin	Arthur, Hon		Lt/QM	k in a	7-11/08,1915	Helles Memorial
Farrell	Thomas	12884	Private	k in a	09/09,1915	Helles Memorial
Fell	Alfred.	9758	L/Sgt	k in a	09/08,1915	Helles Memorial
Fern	Thomas	13251	Private	d o w	10/08,1915	Helles Memorial
Fletcher	Francis William	13006	Private	k in a	09/08,1915	Helles Memorial
Ford	Austin Thomas	12706	Private	k in a	09/08,1915	Helles Memorial
Frith	John Peter	12559	Private	k in a	09/08,1915	Helles Memorial
Gamble	Thomas	13379	Private	k in a	09/08,1915	Helles Memorial
Gibbons	Fred	19840	Private	k in a	15/10,1915	Helles Memorial
Gilham	John William.DCM	6115	A/Sgt	k in a	09/08,1915	Helles Memorial
Glover	Harry	18080	Private	k in a	09/08,1915	Helles Memorial
Goodband	Christopher	13557	Private	k in a	28/09,1915	Helles Memorial
Grant	Charles Henry	13056	Private	k in a	27/11,1915	Helles Memorial
Gundry	Benjamin	22515	Private	k in a	09/08,1915	Helles Memorial
Hall	Arthur	12579	Private	k in a	09/08,1915	Helles Memorial
Hall	George	12711	Private	d o w	25/08,1915	Helles Memorial
Hallam	James Arthur	20343	Private	k in a	09/08,1915	Helles Memorial
Hallam	Walter Pemberton	13071	Private	k in a	09/08,1915	Helles Memorial
Hancock	Cyril	12607	Private	k in a	09/08,1915	Helles Memorial
Harris	Leonard	12408	L/Cpl	k in a	09/08,1915	Helles Memorial
Heap	Francis William	12493	L/Cpl	k in a	25/08,1915	Helles Memorial
Hemming	Frank	13283	Private	k in a	09/08,1915	Helles Memorial
Hempshall	George	13191	Private	k in a	09/08,1915	Helles Memorial
Hemsley	Francis	16996	Private	d o w	11/08,1915	Helles Memorial
Hewitt	George	3999	Private	d o w	09/08,1915	Helles Memorial
Hill	John George	18016	Private	k in a	09/08,1915	Helles Memorial
Holliday	Clarence Percy	13558	L/Cpl	d o w	06/10,1915	Helles Memorial
Hood	Reginald Smith	12418	Private	k in a	09/08,1915	Helles Memorial
Hopkinson	William	22510	Private	died at sea	25/10,1915	Helles Memorial
Hopwood	Robert	18046	Private	k in a	09/08,1915	Helles Memorial
Howard	Frank Edward	13035	Private	d o w	19/08,1915	Helles Memorial
Hudson	Charles S	13186	L/Cpl	k in a	09/08,1915	Helles Memorial
Hudson	George Henry	17824	Private	k in a	22/09,1915	Helles Memorial
Humphreys	William D	13883	L/Cpl	k in a	09/08,1915	Helles Memorial
Hunt	Alfred James	23038	Private	d o w	15/10,1915	Helles Memorial
Ives	James	12523	Private	k in a	09/08,1915	Helles Memorial
Jackson	William	27863	Private	k in a	09/08,1915	Helles Memorial
Johnson	William	13096	A/Sgt	k in a	09/08,1915	Helles Memorial
Kennett	Frederick William	12968	Private	k in a	09/08,1915	Helles Memorial
Kirk	John James	22505	Private	k in a	09/08,1915	Helles Memorial
Knowles	William	12893	Private	k in a	09/08,1915	Helles Memorial
Lakin	William	3981	Private	k in a	09/08,1915	Helles Memorial
Leeson	Frank	21274	Private	k in a	09/08,1915	Helles Memorial
Legge	John M	14050	L/Cpl	k in a	09/08,1915	Helles Memorial
Lenton	John William	17935	Private	k in a	09/08,1915	Helles Memorial
Lilliman	Joseph	12833	Private	k in a	09/08,1915	Helles Memorial

Loane	Samuel	27857	Private	k in a	09/08,1915	Helles Memorial
Lomax	Louis	12488	Private	k in a	09/08,1915	Helles Memorial
Lovell	Arthur	13263	Private	k in a	21/08,1915	Helles Memorial
Ludlam	Geo	12483	Private	k in a	09/08,1915	Helles Memorial
Luntley	Geoffrey	12615	Private	k in a	09/08,1915	Helles Memorial
Mahoney	John	12922	Private	k in a	04/10,1915	Helles Memorial
Mallinder	Thomas	12903	Private	k in a	04/09,1915	Helles Memorial
Martin	James	13903	L/Cpl	k in a	09/08,1915	Helles Memorial
Maskrey	Francis	12590	A/Cpl	k in a	09/08,1915	Helles Memorial
Mayfield	Horace	12614	Private	k in a	09/08,1915	Helles Memorial
Mayo	William Charles		Lt	k in a	7-11/08,1915	Helles Memorial
Michie	James Halley	12605	L/Cpl	k in a	09/08,1915	Helles Memorial
Mills	Samuel	12797	Private	k in a	09/08,1915	Helles Memorial
Milward	Walter	6090	CSM	d o w at sea	29/08,1915	Helles Memorial
Moorcroft	Edgar	13027	Private	d o w at sea	02/09,1915	Helles Memorial
Noble	Henry	13243	Private	k in a	09/08,1915	Helles Memorial
Oates	James	22149	Private	k in a	04/10,1915	Helles Memorial
Pass	Morris E	23290	Private	k in a	09/08,1915	Helles Memorial
Pass	William	18068	Private	k in a	19/08,1915	Helles Memorial
Pell	Sydney Ambrose	12445	Private	d o w at sea	02/10,1915	Helles Memorial
Pepperdine	Frank	12506	Private	k in a	21/08,1915	Helles Memorial
Perrin	Charles	13161	Private	k in a	01/09,1915	Helles Memorial
Poultney	Arthur	13256	Private	k in a	21/08,1915	Helles Memorial
Rabbitt	Harry	27861	Private	k in a	21/08,1915	Helles Memorial
Randall	Charles Deschamps		Captain	k in a	7-11/08,1915	Helles Memorial
Rawlins	Edward	12736	Private	k in a	09/08,1915	Helles Memorial
Rhodes	Harold	18034	Private	k in a	09/08,1915	Helles Memorial
Richards	Arthur	12468	L/Cpl	d o w	10/08,1915	Helles Memorial
Riley	James	13342	Private	k in a	09/08,1915	Helles Memorial
Robinson	Frank	13268	Private	k in a	09/08,1915	Helles Memorial
Rouse	Tom Arthur	13394	Private	k in a	21/08,1915	Helles Memorial
Rudd	James	22514	Private	k in a	09/08,1915	Helles Memorial
Rushe	John	18015	Private	k in a	10/08,1915	Helles Memorial
Ryan	William	12908	Private	k in a	09/08,1915	Helles Memorial
Scott	Fred	12862	Private	k in a	09/08,1915	Helles Memorial
Searle	Sidney William	13105	L/Cpl	k in a	09/09,1915	Helles Memorial
Shaw	Joseph	22513	Private	d o w	15/08,1915	Helles Memorial
Shaw	William	18234	Private	k in a	09/08,1915	Helles Memorial
Simmons	Joseph Price	13270	L/Cpl	k in a	09/08,1915	Helles Memorial
Simpson	Henry	16971	Private	k in a	19/08,1915	Helles Memorial
Smith	George Henry	20340	Private	k in a	19/08,1915	Helles Memorial
Smith	James	12834	Private	k in a	21/08,1915	Helles Memorial
Smith	James William	12949	Private	k in a	21/08,1915	Helles Memorial
Smith	Leonard	12897	Private	d o w at sea	13/10,1915	Helles Memorial
Smith	Sidney.	12976	Private	k in a	09/08,1915	Helles Memorial
Smith	William	12701	Private	k in a	09/08,1915	Helles Memorial
Spink	Alfred Henry	18031	Private	k in a	09/08,1915	Helles Memorial
Spray	James	13229	Private	k in a	09/08,1915	Helles Memorial
Squires	Roger Dewar		Captain	k in a	07/08,1915	Helles Memorial
Stacey	George	13599	Corporal	k in a	09/08,1915	Helles Memorial
Stead	George	13359	Private	k in a	09/08,1915	Helles Memorial
Stevens	George Edward	13346	Private	k in a	09/08,1915	Helles Memorial
Sutton	Horace Josiah		2/Lt	d o w at sea	24/11.1915	Helles Memorial

Sweeney	William	12436	Private	k in a	09/08,1915	Helles Memorial
Thomas	Harry	12503	L/Cpl	k in a	21/08,1915	Helles Memorial
Turpie	Arthur John	6029	A/Cpl	k in a	21/08,1915	Helles Memorial
Turton	Arthur	5066	Private	k in a	14/10,1915	Helles Memorial
Turton	Albert Edward	13934	Private	k in a	09/08,1915	Helles Memorial
Vick	Frank	13108	Private	k in a	09/08,1915	Helles Memorial
Wallace	Francis George	20863	Private	d o w at sea	13/11,195	Helles Memorial
Ward	Albert Ernest	13073	A/Cpl	d o w	03/10,1915	Helles Memorial
Watkin	Herbert	12656	Private	k in a	21/08,1915	Helles Memorial
Watson	Frederick Mark	6584	Sgt	k in a	09/08,1915	Helles Memorial
Welbourn	Samuel	12401	Private	k in a	09/08,1915	Helles Memorial
Wells	Frederic Charles	12355	L/Cpl	k in a	09/08,1915	Helles Memorial
Whittaker	Walter	12458	Private	k in a	04/10,1915	Helles Memorial
Whittemore	George William	13657	Private	d o w	15/10,1915	Helles Memorial
Wigmore	Elijah	12873	Private	k in a	09/08,1915	Helles Memorial
Wilcockson	Tom	13150	Private	k in a	09/08,1915	Helles Memorial
Williams	Arthur	12573	A/Cpl	k in a	09/08,1915	Helles Memorial
Wills	Arthur George		Lt	k in a	07/08,1915	Helles Memorial
Winchcomb	W T	17805	Private	k in a	09/08,1915	Helles Memorial
Winnard	Wilfred	20306	Private	k in a	09/08,1915	Helles Memorial
Womack	George Lewis	12966	Private	k in a	21/08,1915	Helles Memorial
Worth	Lewis	12846	Private	k in a	09/08,1915	Helles Memorial
Johnson	Joseph	13057	Private	d o w	14/11,1915	Hill 10 Cem Suvla
Hazelwood	William Charles	22977	Private	d o w	23/11,1915	Hill 10 Cem Suvla
Button	Noel	13021	Private	died	01/11,1915	Hill 10 Cem Suvla
Brackner	George	13908	Private	died	25/10,1915	Hill 10 Cem Suvla
Foley	Ernest Henry	12721	Private	d o w	23/08,1915	Lala Baba Cem
Bunting	Owen	13275	Private	d o w	11/08,1915	Lancashire Landing
Parkin	Arthur	7750	Private	died	19/01,1916	Lancashire Landing
Trotman	Sidney William	21454	Private	died	21/01,1916	Lancashire Landing
Ball	George	12704	Private	d o w	10/09,1915	Pieta Military Cem
Britland	Robert Charles	12779	Private	died	16/09,1915	Pieta Military Cem
Chambers	William	23157	Private	died	06/12,1916	Pieta Military Cem
Chanter	Henry	12571	Private	d o w	01/09,1915	Pieta Military Cem
Colton	Harold	12617	Private	died	26/11,1915	Pieta Military Cem
Dilkes	Arthur	25557	Private	d o w	19/01,1916	Pieta Military Cem
Edgson	James Herbert	21261	Private	d o w	13/09,1915	Pieta Military Cem
Grice	Levi	12515	Private	died	30/12,1915	Pieta Military Cem
Howitt	Alfred	12988	Private	died	16/09,1915	Pieta Military Cem
Hughes	John	22715	Private	died	04/10,1915	Pieta Military Cem
Derbyshire	George	23663	Private	died	18/10,1915	Portianos Mil Cem Lemnos
Barfield	Daniel	6076	Private	k in a	24/07,1915	Redoubt Cem, Helles
Carter	George E.	13403	Private	k in a	28/07,1915	Redoubt Cem, Helles
Fielding	George Rudolf		Major	k in a	24/07,1915	Skew Bridge Cemetery

There are other men who died of wounds once back in the United Kingdom. It is not an easy undertaking to find these men. I have though listed below two men who I am confident received wounds whilst at Gallipoli -:

10851 Private Percy Mason died 12 January 1916 – Q.393 (Screen Wall) Manchester Southern Cemetery.
12570 Private Arthur Willies died 24 September 1915 – Norton Cuckney (St Mary) Churchyard.
Also on the Roll of Honour is 2/Lt Paull, Frederick Major, killed, 27 November 1915 and his unit is given as 14th Battalion Sherwood Foresters. At the time of his death he was attached to the 9th Battalion.

Private ARTHUR POULTNEY, of Matlock, who is with the Sherwood Foresters.

13256 Private Arthur Poultney is named on the Helles memorial. He has no known grave.

MANSFIELD MAN'S THRILLING EXPERIENCE

RESCUING THE WOUNDED.

Writing to his wife and mother in Forest[e] road, Thorneywood, Nottingham, Private Wi[lliam] E. Smith, 9th Sherwood Foresters, gives [a] thrilling account of his experiences, while re[s]cuing the wounded in Gallipoli.

In civilian life Private Smith is a mine[r]. Born in Briar-street, Nottingham, he has live[d] since his marriage in Chaucer-street, Mans[]field, and worked at the Creswell Colliery. [It] was in this connection that he qualified him[]self for membership of the St. John Ambu[]lance Brigade, and his special knowledge re[]sulted in his adventures as a stretcher-bearer. The perilous nature of this task is generall[y] known by this time. One has to lie down a[t] full length to bandage the fallen with any[]thing approaching a measure of safety. Smit[h] had the misfortune to lose his bearings whils[t] away from the British trenches, and after [a] time made the alarming discovery that he had crawled in amongst the enemy's lines.

He managed to conceal his presence, how[]ever, by spending two weary days and nights without either food or drink. Meanwhile Smith was definitely reported by the British to have been killed in action, and the com[]rades he first encountered on his return were more than a little startled by the appearance of what they took for a moment to be his ghost. The officers told him he was one of the luckiest men on earth to return alive. He was injured in some manner in the scramble back to safety, and now lies in hos[]pital.

In a letter written before his great adven[]ture, Pte. Smith described his experiences in the trench. He wrote: "We are in the trenches again now. We came in again on Friday night, after a five day's rest, which we were ready for. It is all right in the trenches. After you get used to the shrap[]nel and shell fire, you take no notice of it at all. I am sitting back writing this, waiting for them shouting 'Stretcher-bearers!' Then you have to go out in the open. Of course, it is pretty hot work then. It is no soft job, ours, when there is a charge on or a bom[]bardment, like it was yesterday. You could not see anything but smoke, and the noise was doubly deafening. We were a bit busy, but I bet the Turks were more than us, for we did not half give them some lead. All that you can hear when the shells are coming is a fizzing noise—and then the ground goes up, and anything else that is there. Well, it has got to be done. It will be a good job when it is all over, but we have got some good officers and gunners."

Mansfield and North Notts Advertiser 10 September 1915. Private William Smith and related his lucky escape as a stretcher bearer at Gallipoli in a letter to his family.

Sherwood Foresters 26 Sept. 1914 ; trained at Belton Park, Grantham, with his battalion, where he was a member of the team which won Earl Brownlow's Cup in the 33rd Infantry Brigade Sports in March, 1915, and Frensham, near Farnham ; served with the Mediterranean Expeditionary Force at Gallipoli from July, being Assistant Transport Officer, and Bombing Officer to his battalion ; superintended the landing of the Regimental Transport at Cape Helles, after which he joined his battalion in the trenches before Achi Baba on the 25th ; was wounded there the following day, when, as he was about to snipe the Turkish trenches, the enemy's marksman fired first, hit the muzzle of his rifle just as he was taking aim, smashing it, and drove the splinters into his left eye, and as he was attending to his wounds, the Turk put another bullet through the loophole, which pierced his left shoulder. He was operated on at the Base Hospital at Cape Helles, but considering himself fit for duty, rejoined the battalion on 1 Aug., and took part on the night of 6–7 Aug. in the landing at Suvla Bay, when his battalion landed on the beach, south of Lala Baba, without opposition ; advanced with his battalion up the Anafarta Valley, towards the village of Biyuk Anafarta on the 9th, Lieut. West leading the advance with his platoon on the left of the battalion. His battalion filled the two-mile gap between Chocolate Hill on the left and Anzac on the right entirely unsupported. At about 9 a.m. the battalion came under heavy machine-gun and rifle fire, and sustained heavy casualties, which stopped their advance, and in the evening they had only 4 officers and 319 men left out of 750 that went into action in the morning. There is considerable conflict of evidence as to what occurred to Lieut. West. It seems fairly established that a rumour was very general amongst the battalion that he was killed at the head of his platoon, with nine bullets through him during the advance about 9 a.m., although some assert that he fell wounded only, and did not die until after nightfall. It is on these reports he seems to have been included in the list of killed. But it has since been clearly established by many reliable witnesses that, on the officers of the rest of his company becoming casualties, Lieut. West was called for to take command, which he did, crossing over from the left of the battalion to the right about 11 a.m. ; that about 2 p.m. the Turks were reinforced and came up in overwhelming numbers, and that Lieut. West, to avoid their being surrounded, took some men away to the right of the position. He and the me that went with him were never seen again, as most of the rest of the battalion retired on the supporting company, about a quarter of a mile in the rear, at 4 p.m. The whole battalion testifies to the bravery, fearlessness and popularity of Lieut. West, and the respect in which he was held by both officers and men, and a brother officer said that there was not one of his men but would have sacrificed themselves to save him. He was a keen all-round sportsman, and while at school won the Eastty Cup, for the best athlete in the school, two years in succession, 1913–14 ; gained his football colours in 1910, playing for the School XV. for five years, 1910–14 ; was captain of his house ; shot in the Bisley team for the Ashburton three times, 1911–12–14, making a good score in 1912 when the Whitgift School secured third place, and in 1914 won the Banks Cup for the highest score of his school in the Ashburton ; *unm.*

William West.

Lieut. William West's entry in De Ruvigny Roll of Honour.

Three men from Aston-On-Trent would also be mentioned in the local Newspaper-

Derby Daily Telegraph. 23 August 1916.

'Aston-On-Trent losses in the War
In the early period of the war there were very few villages in Derbyshire where more young men enlisted in the Army in proportion to its population than Aston-On-Trent. Of these five have lost their lives in the service of their country…

Private William Smith enlisted in August 1914 on the outbreak of war. He was in the Sherwoods and after training at Grantham was sent to the Dardanelles, where he arrived on July 18. One day early in August he was going to fetch water with a comrade, W. Whittaker (since killed), when he was shot by a sniper. He was 22 years of age. His parents, Mr. And Mrs. Richard Smith, have two other sons serving in France. Last week the news was received that one of them, Private Ernest Smith, was wounded on July 8 this year, a bullet passing through his right side.

Private W. Whittaker enlisted in the Sherwoods in the first week of the war, and went out with the Mediterranean Expeditionary Force. He was killed in action in the Dardanelles in the first week in October 1915. In a letter to his relatives his sergeant paid a touching tribute to his soldier-like qualities. He concluded: " I was with him when he passed away in peace with a smile on his face. His last thoughts were for you all at home". He has two brothers now serving in the Army.

Private William Howard was an adopted son of Mr. And Mrs. Orton, and enlisted in November 1914. He was previously employed by Mr. Moss, of Aston. He went to the Dardanelles, where he died of Dysentery on Sept. 15th, 1915. The Chaplain wrote to his friends at Aston and said he passed away peacefully to rest, and was buried at sea. He was 19 years of age.'

C.S.M. Walter Milward – After the taking of Chocolate Hill the battalion had considerable casualties including Sergeant Pickford and C.S.M. Milward. Both men had been seriously wounded and

Reg Ecclestone, November 1916.

Walter had shrapnel wound from an exploding shell in his right arm. The wound did not receive proper attention for nearly four days due to the difficulty of moving the wounded down to the base, as the Turkish forces still held the heights overlooking the main beaches, constantly shelling the rear areas. When Walter finally reached the Hospital ship H.M. Soudan, lying off shore, gangrene had set in. He was able however, to arrange for a dictated letter to be sent from his bedside after the amputation of his right arm. Sadly his condition grew worse as the gangrene spread and he died. He was buried at sea off Malta on 29th August 1915. Sergeant Sage would give his version of the action on his return to England after the Armistice.

(My sincere thanks to Jack Bagshaw Milward and Hilary Hillier for allowing me to use extracts from Walter Milward – Soldier and Coal Miner 1874-1915)

One young soldier 12761 Private Reg Ecclestone was moved to write a poem about the experience, which was accepted, by the King and Queen:

Most graciously accepted by their Imperial Majesties the King and Queen, and by Her Majesty Queen Alexandra.

The Landing at Suvla Bay.

You may talk of Balaclava,
And of Trafalgar Bay,
But what of the Eleventh Division
Who landed at Suvla Bay ?

Their part of Kitchener's Army,
Who had left mothers, children, and wives,
But they fought for England's freedom,
Fought for their very lives

It was on the 6th of August
They made that terrible dash,
As the Turks upon the hillside
They were trying our boats to smash.

The order came " Fix Bayonets ! "
As out of the boats we got,
Yet every man was a hero
Who faced the Turkish shot.

Ships' sides and funnels were shattered,
And the sea in some parts red,
But the lads fought their way to the shore,
To the beach that was covered with dead.

Then creeping at length up the hillside,
While shot and shells fell around.
They made their last desperate effort,
And charged the Turkish ground.

The Turks began to tremble
When they saw the bayonets play,
Then they turned their backs on the British
And returned from Suvla Bay !

There were Lincolns, Dorsets and Staffords,
The Border Regiment too,
The good old Sherwood Foresters,
And the R.A.M.C. true.

Then came the gallant Manchesters,
With the Fusiliers by their side,
Those trusty lads from Lancashire
Who filled our hearts with pride.

The Yorks, East Yorks and West Yorks,
And Yorks and Lancs., as well,
All fought for the honour of Britain
And with the bravest fell.

The Fighting Fifth were at it,
Northumberland lads, you know,
While the Duke of Wellington's did their best
Driving back the foe.

Far away up the hillside,
Buried 'neath the Turkish clay,
Lie sons of Britain's heroes
Who landed at Suvla Bay.

So remember the Eleventh Division,
Who are all volunteers, you know,
They fought and died like Britons
While fighting their deadly foe.

Composed by Signaller R. ECCLESTONE,
9th Sherwood Foresters : 11th Division.

Chapter Three

1916 – The Year of the Somme

BEFORE THE 9th Battalion moved to France and the Somme, they would spend the first half of 1916 recovering from their four months on Gallipoli. The battalion had suffered extremely badly in its first campaign with many of its officers and men becoming casualties. The Battalion had been hard hit during its sojourn in the Dardanelles. The grievous losses of the Battalion had occurred during a few August days but since that time disease and trench wastage (A not to pleasant army term for casualties), had further weakened it. It was in desperate need of rest and relaxation. In effect it was a new battalion in all but name, such had been its losses. There would have to be time for training in readiness for the battles ahead.

The whole of the 11th Division of which the 9th Battalion was a part would find itself in Egypt and on the Suez Canal.

January to July 1916

Whilst the Battalion War Diaries before July 1916 have been lost, other documentary evidence did survive. Obviously this does not give a day-to-day account of the battalions 'doings' and can in no way give a complete picture. The 33rd Brigade War Diaries do though give strong pointers on the Battalions movements and duties during this period.

Colonel Scothern's notes only give the briefest glimpse of the battalion's tasks for this period in Egypt. Either it was an extremely quiet period or he found it less than interesting. That said he did sum up the battalions stay in Egypt perfectly.

> *"The time spent in Egypt may not have been full of honour and glory, but it served its purpose as the men were given the opportunity of resting after the arduous campaign on Gallipoli, and to prepare themselves for the fighting which lay before them on the Western Front. Opportunities were given to the Officers and Men to see some of the country, and leave was granted to Cairo & Alexandria."*

It is probable that the men had seen enough honour and glory to last them a lifetime.

One wonders what these men of the East Midlands made of this 'alien' country and its people. It would have no doubt have been interesting to talk to such men as the 'teetotal, non-smoking, Methodist Fred Greaves (later to win a Victoria Cross). No doubt though, he like all the soldiers, made the most of their free time in both of these cities. In fact Fred Greaves mentioned to his daughter that he had swam in the Nile. Edward Wood also remembered bathing in the Nile and on returning to shore, someone had stolen his uniform and this is a possible reason for him being returned to the rank of private from that of Lance Corporal. Edward also remembered visiting the Pyramids with others of the Battalion. Other men such as Joseph Hazlewood were just happy to have survived Gallipoli and after the war he would tell his family *'Where I served 1914 war – Suvla Bay, Turkey, Mudros Island Greece, Alexandria Egypt, Suez Canal, Sinai Desert, Then came to France June 1916, went to France 4 times, all for 6d a day'* Joseph would serve in 9th Battalion followed by 1st, 15th and 2/5th and survive the war. He would die whilst resident at the British Legion Home, Galanos House, Warwickshire in 1982.

Before the Battalion embarked for Alexandria, they spent a few days on Imbros and took part in Brigade training.On 28th January the Brigade were ordered to embark for Mudros and from there they were transhipped for Alexandria. The battalion along with The 7th Battalion South Staffordshire

Regiment embarked on 29th January. It was noted that the voyage was uneventful with no enemy submarines reported or sighted. By 3rd February the whole Brigade was concentrated at Sidi Bishr Camp at Alexandria.

The Brigade War diary also gives the strengths of the various battalions as at 1st January 1916 and 13 January 1916. It is worth noting all of the battalions to show just how badly they had suffered whilst on Gallipoli.

The usual establishment for an Infantry battalion was in the region of 1000 men but at this time none of 33rd Infantry Brigades four battalions came even close to this number.

1st January	Officers	other ranks
Brigade Headquarters -	4	47
6th Lincolns -	20	577
6th Borders -	21	384
7th South Staffs -	21	653
9th Sherwood Foresters –	23	753

Despite the drafts of new untried men, the battalion was still under-strength.

It would take much time and effort to re-mould the Brigade into a fighting unit.The battalion continued with Brigade training at Sidi Bishr Camp and Abouker until the 18th February and by this date, it was up to full strength, having 30 officers and 991 other ranks. On the 19th February, the Brigade received orders to proceed to the Suez Canal as part of the defensive force. The Suez Canal was a vital artery for the movement of men and materials and the area would also become the springboard for later attacks into Palestine. Brigade headquarters proceeded to Ballah and the canal defences, with a view to relieving the 92 Brigade, 31st Division. The defences to be taken over consisted of a number of defended localities which were some seven miles from the canal itself. Immediately to the rear of these localities were situated a number of strong points. 68th Field Company, Royal Engineers and the 6th (Pioneer) Battalion, The East York's Regiment accompanied Brigade Headquarters in order to prepare the area. The Brigade Headquarters task was to reconnoitre the front line and support trenches. Arrangements for feeding, watering and supplying the Brigade were also made.

It was no simple task to move and supply over 4,000 fighting men and their support troops.

In the meantime the battalions of the Brigade, including the 9th Battalion continued with their training.

On 23rd February, Major W R Thornton (Royal Berkshire Regiment) reported to Brigade and took command of the 9th Sherwood Foresters.

An entry in the War Diary at that time noted that on 29th February 1916 the strength of the Battalion was 33 officers and 976 other ranks. Nothing unusual in that but the date tells the reader that 1916 was a leap year.

On the 3rd March 1916 was a significant day for some men of the 9th Battalion The Sherwood Foresters. They would leave the Battalion but not the Brigade.

The War Diary states '*3rd March 1916 Sidi Bishr – On this day the 33rd Machine Gun Company (Capt Snell, 6 Lincs Regt) was formed. The Officers, N.C.O.s and men were taken from the existing Regimental Machine Gun Sections and Regimental Reserve Sections and transferred to the Machine Gun Corps*' thus heralding the birth of a new Corps in the British Army.

One of the 9th Battalion men who would transfer was 17329 Private Edward Harris. He had joined the battalion on 24th August 1914 and been with them through Gallipoli. He would now be re-badged under the new Machine Gun Corps with the number 9672. Edward and the other men would though continue with the Brigade.

On 8th March the Brigade began its move to Ballah West and Ballybunion. Ballybunion was the railhead for a light railway between the two, which were some 6 miles apart. The 9th Battalion did not begin its move until 12th March and they would be located at Ballah East, taking over the canal defence posts, bridgehead defences and a post at K. 50.8. They would remain in this general area until the end of June 1916. By this time Major Thornton had been promoted to Lt-Col and the battalion settled in to a routine of defence.

Once the battalion had established itself at Ballah East on the canal bank they set about organizing a system of patrols along the East bank of the Suez Canal.

The battalion had no reports or sightings of enemy movements during this period.They continued with their task of constructing defence lines and at the same time established a system of patrols along the East Bank of the Suez Canal. The work continued throughout March and the heat was intense, which led to a drastic alteration of working hours. The hours of work each day were recorded as

Appendix A (below) – General Tactical and administrative instructions for Ballah Bridgehead and Ballah half section from the Brigade, tasked the 9th Battalion with the following:

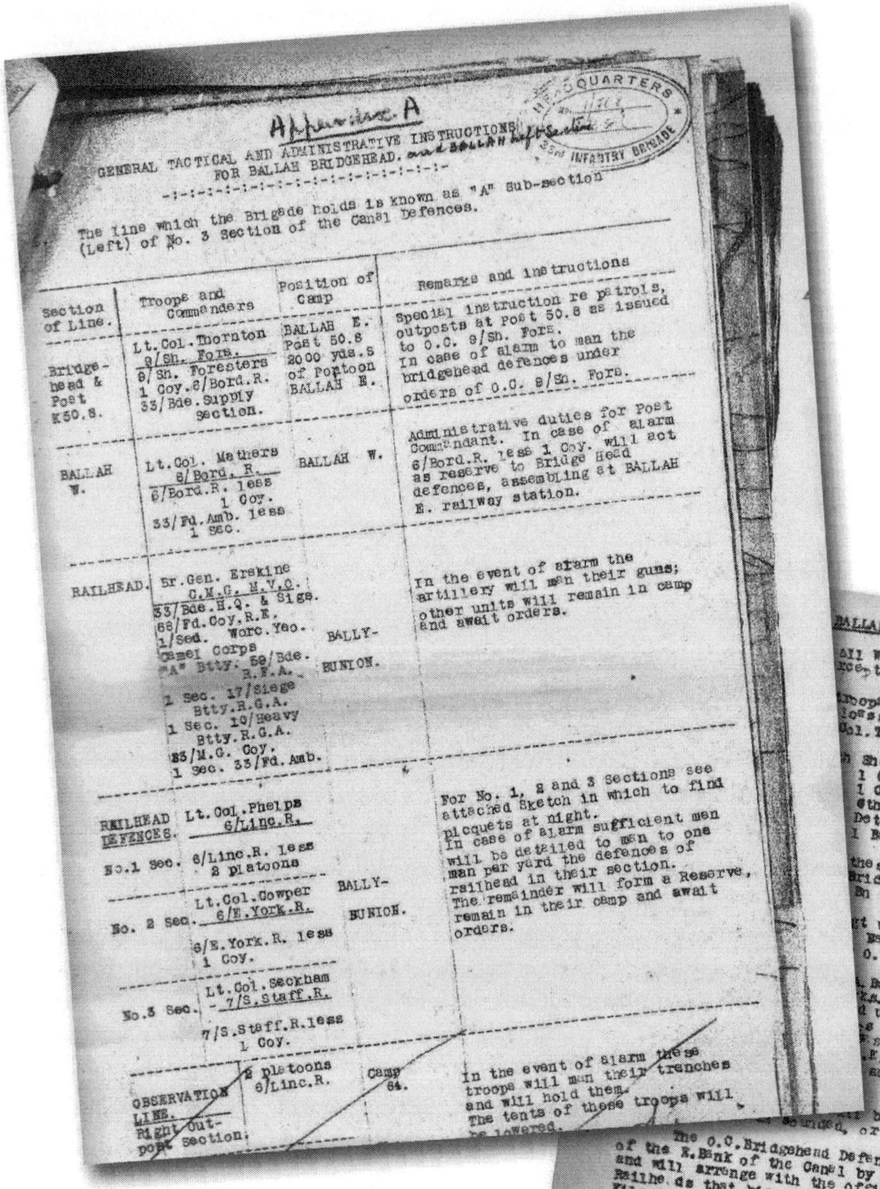

Appendix A

GENERAL TACTICAL AND ADMINISTRATIVE INSTRUCTIONS FOR BALLAH BRIDGEHEAD. and BALLAH half section

HEADQUARTERS 33rd INFANTRY BRIGADE

The line which the Brigade holds is known as "A" Sub-section (Left) of No. 3 Section of the Canal Defences.

Section of Line.	Troops and Commanders	Position of Camp	Remarks and instructions
Bridge-head & Post K50.8.	Lt.Col.Thornton 9/Sh. Fors. 9/Sh. Foresters 1 Coy.6/Bord.R. 33/Bde.Supply section.	BALLAH E. Post 50.8 2000 yds.S of Pontoon BALLAH E.	Special instruction re patrols, outposts at Post 50.8 as issued to O.C. 9/Sh. Fors. In case of alarm to man the bridgehead defences under orders of O.C. 9/Sh. Fors.
BALLAH W.	Lt.Col. Mathers 6/Bord. R. 6/Bord.R. less 1 Coy. 33/Fd.Amb. less 1 sec.	BALLAH W.	Administrative duties for Post Commandant. In case of alarm 6/Bord.R. less 1 Coy. will act as reserve to Bridge Head defences, assembling at BALLAH E. railway station.
RAILHEAD.	Br.Gen. Erskine C.M.G. M.V.O. 33/Bde.H.Q. & Sigs. 68/Fd.Coy.R.E. 1/Sqd. Worc.Yeo. Camel Corps "A" Btty. 59/Bde. R.F.A. 1 Sec. 17/Siege Btty.R.G.A. 1 Sec. 10/Heavy Btty.R.G.A. 33/M.G. Coy. 1 Sec. 33/Fd.Amb.	BALLY-BUNION.	In the event of alarm the artillery will man their guns; other units will remain in camp and await orders.
RAILHEAD DEFENCES.	Lt.Col.Phelps 6/Linc.R.		For No. 1, 2 and 3 Sections see attached Sketch in which to find picquets at night. In case of alarm sufficient men will be detailed to man to one man per yard the defences of railhead in their section. The remainder will form a Reserve, remain in their camp and await orders.
No.1 Sec.	6/Linc.R. less 2 platoons		
No. 2 Sec.	Lt.Col.Cowper 6/E.York.R. 6/E.York.R. less 1 Coy.	BALLY-BUNION.	
No.3 Sec.	Lt.Col.Seckham 7/S.Staff.R. 7/S.Staff.R.less 1 Coy.		
OBSERVATION LINE. Right Out-post Section.	2 platoons 6/Linc.R.	Camp 64.	In the event of alarm these troops will man their trenches and will hold them. The tents of these troops will be lowered.

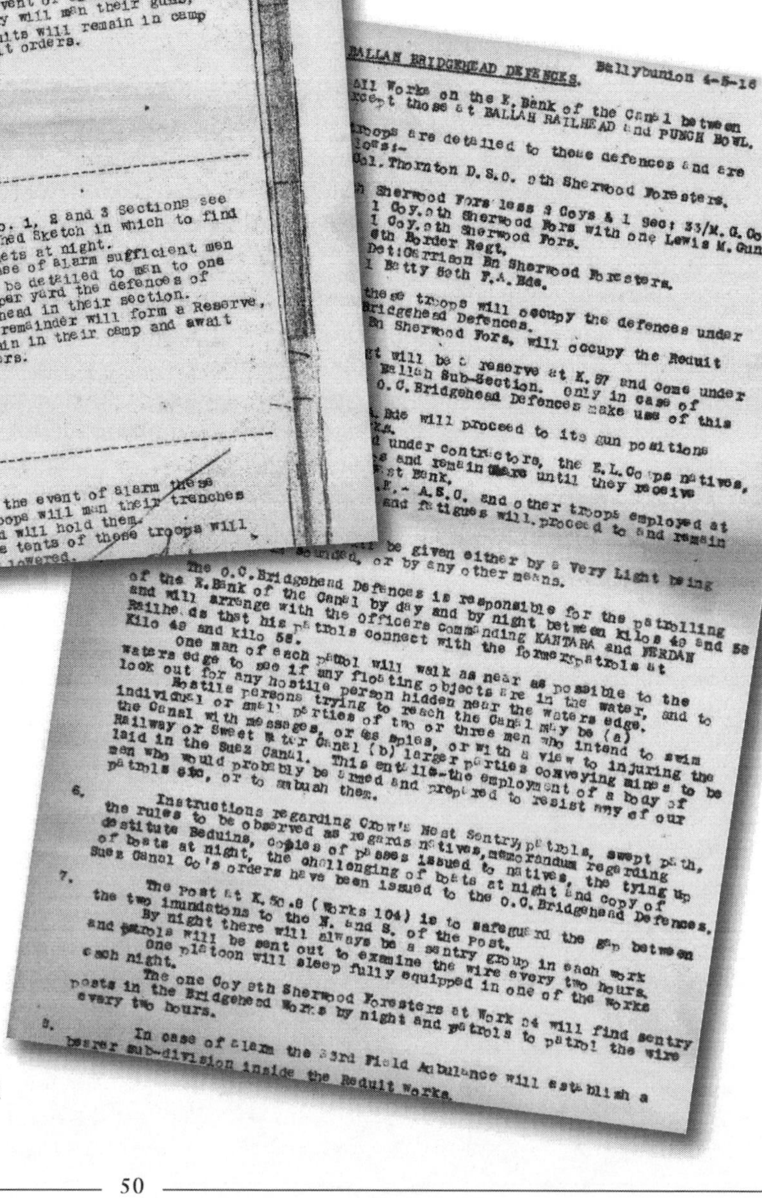

BALLAH BRIDGEHEAD DEFENCES. Ballybunion 4-5-16

All Works on the E. Bank of the Canal between [...]cept those at BALLAH RAILHEAD and PUNCH BOWL.

[...]troops are detailed to these defences and are [...]lows:-

[...]Col. Thornton D.S.O. 9th Sherwood Foresters.

[...] Sherwood Fors less 2 Coys & 1 Sec: 33/M.G.Coy.
1 Coy.9th Sherwood Fors with one Lewis M.Gun.
1 Coy.9th Sherwood Fors.
6th Border Regt.
Det:Garrison Bn Sherwood Foresters.
1 Btty 59th F.A.Bde.

[...] these troops will occupy the defences under [...] Bridgehead Defences.
[...] Bn Sherwood Fors. will occupy the Reduit [...]

[...]t will be a reserve at K.57 and come under [...] Ballah Sub-Section. Only in case of [...] O.C.Bridgehead Defences make use of this [...]

[...] Bde will proceed to its gun positions [...]
[...]d under contractors, the E.L.Corps natives, [...]s and remain there until they receive [...]st Bank.
[...]F.- A.S.C. and other troops employed at [...] and fatigues will proceed to and remain [...]

[...] be given either by a Very Light being [...] sounded, or by any other means.

The O.C.Bridgehead Defences is responsible for the patrolling of the E.Bank of the Canal by day and by night between kilos 40 and 58 and will arrange with the officers commanding KANTARA and FERDAN Railheads that his patrols connect with the former patrols at Kilo 48 and kilo 58.

One man of each patrol will walk as near as possible to the waters edge to see if any floating objects are in the water, and to look out for any hostile person hidden near the waters edge.

Hostile persons trying to reach the Canal may be (a) individual or small parties of two or three men who intend to swim the Canal with messages, or as spies, or with a view to injuring the Railway or Sweet Water Canal (b) larger parties conveying mines to be laid in the Suez Canal. This entails the employment of a body of men who would probably be armed and prepared to resist any of our patrols etc, or to ambush them.

6. Instructions regarding Crow's Nest Sentry, patrols, swept path, the rules to be observed as regards natives, memorandum regarding destitute Beduins, copies of passes issued to natives, the tying up of boats at night, the challenging of boats at night and copy of Suez Canal Co's orders have been issued to the O.C.Bridgehead Defences.

7. The Post at K.50.8 (Works 104) is to safeguard the gap between the two inundations to the N. and S. of the Post.

By night there will always be a sentry group in each work and patrols will be sent out to examine the wire every two hours.

One platoon will sleep fully equipped in one of the Works each night.

The one Coy 9th Sherwood Foresters at Work 94 will find sentry posts in the Bridgehead Works by night and patrols to patrol the wire every two hours.

8. In case of alarm the 33rd Field Ambulance will establish a bearer sub-division inside the Reduit Works.

Ballah Bridgehead Defences

7-00 a.m. to 11-00 a.m. and 4-00 p.m. to 6-00 p.m. and no doubt the men found the heat a pleasant change from an East Midlands Spring.

The battalion continued to take in reinforcement drafts for training purposes with the establishment being exceeded by some 400 men. On 31st March 1916 the Battalion had on its establishment 43 officers and 1401 other ranks.

The battalion settled itself into the usual routine of army life – working on trenches and training. The Bridgehead defences at Ballah East and West, on the banks of the Suez Canal continued to be improved during April.

An interesting link between Egypt and Ypres can be found in the diaries of 22 April 1916, with the mention of Ferdan and Ferdan Railhead. During 3rd Ypres, The Battle of Broodseinde, 4 October 1917, the battalion attacked a machine gun post at Ferdan House and after its capture, made it Company Headquarters.

During the period 23rd to 24th April there was enemy action in the area when 52nd Division located on the left flank came under attack from about 100 men. A later report mentioned the Turks advancing in force and men of C Squadron, The Warwickshire Yeomanry being tasked to patrol the area, although the 11th Division front was reported to be all clear throughout the period.

On 1st May the battalion strength was still well over establishment, standing at 44 officers and 1399 other ranks.

The work of improving the defences and wiring, continued apace and it is clear from the diaries that the enemy was becoming more active and building up its troop numbers in the area. For no apparent reason, on 15th May the 9th Battalion and the 7th Battalion South Staffordshire regiment exchanged camps and duties. This was possibly to ease the boredom but could have had something to do with the weather. It was noted on this day that the ' weather became very hot – 114 degrees in the shade owing to the Hamuen wind. Working and training hours curtailed'. This is possibly why the period 15th to 31st May reports little of note. Usually giving ' Nothing to report. No signs of enemy who is reported to have reduced the number of troops near us'.

The month of June would be the Battalion's last in Egypt and after six months of relative peace and quiet, they would be going to France and eventually the Somme. At the beginning of June the battalion's strength was 43 officers and 1390 other ranks and for the next couple of weeks work and training continued.

Roll of Honour

2902, Private, DESSAUR, Myer, died, Egypt, 5 February 1916, and buried at – Alexandria (Chatby) Military Cemetery, grave E. 19. Myer left a wife Elizabeth.

23288 Private BOOTH, Thomas, died, Egypt, 22 April 1916, and buried at –
Ismailia War Memorial Cemetery, grave B.77. Thomas was born and lived in Heanor Derbyshire.

22195, Private, SMEDLEY, John, died, Egypt, 13 May 1916, and buried at – Alexandria (Hadra) Cemetery, grave D.8. John was born at Derby but living with his parents prior to joining the Battalion.

All three men died of illness.

Then on 17th June, the Division received its orders to proceed to France, with advanced parties of 125th Brigade, 42nd Division arriving to relieve them. The first order of the day was to get the Battalion back down to its normal establishment and therefore men attached for training were withdrawn and sent to rejoin the base details at Sidi Bishr. This left the 9th Battalion with its normal establishment of 34 officers and 995 other ranks.

Between 22nd and 23rd June, the 125th Brigade, 42nd Division relieved the 33rd Brigade (125 Brigade order no 151 and 33 Inf. Bde. order No 12. The 6th battalion Lancashire Fusiliers relieved the 9th battalion at 3.25am on 23 June. The 9th Battalion then marched to Ballybunion at 5.00am where 7th South Staffs provided their meal, in this case, tea. Luckily for the battalion their kit was transported by train.

On 26th June the move to France began with the 9th battalion entraining for Alexandria from where they would embark ship.

It is here that brigade and Battalion diaries differ as to what happened. The 9th Battalion diaries, which begin on 1st July 1916, give mention to the H.T. Oriana whilst the Brigade diary for 28 June gives the H.M.T Minnewaska. The Brigade diary also states that after embarkation, the ship remained at Alexandria Harbour with the men on board until 2nd July. The battalion diary mentions that the H.T. Oriana made a two-hour stop over at Malta on 1st July and passed Sardinia on the 2nd. Both war diaries are actually correct as Battalion Headquarters along with 'A' and 'B' Companies sailed aboard H.T. Oriana. This part of the battalion had strength of 20 officers and 526 other ranks. The other two companies 'C' and 'D' followed a few days later and their arrival was mentioned in the battalion diary. Colonel Scothern notes give the full picture though

'Embarkation was carried out directly after the return to Alexandria, Batt. H.Q. with A and B Coys. Sailing on H.M.T. "Oriana", C and D Coys. Following on the H.M.T. "Minnewaska"'

9th Battalion Battle insignia worn on the rear of the collar. It was chosen because the battalion was 4th in line of precedence within the Brigade.

THE SOMME

On the 1st July 1916, the British Army suffered its greatest number of casualties in any one day as the Service (New Army) battalions were thrown against strongly defended German positions. The Service battalions with its 'Pals' troops saw their first and for many thousands, their last attack. As the heavily laden men advanced shoulder to shoulder on that summer's morning, the 9th Battalion were making a stop over at Malta, as they journeyed to France and what would be two and a half years of trench occupation interspersed with involvement in some of the major offensives. They would take their place on the Somme in early September and fight in and for trenches made famous during the Campaign – Constance, Hessian, Zollern and Joseph.

Prior to that though they would train and hold the trenches in the vicinity of Arras. Many of the men who now served in the 9th battalion had never fired a shot in anger but those who had survived Gallipoli would be on hand to show them the ropes.

The arrangements at Marseilles were less than army like and certainly less than the battalion expected. The H.T. Oriana arrived at 7-00pm and the war diary noted, "Receive disembarkation orders which are very vague". Vague or not, the next morning at 7-00am H.Q., along with A and B Companies disembarked and proceeded to the Railway station some 600 yards away. They shared the train with 6th Battalion York and Lancashire Regiment. By 8-30am they were loaded and ready for the off and so began a 28 hour train journey through the French countryside. It would seem that the journey was far from pleasant as the rain fell and arranged halts were insufficient for the Battalions needs. The conditions on a packed troop train for 28 hours can only be imagined.

Eventually at 12-15am on 6th July, they arrived at St Pol and de-trained. 20 officers and 526 other ranks then marched to their new billets in Petit Houvin, which is some 30 kilometers from Arras. On the 7th July 'C' Company arrived with strength of 4 Officers and 197 other ranks, detraining at Frevent and marching to Buneville. On the following day, H.Q., 'A' and 'B' Companies moved to Buneville, once there they received some training, which turned out to be a route march through the French countryside. This would not have impressed the men as the conditions of their boots were described as 'very bad'. It has to be presumed that the men had been issued 'Western Front' kit, replacing their desert kit. If this was the case, the men's boots would be new and to say the least uncomfortable! Army boots needed breaking in and this could be done in various ways, although urine seemed to be a favourite way of softening them. Even so blistered feet were a common occurrence.

On Sunday 9th July, 3 officers and 231 other ranks proceeded to St Pol where they acted as 3rd Army Headquarters guard, under Captain Stevenson until the 14th. On 10th July 'D' Company made up of 6 Officers and 231 Other Ranks detrained at St Pol and proceeded to the billets at Buneville, arriving at 9-30am By this time the Battalion was all but complete after its move from Egypt. It would be the 14th before the 2 Officers and 27 Other Ranks who made up the transport section eventually rejoined the battalion.

On 12th Lt Critchlow assumed command of 'D' Company. The 13th saw the G.O.C., 11th Division who at this time was Lieut-Gen. Sir C. Woollcombe inspect the Battalion before its move nearer the front.

No sooner had the battalion reformed, than it was on the move again, only this time closer to the Arras front at Agnez Lez Duisans. Immediately the preparations were under way for the battalion to get accustomed to their new surroundings and the trenches they would occupy for several weeks.

On 16th, 8 Officers and 323 Other Ranks under the command of Captain Smeeton proceeded to billets at Arras where they provided working parties for 68th Field Company, Royal Engineers. This Field Company being part of the 11th Division.

On 17th the men continued with their training and there were a number of changes. Captain Stevenson took over command of 'B' Company from Captain E.T. Stevens. Capt E.T. Stevens meanwhile, along with 2/Lt Levene and 14 Other Ranks moved to the Trench Mortar Battery. By this period the Stokes Mortar was widely available and Battalions had men trained and equipped with them.

On the 18th at 12 noon, the battalion's time on the front line began in earnest, when 4 platoons, consisting of 4 Officers and 159 Other Ranks went into the line near Arras. They spent 48 hours shadowing men of 9th King's Royal Rifles, 42nd Brigade and the following day had their first casualty on the Western Front, with one Other Rank being wounded. The remainder of the Battalion spent the time carrying out more training in readiness for the forthcoming trench occupation.

On 20th July 1916, 17010, Private Alexander Payne of 'D' Company died in Southampton and was buried at Southampton (Hollybrook) Cemetery, grave B.2.5. He was a Derby man, married and aged 30 years. He died of illness and not the result of wounds. On 21st July the platoons shadowing the King's Royal Rifles returned as did the men from the Arras working parties. Lt Everard returned to the battalion after leave in the UK.

The Battalion strength on 22nd July was 28 Officers and 736 Other Ranks, which were some 250 men under establishment. The War Diaries give no reason for this, which is surprising, as on 18th and 19th July, the 8th Battalion South Staffordshire Regiment received reinforcements. On the, 18th, it was 83 men from 9th Battalion, The Lincolns and North Staffs. The following day saw 223 Other Ranks, all from the Notts and Derby Regt. The 8th South Staffs had suffered casualties of 25 officers and 320 Other Ranks whilst attacking between the 9th and 11th July. The Arras line was seen as a fairly quiet one and it was not unusual to loan men to other units, particularly as at this time many Battalions had been decimated during the first few days of the Somme fighting.

On the same day there was a newspaper announcement of the death of an ex-9th Battalion man.

The Derby Daily Telegraph on that day had the following -:

> **'Derby County Grounds man Killed'**
> *'Private Fred Edmonds, fourth son of Mr. & Mrs. Edmonds of 120, Shaftesbury Crescent, Derby was killed in action on July 9 1916. He went out with the Sherwood Foresters to the Dardanelles and was wounded in the landing at Suvla Bay.After being in England some little time he was drafted to France, where he was attached to another battalion of the Sherwood Foresters. Private Edmonds was very well known in Derby, as he was grounds man for the Derby County F.C. for a period of nine years. It was the painful duty of his brother (Private W Edmonds) to break the news to his parents'*

Also on 22nd July Major. A. E. Scothern returned from UK leave and assumed command of 'D' Company the following day. There was also mention of 'Heavy bombardment in South' and this was no doubt the start of the next phase of the Somme Campaign – The Battle of Pozieres.

An unusual note in the diary for 24th July – 'One Other rank on leave, to 30th inst'. Whilst Officer leave, both going and returning was usually mentioned, it was not the case for Other Ranks. The Battalion was now ready for the move to the front line at Arras and Col Scothern states:

> *'The line was taken over on the 28th (July), and held until August 18th. It was a very quiet sector an almost ideal one, in which to settle down. The Somme battle had now passed through its opening stages and the 11th Division was brought back for training to take its part in the struggle'*

Whilst a number of the men had learned their trade at Gallipoli, the replacement drafts had not as yet seen action. Neither did they know the survival techniques used by the 'old sweats' in the trenches where the slightest error in judgment could be your last and only time in the front line could give you an edge.

What conditions did the men face? They were more often than not, wet, cold, weary and hungry. They survived on cold food, usually Bully beef, biscuits, cheese, and plum and apple jam. The water was often carried in old petrol tins (Jerry –Cans) and had a taste and odour of fuel with a thin film on top of it. Skin disease was normal as the men rarely saw fruit and vegetables.

The ration dumps for the Division were up to ten miles behind the lines and usually by a convenient railhead. Every morning, transport (usually horse-drawn) would move supplies to the battalion stores area. Here they would be sorted and usually put into empty sandbags for Platoons and Sections. The supplies would then be taken to the support trenches by pack mule or light railway and from here the ration parties would take them via the communications trenches to the front line. Of course on many occasions, shelling or an active sniper would mean no food at all.

The men lived side by side with a multitude of rats, unburied bodies, body parts and the detritus of war. In winter men would be swathed in great coats, balaclavas and anything that would help keep the chill away. Despite this, the men would be constantly cold. After a tour of duty in the front line, the men of the battalion would be exhausted, both physically and mentally. Illness and disease were a constant threat in the trenches and the war diary mentioned such things as measles and diphtheria. Trench Foot was classed as a self-inflicted injury and the men could face dire consequences if they succumbed. The men were issued with whale oil and in theory had to rub it into the feet daily. Being in the front line, especially in areas such as the Ypres Salient, sometimes made this exercise impossible.

Trench Fever was a debilitating disease contracted by troops who were engaged in long-term trench warfare. It was more prevalent in warmer areas or in the case of the western front, warmer periods. Men had symptoms similar to Influenza or Typhoid and although most recovered, they usually ended up in hospital for several weeks. It was not until 1918 that the cause was established – the excretions from the ever present lice, which were a permanent part of trench life.

This then was what the 9th Battalion had to look forward to until November 1918 and of course a number of major offensives.From 25th July, the move into the front line began with an advance party of 7 Officers and 33 Other Ranks. The following day the Lewis Guns and 17 Other Ranks moved out, closely followed by the advanced party of snipers. One officer and one other rank were detailed to the Field Company R.E., but no reason was given. Although it is possible they were concerned with the mining operations in that part of the front line.

Just after midday on 27th more men moved out, with 6 mining shifts and 2 carrying shifts, comprising 8 N.C.O.'s and 52 men proceeding to the trenches. Then five men were sent to the Light Trench Mortar Battery at Arras, and at 10-30pm, the Lewis Gunners and 'A' Company set out for the trenches, with the remainder of the Battalion leaving at 5-minute intervals. This proved to be a difficult journey as the battalion's column was held up by transport of the 8th Northumberland Fusiliers and the Leicestershire Regiment. Between Dainville and Arras, a distance of under three miles, a full hour was lost.

By 1-00am on 28th the Battalion arrived at Arras station and by 4-25am the relief was complete with 'A' and 'D' Companies in I.R., 'C' Company in support and 'B' Company held in reserve. A total Battalion strength of 26 Officers and 646 Other Ranks were holding the various sectors of the front line. It would seem that the German's gave the Battalion a couple of days to settle in to their new surroundings as the diary mentions little of note.

The 29th July has the following 'Casualties 2 Other Ranks. All quiet, false gas alarm, wind North.'

The 30th saw 1 Officer and 20 other ranks rejoining the Battalion from 3rd Army Headquarters. 2/Lt Bowyer and 2/Lt May reported to the Battalion and were taken on strength, being posted to 'A' and 'B' Companies respectively. Meanwhile Lt. Waller and one NCO were sent to Gas School at Gody.

On 31st July at 1-20am a party of six German's raided sap 15 and one other rank was wounded. Probably this man was 12508, Private Smith who died of wounds on 31st July and is buried at Avesnes-Le-Comte Cemetery Extension, some 20 kilometres from Arras. Private Smith had the unwanted distinction of being the first 9th Battalion man killed on the Western front.

Also on the 31st, Major Gater proceeded on leave and he would return on 12th August but only for three days. On 15th August Major Gater left to take command of the 6th Battalion Lincolnshire Regiment who were part of the same Brigade. This officer would eventually command a Brigade in 1917.

Between Tuesday 1st August and Friday 18th August, the Battalion would hold the line in this area and according to the Diary, it was a quiet time and the 'trench wastage' (Army term for men killed in trenches) would seem to agree with this. Even the weather seemed to be kind with some very pleasant, hot days.

The month of August began with continued assaults on the Somme front and the 9th battalion would take its part soon enough.

Between the 1st and 5th of August the trenches remained fairly quiet, which gave the battalion an opportunity to bed itself in to Trench warfare, Western Front style. During the hours of darkness, wiring parties and patrols carried out their work as silently as possible. The slightest sound being magnified greatly and the fear of discovery being constant, that it would bring down machine gun and artillery fire on the exposed men. Even picking out features and the other men in the darkness is an art to be learned. Firstly the eyes have to become accustomed to the darkness and then men have to look at things with a sideways glance. In this way they can get their 'night-vision' and pick out features and men with more ease.

The War Diary on the 1st August gives mention to aeroplane activity and 105mm shells falling in the area 1.57 & 58 (sheet 51B France 1/40,000). At 9-30am on 2nd, the G.O.C. (General Officer Commanding, who at this time was Lieut-Gen. Sir C Woollcombe), the 11th Division visited the men in the trenches. He had taken over command of the Division on the 4th July 1916 and this was probably his first contact with the battalion. No doubt the cynics in the battalion would see this as proof of the area being a 'quiet sector'. There was more aerial activity than anything else, as the Germans attempted to ascertain the British strength in the Arras area of operations. They would also use aeroplanes to spot for the artillery of course in conjunction with balloons.

The 4th, 5th and 6th were rated as quiet, although H.E. shells (High Explosive) fell near battalion H.Q. Only one casualty is mentioned on 5th August, with the man being wounded. There is no mention however of any men being killed on 6th August but Thomas Manderfield of Barrow on Soar Leicestershire did indeed pay the supreme sacrifice on that day.

22845, Private Thomas Manderfield was killed on 6th August 1916 – commemorated on the Arras Memorial, Bay 7. He was the first 9th battalion man commemorated on the memorial. The fact he is commemorated and not buried, would point to him being killed by shellfire. Normally in a quiet sector men would be taken back and properly buried.

At least two 9th Battalion men were killed in action whilst attached to the 8th South Staffs. The 8th Battalion South Staffordshire Regiment were part of 17th Division, XV Corps. 11054, Private John Henry Scott a native of Lincoln aged 32 years, son of the Late Mr. and Mrs. S Scott of Lincoln is buried at Peronne Road Cemetery, Maricourt, and grave IV. C. 30.

During the night of 6th/7th August, the 8th Battalion was in support at Delville Wood. They came under shelling during the day and were also tasked to take up rations to the Border Regiment holding the front line.

Casualties were estimated at 20 other ranks and one of these was John Henry. John was originally in the 1st battalion Sherwood Foresters but had transferred to the 9th.

The 9th also saw another young man die whilst attached to the 8th South Staffordshire's. James Walters was sixteen years of age and had served with the battalion from the age of 15. He had seen action at Gallipoli and at the time of his death, his mother was in the process of getting him out of the army. Sadly she would be to late.

25793, Private James Walters aged 16 years died on 9th August 1916 and is buried in Delville Wood cemetery, grave IV. F. 6. His headstone gives his age as 17 but this is incorrect and will be changed in due course.

James Walters. The youngest man in the battalion to die and his grave at Delville Wood.

During the 9th August the 8th battalion were ordered to the relief of the Border Regiment in the front line trenches and by 4-00 a.m. this had been completed. Whilst this was in progress, a report from 'B' Company came in saying two platoons were buried in a trench, which had been destroyed by a Minnenwerfer (known as a Minnie – a very effective German trench mortar). By 5-40pm the first casualty reports came in with one officer and 18 other ranks wounded and 3 other ranks killed. By 6-00pm the casualty figure was 13 other ranks killed, 47 wounded and 5 missing. James Walters was one of these men and he was placed in a blanket with a comrade and quickly buried. After the war Delville Wood Cemetery was made and graves from a number of battlefield cemeteries where concentrated, one of these men being James Walters

Another man to die whilst on attachment was 23398 Private Abraham Ward, a native of Nottingham. He was killed in action while with the 7th Battalion Lincolnshire Regiment on 9th August and is commemorated on the Thiepval Memorial, having no known grave. It is likely that he lies in an 'Unknown British soldier's' grave in Delville Wood cemetery.

The 7th August saw five new officers taken on strength – 2/Lts Farrand, Young, Wilmot, Phelps and Abbott. Intriguingly a note said ' Two transport men met with a mishap', but just what this mishap was will never be known.

Between the 8th and 12th August, if the War Diaries are to be believed, nothing much happened. Looking at the deaths for this period shows the limitations of War Diaries and of the person making them out. Some are full of information and an excellent guide to the 'doings' of the battalion, others like the 9th Battalion at this time, leave much to be desired. During the same period, The 8th Battalion South Staffordshire Regiment, to which men of the 9th battalion Sherwood Foresters were attached, gave movements, times and other units, thereby giving a much better picture. No doubt the families of the men killed during those days would not consider that nothing much happened.

The period from 9-00am on 8th until 10-00am on the 9th saw a continuous gas alert. The the men worked whilst wearing gas masks and in a higher state of alert. This would normally happen at dawn and dusk, when the men 'stood-to' ready for any attack or fighting patrol, which may have occurred. The 10th saw a British bombardment of Beauran, which was usually met with a robust reply from the enemy artillery. There was also a small amount of rain! By looking beyond the war diaries, it is possible to ascertain exactly what, 'quiet' and 'very quiet' really meant on the Western Front. On 8th August, three men had been killed in action and along with the five men killed on 9th August are all commemorated on the Arras Memorial:

8th August 1916 –

19132, Private William R. Wheatley, aged 26 years, of Ockbrook, Derby.

40776, Private Herbert Coulam, aged 39 years, of Barton-on-Humber, Lincs.

40741, Private Charles Chapman, of Stamford, Lincs.

Note that the two Lincolnshire men's service numbers are only 35 apart and it is likely they trained together.

9th August 1916 –

19800, Private V Clarke, of Cresswell, Derby's. Formerly 11528, Leicestershire Regiment.

19418, Private George Davenport, aged 25 years of Longton, Stoke-on-Trent,

19677, Private Colen Hayes, of Fenton, Staffs.

13542, Private Samuel Langston, of Rotherham Yorks.

5009, Private William Wragg aged 21 years, of Hoveringham, Nottingham.

During the period 1st to 18th August, the battalion had eight men killed, which was indeed a very low total, particularly when compared to the losses a few miles away on the Somme front.

The remaining six days of the battalions stay on the Arras front continued quietly. The enemy shelling became more active and the battalion put out patrols to check on the German positions and attempt to take prisoners, as intelligence on the enemy was always required. On 16th a patrol of 'A' Company did come across a 'Hun' working party and bombed it with grenades, although the results of this attack were not known.

On the 17th August, officers of the 13th Northumberland Fusiliers visited the trenches to prepare to relieve the 9th battalion, the following day. The Germans, as was usual at such times, knew a change over was due and shelled Arras. The German machine-gunners added to the discomfiture, in the hope of catching the unwary during the changeover period. The changeover period was particularly fraught with danger as men went to and fro along the communication trenches. The enemy artillery, machine-gunners and snipers were always active at such times. The slightest relaxation by the troops whilst leaving the trench line could result in a wound or death, although not in this instance.

Finally on the 18th August, it was time for the battalion to leave their quiet sector and prepare for its participation in 'the great struggle' on the Somme. This campaign had continued throughout July, August and into September. The majority of the objectives of 1st July remained firmly in German hands and it would be November before a halt was finally called. The battalion had nearly three weeks to prepare for their entry into the Somme front line. When the battalion got there, it would once again give a good account of itself.

Returning for a moment to the 18th August, the 13th Battalion Northumberland Fusiliers arrived to relieve the battalion and except for a few Whizz-bangs, accompanied by trench mortar shells, all was quiet. By 5-00am all of the Companies along with the specialist groups (Machine-gunners, Trench Mortars and Snipers) were located near battalion H.Q. At 8-30pm the battalion moved off to Berneville with H.Q. leaving first, followed by each Company. The War Diary stated '11-00pm Head-quarters arrives Chateau Berneville, 1 hour before Lancashire Fusiliers' whether this was a race for the best billets is not stated but it seems an odd entry. The 9th (Service) Battalion, the Lancashire Fusiliers were in the same Division but 34th Brigade. It is possible inter Brigade rivalry was the reason for this entry in the diary. There was always a healthy competition between battalions from different Regiments and it engendered 'Esprit de Corps'. By 11-55pm. the battalion was settled in the billets at Berneville, the move made without a hitch. Not that the battalion would stay long, as the move to billets further back would begin the following day.

The Divisional headquarters was located at Gouy-En-Artois and on the afternoon of 19th August, the battalion moved there. The period from 20th to 28th August would be taken up with training and fighting off illness. At any time when a large body of men were gathered together, the likelihood of contagious illness was always there. Many diseases which today are rare and classed as minor, were life threatening 90 years ago.

Sunday 20th August was given over to rest and church parade, which was held in the Divisional School hut!

On 21st, 2/Lt Munday, a solicitor in civilian life returned from leave. In 1918, the then Captain Munday, M.C., would act as the 'soldiers friend' in the Courts Martial of Private A Briggs. Two new officers joined on the 22nd, they being Lieutenant Hind and 2/Lt Hargreaves, although five days later Hargreaves would be seconded to Divisional Headquarters. A Brigade conference took place, whilst the other ranks continued their training for the forthcoming battles. This training would continue until the move forward on 29th, when the specific battle rehearsals would commence. The Brigadier Commanding, 33rd Infantry brigade on 23rd August, inspected the battalion.

The first mention of illness was on 26th August as 2/Lt Fowler was sent to hospital suffering from Diphtheria. It has to be presumed that the illness had also struck among the other ranks as on 27th, Church parades were cancelled on account of Diphtheria. On 28th 2/Lt Ackroyd was also sent to hospital as the Diphtheria continued to thin the ranks of the battalion.

On 29th August the battalion began its move towards the front line area on the Somme. Although not everyone in the battalion would make the move from Gouy-En-Artois, to Estree-Wamin. Firstly the N.C.O.s were held back for a Lewis Gun course, whilst 2/Lt Scott and two servants were left behind in isolation. Presumably they either had Diphtheria or were suspected of having it. Finally 2/Lts Cudlip and Abbott were sent to hospital, to join the ever-growing list of incapacitated officers – not the best preparation for the forthcoming battle.

The battalion completed its move by 4-00pm with battalion H.Q., at map reference H23.b.7.7, ref. 51c France, 1/40,000. The only other item of note seems to have been the weather, with heavy rain commencing at 4-30pm and seemingly continuing throughout the next day. The men being given various lectures on 30th August as it was too wet to attempt any outdoor activities. The 31st would be for most of the men the highlight of the month as it was 'bath-day' in Bois de Robermont. The opportunity to at least remove some, if not all of the trench grime and to wipe out a few hundred lice was not to be missed. It was an impossibility to be lice free but for a few days afterwards, the numbers would be manageable. So began September and the battalion would be fully involved in the latter battles of the Somme campaign.

By the end of September many of men will have died their King and Country, in reality this sacrifice was made for their pals in the battalion with little thought of King or Country.

On 1st September the battalion took part in a Brigade scheme (Training exercise) at Estree-Wamin and the following day they entrained at Frevent for the journey to Acheux. It would take them five hours to make this relatively short journey.The battalion was now in the rear area of the Somme battlefield. The French called it 'the Zone of Occupation' and civilians could remain but military rules and requirements came first.

The diary of Sunday 3rd September mentions nothing with the entry 'Sunday, Wet'. For two ex 9th battalion men though Private George Padgett and Private David Hampson, it would be their last day. They were attached to the 17th battalion at the time.

18744, Private George Padgett, aged 28 years of Rutland Street; Derby is buried in Knightsbridge Cemetery, Mesnil-Martinsart, and grave F7.

Likewise 12932, Private David Hampson, aged 33 years of 31 Shaftesbury Street Derby. He is also buried in Knightsbridge Cemetery, Mesnil-Martinsart, and grave F 19.

An obituary in The Derby Daily Telegraph, Tuesday 26 September 1916 who's publication date would coincide with many of his former comrades also laying down their lives read as follows –

'Local Roll of Honour
Derby Family's Second Bereavement
News has been received by his parents who reside at 31, Shaftesbury Street Derby of the death of Private David Hampson, of the Notts and Derbyshire regiment. He joined the colours at the outbreak of the war and was sent out with his regiment to the Dardanelles where he took part in the landing at Suvla Bay. After being invalided home with dysentery, Private Hampson again volunteered for active service and was sent out to France, where he was killed in action on September 3rd. His only brother was killed in action in France at the commencement of the war at the age of 19. Private David Hampson was 33 years of age, unmarried and resided at the address above mentioned.'

September was the decisive phase of the Battles of the Somme with the British amassing all reserves to smash the German lines, or at least that was the aim. The Thiepval area and Mouquet Farm and been attacked by thousands of troops and each time ended in failure. The Germans had machine gun posts in every shell hole and looked down on the British troops.

The scene was set for the Battle of Flers-Courcelette between 15th and 22nd September, followed by the Battle of Morval 25th to 28th and Battle of Thiepval 26th to 28th. The Canadians would take part of Mouquet Farm on 16th but the glory of its final capture would go to the 11th Division, of which the 9th battalion was a part. The ultimate objective of the 11th Division was Hessian Trench and they would have tank support.

The Germans had fortified and strengthened the trench system between Thiepval and Mouquet Farm. This was the area of Schwaben Trench and Joseph Trench and the 33rd Brigade's frontage ran west from Mouquet Farm and along the upper reaches of "Blighty Valley".

The 4th would be taken up with lectures and battalion attack training before the move into the front line.

The next day saw the battalion move to billets at Bouzincourt whilst 2/Lt Phelps along with seven other ranks left for the Lewis Gun School at Etaples. This seems to be an odd decision as the battalion would move into the front line on the following day. On 6th at 3-00am the battalion moved into the trenches at Ovillers, one of the original targets on 1st July but not taken until September. They relieved the 13th battalion Cheshire Regiment, 74th Infantry Brigade. Whilst no mention of casualties is given in the war diary, there would be one death.

12942, Private Charles Thomas Hudson aged 23 years of 'C' Company of Rivett Street Derby, buried at Bouzincourt Communal Cemetery Extension, grave I.F.8. A dressing station was based here for units at Thiepval and around the Leipzig salient, 3 miles to the east. Although at this time it was also used for the internment of soldiers killed in action and brought back from the line, Charles was one of these men.

Between the 7th and 23rd September the battalion would be in the front line trenches or the reserve line south of Thiepval. This area was on the left of the Albert-Bapaume road and the men would use Nab Valley to access it. Nab and Mash valley along with Crucifix Corner would become well known places to the battalion.

British Divisions had suffered grievous losses in this area on and after 1st July. In fact near here the 11th battalion Sherwood Foresters as part of 70th Brigade had attacked on 1st July with disastrous results. The 11th battalions objective on that day had been Mouquet Farm, which was over a mile to the German rear. The 11th battalion was told it would be a walk over and that the field kitchens would bring them lunch at Mouquet Farm. Few men even reached the German barbed wire that day and the Brigade had 1,987 men killed or wounded. Mouquet Farm would eventually fall to the 11th Division and 9th Sherwood Foresters on 26th September. The

11th Battalion objectives of the 1st July would finally be taken by their sister battalion, the 9th, nearly three months later.

The battalion's time in the front line between 6th and 12th September was rather lively and the casualty list bears this out. The war diary of 7th shows them in the trenches with active artillery from both sides. Captain Smeeton was wounded along with two other ranks. Only one man was shown as being killed but also neither of the two wounded men survived their injuries.

22916, Private Walter Russell Adcock, aged 23 years, of Beeston; Notts is buried in Ovillers Military Cemetery, grave I.E. 32.

Plot I has burials from August 1916 and a number of 9th battalion men are here.

22738, Private Fred Carter, aged 21 years, of Sutton-in-Ashfield; Notts has no known grave and is commemorated on the Thiepval Memorial to the missing.

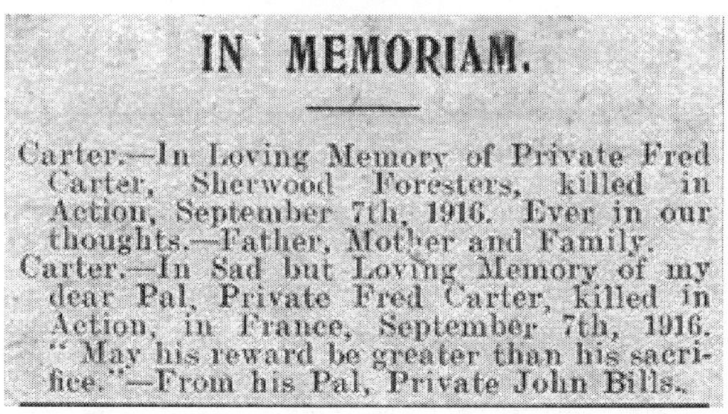

IN MEMORIAM.

Carter.—In Loving Memory of Private Fred Carter, Sherwood Foresters, killed in Action, September 7th, 1916. Ever in our thoughts.—Father, Mother and Family.
Carter.—In Sad but Loving Memory of my dear Pal, Private Fred Carter, killed in Action, in France, September 7th, 1916. "May his reward be greater than his sacrifice."—From his Pal, Private John Bills.

12759, Private Sam Hollyoak, aged 28 years, of Newbold, Chesterfield, Derbys has no known grave and is also commemorated on the Thiepval Memorial to the missing.

The Memorial panels to all of the 9th battalion men are on pier and face 10C, 10D and 11A. A number of officers and men were killed and wounded between 7th and 12th and at times the War Diary entry differs from that of other sources such as the Commonwealth War Graves Commission.

The diary has Lieutenant Everard as being killed with four other ranks on 8th and this date is mentioned in other sources but the CWGC have his date of death as 7th. . These discrepancies occur on a regular basis and show the problems the authorities had dealing with the mass of bodies during major campaigns such as the Somme.

Lieutenant Clement Charlie Everard, aged 36 years, of Bristol is buried in Bouzincourt Communal Cemetery Extension, grave I.F. 10

On the 8th the battalion continued to be plagued by enemy artillery with the British artillery giving as good as it got. 2/Lt Ottewell joined the battalion from base and the weather still held. In fact the weather for September was very good, as Friday 8th had temperatures up to 70 deg F, warm but overcast until early afternoon.

The heavy artillery barrage against the battalion's front continued throughout the next few days and on 11th and 12th a large number of tear gas shells mixed with poisonous gas shells exploded in their trenches. The Germans knew that an assault by the British in this sector was imminent and the constant and heavy shelling would disrupt any preparations and catch men in the open. On 9th 'C' Company relieved 'D' and 'B' relieved 'A' in the firing line at 8-00 a.m. The battalion's casualties began to mount as the enemy artillery barrage continued and the Headquarters dugouts were shelled causing a number of injuries. The War Diary of the 10th had an interesting comment and one that was used for the first time by the battalion – '2/Lt Farrand to hospital (shell shock)'. It is also worth noting that the said 2/Lt Farrand had only been with the battalion since 7th August 1916 and there is no record of him returning to the battalion in 1916. As he left for hospital, 2/Lts Cullin and Birtill reported their arrival.

The 11th and 12th saw concentrated gas attacks by the enemy. The diary states as follows -:

'11th. Artillery active all day. 8pm to 12 midnight, Enemy send over large number of tear shells, which passed over our trenches'. This comment ties in with the enemy trying to harass troops to the rear who were getting in position for the forthcoming attack.

'12th. 4am to 6am Enemy send over large number of tears shells which exploded in our trenches. It was suspected that poisonous gas shells were mixed up with these. Gas helmets were worn and no casualties occurred. 6a.m. Relieved by 6th Lincoln Regiment in trenches and moved into reserve dug-outs vacated by 6th Borders'

The Germans who still held the ridgeline could see all of these movements and knew where and when to target the British troops.

The battalion was now in reserve at Ovillers and Donnets Posts – a slightly quieter area than their previous location. The Battle of Flers-Courcelette began on 15th and continued until 22nd, whilst the battalion would not take a lead roll, they would support other Brigades of the Division.

Returning to the casualties for the period -:

8th September –
2/Lt Egerton, mentioned in the War Diary as being wounded, on 9th, whilst other sources give the date of death as 8th, although the timing of the official death were often delayed. It was unusual to have it a day early.
2/Lt Bertram Gustavus Egerton. Aged 33 years of Highgate London is buried in Bouzincourt Communal Cemetery Extension, grave I F 11. He died of wounds.

He was also mentioned in 'De Ruvigny's Roll of Honour', and this gives more information on the man himself.

'Egerton, Bertram Gustavus, 2nd Lieut, 9th (Service) Battn. The Sherwood Foresters (Nottinghamshire and Derbyshire Regt.) 2nd s, of Gustavus Robert Egerton, of Royston Mansions, Highgate, N.; b. London, 4 Oct 1881; served throughout the South African War 1899-1902, with the Rough Riders (Queen's Medal with four clasps and the Yeomanry Efficiency Medal); rejoined the Rough Riders, with his former rank of Sergt, after the outbreak of war in Aug. 1914; went to Egypt 12 April 1915 and while there was sent to the School of Instruction at Zeltoun, being gazetted 2nd Lieut. Sherwood Foresters 10 Oct. 1915 and served with that Regiment at Suvla Bay; returned to Egypt after the evacuation in Jan. 1916, where he acted as Wharf Master on the Canal, until his regiment left for France 28 June, and died at Bouzincourt 8 Sept. following, from wounds received earlier in the day. Buried in the Communal Cemetery Extension, Bouzincourt. His Capt wrote; 'His death leaves a gap that will not easily be filled. He was a grand colleague to work with – brave, cheerful and very efficient.'

21558, Private E Kitchen, aged 21 years of Mansfield, Notts, killed in action and buried in Ovillers Military Cemetery, grave I.C. 22.
22942, Private William Sharpe, of Hodthorpe, Derbys, killed in action and buried in Ovillers Military Cemetery, grave I. C 21. These two men are buried next to each other

The other three men, who died on the 8th, all succumbed to wounds.

13240, Private Thomas Francis Jerram, aged 20 years of Derby; buried in Bouzincourt Communal Cemetery Extension, grave I.H. 1.

8516, CSM, Arthur Claud Cecil Basham, aged 28 years of Suffolk, buried in Varennes Military Cemetery, I. A. 35. The Cemetery is situated in what was the rear area of the battlefield.

11749, Lance Corporal E V Kennedy, is buried in Warloy-Baillon Communal Cemetery Extension, IV. A. 1. An Advanced Operating Centre was situated here during the Somme campaign.

The Diary between the 9th and 12th gives the total number of men killed as seven, with six on 9th, and one on 10th September. Whilst the CWGC does record seven deaths in the battalion, the dates vary slightly.

9th September –
19908, Lance Corporal, R Marsh, Formerly 12201 Leicestershire Regiment is buried in Ovillers Military Cemetery, I. C. 20. He was born in Yorkshire, enlisted at Chesterfield and gave his abode as West Bromwich.

10th September –
24669, Private, H Hopcroft, of Radford, Notts, He is buried in Ovillers Military Cemetery, I. C. 19.

11th September -
11783, Private Thomas Barker, aged 21 years of Nottingham is buried in Ovillers Military Cemetery, I. B. 26.

22151, Private J R Staniforth of Ilkeston has no known grave and is commemorated on the Thiepval Memorial to the missing.

25580, Private Frank Hollis of Worksop, Notts has no known grave and is commemorated on the Thiepval Memorial to the missing.

20859, Private A E Crump of Worcester is buried in Ovillers Military Cemetery, I. B. 23.

13th September –
20415, Private Sidney Baker of Somercoates, Derbys, died of wounds and is buried in Ovillers Military Cemetery, I B 27.

The period between the 13th and 17th September was one of waiting and reacting to the attacks made by 32nd Brigade, along with the 6th Lincolns and 6th Borders.

The 13th was relatively quiet until 4.pm. when a massive artillery bombardment commenced. On 14th the British artillery worked over the German trenches in preparation for an attack by 32nd Brigade who knew that this area was one of the toughest nuts to crack. For the first time, the new 'wonder weapon', the tank would be employed but with mixed results. Another innovation was a creeping barrage of artillery to protect the advancing troops and this no doubt saved many lives in front of the fortresses of Mucky (Mouquet) Farm and Thiepval. For the artillery to work effectively though the scope of attacks had to be limited and the tactics of 'bite and hold' became the norm. Troops would not be asked to advance beyond the range of the protecting artillery screen. Whilst this type of advance had advantages it was also slow and gave the Germans time to prepare a new line.

The 14th saw a heavy British artillery barrage to prepare for the advance by 32nd Brigade and this attack successfully took all the objectives. The battalion, in reserve stood to at 6 pm in readiness to support, if needed. The following day 'C' Company was moved forward to support 6th Border Regiment who had advanced slightly. In this Captain Harding was slightly wounded but continued with his duties. The remainder of the battalion moved from reserve, into the support dugouts and found little enemy artillery fire in their area. The 16th was another day of support as the 6th Lincolns attacked under a heavy bombardment at 5 pm and occupied Constance Trench without any resistance. 'D' Company moving up in support of the 6th Lincolns during this action and whilst the War Diary did not mention it, one other rank was killed.

34774, Private Walter Dawson, of Radcliffe on Trent, Notts is commemorated on the Thiepval Memorial to the Missing.

At noon on 17th the battalion moved its position slightly to the left in order to support the 6th Border's. They took over the dugouts previously manned by the 6th Borders and awaited orders. At 6 pm these orders came and the battalion moved into the support line to reinforce the 6th Borders in case a German counter attack was mounted.

The 18th saw more Brigade orders issued and the battalion was tasked with relieving the 6th Lincoln Regiment before 11 pm. Despite some fine weather in the previous days, the trenches were knee deep in mud. It had rained all day with some 13mm falling over the battlefield, turning the roads into a muddy slime and the trenches into mud holes.

The rain continued the following day and adding to the battalion's discomfort, the enemy put down a heavy barrage of whiz-bangs (Small caliber German shell, also called pipsqueaks) and High Explosive shells on Constance Trench. Two other ranks being killed and four wounded in this barrage.

14106, Private Edward Fines

14106, Private Edward Fines, aged 26 years of Old Radford, Notts, and I.C. 17 (pictured above).

The two men, who lived and fought together, now lie side by side in Ovillers Military Cemetery.

The battalion was ordered to take Joseph Trench and Operational orders issued. The Companies were lined up ready for the attack but at 2 pm the attack was postponed.

On the 20th according to the war diary, the line was still being shelled, 2/Lt Downman and five other ranks killed and twenty-five men wounded. At 7 am orders were received that the 6th Lincolnshire Regiment would relieve the Battalion. Arrangements were made but at 12noon the orders for relief were cancelled. No reason for this change was given but the situation along the whole of the between Thiepval and Pozieres was fairly fluid as the British troops positioned themselves for the main attack on 26th. The War Diary for 21st gives casualties as 3 other ranks killed and 25 wounded.

Sources give one officer and six other ranks dying

on 21st and one of these was probably wounded prior to this date. There are no deaths mentioned for 20th, although again the conditions in which the diary was being kept must be taken into account. Either taking notes in a poorly lit dugout or writing from memory some days later after serious fighting cannot be conducive to accurate reporting. The weather on Thursday 21st was slightly better and although the trenches were drier, they were still full of sticky, clinging mud. Constance Trench was still getting a fair amount of attention from the enemy artillery.

13151, Private, John William Wadley of Eckington Yorks, Died of Wounds and is buried in St.Pierre Cemetery, Amiens, IV. C. 9

Second Lieutenant Bernard Vincent Ridout Downman aged 20 years; a native of Derby is buried in Bouzincourt Communal Cemetery Extension, I.H.8. All sources except the battalion War Diaries refer to him, as "9th Bn. Attached to the 13th Bn." This was obviously not the case as the 13th Battalion was the reserve based in England.

His death is mentioned in the 'Local Roll of Honour page in the Derby Daily Telegraph dated Tuesday September 26 1916' The day when so many of his fellow 9th men were attacking. His obituary being above the one of Private Hampson mentioned on the 3rd September.

"Derby Clergyman's son Killed. We offer our sympathy to the Rev. F. P. and Mrs. Downman, of Hartington Street, Derby, in the bereavement which had overtaken them by the death of their youngest son, Second-Lieut. Bernard Vincent Ridout Downman, of the Sherwood Foresters. The War Office have notified the family that he was killed in action on September 22. The gallant officer was educated at Derby school and St. Cuthbert's Worksop, before proceeding to Cambridge with a view to taking Holy Orders. He was an undergraduate when war broke out and at once joined the University O.T.C. (Officer Training Corps). The following February, on attaining his 19th birthday, he was given a commission in the Sherwood Foresters, completing his military training at Lichfield. In January of this year he was sent out to join his battalion in Egypt, being transferred to France in June. Another of Mr. Downman's sons is a prisoner of war in Germany, having been wounded before he was captured"

22210, Lance Corporal George Winstanley, aged 26 years, of Bolton; Lancs is buried in Ovillers Military Cemetery, I.B. 17.

4645, Lance Corporal J S Sellers, of Nottingham is buried in Ovillers Military Cemetery, I.B. 18

4687, Private Frank Henry Smith aged 20 years, of Ripley, Derbys is commemorated on the Thiepval Memorial.

14105, Lance Corporal T. Moore of Nottingham is buried in Pozieres British Cemetery, Ovillers-La-Boisselle.

12630, Private William Winfield aged 25 years of Derby, Died of wounds and is buried in Warloy-Baillon Communal Cemetery Extension.

The 22nd would see the battalion being relieved at midnight by the 6th Yorkshire Regiment (32nd Infantry Brigade) and although the day was quiet, another 8 casualties were suffered, two of these men being killed.

19017, Private Ernest Sanders aged 18 years of Longton, Staffs is buried in Ovillers Military Cemetery, I.C. 14

21087, Private H E Swift, aged 27 years of Worksop, Notts is commemorated on the Thiepval Memorial.

By 3am the relief was complete and the battalion proceeded to a mixed camp of huts and tents at Mailly-Maillet. The men would have a couple of days before taking their place in the Battle of Thiepval.

Four men are shown as dying on 23rd September and two of these as killed in action. These men are probably the ones mentioned in the War Diary a couple of days earlier.

The two men killed in action are both commemorated on the Thiepval Memorial.

15137, Private Thomas Henry Cowling aged 20 years of Worksop, Notts

13610, Private Reginald Page aged 21 years of Derby. Reginald was part of 'A' Company

26656, Private William Allen aged 35 years who enlisted at Sheffield but whose parents lived in Saxilby, Lincs, died of wounds and is buried in Aveluy Communal Cemetery Extension. J 27

20301, Private H Harrop aged 23 years of Bestwood Park, Notts, died of wounds and is buried in Warloy-Baillon Communal Cemetery Extension, II. B. 5

The Battalion War diary -:

24th September 1916 – Battalion at Mailley-Maillet. No parades held during the morning. New clothing etc issued. 2.30 pm – Brigade scheme – rehearsal of forthcoming attack on Thiepval.

(Note – On 24th July 1916 II Corps of which 11

Division was a part took over the front and divisions of the X Corps)

The Battle of Thiepval, 26th to 28th September 1916.

The 9th Battalion would once again be taking part in a major battle and would enhance its reputation as an excellent fighting unit, which could be relied on to get the job done despite the cost. By the end of the battle nearly 100 men of the battalion would be dead or dying of wounds with over 200 others suffering wounds. As the men marched to their allotted jump off point they would have seen others busy digging graves in readiness for the battles dead. The men hoped that they would survive but knew what faced them. The men who had already survived Gallipoli would think that they stood a better chance than the new men but shellfire was indiscriminate and you needed luck to come through. Many men hoped for a 'blighty' (Wound needing repatriation to the UK) and some respite from trench life, although some wounds would blight men's lives and cause early death.

It is important to use all possible sources and to report all of these accurately. Therefore Lt-Col Scothern's notes and the C.O.s (Lt.Col Thornton) report of the battle to H.Q. 33rd Infantry Brigade will be used in full. The war diaries give little information but will be used to supplement.

25th September – The eve of the Battle. From 9am to 12 noon the men attended the bathing parades although it may have been better to bathe before getting new clothes and not the day afterwards. The battalion was also under orders to move at short notice and at 3.30pm they set of for Ovillers Post. Teas were at Martinsart Wood at 5pm, and at 8pm the battalion moved off to Ovillers, which was reached at about 10 pm. The packs, which had been sent earlier in lorries, were distributed. In addition, bombs, flares, sandbags, rockets, entrenching tools and extra 100 rounds of small arms ammunition were issued to each man. This took a good deal of time to complete.

Constance Trench – Trenches – Hessian and Zollern – 26th September

The first part of the War Diary has 3.30 pm relief of 6th Yorks completed. This should have read 3.30am the Battalion relieved the 6th Bn Yorkshire Regiment in Constance trench, prior to the attack on the German trenches.

Tea got up with greatest difficulty.

11.30am – Ready, 12.35pm Go Over, 12.28pm 1st Objective, 1.17pm 2nd Objective gained 'B; Coy, 1.45pm 2nd Objective gained 'A' Coy, 2.30pm 3rd Objective gained, 2.45pm Battalion H.Q. move to Zollern trench.

27th – Hessian and Zollern – 10am Received order to go to Joseph trench. 3pm Coys in Hessian return to Joseph trench.

28th – Joseph Trench – Fatigues and consolidation of Joseph trench.

29th – as previous day.

Lt.Col Scothern notes:

"Thiepval – (Sept. 26th 1916)

On Sept. 25th the battalion left Mailly Maillet, and moved up to the line via Ovillers, taking over Constance Trench, the jumping off point, in the early morning of the 26th. Tools and bombs had been picked up at Ovillers Post, and by midday everything was ready.

Punctually at the Zero Hour 12.35p.m, the 9th Sherwood Foresters moved forward under the barrage with the 6th Border Regiment on their left. In ten minutes time the first objective had been taken, and the battalion had captured 95 prisoners, 3 Machine Guns and one Trench Mortar. 'D' Company was leading Company with 'A' and 'B' Companies in support. Several casualties had occurred through over eagerness, the men pressing forward too much into the barrage.

The 6th Borders had been equally successful, and at 12.59 p.m. the Sherwood Foresters moved forward to take the second objective – Zollern Trench. 'A' and 'B' Coys were now in the van, and again casualties were caused by over-eagerness. Zollern Trench was reported occupied by 1.17p.m. Considerable enemy opposition was met with here, and many casualties amongst officers and men occurred. Two platoons of the Support Company in the first objective were ordered up to reinforce Zollern Trench. The captures by the battalion in this trench amounted to nearly 200 prisoners, 3 Machine Guns and 3 Trench Mortars. Some excellent work was also done here in clearing Midway Trench by a special bombing party.

A halt of one hour was made at Zollern

Trench before proceeding to the third objective – Hessian Trench. This was fortunate, as the Brigade in the right had failed to get up.

Two companies continued the attack, but only the left portion of the 3rd objective was taken. The credit for this belonged to the Sherwood Foresters, and one officer and 45 other ranks of the enemy were taken prisoner. Eventually the greater portion of what was left of the battalion seems to have crowded into this portion of Hessian Trench, and tough with Zollern was opened via Midway Trench.

The Brigadier's report on the operations may be here quoted: – "The manner in which Hessian Trench was tenaciously held during the night 26/27th September by the 9th Sherwood Foresters reflected the greatest credit on that Battalion as it was without touch on its right and left with anyone except the enemy".

Early in the morning of the 27th, a bombing attack by the enemy was successfully repulsed, whilst a bombing party of the Sherwood Foresters, who had not by any means lost their aggressive spirit, gained some ground to the right in Hessian until stopped by Machine Gunfire. During these attacks the enemy's 'egg bomb' was a source of annoyance as it outranged ours.

At 3.00 p.m. the 6th Borders successfully attacked the remaining portion of Hessian, and took over the whole of the trench shortly afterwards, the Sherwood Foresters returning to Joseph Trench.

The Battalion had lost heavily, but could be proud of its record, as it had pushed forward regardless of the fact that its flanks were 'in the air'. And had held on to its objective until the battalions on the right and left had come up. It had captured 341 prisoners, 6 Machine Guns and 4 Trench Mortars, but had suffered considerable losses.

The casualties from Sept. 26th to 30th inclusive were: -

	Killed	*Wounded*	*Missing*
Officers	*4*	*10*	
Other Ranks	*48*	*275*	*26*

To appreciate the facts properly it must be remembered that the battalion was attacking a very strongly fortified position defended by a determined enemy. The Germans fought their Machine Guns to the last moment, and in the first objective, the crews were killed to a man. This only enhances the value of the work done. It would seem that despite training being carried out to follow the new creeping barrage, the men got too close. In the heat of battle this was an understandable thing to happen. Valuable lessons were learned though and the creeping barrage would save many lives in future battles. Midway Trench, which is mentioned, was actually Midway Line, a Trench that linked Mouquet Farm to the Schwaben Redoubt.

There was a good reason for the 9th battalion flanks being 'in the air' as elements of 34th Infantry Brigade were decimated. The 8th Northumberland and 9th Lancashire Fusiliers attacked around Mouquet Farm and took their first objective but the 5th Dorsets in support were caught in a German artillery barrage as they moved up, suffering a large number of casualties. The Northumberland Fusiliers faced strong resistance and they had to dig in, having only one officer and some 50 men left. The Lancashire Fusiliers fared no better as they lost heavily, flanking fire coming from the Zollern Redoubt. They also faced very stiff opposition when in the Midway Line. Again only one officer and a few men made it to Zollern Trench. Even the 6th East Yorkshire Pioneer Battalion was thrown in to stabilize the situation. The 53rd infantry Brigade of the 18th Division attacked on the 9th Battalions left took their portion of Zollern Trench but after a couple of hundred yards of further advance were driven into shell holes by the weight of fire.

Officer Commanding 9th Battalion – Lt.Col Thornton – Report on battle.

9th. (Ser) Bn. The Sherwood Foresters.
To: – H.Q. 33rd. Infantry Brigade.

Ref. Your 3/01/47. The following is submitted for the information of the G.O.C.: -

On September 25th, in accordance with orders received the Battalion proceeded via Martinsart, where tea was served, to Ovillers Post which was reached about 10p.m. and where packs, which had been sent on in lorries, were distributed, also bombs, the extra 100 rounds S.A.A. per man, flares, sandbags, rockets and tools; this was a lengthy proceeding.

The Companies then moved up to Constance Trench in the following order;

'B' Company – Captain A Stevenson; 'A' Company – Captain A A Schweder; 'D' Company – Lieut J Critchlow; 'C' Company – Captain R H Gregory, orders being to occupy

the whole length of the trench until the hour for forming up.

Some delay was caused by a policeman mistaking his orders and refusing to allow 'B' Coy. To enter an 'Up' communication trench at point 62, the result being that this Company went round by Brimstone Trench and entered Constance Trench by the new communication trench on the right.

The Battalion was not reported as having taken over till 3.30 a.m. September 26th. The men were issued with a 'M & V' ration and tea was sent up during the morning.

At 10.15 a.m. companies commenced moving into position and by 11.30 a.m. reported that movement was complete. They were formed up as under –

'B' Company on right– 2 platoons in two waves against front side of Constance trench. 2 platoons in two waves against rear side of Constance trench.

'A' Company in centre, 'D' Company on left. Both of these companies formed similarly to 'B' Company.

The trench occupied by the above 3 Coys. Extended from R 33 a 54 to R 32 b 70.

'C' Coy. Was moved up with its right resting on Point 70 ready to move in as soon as the fourth attacking wave had left the trench.

Battalion H.Q. was at point 70.

In accordance with 33rd Brigade order No: 35, and addenda to same, which latter were received at 8.10. a.m.:

The three assaulting Companies moved off by whistle signal at Zero 12.35 p.m., and moving forward occupied the first objective. A message was received at Bn. H.Q. by runner from O. C. 'A' Coy. sent off at 12.48 p.m. that first objective had been taken. O. C. 'B' Coy. also reported to same effect. The O.C. 'D' Coy. was wounded and no message was received from this Company but it was observed to be in its objective.

During this advance, the right Coy. ('B') pressed to close into the barrage and small parties had to come a short way back and casualties occurred through this.

Captures during this advance were: -

2 Machine Guns R 32 b 88; these continued firing up to the last moment and the teams were killed to a man by 'D' Coy.

1 Trench Mortar R 27 c 34.

95 Prisoners – also one Machine Gun at R 32 b 76.

At 12.59 p.m. the assaulting companies again moved forward towards Zollern trench, the 2nd Objective, and a specially chosen bombing party under 2/Lt J.R. Crawford went forward to clear Midway line from R27c54 to R26 b 86.

Companies again pressed forward into the barrage and there were again casualties on this account.

O. C. 'A' Coy. in a report sent off at 1.45 p.m. stated that his company was in Zollern trench, that the trench was in good condition and that he wanted more officers as both his subalterns had been wounded.

As soon as the assaulting companies left the first objective, 'C' Company, which had moved up Constance trench, went forward in four waves and occupied the first objective, two platoons of the 7th S. Stafford Regt, taking the place of 'C' Coy.

Seeing that the assaulting companies had suffered many casualties, at 1.7 p.m. the O.C. 'C' Company was directed to reinforce with two platoons; this he did.

Captures in Zollern trench amounted as far as can be ascertained to close on 200 prisoners; one machine-gun at R26a 83 and two machine-guns at R26b85.

The special bombing party mentioned above worked from R27c54 up trench to R27c57 thence along Midway Line. The officer in charge, 2/Lt J.R. Crawford, since died of wounds, reported many dugouts full of enemy who refused to come out; these dugouts were bombed.

Shortly after it was known that Zollern Trench was occupied, orders were given to run out a line, in order that Bn. H.Q might move there as soon as the third objective was taken. Zollern Trench not being in sight of Point 70 Constance Trench, the actual advance of the two assaulting companies could not be seen, but from information obtained it started too soon by some 3 or 4 minutes. It is likely that this was the reason for the men being caught in the artillery barrage.

In a message, timed 2.38 p.m., O.C. 'A' Coy. wrote from Zollern Trench saying that:

'B' and 'D' Coys. had gone forward to attack Hessian, also part of 'C' Coy. and asks for reinforcements as he is too weak to hold Zollern along the whole length; the message further states that many prisoners had come back to Zollern from Hessian. The same officer

reported later that 3rd objective had been taken, that O.C. 'B' Coy. had asked for reinforcements and that he was moving up 'A' Coy. to Hessian and would leave flying patrols in Zollern.

A message was also received from O.C., 'B' Coy. that 3rd objective was taken and reinforcements urgently needed, and that there was no one up on our left. No report from 'D' Coy.

Captured in Hessian: 1 Officer and 45 other ranks.

A message sent to 7th. S. Staffords about 3 p.m. asking for reinforcements to be sent up to Zollern Trench; exact time of message cannot be read a carbon copy is very indistinct

(The 7th S. Staffords were left to mop-up and they also cleared the Midway Line. Four Platoons were sent in support to Hessian Trench and they helped repel a bombing attack)

Battalion H.Q. moved forward towards Zollern about 2.45 p.m. following the cable which it was hoped would have by then reached that place. On arriving about R 26 d 46 the signalers were found at a standstill having run short of wire, at the same time a runner brought a report that the Medical Officer was wounded; the whole party then came under M.G. fire from Stuff Redoubt and several casualties occurred.

The Bn. H.Q. was then withdrawn to Constance to give the signallers more time to get into Zollern, and to get once more into communication with Bde. H.Q.

At 3.23 p.m. a message was sent to Bde. That all four Coys. Of the Battn had moved into Hessian and that a company of the 7th. S. Staffords was being sent to reinforce Zollern.

About 4.50 p.m. no communication wire having been obtained with Zollern, Bn. H.Q. again went up and found the signallers close to Zollern but still short of wire. Bn. H.Q. moved into Zollern and more wire coming up shortly, communication to the rear was established.

Reports received from Capt. R. H. Gregory in Hessian trench asking for S.A.A. (Small Arms Ammunition) *bombs and reinforcements – two platoons of the 7th S.Stafford R. were sent up, and SAA and bombs got up later. Just before dark a party of 50 men was observed to be coming back into Zollern trench for Hessian trench. On enquiry they were found to be a company of the Suffolk Regt. who had been lying in a shallow trench in front of Hessian and had returned as soon as it was dark.*

During the night the enemy was very active in sniping and collected in some numbers in the right end of Hessian trench.

The night passed without further incident and ammunition, bombs, flares and water were sent up to Hessian by Midway Line, which was in a very bad condition.

September 27th; At daylight the situation was unaltered: at 8 a.m. I went up and inspected Hessian; 120 men of the Sherwood Foresters and 70 of the 7th. S. Stafford R. were there and it was my opinion that there were too many men in the trench; at this time a bombing party on the right of Hessian gained ground to the right until they came to two enemy Machine Guns; on the left the enemy was carrying out a bombing attack and as both officers of the 7th. S. Staffords had been wounded I directed Capt. Gregory to send an officer to drive back this attack…this was done by 2/Lieut E.H.F. Abbott with great difficulty as the enemy's egg bombs outranged him.

About 10 p.m., in accordance with orders from 33rd. Bde. Bn. H.Q. moved into Joseph Trench and the companies in Hessian came back there at about 3 a.m., having been relieved by the 6th. Border Regt.

For the rest of the day and night beyond shelling nothing to note.

September 28th. : – Consolidation of Joseph Trench, bringing up ammunition and collecting bombs, clearing the trench etc. Constantly shelled throughout the day.

September 29th. : – The battalion was employed on various fatigues from 3 a.m. till 11 p.m.; about 8 p.m. orders received to be ready to go up to Zollern to reinforce the 6th. Lincoln Regt. if necessary. The O.C. 6th. Lincoln R. who kept in close touch throughout the night did not require this assistance. Heavy shelling from 3 p.m. to 6 p.m.

September 30th. ; – Nothing of note occurred; consolidation carried on with; heavily shelled at intervals. At 7 p.m. relieved by 1st. Wilts Regt. And marched to Heduville.

So ended the battalions participation in the battle of Thiepval and once again they had suffered heavily but had got the job done. General Sir Hubert Gough Commanding reserve Army (later to become Fifth army) sent the following dispatch: -

> *"The following message received today from General Sir H. Gough Commanding Reserve Army by the G.O.C. 11th Division is to be communicated to all ranks, begins –*
>
> *My best congratulations to you and your Division on their gallant fighting today and throughout the successful operations in which you have been engaged since the capture of the Wonder Work. Your (You) have all done splendid work. Ends"*

Private Alfred Scott was by this time in hospital recovering from wounds and he also got the news of the battalion's efforts. He stated ' While I was in the hospital our Sgt Major was brought in, and he told me our battalion had the honour of capturing Thiepval'. (Derby Daily Telegraph, October 1916). It is more than likely that the Sgt Major was CSM Pickford of Leek, Staffs who died of wounds, at home on 23 October 1916.

The Brigade suffered over 600 casualties and more than half of these came from 9th battalion. The newspapers would once again be full of casualty lists and families would mourn their men. One man died on 26th September of wounds received earlier in the month. 12434, Private Tom Hutchinson, of Sherwood Notts, and is buried in Etaples Military Cemetery. His brother Harry had emigrated to Australia and would join the 46th Battalion A.I.F. He would be killed on 3 April 1918.

Only one man was killed whilst the battalion made its way to the front line on 25th September. 6991, Lance Corporal James Hillyard of Nottingham is buried in Norfolk Cemetery, Becordel-Becourt, and grave II A 36.

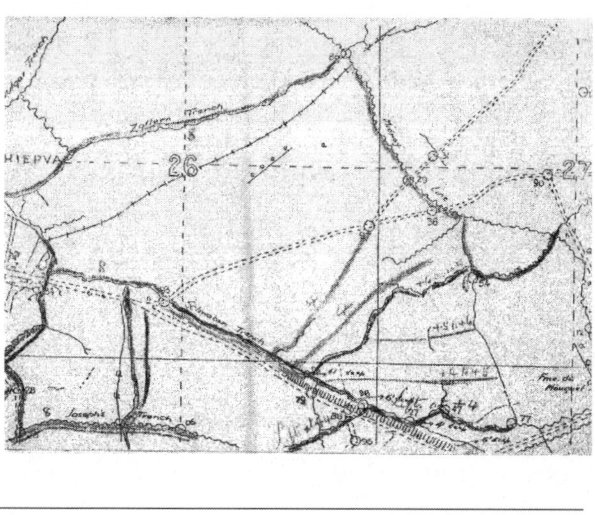

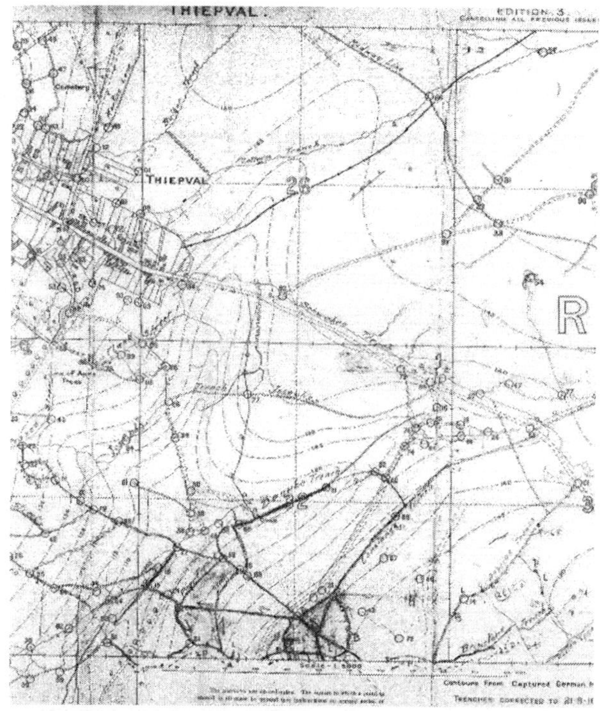

Surname Given Name Number

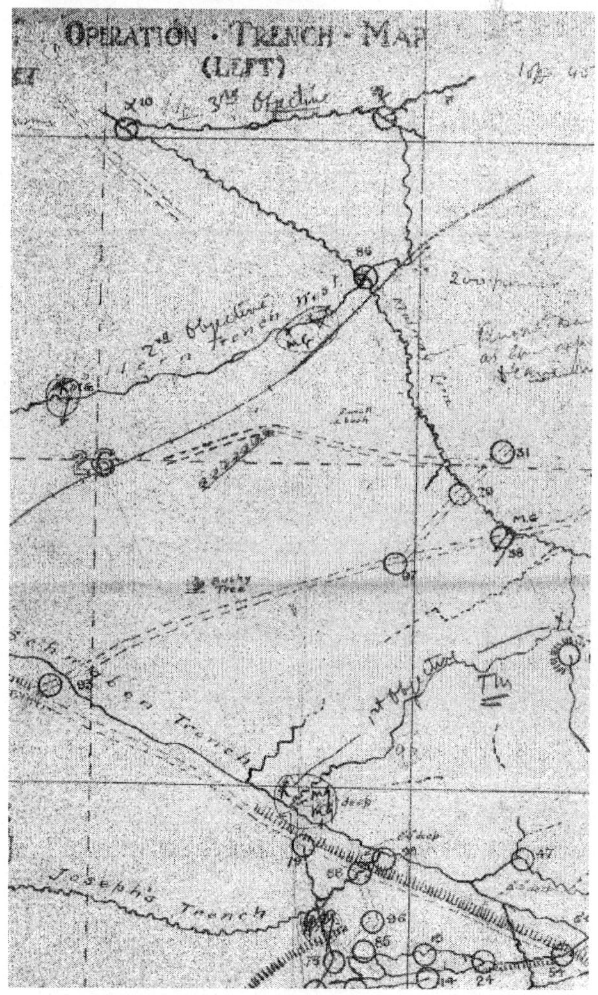

Maps showing the area of attack at Ovillers, taken from Brigade Orders and showing the trenches which were to be assaulted.

Roll Of Honour – Battle of Thiepval 26th to 28th September 1916.

The Following men are all commemorated on the Thiepval Memorial to the missing.

The Memorial is situated on the battlefield and close to the trench system where so many of the 9th battalion died or received wounds.

Rank	Born	Enlisted	Date died			
Allsop	Thomas	18452	Private	Tamworth Staffs	Mansfield	26-Sep
Armstrong	John G	23163	Private	Clay Cross	Clay Cross	26-Sep
Ault	William	22789	Private	Unknown		26-Sep
Baker	Frederick	19251	L/Cpl	Derby		26-Sep
Baker	Willie	13111	Private	New York, Yorks	Retford	26-Sep
Barlow	Walter	25398	Private	Brimington Dbys	Chesterfield	26-Sep
Bennett	Henry	24265	Private	Grassmoor Dbys	Chesterfield	26-Sep
Berry	Albert	13704	Private	Nottingham	Nottingham	26-Sep
Blakeway	Benjamin	12472	Private	Walsall Staffs	Mansfield	26-Sep
Briggs	Ernest	12416	Private	Derby	Derby	26-Sep
Brown	Sydney	13419	Private	Mexborough Yorks	Worksop	26-Sep
Carter	Charles	17796	Private	Hednesford Stfs	Mansfield	26-Sep
Causer	Thomas	20366	Private	Birmingham	Birmingham	26-Sep
Cockayne	Walter	20698	Private	Nottingham	Nottingham	26-Sep
Cooper	William	12962	Private	Staveley Dbys	Chesterfield	26-Sep
Croucher	George	23083	Private	Church Gresley	Burton	26-Sep
Daft	Arthur Frederick	10951	Private	Radford, Notts	Derby	26-Sep
Ede	Fred DCM	12770	A/Sgt	Retford Notts	Nottingham	26-Sep
Ellis	William	16826	Private	Nottingham	Nottingham	26-Sep
England	Edwin	22645	Private	Alfreton	Nottingham	26-Sep
Flint	Henry E	11010	L/Cpl	Burton on Trent	Nottingham	29-Sep
Forbes	John	13106	L/Cpl	Co.Westmeath	Derby	26-Sep
Freeman	Walter	19219	Private	Nottingham	Nottingham	26-Sep
Fretwell	Ernest	13159	Private	Eckington Yorks	Mansfield	26-Sep
Furness	Walter	24704	Private	New Whittington	Chesterfield	26-Sep
George	William Henry	14367	Private	Hasland Dbys	Chesterfield	26-Sep
Glover	Fred	3686	Private	Nottingham	Nottingham	26-Sep
Gregory	James William	25206	Private	Selston Notts	Nottingham	26-Sep
Hadman	John William	23200	Private	Hucknall Torkard	Mansfield	26-Sep
Hartshorn	Charles	21540	L/Cpl	Brownhills Stfs	Chesterfield	26-Sep
Hind	Jesse Francis Montague		Lieut			27-Sep
Hodson	Benjamin	19857	Private	Birmingham	Chesterfield	26-Sep
Holmes	Charles Edward	23045	Private	Westwood Notts	Sutton in Ashfield	26-Sep
Hone	James Henry	14311	Private	Birmingham	Chesterfield	26-Sep
Horlock	Henry	6924	L/Cpl	Christchurch Lncs	Kinsale Co Cork	26-Sep
Jones	William H	6596	Private	Brampton Dbys	Chesterfield	26-Sep
Kirkham	Harry	24023	Private	Calverton Notts	Ilkeston	26-Sep
Knight	George	13846	Private	Codnor Derbys	Derby	26-Sep
Leavesley	Horace	12400	Private	Nottingham	Nottingham	26-Sep
Liley	J	12608	Private	Collingham Notts	Welbeck Notts	26-Sep
Lloyd	John	19054	Private	Dawley Green Salop	Mansfield	26-Sep
Longdon	Herbert	15772	Private	Leeds	Derby	26-Sep
Lowe	George Henry	7046	Private	Queensborough. Leic	Derby	26-Sep
Marks	William	15002	Private	Worksop Notts	Worksop	26-Sep
Marsden	George	21502	Private	Mansfield	Mansfield	26-Sep
Page	John	21205	Private	New Houghton	Mansfield	26-Sep
Parry	Edward Richard	22158	Private	Newthorpe	Chesterfield	26-Sep
Pearson	Peter	15335	L/Cpl	Mansfield	Mansfield	26-Sep
Perotti	Ben.	22908	Private	Nottingham	Nottingham	26-Sep
Pierrepont	Bertram	24174	Private	Ilkeston	Ilkeston	26-Sep
Richardson	Robert	7018	Private	Walsall Staffs	Derby	26-Sep

Surname	Given Name	Number	Rank	Born	Enlisted	Date died
Riley	Percy	12404	Private	Hucknall Torkard	Nottingham	26-Sep
Rimmington	Walter G	11761	A/Cpl	Louth Lincs	Nottingham	26-Sep
Sansom	Albert	4409	Private	Nottingham	Nottingham	26-Sep
Schweder	Archibald Alan MC		Captain			26-Sep
Sewell	Herbert	21588	Private	Blyth Notts	Retford	26-Sep
Shaw	Arthur	12485	Private	Derby	Derby	26-Sep
Shawcroft	John	20828	Private	Clay Cross	Chesterfield	26-Sep
Shepherd	Joseph	18579	L/Cpl	Clay Cross	Ilkeston	26-Sep
Shirley	Charles	21789	Private	Hartington Dbys	Derby	26-Sep
Smedley	Samuel George	25908	Private	Eckington Yorks	Worksop	26-Sep
Stenson	Garnet	23126	Private	Derby	Nottingham	26-Sep
Straw	Ernest	12648	Private	Long Eaton	Derby	26-Sep
Thompson	William	23046	Private	Chesterfield	Chesterfield	26-Sep
Turner	Joseph	23340	Private	Grassmoor Dbys	Chesterfield	26-Sep
Undy	William Henry	9719	Private	Attercliffe Yks	Chesterfield	26-Sep
Vickers	George Hartley	18370	L/Cpl	Ashford in water	Chesterfield	27-Sep
Wakefield	James Parks	12907	Private	Tupton Derbys	Chesterfield	26-Sep
Waplington	Arthur	27044	Private	Nottingham	Nottingham	26-Sep
Ward	Joseph	19549	Private	Pleasley Notts	Mansfield	26-Sep
Whitehouse	William	27786	Private	Alvaston Derbys	Derby	26-Sep
Wilkinson	William	13367	L/Cpl	Retford Notts	Retford	26-Sep
Wilkinson	John	13306	Sgt	Awsworth Notts	Clay Cross	26-Sep
Worker	James	20006	Private	Wombwell Yks	Chesterfield	26-Sep

Information taken from the Commonwealth War Graves Commission website and cross referenced with 'Soldiers Died in the Great War 1914-1919, Part 49. The Sherwood Foresters (Nottinghamshire and Derbyshire Regiment)

The Derbyshire Courier dated 28th October 1916 gives mention to one of the above men.

Hasland Soldier Killed

"Mr and Mrs Joseph George, 18 Park Hill Cottages, Hasland received official notice from the War Office on Saturday that their second son Private William George, Sherwood Foresters was killed in action on 28th September. The parents had received no news from their son for a month and had grown anxious as to his fate for he had corresponded regularly previous to that time. Lance Corporal J. Guest also of Park Hill was in the same charge where he was wounded and he has been home on sick leave but could throw no light on what had befallen Private George although they were on the parapet together. The sad news was followed by a letter on Tuesday morning from Corporal Willis of the deceased's Platoon conveying the sympathy of all his comrades to the bereaved parents and stating that Private George was much respected and died a hero serving his King and country. The deceased soldier who was 21 years of age enlisted on 7th September 1914 and went to France in March 1915. He was wounded on 8th May of the same year and after regaining convalescence was drafted to Egypt on 25th October where he remained until early in July 1916 when he was again transferred to France."

The *Derby Daily Telegraph* also mentioned Lieut. J. F. M. Hind who was killed on 27th September.

25908 Private Samuel George Smedley, killed in action 26/09/191

Local Roll of Honour

Sherwood Officer Killed

"Lieut. J. F. M. (Monty) Hind, killed in action, was the only son of Mr. and Mrs. J. W. Hind, of Fairlawn, Sherwood and was 23 years of age. He was educated at Aldro, Eastbourne, Rugby, and Oriel College, Oxford where he passed the Final History School in the summer of 1914. He had entered the Inner Temple, but when war broke out he at once applied for a commission, being gazetted to the Sherwood Foresters. He went out to Gallipoli with his battalion at the end of June 1915, and took part in the landing at Suvla Bay, where the battalion suffered heavy losses, he being severely wounded in two places. On January 1st last he joined the reserve battalion, and on Easter Sunday he sailed for Egypt. Towards the end of June he left for France in command of detachments. His uncle, Lieut-Col. L. A. Hind, M.C., of the Robin Hoods, was killed in action last July.

The above piece differs from the War Diary of 21st August 1916, as it states –' Lieut Hind and 2/Lt Hargreaves joins for the first time'

On the same page of the newspaper there is mention of a 9th battalion officer wounded.

Another Sherwood Officer Wounded

'Second-Lieut. G. E. King, of the Notts and Derbyshire Regiment, who is in a Leicester hospital recovering from a gun-shot wound, is the only son of Mr and Mrs. J. E. King, of 59 Forest Road, Nottingham. He had been to Gallipoli and Egypt before he went to France some months ago, and was given his commission in March'

Although the majority of the men killed have no known grave, a few are buried in cemeteries nearby. Others who died of wounds are buried near hospital centres and one at home.

26 September 1916
10521 Private Harold Walker of Bottesford, Notts, killed in action and buried in Ovillers Military Cemetery, grave I. E. 39.

Regina Trench Cemetery, Grandcourt.
The men buried here would have been initially interred near the front line in a small battlefield cemetery. After the armistice graves from many smaller cemeteries were concentrated here.

19240 Private Alfred Antcliffe, aged 20 years of Heanor, Derbys, killed in action, grave IX. F. 18.

20892 Private Thomas Chambers of Bulwell, Nott's, killed in action, grave VII. H. 28

23089 Private P C Colton, aged 26 years of Nottingham, killed in action, grave IX. F. 17.

18610 Private Thomas Hammersley of Longton, Staff's, killed in action, grave IX. F. 26.

21832 Private Alexander Jones of Harthill York's killed in action, grave VII. L. 4.

13328 Private William Tarr of Ollerton, Nott's, killed in action, grave IX. F. 5.

Pozieres British Cemetery, Ovillers-La Boisselle
This is another small battlefield cemetery that was greatly enlarged after the armistice. One of the 9th battalion men was probably buried here during the battle and his grave destroyed later on. He is commemorated under a special memorial in the cemetery. His headstone will have either 'Known' or 'Believed' to be buried in this cemetery.

22680 Private John Thomas Larkin Burrows of New Sawley, Derby's, killed in action, grave IV. D. 16

12369 Private Ernest Buxton, aged 24 years, of Great Grimsby, Linc's, killed in action, grave IV. B. 50.

23711 Private George Robert Farby aged 22 years of Barlborough, Derby's, killed in action, grave IV. D. 29. George was the best friend of Fred Greaves V.C. The night before the attack he asked Fred to contact his Mother because he expected to die. As they went over the top on 26th, George was shot dead.

He is commemorated on the Barlborough memorial.

See the note at the bottom – Corporal Fred Greaves V.C. Fred's service number was 23715, only four away from George's.

21515 Private W Jacques of Doncaster, York's (Born at Carlton Nott's), killed in action, grave IV. C. 25.

13094 Private William Herbert Keel, aged 27 years who enlisted at Worksop, Nott's, killed in action, grave – Special Memorial.

11675 Private C Trelfa of Derby, killed in action, grave IV. B. 22.

Contay British Cemetery, Contay

This cemetery was next to Casualty Clearing Stations and the majority of men died of wounds. The cemetery today is arguably the most beautiful situated in this area.

20359 Corporal Robert Bainbridge aged 37 years of Ripley Derby's, killed in action, 28 September 1916, grave II. D. 11 (It is more likely that he died of wounds).

15760 Private Bickley Calladine aged 20 years of Normanton, Derby's, died of wounds, 27th September 1916, grave II. D. 21.

20118 Private Thomas Connor of Castle Bromwich, Staff's died of wounds, 27th September 1916, grave II. C. 26

23244 Private Benjamin Clarke of Kedlington Suffolk, died of wounds, 1st October 1916, grave I. E. 2

Puchevillers British Cemetery

Another cemetery situated next to Casualty Clearing Stations.

2867 Private William Charles Brown aged 25 years, died of wounds, 28th September 1916, grave IV. E. 35. (Again records vary – Soldiers Died has born Sneinton, Nott's whilst the CWGC has his abode as Newcastle-on-Tyne, Native of Sheffield)

25010 Private William Fowke aged 37 years of Belper, Derby's, died of wounds 27th September 1916, grave IV. E. 19

5064 Private F. Morley, enlisted at Nottingham, died of wounds, 27th September 1916, grave IV. E. 23.

22931 Private William Pearson aged 24 years of Derby, died of wounds, 28th September 1916, grave IV. E. 26.

19233 Private John William Armstrong of Huthwaite Nott's, died of wounds, 28/09/1916, grave IV E 25.

21189 Sergeant John William Walker of Belper Derby's, died of wounds, 29th September 1916, grave V. B. 10.

6730 Private Frederick Marriott of Sutton-in-Ashfield, Nott's, died of wounds, 3rd October 1916, grave V. C. 19.

Warloy-Baillon Communal Cemetery Extension.

An Advanced Operating Centre was here in 1916. 23878 Private A. W. Price of Radford, Nott's, died of wounds, 27th September 1916, grave IV. B. 13

Cerisy-Gailly Military Cemetery

Plot III, within which our man is buried was concentrated after the armistice and includes a number of graves cleared from the Thiepval area. Cerisy sits on the river Somme.

19709 Lance Corporal Joseph Thomas Ibbett aged 23 years of Radford, Nott's, killed in action, 26th September 1916, grave III. F. 14. He was no doubt quickly buried just after the battle, either in a shell hole or part of a trench. He was one of the few identified when re-internments commenced after the armistice.

Blighty Valley Cemetery, Authuile Wood

This cemetery has a number of 11th battalion Sherwood Foresters who were killed attacking on 1st July 1916.

Second Lieutenant John Russell Crawford aged 21 years of Whitley Bay, 13th battalion, attached 9th battalion, died of wounds, 27th September 1916. His grave was later destroyed by shellfire and he is commemorated under Special memorial 20.

Lonsdale Cemetery, Authuile

This cemetery is just south of Thiepval and was again enlarged after the armistice.

20220 Private William Horace Vickers aged 21 years of Nottingham; killed in action 27th September 1916, grave X. G. 3. William would have been re-interred in this cemetery after the armistice.

Bouzincourt Communal Cemetery Extension.

Captain Alan Stevenson aged 29 years of Manchester, 13th battalion, and attached 9th battalion, killed in action, 26th September 1916, grave I. H. 16. He was the son of a vicar. This cemetery was in a rear area and it is more likely that he died of wounds, although it was not unknown for men to bring their officer back for proper burial. The battalions base after the battle was only a couple of miles from Bouzincourt.

A.I.F. Burial Ground, Flers

Australian Force Burial ground, Flers is some six miles from the area in which the 9th battalion were fighting. This man's burial shows the difficulty of connecting a battle in one particular area with a man buried there. It is likely that when in 1927 Thiepval Memorial to the Missing was decided on for the main memorial, he was re-interred at the A.I.F., Flers. Many graves had to be moved to accommodate the Thiepval Memorial.

Plot XV also has men from the 1918 Thiepval battles, which gives added credence to the re-internment theory.

19614 Private Percy Bacon of Mansfield, Nott's, killed in action, 26th September 1916, grave XV. O. 21.

Connaught Cemetery, Thiepval.
The wood behind the cemetery was known to the troops as Thiepval Wood. The cemetery is situated close to the old 1st July front line.
19756 Sergeant George W. Bell aged 22 years, 'D' company of Worksop, Nott's, killed in action 26th September 1916, grave VI. E. 8.

Base Hospital cemeteries
Wimereux Communal Cemetery
It is the civilian cemetery and in the northern part of the town. The headstones are unusual as they lay flat and this is because of the sandy soil. It also has a famous grave as Lieutenant- Colonel John McCrae is buried here. In 1915 at Essex Farm Dressing Station, near Ypres, he wrote 'In Flanders Fields'.

21197 Private William Edward Maxey aged 21 years of Selston, Nott's, died of wounds, 2nd October 1916, grave I. R. 1A.

24240 Lance Corporal Alfred Wheatley aged 27 years of Derby, died of wounds, 1st October 1916, grave I. Q. 27A.

Etaples Military Cemetery
This is the largest Military cemetery in France.

12703 Private Leonard Lawley aged 20 years, a native of Birmingham, died of wounds, 14th October 1916, grave VIII. A. 2A.

13079 Sergeant Edward Richardson aged 23 years of Bulwell, Nottingham, died of wounds, 2nd October 1916, grave XI. D. 2A

Boulogne Eastern Cemetery
This is a large civilian cemetery to the east of Boulogne town centre.

23368 Private Samuel Edward Hyde of Burton-on-Trent, died of wounds, 3rd October 1916, grave VIII. C. 170.

23392, Private Douglas Duncan Claude Watson of Sheffield, died of wounds on 5th October 1916, grave VIII. C. 170 (The same grave reference as Sam Hyde)

15768 Private James Trickett of Whaley Bridge died of wounds on 3rd October 1916, grave VII. C. 166

23227 Private George Evans died of wounds on 2nd October 1916, grave VIII. C. 168

Buried at Home
On 2nd October 15928 Private Harry Cutts aged 19 years and from Bolsover Derbyshire died at home of wounds. He is buried in Bolsover (St Mary) Old Churchyard and grave 166. A couple of days earlier one of Harry's pals had also died of wounds and was buried in Bolsover (St Mary) New Churchyard. 24497 Private Horace Tom Cowley aged 30 years had served with Harry on Gallipoli. Both had been wounded during the Somme fighting and Horace died on 30th September 1916 and had been in 'C' Company. 12676 L/Cpl William Abbott also wounded during the Somme fighting died on 20/10/1916 and buried close to Tom Cowley.

9031 Company Sergeant Major David Pickford of Leek, Staff's is buried at Leek Cemetery, grave 7080. He died of wounds at home on 23rd October 1916.

Two other men were in the 9th battalion but at the time of death attached to other battalions.

Thiepval Memorial – 17th battalion – 6112 Sergeant Moses Holloway of Derby, killed in action, 9th October 1916. On that day the 9th battalion were at rest in Mensil Domqueur. The 17th battalion, which was part of 34th Division, attacked the Schwaben Redoubt. The 9th battalion were enjoying a soccer match that day. The medal rolls for the 9th show him as being a Private and then Acting Sergeant whilst with them. As the Medal rolls show no other battalion it is likely that he was attached to the 17th battalion, possibly staying behind when the 9th battalion moved out on 30th September.

Peake Wood Cemetery, Fricourt – 'A' Coy. 11th battalion – Captain Richard Jefferys Nicolls aged 22 years of Bottesford Rectory, Nott's, killed in action, 1st October 1916, grave C. 24. Captain Nicolls was on attachment to the 11th battalion from the 9th Battalion. The 9th were at this time arriving at Acheux after their time in the trenches.

The battalion would spend over a month away from the dreaded Somme battlefield but would return soon enough. They had been re-blooded and paid a high price but once again acquitted themselves well in battle. The battalion would once again have to be strengthened after its losses and no doubt some who had survived Gallipoli and the Somme must have wondered how long their luck would last.

Colonel Scothern gave a short paragraph for this period, 30 September to 21 November 1916. In fact he only managed some thirteen lines between 30th September and the end of the year.

> *"On September 30th, the battalion was relieved by the 1st Wilts (Wiltshire regiment, 7th Brigade), and marched to billets in Hedauville. From Hedauville the battalion marched to Acheux, entraining there for Candas, thence proceeding by a series of*

marches to Mesnil Domqueux. The stay here, lasting until Nov 11th, was spoiled by rain, but a good deal of training was carried out nevertheless".

In essence the paragraph does not give the reader very little information, nor does it convey the daily hardships endured by the men. Whether the men marched or travelled by train, the journey would have been an unpleasant one. Marching many miles each day in hobnail boots, carrying a full pack and wearing (or carrying) a soaked greatcoat was exhausting for men already pushed beyond the limits of human endurance in battle. Rail travel may have been less tiring on the body and feet but was no first class jaunt watching the countryside going by. Wagons were the mode of transport and each had inscribed on the side "Chevaux 8 or Hommes 37-40". The men would sleep packed like sardines on the floor of the wagon with only bully beef and hard tack biscuits to sustain them. Troop trains were also laboriously slow and it could take many hours to reach their destination. On leaving the cramped troops train, the men would have yet another march to their new billets.

The War Diary entries for October would tell of travel and training with the immortal soul catered for as well. The Battalion would also take part in various sporting activities.

On 1st October at 8.45 a.m. the whole battalion left Hedauville and moved to Acheux, arriving at 10 a.m. This move was a march and in terms of distance very small being around five miles between the two places. On arrival they had the luxury of being billeted in huts but their stay would not last long. In fact the next morning they were on the road again. Under modern conditions the journey between Acheux and Boisbergues is a fairly easy one and with the latest G.P.S. systems it is also idiot proof. In 1916 it was anything but straightforward and took the battalion seven hours. Administration order No 5 saw the battalion entrain at Acheux-Varennes station at 3.30 p.m. Unfortunately the battalion had spent two hours waiting in the rain prior to entraining and therefore nearly 1000 very soggy men had to endure a three and a half hour train journey to Candas. Upon arrival at Candas the battalion still faced a march of over three hours to their billets at Boisbergues. Once again the rain fell heavily and the men's various pieces of equipment would weigh heavily. There is no doubt that the men would have been pleased to have seen their beds on that particular night.

There is no mention of wooden huts as billets, so it can be assumed that bell tents were once again used. A total of 22 other ranks joined the battalion at Boisbergues as reinforcements for the losses sustained during the last battle. One of these was 2521 George Astle who had been renumbered as 70800.

The 3rd October would see the battalion on the move yet again under 33rd Brigade operational order 38 and the destination was Agenville. The first line transport moved out during the morning and then returned to make a second journey. It took a great deal of operational skill and much transport to move a Battalion numbering upwards of 1000 men. It was more than likely that the transport would carry the majority of the men's personal equipment, which no doubt made the three and one half hour march more bearable. It has to be remembered that the battalion had fought a gruelling battle only days previously and the physical and mental fatigue would still be with them. The battalion arrived at Agenville at 4.50 p.m. Another 26 other ranks joined as reinforcements and whilst these men would replace the dead from the previous battle, more would be needed to cover wounded and missing. Once the battalion had settled in to its training area, the process of replacing losses would be completed. A number of men previously with the battalion would return after their wounds had healed but new men would also be needed.

The 4th October was a confused day with Brigade sending movement orders and then countermanding them. The C.O. inspected the 48 other rank reinforcements at 11 a.m., and no doubt gave them a pep talk, which would include the achievements of the battalion thus far. A wire was received at 12.30 p m., outlining yet another move which would take the battalion to Mensil Domqueur. At 5 p m the orders duly arrived detailing H.Q., and two companies to Maison Roland and two companies to Mensil Domqueur. The men prepared for the forthcoming move but at 10 pm., it was all change again as the orders were cancelled and new instruction saw the whole battalion moving to Mensil Domqueur. Such periods of confusion were commonplace as Staff Officers at Corps H.Q., 'juggled' their resources. Not that this endeared them to the P.B.I. (Poor Bloody Infantry) for whom each set of orders meant more work. Mensil Domqueur being situated northwest of Amiens and not far from the Doullens to Abbeville road.

On 5th October the battalion duly moved from Agenville to Mensil Domqueur, although it did so without the forty-eight reinforcements. These men proceeded to Gramant for yet another inspection and pep talk. On this occasion it would be the G.O.C. (General Officer Commanding), the 11th Infantry Division who at this time was Lieut-Gen. Sir C. Woollcombe who had taken over on 4 July 1916 and would lead the Division until December 1916. The reinforcements left at 8.30 am for their 10 am 'appointment with the G.O.C. Meanwhile at 10.30 am the rest of the battalion left Agenville, arriving at Mensil at 11.20 am. They proceeded to settle in to the village and make preparations for a period of training. Despite the battalion's success, the last battle had shown that work was needed on creeping barrages. A number of men had been killed and wounded getting to close to the barrage.

The 6th October saw training in the morning followed by a parade in the afternoon in order that the G.O.C., 33rd Brigade could give an address. This would be the normal 'pep talk', praising the men's efforts in the last battle, telling them how their actions had brought closer the downfall of the German Army and urging them on for battles yet to come. The usual scene would see the G.O.C., astride his charger with the Brigade gathered around him.

The following day, training was interrupted yet again with yet another talk, this time by G.O.C., II Corps. The morning training proceeded as normal with various elements of the battalion honing their skills – Lewis gunners, bombers, snipers and riflemen. At 3 pm whilst the men trained, the G.O.C. inspected them and then at 3.15 pm he addressed the Brigade. No doubt the address followed the lines of the previous day with much praise for the Brigades efforts.

During the fighting of 26th September, 2/Lt E.H.F. Abbott had been slightly wounded but he had remained with the battalion. By 7th October his wound was such that he had to be admitted to hospital for treatment. Infections were common during the war and the slightest wound could become infected and if not treated immediately even gangrenous. At 9.20pm, Lt-Col W.B. Thornton D.S.O., officer commanding proceeded on leave to England. Officers had regular leave, either in France to enjoy the pleasures of such places as Paris or to England. Other ranks were rather less fortunate with leave being short and infrequent. Leave could be a once a year occurrence for other ranks and with the leave period beginning when they left the unit, it could also be very short as travelling to the East Midlands in 1916 could take several days. Many men though preferred not to return home, as it seemed more alien than the front line at times. Family and friends could have no comprehension of the horrors and deprivations of trench life. It was therefore an easy option to remain in France or Belgium where they could make use of the Corps rest camps, visit Estaminets with friends or venture in to Paris with comrades.

Sunday 8th October saw church parade for Wesleyan and Catholics and no doubt Fred Greaves would have attended and offered up a prayer for his dead friend George Farby.

At 10 am four men proceeded to the 11th division rest camp for a well-earned break from the rigours of the war. Although the term 'rest camp' was somewhat ambiguous as the men would still be under the control of the army and parades and organized sports would keep the men active. At 4 p.m. the battalion was once again brought up to strength with the arrival of 2/Lt C. W. Tarlton and 364 other ranks as reinforcements. The arrival of over four hundred reinforcements since the beginning of October shows the extent of losses during the battalion's successful attack around Mouquet Farm. The Divisions honour of taking this infamous farm had come at a high price. A number of the NCOs and men who arrived as reinforcements had previously served with the battalion. No doubt these men had suffered wounds or illness in Gallipoli and were now rejoining their old comrades.

The Battles of the Somme still raged and men were constantly needed to reinforce other hard pressed Regiments fighting. Therefore a draft of one officer and one hundred and eighty three other ranks under the Sherwood Foresters umbrella was picked out ready for any eventuality that may have arisen. This had happened previously when a draft was sent to the South Staffs in July 1916. Among their number was young James Walters who at age sixteen was killed at Delville Wood. A number of the 9th battalion men would meet their deaths whilst attached to other regiments of Sherwood Forester battalions.

The 9th October saw more training in the morning but the afternoon was given over to recreation. At 2.30 pm the battalion's soccer team took on the 6th Lincoln's and came out victorious, winning by a margin of five goals to four. The Divisional band was also drafted in to play before and after the game. No doubt all the songs made so famous in those days were sung with gusto. Sport had always been an important part of army life as it was seen as an important tool for character and team building. It also gave the men something to think about when out of the trenches other than the war and training. Engendering a feeling of competition between regiments also helped when the fighting recommenced as 'Esprit de Corps' would make them want to 'out do', other troops fighting alongside them.

The day also saw another death as 12866. Private Arthur Watkinson Died of wounds at home. Arthur was aged 19 years and is buried in the family grave at Worksop, Notts

The 10th saw more training as the men were prepared for the next battle and the 'newbie's' were integrated into the battalion set up. The campaign season was not yet over on the Somme and would not end until the weather made offensive actions impossible in mid November. The 10th also saw the start of a possible major cause for concern as a case of measles was notified. Any infectious disease could spread rapidly through such a large body of men who lived and worked so closely together. When the deprivations of war were added – unsanitary conditions, lack of sleep, rats, lice, living in trenches and poor nutrition, disease could spread rapidly.

12866 Private Arthur Watkinson

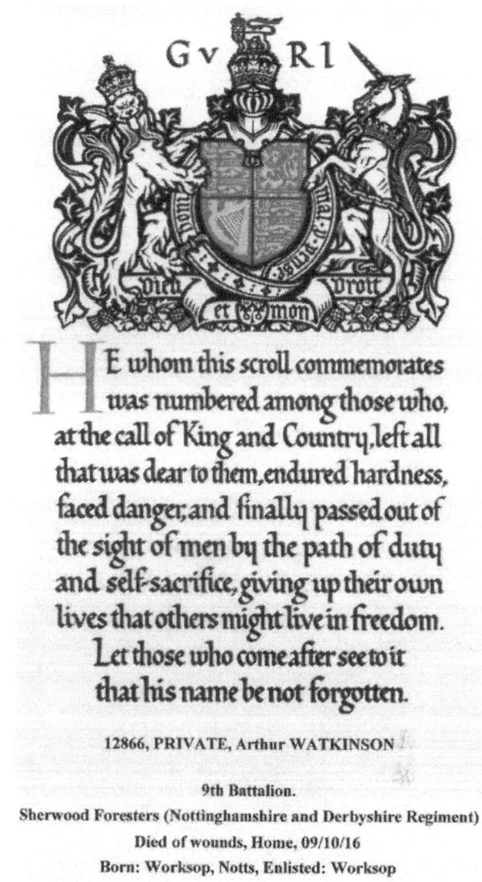

G v R I

HE whom this scroll commemorates was numbered among those who, at the call of King and Country, left all that was dear to them, endured hardness, faced danger, and finally passed out of the sight of men by the path of duty and self-sacrifice, giving up their own lives that others might live in freedom.
Let those who come after see to it that his name be not forgotten.

12866, PRIVATE, Arthur WATKINSON

9th Battalion.
Sherwood Foresters (Nottinghamshire and Derbyshire Regiment)
Died of wounds, Home, 09/10/16
Born: Worksop, Notts, Enlisted: Worksop

Death Scroll – Issued to the families of all men killed

On 11th two more cases were notified and all of their contacts were put under isolation in an attempt to stop the outbreak. At 4 p.m. the battalion saw the arrival of six new officers with 2/Lts Ince and Campion joining 'A' Company, 2/Lts Smith and Suffolk, 'C' Company, and 2/Lts Trohear and Crowther to 'D' Company. Another batch for the Company Sergeant Major's to turn into real officers before the battalion returned to the trenches.

The 12th saw another case of measles and the whole of the last draft of men were put into isolation. It can therefore be assumed that the MO had identified them as the carriers. The loss of some 364 men so soon after their arrival threw the training program into some confusion. The same day saw 2/Lt Harwood and the R.Q.M.S., proceeding to England on 10 days leave.

The following day saw the battalion soccer team once again victorious as they beat the 6th Borders one nil. It also saw 2/Lt McCormack and one corporal proceeding on leave.The 14th showed a change in training as the battalion prepared once again to move into the trenches. The battalion carried out an attack in cooperation with the 6th Borders, although for 1916 at least, the 11th Division would see no more battles. It would though return to the trenches. Another officer 2/Lt Cudlip and one sergeant proceeded on leave and more cases of measles were notified.

Private Haslam was by this time in hospital in England. He would not return to the Battalion but join the Labour Corps.

'The Derbyshire Times, Saturday October 14 1916. Chesterfield Casualties

News had been received that Pte. Frank HASLAM, son of the late Mr Jas. HASLAM M.P. for Chesterfield, has been admitted to the Military Hospital at Colchester, suffering from wounds received in action on the Somme Front after 16 months fighting. Pte. HASLAM had seen service in the Dardanelles for 12 Months, and then was sent to France. He is progressing favourably and writes in appreciative terms of the treatment he is now receiving. Pte. HASLAM has not yet seen the monument that was erected to the memory of his father by the Derbyshire Miners' Association, as he left England the day following the statues of Messrs HASLAM and HARVEY were unveiled. Aged 31, he is in the Sherwood Foresters, and formerly worked as a mechanic for the Grassmoor Co. Ltd.'

Sunday 15th was a fairly quiet day with church parade services and rest. It also saw 2/Lt Richardson and one private proceeding on leave.

The 16th would see Lt & Adjutant Nason and one private proceed on leave whilst the remainder of the battalion continued training. A Brigade scheme (exercise) practicing attacking three objectives was carried out. As previously stated a Brigade was made up of four battalions (until reorganization in 1918) and it was the norm for three to attack whilst one remained in reserve. After the scheme, the battalion continued its specialist training. The disaster, which had befallen the British army in July 1916, had been a steep and costly learning curve and in some areas changes had been slow but changes were being made. Specialist teams were used for specific tasks during attacks and every man had to be well versed in his own task.

The 17th October saw the battalion at Maison Roland, digging trenches in preparation for a practice attack and the following day the practice attack was carried out. This was another change as men were given the opportunity to rehearse for an attack. Two other ranks proceeded on leave and worryingly a case of Diphtheria was found in the battalion.

Whilst the battalion trained, one of its ex members would die whilst in the 2nd Battalion. 22072, Private George Irvine Jinks aged 20 years the son of Alfred and Sarah Jane, Shirebrook, Notts is commemorated on the Thiepval Memorial.

On the 19th 2/Lt Suffolk and 115 other ranks proceeded to Authieulle to relieve a party from 6th Lincolns. These men would be kept close to the front line and used for working parties. They could also be drafted in to the front line if the need was urgent. 2/Lt Barter and one private proceeded on leave.

The 20th was a mixed day with training cancelled in the morning due to rain. As the men would be expected to occupy trenches and mount attacks in any weather, it seems strange that rain should prohibit training. Specialist training was carried out in the afternoon and the diary consistently showed that more and more emphasis was put on specialist training as the tactics of war changed. The Brigade also formed for a Ceremonial parade and the G.O.C. presented Military Medals of which several were to 9th battalion men.

The following day saw more specialist training with intensive digging, rapid wiring etc. Taking a trench in battle was only half of the job and keeping it was usually much more difficult. The trench had to be secured, wired, fire steps built facing the enemy and preparations made for the inevitable counter attack. Many a potential victory had been lost as counter attacks caught the men unprepared. Meanwhile the officers carried out revolver practice, although by this time many preferred carrying a rifle into battle. Looking like an officer in battle made you an obvious target for snipers.

The following day, 22nd October saw church parade, which was a compulsory activity. Not that the men would have objected as since the British armies birth, church parade was seen as a 'cushy number' (easy time) by most. Two more other ranks proceeded on leave, which with the forthcoming actions looming, could well be their last. The officers spent the afternoon practicing with their revolvers once again. Many of these officers were new second lieutenants and only attached to the battalion for training purposes. The Lewis gunners were also given the opportunity to practice their deadly trade.

Monday would see nine of the attached officers leave for their new battalions and brigades. At 8-30 am they proceeded to H.Q., 32nd Brigade (also 11th Division) to join the 6th Battalion York and Lanc's Regiment. Two more other ranks proceeded to the UK on leave. The remainder of the battalion would continue training in preparation for front line duty on the Somme. Between 9 am and 1 pm and 2.30 pm and 4 pm, the battalion trained in all elements of warfare. At 6 p.m. the battalion received movement orders from 33rd Brigade HQ. They were to move into new billets at Bonneville. The battalion spent two hours preparing for this move but at 8 pm a message was received postponing it. This again was a regular occurrence during the Great War.

The 24th and 25th would follow the usual routine whilst out of the line with more training as the lessons learned in the Somme battles were acted upon. Rapid wiring, intensive digging, musketry and specialist training continued to be practiced over and over again. All of the soldierly arts had to become second nature to all of the men as they attempted to get the slight edge that might defeat the enemy. Also on the 24th, the proposed move was once again put on hold and the 25th saw two other ranks proceeding on leave.

The battalion specialists took part in a combined scheme giving the bombers (grenades) Lewis

Gunners, snipers and trench mortar sections the opportunity to practice working in unison whilst supporting the rest of the battalion in an attack. This type of attack would become ever more important in 1917 as the German Army retreated to the Hindenburg line. Methods of attack would have to be completely different and every arm of the battalion would have to learn new methods of fighting. Confidence in comrades was essential for a successful attack as one weak link could spell disaster for the whole battalion. Meanwhile the Companies had a pleasant route march to keep them entertained! The latest additions to the battalion were put through their paces with personal weapon training. The battalion was also inspected by the Commanding Officer during the afternoon of 25th. Whilst out of the line the men could look forward to many and varied inspections with every part of the body, kit, weaponry and uniform coming under scrutiny at one time or another. Captain L. D. Goldie reported for duty on 25th bringing with him four other ranks reinforcements.

The 26th October saw some respite from training but only because it rained heavily during the morning. Interestingly on the Somme battlefield only 1mm of rain was reported that day. The afternoon was given over to Musketry, more inspections and specialist training.

The morning of Friday 27th saw the whole Brigade taking part in a tactical route march taking in the delights of Fransu – Franqueville – Chausses – Brunehaut and Maison Roland. This was followed by a foot inspection! The Divisional band was in the village of Mensil during the afternoon playing a selection of music for the troops and locals alike. Two other ranks proceeded on leave but there is no record of whether they took part in the mornings stroll in the countryside.

The following day began as per normal with training from 9 until 1pm but then the men were given the luxury of a 'half holiday' and no doubt some men took the advantage of visiting a local Estaminet to sample the watered down French wine and beer. The day also saw the return from leave of 2/Lts McCormack and Harwood and one Corporal.

The weather continued to be a problem on Sunday 28th October with Church parade having to be cancelled. The weather in the area over that weekend was indeed very wet with 8mm of rain on Saturday and 7mm on Sunday. As the army did not usually concern itself with weather, it can only be assumed that the said Church parade was due to be held in the open air. 2/Lts Richardson and Cudlip, returned from leave along with three other ranks at 8 pm. Twenty reinforcements also arrived during the day from the 14th Infantry Brigade Depot. One of these was 70800 Private George William Astle who had served with 2/6th battalion since 9th October 1914. George would finish the war with the 12th Battalion.

The next two days saw the training intensify with both mornings taken up with practice attacks near Bois-de-Ribeaucourt. This even today is a large area of grassland and woods. For some reason 'open warfare' practice attacks were made but as the Somme battles had been anything but 'open warfare', it is difficult to see the reason for this, unless battalions were being prepared for 1917. In the event it would be nearly two years before the British army would see true open warfare. Afternoons were taken up with musketry, company training and yet more inspections. On the 30th Lt. And A/Qr (Acting Quartermaster) Mr Prosser left for leave. The following day saw 2/Lts. Russell, Burton, Campion and Rees rejoin the battalion from secondment at 32nd Brigade.

November would see the Battles of the Somme come to a stuttering end as the weather finally got the upper hand. The 9th battalion would not be called on again to attack on the Somme in 1916 but they would hold the front line trenches and suffer casualties.

Colonel Scothern's notes for November through to the end of the year were once again brief:

> *"The battalion moved to Coulon Villers on Nov 4th on November 11th, the return journey to Hedauville was commenced and taken in easy stages, the route being via Montrelet. On the 18th it moved to Martinsart Wood, being attached to the 37th Division, but the next day orders were received to go back to Hedauville, and proceed next day to St Pierre Divion. The next two days spent in continual movement, the line finally being taken over on November 25th, N.E. of Beaumont Hamel Station. This sector was fairly lively, and a working party detailed to dig a trench in front of our old line was caught in an enemy barrage and suffered severely. On 30th the 6tj York and Lancs, relieved the battalion which moved back to Englebelmer, remaining there for just over a fortnight, working on the roads and cutting brushwood in Aveluy Wood. On December 17th the line at St Pierre Divion was taken over, and from then until January 19th 1917 the time was spent either in the line or at Englebelmer".*

Not only were Col Scothern's notes short and lacking in detail, they also differ from the battalion war diaries, which causes confusion. None of his dates match those of the diary but it is possible his notes were compiled much later. Although for an officer who would one day become the C.O. of such an efficient battalion, it would seem unusual that his notes are not more precise.

Wednesday 1st November was a day that all ranks had looked forward to – bath day. The opportunity to say goodbye to a few hundred lice and for at least a few hours feel really clean. Sadly the lice would soon return, as would the grime.

Not that bath day was a case of stripping off and jumping into lovely hot water. Firstly they had a march of 5 miles to the bathing area at Domart and men set of in parties at intervals of one hour for their bath. This process continued from 6 am until 2 pm and the sight of hundreds of men marching from Mesnil to Domart must have intrigued or bemused the local French population. Once the ablutions had been completed and the men were spick and span, they were inspected at 2.30pm. The 2nd saw the cancellation of yet another route march due to rain and it has to be wondered if the battalion had its own rainmakers, although it is hardly surprising to get much rain in November.

The battalion was treated instead to lectures on various topics such as Musketry and gas helmet drill. Both of these topics vital if you were to stay alive whilst in the front line and it would not be long before the battalion started its move towards the front line.

Divisions who at this time were still involved in attacks and raids on the Somme front would need relieving in the not to distant future.

The 3rd would see another pleasant stroll for the battalion with a morning route march, which followed the same route as the previous week. On this occasion an advanced guard was deployed ahead of the battalion. The battalion returned in the afternoon to more Musketry, Bayonet fighting and allied training.

The Battles of the Somme were still taking place but as the weather worsened it would not be long before a halt would be called and the winter finally stopped troops from both sides in their tracks. It would then be a case of surviving the elements throughout the winter.

Between 9-30 and 10-30 am on 4th, the General Officer Commanding 33rd Brigade inspected the battalion, after which they continued with their training programme. The men would know that a move to the front was not far off as the GOC usually inspected when the battalion left the line or were ready to re-enter it.

Although as the weather deteriorated and the onset of winter curtailed offensive actions, it was unlikely that the training would be put to use until the spring of 1917 at the earliest.

Sunday 5th saw Church parade services and little else, which was another sign of things to come as the men were rested in preparation for front line duty.The 6th to the 10th, were days of training in the art of war as the men honed their skills ready for the forthcoming move to the front line. The G.O.C. 33rd brigade inspected the men's billets on the afternoon of the 7th. The various inspections of men, kit, and accommodation were all designed to evaluate the battalion's readiness for front line duty. The 9th battalion on this and all occasions would prove to their G.O.C that they were once again more than ready for whatever he had in mind for them.

On 8th 'B', 'C' and 'D' Companies spent the day on the ranges at Cramont, zeroing their weapons and sharpening their aim. The morning of the 9th was taken up with a short route march from Domqueur to Fransu and return which was a mere 5 miles.

The 11th saw the battalion leave Domqueur and move to new billets at Coulonvillers, a march of some 5 miles once again. The majority of their kit would have been taken on the transports and no doubt the men would be singing the wartime favourites as they marched through the countryside. The day though was frosty with a temperature of 55 deg F; it was misty with low cloud covering the area. Did the men know that they were within 10 miles of another famous battle site, that of Crecy, doubtful as they had other things on their minds.

They would have expected to remain at Coulonvillers for one night before continuing to Montrelet but this was delayed. The men attended Divine Services on the morning of the 12th and the G.O.C. 33rd brigade joined them (Always a bad sign). At 3.0 pm Brigade movement order 140 arrived, advising of a move but B.M 146 cancelled this at 7 pm.

Juggling Brigades and Divisions was no easy task for the movement officers.

To keep the men active a route march was organised for the morning of the 13th. Then at 5 pm., new orders arrived for the move to Montrelet. Anyone in the battalion who had seen a map would have known that they had marched in the opposite direction when going to Coulonvillers thus adding a few more miles to the march.

On the 14th the move from Coulonvillers to Montrelet, a distance of roughly 12 miles, was begun. At 9-15 am they marched from Coulonvillers to join the other battalions of the brigade and thence to Montrelet. The sight of some 4000 men marching in column of threes must have been wondrous, as they marched through the French countryside, their hob nail boots resounding on the paved roads. After the quiet times of recent weeks the men knew that it was back to the Somme and many must have wondered what horrors awaited them. No doubt some would get 'the feeling' that they would not return and the bullet or shell with their name on it was awaiting them. Others would decide that they would survive unscathed. For all though, they knew what to expect and no man would be under any illusion as to what awaited them. The Brigade arrived at Montrelet around 4 pm and the next few hours were taken up with settling in to the new billets. No sooner had this been accomplished than orders were received to move to Vadencourt. It has to be pointed out that during the period attacks were still being made in the forlorn hope that a final breakthrough could be made. By the 19th offensive actions would cease but until then units would be constantly on the move as GHQ sought to gain an advantage.

On Wednesday 15th the battalion moved out of Montrelet at 9-45 am en route for Vadencourt, some 12 miles away and whichever route they took, they would pass a number of British War Cemeteries and know that some of their old pals lay in them. The battalion arrived at 4-30 pm and settled in once again. At 8-30 pm orders were received to relieve men of the 96th Brigade, 32nd Division in the Schwaben Redoubt an area well known to the battalion from the September battle. On the morning of 15th the 32nd Division had relieved the 2nd Division and after a strong German counter attack on the 16th Gird Trench was lost. It was possibly for this reason that at 7-30am on 16th 33rd Brigade operational order No 42, cancelling the move was received, although the battalion was ordered to remain on stand-by pending further orders from Brigade. At 12 noon the battalion was ordered up to Hedauville, arriving at 3-30pm. A move of only 4 miles but one closer to the action and only some 5 miles from the front line. The men though still had the luxury of living in billets, although it would seem that the previous occupants had left them in somewhat of a mess. The 17th was taken up with clearing up the billets followed by physical training. 2/Lt Smith rejoined the battalion after a spell in hospital, no doubt pleased to be back before the battalion went into the line. At 9 pm a wire arrived ordering the battalion to be prepared to move at a moments notice from 7 am on 18th and at 11.45 pm operational order No. 43 was received regarding a probable move into the front line. The 18th and 19th November would see the final attacks of the Somme offensive and reserve Divisions would always be on standby for the big breakthrough.

On the 18th at 11 am, the movement order arrived, with operational order No 43, instructing the battalion to move 'at once' to the camp located at Q. 32.c. near Martinsart. The old sweats would be apprehensive, constantly checking weapons and equipment as they marched towards the sound of the guns and that sound was deafening as shells of all calibre rained down, not only on the front line but rear areas as well. A mixture of shelling and heavy rain had turned this chalk-based area into a quagmire and men cursed as they struggled through it. Every muscle and sinew would be straining as they struggled under full packs. The men who had joined whilst the battalion was at rest experienced for the first time the sights and sounds of modern warfare. Many were the new conscripts whom for whatever reason had not been swept along in the early fervour of war and volunteered. Others who had returned after earlier wounds had healed would wish to be anywhere but on the Somme. Others would relish another opportunity to have a go at the Hun. Eventually at 2pm the battalion arrived in camp and were quartered in bivouacs and tents. They were put under the orders of 37th Division who were involved in the last faltering battle of the Somme offensive, as each side fought for the best position before the onset of winter.

The 37th Division were involved in the final attack on Saturday 18th November. The temperature was 54 deg F and there was 8 mm of rain during the day, which turned to sleet and snow during the night. The 37th Division as part of V Corps attacked north of the River Ancre. Whatever the General Staff had planned for 11th Division in support, it would not happen as overnight a gale blew up after the previous, snow, sleet and rain. Even the most optimistic in the general Staff had to except that the Somme offensive was at last over and trench occupation until the spring was the order of the day

The 19th would see the weather as the winner and the Somme Campaign finally ground to a soggy end after over four months of toil by the Allies and objectives of the 1st July still lay somewhat distant. At noon on 19th, the battalion received orders to return to Hedauville and they duly arrived at 3.15pm to be billeted in huts. The battalion had spent five days marching from one location to another, having little idea of when or if they would be called upon to

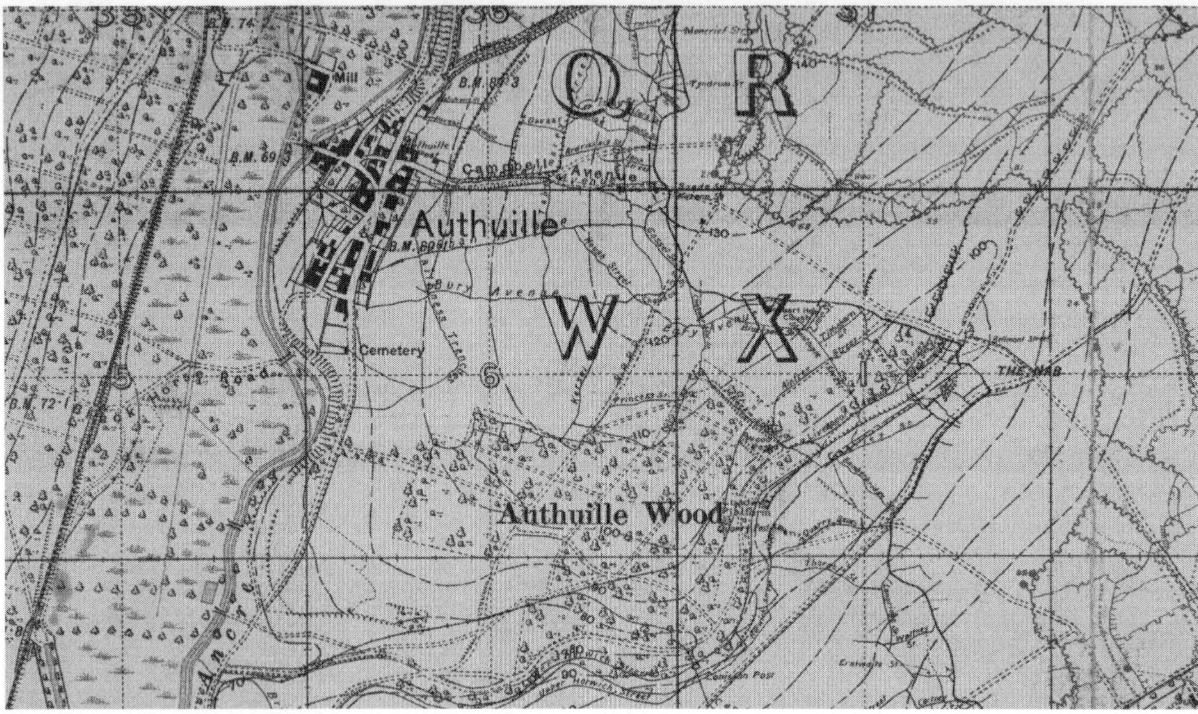

Orvillers 57d S.E.4 – 1916

fight. In the event their mini tour of France had been a fruitless and possibly pointless one but as every soldier soon learnt ' Ours is not to reason why'. Once at the hutted camp they would no doubt have been looking forward to a good nights sleep. This was not to be, as at 11.30 pm, movement orders arrived detailing a move to dugouts at St Pierre Divion, one step away from the front line trenches and the battalion's home for ten days. Eventually at 1.30 am on 20th battalion orders were issued and preparations made for the move. The men could then bed down for a few hours sleep before move off at 9 am. The transport moved directly to St Pierre Divion, whilst the battalion moved first to Authuille, arriving at 12.30 pm, where brigade HQ was set up at Q. 18 .a. 80 and battalion HQ at Q 36. c. 88.

An intriguing line in the war diaries followed '5.0 pm, Orderlies find Bde H.Q., No orders received' did this mean that battalion could not find the Brigade location or disorientated orderlies got lost! The reason will forever remain a mystery but after the movements of the previous days, an orderly could hardly be blamed for having little clue as to his location. Whatever the reason once the orderlies did find brigade HQ, no orders were forthcoming. At 7 pm., the battalion transport finally arrived after they had visited St Pierre Divion to drop off stores in the area of the battalion's front line trench occupation.

The following morning, 21st saw the battalion moving into the front line, under 56th Brigade operational order no 134. The 56th Brigade had one of their battalions, The King's Own occupying the front line and would coordinate the movements of all battalions involved. What the men would be only too aware of though, is that they faced a dangerous few hours. The period when one unit was relieving another was fraught with extra dangers on top of the usual ones. The enemy would be well aware that Brigades were rotating in their area and in most cases knew exactly which battalions of which regiments would face them. Artillery and snipers would be active as they attempted to 'take out' the men new to trench warfare or the men who did not concentrate enough. They also had a larger number of targets to aim at as men crowded in support and front line trenches. It was always fun on both sides to give the new men a warm welcome.

Forward dugouts, support, communication and front line trenches had to be taken over in such a way that the opportunity of a surprise attack by the enemy was negated.

The movement would be carried out in stages to minimize the dangers of an attack or heavy barrage causing havoc. Therefore at 10.45am the battalion-received orders to relieve the 2/7th Battalion The Worcestershire Regiment, 183rd Brigade, 61st Division in the dugouts at St Pierre Divion. The move commenced at 11.30 am and was successfully completed by 2.15 pm, at which time the 2/7th Worc's would move back to Authuille. Phase two began at 4.45 p.m. as the battalion proceeded to relieve the 7th Battalion Royal Lancaster (King's

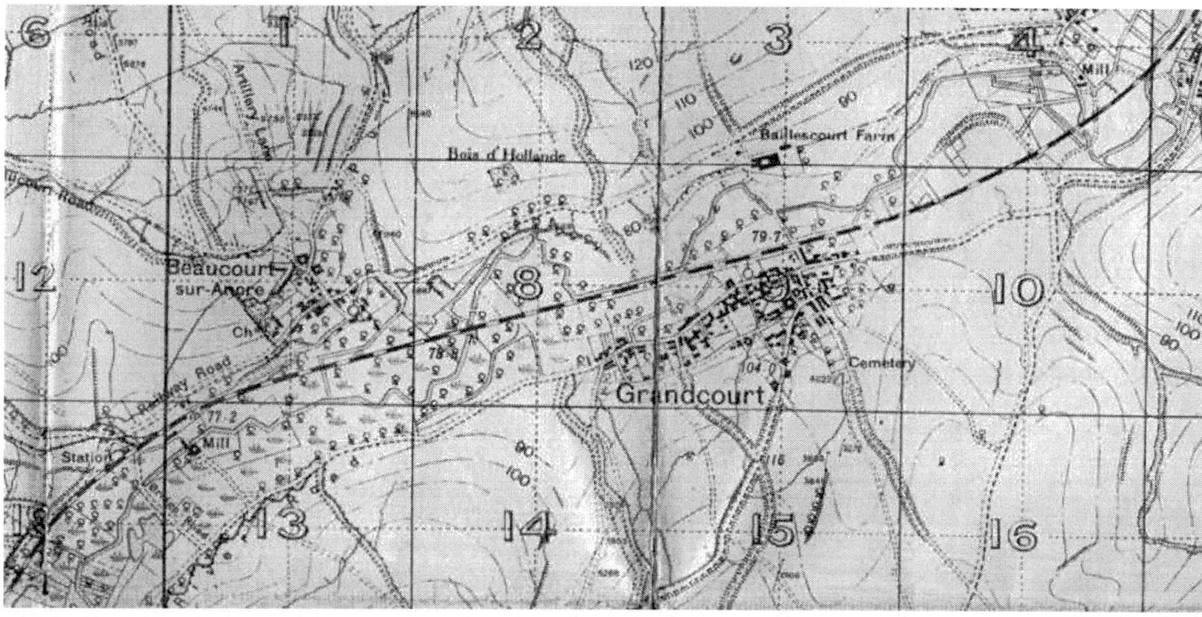

Beaumont Hamel 57d .S. E. 1 – 14th October 1916

Own) Regiment, 56th Brigade, in the support trenches and in the front line.

The battalion front extended from R. 14. a. 59 to R 12. c. 06, with a forward post established by 2/Lt Ottewell at R.8.c.46.

During the relief the battalion would have one other rank killed but by 9 pm they had settled into their positions.

On checking both the Commonwealth War Graves Commission and Soldiers Died in the Great War it was found that no man from the 9th battalion was listed as dying that day or indeed any day until 24th November. After some detective work, it was found that one 9th battalion man was listed as being killed on 22/1/1916 and buried at Connaught Cemetery, Thiepval. If this man was indeed from the 9th battalion, then he could not have been killed on that date and buried on the Somme. The battalion being in Egypt from January to June 1916 made this impossible. On contacting the CWGC, the following was established –

Private F Robinson's battlefield grave was found in October 1919 at location 57d. R. 14. a. 9. 1. His grave had a cross with name, number, unit but no date of death.After tracking down his death certificate it was obvious that Private Fred Robinson, killed 22/11/1916, and the one other rank killed on 21/11/1916 were one and the same. The CWGC have amended his details on their casualty lists to read 17th Bn attached 9th Bn.The headstone will be amended to give his correct date of death when next it is repaired or re-etched.

Therefore 26774, Private Fred Robinson, aged 24 years buried at Connaught Cemetery, Thiepval, and grave VIII. F. 2 now has the correct date of death and is also listed amongst his 9th battalion comrades.

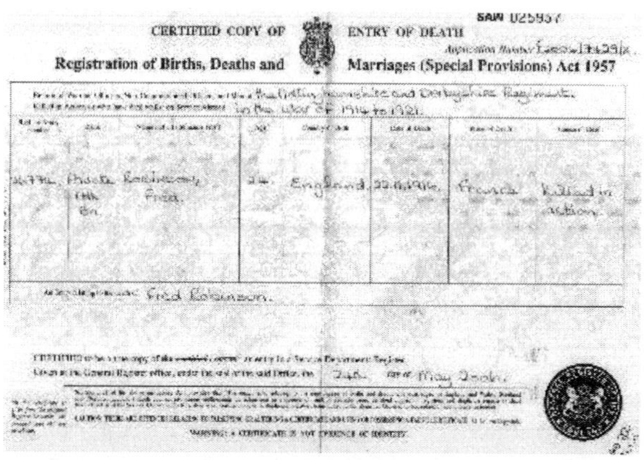
CERTIFIED COPY OF ENTRY OF DEATH
Registration of Births, Deaths and Marriages (Special Provisions) Act 1957

26774	Private Robinson Fred 17th Bn	24	England	22.11.1916	France	Killed in action

Fred Robinson

Fred Robinson's death certificate

The battalion would spend the 22nd November with their heads firmly down as the enemies artillery was extremely active. The day saw 10 other ranks being wounded, although with deaths in the following days, it is impossible to state whether any of these men eventually succumbed to their wounds.

The battalion was relieved at 6.0pm that evening by the 11th Bn Manchester Regiment of 34th Brigade. By 10.45 pm the relief had been accomplished without any further casualties and the men settled in to dugouts in Thiepval Wood, although this was known as Authuille Wood to the French. The battalion being in the vicinity of 'Paisley' Dump.

On 23rd the battalion moved to dugouts at Paisley dump arriving at 12.20pm and at 2.0pm, H.Q., 'C' and 'D' Companies proceeded to dugouts north of the Ancre River at Beaumont Hamel which was the old German reserve line. During this move 2/Lt Campion sustained wounds.

The 24th November would be another day of loss for the battalion and show just how dangerous, 'working parties' could be. At 2.0pm 'A' and 'B' Companies moved to dugouts in the old German Support line and at 5.0pm a working party made up of 100 men from each Company set out to dig a new trench which would be forward of the British 1st Line and situated north of Beaumont Hamel. The German's seeing something was happening sent over a heavy artillery barrage, which resulted in shells landing amongst the 200 men with devastating results. The war diary mentions that 2/Lt Crowther and eight other ranks were killed immediately and 2/Lt Rees and eighteen Other Ranks being wounded. It is difficult to give a precise number of men who would die of wounds but from 25th November to 30th the war diary mentioned only 8 casualties but no deaths.

The actual deaths for the 24th were eventually listed as twelve and in the following week another fourteen men died. Some of these would not have been as a result of the 24th shelling but undoubtedly others were.

The twelve listed as being killed on 24th November 1916:

Thiepval Memorial

8576, Company Sergeant Major Richard Bailey, aged 35 years and a native of Stafford and the son of William Bailey and husband of Annie Elizabeth.

70810, Private Herbert Burrows was a Nottinghamshire lad through and through, born in Stapleford, enlisted at Beeston and living at West Bridgeford prior to the war.

50619, Private Harry Dent, was a 22 year old from Lincolnshire and the son of Mrs. Mary Dent.

The remainder of the men would at least have a burial and lie in Hamel Military Cemetery, Beaumont Hamel.

71070, Private William Richard Alexander, aged 25 was the son of Thomas and Ellen of Lingwood, Norwich, enlisting in Norwich. He is buried in Plot II, Row F, and grave 6.

70997, Private Samuel Bell was born and raised in Leicester and had previously served as 27038 in the Leicestershire Regiment. He is buried in Plot II, Row E, and grave 2.

70859, Lance Corporal Samuel Barton was aged 31 years and before the war a schoolmaster in Sutton St, Edmund Lincolnshire. No doubt his students would have been sad but extremely proud when they heard of his death. He was the son of Mr. and Mrs. Robert Barton of Holbeach Lincs and the husband of Marjorie. He was formerly 26910, in the South Staffordshire Regiment. He lies next to Private Bell in grave II. E. 3.

25367, Private William Bradley was 23 years old and a Derbyshire man, the son of Francis and Maria of 46, Higham, Alfreton, Derbyshire. He is buried in II. C. 7

Second Lieutenant William Osborne Crowther had only recently joined the battalion and his CWGC details show him as 3rd Bn. Attached 9th Bn. The 3rd battalion was the reserve based in Derby and 2/Lt Crowther had been commissioned for less than four months. He was 19 years of age and the son of Allan and Sarah Ellen of Altofts, Normanton Yorkshire. He is mentioned in De Ruvigny's Roll of Honour thus –

> *'Crowther, William Osborne, 2nd Lieut. 3rd (Mil) Battn. The Sherwood Foresters (Nottinghamshire and Derbyshire Regt.), 3rds, (son) of Allan Crowther of Habit Royd, Altofts, by his wife Sarah Ellen dau. Of Richard Williams of Holyhead; born Altofts, 24 Sept 1897; educ. Normanton Grammar School; joined the Leeds University O.T.C. in Oct 1915, and finished his training at Trinity College, Cambridge; obtained his commission in Aug. 1916 and was afterwards attached to the 9th (Service) Battn. Of his regiment; served with the Expeditionary Force in France and Flanders, and was killed by a shell while in charge of a working party 24 Nov. 1916. Buried in Hamel Cemetery. Lieut-Col Thornton wrote -: He was very popular with his brother officers and his men, and we have suffered a great loss in his death, for he was a very promising and gallant young officer, and one who did his duty fearlessly.'*

2/Lt Crowther is buried in Plot II, Row F, and grave 2.

22913, Private Samuel Goddard aged 33 years, the son of W and Eunice, a native of Ruddington, Notts is buried in II. F. 5

70992, Private Allan Smith was formerly 27085, Leicestershire Regiment and a native of Leicester. He is buried in II. F. 7.

51975, Private Bert Taylor was a Lincolnshire man born in Friskney and he is buried in II. F. 4.

70989, Private Harold Duncan Taylor was a Leicester 'man' formerly 22742 Leicestershire

Regiment. He was aged 19 years and the son of Mr. C H and Mrs. M A Taylor of 7 Cecil Gardens Leicester. Soldiers died in the Great War list him as dying on 12/11/1916 but this was obviously a misprint. He lies in grave II.E. 4.

From the 25th, the battalion would be once again in the front line trenches and whilst mention was made of men being wounded, the war diarist did not list any killed. The CWGC records though show nine men 'killed in action' between 26th and 29th.

At 5.0pm on 25th the battalion relieved the 6th Bn Border Regt in the front line North East of Beaumont Hamel Station. The relief was completed by 11.0pm with four other ranks being wounded.

The following day was seen as being quiet but the conditions in the trench line and rear area had deteriorated as winter set in. It was very wet all day and the mud was a constant problem, so much so that the battalion had problems getting their rations and water up. Trench occupation in the front line was a nightmare during the winter months and the men would spend five days living like their constant companions the rats. If they were lucky a Dixie full of stew would make it from the rear but usually it would be hard rations of biscuits and tinned bully beef. The men would be caked with mud and covered in lice, but woe betide any man who contracted trench foot which was seen as a self inflicted injury. The toilet would be a dugout with a piece of wood across the hole and anything handy would be used as toilet paper. The men would stand to at dawn and dusk, which was a favourite time for attacks. In between watches they could read letters from home and write them. All the time though would be the stench of death, decay, cordite and gas. The night was a time of trench repair, extending saps and raids into no man's land. Three 9th Bn. men are listed as being killed in action on 26th although the war diary only mentioned 2/Lt Briggs being slightly wounded but remaining on duty. Surprisingly an officer who was not even with the battalion would get a mention in the war diary. Lt. And Q.M. Prosser, DCM, being killed at Mesnil, which was the main artery into the battlefield and approximately a mile from the front. It was though constantly shelled by the enemy and it is possible that Quartermaster Prosser was caught in the shellfire.

Q.M. Prosser was at the time attached to the Worcestershire Regiment with a further attachment to the Border Regiment. Albert Victor Prosser had enlisted in the Border Regiment and had previously served in the Boer War. He was Company Quartermaster Sergeant (regimental number 20028) in the 6th Bn Border Regiment and recommended for a Victoria Cross for gallantry at Suvla Bay, Gallipoli, eventually being awarded the DCM. He had gone out under heavy fire into burning bushes to rescue his wounded Colonel. The Colonel was shot and killed whilst the CQMS was carrying him, but Prosser went on to safely rescue thirteen others at this time. He was commissioned into the 4th Bn The Worcestershire Regiment as a 2/Lt, on 21 October 1915. Acting Quartermaster, Lieutenant, attached to 9th Battalion Sherwood Foresters and killed in action at Mesnil on 26/11/1916. He was awarded the DCM, QSA (Queen's South African medal), 14/15 Star, British War Medal, Victory Medal, and Serbian Cross of Kara George 1st Class with Swords.

Lieutenant Albert Victor Prosser DCM, aged 41 years husband of Ellen Elizabeth is buried at Mesnil Communal Cemetery Extension, grave II. B. 18.

70883, Private John William Lloyd aged 28 years husband of Martha a native of Wolverhampton and formerly 26742 South Staffordshire Regiment is commemorated on the Thiepval Memorial.

22298, Private John William Leivars, aged 36 years, husband of Lilly and a native of Old Sawley; Derby is also commemorated on the Thiepval Memorial.

The 27th was seen as a quiet day in the trenches but not so for two men. Things seem to have livened up as dusk fell though as at 6 pm the outpost party of 'B' Company sighted a strong enemy patrol. The outpost party used their rifles to good effect and dispersed the enemy patrol, inflicting heavy casualties. Six of the enemy walked over and handed themselves in to 'D' Company.

17661, Lance Corporal William Barratt, who was born in Worcester, living in Falmouth Cornwall prior to the War, had enlisted in Nottingham. He is commemorated on the Thiepval Memorial.

32279, Private Herbert Spencer a native of Ilkeston Derbyshire is also commemorated on the Thiepval Memorial.

Except for the enemy firing Gas shells at 4 am and 8 pm, the 28th was relatively quiet. No casualties were reported and no doubt the men were able to 'relax' in the trenches. At 1 am a retaliatory Gas shell barrage was fired by the British Artillery to keep the Germans on their toes. The 6th Bn Yorks and Lancs (32nd brigade) officers arrived at about this time to sort out the details of the relief, which would take place that evening. The 6th Y & L, Commanding officer, Adjutant and Sniping Officer were in attendance for this meeting. The 9th battalion H.Q. was moved to a new dugout at R. 7. a. 03 in preparation for the move. The Germans were also well aware that it was change over time, therefore, 10 am and 5pm saw a rather noisy barrage, which for a number of the men would be their last 'noisy barrage'. The war diary mentioned 8 other ranks casualties for the period.

The relief did not go according to plan but it rarely did as men attempted to negotiate mud filled trench systems on cold dark nights. At 6 pm the first relief party had negotiated the mud and shells to arrive. Then the relief was held up as firstly the 'A' Company guides lost their way and then the York and Lancs. men heading for the dugouts when they should have headed directly for the advanced posts. The cursing from the 9th Bn men can be imagined. Eventually at 3.05 am, on 30th the relief was completed and the men could relax in the knowledge that they had survived yet another stint in the front line. They first had a stop at the battalion cookers for some well-earned hot food and drink. No casualties had been reported whilst the actual relief took place and at 4.30 am H.Q. arrived and at 6.15 am the battalion arrived at Englebelmer, followed at 7.0 am by the men from the advanced posts. The rest of the day was taken up with rest and cleaning up of kit. The men would spend the first days of December 1916 at rest, although in the Great War this was a relative term.

Five of the eight casualties mentioned on 29th had been killed in action and the other three died of wounds.

71047, Private Joseph Claud Baker, aged 28 years; son of Joseph and Emma of Folkestone, Kent is commemorated on the Thiepval Memorial.

25299. Private Henry Bentley was born at Rhyddings, Yorkshire and is commemorated on the Thiepval Memorial.

21714, Private Joseph De Banke aged 22 years, son of Thomas and Sarah and a native of North Wingfield, Derbyshire is commemorated on the Thiepval Memorial.

45933, Private George Frederick aged 24 years, son of Priscilla and of Kegworth Derbyshire is buried at Serre Road cemetery No. 2, grave XVI. J. 7.

70953, Private Victor Hugh Simpson aged 19 years, son of John William and Hannah, Ingoldsby Grantham Lincs and formerly 26951 South Staffordshire Regiment is commemorated on the Thiepval Memorial.

19577 Private James Henry Rushton, MM, aged 26 years and son of William and Elizabeth of Normanton York's, died of wounds on 2 December 1916 and is buried at Contay British cemetery, grave VIII. C. 12. He was awarded the Military Medal whilst serving with the 10th Bn and the London Gazette mentions – 21.10.1916. – For gallantry and devotion to duty when in the attack on Delville Wood on 7th and 8th August 1916.

He is buried at Contay British cemetery, grave VIII. C. 12.

70898 Private James William Truss, aged 32 years and husband of Rose Ellen of Holbeach, Lincs was formerly 26954 South Staffordshire Regiment, died of wounds on 3 December 1916 and is buried at Puchevillers British Cemetery, grave VI. C. 15.

46204, Private Wilfrid Smith aged 24 years and husband of Hilda was born in Wisbeach, Cambs. He died of wounds on 4 December 1916 and is buried at Contay British cemetery, grave VIII. C. 18.

On 1st December 1916 the battalion could be found at Englebelmer (Map 57D S.E. 1/20.000) and although out of sight of the front line, they were not out of sound. Neither would there be much time for rest and relaxation, as working parties were always needed for a variety of tasks. The battalion was only some 4 miles from the front line and well in range of the German artillery. The main task for the following days would be working parties on the Englebelmer to Martinsart Road with 200 other ranks being sent each day. When not working on the road the usual kit cleaning and inspections took place.

Sunday 3rd December saw voluntary church services and no doubt this was preferable to working on the road. At 10 am the battalion was inspected by the G.O.C. 11th Division, after which Lt. Col. W. B. Thornton D.S.O. proceeded on thirty days leave.

The 4th to 16th December would see the men working on the roads or cutting brushwood in Aveluy Wood. This would be a half-day exercise giving the men plenty of time for more cleaning but also the opportunity to rest and write home.

On 4th the Divisional Gas N.C.O's inspected all the battalions gas helmets in preparation for the next front line occupation. The day would also see the 23005 Private George Hopkinson, aged 24 years, succumb to his wounds at Rouen. He had enlisted in February 1915 and was the son of George Henry and Sarah Patience of Alfreton Derbyshire and is buried at St. Sever Cemetery Extension, Rouen, grave O. III. I .4.

On 5th the C.O. Company commanders and one N.C.O. per Company proceeded to the trenches near St. Pierre-Divion, to reconnoitre them for later in the month. At 3 pm the C.O inspected the battalion and no doubt mentioned the 'joys' they had to face in the non-to distant future.

The 6th, 7th and 8th saw more fatigue parties working on the roads but more importantly for the men, the 6th was bath day. Another opportunity to rid themselves of lice for a few hours and have their uniforms deloused. If a man was lucky he could get one of the first baths with hot clean water but the majority would step into water used many times over. At least the caked mud and aroma of the trenches would be cleaned away for a few days, although living under canvas on a mud covered Somme would soon see the grime return.

The 6th would also see another man succumb to wounds at the base hospital.

9015 Private Charles Gilman aged 32 years, son of William and a native Nottingham, is buried at St Sever Cemetery Extension, Rouen, grave O. III. G. 8.

The 9th was once again a morning of fatigues on the roads in the never-ending battle to keep the transports moving. In the afternoon 2/Lt E. D. Smith and a party of 25 other ranks proceeded to Thiepval as a working party. In the late evening at 10 pm 35 reinforcements arrived to replace the men recently killed and wounded. It is doubtful that by late 1916 many of these men would have been from East Midland counties and no doubt some would have been conscripts.

Sunday 10th saw voluntary church services for the C of E men and at 11 am the Non-Conformists attended church parade. Many of the men from Nottinghamshire and Derbyshire would have been raised as Methodists as the East Midlands had a strong tradition in Non-Conformism.

The 11th until the 16th would see more fatigue parties of varying kinds. Work continued on the roads and a number of men worked in Aveluy Wood cutting brushwood. On the 15th and 16th the battalion would once again be allotted baths and no doubt the men took full advantage. The opportunity to bathe twice in a couple of weeks would not be missed. Being located so close to the front line would mean that ablutions would be primitive to say the least. The 15th also saw the return of 2/Lts N.G. Smith and S.M. Ince from hospital and just in time for the battalions return to front line duty.

The 17th December would see the battalion returning to the front line for nine days. The relief of the 7th South Staffordshire Regt began at 12 noon, although the advance parties moved off at 10 am. The trench line was at St. Pierre Divion on the Hansa Line and at 12noon, 'A' and 'B' Companies moved off, followed at 2 pm by 'C' and 'D' Companies. The relief was completed without incident by 7.15 pm and battalion HQ was set up at Q.24.c.4.1.

The first company to occupy the front line was 'B' with 'A' company taking up position in the Hansa Line. The remainder, 'C' and 'D' would be in the reserve dugout, which was located near battalion H.Q. The battalion settled in for another period of patrolling, repairing the front line trench and always being on the alert for enemy activity.

Captain Piper's stay though would be a short one as on 18th he proceeded to the Fifth Army School. For the front line, it was a quiet and uneventful day and good work was done on deepening the trenches. Work was also carried out on trench drainage, which

Beaumont Hamel, 57d .S.E.1 – 14th October 1916

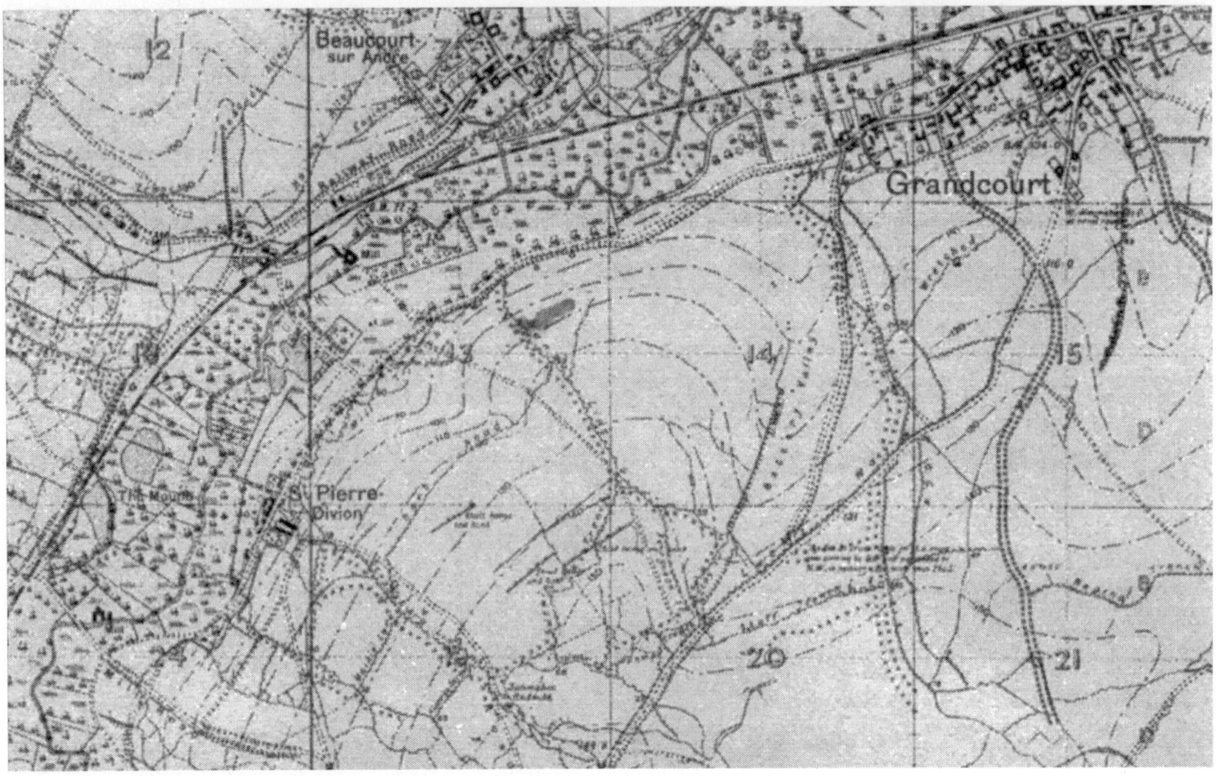

Battalion location 17th to 25th December 1916.

was always a problem. Working in a trench was no mean feat when battle readiness had to be maintained at all times. The men would wear their webbing and equipment at all times, with their personal weapon never far away. They would have iron rations in their haversack but would hope that the ration parties would make it each day. Rations such as hard tack biscuits and corned beef were for emergency use. On the first day men would also be carrying whatever rations they had not used up and they might have had some bread or cold bacon left. Despite the mud and rain the men had to keep their weapon as clean as possible at all times. A jammed rifle could not only lead to the death of a man but would also put his mates in jeopardy.

The 19th saw the men revetting and working on trench drainage – Repairing the trench sides was an almost daily routine as artillery caused cave ins. Carrying parties also had to be found from the Companies in reserve and the Royal Engineers needed fatigue parties for their work. The interesting note shows how the men could get used to anything – 'Enemy Artillery normal'. It is difficult to imagine how anything could be classed as 'normal' in trench warfare but the men got used to the deprivations, the noise, and the constant nearness of death or maiming. At 8.pm the inter-company relief took place and the men of 'A' company moved into the front line whilst 'B' company moved to the Hansa Line (see map above). During this relief 2/Lt Odell was wounded and one other rank killed. The other rank was 22635, Private Edward Robinson of East Drayton, Nott's who is listed as killed on 20th December and is buried at Hamel Military Cemetery, Beaumont Hamel, and grave II. F. 1.

The 7th South Staffordshire's had reported enemy activity on the Hansa Road at a house and it was thought that a machine gun emplacement was being constructed. An Officer's patrol went out but could not even find the house let alone a machine gun post.

At 2.15am on 20th December a patrol of one Sergeant and three other ranks from 34th brigade went out to their forward piquet but did not report to said piquet. Neither did they report to the British front line. They were posted as missing but a search would be made for them. The area between both front lines and their forward posts and piquet's was always a dangerous place. Patrols were often sent out to either get intelligence, take prisoners or mount raids. On many occasions a small patrol could be confronted by a larger enemy patrol and be either killed or taken prisoner. Once again the enemy artillery was normal and work carried on in the trench system revetting, drainage, and the laying of duckboards to improve the trench were all carried out by the men. Meanwhile more men assisted the Royal Engineers and carrying parties moved the essentials of war to the front line.

The 21st would again see work done on the trench system and the enemy artillery once again acted in a 'normal' manner. During the winter months men on both sides were more concerned with making life as comfortable as possible in the trench system, with an attitude of 'live and let live' being the norm. In the evening at 9.15 pm the inter company relief's took place once again with 'A' and 'B' companies returning to the reserve dugout and 'D' company taking over the front line, whilst 'C' moved to the Hansa Line. The men of 'A' and 'B' companies would find that the reserve dugout was no safer than the front line though. At 7.15 am and 6.30 pm officer patrols went out once again to search for the missing patrol but no trace was found. It would be clear that they were either dead or prisoners but for the families it was a case of not knowing as the men were listed as missing in action.

At 1 am on 22nd an officer's patrol reported an enemy post on Hansa Road at point R.8.d.22. (see map), and working parties were heard in the area but they could not locate the house mentioned by 7th South Staffs. The usual work on the trench system was carried out and the diary mentions 'Day quiet' although three of the men may have disagreed when shells fell near the reserve dugout. The diary mentions three other ranks as being wounded and two of these would die of wounds a few days later.

The 23rd would see the search for the enemy house end as an officer's patrol of Hansa Road at 11pm found the post. The house was in fact a shrine with crucifix but in the South Staffs defence many of these shrines are similar to a small house. It was evidently a small post as traces of a dugout were found along with sandbags and ammunition boxes. It had though been demolished by gunfire and no longer a threat. It was found at point R. 14. a.69 Christmas Eve saw the work on the trenches continue and at 7 pm 'B' company moved to Hansa, whilst 'C' would occupy the front line. No doubt the men would think of home and happier times but also wonder just how much longer the war would grind on for. Would they see another Christmas in the trenches or indeed would they see another Christmas at all.

Christmas day would see the battalion relieved by 7th South Staffordshire's and a move back to Englebelmer, although it would be late that night before every man reached the relative safety of the camp. At 8 am the German artillery was once again normal and the British artillery described as 'quiet' although they did send a bombardment over at 8 am, 12 noon and 3pm, which was no doubt meant to remind the Germans that this day was just, like any other. The first company of the 7th South Staffs who would take over the front line arrived at 2.40pm and by 6pm the relief was completed without any casualties. By 6pm the first men of the battalion were at Englebelmer but it would be 11.15 pm when 'C' company finally made it.

Two of the three men wounded on 22nd December died on 25th.

70962 Private William Edward Bates aged 26 years and the husband of Ida from Leicester was formerly 24166 Leicestershire Regiment. He is buried at Varennes Military Cemetery, grave I. F. 15.

12372 Private William Tyndall Buckley was 19 years of age and a native of Wadsley Sheffield. His mother Emma would never see her young son again. He is buried at Etaples Military Cemetery, grave XX. L. 2A.

The remainder of 1916 would be spent out of the line and employed in fatigues and inspections.
The 26th was given over to rest and recuperation and of course kit and clothes cleaning. A time possibly for the men to read letters from home and to open Christmas parcels. A time to write to the family and then just sleep or if really lucky, visit an estaminet for a good meal or a glass or two of French wine.

The 27th to 30th saw the Companies interchanging duties as listed:

27th – 'A' and 'B' Coys. Road fatigues. 'C' and 'D' Coys. Kit inspections etc.
28th – 'C' and 'D' Coys. Road fatigues. 'A' and 'B' Coys. Kit inspections etc.
29th – 'A' and 'B' Coys. Road fatigue. 'C' and 'D' Coys Gas Helmet Drill etc and baths.
30th – 'C' and 'D' Coys. Road fatigue. 'A' and 'B' Coys. Training Gas Helmet Drill etc.

It is to be presumed that on the 29th, all the battalion got their baths and not just 'C' and 'D' Companies. The 31st saw the fatigues continue with a break at 10.15 am for a Church of England service in the Church Hut. The non-Conformists would have a parade service in the Church Hut later that day. 2/Lt Trohear was sent to hospital but no reasons were given.

So ended the year 1916 for the battalion and they had once again 'done their bit'. The year had started quietly but from July they had showed their metal on the Western Front. The year 1917 would see more glory for the battalion but more of its men pay the supreme sacrifice for their country. They would hope that 1917 would be the decisive year and that before its end normal life could be resumed.

Chapter Four

1917 – Messines and 3rd Ypres

THE YEAR 1917 would see the 9th battalion on the Ypres Salient as the focus moved from the Somme. They would once again fight valiantly and suffer large losses but the reputation of the battalion would grow in the mud and rain of 3rd Ypres.

The 11th Division of which the battalion was a part had gained a reputation for tenacity in attack and was used in major offensives. Other Divisions without such a reputation would be used mainly for trench occupation. This was though a double-edged sword as the Division would spend much time out of the line in training but would spearhead attacks. A study of the 9th battalions war deaths shows that the majority came from offensive operations and very few from trench occupation.

Colonel Scothern's notes saw the period from January to May as a quiet time with the battalion involved in training as it prepared for the next major offensive. He devoted two lines to January:

'The Division was relieved and moved out to rest, the battalion going back to old quarters in Coulon Villers. Time passed uneventfully here, the usual training with plenty of sport carried on'

A further three lines for February, ' February still found the Division at rest, but in the middle of the month a move was made to the district near Doullens, Batt H.Q., 'B' and 'D' Coys, going to Famechon, 'C' Coy to Sarton and 'A' Coy to Freschvillers. Here there was a great deal of work done on the railways, most of the time being spent on this'.

The period March through to the end of May was given a slightly longer piece, ' On March 24th the battalion concentrated at Orville, and settled down to serious training once again. This training was hard and thorough, and was devoted mainly to practice in the attack and night operations. It continued until April 4th, when a move was made to Vauchelles, training again being resumed. This place was vacated on April 19th, when the march to Bapaume commenced. On April 24th, the battalion, very fit after its long rest, relieved the 5th Australian Bn, near Morchies. The battalion was not destined to remain here long, as after a short spell in the trenches near Veluwood, it was relieved and moved to a new camp near Montauban, moving again the next day to Fricourt.

On May 18th the battalion entrained at Albert, arriving at Caestre the following day minus 6 officers and 50 men who were left at Abbeville, owing to the train, following a usual playful habit, pulled out without warning. These eventually arrived a day later. On the 24th a move was made to West Outre (Westoutre). The battalion was now to apply the training it had undergone during the early part of the year, as the 33rd Brigade was one of those selected to take part in the attack on the Messines Ridge.'

As usual, Colonel Scothern gave a concise version of the battalion's movements and 'doings' for the period.

January 1st 1917 saw the battalion at Englebelmer, where 'C' and 'D' companies continued working on the roads, whilst 'A' and 'B' companies had a day of training.

Sir Edmund Blunden who had been based at Englebelmer several times during 1916, described the village thus '... Pretty Englebelmer' the battalion diary made no mention of the village or how pretty it was. Although after the Somme campaign there was little of the village left to be pretty or otherwise.

On the 2nd, the battalion left Englebelmer for

another stint in the front line at St Pierre-Divion, under 33rd Brigade Operational order No 52, battalion Operational order no 2 and 7th South Staffordshire Regiment O.O No 1.

The battalion relieved the 7th South Staffordshire's at St Pierre-Divion with, 'C' and 'D' companies leaving Englebelmer at 1 pm, followed by 'A' and 'B' companies at 2-30pm. By 6-30pm the relief was complete, with battalion HQ set up in a dugout at point Q 24. b. 41. Companies 'A' and 'B' occupied the reserve dugouts, whilst 'C' Company occupied Hansa Trench and 'D' Company the Canal and Ferdan Trenches. The night remained quiet and no casualties were suffered.

The enemy would not remain quiet for long though and on the 3rd the battalion were on the receiving end of a particularly heavy barrage with both Cockshy and Ferdan trenches being targeted intermittently between 12-30 and 3-30, High Explosive and shrapnel being employed by the enemy. Shrapnel was particularly nasty as large pieces of red hot metal flew about hitting men indiscriminately. Bullet wounds were usually clean whereas shrapnel would leave gaping wounds of varying sizes.

The men meanwhile worked on improving the trenches, which was a never-ending task as artillery constantly dislodged sand bags and caused cave-ins along the front. Carrying parties and men for wiring were also needed. The duties in front line trenches were not just ones of keeping the enemy at bay.

An officer patrol (*patrol led by officers*) was sent out to point R. 14. d. 62, to ascertain if the Germans had any form of post at that location but none was found and no casualties were reported in the war diary.

The 4th to the 9th followed much the same pattern, which was typical of winter trench warfare. Despite modern weaponry all sides stuck rigidly to the 'Campaign season', which normally saw offensive operations from the spring through to the onset of winter. Logistics at the time had not caught up with weaponry and winter movement of all that an infantry battalion needed was fraught with difficulty. Not that sitting in a wet or frozen front line trench was a soft option and just surviving the elements was enough for most men. The enemy would shell occasionally with the usual Royal Artillery riposte. Snipers were a daily curse and the slightest error could result in sudden death. The British High Command also liked to keep the enemy on their toes and patrols into No Mans land were a regular feature of front line life. Food was usually cold and water was scarce. Rats and lice lived alongside the men and there was always the smell of war – the cordite, gas and decomposing bodies.

The war diary noted 'Enemy artillery normal', although how anything could be classed as normal in the Great War would be difficult to comprehend. No doubt over the previous two years even the most abhorrent occurrences became normal. Another officers' patrol was sent out and found enemy wiring in Battery Valley, which led from St Pierre-Divion to Grandcourt. Work continued on trench improvements, repairs and wiring which would at least keep the men warm. As ever whether in the line or reserve, daily-carrying parties also had to be found from the men occupying the reserve dugouts.

The diary mentioned aeroplane activity by 'Our Air Force' as by this time all arms cooperation was increasingly regular. Patrols were also sent out to liaise with the piquet of the left Brigade at R. 8.c.56 and also across Battery Valley. It was obvious that the enemy activity in and around Battery Valley was a cause for concern and the areas needed patrolling on a regular basis.

The only casualties mentioned in the war diary were on the 8th January, when four men received wounds and one was killed.

No records show any man dying on the 8th January, although there is a death recorded for the 18th. The Commonwealth War Graves Commission as the official date of death.

70987, Private Arthur Shillaker had previously served as 27295 in the Leicester's.

Officially he died on 18 January 1917 and is buried at Hamel Military Cemetery, Beaumont-Hamel, and grave II. C. 2. He was a native of Leicester.

On 10th January under Brigade operational order No 53, battalion OO no 2, 7th South Staffordshire's relieved the battalion at 2 p.m. By 10 pm that evening the relief had been successfully completed and the battalion returned to Englebelmer.

The only casualty mentioned during the relief was 2/Lt C.E. Barter who was wounded. The battalion would remain at Englebelmer until 14th January, the usual round of inspections, fatigues and equipment cleaning being the order of the day. The men also had the opportunity to warm up after trench duties undertaken in freezing weather.

It must be said at this point though that the writers and poets of the Great War painted a picture of life in the trenches and the camps just behind the line from their own middle or upper class experiences prior to the war. Many of the other ranks had come from the mines, industrial cities or farms and life was not dissimilar to that at home. Out of the line the men had good food, medical facilities, sports, canteens, band concerts and the local hostelries. Even the time of trench occupation with the constant aromas of death and cordite, the rats, lice, basic latrines would eventually seem almost normal.

The 14th January being a Sunday was 'voluntary church services' but as every soldier who has ever served knows, for voluntary read compulsory. Men not attending would find themselves volunteered for fatigues and even a boring sermon from the padre was preferable to repairing roads.

On 15th, Under Administrative order No.8, Brigade O.O. No 54, Battalion O.O. No 3 an advance party consisting of Lt Sharwood and 14 other ranks proceeded to Coulonvillers to arrange billets.

The battalion returned to the front line in the area of St Pierre-Divion, knowing that if they survived the next five days of trench life, they would be out of the line and in comfortable billets for a time. All would hope that the bullet or shell with their name on it would not strike. At 1.30 pm the battalion moved off to relieve their sister battalion the 7th South Staffs in the trenches north east of St Pierre-Divion. By 8 pm the relief had been completed without any mishaps. Whilst trench occupation was after 'going over the top', the most dangerous time for any battalion, the period of relief was one of great tension. Silent movement of a large body of men, carrying all of their equipment was not an easy task. To add to their problems, the Germans opposite would know the relief was due and an artillery barrage on the communications trenches would often result. Snipers would also be on their toes looking for any man who would make an easy target. It would be a relieved body of men who eventually settled into the front line despite its inherent dangers.

Trench warfare followed a fairly set routine, particularly during the winter months. Neither side wanted to be too aggressive as in most cases life was quiet, and just surviving the elements was the major concern. A fairly set routine would follow and it was easy for a man to relax with fatal consequences. Artillery and trench mortars were indiscriminate but snipers were always on the look out for the unwary.

The normal routine would be five days in the trenches, five days in reserve and five days at rest. Although as the war diaries show – rest was a relative term. Men were always required for fatigue parties, either in the rear areas, communication trenches or even at times in the front line.

Between the 15th and 19th January the battalion found itself garrisoning a new post just to the left of Ferdan Trench. (The battalion came to know the name Ferdan well – It was a name used for an area in Egypt, a trench on the Somme and in 1917 they would attack Ferdan House near Poelcappelle)

The routine of front line occupation was carried out as normal despite the freezing weather. Living in a trench in sub zero temperatures would have been a test of endurance for men on all sides. The battalion still carried out fighting patrols across Battery Valley towards the O.G.1. (Old German Line 1) and also liaison patrols to the left Brigade at R.8.c.56. The usual trench improvement work was also carried out during this period. Shelling by both sides was fairly sporadic and the casualty figure mentioned was 5 men, whilst out on patrol. Two of these men probably died of wounds later in the month.

On 19th under 33rd brigade O.O. No 55, battalion O.O. No 4, the long awaited relief was ordered. Not before time either as the weather had deteriorated with the snow falling and the temperature plummeting. Not surprisingly the activity on both sides was quiet as surviving the extreme cold was of a greater concern than attacking the enemy. At 1 pm 2nd battalion Royal Marine Light Infantry relieved the battalion and the move was made to the billets at Englebelmer, the relief being completed by 8 pm that evening and the men safely in billets. The battalion would soon be able to relax completely away from the front. The 20th saw the battalion under O.O. 56 – No 5 leave Englebelmer for Puchevillers. At 2 pm the men were moved by bus to Puchevillers and by 6-30 pm the battalion had settled into its new billets which consisted of huts and tents. The weather was still extremely cold and no doubt the men allotted tents looked on in envy at the men in huts. Bus travel in 1916 was not a particularly pleasant experience during winter months. Solid tyres on frozen ground and an open upper deck made for a fairly uncomfortable ride, although it was marginally better than the alternative, which would have been marching.

As the battalion settled in yet another of their number succumbed to his wounds and died at the 11th Casualty Clearing Station in Varennes.

3680, Private Harold Leslie Tyers a native of Nottingham, aged 22 years was no doubt one of the casualties of 18th January. He is buried at Varennes Military Cemetery and grave I. F. 70.

The following day under O.O., No 57 – No 6 the battalion marched with the Brigade group to billets at Longuevillette. The march commenced at 10-00am and the battalion finally arrived at 4-30pm. The distance between the two villages depending on the route would have been between 10 and 15 miles, the progress through the frozen rear areas of the Somme being incredibly slow for such fit men. The battalion transport though was delayed due to the frozen state of the roads. The men would have had a cold wait for their kit to arrive.

21271 Arthur H. Chambers left the Battalion on 21st and proceeded to England to be commissioned. He would serve as a Lieut. In the 2/5th battalion and receive wounds in September 1917 and March 1918 becoming a Prisoner of War on 21st March. The 22nd saw the battalion on the move again as under O.O. No 7 the brigade moved to its designated rest area. The destination was Coulonvillers, which was an area they all knew well, and near Abbeville, which could be easily reached, should a man get the time for a spot of leave. Officers could look forward to leave in Blighty or a few days in Paris.

The battalion could now settle in and recover from their recent hardships before preparing for the next offensive, which would come soon enough. The first couple of days would be taken up with the usual work of cleaning and inspections. Weapons had to have a good clean to remove the mud and grime of the trenches. Personal kit was also caked in mud and was in need of a good clean. The weather remained extremely cold with hard frosts. Inspections would be carried out to ensure that all weaponry and personal kit was up to scratch and woe betides any man who did not have spotless kit, despite the weather and conditions.

The 26th/27th was taken up with Platoon training and at this time the lessons learned from the Somme campaign would be worked on. The 28th was a Sunday and whilst the Church of England men had a voluntary service, the Non-conformists attended church parade. No doubt Fred Greaves V.C. a staunch Methodist would have attended.

On the same day another battalion man succumbed to his wounds.

70901, Private Herbert Wardle aged 21 years, died of wounds and was buried in Doullens Communal Cemetery Extension No 1 in grave IV. G. 10. He had previously served as 26960 in the South Staffordshire Regiment. The period from 29th January until 14th February would see the battalion undertaking various types of training – Platoon, Company and the like in readiness for their next stint in the front line. Not that the period was all work and no play as sport was always an important part of Army life. It was seen as good for character and team building whilst adding inter unit rivalry. Football matches were a regular pastime for the men with inter company matches and also games against the other battalions in the Brigade.

Working parties also had to be found for various tasks and the battalion would spend some time working on the local firing ranges and building a new assault course complete with trenches. There were some highlights during the rest period and on 31st January the G.O.C. (General Officer Commanding), the 11th Division; Lieut-Gen Sir C. Woollcombe inspected the battalion whilst they trained.

The 7th February would have been of particular interest to all of the men when they marched to Cramont for bathing as it meant a few lice-free days to look forward too before the itching would start again. For two men the 9th February was also a special day when they received award ribbons for Gallantry medals. A composite Company under Captain Harding attended an Honours and Awards parade at 2.30 pm. Two Staff officers were in attendance – D.A.A. (Deputy Assistant Adjutant) and the QMG (Quartermaster General).

Sergeant Blurton received his DCM ribbon for his actions on 27 November 1916 for conspicuous gallantry in action north east of Beaumont Hamel. He displayed great courage and determination in holding an advanced post against a strong party of the enemy, killing many of them and capturing several prisoners. Private Bark received his MM ribbon for his actions on the same date. He held an advanced post against a strong party of the enemy, killing many of them and capturing several prisoners Bark would die of wounds on 2 May 1918

The same day 56418 Private Walter Sweet aged 38 years died at a Stationary hospital in Abbeville. He is buried in Abbeville Communal Cemetery Extension and grave II. C. 8. Walter was a native of Nottingham.

The 11th February saw a special Platoon chosen by the Brigadier General of 33rd Brigade being inspected by the Divisional Commander at 10-15 a.m. This honour would reflect on the whole battalion and shows the high regard in which they were held.

Training continued and a special Platoon from 'A' Company demonstrated the new attacking ideas, which had been put in place. Much more emphasis would be on Platoon autonomy and Platoon commanders were given the opportunity of thinking on their feet instead of awaiting orders from higher echelons. The 15th February saw the Battalion on the move again and at 9-30 a.m. they marched with the Brigade group from Coulonvillers to Candas, a distance of some 12 miles. They arrived at 2 p.m. and they settled into new billets but the stay would be a short one as at midnight Brigade O.O No 59,

Battalion O.O. 8 and Brigade, O.O. No 60 were received detailing a move the following day. 2/Lt E. D. Smith though had remained at Coulonvillers, taking on the post of Town Major.

Once again the stay would be a brief one as at midnight on 15th orders were received for a move the following day. Brigade O.O. 59 and 60 and battalion O.O. 8, detailed a move to Famechon some 20 miles distant and closer to the Somme front line. No doubt many of the men expected to be in the front line trenches before to long.

Battalion O.O. No 9 instructed the battalion to have advance parties moving off at 8-30 am to take over the work and billets in the Authie area. The remainder of the battalion was to be split and moved to areas close to Famechon or in the Town itself. At 9 am the Battalion less 'A' company left for their respective areas with H.Q., 'B' and 'C' Companies marching to Famechon and arriving at 2.30 pm. In the meantime 'C' Company marched to Sarton, which was approximately five miles less. At 10 am 'A' Company set off for their destination, which was Freschvillers, a mere 12 miles stroll from Candas.

The battalion found itself spending the remainder of February and much of March on railway construction.

The 17th had the entry '7.0 am to 5-30 pm. All available men on work for new railways'. This was the new Authie Valley Railway under construction to make movement of supplies and men easier to the new front line. During the period life carried on as normal within the battalion but the emphasis was always on the Railway and its construction. The 18th was a Sunday and H.Q., 'B' and 'D' Companies had a rest day unlike 'A' and 'C' who had to find working parties for the day. It is possible that on one of these working parties

It is possible that on one of these working parties 27040 Private Albert Edward Cresswell aged 36 years, of 'C' Coy, received the injuries which meant he died later in the day. He was a native of Nottingham and is buried at Puchevillers British cemetery and grave V. A. 6.

The following day two officers and 50 other ranks arrived as reinforcements for the battalion.The 22nd saw a football match take place between the battalion and the 7th South Staffordshire's, resulting in a victory 4 goals to 3 in the battalions favour. The 23rd saw one new officer arrive and the following day Captain Scott returned from hospital.

The 24th saw the death of 70887, Private Charles Lewis, aged 30 years and a native of Lincolnshire. He is buried at Warlincourt Halte British Cemetery, Saulty and grave V. B. 8.

Sunday 25th saw only two platoons working but the following days it was once again 'all hands to the pump'. Before the month was out another four officers and 21 other ranks arrived as reinforcements.

The month of March began with all of the battalion working a ten-hour day on the railways. Each Company worked in a different area, with 'A' Coy, at Freschvillers, 'C' Coy. At Sarton, H.Q., 'B' and 'D' at Famechon.At 8 pm on 4th orders were received that no further work was required on the Authie Valley Railway and the battalion could look forward to some rest. This was short lived though but at least the men could spend the 5th resting and using the baths. The men would have little in the way of real rest as cleaning up and inspections were also held.

On the 6th saw the men trained in Companies and trying out the new formations for attacks. Specialists were being used more – bombers (Grenade throwers) and machine gun sections. The newly formed Machine Gun Corps was also being integrated into battle tactics. Although the diary does not mention what the new tactics were I believe that they meant this. The men were also being taught to move in sections and to cover other sections as they moved forward. Much had been learned after the abject failure of the 1st day of the Somme. The afternoon was taken up with inspections and recreational training. From 7th until 23rd the battalion would be back working on the railways with a half day for baths and recreation being the only respite.

A number of officer movements took place during this period -:

The 7th saw Major Scothern and Captain Harding proceed on four days leave in Paris. On the 8th, Lieut, Harwood returned from Hospital and on the 10th Lieut. C H Sands was transferred to the Royal Flying Corps. The 11th saw Captain L. D. Goldie transferring to the 12th (Labour) Battalion, Duke of Cornwall's Light Infantry.

On the 12th 2/Lt L.H. Phelps rejoined the battalion from hospital and the 14th saw 2/Lt L.A. Loup transferring to the Indian Army.On 11 March 12568 Corporal Thomas Milner aged 23 years a native of Mansfield Nott's was killed in action. He was a member of the 2nd battalion but had initially served with the 9th. He is buried at Philosophe British Cemetery, Mazingarbe and grave I. M. 44. As will be seen later a number of 9th battalion men are also buried at this cemetery.

Finally on 24th March the Battalions labouring stint on the Authie Valley Railway was over and a return to training could be made.The battalion concentrated at Orville under Brigade operational order No 61, Battalion O.O. No 10. At 10.45 a.m. H.Q., D & D Companies moved from Famechon and by 2 pm, all Companies had arrived at Orville and settled into billets.

Between the hours of 3pm and 8 pm, the battalion was detailed for baths, which were much needed after the recent weeks of toiling on the railway construction. The next day was a Sunday and given over to voluntary Divine services, followed by the remainder of the men getting their baths and a change of clothes. The billets and men's kit were inspected and everything would have to be spotless whilst the battalion was at rest. In the British Army, cleanliness was indeed next to Godliness and woe betides any man who had unclean kit.

The 26th would see training commence in preparation for the coming campaigns of 1917 when it was hoped that the enemy would be defeated. Many lessons had been learned from the Somme campaign and these had to be practised over and over again so that the officers and men would be ready for any eventuality in battle.

Interestingly the mornings training for 26th was delayed owing to rain although the time was utilised for lectures. The training eventually got under way in the afternoon and consisted of two hours of practise attacks.The day would also see Lieut. Harwood and three other ranks departing for Calais to act as instructors at the Divisional training unit.

The following four days were taken up with a variety of lectures and more training.The Allied offensives of 1917 were about to begin with the Battles of Arras from 9th April, although 11th Division would not be employed until The Battle of Messines in June. The intense training would be aimed at Messines and the sought after breakthrough. New tactics would be practised again and again until the officers and men could do them in their sleep. This again shows how the British forces had moved on since 1916, with all arms working in unison to get the job done.

The 27th saw company training all day and at 5.34 pm all the battalions officers attended a Regimental exercise at Bois Brule. The following three days consisted of more Company training. Specialist training was also undertaken, along with Gas Helmet Drill and firing practice. The men were tested on control and direction of fire, rapid loading and marching in artillery formation with advanced guards. All this training concentrated on a rapid breakthrough attack followed by open warfare. Whether this was an exercise in boosting moral or there was an actual belief that an entrenched enemy could be beaten back remains unclear. On 29th at 5.30pm 33rd Brigade Commanding officer gave the men a lecture wason 'Open Warfare' and it can be assumed that the battalion was being prepared for rapid deployment if the Battle of Arras succeeded. It would though be some considerable time before 'Open Warfare' would be seen. The following day 'the Battalion attack' was practiced on four lines of trenches whilst the specialists honed their own skills. The 30th saw a route march in artillery formation with an advanced guard put out which again was part of the 'Open Warfare' preparations.

April 1st was a Sunday and the men attended church services with the C of E service at 10-30 am, followed by the Non-Conformist and Roman Catholic ones at 11.30 am.

Major A.E. Scothern left for Aldershot to attend a Senior Officers course, with Captain S.H. Piper taking over as the second in command of the battalion.Major Scothern's absence may explain the error in his notes for April 1917.

He wrote '...until April 4th, when a move was made to Vauchelles, training again being resumed. This place was vacated on April 19th when a march to Bapaume commenced. On April 24th the battalion, very fit after its long rest, relieved the 5th Australian Bn. Near Morchies. The battalion was not destined to remain here long, as after a short spell in the trenches near Veluwood, it was relieved and moved to a new camp near Montauban, moving again the next day to Fricourt.'

As will be seen the War Diaries for the month differ from the above. From 2nd to 11th April the training continued apace as the men continued their preparations for the next assault. Company and battalion training concentrated on 'Open Warfare', men using artillery formations, throwing out patrols and consolidating positions once taken. Meanwhile the specialists such as bombers, snipers and machine gunners continued with their own training.

The 7th saw the men practising forming up on tapes for night attacks on two lines of enemy trenches and then consolidation. As with all Army training a pamphlet was produced giving details of how to consolidate trenches and localities after assault and capture, including notes on 'rapid wiring'. All details were given, including the number of men needed for each type of wiring in front of the trenches. The men trained and trained so that when a position was taken it would be an automatic response when throwing out a wire in front of them.

The first paragraph of the notes:

> *'The capture of a system of hostile trenches is an easy matter compared with the difficulty of retaining it. A thorough knowledge of the principles, a careful study and correct use of the natural features of the ground, and a detailed preparation and organisation of the work, are necessary; but success will only result if there is also an absolute determination on the part of all ranks to get the work done promptly at all costs'.*

Sunday 8th saw parade services for Divine Worship and any man missing the said parade could be punished heavily. The King's Regulations stated that deliberately missing a Divine Service parade was punishable by Field Punishment No 1 (FP No1). This consisted of the man being tied to a fence or wagon wheel for a couple of hours each day for the length of the sentence. Captain J Critchlow who had been wounded in the attack of 26 September 1916 returned to the battalion and 15 other ranks arrived as reinforcements from the base at Etaples.

The 9th was once again a wet day, which curtailed training, as the ground was too wet to practice, attacks. Perhaps practise attacks over sodden ground would have been a useful preparation for the battles of Ypres later in the year. The Companies were instead treated to a short route march in the rain during the morning. The afternoon was once again taken up with specialist training and company attacks. The 10th saw 2/Lt Ottewell leave for Newark in England and a course of instruction in Field Engineering. The remainder of the battalion once again practiced attacking in various forms with emergency formations and rapid loading taking the fore.

The 11th April would see the battalion on the move but not before another practise attack was undertaken. At 11 a.m. orders were received from Brigade for the troops to return to billets and prepare for a move at short notice. The same day saw flanking operations to the Arras Offensive begin near Bullecourt and there is little doubt that 11th Division was put on alert for follow up operations. At 12 pm Brigade sent orders to carry on with training around the billets but later at 2 p.m. the order to discontinue training was received. Brigade also stated that the battalion would move within the next few hours. At 4 p.m. the battalion received its marching orders to move to Vauchelles-Les-Authie (B.M. 231) and at 5.45 pm the move from Orville commenced. The whole Brigade marched from Orville to Vauchelles-les-Authie and by 7.45 p.m. the battalion was settled in its new billets.

The 12th was a quiet day and the men had the opportunity to clean up equipment and clothing, followed of course by the usual inspections.

The day also saw 13567 Private John Walter James succumb to his wounds at the base hospital in Boulogne. John was a native of Worksop, Nott's aged 30 years and is buried in Boulogne Eastern Cemetery, grave IV.D.8.

The 13th and 14th saw training continue that pointed to a failure to make a breakthrough followed by open warfare. The battalion therefore had a more leisurely approach to the front line. Night operations were once again a feature of the training as the men practiced forming up on tapes. On the 15th the rain once again caused havoc with the training schedule. Being a Sunday the men attended voluntary Divine Services at 6.30 p.m. and during the day Major M.J.D. Grimes and 63 Other Ranks reinforcements arrived. The 16th was another day of training with the emphasis once again on Open Warfare. It was obvious that the General Staff expected that the Arras offensive would lead to a breakthrough, followed by 'Open Warfare'. The 17th was yet another day of heavy rain and training was curtailed with the men being given lectures in the billets. Between 2.30 p.m. and 4.30 p.m. Open Warfare was resumed. The 17th also saw another man die although in the case of Ernest Scattergood it was from illness.

61560 Private Ernest Charles Scattergood aged 38 years died at home in Nottingham and is buried in Nottingham General Cemetery.

An interesting note on the 18th shows that new methods of warfare evolved throughout the war. Experiments were carried out using rifle grenades to cut wire and destroy wire obstacles. The Somme battles of 1916 had shown that artillery did not always cut through the wire and something new was needed. The experiment was successful and would be adopted for emergency use in an assault. Meanwhile the battalion continued with its training and the men took part in a route march with advanced guard formations. Specialist training was also undertaken and in this case it was musketry drill.

The 19th would see the battalion on the move again with a short march of 14 kms to Bouzincourt. Under 33rd Bde. O.O. No 62. Battalion O.O. No 11, the battalion along with the rest of the Brigade left at 10.15 for the short march to the new quarters. They arrived at 3 p.m. but were not impressed with the new quarters, which were found to be in a dirty condition and bad state of repair. This is surprising as they were huts and usually they would be kept clean and in good order. There is a possibility that the huts had previously been occupied by French troops who were not the best for cleanliness. The battalion would not remain long though as the move towards the front line continued after a brief stopover. The Battalion had been tasked with relieving the 31st Australian Battalion at Bapaume.

At 9.30 a.m. on 20th the advanced party which consisted of 2/Lt Suffolk (Intelligence Officer), One N.C.O. from each company and one from Battalion H.Q., proceeded to Bapaume in order to take over the shelters, stores etc. from 31st Australian Battalion. Under 33rd Brigade O.O. No 63/64, Battalion O.O. No 12/13, the battalion had been detailed to relieve the Aussies in the front line. At 1.30 pm the remainder of the battalion marched to Courcelette arriving at 5.30 p.m. They marched along the old Roman road between Albert and Bapaume and passed Thiepval. Many of the men would remember the vicious fighting of September and the friends and comrades who lay in the area. They saw the thousands of wooden crosses as they marched and wonder if this time their number would be up. The German army had retreated to the newly constructed Hindenburg line and left the landscape in ruins with anything of use destroyed.

The 21st saw the battalion complete the march to Bapaume and the relief of the 31st Aussie Battalion. The battalion vacated Courcelette at 9.45 a.m. and marched the 10 kms, reaching Bapaume at noon and relieving the 31st Aussie Battalion.

The Companies were distributed as follows (reference – Map France 57c N.W. 1/20,000, edition 6A) – Battalion H.Q., 'A' and 'D' Companies were located along the Bapaume to Peronne road in ruined houses, in square H.34.c. 'B' Company in ruined mills at H.34.d45., and 'C' Company in ruins at Bancourt H.36.a.84.

The following two days would see some work but mainly for the men was the pleasure of the baths. Although it would seem from the diaries that 'B' company missed out on this pleasurable experience. The morning of the 22nd saw the men cleaning up and having inspections. Between 2.30 and 4.30 'A', 'D' and H.Q., Companies had hot baths. The following morning 'C' Company bathed before joining 'B' company to work on the ANZAC Light Railway near Beugny, which was some 4 Kms east of Bapaume towards the front line. At 10.15 the CO and Company commanders set out to reconnoitre the trenches occupied by the 5th Australian Battalion near Morchies.

The 24th saw the battalion return to the front line and much work was needed on the new trench system. The German retreat to the Hindenburg line had only just been completed and Bapaume had been in British hands since 17th March. The German artillery would have been ranged on every part of the area in and around Bapaume, whilst much of the infrastructure had been destroyed during the retreat. The British not only had to hold the new line but also turn this desolate area into a functioning base for operations.

Under 33rd brigade O.O. No 63.d 22.4.17, the battalion was ordered to relieve the 5th Battalion Australian Imperial Force (A.I.F.) where they became Brigade reserve at various locations under battalion O.O. No. 14. At 1 p.m. the Transport column, reserve officers, specialists and N.C.O.'s moved off to the transport lines situated north east of Fremicourt (Map 57c N.W. ref I.20.b). At 5.30 p.m. the Battalion H.Q. arrived at I.17.a. 34 and commenced digging shelters in the sunken road situated there. The remainder of the battalion arrived at hourly intervals with 'A' and 'B' Companies at 7.30 p.m., 'C' Company at 8.30 p.m. and finally 'D' Company at 9.30 p.m. By 9.35 p.m. all of the battalion was situated in its correct area of operation. The stay for some would be short lived though as the Germans immediately laid down a heavy barrage resulting in Battalion H.Q., along 'B' and 'C' Companies withdrawing to point I.21.d.86 (Map 57c N.W.), which was south of the Railway Embankment. Luckily for the battalion, no casualties were sustained during the barrage.

By 25th it was obvious that the German artillery had every inch of the area ranged and at noon the Transport lines and Quartermaster Stores were also shelled and forced to move to point I.20.d. At 7.30 p.m., H.Q., 'B' and 'C' Companies moved again to C.30.d.45.

As the area had just been occupied no trench system existed and a series of posts covered the area. These would be built upon in the coming weeks to form a complete trench system.

The final disposition of the battalion on the night of 25th/26th of April was a follows:

Map 57c N.W. 1.20,000 –
Battalion H.Q., – C.30.d.45 – 'A' Coy, H.Q. and three platoons at I.17.b.50 to 56. – One platoon of 'B' Coy. In post three at J.4.c.Coy. H.Q at J.2.b.28.
Two sections of 'B' Coy. In post 4 at J.3.b.64
Two sections of 'B' Coy. In post 5 at J.26
One Platoon of 'B' Coy. At Battalion H.Q.,
Two sections of 'B' Coy. In post 6 at D.25.b.61.

'C' Coy. On right of battalion H.Q. in square C.30.d
'D' Coy. On road J.1.d. 40 to J.1.d.15.
Coy. H.Q. at J.1.d.40

The above shows the problems when a trench system is not in place and various sections are spread amongst the posts. The veterinary officer was called upon to shoot a mule, which was wounded whilst transporting rations to the men. At noon 2/Lt C.R. Cook reported from 14th Infantry Brigade depot. At 10 p.m. 'B' Company found working parties to be used in improving five of the posts. 2/Lt C.A.B (surname) rejoined his company from echelon 'A'.

The following days were taken up with improvement work on the posts and shelters. The posts needed wire in front of them, S.A.A. and bombs within them. All Companies constructed shelters with two huts being built for H.Q. The 33rd Brigadier General visited Battalion H.Q., twice on 27th to see how things were progressing. At 9-30 p.m. on the 27th the Strombus Horn sounded for a gas alarm but this proved to be a false alarm. On the 28th the Battalion made a gas attack but otherwise the day was quiet. The village of Morchies did get its usual shelling by the Germans but no casualties were reported. The Companies continued to work on the posts as the line slowly took shape.

The 29th dawned and the weather was dry, sunny and fine. Battalion H.Q. was a camouflaged as there was much aerial activity locally. A large number of British machines were seen overhead during the day. The enemy artillery had a quiet day and this was possibly because of the British aerial Activity. At 3.p.m. arrangements were put in place for the 8th Northumberland Fusiliers (34th Brigade, 11th Div) to relieve the battalion. The men continued with the work of improving posts, wiring and moving ammunition forwards. During the night of 29th/30th the men put up 300 yards of wire in front of the positions and this was no mean feat in the conditions that prevailed.

Advanced parties from the Northumberland Fusiliers arrived during that night. Arrangements were also made to relieve the 11th Manchester Regiment (34th Brigade) in the reserve Brigade line (33rd Brigade O.O. No 64, Battalion O.O. No 16.) Captain W. B. Vann reported his arrival and the day was again quiet with only aerial activity to report.

May 1st saw the battalion relieved by Northumberland Fusiliers and by 12.05 a.m. this had been completed. In turn the battalion relieved the Manchester Regiment men and this was completed by 1.25 a.m. As usual the enemy knew that the relief was in progress and sent over some tear gas, although only a slight smell of gas reached the battalion. The battalion, were now in the trenches near Morchies, which were known as the Beaumetz-Morchies line, although once again this was a collection of posts and the battalion was deployed as follows:

Ref. Map 57C France 1/40,000 –

H.Q. at I.12.a.35, 'B' Coy. At I.5.c. 'C' Coy. I.6c.5.8. 'A' Coy. I.11.d.59. 'D' Coy. J.14.a.2.8.

The battalion sections would garrison the various posts, although 'A' Coy, were tasked with supplying escorts for the Australian Artillery Batteries nearby. The men settled in to their new surroundings with only the daily aerial activity as a diversion.

The 2nd would see some of the men bath and get a change of underclothing, which was no doubt the highlight of the day. A total of 125 men were given the luxury of bathing with 45 visiting the Brigade baths at Beugny and 80 at the Battalion baths situated at the transport lines at Fremicourt. At 7.pm. the enemy heavily shelled the British artillery batteries and two other ranks from 'B' Company were wounded.

The 3rd would be a busy day, which would also see the battalion lose more men. At 3.45 a.m. the British Artillery opened up with a barrage on the enemy lines in the vicinity of Bullecourt in preparation for the battle which would take place from 3rd to 17th May. The battalion continued to strengthen their trenches and cut shelter slits into the various posts on the front. Wire was also put up in front of the trenches and splinter proof covers erected on the shelters. Recesses were cut to store S.A.A. and bombs in preparation for a possible counter attack, whilst "B" Company worked on the defences at Morchies. At 9a.m the CO visited the transport lines at Fremicourt, as did another 80 men for their bath and clean underclothes. 2/Lt Booth gave bombing instruction to three sections from 'A' and 'B' companies near Beugny. These took place at 11 a.m. 3 p.m. and 4 p.m. At noon the enemy commenced shelling the British batteries in the valley near Morchies with gas shells containing Phosgene and Prussic acid. One shell fell between the Battalion H.Q., dugouts but luckily the wind carried the gas away and no casualties were sustained. Samples were immediately taken from the shell hole and sent to the 11th Division Gas Officer for analysis. An enemy High Explosive shell hit the road close to 'B' Company and this caused the death of two men and the wounding of three others. Unusually for the war diaries one of the men was mentioned by name – Sgt. Denman. At 8 p.m. the enemy counter attacked at

Bullecourt and the battalion was ordered to prepare itself to reinforce if necessary but in the event the enemy attack failed.

Although both men killed on 3rd were buried, their graves were subsequently lost and they are both commemorated on the Arras memorial.

12685, Sergeant John Widdowson Denman a native of Chesterfield, Bay 7 Arras Memorial.

61531, Private George Arthur Widdowson, aged 19 years of Brampton, Chesterfield, and Bay 7. Arras Memorial.

Interesting that both men have 'Widdowson' in their names and are from Chesterfield. Much work was carried out on the night of 3rd/4th with trench improvement, revetting of shelters and construction of latrines. The wire in front of the posts was also thickened whilst 'B' Coy. continued working on the defences at Morchies. An unusual note was made in the diary – '10.30 a.m. Adjutant visits transport lines for bath and rest' but no mention is given as to why he above all others needs a 'rest'. It is doubtful he got his rest as the enemy used a 9.2" heavy Gun on the transport lines whilst he was there. At 9.30 p.m. the C.O. and Company Commanders proceeded to the H.Q., of 6th York and Lancaster Regiment (32nd Brigade) to arrange the relief of the battalion on 6th. Captain C.G. Waddington R.A.M.C. was taken ill and replaced by Capt Laurie.

Again an unusual entry for the diaries – 'Sgt Denman and 1 O.R. (Pte Widdowson) 'B' Coy, buried near 'B' Coy H.Q. Service conducted by Rev. C.F. Barnes'. It is obvious that Sgt Denman was a well-respected N.C.O. within the battalion. The day was very quiet and men were released for baths once again, with 75 visiting the Brigade baths at Beugny and 80 the battalion baths at Fremicourt.

Another man would die of his wounds that day probably sustained on 3rd.

70946, Private Walter Taylor aged 31 years and a native of Butterwick Lincolnshire had previously served with the South Staffordshire regiment (26856). He is buried at Grevillers British cemetery, grave III. D. 14, where it says on his headstone "He did his bit, until he was hit, now let him rest in peace.

The 5th was a very warm and very quiet day and the men continued the work of strengthening dugouts, shelters and posts. The C.O. visited the C.O. of 6th Yorkshire Regiment (32nd Brigade) at 2 p.m. to arrange for the relief of that battalion by the 9th Bn, on the night of 6th/7th May. The British artillery again put over a heavy barrage in the direction of Bullecourt at 4.30 p.m. and 10.30 p.m. The Brigadier General visited Battalion H.Q. to observe these barrages, which lasted for half an hour on each occasion. The 6th would see the battalion on the move again under Brigade O.O. No. 65 and Battn O.O. No. 17. The weather was hot and the day was a quiet one with little activity from the enemy. The 6th York and Lancaster Battalion relieved the battalion who in turn moved out to relieve the 6th Yorkshire's in the front line north east of Hermies. Firstly at 2 p.m. the battalion transport moved from Fremicourt to Velu Wood. Second to move was 'A' Company who once relieved in the Beaumetz-Morchies line, proceeded to Velu Wood and after having a hot meal moved off to relieve 'A' Coy. 6th Yorks. At 8.20 p.m. 'B', 'C' and 'D' Companies were relieved and moved off to relieve 'D', 'C' and 'B' companies, 6th Yorks. Finally at 8.40 p.m. Battalion H.Q., was relieved and moved off to relieve Battalion H.Q. of 6th Yorks.

At 11 p.m. on 6th the Battalion HQ was in position and settled in for its five-day stint in the front line, although this would be extended to eight days. The Companies took a little longer to arrive and settle into their allotted trenches with 'D' Coy. arriving at 12.20 am on 7th, followed by 'C' Coy. at 1.05 a.m., 'A' Coy. 1.30 a.m. and 'B' Coy. 3.40 p.m. The enemy remained fairly quiet although a few aerial torpedoes and shells were deployed against the battalion but the British artillery soon quietened them. The C.O visited the positions of 'A' and 'B' Companies during the day. Captain Vann reported to 11th Division for new duties, whilst Captain S.H. Piper proceeded on leave.

The next few days would see the battalion in the usual front line routine with little sleep or hot food, constantly on the alert and the never-ending work of improving the positions. Hermies had only been in British hands since the 9th April and the trench system was therefore a rudimentary affair. The 8th was fairly quiet and the weather was showery with a light variable wind. This would at least negate the possibility of gas attacks. Machine Gun fire and vane bombs were used on 'C' Companies No 7 post at K.19b.8.5. Likewise 'A' Company was fired on with aerial torpedoes at 5 p.m. No casualties were incurred during the day. At 6 p.m. Lieut, D.G. Brook and 2/Lt Bowyer arrived at the transport lines from the Divisional base.

The 9th would see more work carried out but little enemy activity although 'C' company was shelled intermittently by an enemy 77 mm gun which resulted in 2nd Lt. Dean and one other rank being wounded. Likewise 'A' Company came under fire from aerial torpedoes and rifle grenades and this resulted in one other rank being killed and five wounded.

70952 Private Harry Shaw is actually commemorated as dying on 10th May. He was 27 years old and a native of Walsall, Staffordshire. He was formerly 25645 in the South Staffordshire Regiment. He is buried at Hermies British Cemetery, grave A.16.

Two of the wounded would succumb to their wounds a couple of days later.

70801 Private Frederick John Milward who was born at Mayfield Staffordshire died of wounds on 11 May 1917. He is buried at Grevillers British Cemetery, grave IV.E.12.

22989 Private George Bailey who was born at Chesterfield died of wounds on 11 May 1917. He is buried at Grevillers British Cemetery, grave IV. E. 16.

An article appeared in The Derbyshire Times dated Saturday 2nd June 1917.

Hasland Family's Patriotism

A Hasland family have an enviable record on patriotism. Mrs Bailey of 21 Grove Street Hasland, has had news from Lichfield to say her third son Private G. Bailey of The Sherwoods died of wounds on May 12th at a clearing station in France. He enlisted on February 6th 1915 and went to the Dardanelles. Returning he was sent to France in July 1916. Wounded on the Somme on September 25th he was sometime in a London hospital. He returned to France in March last. Before enlistment he worked at the Glapwell Colliery.

Another son Private F. Bailey was wounded on May 25th in the left arm and is now in a Bradford hospital. He has been previously wounded this year. Before enlistment he worked for Messrs. N. Atrill Ltd., Coal Merchants, Chesterfield. A third son Gunner F. Bailey R.F.A. is over on leave after being in France nearly two years. He was formally a pony driver at Grassmor Colliery. The eldest brother Private T.M. Bailey, Welsh Regiment, is now in Salonica.

The 10th was again a hot day and work continued improving the positions. Arrangements were also made with 6th Lincolns (33rd Brigade) for the Battalions relief although the following day this was cancelled. A patrol consisting of one N.C.O. and five men went out from post No.8 which was on 'C' Companies front. They reported seeing a German Machine Gun and vane bomb thrower in an enemy post some 70 yards away. No doubt this would get attention from the British artillery at some point. The 11th to the 14th May were much the same with a great deal of work carried out on improvements and thickening the wire obstacles in front of the trenches. The enemy remained reasonably quiet during this period. There was some aerial activity and the enemy artillery occasionally shelled but no casualties were sustained. In particular 'A' Company was kept on its toes with aerial torpedoes, vane bombs and whizz-bangs. Likewise the enemy sent some 30 77mm shells which landed near No. 7 Post which was occupied by 'C' Company. At 6 p.m. on 12th, Captain E Bourdas arrived from the Divisional base. Finally on 14th May under Brigade O.O. No. 68, Battalion O.O. No.18, the 4th Royal Berkshires relieved the battalion.

The same day another 9th Battalion man would die although the CWGC have him as being in the Depot Regiment. He was though in the 9th battalion and no records show him being transferred.

12902, Lance Sergeant William Barber, aged 26 years, born at Duckmanton Derbyshire died on 14 May 1917 and is buried at Duckmanton Church Cemetery.

The relief of the battalion was completed by 1.15 a.m. on 15th May and the Companies stopped for a meal at Velu Wood prior to marching off independently to Camp at Beaulencourt and by 8 a.m. the men were settled. So would start the move northwards into Belgium and the battles of Messines and Ypres.

Under Battalion O.O. No 19 Sgt Cornelius proceeded to Aveluy and joined the advanced party, which was leaving for the new Brigade area that was near Hazebrouck. At 2.30 p.m. the battalion moved to the Brigade camp near Montauban and by 6.30 p.m. they had all settled in to the huts. (Map ref. Lens 11 and Amiens 17, 1.100,000).

On the 16th the battalion spent the morning cleaning up and being inspected before moving to the Brigade camp at Fricourt under Battalion O.O. No.20. By 4.15 p.m. the battalion was settled into its new accommodation although the stay would not be a long one. Three 2/Lts, May, Phelps and Smith attended interviews with a representative of the Royal Flying Corps with a view to joining as observers.

The following day would be one of rest with the men also cleaning up their kit and weapons. 2/Lt Suffolk and Capt. Scott where granted leave for England whilst 2/Lt Clayton arrived from Calais. The Adjutant would have a hectic day and at 10 a.m. he reported to Albert Station to arrange entrainment of the battalion to a new area near Hazebrouck. It was no mean feat to move a battalion upwards of 1000 men plus transport by train in 1917. At 3 p.m. 'B' Companies day of rest ended when they were detailed as the loading party and moved off to Albert.

On 18th (under Brigade O.O. 71 and entraining instructions. Battalion O.O. No.21) at 11 a.m. the transport moved off to entrain at Albert, followed at noon by H.Q., 'A', 'C' and 'D' Companies moved off to entrain at Albert. At 4.07 p.m. the train left Albert and made its slow progress to Caestre situated just north of Hazebrouck. At Abbeville 6 officers and 50 other ranks were left behind when the train without any notice moved off. The remainder of the battalion arrived at Caestre on the 19th at 5.30 a.m. and then marched to new billets near Godeswaersvelde (God Wears Velvet) some 5 Ks away. The area was in the vicinity of the Mont des Cats and the Abbey housed a British Hospital. It is doubtful that the men had the opportunity to test the excellent Trappist beer brewed there though. By 8 a.m. the Battalion less its stragglers and 'B' Company had settled in to their new surroundings which was part camp and part farm buildings. Meanwhile at 4.a.m. 'B' Company, the loading party entrained at Albert for their thirteen-hour journey eventually arriving in Caestre at 5. p.m. and were settled in camp an hour later. They were accompanied by the 6 officers and 50 other ranks stragglers who had missed the train.

Sunday 20th would be a day of rest, inspections and Church services. The weather was also fine although being Flanders this could change rapidly. The following day 'B' company was on the move again as at 3 a.m. orders were received for one company to proceed as an advanced party to a new billeting area near Westoutre. The billeting party were ordered to report to Brigade H.Q., at 9 a.m. on bicycles. (33rd Brigade No4/01/35) and at 8 .10 a.m., 'B' Company proceeded as advanced party to arrange a camp at M.21.a.5.9. (Map Ref. 28 France 1/40,000). At least 'B' Company would have a pleasant cycle ride though the lanes of Flanders prior to starting work on the camp.

The 22nd should have been a day of training but the Flanders weather had other ideas and a day of constant rain scuppered the Brigades plans, although at 11.15 a.m. the G.O.C. (General Officer Commanding) Second Army, General Sir Hubert Plumer inspected the battalion in their billets. Other than that the men had a relaxed day by World War 1 standards. The following day it was back to normal with a route march of three and a half hours through the Flemish countryside which whilst mainly flat did contain locally the Hills of Monts des Cats, Mont Rouge, Noir and Kemmel. They would see the ridge of Messines and those surrounding Ypres, but all were in enemy hands. Within a couple of weeks though the Messines Ridge would be under British control. There would be crops growing in the battalions' area, particularly hops for the brewing of strong Trappist ales. Also close by was the aerodrome at Abeele which often received the attentions of enemy aircraft and shells. Despite the nearby sounds of war the men would have had a pleasant march through the Flanders countryside. The afternoon was again taken up with drill, which included rapid loading, gas helmet and visual training.

During the forthcoming battle of Messines, 33rd Brigade would come under IX Corps and Lt-Gen Sir Alexander Hamilton-Gordon and would be the reserve assault division for phase two of the battle. They would be working with 16th (Irish) Division, 19th (Western) Division and 36th (Ulster) Division. At 9 a.m. on the 24th, Capt Harding proceeded to the IX Corps front in 16th divisions area, which was around Wytschaete (Whitesheet) to reconnoitre. Two of the mines would be detonated on this Divisional front at Petit Bois and Maedelstede Farm. Meanwhile the battalion moved to a new area some 500 yards south of Westoutre. The march took approximately two hours and by noon the men had settled in to their new surroundings with H.Q., and the transport section billeted in huts. The others were not so fortunate with 'A', 'C', 'D' and part of 'B' companies in tents. The reminder of 'B' Company and the Quartermasters Stores were located in farms. The Battalion was now in their final pre-battle position and would spend the two weeks prior to June 7th, in preparation for their part in the assault.

The 25th would see Major Piper continue the reconnoitring of the IX Corps front with a visit to 36th Division (The War Diary gives 30th Div but this is incorrect) who would take Wytschaete itself and three mines would be blown in this vicinity at Peckham House, Spanbroekmolen and Kruisstraat. Over the next couple of days the men would be given the opportunity to bathe and change their clothing at 19th Division and 33rd Brigade baths. The training continued with particular attention being paid to passing messages and dissemination of information, whilst the specialists would continue with their training. The C.O. and Major Piper continued with the reconnoitring by visiting the 19th Divisional front which extended from the north of Wytschaete to St Eloi. One mine would be blown in this area at Hollandschesschuur. Depending on how the battle went, the Battalion could be sent to any of the three Divisional fronts.

Sunday 27th may was given over to Divine Service Parades, whilst 2/Lt Briggs proceeded on leave. The following four days were a hive of activity as the stores and ammunition needed for the offensive were stockpiled close to the front line. The Battalion would supply working parties for 16th (Irish) Division and also attempt to fit in last minute training. Working parties of one officer and 30 other ranks worked a shift system, which saw them working four hours at a time in the area of Kemmel to unload the light railway trucks which arrived constantly. One party of men worked at Parrett Farm, which was only some 1000 yards from the front line whilst another party was located at point N 21.a.5.4. (Map Ref; 28. S.W. France). The C.O. also inspected the battalion by Company as time permitted. When the men returned to camp they were allowed time to rest before more training was undertaken.

The first two days of June would see the battalion undertake more working party duties, which again entailed off-loading light railway trucks at Parrett Farm and near Kemmel. The Germans knew that an offensive was in the offing and shelled constantly and not being in the front line did not mean a less dangerous time. So it was for 'A' Company on 1st June when one man was killed and one wounded whilst working near Parrett Farm.

70886, Private Tom Larder a native of Strubby Lincs and formerly 26936 South Staffordshire Regiment is the only 9th Battalion man buried at Kemmel Chateau Military Cemetery, grave E 53.

The war diary also noted that all box respirators were fitted with a new extension attachment. Gas warfare evolved throughout the war and respirators were constantly upgraded to neutralize the effects on the men. By 1917 gas shells were the preferred way of delivery as they could target specific areas. A number of units were caught out during the battle of Messines and the aim of slowing down the attack was achieved.

After a day of working parties the battalion-received orders at 10 pm on the 2nd stating that they would be relieved by 34th Brigade the following day. By 8 a.m. on 3rd June the relief was complete and serious training for the forthcoming battle could commence. Once again Sunday 3rd had an entry which showed the importance of religion in the British Army ' 9 a.m. – Sunday – Parade Service for Non-Conformist Service'. Nottinghamshire and Derbyshire being strongholds of Non-Conformism would see a large number of men attending. The 4th, 5th and 6th would be taken up with more last minute training. Whilst the men would know that they would soon be fighting, they would not have any idea as to the scale of the mines that would be blown on 7th June. Specialists honed their skills and the other men practiced their bayonet fighting. Rapid wiring was also practised, as the men would have little time to consolidate a newly taken trench before a German counter attack. The Brigade attack was practised so that every man knew his role. Officers and NCOs would pore over a mock up of the battlefield showing every trench, strongpoint and point of reference. They would also need to have the exact timings of the creeping barrage. Too close as on 26th September 1916 and casualties would occur, to far back and the enemy infantry would be waiting. It has to be said that General Plumer had left nothing to chance and the Battle of Messines was probably the best planned and executed of the whole war. For two years Sappers had been tunnelling under the Messines ridge and when the mines exploded many German soldiers were literally vaporised and others buried in the subsequent fall out of earth. An artillery barrage of some 2,230 guns and howitzers then opened up in a crescendo of noise. At the same moment some 700 Machine Guns and 400 Mortars opened in support. As morning turned to afternoon on the 7th, Gen Plumer and his staff had the satisfaction of knowing that all had gone to plan and by WW1 standards with fairly light casualties.

The second part of the battle would see the 33rd Brigade, including the 9th battalion engaged. The battle to capture the Oostaverne line and Sehen-stellung was to begin at 3.10 p.m. Unfortunately the Battalion was late arriving and the Australians who were ready and in position several hours before the battle suffered many casualties. It was not through the fault of the Battalion but movement orders had arrived late. They had marched during the night from Kemmel and were then rushed forward in a forced march on a hot June day. This was not the best preparation for a forthcoming assault and it was decided to use troops from 19th Division who were considerably closer to the front line. The Australians attacked and duly took their objectives but at considerable cost. The 33rd Brigade, which should have attacked north of the Australians, had still not arrived. Eventually the brigade with twelve tanks took over part of the Australian line once they had arrived. By 11th June the battle was effectively over as the Germans withdrew to a more tenable line. Despite gaining all three of its objectives, Messines was yet another example of the British not pressing home its advantage. It did though pave the way for the Battles of Ypres, universally known as Passchendaele. Delays, the weather and a change in German tactics would see the victory of Messines followed by the horrors of Ypres.

Finally on 6th June at 10 a.m. the C.O. held a conference with all Company Commanders and outlined the orders for the forthcoming operations. The remainder of the day was taken up in issuing trench equipment to the men. General preparations for the active operations also took place. The men would also prepare themselves for the following day and wonder if they would survive. At 11.30 p.m. the Battalion moved to the G.H.Q. III line at N.1.46.77, Map 28 S.W. France, arriving at 1.30 a.m.

The traffic on the road was light and although the enemy had used gas shells in the area, the gas was not strong enough to cause any problems. On arrival Rifle grenades, bombs and tools were drawn and immediately issued to the Companies. All that remained was the waiting for the battle to commence. The battalion would not be going over the top at zero hour, which was at 3.10 a.m. but would be in reserve to exploit any advances made by 16th (Irish) Division to which they were attached for this battle.

It is important to record the Battalion's efforts in the Battle of Messines as fully as possible; therefore both Col Scothern's notes and the C.O.s narrative of events until 11th June 1917 are below.

Colonel Scothern's notes 6th to 11th June 1917.

'For the forthcoming attack on the Messines ridge, the 33rd Brigade was attached to the 16th (Irish) Division, and on June 6th took up a position in and near what was known as the G.H.Q. 3rd line. Its role was that of 'exploiting a success' and as far as the Sherwood Foresters were concerned this meant waiting for orders. When all the objectives were taken (five in all) the battalion was to push forward and capture Oostaverne Village and the Mahieu Farm line.

Dawn on June 7th was a particularly fine one, and advantage was taken of the absolute quiet prevailing to have an early breakfast. Suddenly there were terrific explosions as the mines were exploded, and simultaneously a heavy barrage opened from our guns. The secret of the mines was well kept, as the explosions came as a surprise to the whole battalion.

The attack was a complete success, but for some reason or other no orders reached the 33rd Brigade, and at midday the men settled down to dinner. At 1.30 p.m. orders were received to follow the retreating army (German) at all costs, and the battalion set, companies moving in file. By this time the day was very hot, and as movement was necessarily very fast, the men, carrying heavy loads as they were, became exhausted fairly quickly, but stuck it splendidly, and reached the Messines ridge in good time, passing guns going up,

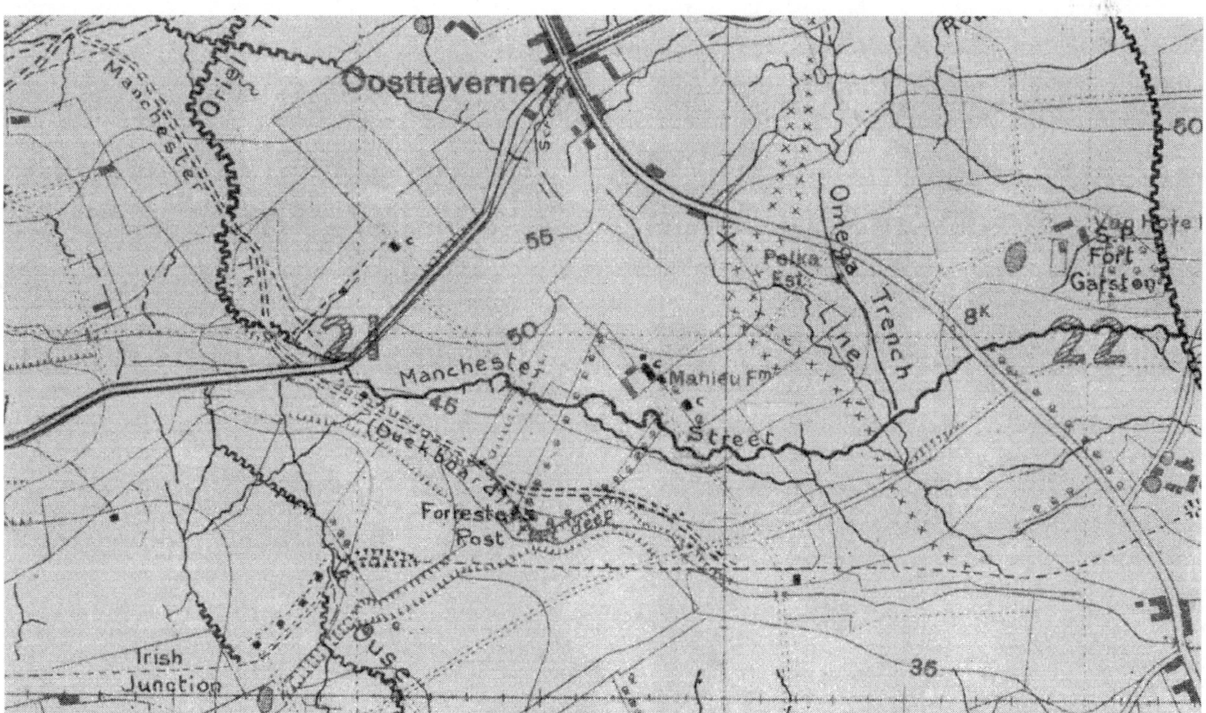

Oosttaverne and Mahieu Farm

prisoners coming down, and all the confused medley of a modern battlefield en route.

The Ridge was reached without incident, but at this juncture a low-flying aeroplane came over, and as a result of this, shortly afterwards the Germans opened a fierce barrage with their heavy guns. This shelling increased and the battalion was forced to break up into artillery formation. A rather peculiar incident occurred here. One company in file, with Company Headquarters leading, closely followed by a platoon, were advancing, when one shell killed or wounded all the Company Headquarters leading, and six men leading the leading platoon, but left the Coy. Commander and the platoon Commander unhurt.

It had been arranged that when the 33rd Brigade advanced, movement should be carried out under a barrage (creeping barrage for protection) By this time it was evident that the barrage had fallen but gone on. Accordingly there was nothing to do but push on, and this was done 'B' and 'C' Coys. Leading. The Mahieu Farm line was reached without opposition, though 6th Lincolns had some trouble. The men immediately began to dig in, and patrols were pushed forward. These patrols found no enemy in the vicinity, and the line was advanced slightly, and consolidation of the positions began, with 'B' and 'D' Coys in front, and 'A' and 'C' Coys in support.

The Borders and Lincolns had come up on the right and left respectively and the work of consolidation was carried on without interference. The casualties up to this point had been fairly heavy, the forward companies suffering the most.

The evening of the 7th passed without incident accept that our own heavy guns were firing short, and one shell completely demolished a hastily constructed strong-point that had been put up.

Patrols were out during the night and reported the enemy massing in some dead ground about 250 yards away. The battalion commander was informed, and he got in touch with the artillery straight away, a particularly accurate shrapnel barrage was put down at 3 p.m. The enemy ran in all directions, but it is extremely doubtful whether any escaped.

At 6 p.m. the enemy put down a heavy barrage on the whole front. This luckily just missed the two front companies, falling just behind. Under cover of this the German's counter-attacked, but not on the actual front of the battalion, speaking volumes for the effectiveness of the artillery work earlier in the afternoon.

The counter-attack was a failure all along the front, and the rest of the night was quiet, being spent on our side in patrolling and consolidating. The Battalion was to be relieved on the night of the 11th by the Northumberland Fusiliers, and preparations were well advanced, when the enemy again dropped a heavy barrage at 6 p.m. Nothing developed from this however, and when calm had been restored the relief was proceeded with, and the battalion went back into reserve in the old front line.

The material captured by the battalion included 29 Field Guns, one 4.2 Howitzer, 3 Trench Mortars, several Machine Guns and such odd trophies as drums, bugles and bicycles.

The battalion remained in reserve for some days, salvaging and clearing up the ground in the vicinity, finally moving on June 18th, to a camp near Danoutre (Dranoutre), and next day commenced a lengthy march lasting several days to the training area at Est Mont and Quest Mont.'

The CO produced a narrative of events from 11.30 p.m. on June 6th to 6 a.m. on June 11th 1917.

'June 6th.

11.30 p.m. battalion marched to G.H.Q. III Line arriving at 1.30 a.m. June 7th. No obstruction from traffic on road; the area passed through had been shelled with gas shells but the gas was not strong enough to hurt. Rifle grenades, bombs and tools were drawn and issued to Coys. At once.

June 7th.

3.10 a.m. Zero – Mines exploded and intense barrage fire opened. Breakfasts 5.45 a.m. – rations for the day were issued and men instructed to rest.

9.30 a.m. – B.M.S. 266/32 re barrage was received.

9.45 a.m. – reports from Heavy Artillery that BLUE LINE was taken. Later reports re taking BLACK and MAUVE Lines were received.

12 noon – Orders (B.M.) to move to VIERSTRAAT SWITCH received and Battalion moved off at 12.30 p.m.

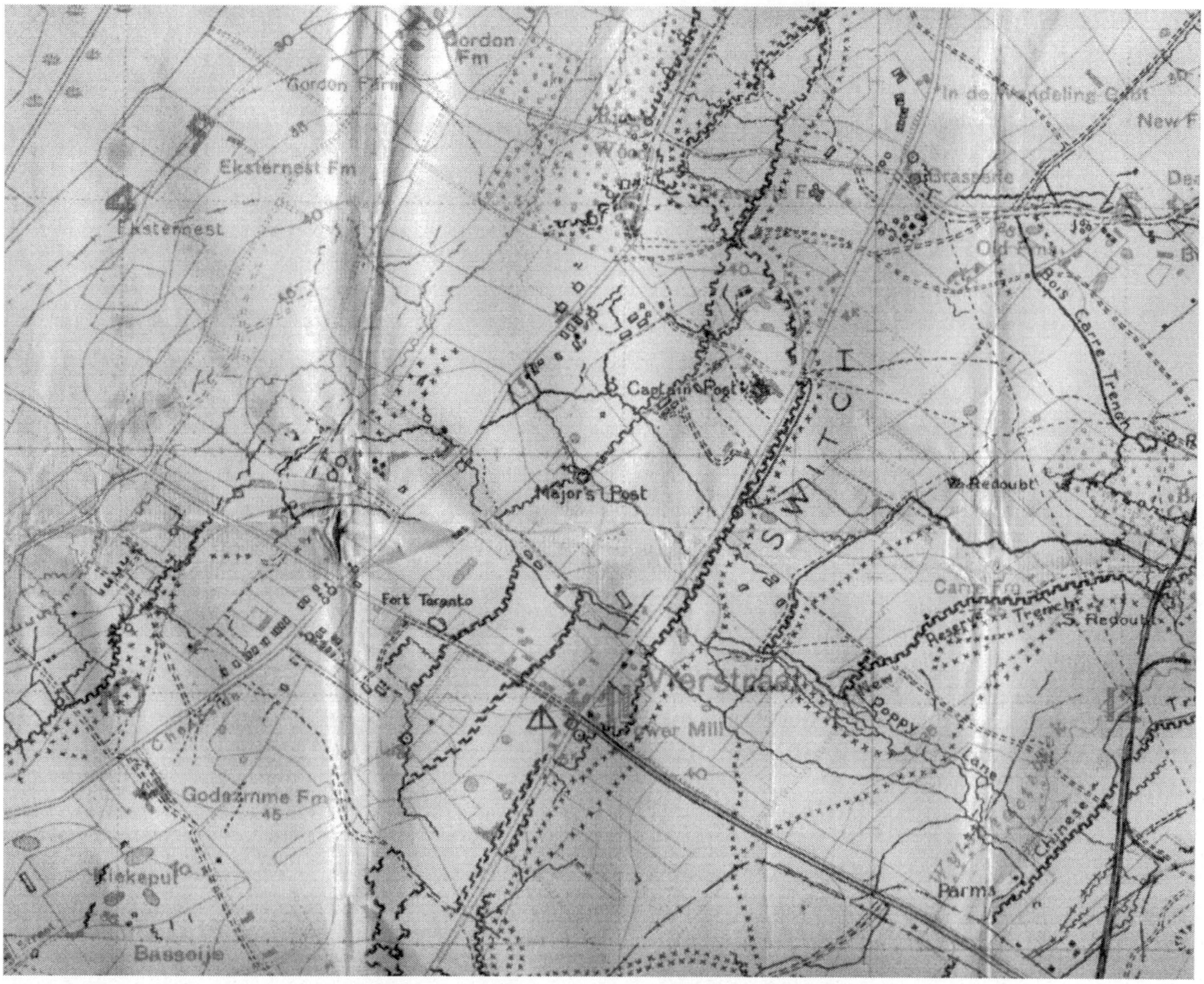

Map of Battalion Advance at Messines – moving to the Vierstraat Switch

12.50 p.m. – Received by cyclist orderly A.C.D.1 containing orders to move to CHINA WALL (Trench system) – C.O. to report at Bde, H.Q. at S.p. 13. The weather was very hot, and this combined with the heavy loads carried by the men, made marching a very slow process. The head of the Battalion reached CHINA WALL at about 2.10 p.m. There was much delay crossing YORK ROAD to CHINA WALL owing to old wire entanglements and trenches. With reference to the above it may be useful to point out that A.C.S. 1 contained a reference to a previous message B.M.S. which had not been received – this latter message was delivered to the C.O. by 2/Lt Smith of the 6th Lincoln Regt. at about 2.30 p.m.

Instructions were issued verbally to O.C's Coys. In accordance with those detailed to C.O. by the Brigadier General Commanding (Brig A.C. Daly). These were: – That the Battalion was to move with all speed to its proper position of deployment, the line O.20.d.8.9 – O.20.d.8.2, and take over its proper position in the attack from 7th South Stafford's Regt. should there be time to do so before Zero hour, failing this to move in support of that Battalion, and having got in touch with its O.C. to move to a selected position in reserve. It is strongly insisted in these instructions that speed was essential.

The Coys. were ordered to follow Battn. H.Q. up on to the Wytschaete Ridge with the intention of forming artillery formation; two lines of Coys. each in four lines of sections under cover of the ridge before advancing down the forward slope.

The advance started at 2.10 p.m. narrow tracks only being available. Owing to the heat the men were considerably distressed, a few men fainting. When the head of the Battn. Was about half way up the ridge a considerable barrage fire of 5.9' was opened and casualties occurred. Many other small parties were moving up at the same time and kept getting mixed up with the Battalion. A halt was called near SOUTHERN BRICKSTACK to enable the Battalion, which was considerably straggled out, to close up. Owing to the broken nature of the ground and the necessity for shoving on, it was decided not to attempt an advance in artillery formation but to continue the advance; the companies being in file, the signal was passed to advance. OBVIOUS TRENCH was crossed about O.19.c.77 and the advance continued to road O.20.25.10. By this time the Companies had become scattered owing to the presence of other troops crossing through them and also fairly persistent shellfire. Battn. H.Q. and one Platoon then moved direct to O.21, central arriving there about 4.15 p.m. (see map B below) This spot was selected, as it was thought that being open ground and a good view it would be easier to pick up and reform the Battalion. This proved a difficult matter owing to the congestion of troops on the ground.

By 7 p.m. the Battalion with the exception of stragglers was collected and formed – 2 Coys. on the MAHIEU LINE and 2 Coys. in reserve about O.21.central. Orders to dig in were issued.

Communication was at first very difficult as the Headquarters pigeon man was blown up with his pigeons by a shell and Coy. Pigeons could not be found. A message timed 4.30 p.m. No. V.R.L. 10 informing Brigade of the state of affairs was given to 2/Lieut. Colbeck R.F.A. who undertook to dispatch it through Corps by the artillery line. Subsequently this message was returned, he having been unable to send it. At 6 p.m. the adjutant saw and discussed matters with Lieut. Col. SECKHAM. The position was that the ODOUR ODONTO TRENCH throughout its length on the Battalion front was held by Australians, Gloucester's and odd parties of Dublin Fusiliers, North Stafford's, etc there were also tanks with Lewis Guns right up to the trench.

With the exception of shelling the night was quiet. About 10 p.m. our Heavies put a number of shells into squares 21, 22, killing 2/Lieut. GILLAT, R.E. and others working in Forester Post. Transport Officer arrived with rations, which were sent at once to Companies (12.20 a.m. 8th June).

JUNE 8th

6.30 a.m. A British plane brought down north of OOSTTAVERNE, and in reference to this it should be pointed out that a message dispatched from brigade re lightening flares in front line at 6 a.m. for this plane was received by Battn. H.Q. at 8.20 a.m. At 4.10 a.m. BM. 14 was received and instructions issued for a reconnaissance of the line. The relief of the line allotted to the Battalion was completed shortly after 4 p.m. A line was run out to the Australians early in the morning, as it was found that they had no means of communication except by runner, which was rendered difficult by sniping – a number of the enemy were hiding in shell holes in front of this line, a few of these were killed and a few brought in as prisoners.

10.55 a.m. enemy was reported attacking in front of ODOUR TRENCH; barrage was asked for and put down very quickly. The enemy on and off all day barraged the area O.21.

8.50 p.m. A heavy barrage started by British Artillery on the left of the battalions' front. The enemy opened a barrage all along their front, what appeared to be an enemy counter-attack in the direction of O.28 central was observed, 200 or 300 men were seen to come over the ridge and were checked in our barrage. Later, charged by a small party of our troops and driven back. It was getting very dark and difficult to see. No warning had been given as to the cause of the barrage, the Battalion was directed to stand to and the reserve Company ordered to be ready to move up should it be necessary to counter-attack.

9.30 p.m. 2/Lieut MAY wounded. About 11.30 p.m. the situation quietened down. Constant communication was maintained by wire with 'B' and 'D' Coys. who reported all correct.

JUNE 9th

12.10 a.m. Rations arrived and sent up.

Intermittent and pretty heavy shelling of O. 21 central with 5.9's which continued throughout the night. Capt. GREGORY reported killed while in Forester Post. 2/Lt COOK killed in ODOUR TRENCH about the same time.

2.30 p.m. A.C.D. 14 arrived – arrangements made accordingly.

8.20 p.m. A.C.D. 14 cancelled.

9.00 p.m. Arrangements made for 'D' Coy. on left ODOUR TRENCH to co-operate with 7th King's Own in advancing their line at 11. p.m. – these arrangements postponed. The night was quiet, rations were sent up to frontline.

JUNE 10th.

11 a.m. arranged relief with 7th King's Own.

2.30 p.m. Conference of C.O's – V.R.T. V.R.L. V.R.A. re relief arrangements.

MAHIEU – OOSTTAVERNE shelled at intervals by our artillery during the day also the front line.

10.20 p.m. Both sides opened heavy barrage – Germans sending up many double star red lights and green lights. The enemy barrage remained intense till 11.40 p.m. both the artillery and Brigade wires were cut. Battalion line to front Coys. remained intact. The barrage died down about 12.15 a.m. on June 11th.

JUNE 11th.

Relief of Battalion completed by 8th Northumberland Fusiliers by 3.40 a.m. The relief of the line handed over to 56th Brigade was carried out early on the evening of the 10th.

Amended casualty list and recommendations for immediate reward will be forwarded.

Lieut.Colonel
Commanding 9th Sherwood Foresters.
11th June 1917.

So ended The Battle of Messines for the battalion. It had started with confusion and lost orders but eventually despite communication problems the Battalion did its job. It was three miles from the front line at Zero hour and released an hour late, adding

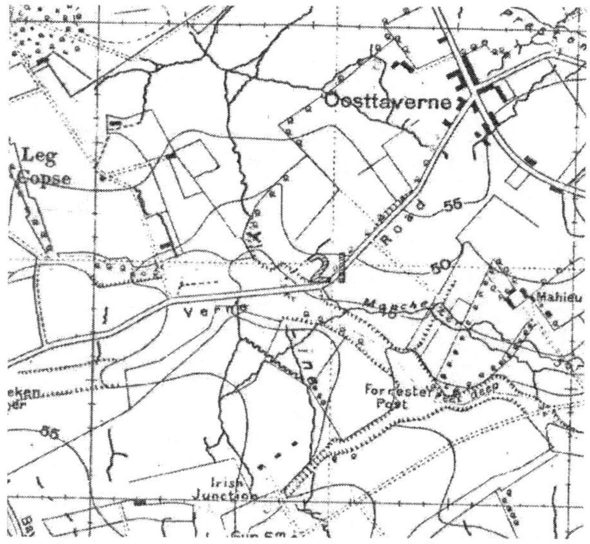

B. -O.21 – Location of battalion once advance was completed

to this the German Artillery fire and difficult ground saw the delay grow. The 9th did not arrive until some 30 minutes after the afternoon zero hour but General Plumer had given his commanders much more autonomy in battle and 57th Brigade stepped in to cover 33rd Brigade. This left the 33rd Brigade with a 1200-yard front to take instead of 1,800 yards. The Brigade attacked Joye Farm and Van Hove Farm assisted by four tanks and after a brief enemy resistance occupied both.

The battalion proceeded to shelter trenches at N.23.c (28 France) and the day was spent cleaning up, re-organising and improving the shelters, which they occupied.

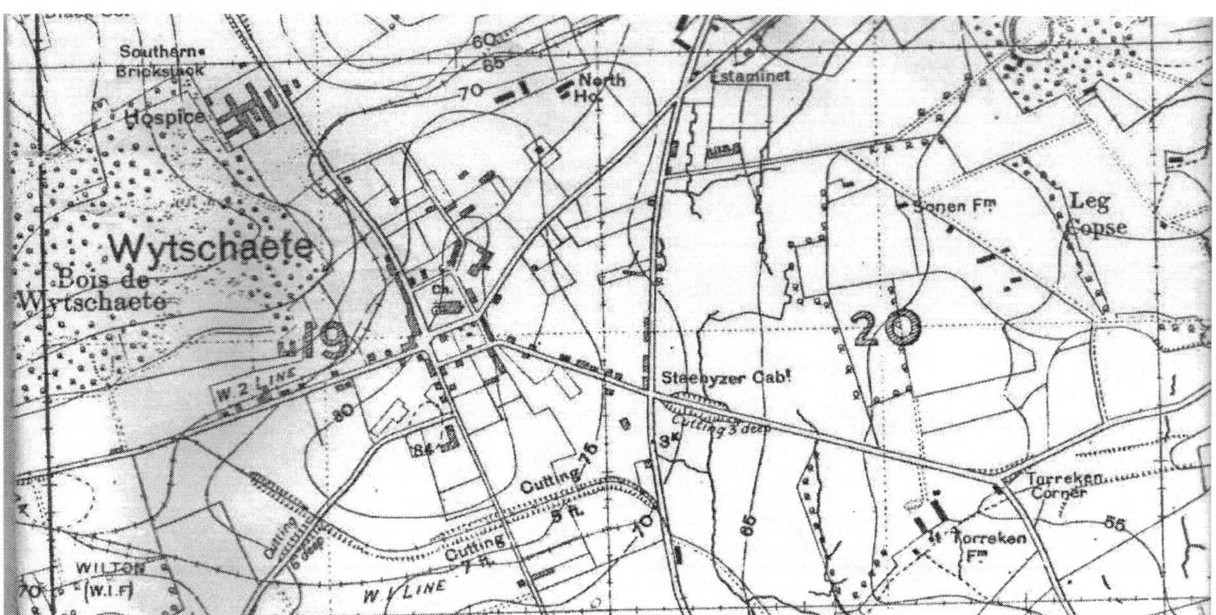

A- The Battalion advance in the afternoon of 7th June 1917. Southern Brickstack area near Torreken Corner.

They had suffered lightly by WW1 standards but twenty-five families would soon receive news that their man would not return home. Over a hundred men were wounded during the Wytschaete Operations and some would never return to the Battalion.

9th Battalion men killed during Messines

07/06/1917:

71022, Private William Barker, enlisted Derby and Commemorated on The Menin Gate panel 39-41. William's family sought the help of the Red Cross in finding their man. The British Red Cross and Order of St. John, Enquiry List No 14. 1917 for men wounded & missing which contained enquiries up to July 20th 1917 was printed August 1st 1917. Four 9th Battalion men were mentioned of which William was one.

4913 Private Isaac Curtis 'C' Coy. Aged 34 years and a native of Nottingham left a wife Frances and he is also commemorated on the Menin Gate at Ypres.

14235 Private Henry (Harry) Green aged 20 years of age and the son of Charles William and Annie. He was born in Sheffield and the family lived at Alfreton when he enlisted. He is buried in Wytschaete Military Cemetery, grave I. C. 9.

The inscription reads –' Some day sometime, Our eyes shall see, The face we keep in memory. Harry had enlisted early in the war between 28 August and 4 September serving with the Battalion throughout.

76267, Private Robert McNeil aged 33 years had previously served as 404175 in the Highland field Company R.E. He had enlisted at Dundee although his home was given as Ilford Essex. Robert was a married man living in Canada in 1914 but on the outbreak of war he returned to England to join the Royal Engineers. His wife was left at home in Chilliwack, British Columbia, Canada. He has no known grave and is commemorated on the Menin Gate panel 39-41.

71011, Private Herbert Pratt aged 27 years was the son of Alfred and Mary Ann of Hinckley Leics.

14235 Private Harry Green and his grave at Wytschaete Cemetery

He was in 'C' Company at the time of his death. He is also commemorated on the Menin Gate.

23065, Private William Whyler a native of Nottingham is also commemorated on the Menin Gate.

08/06/1917 –

On 8th June 1917 The Battalion would have one fatal casualty

20419 Corporal Arthur Marshall was a native of Clowne Derbyshire and has no known grave. He is commemorated on The Menin Gate, Ypres.

9th June was the Battalions costliest day of the battle with two officers and nine other ranks dying. All the men who died are commemorated on the Ypres (Menin Gate) Memorial and have no known grave.

Second Lieutenant Cyril Ramsay Cook had been with the Battalion since 25th April 1917 and he was still termed as 4th Bn attached to 9th Bn. He was 19 years of age and Messines would be his first and last Battle.

It is worthwhile putting the full entry in De Ruvigny's Roll of Honour in the history as the response to his death by his Sergeant are most interesting.

'Cook, Cyril Ramsay, 2nd Lieut, 9th (Service) Battn. The Sherwood Foresters (Nottinghamshire and Derbyshire Regiment), eldest son of Frank Cook of Endcliffe Caterham Valley County of Surrey, by his wife Sybil daughter of the late Hugh Francis Ramsay of Hankow, China; born Upper Warlingham County of Surrey, 10 February 1898: educ. Marlborough College; was a member of the Nottingham University O.T.C., and later underwent training at Christ's College Cambridge; obtained a commission in Feb 1917; was sent to Sunderland to the 4th (Territorial) Battn. Sherwood Foresters; served with the Expeditionary Force in France and Flanders, and was killed in action at Messines 9 June 1917. Buried there. His Commanding Officer wrote; ' I am told by his Company Commander that death was instantaneous. He had only been a short time with the battalion, but had made his mark, and was a splendid officer, who had the entire confidence and trust of his men. As his Commanding Officer, I had the very highest opinion of him, and he is a sad loss to us. He was buried close to were he was killed, and his grave marked and the exact locality sent on to the Graves' Registration Office... Your son struck me as being the exact type of what a young officer should be, and his Company Commander was full of his praises to me in the recent operations, and a brother officer;' I should like to tell you that in spite of the short time your son was with us, he was extremely popular, and when it came to the actual work in action, I can assure you, his coolness and the thoroughness of his work was, in one of so little experience, utterly phenomenal. He only came to my company on the day he went up the line, through one of my officers being suddenly sent for to join the Flying Corps, but he lost no time in getting a thorough grip of his N.C.O.'s and men. There was one very extraordinary incident in connection with his death. He was in the front line, talking to his to his platoon sergeant; as far as I can remember, at about 1 a.m., when he was hit by a piece of shell and instantaneously killed. His sergeant, who had already won the Military Medal for gallantry early in the war, pounced on him immediately, took his revolver off him, and shouting something about 'I'll avenge you, sir, I'll kill some..' was away over the parapet before anyone could stop him. Of course, nobody expected to see him again, but he returned in about an hour's time with an empty revolver and obviously quite mad.' His Chaplain wrote ' The moment he joined he leapt straight into our hearts. We all knew we had a good boy, and he immediately took his place in all fun and gaiety. He was so full of life and enjoyment, and with it all so thoroughly good and clean and wholesome.... He was extraordinarily popular, and we shall greatly miss his cheerfulness and good looks'.

Such praise given for a young man who had been with the battalion but a few hours in battle.

57110 Private Frederick Elliott was a native of Ironville in Derbyshire.

Another 19 year old to die was 4574 Private Arthur Fox, a native of Nottingham. His mother Ann would have no grave to visit.

5888 Company Sergeant Major Frood was a Londoner. He was a 1st Battalion man serving with 'A' Company when they crossed to France on 4 November 1914 and was wounded on 15 January 1915. On recovery he was in the 3rd Reserve Battalion before being posted to the 9th Battalion on 25 October 1915. He had served in the 2nd Battalion in 1899 with the rank of Boy Soldier.

Captain Gregory MC

Captain Reuben Henry Gregory MC proceeded to France with 'B' Company, 10th Battalion in July 1915. Whilst in the trenches south of Ypres on the night of 27/28th August 1915 he was wounded in the foot.

14721 Private John Thomas Harris was a native of Eckington, Yorkshire, aged 43 years.

76224 Private John McCraith was a native of Scotland and had formerly served as 404441. Highland Field Company, Royal Engineers.

56012 Private Henry T Parr was another native of Nottingham.

70938, Private Charles Price was 34 years of age. He was a native of Norbury, Salop and formerly 25708, North Staffordshire Regiment. His widow Margaret named her house 'Sherwood' in his honour.

76329, Private James S. Westwater was a native of Scotland and formerly 9912, Highland Royal Engineers.

10/06/1917 –
Four men would be killed on this day.

70966, Lance Corporal A Dunkley was formerly 24059 Leicestershire Regiment and a native of Leicester. He is buried at Wytschaete Military Cemetery, grave I. D. 5.

26931, Private Arthur Sibbring aged 32 years was born in Nottingham but living with his family in Stockport Cheshire before the war. He is buried at Irish House Cemetery, grave A. 14.

28648, Private Samuel Henry Smith aged 30 years was a native of Borrowash Derbyshire and living in Manchester before the war. His family desperate for news approached the British Red Cross when he was posted as missing. They hoped he might be a prisoner of war. Samuel like many of his comrades is commemorated on the Ypres (Menin Gate) Memorial.

70991, Private Albert Hardy Sutton was a Leicester man and formerly 26170, Leicestershire Regiment. His name also appears on the Menin Gate.The final four men to died would succumb to their wounds at Bailleul and all are buried at Bailleul Communal Cemetery Extension (Nord)

10/06/1917 –

31598, Private Alphonso Matthews was 21 years of age and a native of Nottingham. Also known as Alfred he is buried in grave III. C. 25.

11/06/1917

71002, Private Walter Bayliss aged 30 years was a native of Leicester and formerly 27070, Leicestershire Regiment. He left a wife Clara and is buried in grave III. C. 47.

70927, Private Harry Holmes was formerly 2571, North Staffordshire Regt and is buried in grave III.C.75.

76261, Private Francis B McFarlane was 26 years of age and a native of Scotland

He was formerly 404070, Highland Field Coy. R.E. He was the fourth ex Highland Field Coy. man to die during Messines and he is buried in grave III. C. 56.

The 12th June saw the Battalion near Kemmel were the reserve personnel, 'A' and 'B' echelons rejoined the battalion. The men were given time to rest and the battalion reorganised in readiness for its next task. The enemy shelled the area intermittently from 2 p.m. until 5 p.m. but no casualties occurred.

The following four days would be taken up with salvage work, which was notoriously dangerous. Shells, Bombs and all manner of munitions had to be recovered and checked for future use. Many men had been wounded or killed doing this work in the past and sadly the battalion would also suffer. The battalion worked an area in square N. 23. b. just below Vandamme Farm during the 13th and 14th. Each Company provided 75 other ranks for the task. At 11 a.m. on the 13th the Brigadier General visited battalion H.Q. No doubt he arrived to congratulate the battalion on its efforts during the Messines attack and subsequent 'victory'. At 2.30 p.m. Major Piper

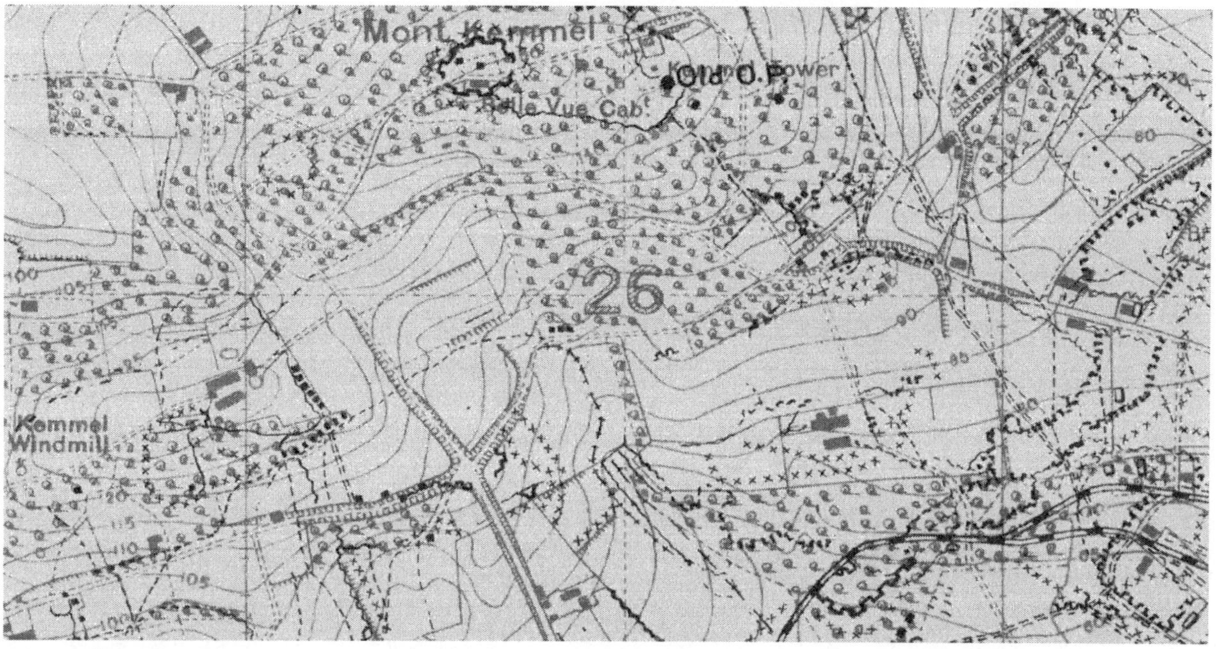

Map ref N. 26 – The camp was probably the unnamed buildings just north of Cupola Dugouts.

left to reconnoitres the site of a proposed new camp some 500 yards S.E. of Kemmel (N. 26 to 90) in readiness for the battalions next move. At 7 a.m. on the 14th the Battalion moved to the new camp

The 15th saw all Companies working from 7am to noon and 3 to 5 p.m. on salvaging but they had moved to sub square 'd' in N.23. the Banff Dugouts area. During the day the men were given the opportunity of visiting the baths at Dranoutre where they received a hot bath and a clean change of underclothes.

Disaster would strike the Battalion on 16th whilst the men continued with the salvage work. A Trench Mortar Bomb, which had been salvaged suddenly exploded, and three men from 'B' company were killed instantly.

All three men lie next to each other in Irish House Cemetery, which was begun in June 1917 by the 16th (Irish) Division and took its name from a small farmhouse nearby. This is a true Battlefield cemetery with just 117 graves.

10536, Private Ernest Bond was a native of Newark; he is buried in grave A.3.

12413, Sergeant Frank Clayton was born in Bradford Yorkshire but living in Lancashire.

51664, Private Harry Strickson aged 33 years was a native of Spalding Lincs.

Sgt Clayton and Private Strickson are buried in grave A.4.

Colonel Scothern, noted:

'The battalion remained in reserve for some days, salvaging and clearing up the ground in the vicinity, finally moving on June 18th, to a camp near Danoutre (Dranoutre), and next day commenced a lengthy march lasting several days to the training area at Est Mont and quest Mont.'

The 17th was a Sunday and the men had the opportunity to rest and attend church. On the 18th the battalion began its long march to the training area and orders were received to move at short notice (under Brigade wire B.C. 100 O.O. No 26 Bde. No 75.). At 4.30 p.m. they moved off to the new camp near Dranoutre (Map Ref M. 23.c.0.3. Sheet 27 France) and by 6.30 p.m. the men were settled into their new surroundings after a march of only some 4 kms. The morning of the 19th was taken up with rest and cleaning up in preparation for the next move and at 5. 25 p.m. that move was made. Another short march of some 5 kms to a camp at Schaexkem, near St. Jans Cappel, arriving at 7 p.m. (O.O. No 27. Bde. No 76) (North- West of Bailleul).

The move on the 20th commenced at 9 a.m. and the men marched approx 14 kms to billets at Rouge Croix on the outskirts of Hazebrouck (Hazebrouck map. Sheet 5A) (O.O. No 28. Bde. No. 77). Next day was one of rest, cleaning up, inspections and specialist training. With so much going on it is doubtful much rest was had, although 'rest' was a much-abused word in the Army. Lt. Col W. B. Thornton, D.S.O. proceeded on leave to England and Major Piper assumed command of the Battalion.

At 7.20 a.m. on 22nd the battalion continued its move with a march of some 6 kms to St. Sylvestre –

Cappel on the Cassel road. This short hop was completed by 9 a.m. and the men settled into their latest billets (O.O. No. 29.) An early start the following day saw the men off at 5.30 a.m. and marching to Renescure, just south of St Omer, arriving at 10 a.m. after a march of some 15 kms. The men could then relax in preparation for their final days march from Renescure to Ouest Mont and Est Mont. The 24th saw the battalion leaving for Ouest Mont and Est Mont training Area at 5.30 a.m. and by noon the men were settled in their new billets which would be their home until 10th July. On arrival two officers and six other ranks reinforcements joined the battalion. These would replace the men lost during the Messines operations.

Between 25th June and July 11th intensive training would be the order of the day in preparation for the forthcoming operations north of Ypres. A daily training regime was set up and there is little doubt that the men would know that a major offensive was in the offing. Reinforcements continued to arrive with 44 Other Ranks at 6. 30 pm on 25th and 14 O.R.'s on 26th.

On 28th June Capt W.M. Robinson and 2/Lt W.W. Odell proceeded on leave.

In preparation for forthcoming actions the Divisional Gas NCOs' inspected all of the Box respirators and P.H. Helmets. Only one day of training was lost to rain and that was 30th June although there were plenty of indoor activities to keep the men occupied.

Finally for June the monthly returns were attached.

The 9th (S) Bn. Sherwood Foresters strength table. Details of casualties etc

		Officers	O.Ranks
1. Strength –	On 1st June-	38	997
	On 30th June-	36	951
2. Reinforcements.			
	Total during month	2	145
3. Casualties. –			
	Killed	2	18
	Wounded	2	115

(During the Wytschaete Operations.)

Other casualties during Month.

Killed	4
Wounded	1

So ended another month for the Battalion.

July 1917 would see the British attempt to push the German Army off the ridges that surrounded Ypres. On two occasions the Battalion would find itself caught up in what was officially The Battles of Ypres 1917, 31st July – 10th November but what would forever be called 'Passchendaele'. The Battle of Langemarck 16th to 18th August and the Battle of Broodseinde on 4th October would see many heroics and the ultimate honour for the battalion. Prior to the battles though the Battalion would spend an uncomfortable time in the line in front of the Yser canal. They would lose more men than in the Messines operations but enhance their growing reputation as a tenacious fighting unit.

Prior to the forthcoming operations though the men had to train and there was also the small matter of the Brigade Horse Show to prepare for. Each battalion would keenly contest every event and the men would also be happy to have an afternoon of total relaxation.

The 1st July was a Sunday, the men could rest in preparation for the training ahead and attend divine service. The following day training began in earnest and Lt. Col Thornton returned from his ten days leave. Major A.E. Scothern returned from his Senior Officer's course in Aldershot. 2nd Lts A.H. Pickard and F.T. Tourt arrived from base along with four Other Ranks to reinforce the Battalion. The usual training methods known so well to the battalion were gone over again and again. Specialists practised their various specialties such as bombing, sniping and machine gun fire. From midnight on 4th to 6 am on 5th night operations were practised with the men forming up at night on taped lines in preparation for dawn attacks. Between 11 and noon the men had inspections and physical training before the much-awaited Brigade Horse Show. Captain and Adjutant W. Nason proceeded on leave, so missing the excitement. The Horse Show took place on the afternoon of the 5th and the Battalion did well in several areas with First prizes in best turn out for – Travelling Kitchen, G.S. (General Service) Limber and Pack Horse. Whether the Kitchen was efficient as well as best turned out was not recorded. The 6th/7th and 9th saw more training with Sunday 8th given over to rest and divine services.

Monday the 9th July would see another ex 9th Battalion man die.

12814 Private Herbert Brocklehurst was serving with the 10th battalion on the Arras front. It was seen as a quiet area but not for Herbert and he was killed in action and buried at Sunken Road Cemetery, Fampoux and grave I. B.11.

The 10th saw Company Commanders and one other Officer per Company proceed to XVIII Corps School for a special course of instruction dealing with the forthcoming operations north of Ypres. This course would be of four days duration and amongst other things the Officers would peruse a mock up of the battlefield area they were to fight in. By mid 1917 the planning of offensive operations had become a fine art although the usual 'Fog of war' could scupper the best of plans and usually did. The Germans would employ new defensive tactics during the Ypres Operations, which included the use of strong points such as old farms and concrete bunkers. These 'outposts' could cover each other with machine gun fire but they all had to be taken and slowly British tactics evolved for overcoming them.

The 11th saw the commencement of the move back to the salient and the Battalion was under no illusions as to the task ahead. The Battalion would be located near Poperinghe at a camp located – Map 28 1:40,000 A 30. d. 19. After a morning of training the men made their preparations. The following morning between 10 a.m. and noon the Battalions transport moved off whilst at 2.15 p.m. 2/Lt Briggs and the advance party entrained at Watten station. They would take over the camp in readiness for the Battalions move the following morning. At 6 a.m. on 13th the Battalion moved off to Watten Station and entrained for Poperinghe. This short journey took seven hours but was preferable to the alternative of several days marching. Between 1 p.m. and 3 p.m. the Battalion settled into its new surroundings although the stay would be brief. The 14th would see the men making final preparations for their spell in the front line just north of Ypres and 33rd Brigade would be responsible for holding the whole of XVIII Corps front whilst preparations for the Battle of Pilckem on 31st July were made.

Col. Scothern would call this a 'sticky time' and how right he was:

> *"... on July 13th when a move was made by train to Poperinghe, the Ypres salient being the ultimate destination. So commenced what one would call a "sticky time". On July 15th the 33rd Brigade took over the whole front of the 16th Corps (actually 18th Corps), the 9th Sherwood Foresters taking part of the front line, and having Lancashire Farm as Batt. H.Q. The line was in very poor condition and the weather made matters worse. Generally speaking the days were quiet, but the enemy artillery fire at night was very heavy, and consisted of a high proportion of gas shells.*
>
> *The battalion was relieved by the 6th Lincolns on 17th, and moved back to reserve on the Yser Canal Bank, Very strong working and carrying parties had to be found from here, and reserve was far from being a sinecure, the enemy shelling hampered the work very considerably. On 19th 'A' Company went back from the line to prepare for a raid, and the remaining three companies proceeded to relieve the 6th Borders in the centre sub sector.*
>
> *Artillery activity during the next four days was very great, but several useful patrols in the locality, which 'A' Company were to raid, were carried out, and the enemy wire there thoroughly examined.*
>
> *On the 24th 'A' Company came up to the Canal Bank, and when evening fell moved up to their jumping-off point, Hornby Trench. This process proved very difficult, as gas helmets had to be worn all the way, and the enemy shelling was very heavy. In fact, the Company only just managed to get into position by the time the barrage opened.*
>
> *The raid commenced at 4.30 a.m., and was brilliantly successful. Eight prisoners were captured, at least 40 of the enemy killed, and much information of value obtained. The casualties of the raiding party only numbered eleven (including one officer), all wounded.*
>
> *The battalion returned to the Canal Bank on the 26th. The last few days in the line had been very trying, and the casualties' heavy. Orders were received on the 28th to move back to 'O' Camp and thence to 'H' Camp."*

The Battalion would suffer almost 100 casualties during their fourteen-day tour of duty. The Officers' and NCOs proceeded to a location just outside the camp and studied the model of the Corps front in preparation for the deployment. At 10 a.m. the Commanding Officer and Signalling Officer proceeded to the front line and reconnoitred the area, which the Battalion would take over. At 8.30 p.m. on 14th the Lewis Gun sections under the Intelligence Officer moved out to relieve their counterparts in the front line. The relief was completed with no reported casualties.

The Company Commanders moved off at 2.30 p.m. on 15th to reconnoitre the front line which the Battalion would hold. Battalion H.Q. left camp at 7.30 p.m. to relieve the 7th Argyle and Sutherland Highlanders and 4th Gordon Highlanders of 51st (Highland) Division. The Battalion would be holding a two-battalion front at a time when the enemy knew something was in the offing. An already difficult job would be made doubly difficult and the men would be under no illusion as to the task ahead.

By 12.30 a.m. on 16th the relief was completed by all Companies and the battalion were in trenches north of Ypres.

Dispositions were as follows -:
Battalion Headquarters at C. 25.b.2.5 – Near canal

The day was a quiet one although the British aeroplanes were busy towards the evening. Aerial photographs were needed before the Battle of Pilckem began on 31st July. The enemy Artillery and Trench Mortars were very busy during the night, no doubt a welcome for the new battalion by the enemy. Casualties were given as three other ranks killed and sixteen wounded whilst the 17th had one killed and

Advanced Battalion Headquarters at C. 14.c.1.2, which was Lancashire Farm. The front held by the Battalion was from C.13.b.9.2 to C.15.c.7.6. The map shows the area from Ypres canal to La Belle Alliance

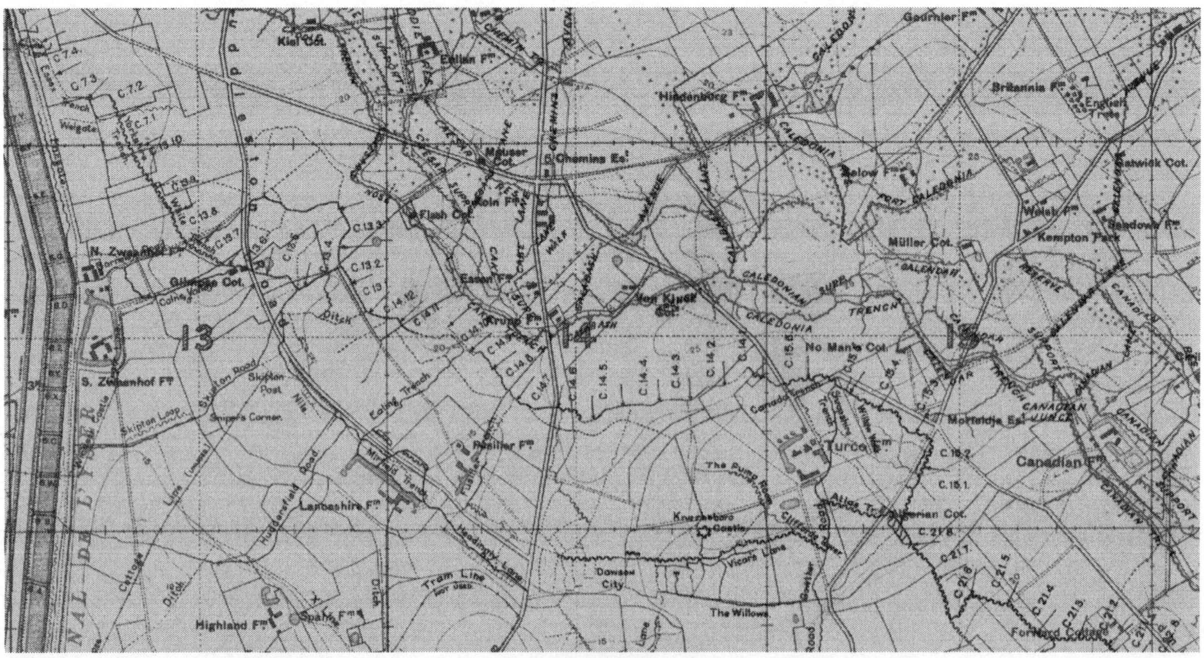

Map Belgium 28 N.W. The front line in the Battalions area of operation

three wounded. Only one man is officially listed as being killed on the 16th and three on 17th. and two of the wounded men also died on the 17th.

Four of the men are buried at Essex Farm Cemetery next to the Dressing Station made famous by John McCrae and his poem 'In Flanders Fields'.

16/07/1917

31282, Private Richard Darby aged 19 years of 'D' Company, enlisted at Nottingham and lived in New Basford Nott's. He is buried in grave I.P.1.

17/07/1917 –

18271, Private William Foster enlisted at Nottingham. He is buried in grave I.P.2

81570, Private Ernest Taylor aged 27 years, a married man from Belper Derbyshire. He is buried in grave I.P.2 and his headstone had the inscription 'Father in thy gracious keeping, Leave we now thy servant sleeping'.

The two men do have separate headstones but were buried shoulder to shoulder in one grave.

24414, Lance Corporal Henry Rodgers was born In North Wingfield, Derbys and he is buried in grave I.P.3

The two men who died of wounds are buried at Dozinghem Military Cemetery, which was the location of the 4th, 47th, 61st and 63rd Casualty Clearing Stations. It is located at Westvleteren and the name 'Dosing hem' was given by the troops. Nearby are the cemeteries of Mendinghem and Bandagehem.

22605, Private John Edward Wornes was a native of Brimington, Derbys, and is buried in grave I.D.15.

15372, Private Edward Pettit aged 30 years was born in London but living near Mansfield prior to the War. He is buried in grave I.D.16.

At 11.30 pm on 16th the enemy bombarded the rear areas with a new kind of gas shell causing violent sneezing, throat irritation and it also affected the eyes. This would have been Blue Cross shells, which was introduced in July 1917 at the same time as Mustard Gas. The shells contained diphenylchloroarsine (DA) as a solid contained in a glass bottle embedded in the high explosive. The detonation was supposed to create a very fine dust, which could penetrate respirator filters and cause intense pain to the sinuses. This was intended to force soldiers to remove their gas masks and succumb to phosgene (Green Cross) shells fired simultaneously. The theory though did not succeed as fact, as the detonation failed to create small enough particles. Only on rare occasions did Blue Cross shells cause serious problems. It is likely that the Battalion was one of the first to be on the receiving end of these shells.

The 17th was seen as a normal day with Artillery active on both sides. The Adjutant rejoined the battalion after his spell of leave. At 8 15 p.m. the Battalion relief was begun and the 6th Lincolns took over the front line. The Battalion would occupy the dugouts on the Yser Canals eastern bank (BN. O.O. no 33). Battalion Headquarters was located at C. 25.d.3.9 (see map above). It took until 1.20 a.m. on the 18th for the relief to be completed. Only two Other Ranks were wounded during the relief. The Battalion had to find various working parties throughout the day and when time permitted rest and clean up.

The 19th was another day of working parties and one from 'D' Company suffered a number of casualties whilst working at Marengo Dump. The War Diary gives the figures of three killed and four wounded but again only one man is listed for 19th. This is not unusual because the official registration could take place some time after death. In all four men would die as a result of the Marengo Dump shelling.

19/07/1917 –

Ypres (Menin Gate) Memorial.

19191, Lance Sergeant Joseph Hebblethwaite was 24 years of age and lived in Bolsover prior to the War.

20/07/1917-

57234 Private Ernest Cox is officially commemorated on the Ypres (Menin Gate) Memorial. Recent research has queried this because of the following. Between L/Cpl Rodgers, I. P.3. and Private Hill I.P.5, there is a grave with the following ' A private of the Great War, Notts & Derby Regt, 19th July 1917, Known Unto God'.

Ernest was seriously wounded and taken to the 88th Field Ambulance where a sub-section of 33rd Brigade Field ambulance were working. This was only 250 yards from Essex Farm, which was the nearest Burial ground. A dossier has been submitted to the Ministry of Defence concerning Ernest. Ernest was born in Pinchbeck, Lincs but lived in Bulwell Notts.

70837, Private George Hill was only 19 years of age and the son of George and Annie Hill of Wolverhampton. He had previously served as 19857 in the South Staffordshire Regiment. His headstone inscription reads 'Till we meet again'. He is buried in grave I.P.5.

71025, Private Ernest William Hodges aged 21 years Died of Wounds at Canada Farm and is buried

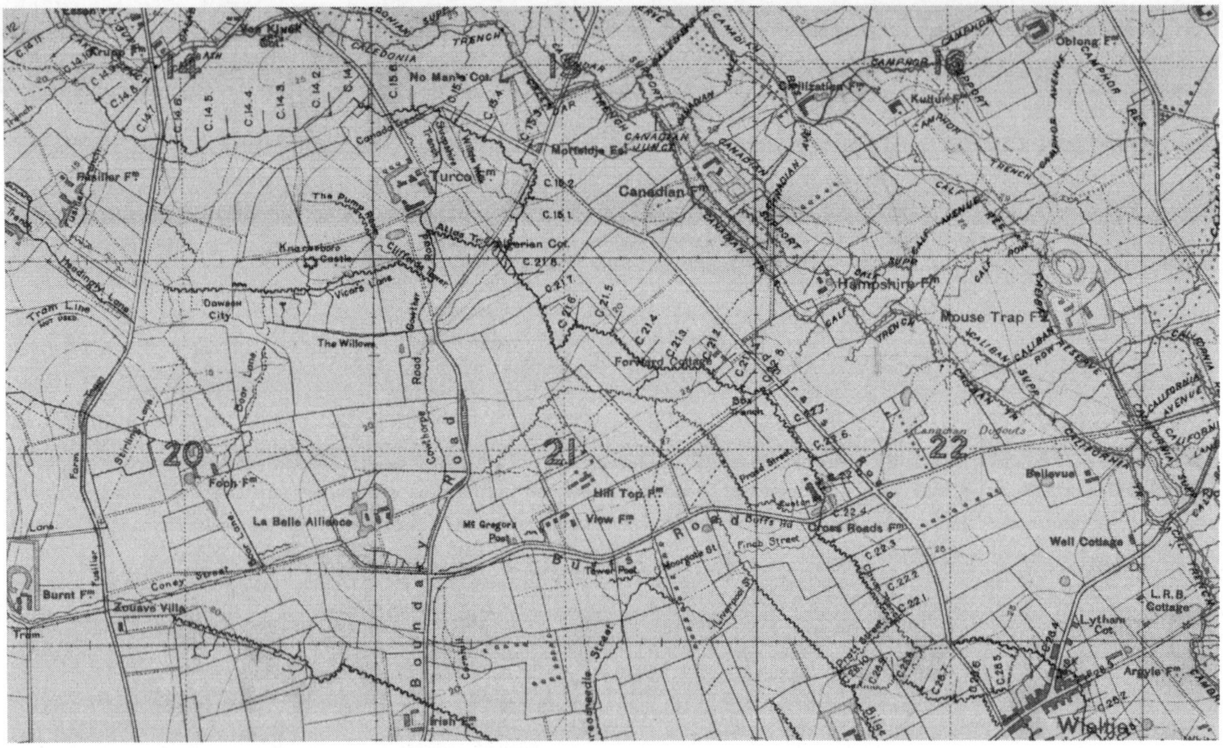

Dispositions of Companies – St Julian 28 N.W.2
(Under Battalion O.O. No. 34 and appendix D) H.Q. – C.20.d.4.5. 'B' Coy. H.Q. C.21.c.0.5. 'C' Coy. C.21.d.1.9. 'D' Coy. C.20.d.5.4.

in that cemetery. He was 21 years of age and a native of Tunbridge Wells Kent. Interestingly he enlisted at Godalming, which was the location of the battalion before Gallipoli. Did he see the Battalion and think 'I want to join them', who knows. He is buried in grave I.F.9 and his headstone inscription reads 'We'll read the meaning of our tears, and then someday we'll understand'

At 4 p.m. on 19th, 'A' Company moved back to the camp at A.30.d for rest and training prior to a proposed raid on Canadian Trench. The camp was probably Anzac Camp south west of Ypres.

The remainder of the battalion found more working parties on 29th before relieving the 6th Borders in the centre sub-sector.

The relief was duly completed by 11 p.m. and no casualties were recorded. A Patrol was sent out by 'C' Coy, along the enemy wire, which was found to be in good condition. This would mean that the British artillery would have to shell it again in preparation for 31st July.

Between 2 and 4 a.m. on 21st 'B' Company in the support line near Hill Top Farm was heavily shelled with High explosives and gas shells. The front line and Canal Bank were also subjected to a barrage of Phosgene gas shells. Between 10 p.m. and 1 a.m. 'A' Company came under artillery attack in their camp south west of Ypres.

Between 6 p.m. and 6.14 p.m. the British artillery put up a practice barrage. A patrol by 'B' Company along the German wire in front of Canadian trench found a thin line of wire concealed in long grass west of Admirals road. Casualties for the 21st were recorded as 2/Lieut F.F. Birtill being wounded along with one Other Rank. Three men were killed and they all lie side by side in La Belle Alliance Cemetery. La Belle Alliance was named after a small farmhouse, which stood nearby (see map above) and there are 60 graves of which 50 are identified. It is probable that some of the 'Unknowns' are in fact 9th Battalion men. A total of 34 men were from 33rd Brigade and of these 14 are 9th Battalion men.

90007 Sergeant Thomas Banton aged 37 years of Selston; Notts is buried in grave C.5.

13472, Private Ernest Funnell was a native of Brighton Sussex who travelled to Chesterfield to join up. The reason for his keenness to join the Sherwood Foresters will probably never be known. He is buried in grave C.4.

71058, Private B Margetts was born in Lenton, Notts. And little else is known of him. He is buried in grave C.5.

The 22nd saw a great deal of enemy Artillery fire and gas shells and H.E. hit the front line from 1 a.m. to 4 a.m. The British Artillery matched the enemy artillery during this period and the noise must have been horrendous. A Patrol was sent out by 'D' Company at 1 a.m. to examine the enemy wire in front of Canadian Trench and they found several gaps in the wire. The Canal Bank received a considerable number of gas shells in the evening. All part of the enemies attempts to disrupt preparations for the forthcoming attack. Battalion H.Q. was also shelled heavily during the night. At 9 a.m. 'A' Company practiced their forthcoming raid near to their camp.

Casualties for the day were given as two Other Ranks killed and fourteen wounded.

The only man officially listed for 22nd was Harry Hughes who died of wounds.

32984, Private Harry Hughes was a native of Whittington Moor, Derbys and he is buried at Essex Farm and grave II.H.4. It is likely that the two men killed on 22nd and the three on 23rd are all listed on 23rd returns. All five men are buried at La Belle Alliance.

The men were buried shoulder to shoulder in this battlefield cemetery and a number have two or three names on one headstone.

23/07/1917 –

53592, Private Arthur Brooks was a native of Nottingham and is buried in grave C.4

23223, Private Thomas Henry Buxton was a Yorkshire man and is buried in grave C.4. It is a front line cemetery and the men were buried in a single trench shoulder to shoulder. After the war the CWGC could not always get single headstones for each man due to the close burials. In this case they would put two mens names on. When you see headstones very close together, often they have two names on them. If the men were unrecognisable they would put either /or on the headstone.

21504, Private Harold Marsh was a native of Sutton in Ashfield, Notts and is buried in grave C.4.

70814, Corporal Charles George Millott aged 22 years was a Mansfield man and in 'C' Company. He is buried in grave C.5 He had started his service in the 1/8th (TF) Battalion with the number 2210. He entered the French theatre of war on 2 March 1915.

"CORPORAL CHARLES MILLOTT.
We have previously announced the death in France of Corporal Charles Millott, the son of Mr and Mrs Millott, 17 Murray St, who was killed in his dugout by a shell on July 25th, at the age of 22 years. The deceased, who before donning khaki, was employed by Messrs Eden and Sons, had experienced about 2-1/2 years of active service, and some two months ago was home on leave. He was in the Sherwood Foresters, as also is his brother William, and the latter sent home the first intimation the parents received of their son's death. Further particulars of the sad occurrence, together with a tribute to his fine soldierly qualities, are given in the following letter which has since come to hand from his platoon sergeant: -

Dear Mrs Millott, and family, – With the deepest sympathy I regret to be one of the people to tell you of the sad death of your brave and gallant soldier son, Charles, who met his death like the good soldier he was, on the 25th. He and I had just been on a ration party, and had been hold up with the Bosches sending gas, and your son had not been back five minutes when he was killed instantly by an enemy shell. He went into his little dug-out, which we shared, and sat down, when the shell came and went right through the top, killing him and wounding seven others, I hardly need tell you how greatly he is missed in his platoon, for he was always so cheerful and happy. He and I were looking after the platoon, having no officer at the time, and I, offer you, on behalf of his platoon, my deepest sympathy. I know it will be a great blow to you, but it might be a little consolation to you to know that he had a proper burial. I went to see the last of him in a little cemetery just behind the place where he died. I had the good fortune to see his brother just as I was coming out, and I pointed out the place to him, so he may have the chance of getting more particulars about him. I have had the parcel today, which you sent your son, and have given it to his section, and thank you very much for the same. As you know the men make it a rule for all parcels to be given to the man's section, if anything happens. Well, I will now close with all the platoon's sympathy.

E C Harwood."

Another article states –

"Killed in a Dug-out.
Fate of Pte, Charles Millott, MansfieldNews has been received this week by Mr. And Mrs. Millott, of Murray Street, Mansfield, that their son, Charles, of the Sherwood Foresters, has been killed in France (actually Belgium); the information being sent by his brother, William, who was also with the Sherwood's at the front.

The deceased, who was home on leave a few weeks ago, was in a dugout when he was struck on the head by the nose cap of a shell and fatally injured. He joined the Army soon after the outbreak of war, when he was employed at the Hermitage Mills and had previously been slightly wounded."

(the author would like to thank to David E Millott for providing the above information)

24514, Private John Henry Petford, was born in Dudley, Worcs and enlisted at Wolverhampton. He is buried in grave C.5.

On the 23rd 'C' Company relieved 'B' Company in the front line. Artillery on both sides was once again very active. A Patrol sent out by 'D' Company found several gaps in the enemy wire in front of Canadian Trench. Despite these gaps it was concluded that the wire would still be a considerable obstacle to an advance. More work would be needed by the British Artillery over the coming week. Casualties were put at three Other Ranks killed (see above) and five wounded.

'A' Company continued to rehearse for the up coming trench raid. The 24th would see Canadian Trench kept under constant observation and a Patrol by 'B' Company found the wire practically cleared in front of the trench itself. The British artillery had done its job well and now it was the Battalions turn as 'A' Company mounted their Trench raid. During the morning of the 24th, 'A' Company moved up to the Canal Bank. At midnight they proceeded to the front line (Hornby Trench) and took up position in readiness for zero. The move up was not without its difficulties as the enemy sent over a constant stream of gas shells. Marching any distance wearing gas masks was not an enjoyable experience and more so when all the equipment for a trench raid also had to be carried. The raid was timed to begin at 4.30 a.m. and would be in effect a practice attack for the 31st.

Meanwhile four men would succumb to their wounds on 24th as a result of the previous few days shelling.

60353, Private Victor Bates aged 20 years and a Derbyshire lad died of his wounds and is buried at Dozinghem Military Cemetery and grave I.I.14. Three graves from Victor is –

19799, Lance Corporal Soloman Burton, MM, was also aged 20 years and lies in grave I.I.17. Solomon's London Gazette entry for his Military Medal was dated 18 August 1917 and it is possible that he never knew of the award.

Two men lie close to each other in Lijssenthoek Military Cemetery. A number of Casualty Clearing Stations were based here and the Railhead of Remy Sidings was behind the Cemetery.

12781 Private George Edward Lloyd aged 21 years was in 'C' Company and a native of Shropshire. He had travelled to Derby at the outbreak of war to join the Sherwood's. He is buried in grave XVI. C. 17A.

56423 Private Arthur Towle was a native of Nottingham and is buried in grave XVI. E. 14.

The War Diary listed four men being killed on 24th although the figure was actually five. Three of the men are buried in La Belle Alliance Cemetery.

31615 Private William Percy Barnes was 21 years of age who was born at Belper in Derbyshire and he is buried in grave C.4.

90002 Corporal Harry Street was 24 years of age and in 'C' Company. Harry was the son of Albert and Sarah Jane and lived in Ockbrook, Derbys. He is also buried in C.4.

70949 Private Arthur Webster was also 24 years of age. He was from Walsall Staffs and formerly 24141 South Staffordshire Regt.

The other two men have no known grave but it is possible that they also lie in La Belle Alliance. They are though like many thousands of others remembered on the Ypres (Menin Gate) Memorial. All of the Sherwood Foresters are to be found on Panels 39-41.

27279 Private George Alexander Sheppard was a Nottingham man.

16193 Private George Taylor Whyman was born at Old Basford Notts.

At 4.30 a.m. on 25th 'A' Company under the command of Captain J. Critchlow began their trench raid. The force was made up of 4 officers and 130 other ranks of 'A' Company assisted by 10 Royal Engineers. The raid was made on the Canadian Trench and Canadian Support Trenches under the protection of a box barrage and Machine Gun barrage. The raid was a complete success and left the enemy with a 'bloody nose'. Eight prisoners and much valuable information were brought back for the intelligence officers. At least forty of the enemy were killed and the dugouts and trenches were wrecked. During the raid 'A' Company sustained casualties of 1 Officer and 10 Other Ranks wounded. Unless the Company in which a man served is mentioned, it is virtually impossible to work out which one he was in. Possibly one of the wounded men in the raid was 26522 Private Frederick Armstrong and he would survive. Two other men would succumb to their wounds the next day could also have served with 'A' Company.

21851 Private John William Nurse was a New Whittington man and attached to the Trench Mortar Battery. He is buried at Vlamertinghe New Military Cemetery and grave V .A. 20.

64358 Private Thomas Keeton was married and a Nottingham man. He is buried at Lijssenthoek Military Cemetery and grave XVI. H. 1.

The enterprise undertaken by 'A' Company would hopefully assist the men going over the top five days later as the Battles of Ypres began with the attack on the Pilckem ridge. After the raid 'A' Company returned to the Canal Bank and then to the camp at A.20.d. They would get a well-earned days rest for their efforts. The remainder of the battalion had a normal day with no casualties. No doubt the enemy were to preoccupied sorting their own defences out during the day to worry about the men opposite them. The enemy though were also putting into practice new tactics for defence, which would cause many problems in the weeks to come. The enemy did though shell Hill Top heavily.

The 26th saw 'A' Company return to the Canal Bank at 3 p.m., taking over working party duties from the 6th Lincolns who would be going up the line that night. The day was a normal one with only the usual shelling to contend with. Only two men were wounded during the day.

At noon on 27th a report was received that a reconnaissance plane had gone up in the morning and could find no trace of the enemy west of the Steenbeck River (Steenbeek Stream) and it was thought that they had evacuated the forward areas. This was actually the new German form of defence using strong points to hold the line and bringing troops forward when needed. In view of this supposed evacuation by the enemy the battalion was ordered to 'stand to' in readiness for a move forward in the event of an emergency. The 6th Lincolns and 7th South Stafford's sent out patrols in the area to gain touch with the enemy. They found the enemy holding certain strong points and positions on the front and withdrew to their own front line.

At 10 p.m. two Lewis Gun teams were sent to reinforce the 7th South Stafford's and Companies were once again ordered to 'stand to'. This new German defence was obviously unsettling British Commanders with their own offensive so soon to begin. The enemy shelled the Canal Bank intermittently throughout the day and the Battalion casualties were two Other Ranks killed and two wounded. The two men killed were listed as dying on 28th July and both are buried at La Belle Alliance Cemetery.

71065 Private Lance Veres was born at Pontypridd, Wales although on the outbreak of war he was at Hucknall Torkard, Notts. He was possibly a miner who had moved looking for employment. He is buried in grave C.1.

71028 Private Robert Hamilton Russell McAusland was a Derby lad born and bred. He was 21 years of age and is buried in grave C.1.

The 28th would be the battalions last day in the trenches in this area prior to The Battles of Ypres, which would commence on 31st. It was thankfully

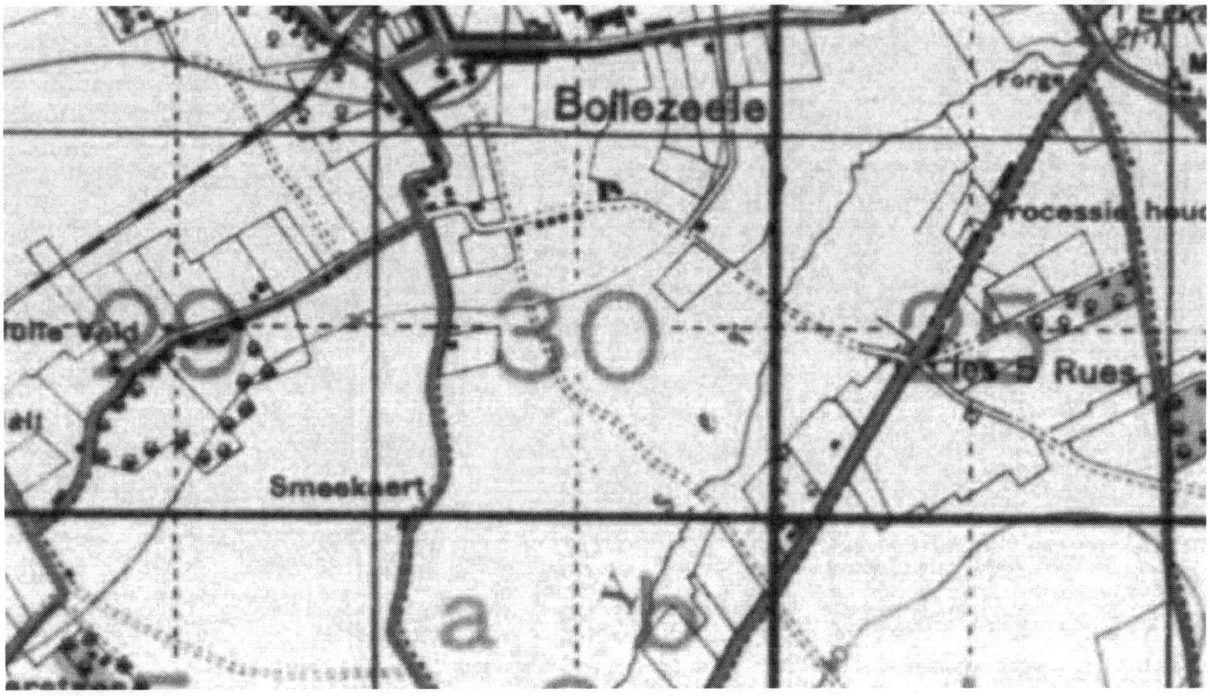

A30 near Ypres

a quiet day after a trying time for the battalion. At 4.30 p.m. the Lewis Gunners returned to the Battalion and orders were received to move to the camp at A.30.d and b. under Battalion O.O. No. 37, Brigade O.O. No. 86 dated 27.7.17.

17941 Corporal Harold E. James Jackson died of wounds and is buried at Lijssenthoek Military Cemetery. He was born in Bedford but living in Stapleford Nott's prior to the war. The inscription on his headstone reads, 'Gone but not forgotten, from his loving Wife & Daughter'. Harold is buried in grave XVI. I. 18A.

He would be the last man to die from this expensive period of trench occupation.

At 1.30 a.m. on 29th the Battalion received orders to move and proceeded to the camp at A.30. d and b. The Battalion experienced great difficulty as the enemy laid down a heavy gas barrage but fortunately no casualties were incurred. By 3 a.m., H.Q., 'B', 'A' and 'C' Companies had arrived in camp but 'D' Company did not arrive until 5.30 a.m. They had marched independently to the camp after being relieved by a Company of the 7th K.R.R.C. (King's Royal Rifle Corps, 14th Division).

Men were given time to rest and clean up on the 30th but ominously for the Battle of Ypres it rained heavily all day. The camp became extremely muddy and an unpleasant place to be and it was no doubt with some relief that at 8 p.m. a move was made to a new camp near St. Jans Ter Biezen, which was between Poperinghe and Watou. There is some confusion as to the name of this camp though as the war diary called it 'N' Camp, whilst Col Scothern gives 'H' Camp. It was located at F.27.a.1.2. (Sheet 27). By 10.30 p.m. the men were in their new camp and could settle down for a couple of weeks of relative quiet.

The 31st saw the beginning of the Battle of Ypres, 1917 and the attack on Pilckem Ridge. It had actually been scheduled for 25th June but postponed. Various reasons were given with General Gough mentioning the late arrival of French Troops. Whilst Sir Douglas Haig mentioned that the British counter battery work was so effective that the enemy had moved back and the extra days would enable Aerial reconnaissance of the new enemy artillery positions. Whatever the reasons, the extra delay would prove fatal for the Campaign. The first day of the battle was certainly successful but the weather was dreadful with heavy rain being a constant problem. The next battle could not begin until the ground had dried out enough for a realistic chance of success.

This would be The Battle of Langemarck on 16th August 1917 and the 9th Battalion would be a part of it.

August 1st to 14th would be taken up with training for the forthcoming attack, although the Battalion would be in reserve during the battle itself. The first four days were taken up with Company training in the vicinity of their billets. The new enemy defensive tactics, which had been discovered during the battalions last few days in the trenches, would need to be counteracted. The men had to learn new

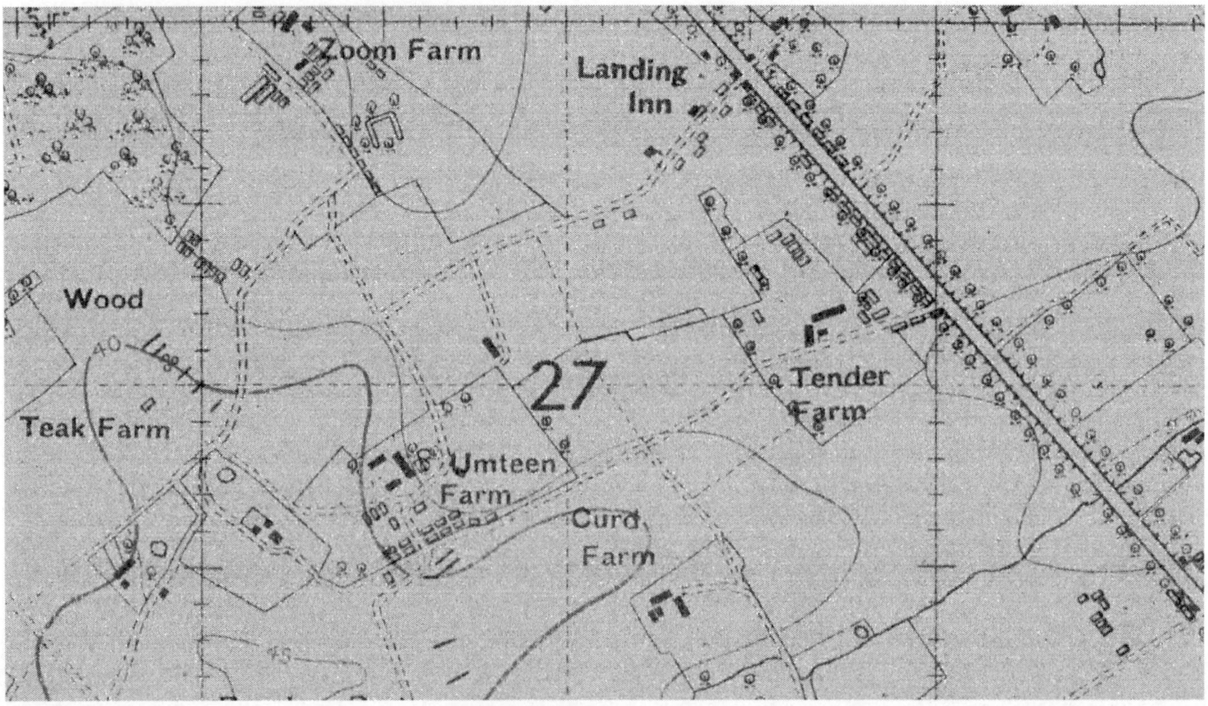

The battalion was based in Zoom Farm (top of map)

strategies for overcoming the concrete bunkers and strong points, which protected the enemy front line. The enemy were sitting on the ridges that surrounded Ypres, giving them uninterrupted views of the Battlefield and British movements. The constant shelling would turn the battlefield into a quagmire as the delicate balance of dykes and streams was destroyed. Every shell hole would be filled with water laced with gas, body parts and all manner of detritus. Every stream had been turned into a muddy river. This is what the Battalion had to train for and they knew it would be just as fraught as Gallipoli and the Somme.

The Divisional Gas officer examined the men's box respirators on 1st and on 4th with all ranks receiving a new issue. No comment was made as to the reason for this change but the Battalion had suffered the new enemy gases during July and filters capable of working with Mustard and Blue Cross gas were needed. It does show the speed in which the scientists could react to new forms of gas.

Sunday 5th was given over to rest and church services which would have been a welcome break for every man in the Battalion.

More training was undertaken over the following two days with the emphasis on Company manoeuvres. The usual inspections were also a regular feature during this period of time. A route march to Watou by 'A' and 'D' Companies was undertaken on 7th with yet another move of camp on 8th. The Battalion less the reserve personnel (Echelons A and B) left camp at 7 a.m., moving to E Camp at A 30 central, arriving at 9 a.m. The reserves moved to Houtkerque, which was northwest of Watou.

The 9th, 10th and 11th saw more Company training, although on each day one Company would be detailed to work on a model near camp. Large sized scale models were used prior to each battle to give attacking troops the opportunity of seeing the lay of the land. Aerial photographs would be turned into a model of the battlefield, with all contours, rivers, concrete bunkers, strong points and enemy dispositions marked. This again showed how battle planning and tactics had evolved as the war progresses.

Training would continue until 13th August, although Sunday 12th was given over to bathing and the issue of clean clothing. A sure sign of a forthcoming battle would be Church services, baths and clean clothing. The British army wanted their men physically and spiritually clean prior to battle. The men were always pleased to have the opportunity to bathe but it was no relaxing hot bath on ones own. Huge tubs full of hot water accommodated up to twelve men at a time. There was a fair drop from the top of these tubs to the water itself. A complete set of underclothing would then be issued but there was no guarantee that it would fit. Men would have to sort out the sizes amongst themselves. Whilst the men bathed, their uniforms were baked in a sort of oven. This would kill lice and disinfect the uniform.

On the 14th the battalion moved up the line once more and left for Siege Junction at 7.15 a.m., arriving there at 7.50 a.m. The new camp took its name from the Junction being called Siege Camp. It is believed that the camp got its name from the Siege Guns located nearby. On arrival the men were issued with their fighting kit and S.A.A. (Small Arms Ammunition).

At 6.30 p.m. a working party consisting of forty Other Ranks led by 2/Lt Odell were sent to Gournier Farm. One man was possibly killed on this working party.

19009 Private Luther Caunt is listed on the CWGC as being killed on 14th August but SDGW has 19th.

Luther was a Sutton in Ashfield man and is buried at Tyne Cot Cemetery and grave LXIV. G. 2.

The following morning Companies trained and carried out practice attacks on sealed pillboxes in conjunction with the 7th South Stafford's. Troops fighting in the early battle of the campaign had come up against these pillboxes and a way of neutralizing them had to be found. Men not yet engaged needed, guidance and practice on the methods used.

The Battalion less the transport, some of the H.Q. detail and Q.M. Stores proceeded to dugouts at the Canal bank east near bridge 4. This area was one of total decay and devastation with vile smells and the canal littered with corpses of men and animals. The shattered remains of wagons and limbers also littered the green mass that had once been a Canal. At 1.10 a.m. on 16th the battalion arrived at the Canal Bank (Yser) and settled down for four hours prior to zero hour which was at 4.45 a.m.

Brigade H.Q. was situated by a lake but no location was stipulated, whilst Battalion H.Q. occupied dugouts on the canal bank. The Battalion was in reserve and zero hour came and went without any orders being received. The men would have heard the crescendo of noise as the battle opened and would wonder when their involvement would begin. Fifth armies main task was to secure the Steenbeek and take Langemarck. The attack had been planned for 14th but time was needed for the ground to dry out. Thankfully no rain fell on 16th but it was still a dull overcast day.

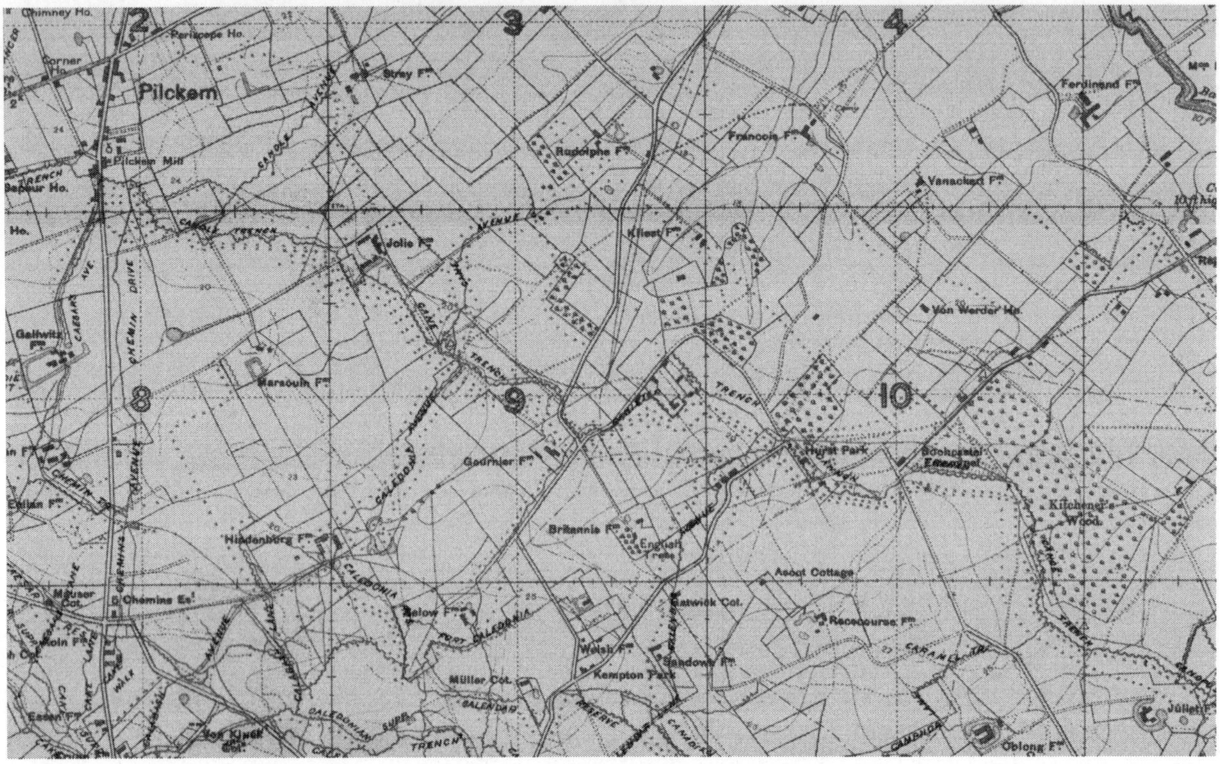

Gournier Farm is in square 9d – the possible location of Private Luther's death

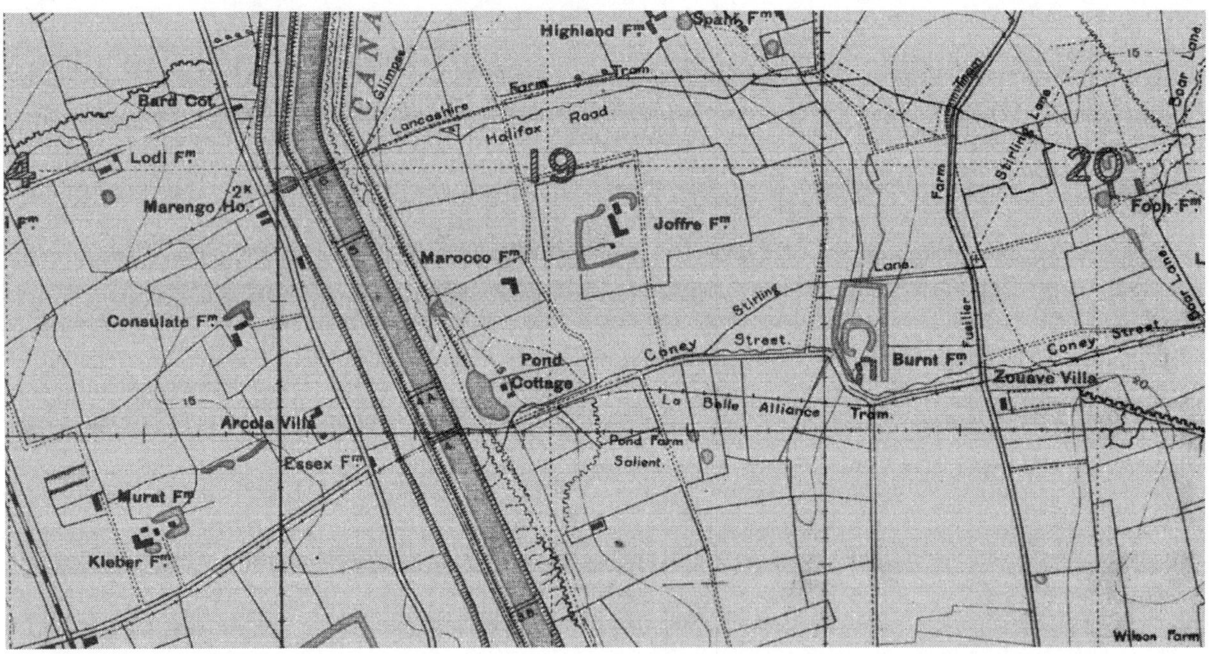

Bridge 4 near Essex Farm

Finally at 6.05 a.m. orders were received for the battalion to move forward at 6.45 a.m. (zero plus 2) and by 8.30 a.m. the move to the old British front line had been completed. At 9 a.m. orders were issued to move to the black line with H.Q. based at Gournier Farm (see map for 14th August) and by 9.25 a.m. H.Q. had arrived. On arrival at the black line at 10.20 a.m., the Companies took up the following positions –

'D' Company – In Cane Trench (Just in front of Gournier Farm)

'B' and 'C' Companies at C.9.b.

'A' Company at C.3.d. – Maintaining touch with 20th Division on the battalions left flank.

At 11.50 a.m. reports came in that the enemy was massing at Poelcappelle in readiness for another attack but nothing came of this. The British Artillery in the area did excellent work in keeping the enemy at bay. At noon guides arrived to take the battalion forward to the Steenbeek if required but in the event the move was not needed. The O.C. of the 7th South Stafford's did send two Companies forward to link with the right hand Division though. At 5.50 p.m. Capt Munday arrived with the ration party which no doubt cheered the men up. Orders were received informing the Battalion that 33rd Brigade would take over the Divisional front with the South Staffs on the right and the Sherwood Foresters on the left. Overnight the battalion remained in position but no movement orders arrived.

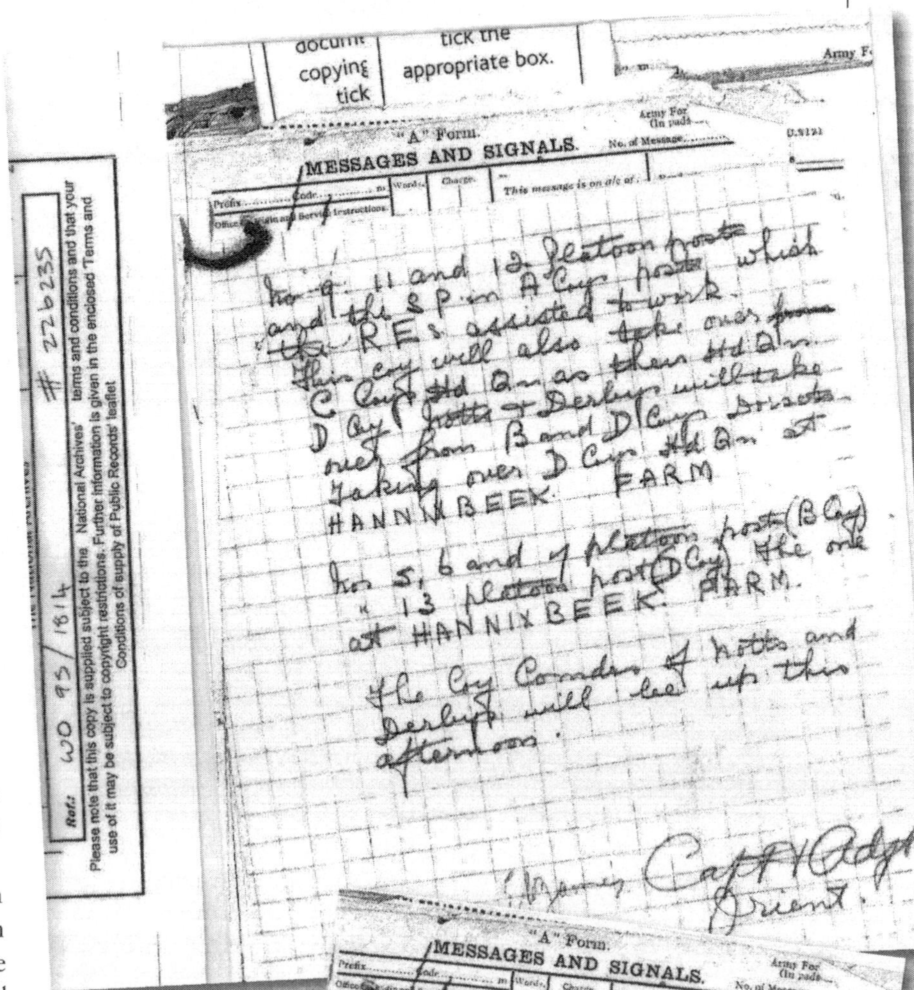
"A" Form. MESSAGES AND SIGNALS.

Ref.: WO 95/1814 # 226235
Please note that this copy is supplied subject to the National Archives' terms and conditions and that your use of it may be subject to copyright restrictions. Further information is given in the enclosed 'Terms and Conditions of supply of Public Records' leaflet

No 9. 11 and 12 platoon posts and the S P in A Coy posts which the R.E.s assisted to work. This coy will also take over from C Coy Hd Qrs as their Hd Qrs. D Coy (Notts & Derbys) will take over from B and D Coy Dorsets taking over D Coy Hd Qrs at HANNIXBEEK FARM

Nos 5, 6 and 7 platoon posts (B Coy) " 13 platoon post (D Coy) the one at HANNIXBEEK FARM.

The Coy Comdrs of Notts and Derbys will fix up this afternoon.

Capt & Adjt Orient.

The only man to die on the 16th is buried at Artillery Wood cemetery. This Cemetery also contains the grave of the Bard Hedd Wynn (Ellis Evans).

21912 Lance Corporal Joseph Eades was 22 years of age and from Baslow in Derbyshire. His headstone has the words 'Of Baslow, Duty well Done'.

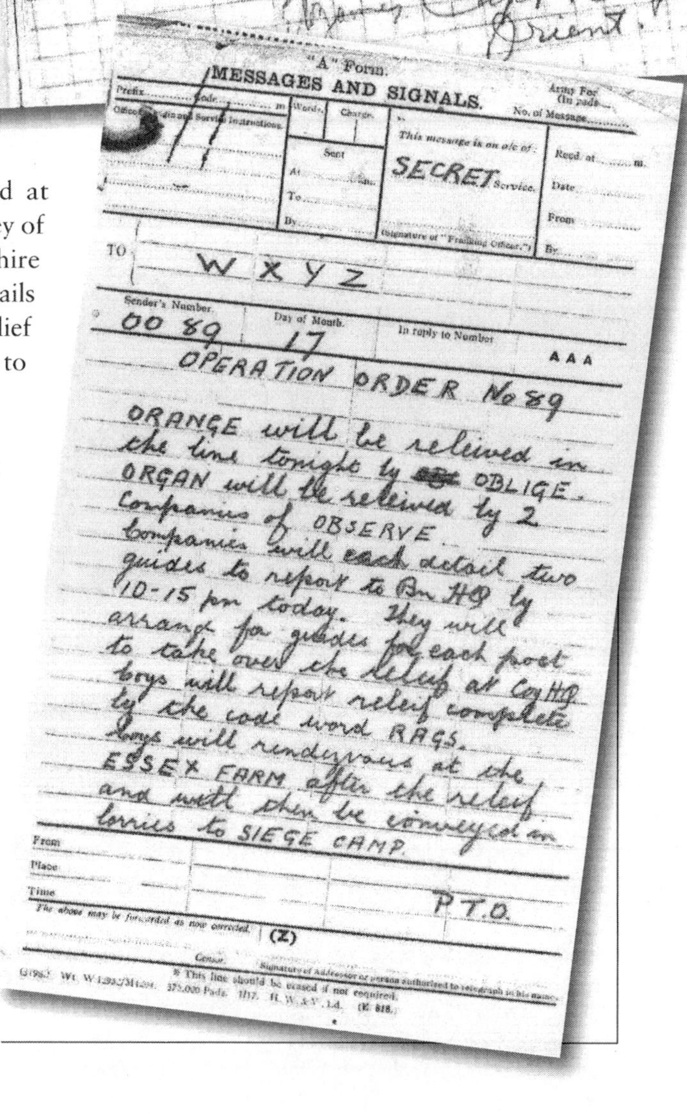
"A" Form. MESSAGES AND SIGNALS.

SECRET

TO WXYZ

Sender's Number: 00 89 | Day of Month: 17

OPERATION ORDER No 89

ORANGE will be relieved in the line tonight by OBLIGE. ORGAN will be relieved by 2 Companies of OBSERVE. Companies will each detail two guides to report to Bn HQ by 10-15 pm today. They will arrange for guides for each post to take over the relief at Coy HQ. Coys will report relief complete by the code word RAGS. Coys will rendezvous at the ESSEX FARM after the relief and will then be conveyed in lorries to SIEGE CAMP.

P.T.O.

At 9.20 a.m. on 17th further orders were received at Battalion H.Q. and the C.O. moved off to see Col. Hanney of the 5th Dorset's and Col. Thurlow of the 9th Lancashire Fusiliers (both 34th Brigade, 11th Division) to arrange details of the relief. By 4 p.m. all of the arrangements for the relief were completed and the men would know that the move to the front line was imminent.

The Operational Orders by Lt.Col Haney, Commanding Orient (Orient – 5th Dorset's), 17-8-17.

The Battalion met its guides at Francois Farm (C.4.c. central) and the difficulties of negotiating the barren wilderness that was the Salient soon became evident. The diary entry read, *'After many wanderings after lost guides battalion finally completed relief by 3.50 a.m. on the 18th inst'*. Incredibly a march of some 3000 yards as the crow flies took nearly six hours. Just prior to the relief the 9th Lancashire Fusiliers had occupied Rat House (U 29.b.) and advanced the line. It was this new line that the battalion took over. This meant that only verbal orders were issued in deploying the Companies. Battalion H.Q. was some 200 yards

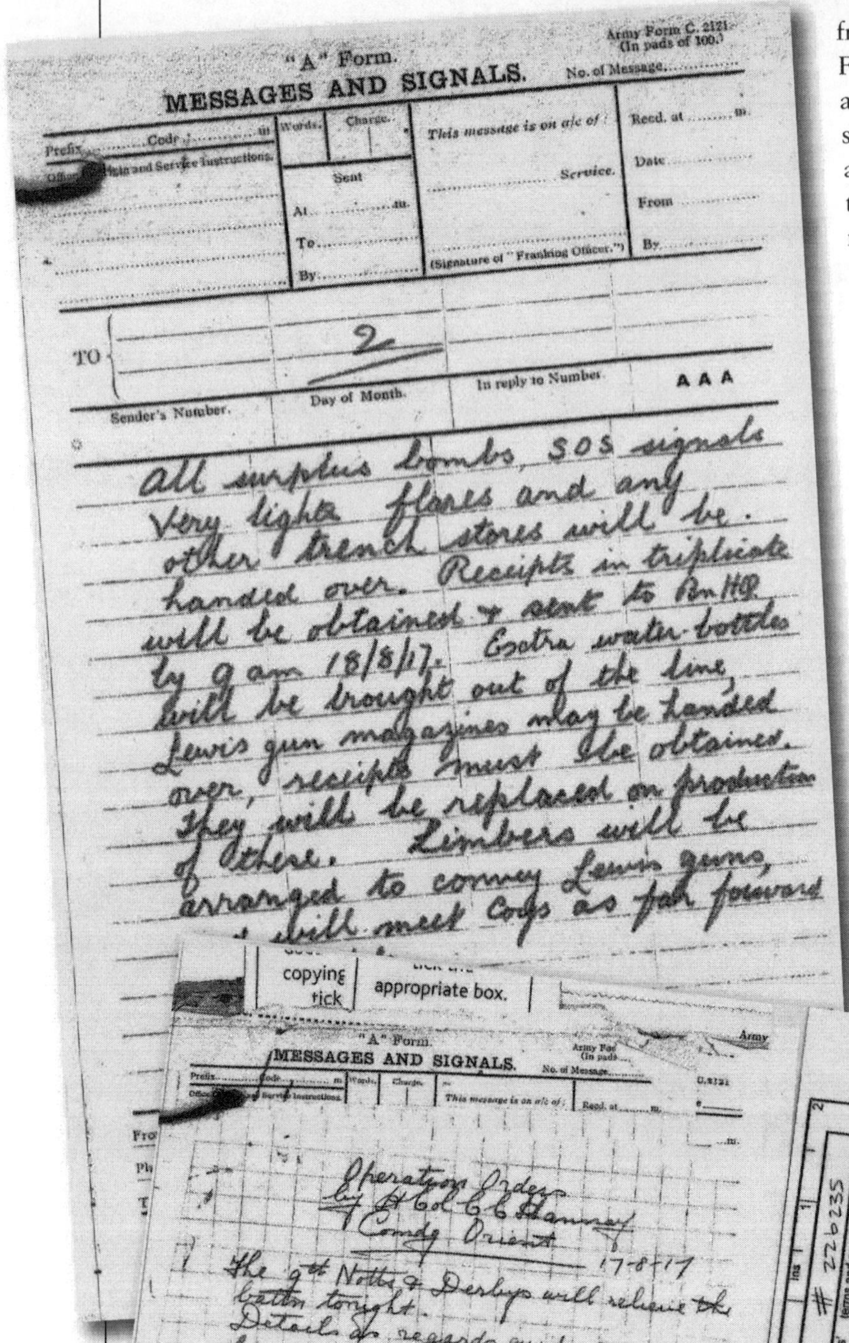

Army Form C. 2121. (In pads of 100.)

"A" Form.

MESSAGES AND SIGNALS.

TO 2

all surplus bombs, SOS signals Very lights flares and any other trench stores will be handed over. Receipts in triplicate will be obtained & sent to Bn HQ by 9 am 18/8/17. Extra water bottles will be brought out of the line, Lewis gun magazines may be handed over, receipts must be obtained. They will be replaced on production of these. Limbers will be arranged to convey Lewis guns, & will meet Coys as far forward

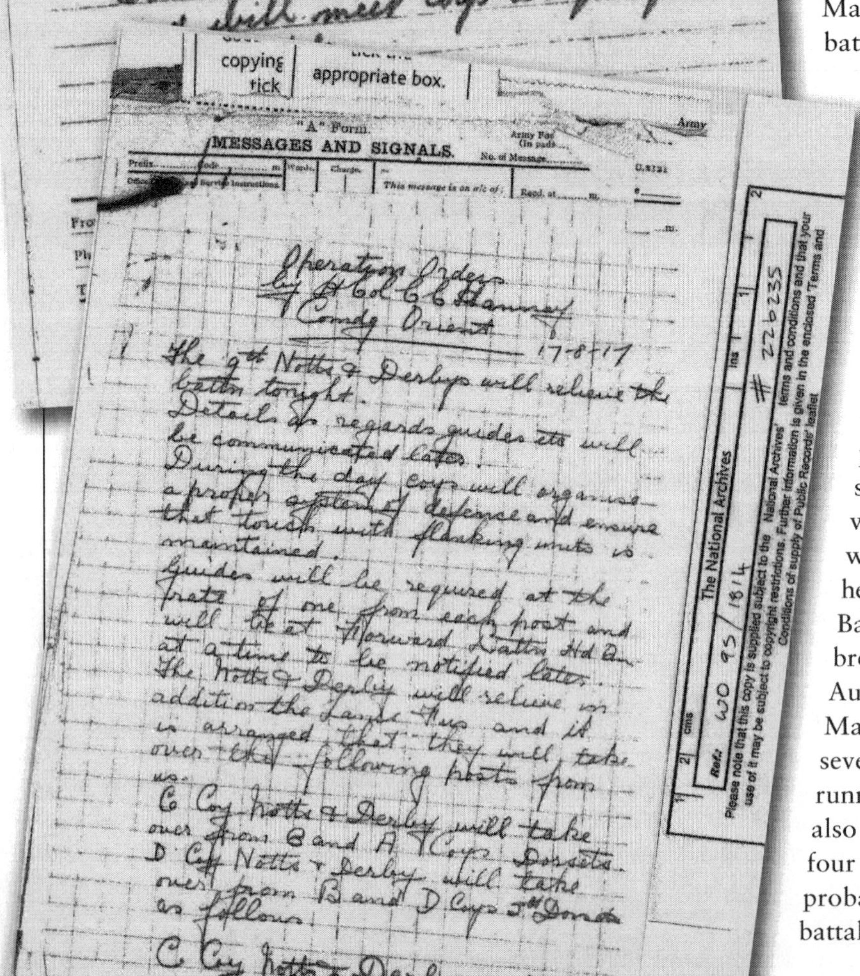

"A" Form.

MESSAGES AND SIGNALS.

Operation Orders by Lt Col [illegible] Comdg [illegible] 17-8-17

The 9th Notts & Derbys will relieve the battn tonight. Details as regards guides etc will be communicated later. During the day Coys will organise a proper system of defence and ensure that touch with flanking units is maintained. Guides will be required at the rate of one from each post and will be at Forward Battn Hd Qrs at a time to be notified later. The Notts & Derby will relieve in addition the Lanc Fus and it is arranged that they will take over the following posts from us. C Coy Notts & Derby will take over from C and A Coys Dorsets. D Coy Notts & Derby will take over from B and D Coys 5th Dorsets as follows. C Coy Notts & Derby will take over from C and A Coys Dorsets

The National Archives. Ref: WO 95/1814 # 226235

from the front line in the area of Haanixbeek Farm. By 3.50 a.m. the relief was completed and the men settled into their new surroundings facing Poelcappelle. It had been arranged that a smoke screen would be put up to aid the relief but the bombs (grenades) did not arrive, so no protection was forthcoming. Despite this the relief was carried out without any difficulty.

Two men were killed on 17th August.

21602 Private Isiah Byfield was born at Walsall Staffs although he enlisted at Mansfield. He is buried in Artillery Wood cemetery and grave IV. B. 16.

18973 Private Thomas Phipps also enlisted at Mansfield, he though was living at Lenton, Notts at the time. He is buried in Bard Cottage Cemetery and grave IV. B. 44

More problems arose at 3.00 p.m. on the 17th – the diary entry read:

'try to find new Battn H.Q. at Machine Gun House at U 29.c.2.2.'

Sadly the diarist did not make plain whether H.Q. itself was relocating to Machine Gun House or members of the battalion could not find H.Q. It was probably the former as there is no mention of such a place on the map and it was possibly a local name not officially used. The nearest buildings in the area were at Partridge Farm. At 3.30 p.m. the enemy conducted its own relief opposite the right of the battalion sector and the Field Artillery were informed but no action was taken. An opportunity to harass and disrupt the enemy was missed. At 5 p.m. Private Austin was wounded by a sniper whilst at Battalion H.Q., but he would survive the experience and the war. At 8.30 p.m. the enemy sent over a heavy artillery barrage which targeted the Battalion H.Q. and could have been brought down by the sniper who had shot Austin earlier. One shell killed three Machine Gunners and wounded six or seven men, plus wounding the Battalion runner Private Pearson. Private Pearson also seemed to survive the experience but four men are listed as killed on 19th. It is probable that the Machine gunners were battalion Lewis Gun men and not from the

Machine Gun Corps. From 11 p.m. onwards the enemy kept up intermittent shelling which continued throughout the night but no casualties were recorded. Men of the 6th Borders brought up rations for the battalion and left them with C and d Companies in reserve at Haanixbeek Farm. From here the two Companies distributed the rations to A and B Companies in the front line.

Three of the men killed on 19th are buried in Tyne Cot Cemetery and one is commemorated on the Tyne Cot Memorial. The names on the Memorial are from 16 August 1917 onwards.

18545 Private John Clifford Taylor was 26 years of age and a native of Ashbourne in Derbyshire. He is buried in grave LXIV.G.1 at Tyne Cot Cemetery.

27733 Private John George Burton was 25 years of age and a native of Sutton in Ashfield, Notts. He is buried in grave LXIV. G. 3.

30354 Private Charles Locke was a native of Nottingham and is buried in grave LXIV. G. 4.

All three men would have been buried near to where they fell and removed to Tyne Cot after the War.

24257 Private Frank Nash was a Borrowash man and he is commemorated on the Tyne Cot Memorial – panel 99-102.

At 6 a.m. on 19th the South Staffs assisted by tanks found The Cockcroft (C.6.a.3.2) unoccupied and 9th Bn H.Q. had a grandstand view from their location at U 29.d.5.2. although the sequence of events as laid out in the diaries was short and sweet:

'Tanks could be seen advancing in front of Mon du Hibou and one was seen to return'.

Martin Marix Evans in his book Passchendaele The Hollow Victory (Pen & Sword military 2005) gives a tankies eye view:

"Coutts attacked the Cockcroft with his 'female tank', leaving the road to get within 50 yards and opening fire with his Lewis guns. The garrison, in spite of the strength of the fortification, abandoned their position after the briefest fights. Coutts supporting infantry, however failed to come up at his signal, and the tank commander was obliged to leave his machine and go on foot to find them. Maison du Hibou fell to Baker's 'male' tank. From the road little was achieved, but Baker left the hard surface and managed to get to the rear of the blockhouse before bogging down. From there his 6-pounders hurled some thirty or forty rounds at the door, forcing the garrison out to be captured by men of the 1/8th Worcesters or shot by Morgan's female tank"

At 9 a.m. it was decided that Machine Gun House would be the new Battalion H.Q. The entry of the 18th seemed to suggest that it had taken a day to find Machine Gun House. It would though be no safer a location than the old H.Q. It took until 5 p.m. to get a telephone wire fixed up at the new location, whereupon the C.O. and Adjutant moved in with the remainder of the H.Q personnel dribbling down during the day. This would be necessary so as not to give the enemy to easy a target especially as snipers were still around. It was though obvious that the old H.Q. was not only in a vulnerable location but also overlooked by the enemy. Between 11.40 a.m. and 1.30 p.m. the old H.Q was heavily shelled and no one could get in or out, although only two servants are recorded as receiving slight wounds. The Germans had had nearly three years to list the co-ordinates of every piece of shelter within their area. Their artillery was ranged in and awaiting the British. At 5.40 p.m. the enemy was seen to be collecting in the vicinity of Bulow Farm (U.30.c.1.5) and the South Staffs were warned, although nothing came of the enemy movement. At 10.p.m. the Battalion received orders concerning its relief by 6th Borders and at 11.pm. two Company Commanders from that Battalion visited the front line to make arrangements for the relief of 'A' and 'B' Companies. At 11 a.m. on the 20th Lt. Col Scothern of the 6th Borders arrived at Battalion H.Q. to make arrangements for the forthcoming relief, after which relief orders were issued to the Battalion.

The Corps heavy artillery opened up a barrage on Pheasant Farm at 4 p.m. and it continued for two hours. The farm would be Battalion H.Q. during the October 4th battle. The Pheasant farm and trench area was being softened up in preparation for the next stage of operations. The enemy retaliated at 4 p.m. with a heavy barrage east of the Steenbeek. They followed this up with yet another heavy barrage at 7 p.m. At 8.30 p.m. Col Scothern (Borders) arrived at Battalion H.Q. Each Company reported to H.Q. that its own relief was complete as they moved back from the front line. Lance Sergeant Tebbutt was killed by a stray bullet whilst passing Battalion H.Q. and like so many men on the Salient his grave was later lost.

13905 Lance Sergeant Albert Tebbutt was 21 years of age and a native of Beeston, Notts. He is commemorated on the Tyne Cot Memorial.

Another man would die that day from wounds received earlier.

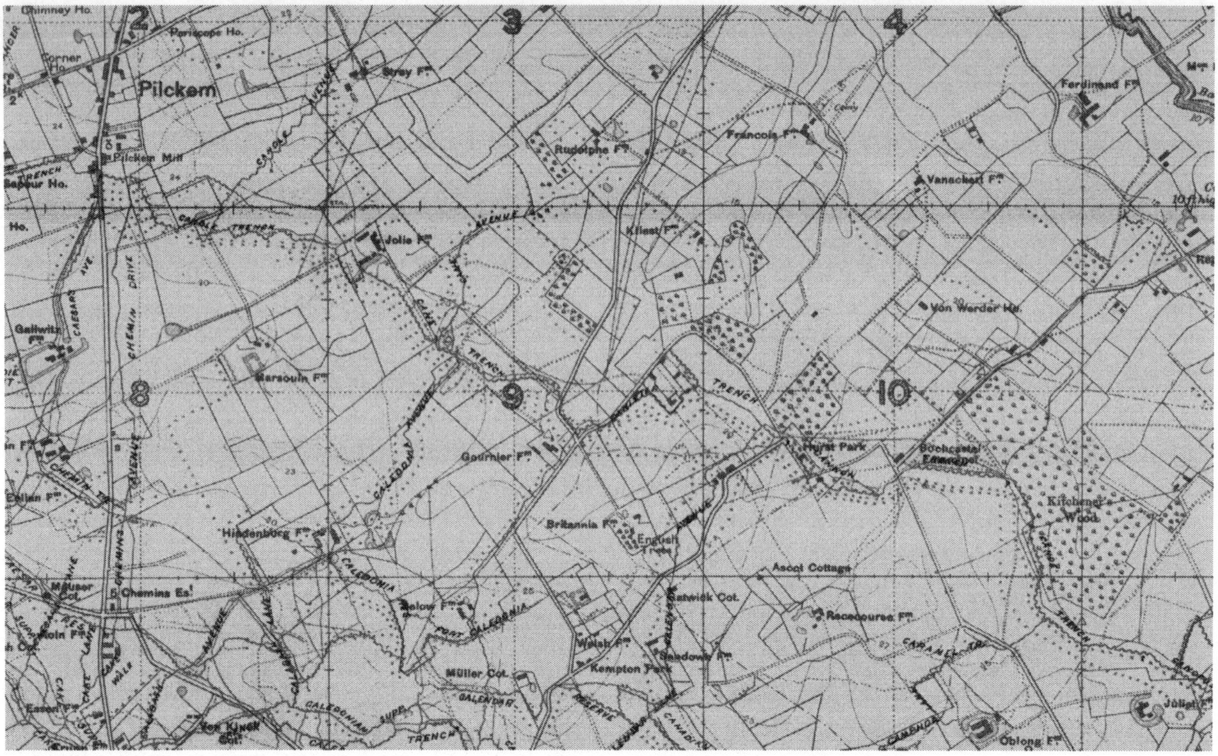

Gournier Farm with Francois Farm and Von Werder House to the North East. The Steenbeek is in the top right hand corner of the map.

10400 Private William Dolphin was 28 years of age and had previously served with the 2nd Battalion. He is buried at Brandhoek New Military Cemetery No.3 and grave I.D.28.

By 12.40 a.m. on 21st the relief was completed, although it would take some time for all of the Companies to reach Gournier Farm. Headquarters had to lay up for 20 minutes after coming under heavy shellfire. They had just commenced their move back when the shelling occurred and it was probable that the enemy had seen the movement particularly as each Company had already passed through. The H.Q. men eventually reached Gournier Farm at 3 a.m. and two of the Companies were already there. It would be 7 a.m. before 'C' Company finally made an appearance.

The Battalion may have been out of the front line but it was by no means out of the firing line. They would be employed in supporting the other Battalions of the Brigade in the line. If anything this was a more difficult undertaking than being in the front line trenches. The men would have to struggle through the clinging mud on duckboard tracks. Many men slipped off the tracks and vanished forever in the Flanders mud.

At 4 a.m. on 21st orders were received to detail carrying parties from Francois Farm and Von Werder House to The Steenbeek, and under normal circumstances two Companies would work and two would rest. The Salient though was anything but normal and the whole Battalion would have to participate. Moving the stores and ammunition to maintain the offensive operations on the salient was nothing short of a nightmare. After weeks of heavy shelling the delicate drainage system was shattered, added to this the wettest summer on record filled shell holes with water and turned the Salient into a quagmire.

Wooden duckboards crossed the battlefield but one slip and a man could vanish in putrid water or become trapped in the clinging mud. It was virtually impossible to move anything other than by manpower and a two-man lift took four men and occasionally as many as eight. During the work 'C' Company had casualties of nine men wounded and one killed. Two men actually died and are both commemorated on the Tyne Cot Memorial.

26189 Private Herbert Arthur Bird was a Nottingham man.

67637 Private David Randolf Waind was just 19 years of age and a Yorkshire lad.

The following day another man died of his wounds and is buried at Lijssenthoek Military Cemetery.

56463 Private Sam Stead of A Company was 40 years of age and a Chesterfield man.

A Brigade order arrived at 10.30 p.m. detailing an advance to Bulow Farm (north of The Cockcroft) and all Companies were ordered to be ready to move as from 5.25 p.m. on 22nd in support of this attack. Zero hour was 4.45 a.m., the advance being made by 6th Lincolns and at 5.15 a.m. the C.O. proceeded to Brigade Headquarters to ascertain how the advance was proceeding. At 5.25 a.m. all Companies stood to in readiness to move off. In the event the advance was a complete success and the Battalion was not called upon.

As darkness fell at 9 p.m. carrying parties from all of the companies were detailed to get stores up to the Steenbeek. At 4 a.m. on 23rd Brigade orders were received detailing the battalion to relieve the 6th Lincolns and the C.O. moved up to the front line to make the necessary arrangements. The Lincolns had been ordered to occupy Pheasant Trench and Vieilles Maisons during the night of 22nd/23rd and if found unoccupied hand it over to the battalion. At 10 p.m. the Battalion moved off following guides to the Lincolns positions carrying with them everything they would need in the way of rations and water for the 24th. The Lincolns reported at 11.30 p.m. that both Pheasant Trench and Vieilles Maisons were occupied by the enemy and in light of this the battalion relieved them at Mon Bulgar. The relief was fully completed by 12.40 a.m. on 24th. The Borders reported at 12.23 a.m. that their section of Pheasant Trench was also occupied by the enemy and it would be up to the higher command to decide if further advances would be made. The daylight hours were extremely quiet and this gave ample opportunity for the observation of the battalion's area of operations. Once again an order received at 5.55 p.m. showed just how difficult conditions were on the Salient. The Battalion was ordered to put up a smokescreen on 26th and at the same time the York's received orders to deliver the smoke bombs. It would take over 24 hours for the York's to collect and deliver the smoke bombs, a task usually lasting no more than a couple of hours. The enemy put down a very heavy barrage at 11 p.m. in answer to an earlier one by the British heavy guns. The Division on the right put up S.O.S. flares but after an hour the enemy artillery ceased without a counter attack materialising. At the time 'A' and 'B' Companies were delivering rations but fortunately escaped the shelling. Both companies were commended for their excellent work, with 'A' Coy. moving rations from Minty Farm to Mon Bulgar and 'B' Coy. from Bulgar to the front line.

The first entry of the diary for 25th stated, " Weather fine" and in the summer of 1917 this was somewhat of a novelty. The enemy continued to shell the Langemarck Road to Mon Bulgar, meanwhile the British 4.5 Howitzers were having problems finding their range. Either that or they did not have the up to date locations of the British infantry as they continually shot short. The diarist was not impressed:

> *"7.45 to 8.15 p.m. – 30 rounds – 1 per minute – fired at Haanixbeek Fm by* **our** *4,5 Hows. 8.15 – 8.35 p.m. – About 10 rounds every three minutes fired at Haanixbeek Fm by our 4.5 Hows. Reported but no effect"*

The battalion had been in that area for days and it seems inconceivable that the Artillery did not know this. In defence of the Artillery though it was possible that worn barrels and not incompetence caused the error but this was no consolation for the P.B.I. suffering on the front line.

The Battalion once again got the rations through to the front line despite heavier shelling and the conditions under foot. No casualties were recorded for 25th August.Once again the Division on the right sent up S.O.S. flares and a heavy enemy barrage ensued in answer to the British shelling. It would seem that the Division on the right had the 'wind up' as nothing untoward happened.

A number of officers arrived during the night as preparations for the attack on the 27th August was made. The fifth army needed to move its artillery up to the Steenbeek but this was no easy matter on the sodden salient and the ridge east of the Steenbeek was still in enemy hands. Therefore only limited operations could be undertaken at the time. The C.O., Adjutant, O.C.s Companies, Intelligence Officer and Supply Officer of the West Yorkshire Regiment all arrived. The O.C. of each Company being sent up to visit the front line and inspect the ground. Meanwhile the senior officers made arrangements for the Battalions relief. More officers arrived including those of the six-inch Howitzer Battery, Light Trench Mortars, Machine Gun Company and 18 Pounder batteries.

At 3 a.m. on 26th two wounded men from the 6th Lincolns were found and recovered from a part of Bulow Farm. One of the major problems of the campaign was the recovery of wounded men and many waited for days, some dying before help arrived. Another batch of officers arrived at Battalion H.Q. with visits from 6 inch Howitzer Officer Col. Coleridge and Brigadier General Price being recorded.

At 4.40 a.m. a smoke barrage was put up on Bulow Farm and the right hand part of 'B' Companies location. This was to test the enemy reaction prior to the attacks on 27th August, although the result was just one anti tank gun opening fire. The Battalion would not participate in the forthcoming assault and at noon on 26th, orders arrived detailing the relief. The C.O. sent orders to the rear for the battalion transport to be ready. The assaults, which took place on 27th, would be the last for almost a month and indeed the German generals thought the British Campaign had ended. Nothing could be further from the truth and the battalion would be back in October to play its part in further attacks.

Officially the Battle of Langemarck ran from 16th to 18th August 1917 but as has been seen further minor operations took place. Lord Haig did though mention the operations in his dispatch of 25th December 1917 '. *On 19th, 22nd and 27th August, positions of considerable local importance in the neighbourhood of St. Julien were captured with some hundreds of prisoners, as the result of minor attacks, conducted under the most unfavourable conditions of ground and weather. The ground gained represented an advance of about 800 yards on a front of over two miles'.*(Paragraph 48 extract Lord Haig's Dispatch 25th December 1917. taken from 'A record of the Battles and engagements of the British Armies in France and Flanders, 1914-1918 by Captain E.A. James 1924)

At 10 p.m. guides were sent out to M Bridge (Yser Canal) to show the new troops the route, although heavy rain once again caused major problems. The heavy clouds and rain left the Salient in total blackness and this delayed the relief. On the return several of the Battalions platoons wandered around aimlessly before finally arriving back.Once again the diary tells the story with few words "10 p.m. Rain hard. – 11.30 p.m. Clears up. – 27th 2 a.m. Rains again. 3.15 a.m. – relief complete."

It had taken over five hours for the men to walk a couple of miles. The rain continued but by 6.53 a.m. the Battalion was settled in Murat Camp. The men could rest and clean up after a torrid few days in the mud of the salient. Men of 32nd brigade would not be resting as at 1.55. p.m. the battle began but on the 9th Battalions old front it was a complete failure except for the capture of part of Vielles Maison. The preparatory work carried out by 33rd Brigade had come to nought, although it was not for the want of trying. It was the weather and not the enemy that had stopped the attack.

Four men from the battalion had died on 26th August and none of them have a known grave. They are all commemorated on the Tyne Cot Memorial within the vast Tyne Cot Cemetery.

11699 Private Reginald Heath was 24 years of age and had previously served in the 1st Battalion. He was born in Gresley Derbyshire but living with his mother in Nottingham prior to enlistment.

28104 Lance Corporal Ralph Hutson was previously in the 17th Battalion and he was a Nottingham man.

5053 Private Mark Toon was a 1st Battalion man prior to his service in 9th. He was renumbered in 1916 to 335053. He was born in Stamford Lincs.

13438 Private John Woodward was a native of Shirland Derbyshire.

After the mud and rain of the past days, the men were sent to the Divisional baths and also issued with clean underclothing. The 28th was a day of inspections, cleaning up and relaxing, which was probably a blessing as it rained all day again. At 6.p.m. orders were received for a move to Brake Camp at A 30 Central.

At 6.50 a.m. on 29th the Battalion moved off and away from the Salient and the horrors it contained. They arrived at 8.40 a.m. and the Companies were put at the disposal of their O.C.s for inspections, cleaning and reorganisation. The following day followed much the same pattern but the 31st would see training begin once again. Physical Training, bayonet practice and specialized training were undertaken. The men had the opportunity to bathe once again, the second time in four days, followed by the issue of clean underclothing. This more than anything shows how the insidious mud and grime of the salient ingrained itself into the men's clothing and skin.

So ended another month for the battalion and all that was left was the monthly reckoning.

August 1917 –

	Officers	OR
Strength on 1st August –	39	894
15th	41	885
27th	39	815
31st	39	1004

Reinforcements joined during month –
217

Casualties during month	Killed	Wounded
	14	50

Two ex Battalion Officers both paid the ultimate price on the 20th.

2nd/Lieut Harold F. Young was with 43rd Squadron Royal Flying Corps and aged 19 years. He is commemorated on the Arras Flying Services Memorial. He had been wounded whilst with the Battalion on 26 September 1916.

2/Lieut Hugh T. Orchard was with 15th Battalion and buried at Villers-Faucon Communal Cemetery.

What did Col. Scothern make of the period from 15th to the end of August?

> *"Siege Camp provided a resting place for one night, and on the 15th the battalion was in dug-outs on the Canal Bank in reserve and readiness to support the 33rd Brigade who were attacking on the 16th. The advance was successful and the battalion moved forward to conform to this, Battalion H.Q. being situated at Gournier Farm.*
>
> *On the night of the 17th the 33rd Brigade took over the Divisional Front. The relief was extremely difficult owing to the darkness. This made it very hard to keep to the duckboard tracks, and as the ground was a little short of a morass; woe betides the unlucky individual who strayed. The guides also lost the way, and it was very late before the final relief was reported finished. Battalion H.Q. were then at Haanixbeek Farm.*
>
> *The 6th Borders relieved on the 20th and the battalion went back to the Gournier Farm area. The enemy shelling in this area was particularly heavy, and the working parties suffered severely. It was not al all unusual at this time for the whole battalion to be on carrying parties, and one had to be a participant to thoroughly realise the terrible conditions under which the men were living at the time.*
>
> *Slight advances of the line were constantly being made and on the 22nd the 6th Lincolns were ordered to take Bulow Farm. The battalion 'Stood to' ready to help, but the operation was successfully carried out, and no help was needed. However, the Lincolns were relieved at Mon Bulgar by the Sherwood Foresters on the 23rd, who were in turn relieved by at the end of three days by the 32nd Brigade.*
>
> *This Brigade attacked the next day, but unsuccessfully, and it was thought that the 33rd Brigade would have to go back again, but this proved without foundation, and the battalion went back to 'O' Camp preparatory to moving back still further for rest"*

The month of September would be a quiet one for the battalion and plenty of sport and recreation would be the order of the day. Training would also be undertaken in preparation for the battalion's next battle. Once again this would be on the Ypres salient when the Battle of Broodseinde was launched on 4th October. The battalion would be tasked with taking Poelcappelle on the left flank. This though was for the future and the men could spend a month forgetting about the war.

Col Scothern wrote:

> *"… The battalion remained at 'O' Camp for a week, and then moved south to Poperinghe to Forth camp. The stay at this camp was one of the pleasantest in the history of the battalion. Afternoons were devoted almost entirely to sport, which embraced cricket, football, Association and Rugby, cross-country running, and a battalion sports meeting. The last named in particular was most successful, being held on a sunny Sunday afternoon with the Divisional band in attendance. The war was forgotten for the time being.*
>
> *On September 11th the battalion moved still further back to the vicinity of Houtkerque training for another attack, and remained there three weeks. Companies were rather scattered, but again the stay was very enjoyable, although the training was hard. Sport was again to the fore, and a well-organised platoon football competition was followed with a great deal of interest. No. 14 Platoon eventually proved the winners, but only after a stiff struggle. The Brigade also held a very successful sports meeting in which the Battalion did well.*
>
> *The training was all devoted to the forthcoming attack on Poelcappelle, and was carried out very thoroughly, several rehearsals on a set stage being gone through. By the end of September, everything was ready, and the battalion moved off to Siege Camp on October 1st in lorries."*

Saturday, 1st September was a fairly relaxed day with some Company training carried out on ground to the east of the camp. During the afternoon the Platoons and Sections were reorganised as the new reinforcements had to be integrated within the battalion structure prior to the real training commencing. The men were also to get new uniforms and as the diary put it ' Fitting of new clothing' took place in the afternoon.Basically it would be a question of the men swapping what was issued to get a better fit after queuing at the QM stores and being given a uniform 'roughly your size'.

Sunday 2nd saw Church services in the morning followed by an afternoon of sport. Football and cricket matches were played on an inter platoon basis but sadly none of the scores were mentioned in the war diary. More than anything it was a time for the men to relax and put thoughts of the war to the back of their minds.

A time for reading letters, writing home and one of relief for surviving once again. After their time on the Salient in July and August the men needed a period of total relaxation and recuperation. The Battles of Ypres had pushed the British Army to its limit, mentally and physically. Moral was not at a high level and British Commanders did not want the French mutinies to spread to their own army. The men would need as much recovery time as possible before the inevitable return to the Salient.

Monday 3rd saw another man die but the cause is unclear. He is buried at Calais Southern Cemetery and a number of General hospitals were based here in WW1.

7351 Private Herbert Fox was 46 years of age and a native of Dewsbury Yorkshire. He is buried in grave H.5.4.

Monday 3rd was a day of training and split into two segments – 9-12 noon and 2-30pm – 4.30pm. Platoon and Company training embraced close order drill, physical and bayonet training, gas helmet drill, musketry and practice attacks. The lessons of the August battles had to be learned quickly in preparation for the next visit to the salient. Ways of combating the new German defence in depth and concrete bunkers had to be devised. The specialists also honed their skills with special training for the Lewis Gunners, Signallers, Grenadiers and Scouts. The Grenadiers used rifle grenades and these were a vital piece of weaponry for trench warfare. They could clear trenches but also be used to break up the counter attacks that always followed an assault. It had always been the case that taking the trench was not the problem, keeping it was.

Orders were received that the Brigade would move to a new camp the following day and at 7.30 a.m. on the 4th the battalion left 'O' camp and moved to Forth Camp (ref sheet 27 square 15b), arriving at 9.30 a.m. The remainder of the day consisted of rest and recreational training. The 5th followed the same pattern as the 3rd with platoon and company training.

Even though the battalion was out of the line and at rest, daily situation reports would arrive from Corps headquarters. For example the 6th September mentioned: -

Artillery – enemy and British.
Air activity- Enemy – machine gunning the front and bombing the rear lines.
Work – Enemy working parties and their positions.
Movement – Enemy movement in the area.
Patrols – British patrols along the trenches. It has to be remembered that the enemy and British held many trenches at the same time. These would have barbed wire blockades and bombing posts.
Weather forecast.
Enemy's defences – The state of his defences.
Infantry activity – Any patrols or raiding parties would be noted.
Aircraft – This was put in to specifically note a new enemy Tri-plane and the fact that it had been mistaken for a British plane.
Identification of the Enemy's units – This mentioned a body being recovered and his uniform being that of the 1st Res. Coy. 18th Pioneer Regiment.

Information from the British front – Photographs had shown the British line to be continuous between Dadizeele and Menin.

Aeroplane Photographs were listed so that units could indent for them if needed.

If the battalion was called upon in a hurry they would have all the information needed at hand to occupy any area of the front.

The following four days were set aside for recreational training with various sports and games being contested. No doubt the inter platoon football matches were popular and keenly contested. The period culminated on Saturday 9th with the battalion sports day and adding to the festivities was the attendance of the Divisional band between 3 and 4.30 p.m. The following day was given over to divine services and rest. All of the men would have appreciated the opportunity to relax totally for those few days.

At 10 a.m. on 11th the battalion moved to a new billeting area near Houtkerque, which was east of Poperinghe.

On arrival at 1.30 p.m. the disposition of the battalion was as follows:

Battalion H.Q., 'A' Coy and two platoons of 'D' Coy in farm buildings and tents at E. 19.b.1.5. – Gig Farm on map above.
'C' Company and transport lines in farm and tents at E.19.c.6.1. – Ralph Farm on map
'B' Company in Farm and tents at A.20.c.1.9. and 'D' Company – 2 platoons in farm at A.24.d.7.0. (Should they be D and not A?)

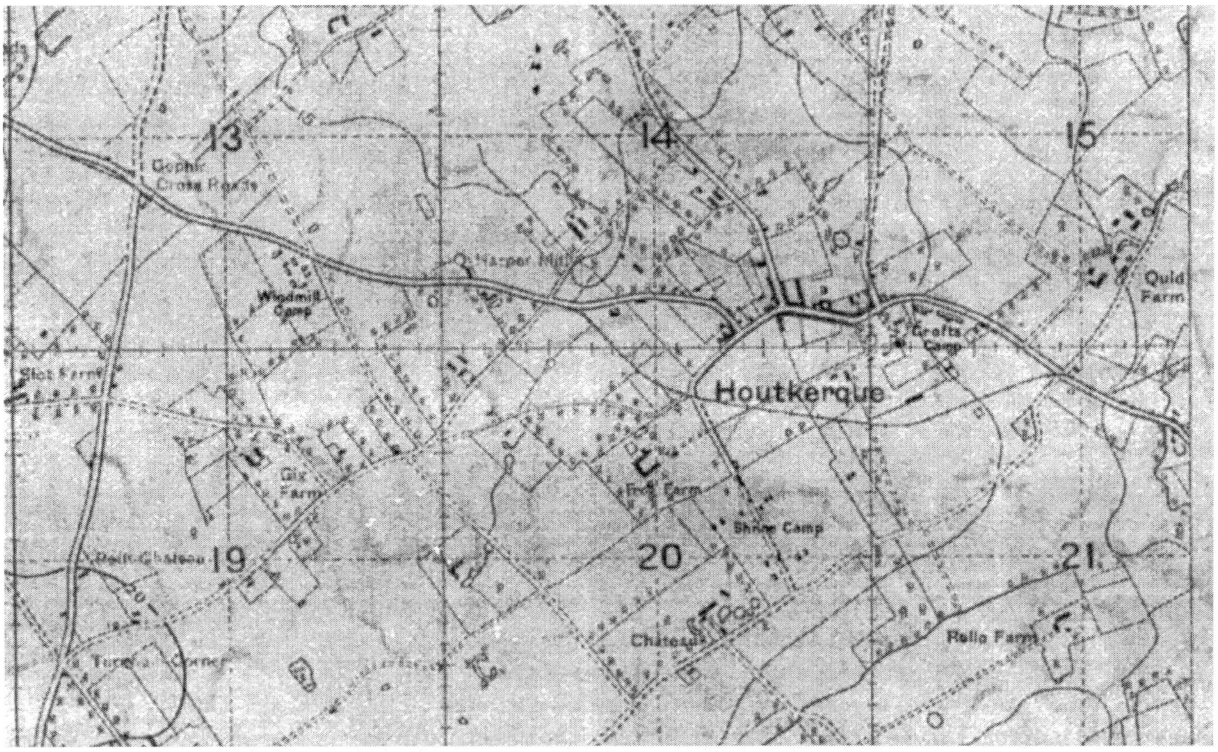

The battalion would remain at these locations until the end of September and training would continue in preparation for the forthcoming battle. A combination of platoon, company and battalion training was carried out. Recreational training with inter platoon football and route marches of between 7 and 8 miles also kept the men fit. The officers took part in a regimental exercise on 20th giving them the opportunity to work closely with their opposite numbers in the other battalions of the brigade.

Time was also given over to night operations – forming up for night attacks on taped lines, message sending and night movement.

Sunday 23rd saw the men attend divine service followed by a visit to the brigade baths. The training continued and emphasise was put on the battalion attack which was practised on three days prior to a rehearsal with the 7th South Staffs. The 27th saw all surplus personnel for the next operation move to the 11th Divisional Depot at Houtkerque. In the meantime the remainder of the battalion continued practising with the 29th seeing the last day of training:

29th September 1917-

9-10am – Physical training, Bayonet Fighting.

10-12 noon – Companies rehearse attack to be made in forthcoming operations.

1.30-4.30 pm – Rehearsal of Battalion attack.

9 pm – Night operations – forming up for the attack on taped lines.

Sunday 30th September –

10am – Rehearsal of Battalion attack with 7th South Staffordshire Regiment.

The quiet month of September had ended and the battalion was once again ready to enter the fray. Within a week some 250 men would be casualties but the village of Poelcappelle would be taken and one man would have won the ultimate accolade given by the British Military.

Col. Scothern wrote:

"October 3rd was uneventful except that the enemy put down a heavy barrage at 5 a.m. At 8.30 a.m. tapes marking the forming up positions were laid, and the battalion moved off on these at 1 a.m. on 4th.

The straggling village of Poelcappelle was the objective, and considerable trouble was expected from Pillboxes and machine gun emplacements.

The whole operation however had been carefully rehearsed on ground marked to represent the exact scale, and methods of dealing with the known machine gun nests devised, so that the men had the fullest confidence in themselves.

'A' Company and half of 'B' Company led the attack, which commenced punctually at 6 a.m. Just before Zero hour the Germans put down a heavy barrage which fortunately

missed the first wave, though the supporting companies suffered somewhat from it.

The first objective was successfully reached after some stiff fighting, and there halted for one hour. 'D' Company and the rest of 'B' Company then pushed on, and reached the second objective by 10 a.m., 'D' Company having considerable trouble at Ferdan House.

The casualties were rather heavy, and by this time there was only one unwounded officer left. The N.C.O.'s however, rose to the occasion and the positions were rapidly consolidated.

For some time matters were quiet, but in the afternoon the enemy delivered a heavy counter-attack on the Brigade on the left, whose troops fell back. The 9th Sherwood Foresters, true to their traditions, stuck to their positions although exposed to heavy flanking fire, and by throwing out extra posts, formed a defensive flank, and temporarily restored the situation.

The lost part of the line was eventually regained. The night of 4/5th was exceptionally quiet, and the next day there was only intermittent shelling.

The battalion was relieved on the evening of the 5th by 6th Borders. This was delayed for some time owing to shelling and the darkness but when the men got up matters were easier, and relief proceeded without a hitch. Companies moved back to the area around Cane Post where in the words of a participant 'We were fairly comfortable considering everything'. Here they stayed until October 7th when they were relieved, and the battalion proceeded to Siege Camp'.

On October 1st the battalion left Houtkerque at 8-30 am and proceeded by bus to Siege camp, arriving at 12.30 pm. (Sheet 28 NW Belgium B.20.d.7.6.). The men spent the remainder of the day resting. The C.O. proceeded by bus to visit trenches although it is doubtful a bus could get any closer that the Canal Bank. Major S.H. Piper would take no part in the forthcoming battle and proceeded to England on Senior Officers Course.

The following morning at 2am the Trench equipment was issued and packs etc dumped, in general getting ready for the move forward.

After a fairly dry September the rain also began to fall on 2nd and grew gradually worse as the days passed. From the afternoon of 4th, heavy rain fell for almost a week and it was probably this that dissuaded the enemy from counter-attacks.

The Battalion proceeded by Company to relieve 32nd Brigade in left sector of 11th Division front as per the Relief Table, A and B Companies to the front line, D Company to Cane Post and C Coy to the Canal Bank. HQ – Dog Houses V 29 B 9. 3 (Cane Post C.9.a)

By 9.40 pm the relief was completed without any problems.

At 5 am on 3rd the enemy put down on the line Dog House – Below Farm a fairly heavy barrage. This line was the reserve line some 300 yards behind the front. Final arrangements for attack were made during day and then it was a question of waiting until zero the following morning. Also after the enemy barrage on the reserve line there was a fair amount of praying that the same would not happen to them.

The first man to die in the battalion during this period was –

70230 Private John Reginald Cory, who was living in Mitcham Surrey but had enlisted at Chesterfield, He like so many of the men killed during the battle is commemorated on the Tyne Cot Memorial.

At 6.30 pm Captain J Critchlow MC, Lt Bowyer, and the Scouts put out tapes for Battalion to form up on.

The day of the battle dawned early for the battalion and at 1 am they moved to form up on tapes for attack as per O.O. No 50.

Boundary on left adjusted with S.L.I (1st Bn. Somerset Light Infantry 11th brigade, 4th Division) and on the right with 7th S Staffs.

At 4.52 a.m. the Battalion formed up in readiness for Zero and Brigade was informed. Battalion HQs established at Pheasant Farm. At 6 am Zero the British artillery opened up with a massive barrage. The artillery had been firing practice barrages for a number of days to confuse the enemy and unlike the early battles no extended length barrage was used. The men would move forward under a protective barrage instead. – ***See narrative of events.*** Ten tanks were also assigned to the 11th Division attack and although the enemy were driven out of Poelcappelle they would infiltrate back into parts of this sprawling village. Efforts would be made on the 9th October to rectify this but with no success and heavy casualties.

Rations where sent up by line party to Companies but were rather short on arrival. The men would not have been best pleased by their colleague's efforts but they did have iron rations to keep them going.

(At this point the narrative of the battle by the Commanding officer 9th Sherwood's will be inserted. Followed by 33rd Infantry Brigade Operational Orders for October and then the diary will be recommenced)

9th Service battalion The Sherwood Foresters.
To; Headquarters,
33rd. Brigade.
Narrative of Events During Recent operations.
On the morning of October 4th, the battalion was forming up for attack on 'A' and 'B' lines by 4.50 a.m. The forming up was carried out without incident – a strongish breeze was blowing and a slight drizzle prevailed.

The battalion was formed to attack the two objectives on a three-platoon front, as under: -

For first Objective:

LEFT – "A" Company in two waves of two platoons each.

RIGHT- Two Platoons of "B" Company in two waves of one platoon each.

For Second Objective: -

LEFT – "D" Company in same formation as above.

RIGHT – Two platoons of "B" Company in same formation as above.

The Reserve Company, formed up in artillery formation about U. 30, a. 1. 4.

Platoons of first waves were formed in two lines of sections in file with a screen 20 yards in front of section columns.

Platoons of second waves were formed up as above but without the screen of scouts.

At 5.30 a.m. the enemy began to shell the area between PHEASANT FARM and SNIPE HOUSE causing considerable casualties to the Reserve Company.

The guns opened exactly at 6 a.m. and leading Companies at once moved close up to the barrage.

No serious opposition was encountered on the way to the first objective and by 7.18 a.m. "B" Company on the RIGHT had reported capture of 1st. objective and that the company was in touch on both flanks.

During the advance on the first objective all four platoons closed up to barrage in one wave and kept if anything rather two (his spelling) close to the barrage. The company experienced difficulty in keeping direction partly owing to the darkness and partly to the fact that the troops on our RIGHT inclined away rather to the right. The Company Officers found great difficulty in rectifying this.

On the LEFT of the Company Front, the enemy were cleared out of some consolidated shell holes after slight resistance. The Company reached the first objective right on top of the barrage – the two half companies were sorted out with little difficulty. Two fortified shell holes were found on the objective each holding a Machine Gun; the enemy ran back taking the locks with him. (These two machine guns were claimed by an officer of the Somerset L.I. whose company had straggled along behind our attacking Companies. There was no officer of the Battalion present at the time and the N.C.O. in charge gave up the guns)

The two platoons for the second objective moved up to the protective barrage whilst the other two consolidated.

Meanwhile, "A" Company on the LEFT moved forward. 2/Lieut J Adamson M.C., the Acting Company Sergeant Major, and two platoon sergeants were hit. This Company also experienced slight loss of direction, but as the light became stronger it was rectified. On topping the rise the Company came under Machine gun fire and a number of men were hit. Men could not see the barrage owing to the wet ground and a number tried to get near H.E. bursting on the ground; this caused some casualties.

Three machine guns were met in shell holes; in two cases the enemy picked up the gun and ran back with it.

After the first quarter of an hour rifles began to jam with mud and wet, otherwise more of the retiring enemy would have been killed.

The enemy seemed disinclined to surrender but ran back before the advancing troops got to within 20 yards, in nearly all cases leaving their rifles behind them.

There was no fighting at close quarters.

Very good use was made of captured machine guns and our own Lewis guns against the retiring enemy.

The Company noticed that the enemy had a trick of lying quiet while our troops passed over, after which they would get up and surrender to the stretcher-bearers.

The Company reached its objective and found the large concrete emplacement at V 19 a. 5.1. It was found to be occupied with 2 machine guns on top and two on the flanks outside. Corporal Greaves accompanied by Sergeant Terry, seeing that there was no time to deal with it in any other way, rushed forward and threw a bomb inside. Five men inside surrendered but in the rush 20 others ran back. Four machine guns were in this emplacement. Posts were pushed out under the protective barrage.

On the barrage moving forward, the two rear platoons of "B" Company on the RIGHT moved in good formation and direction was easily kept. Two fortified shell holes were found with a machine gun in each; the enemy ran back taking the locks with him.

The final objective now being taken, the half company quickly dug in under fire of snipers and machine guns. Communication was established with a Tank at V. 19. b. 6.2. and S.A.A. and Lewis Gun Panniers fetched over to the Company position in the front line.

On the Left of the second advance, "D" Company, which had followed up "A" Company, to the first objective, moved forward to the second and whilst waiting under the protective barrage a number of casualties were caused by Machine Gun Fire from FERDAN HOUSE. By the time the barrage lifted there was only one officer left with the Company.

FERDAN HOUSE was found to be occupied by one machine gun team and a Trench Mortar Battery; these were all either killed or captured.

On reaching the final objective posts were put out and touch established with the Somerset L.I. and "B" Company. Captain J. F. Mc.Cormack was killed putting out the front line posts. C.S.M Betesta established Company Headquarters at FERDAN HOUSE and sent patrols up to the protective barrage.

Shortly after 1p.m. the Somerset L.I. on our LEFT retired about 400 yards and were followed up by a line of Germans and some snipers who fired across our positions. During this period, Sergeant Carlisle of "D" Company organized small groups of two different regiments from the Brigade on our left and eventually succeeded in establishing touch on the flank. He also brought two captured machine guns and two Lewis guns to bear on this attack. During this period, "D" Company's posts were not moved, but later when the Somerset L.I. came up again the three posts on the LEFT were withdrawn about 100 yards in order to keep in touch.

2/Lieut: W.J. Trenaman was sent from "B" Company to take command of "D" Company. On his being wounded later in the afternoon, Lieutenant R. V. Bowyer was sent up from Battalion Headquarters to take over command.

About 3 p.m. it was reported that a shell had burst in "B" Company's Headquarters severely wounding Capt. E.W. Grimsdale. Also about the same time came across the news that Captain N.G. Smith commanding "A" Company was wounded. Capt J. Critchlow then went up to replace him.

Nothing further of mark followed. During the night an enemy patrol about 6 strong was destroyed by our Lewis Gun and rifle fire.

No effort was made by the enemy to counter attack on our own front line and beyond placing a continuous barrage on the line between ROSE HOUSE and DOG HOUSES no activity was shown by him.

It had been hoped to move Battalion Headquarters to ROSE HOUSE, but this place was found to be nothing but a heap of ruins, and as the only available accommodation was urgently required for Companies, no attempt was made to move forward of PHEASANT FARM.

Early in this action, the Reserve Company, which had at first become scattered in shell holes owing to the enemy barrage, moved up to the ROSE HOUSE line and kept in closest touch with the front Companies.

By 8 a.m. messages were being received from a Signal Station at ROSE HOUSE, and by 8 a.m. communication with the front line Companies had also been established.

Lt.Col W. B. THORNTON, D.S.O.
7th October 1917. Lieutenant Colonel.
Commanding 9th. Bn. The Sherwood Foresters.

Message form –
From front.
I am at V.19. b. 2.4
I am at V.19. b.2.4. and am consolidating.

Am held up at V. 19. b.2.4. H G. at V 19. h. 8.6.
I am in touch with Shropshires on left
I am not in touch in – ?????
Hostile ????? active V 19. h. 8.6.
Time – 10 am
Date 4 Oct 1917.
Platoon (crossed out) Now Section
Company 33rd G Coy. Signed (possibly) G N Mc Kiever.
Also has Wounded in heart at?
Very Badly Wounded reported to D Holt.

APPENDIX 1

Summary of Casualties.

	O.	*ORn*
Effective Strength, 1st Oct, 1917	*38*	*995*
Drafts joined	*7*	*141*
Total	*45*	*1136*
Casualties	*15*	*234*

Effective strength Oct, 31st 1917	*30*	*902*
Casualties	*O.*	*OR*
Killed	*3*	*38*
Wounded	*8*	*181*
Missing	*1*	*9*
Evacuated	*3*	*6*
(Struck off Strength)		

Officers Killed: Capt. J.F. Mc Cormack, Lieut. O. St. M. Jones,
2/Lt. E.D Smith
Oct. 4. 1917.

Officers Wounded: 2/Lt. Thurburn, Lt Kingdon, 2/Lt Gallimore, Capt N G Smith, 2/Lt, J Adamson, 2/Lt. Trenaman, Capt. C E Scott, Capt. E. W. Grimsdale.
Oct. 4 1917.

Officers Missing – 2/Lt W. W. Odell (Records show him as killed and on memorial, unknown grave)

Evacuated – Major A.E. Scothern, Major S. H. Piper, 2/Lt Pickard
Struck off strength.

Officers Joined – 2/Lts. Hudson, Archer, Cooper, Schur, Francis, White and Smith
24 and 25 October 1917.

Officers on leave – Lt. Col. W.B. Thornton, D.S.O. Capt. J.C. Critchlow.

33rd Infantry Brigade Instructions for Operations October 1917.
On 4th October 1917 the Battle of Broodseinde, part of 3rd Ypres (Passchendaele) began. The 9th (service) Battalion The Sherwood Foresters took part in an attack on Poelcappelle.

B/N/SR/19 Copy No 4 27-9-17
Ref POELCAPPELLE
Sheet 1/10,000
33rd INFANTRY BRIGADE INSTRUCTIONS
For OPERATIONS – Sept/October 1917.
PREAMBLE

1. *Plans for the forthcoming operations by 33rd Infantry Brigade, discussed at Brigade Hd, Qrs on 24th instant, will be issued from time to time in the form of instructions.*

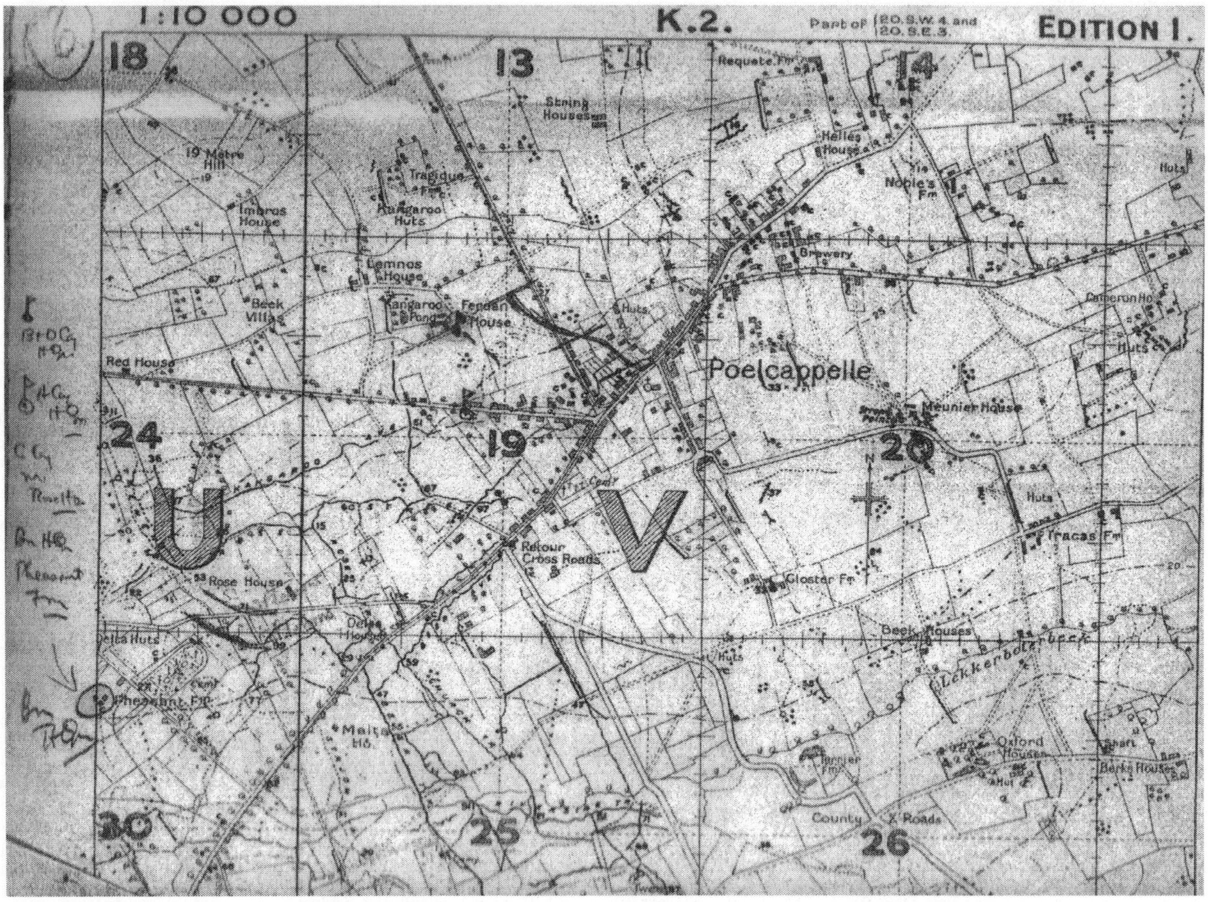

Battalion and Company H.Q's on 4th October 1917. Pheasant Farm and Ferdan House.

Copies of these instructions as necessary will be issued under: –

6th Lincoln R. Copy No.1
6th Border Regt. Copy No 2.
7th South Staffordshire Rgt. Copy No 3
9th Sherwood Foresters Copy No 4
33rd Machine Gun Coy. Copy No 5
33rd L.T.M. Battery Copy No 6
C.R.A. 11th Division Copy No 7
11th Division Copy No 8
33rd Bde Supply Officer Copy No 9
A.D.M.S. 11th Division Copy No 10
Brigadier General Comdg. Copy No 11
Staff Captain Copy No 12
Intelligence Copy No 13
Signals. Copy No 14
34th Infantry Brigade Copy No 15
Office. Copy No 16
32nd Infantry Brigade. Copy No 17

2. The following Appendices as necessary will be issued with these Instructions:
Appendix A. – Artillery Arrangements.
Appendix B. – Machine Gun Arrangements.
Appendix C. – Trench Mortar Arrangements.
Appendix D. – Signal Arrangements.
Appendix E. – Co-operation of Tanks.
Appendix F – Co-operation of Special Coy, R.E.
Appendix G. – Contact Aeroplane arrangements.
Appendix H. – R.E. Arrangements.
Appendix I. – Intelligence.
Appendix J – Reports to be rendered by Brigade (Units during Operations)
Appendix K. – Administrative Instructions.
Appendix L. – Table of weights to be carried by troops in action.
Please acknowledge. G. DeClair, Capt, Brigade Major, 27th September 1917, 33rd Infantry Brigade.

SECRET Copy No 4
33rd Infantry Brigade Order No.100. 3/10/17.
Ref POELCAPPELLE Map 1/10,000

1. *On a date and an hour to be notified later, the 11th Division will attack the enemy opposite their front.*
2. *The 11th Division attack will be carried out by 34th Infantry Brigade on the right and 33rd Infantry Brigade on the left. The 11th Inf. Bde (4th Division) will attack on the left of the 33rd Infantry Brigade.*
3. *The 33rd Infantry Brigade will attack on a two Battalion front – 7th South Staffs Regt on the right and 9th Sherwood Foresters on the left.*
4. *The attack will be made under an artillery barrage and will be carried out in accordance with 33rd Infantry Brigade Instructions, which have been issued to all concerned.*

5.(a) The Objectives will be –
1st Objective:- The RED DOTTED LINE – V.25.b.95.05 – V.19.d.24.20 – V.19.a.22.28 – on which there will be a pause for approximately 1 hour and 10 minutes.
2nd Objective:- The RED LINE – V.26.a.77.53. (on LEKKERBOTERBEEK) V.20.c.12.86 – V.19.b.77.41 – V.19.b.06.88

6. *The boundaries between Brigades and Battalions will be as follows: –*

(1) Between 33rd Inf. Bde (7th S.Staffs and 34th Inf. Brigade (11th Manchester R) – On STEENBEEK at C.5.a.15.10.
On LANGEMARCK ROAD at U.29.d.80.15
On ST JULIAN POELCAPPELLE Road at U.30.b.90.35
Near RETOUR X Roads at V.19.d.27.20
S.E. of POELCAPPELLE CHURCH at V.20.c.10.87.
(2) Between 7th S.Staffs R and 9th Sherwood Foresters –
V.19.b.65.50 – V.19.b.45.20 – V.19.b.25.10 – V.19.c.65.5 – U.24.d.95.15 – U.30.b.5.8.
(3)Between 33rd Inf.Bde (9th Sh. Foresters) and 11th Inf. Bde (1st Somerset Light Infantry); – V.19.b.1.8. = FERDAN HO. (inclusive) to 11th Inf. Bde) – V.19.a.2.2. – U.24.d.45.70 – WHITE HOUSE inclusive to 33rd Inf.Bde – U.29.a.95.25.

Each objective will be consolidated as soon as captured. Strong points will be constructed as detailed in para.14 of 33rd Inf. Bde Instructions.

7. *The closest touch will be maintained with troops on either flank. Troops of 33rd Infantry Brigade will meet troops of 34th Infantry Brigade and 11th Infantry Brigade at the points detailed in para. 16 33rd Inf. Bde Instructions. The meeting of the above liaison parties will be especially reported.*
8. *The role of the 6th Border Regt as Bde Reserve (counter attacking Battn) and 6th Lincoln Regt – Div'l Reserve, as laid down in 33rd Infantry Brigade Instructions will hold good.*
9. *The action of tanks and Contact Aeroplanes as laid down in 33rd Inf.Bde Instructions will be put into effect.*
10. *The action of 33rd M.gun Coy and 33rd L.T.M. Bty as already defined in 33rd Inf.Bde Instructions will be carried out.*

11.(a) 7th South Staffs R and 9th Sh. Foresters will

be formed up in their Battle positions and all arrangements complete for the advance, by Zero minus 1 hour.

11. (b) The necessity of maintaining silence while forming up will be firmly impressed on all rank. Once the troops are formed up, there will be no further movement.

11. (c) The completion of forming up will be notified to Brigade Hd.Qrs by wiring code words as follows: –

7th South Staffs R. "Lieut. ROBINSON"

9th Sh.Foresters "Capt FITZPATRICK"

12 (a) An Officer from 7th S.Staffs.R, 9th Sh.Foresters, 33rd M.Gun Co, 33rd L.T.M.Bty and O.C. Brigade Signals will be at Brigade Hd.Qrs (VARRA FARM) at 8 pm on Y/Z night to synchronize watches.

12 (b) A watch will be sent by O.C. Brigade Signals to H.Q. 6th Border R (CANAL BANK) and H.Q. 6th Lincoln Regt (SIEGE CAMP) at 9.0 p.m. and 9.30. p.m. respectively on Y/Z night for the same purpose.

12 (c) Time will NOT BE SYNCHRONIZED ON THE TELEPHONE

13. Attention is drawn to 11th Div. Battle Standing Orders.

14. The date and hour of zero will be notified later.

Issued at 1.30 p.m. G. DeClair. Capt, Brigade major. 33rd Infantry Brigade.

Copies to: –

No.1 Lincoln R	*No.14. C.R.A. 11th Div.*
No.2 Border R.	*No.15 O.O. Left Group. 11/Div. R.A.*
No.3 S, Staff.R.	*No.16 C.R.E. 11th Div.*
No.4 Sh.Fors	*No.17 A.D.M.S. 11th Divn*
No.5 M.G.Coy	*No.18 32nd Inf.Bde*
No.6 L.T.M.Bty	*No.19 O.C. 'D' Battn.Tanks.*
No.7 11th Inf.Bde.	*No.20 War. Diary.*
No.8 34th Inf.Bde.	*No.21 File.*
No.9 11th Div.	*No.22 XVIIIth Corps Counter Bty*
No.10 B.G.C	
No.11 S.C.	
No.12 I.O.	
No.13 Signals	

A379.

Secret BMS/2/27 Copy no 4

33rd INFANTRY BRIGADE INSTRUCTIONS 27-9-17.

For OPERATIONS Sept/Oct 1917.

Ref – POELCAPPELLE Map 1/10,000 Ed. 3.

1 (a) On a date and at an hour to be detailed later, the XVIIIth Corps in conjunction with the Vth Corps on their right and the XIVth Corps on their left, will attack the enemy's position opposite their front.

1 (b) The XVIIIth Corps attack will be carried out by the 48th Division on the right, and the 11th Division on the left. 4th Division (XIVth Corps) will attack on the left of the 11th Division.

1 (c) The 11th Division attack will be carried out by 34th Infantry Brigade on the right and the 33rd Infantry Brigade on the left. 11th Inf.Bde (4th Division) will attack on the left of the 33rd Infantry brigade.

1 (d) The 11th Division attack will be divided into two phases –

1st Phase – The advance from the BLUE LINE to the RED LINE (B Line)

2nd Phase – The advance from the RED LINE to the GREEN LINE (D Line)

2. 33rd Infantry Brigade attack will be carried out as follows: –

First Phase – Right Attack – 7th South Staffordshire Rgt. Left Attack – 9th Sherwood Foresters.

The 11th Manchester Rgt (34th Bde) will attack on the right of 7th South Staff.R, and the 1st Somerset Light Inf. (11th Bde) on the left of the 9th Sherwood Foresters.

Second Phase Right Attack – 6th Lincolnshire Regt. Left Attack – 6th Border Regt.

The 5th Dorsets (34th Bde) will attack on the right of the 6th Lincoln Regt and the 1st Rifle Brigade (11th Bde) on the left of 6th Border Regt.

3 (a) Each Battalion will be allotted one section of Vickers Machine Guns (4 Guns). This section will be under the direct orders of the Battalion Commander, and will be given definite instructions beforehand as to the positions they are to take up. O.C. 33rd Machine Gun Coy will arrange with Battalion Commanders that the sections of his Company co-operate in all practice attacks carried out by the Battalion to which they will be attached during actual operations.

(b) Two sections (8 Guns) of 33rd Machine Gun Coy will be employed in barrage work during each phase of the operations (Vide Appendix B.)

4 Objectives and boundaries for the above attacks are shewn on the attached map marked M.21/33. (To Brigade Units only)

5. Instructions to the Trench Mortar Battery will be issued later as Appendix C.

6 (a) The formations to be adopted for the attack

will be those agreed upon in recent Brigade Conferences. Battalion Commanders will make a careful study of maps and aeroplane photographs and detail definite units to deal with any known enemy strongholds.

It must be impressed upon the Commanders of these units, that it is their duty to deal with any enemy found in these strongholds and then push forward at once behind the barrage, leaving a small garrison in the reduced strongholds. It is essential that the leading troops keep as close to the barrage as possible.

6 *(b) Every unit will have a reserve.*

6 *(c) It must be impressed upon all ranks that the Rifle and Machine Gun are the first and deadliest weapons of the Infantry in the present type of fighting, and every effort must be made to get forward S.A.A. quickly in order to repel hostile counter-attacks which are certain to be delivered. Special instructions regarding the supply of S.A.A. will be issued later in Appendix K. " Administrative Instructions".*

6 *(d) Subordinate Commanders must understand the value of a local counter-stroke swiftly made against a local enemy counter-attack. This element will be introduced into all practice attacks.*

7. *The attack will be made under an Artillery Barrage, the particulars of which will be forwarded later in Appendix 'A'.*

8. *Battalion Commanders will arrange as soon as possible for a liaison between their own Battalion and battalions of other formations operating on their immediate flank (vide para.2 above). H.Q. of 11th Manchester Regt is at D.16.c.1.9. (sheet 27). And H.Q. of 5th Dorset Regt – D.18.c.2.4. (sheet 27). The locations of Battalions of the 11th Brigade have already been forwarded to those concerned.*

9. *Battalions will each take only 17 Officers into action, and all units will leave out of action (as a minimum) the personnel laid down in the Pamplet – S.S. 133- "Instructions for Training Divisions for Offensive Action".*

10. *Personnel who will not take part in the attack on the actual day will not form part of units during practice attacks.*

11. *A model of the ground over which the Brigade will operate, has been constructed at Brigade Hd.Qrs. Commanding officers of battalions. M.Gun Coy. L.T.M. Bty and Brigade Signal Section, will arrange that all officers and N.C.O.s and as many men as possible, view this model. Each party of other ranks will always be in charge of an officer who will explain the country to his party from the map. Parties will not exceed 30.*

12. *Equipment to be carried by the troops in Battle is laid down in Appendix 'L' (to Brigade Units only)*

ACKNOWLEDGE

G.DeClair, Capt. Brigade Major. 33rd infantry Brigade. 27th September. 1917.

Copies to: – Lincoln R., Border R. S.Staff.R., Sh.Fors., M.Gun Coy., L.T.M.Bty., C/R.A. 11th Div., 11th Division., 33rd B.S. Offr., A.D.M.S. 11/Div., B.G.C., Staff Capt,. Intelligence., Signals., 34th Inf.Bde., 32nd Inf Bdes.

SECRET BUS/2/33 Copy No 4

Ref – POELCAPPELLE MAP 29-9-17

1/10,000.

33RD INFANTRY BRIGADE

INSTRUCTIONS

13 *(a) 7th South Staffordshire Regt and 9th Sherwood Foresters will form up in the area between PHEASANT TRENCH (exclusive) and our present front line (inclusive).*

The boundaries between the Battalions West of our present front line will be: – U.24.d.65.00 – CEMETERY (inclusive to Sherwood Foresters) – PHEASANT FARM (inclusive to Sherwood Foresters) – U.30.a.10.10 – CAT HOUSE.

The forming-up areas will be carefully reconnoitred beforehand. 7th South Staffs R and 9th Sherwood Foresters will form up on lines of tapes and luminous discs which will be placed in position by specially selected parties of N.C.Os and men under an officer in each Battalion. These parties will reconnoiter the forming-up area and also practice laying out the tapes in the back area by day and night beforehand.

13 (b) Constant patrols will ensure that there are no enemy posts or removable obstacles between the forming up positions and the lines on which our barrage comes down at Zero. This barrage line will be 150 yards in front of the forming-up positions. In order to avoid putting the enemy on his guard, the removal of obstacles will take place as late as possible.

14 *(a) The objectives once gained will be consolidated by complete units definitely detailed beforehand and disposed in depth. Strong points will be constructed and garrisoned as follows –*

By 7th South Staffs Regt – in the vicinity of –
Houses at V.19.c.8.1.
House at V.19.c.5.8.
German M.G. Emplacement at V.19.c.35.40.
V.19.c.90.25 (to contain Vickers Gun)
V.19.c.75.50 (to contain Vickers Gun)
V.19.d.6.5. (R.E. to assist).
V.19.d.4.8.
V.19.d.2.9.
V.19.b.60.05.
V.19.b.8.0. (to contain Vickers Gun)
V.19.b.65.20. (to contain Vickers Gun)
By 9th Sherwood Foresters in the vicinity of –
1. V.19.a.3.0, 2. V.19.a.6.2., 3. V.19.a.7.6., 4. V.19.a.8.5., 5, V19.b.0.2.
6. V.19.b.1.6., 7. V.19.b.85.70. 8. V.19.b.35.35. 9. V.19.b.38.25.
10. V.19.b.35.15. 11. V.19.b.30.60. 12. V.19.c.35.33.. 13. U.24.d.65.60. U.24.d.45.75.

14 (b) One half section R.E., each will be attached to 7th South Staffs.Regt and 9th Sh.Foresters to assist in the consolidation of Strong Points at – V.19.d.6.5. and V.19.a.70.45. Infantry parties for these Strong Points will be detailed by Commanding officers before the commencement of operations. The R.E. personnel will be kept at Battalion Headquarters until such time as it is definitely reported that the ground which the strong points are to be constructed has been captured and Commanding Officers are satisfied that consolidation can begin. Careful arrangements for guiding the R.E. personnel to the sites of the strong points must be made beforehand.

15 (This section has been written through with 'Cancelled' but I have included it for historical accuracy)
During the attack by 7th South Staffs regt and 9th Sherwood Foresters, the role of the 6th Border Regt will be one of readiness to deal with any successful hostile counter-attack which the two front Battalions, having used all their resources, have failed to dislodge. The Border Regt. Will not be used to reinforce the battalion in front of them. Close touch will be kept by this Battalion with the situation in front, and routes forward will be reconnoitred as soon as practicable. At Zero minus 6 hours 6th Border Regt will be concentrated in previously reconnoitred positions East and West of the STEENBEKE. After Zero the officer commanding will move his Battalion forward in his own time to the area between PHEASANT FARM and ROSE HOUSE within the Brigade boundaries, so that the whole of his Battalion is concentrated in that area by Zero plus 3 hours. Half-hourly reports as to the progress of this move will be made to brigade Hd.Qrs from Zero plus 30 minutes onwards.
This Battalion will be in readiness to move forward from the area described in the preceding paragraph at short notice, should orders to that effect be received from Brigade H.Q. However, the Officer Commanding is authorized to use his battalion for a counter-stroke without previous reference to Brigade H.Q, should time and urgency of the tactical situation, in his opinion, demand it. Any action taken will be reported to brigade H.Q. at once.
An Officer from among those detailed to go into action will be sent to Brigade Hd.Qrs at Zero hour by this battalion to act as Liaison Officer.
(End of cancelled section)

16. Closest touch will be maintained with troops on the flanks. Arrangements have been made for troops of flank brigades to meet troops of this Brigade as under: –
7th S.Staffs R to meet 11th Manchesters at –
MALTA HOUSE.
POND at V.25.a.9.9.
CROSSROADS V.19.d.40.05.
ROAD JUNCTION at V.19.d.95.90.
9th Sh.Fors to meet 1st Somerset L.Inf at –
TREES AT U.24.d.6.7.
CROSSROADS at V.19.a.3.8.
FERDAN HOUSE V.19.a.7.6.
ON ROAD at V.19.b.05.95.
Special parties will be detailed before Zero to effect the above liaisons.

17. The 11th Division attack will be supported by the Right and Left groups 11th Division Artillery consisting of: –
Right Group – 58TH 256TH, 77TH (army) and 93rd (Army) Brigades R.F.A.
Left Group – 59th, 255th, 34th (Army) and 298th (Army) brigades R.F.A.
STRENGTH 144 Eighteen Pounders.
40 4.5" Howitzers (58 has been crossed out)

18 (a) Barrage Table and further particulars as to the Artillery supporting 33rd Inf.Brigade attack will be published later in Appendix A.

18 (b) Harassing fire and special treatment of enemys' communications will be carried out from now up to Z day.

18 (c) Strong points will be dealt with by the Heavy Artillery, but the general terrain will not be destroyed. The Heavy Artillery have been

asked to give special treatment to the following points between now and Zero –
V.19.b.60.35. Concrete
V.19.b.38.20. Concrete
V.20.a.35.00. Concrete
V.14.c.15.30. Concrete
V.20.a.05.65. Concrete
V.19.a.62.13. Concrete
V.19.c.8.5. Concrete
V.19.b.1.1. Concrete
V.19.b.60.85 Concrete
V.19.b.45.00 Concrete
V.19.d.35.95.Concrete
V.19.a.7.6. (FERDAN HOUSE).
V.19.b.05.95.
AREAS Concrete emplacements etc in area –
V.20.a.05 to V.30.a.5.8.
V.14.c.12 to V.14.c.5.3.
V.19.b..67 to V.19.b.9.4.
V.19.b.88 to V.26.a.5.4.
Area covered by concrete emplacements between junction of roads V.19.b.5.1.

18 (d) The Divisional Artillery will carry out each day short concentrated barrages, varying in intensity, rate and locality.

18 (e) Barrages for the support of the actual attack will be formed in depth, especial attention being paid to localities from which rifle and machine gun fire could be directed by the enemy through the Creeping barrage.

19. The attack will be supported by Machine Gun Barrage of 32 guns from positions about 200 yards in rear of PHEASANT TRENCH, details of which will be issued later.

20. To further demoralize the enemy, opposing the 11th Division, gas will be discharged (wind and weather permitting) towards POELCAPPELLE during the night immediately preceding Zero vide Appendix F. issued herewith.

21. Tanks will co-operate with the 11th Division in the attack. Details will be published later in appendix E.

22. Forward communications will be organized on the plan adopted by the 11th Division during recent operations. Full details as to intercommunication will be published later in Appendix D.

SECRET H.S/3/46 Copy No 4.
3-10-17
33rd Infantry Brigade Instructions.
Herewith new paras. 23 and 24 also addendu to para. 6 (c) – 33rd Infantry Brigade Instructions.
Please Acknowledge.

G.DeClair, Capt, Brigade Major, 33rd Infantry brigade.
Copies – Bde Units. 11th Div. Staff.

Para 23. Coys (Units crossed out) are again reminded of the importance of rendering reports of hostile shelling and any possible short shooting by our own artillery as accurately and in as much detail as possible. Vague reports on shellings do not enable Bn (Brigade crossed out) H.Q. of the Artillery to take any action.

(In margin –'Shelling – report on)

Para.24. Coy (Battalion crossed out) Commanders are reminded of the necessity of watching the flanks. Special troops will be detailed for this purpose, and to attack or mask any hostile posts which may be holding out on the flanks, and are hampering the advance. Those posts, provided that they are adjacent, will be engaged, whether within the Bn (brigade crossed out) area or not.

(In the margin – handwritten – 'Protection of Flanks)
Addenda to Para. 8 (c)

The importance of collecting S.A.A. from casualties will be impressed on all ranks. Slightly wounded men will be made to understand that it is a point of honour for them to hand over all the S.A.A. they have on them, before proceeding to the dressing station; by doing so, they are saving the lives of their comrades.

(In margin – ' Collection of SAA etc from casualities')

33rd Inf. Brigade Dump will be established at SNIPE HOUSE before Zero. The components of this dump will include S.A.A., Grenades, water, Iron Rations, S.O.S. Signals and Stokes shells. Full details of this dump will be issued later by the Staff Captain in Appendix K.

Issued at 3.50 pm 30-9-17 G.DeClair, capt, brigade Major, 33rd Infantry Brigade.
Copies to – Lincoln R., Border R., S.Staff.R., Sh.Fors., M.Gun Coy., L.T.M. Bty., C.R.A. 11th Div., 11th Div., A.D.M.S. 11th Div., Brigadier General Comdg., Staff Captain., Intelligence., Signals., 34th Inf. Bde., 32nd Inf, Bde., O.C. Left group 11th D.A., 11th Inf. Brigade.

SECRET Copy No 4
33rd Infantry Brigade Instructions
APPENDIX A.
Date stamped – 3 Oct 1917 H.Q. 33rd Infantry brigade.
Ref – 1/10000 POELCAPPELLE Map.

Date stamped – Headquarters, 33rd Infantry brigade, 3 Oct 1917.

1. *The attack will be made under an artillery barrage according to the attached barrage table, and will be supported by artillery detailed in para. 17A of these instructions.*

2 (a) *The initial barrage will come down on line V 25c 98.58 – V 25. a 05.55 – U 24 d 15.50.*

2 (b) *The barrage will lift at Zero plus 3 minutes and move forward for the first 200 yards at the rate of 50 yards in 2 minutes.*

2 (c) *After the first 200 yards and up to the protective barrage for the red DOTTED LINE it will move at the rate of 50 yards in 3 minutes.*

2 (d) *It will lift off the RED DOTTED LINE at Zero plus 47 minutes and will reach a protective line from V20 a 30. 30 to V 19 a 85.65 at Zero plus two hours and ten minutes.*

2 (e) *The barrage will move forward again from this protective line at Zero plus 2 hours and 10 minutes at the rate of 50 yards in 4 minutes until it clears the RED LINE at about 2 hours 30 minutes and becomes protective on the line V 26 b 13.82 – V 20 a 00.70 – V 13 d 42.05 at Zero plus 2 hours and 40 minutes., where it remains for two hours.*

All lifts will be of 50 yards

3. *During the pause on the RED DOTTED LINE, the high ground about MEUNIER HOUSE will be masked by a smoke screen*

4. *A gas shell bombardment will be carried out by 60-pdrs. And 4.5 Hows. At the following times:-*

   Zero plus 4 hours 45 minutes to Zero plus 6 hours 45 minutes.

   2. p.m. too 3.15 p.m.

   5.45 p.m. to 7 p.m.

   5. No gas shelling will take place within 500 yards of the RED LINE, i.e. V 19 b 15.80 – V 19 b 80.40 – V 20 a 40.00, or within 1000 yards if the wind is North, North East, East, or South East.

6. *The bombardment will open with H.E. and will then change to gas for 10 minutes, and will move forward in two lifts of 100 yards each of ten minutes interval.*

7. *During the gas bombardments H.E. and shrapnel will be fired in a proportion not to exceed 1 H.E. to 5 Gas Shell.*

8. *If a high wind is blowing the gas bombardment will not take place.*

9. *No other firing will take place in the gassed area during the bombardment.*

10. *O.C. Left Group 11th Div. Artillery will provide one Liaison officer to remain at Bde. H.Q.*

7th S.Staffs. Regt.

9th Sherwood Foresters.

ACKNOWLEDGE G.DeClair, Capt. Brigade Major. 33rd Infantry Brigade.

Copies to: –

Lincolns, Borders, S, Staffords, Sherwood Fors, M.G. Coy, T.M. Batty

11th Div, 11th Bde., 34th Bde., Left Group 11th Div. R.A., B.G.C., B.M., S.C.,

Barrage Map will follow.

SECRET RMB/2/52 2/10/17.

33rd Infantry Brigade Instructions

Para.15 of 33rd Inf. Brigade Instructions is cancelled, and the following will be substituted.

Para 15. During the attack by 7th South Staffs R and 9th Sh. Foresters, the role of the 6th Border Regt will be one of readiness to deal with any successful counter-attacks, which the two front Battalions, having used all their resources, have failed to dislodge.

The Border Rgt will not be used to reinforce the Battalion in front of them.

Close touch will be kept by this Battalion with the situation in front, and routes forward will be reconnoitred as soon as possible.

At Zero, 6th Border Regt will be concentrated in previously reconnoitred positions in the area CANE TRENCH – VARNA FM – STEENBEEK.

The officer commanding 6th Border Regt will move his Battalion forward in his own time to the area between PHEASANT FM and ROSE HOUSE within the Brigade boundaries as follows: –

2 Coys by Zero plus 2 and half hours.

2 Coys by Zero plus 3 and half hours

H.Q. of 6th Border Rgt will be established as follows: –

At Zero in the vicinity of VARNA FARM.

At Zero plus 2 hours at SNIPE HOUSE.

Frequent reports as to the progress of the move of this Battalion to the PHEASANT FM – ROSE HOUSE area will be made to Brigade Hd.Qrs.

This Battalion will be in readiness to move forward from the area described above at short notice, should orders to that effect be received from Brigade H.Q. However, the officer commanding is authorized to use his Battalion for a counter stroke without previous reference to Brigade Hd, Qrs should time and the urgency of the tactical situation in his opinion demand it. Any action taken will be reported to Brigade H.Q. An officer detailed from among those detailed to go into action will be sent to brigade Hd. Qrs at

Zero hour by this Battalion to act as Liaison officer.

New Para.26 6th Lincoln Regt will be in Divisional reserve and will move from SIEGE CAMP to the CANAL BANK, so as to arrive at the CANAL BANK by Zero plus 6 hours.

O.C. 6th Linc.R. will arrange to reconnoiter the accommodation held by 6th Border R on the Canal Bank and in the CANE TRENCH – VARNA FM – STEENBEKE Area and send advance parties to take it over, when vacated by Border Rgt.

ACKNOWLEDGE

Copies to all recipients G.DeClair, Capt, Brigade Major, 33rd Infantry Brigade.

SECRET BMS/2/55 Copy No 4
2-10-17
33rd Infantry Brigade Instructions
Herewith new para. 23 and addenda to paras. 13A.
33rd Inf. Bde Instructions
Copies to all recipients. G.DeClair, Capt, Brigade major, 33rd Infantry Brigade

(a) Para.25 – 1 Platoon 6th Lincoln Rgt will be detailed to act as a carrying party for 33rd M.Gun Coy on Y/Z night. O.C. 33rd M.Gun Coy will –

1. *Inform O.C. 6th Lincoln R direct as to at what hour and where this party will be required*
2. *Provide necessary guides.*

(b) 1 Coy. 6th Lincoln Rgt will be required for carrying during operations. This Coy will probably be required in two parties of two platoons, each under an officer, one party to carry for 7th S.Staff.R, one party to carry for the 9th Sherwood Foresters. However, both parties will be prepared to work in either sector. Officers in command of parties will reconnoitre the forward routes to the Brigade dump at SNIPE HOUSE and thence to Battn H.Q. This Coy will move forward so as to arrive at CANE TRENCH at Zero plus 6 hours. The Company Commander (whose name will be notified to Bde H.Q. as soon as possible) will remain at CANE POST where he will be in telephonic communication with Brigade Hd. Qrs.

Addenda to para. 13 A.

The direction of the advance will be maintained by compass bearings.

The bearings are as follows: –
Right of 7th S, Staffs.R. ..... 56 degrees true
Left of 7th S.Staffs. R. .... 55 degrees true.

The bearing along the forming up line from right to left is 323 degrees true.

SECRET Copy No 4 2/10/17.
33rd Infantry Brigade Instructions
Machine Gun Arrangements. Appendix B.

1. The following Machine guns will be available for the attack: –
32nd M.Gun Coy – 16 guns.
33rd M.Gun Coy – 16 guns.
34th M.Gun Coy – 16 guns.
197th M.Gun Coy – 8 guns.

2. Guns will be disposed as under at zero: –

2 (a) For Barrage –
32nd M.Gun Coy – 16 guns.
*33rd M.Gun Coy – 8 guns.**
197th M.Gun Coy – 8 guns.
To rejoin 33rd Bde on completion of the barrage.
These guns will be in position and ready to fire by zero minus 6 hours.
The position of these barrage guns and their barrage lines will be as shewn on the attached tracing.

2 (b) For the support of attacking Battalions under Battalions Commanders concerned.
33rd M.Gun Co 8 guns.

3 (c) On completion of barrage, these guns will be concentrated by O.C. 33rd M.Gun Coy in the vicinity of HANNIXBEEKE FM.

4 (d) Two of these guns will then be earmarked to go forward with 6th Border Rgt if necessary. On arrival, at HANNIXBEEK FARM one officer from M.G. Co. will be sent to get in touch with O.C. 6th Border R at SNIPE HOUSE.

4 (e) O.C. M.Gun Coy will report to brigade Hd Qrs as soon as possible –
That his guns are concentrated as directed.
That his officer is in touch with O.C. 6th Border R.

M.Gun H.Q. will be at HAANIXBEEK FARM.

Copies to – Bde Units, 34th Inf.Bde., 11th Inf Bde., 11th Division., B.G.C., S.C., I.O., Signals.

G.DeClair, Capt, brigade Major, 33rd Infantry Brigade.

DISTRIBUTION OF TROOPS
(Reference 4th Division Order No. 61)
29th Division – 86th Brigade (assaulting Battn) – 1st R.Dublin Fus.
Blue diamond on back of collar.
Red triangle on sleeve.
4th Division –
10th Brigade –
2nd Seaforth Hrs – Plaid triangle
3/10th Middlesex R. – Red and Yellow triangle. (red forward)

1st R. Warwicks – Green
The Household Bn,
11th Brigade-
1st Hampshire Regt. – Yellow Tiger.
1st Somerset L.I. – Yellow (oblong strip)
1st E.Lancs R – Yellow (oblong vertical)
1st Rifle Bde. – Yellow Maltese Cross
11th Division – 33rd Brigade –
(1st Objective)
9th Notts. & Derby Regt. – White roman four on back of collar
(2nd Objective)
6th Border Regt. – white roman two on green at back of collar.
NOTE: – Distinctive Badges of 4th Division are in every case on upper part of arm.
(Badges were needed, so that in battle, friendly units could recognize each other.)

Returning to the War Diary, on 5th the Battalion H.Q. was located at Pheasant Farm and overnight all the objectives had been held. The enemy sent a pretty heavy barrage over on to the Pheasant Farm line causing more casualties. By 4pm all arrangements for the forthcoming relief were completed and orders were issued for relief by 6th Border Regiment. At 8pm the night was very dark but the moon came out which greatly assisted the guides. At 9-30pm all guides were sent off to their various companies. Once the Battalion was relieved the men proceeded to the Cane Post Area (C 9 a. 28 NW), which was located in Cane trench. Battalion HQ was situated at Cane Post. The Battalion arrived in the Cane Post area by 2 am and Captain Harding was at H.Q. to meet them. The Battalion remained in this location awaiting orders but none came. The reserve officers moved up from the Transport lines to replace the officers killed and wounded in the attack. Heavy rain added to the battalions problems in the evening and the already sodden trenches took in more water.

The 7th would be another day of waiting to see if the relief would come or a return to the front line was necessary. At 8am the Billeting Party under Lieut Harwood proceeds to Eperlecques area, which is north west of St Omer. At 1pm the possibility of Battalion going back to hold line was notified in B M 196. In the event nothing came of this and the men could relax. At 7pm the relieve was decided and the 8th Duke of Wellington's came up to relief the Battalion. The Transport was sent up to collect the Lewis Gun magazines and 1st Line Transport proceeded to the new area.

By 1.30 am on the 8th the relief was complete and the Battalion moved off to Siege Camp arriving at 4 am.

Their involvement in the Battle of Ypres 1917 was over and the three visits to the Salient had been costly. The Campaign would go on until November 10th but other troops would now sacrifice themselves in the mud of Flanders.

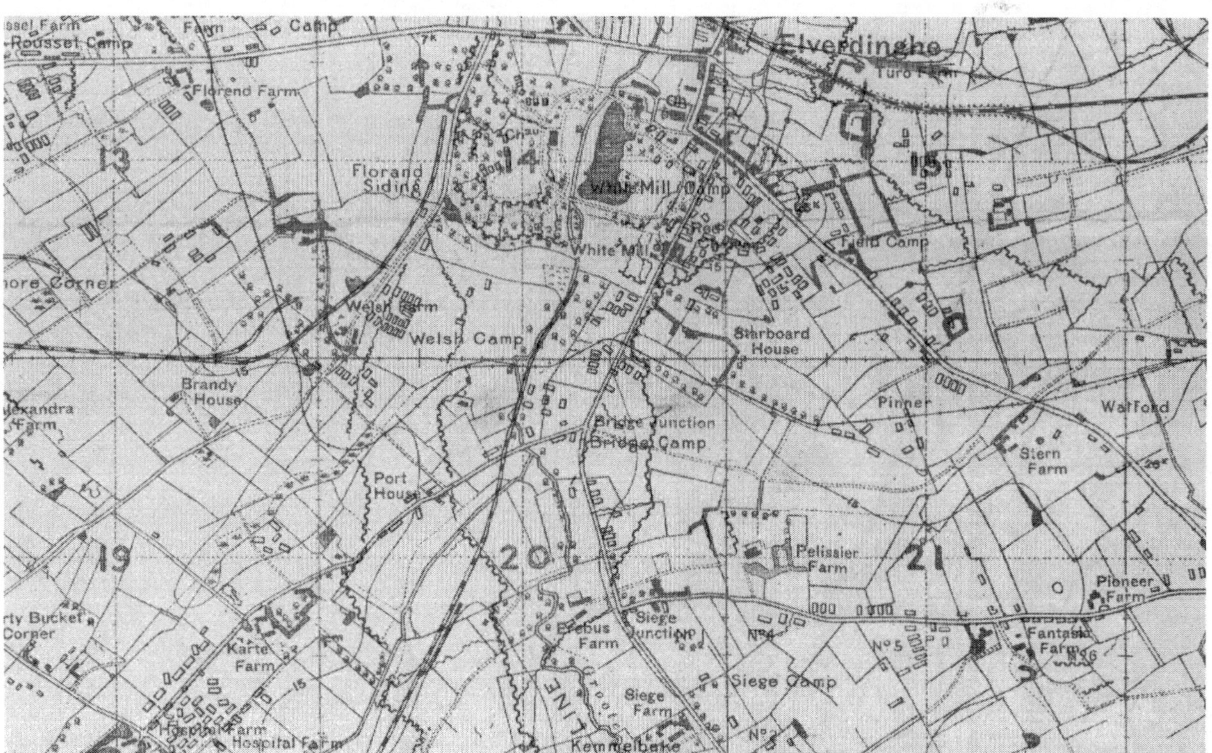

Siege Camp and area. This was the forward area used by troops moving into or out of the line

The majority of the men killed would have no known grave and are listed on the Tyne Cot Memorial. These men are listed below-

Men Commemorated on the Tyne Cot Memorial

Given name	Surname	Number	Rank	Died
Henry	Allen	92176	Private	04/10/1917
Herbert	Allwood	21477	Private	04/10/1917
Frank Arthur	Ash	204433	Private	04/10/1917
Thomas Samuel	Austin	70999	Private	04/10/1917
Frank	Birdsall	92238	Private	04/10/1917
Jonathon Henry	Bartle	82114	Private	04/10/1917
Arthur	Bowler	68053	Private	04/10/1917
George Wild	Bradley	30358	Private	04/10/1917
Thomas Edward	Bullock	92188	Private	04/10/1917
Albert Edward	Buxton	19774	Private	04/10/1917
John Thomas	Careless	19221	Private	04/10/1917
Harry	Cope	31822	Private	04/10/1917
John Reginald	Cory	70230	Private	03/10/1917
Henry	Cowlishaw	23884	Private	04/10/1917
Fred	Crossley	23384	Private	04/10/1917
Robert McKee	Devine	22561	L/Cpl	04/10/1917
Teddy	Fleming	92179	Private	04/10/1917
John.	Fletcher	24149	Private	04/10/1917
George	Glass	71007	Private	04/10/1917
Bernard	Goulding	4839	Private	04/10/1917
Sidney Albert	Grace	70957	Private	04/10/1917
Vernon	Greenhough	26858	Private	04/10/1917
Tom Cash	Hill	12954	Private	04/10/2017
Walter Henry	Hinkinbotham	45379	Private	04/10/1917
Albert W	Hinton	92210	Private	04/10/1917
Thomas Alfred Garlin	Hunt	25944	Private	04/10/1917
Herbert	Jackson	83798	Private	04/10/1917
Oliver St Michael	Jones		Lieut	04/10/1917
Alexander Henry	Keene	51314	Private	04/10/1917
George	Martin	12898	Private	04/10/1917
John Thomas	Mason	70890	Private	04/10/1917
Wiliam Ernest	Maxwell	41993	Private	04/10/1917
Joseph Francis	McCormack		Captain	04/10/1917
George Henry	Mead	12297	Private	04/10/1917
George	Mills	50576	Private	04/10/1917
Charles	Oddey	70267	Private	04/10/1917
William Ward	Odell		2/Lieut	04/10/1917
Stanley	Oldenbittle	27646	Private	04/10/1917
Horace	Painter	11270	Private	04/10/1917
Tom	Poskett	204462	Private	04/10/1917
Claude Alfred	Pymm	204446	Private	04/10/1917
Frank	Reed	15589	Private	04/10/1917
Thomas	Riley	49178	Corporal	04/10/1917
George	Robertson	13565	Private	04/10/1917
William	Robinson	14232	L/Cpl	04/10/1917
Richard	Rowell	92173	Private	04/10/1917
Joseph	Scragg	61482	Private	05/10/1917
Edwin	Simmonds	21129	Corporal	04/10/1917
Charles Dawkes	Simpson	30540	Private	04/10/1917
Thomas A	Sprowell	51438	L/Cpl	04/10/1917
Frank	Thompson	22146	Private	04/10/1917
William.	Turner	92424	Private	04/10/1917
George	West	3145	Private	04/10/1917
Fred	West	28135	L/Cpl	04/10/1917
Harry	White	71012	L/Cpl	04/10/1917
Arthur	Williams	29778	Private	04/10/1917
Edgar Charles	Young	75344	Private	04/10/1917

Lt. Oliver Saint Michael Jones. 4th October 1917. Commemorated on the Tyne Cot memorial.

Two men who fell would have their graves found after the war and were reburied –

Both men died on 4th October 1917.

86411 Private John William Clayton was aged 25 years and from Alfreton. He is buried at Poelcappelle British Cemetery and grave XLVII. C.1. The cemetery was made after the war and some 70% are of 'unknown' graves. It is likely that many of the 9th battalion men killed on 4th October 1917 are buried here.

92192 Private John Coan was a Lancashire man and formerly T/259854 R.A.S.C. He is buried at Tyne Cot Cemetery and grave LIX. E. 7. The largest British War Cemetery in the world also has some 70% of 'unknown graves.

Four men are buried at Cement House Cemetery Langemarck, three died on 4th October and one on 5th. It is likely that these men were caught in the enemy barrage on the reserve line.

24531 Private Jerimiah Nicholls was a native of Hucknall Torkard and is buried in grave III.F.7.

45695 Private John George Scott of 'C' Company was 25 years of age and is buried in grave XI. C. 30. He is listed as dying of wounds and the headstone inscription reads –'A place is vacant in our home, which never can be filled'.

86412 Private Edward Widdowson aged 27 years and off West Bridgeford. He is buried in grave VI.F.29.

12549 Lance Corporal John Richard Birley was 25 years of age and of Staveley. He died of wounds on 5th October and is buried in grave IV. B. 4.

A number of men would reach the major Casualty Clearing Stations set up for the Battles of Ypres 1917.

Twelve men would die of wounds at Dozinghem near Westvleteren.

05th October 1917.

7807 Private Daubney was a Derby man had is buried in grave V.H.7. The Derby Daily Telegraph reported his death on 27 October 1917 –

"M. R., Employee Dies of Wounds
Mrs H. Daubney, 25 Watson Street Derby has received official intimation that her son 7807 Pte. A. Daubney of the Nott's and Derbyshire Regiment has died of wounds received in action. He was admitted to a Casualty Clearing Station suffering from shell wounds to the back and leg, and died on October 5th. Pte. Daubney enlisted in Nov. 1914. He went through the Dardanelles campaign, afterwards going to France, where he served two years. He was last home on leave in February last. He was previously wounded in France in June 1917. Thirty-seven years of age, he leaves a wife and two children. Before enlisting he worked at the Carriage Side, M.R. He went through the Boer War with the King's Royal Rifles, and was in Ladysmith during the siege. He held the Queen's medal with three bars and King's with two bars"

22672 Private Reuben Ellmer who was born at Rotherham Yorks and is buried in grave V.H.17

11709 Sergeant Alfred Thomas Hinkley MM, aged 24 years and a Derby man is buried in grave V.H.14

23318 Private John Thomas Roe aged 21 years was a native of Crich, Derbys and he is buried in grave VII. G.1.

6th October 1917.

79673 Lance Corporal Frederick Henry Buxton aged 25 years and a native of Brampton Derbys is buried in grave V.H.6. The battle on 4th October had been a double tragedy for the Buxton family. Albert Buxton MM who was killed and is commemorated on the Tyne Cot memorial was Frederick's cousin.

18432 Lance Sergeant George Fisher aged 23 years was born at Shelford Nott's and is buried in grave VIII.I.16

26243 Lance Corporal John Henry Smith aged 35 years was the husband of Florence Elizabeth and a Nottingham man. He is buried in grave VII.I.15.

7th October 1917.

73078 Private Edwin Cox was a Birmingham man and formerly 9864 South Staffordshire Regiment. He is buried in grave VII.G.20.

52230 Private William Henry Slater was 35 years of age and a native of Nottingham. He is buried in grave VII.I.8.

9th October 1917.

60314 Corporal Luke Burke was born in Nottingham although living in Shepherds Bush on enlistment. He is buried in grave VIII.G.13.

15th October 1917.

49340 Private Albert Ernest Hart was formerly in the 10th Battalion and born at Fleet Lincs. He is buried in grave XI.I.5.

Three men would arrive at the Casualty Clearing Station at Proven and buried in the adjoining cemetery – Mendinghem Military Cemetery.

5th October 1917.

15198 Lance Corporal Alfred Louis Green MM was a native of Chesterfield and is buried in grave VII.B.36.

07th October 1917.

24972 Private John Edward Betts of Nottingham is buried in grave VII.B.45.

9th October 1917.

13124 Sergeant William Throssell MM, aged 24 years was living at Upper Hartshay, Belper on enlistment. His headstone has the inscription ' Thy will be done from sorrowing Mother, Brothers and Sisters'. He is buried in grave VII. E.46.

Four men would reach Base hospitals near the coast only to succumb to their wounds.

St.Sever Cemetery Extension, Rouen –

73037 Private William John Dale aged 21 years of East Bergholt; Colchester Essex was formerly 24453 Northamptonshire Regiment. He died on 10th October and is buried in grave P.III.F.7B.

Also in the same cemetery is –

71031 Private Henry Joseph Perry aged 34 years who was also an Essex man. He died on 11th October and is buried in grave P.III.F.11B.

One man would die at Boulogne and be buried in the Eastern Cemetery.

14087 Corporal John Guy aged 20 years from Carrington Notts is buried in grave VIII.I.54.

Finally one man made it as far as Etaples and is buried at the Military Cemetery in grave XXX.D.5A.

92130 Private George William Bannister was from Bradford Yorkshire.

As Col Scothern had mentioned:

"By this successful operation, the battalion had materially added to its honours"

23715 Acting Corporal (Later Sergeant) Fred Greaves actions on 4th October 1917 would win him the ultimate accolade of a Victoria Cross. Fuller details about Fred and the action will be seen later. The citation – London Gazette dated 26 November 1917.

'His majesty the King has been graciously pleased to approve the award of the Victoria Cross, for most conspicuous bravery, initiative and leadership when his platoon was temporarily held up by machine gun fire from a concrete stronghold. Seeing that his platoon commander and sergeant were casualties, and realising that unless, this post was taken quickly his men would lose the barrage, Corporal Greaves, followed by another Non-Commissioned Officer rushed forward regardless of his personal safety, reached the rear of the building, and bombed the occupants, killing or capturing the garrison and taking four enemy machine guns.

It was solely due to the personal pluck, dash and initiative of this Non-commissioned Officer that the assaulting line at this point was not held up, and that our troops escaped serious casualties.

Later in the afternoon, at a critical period of the battle when the troops of a flank Brigade had given way temporarily under a heavy counter-attack, and when all the officers of his company were casualties this gallant Non-commissioned officer grasped the situation quickly. He collected his men, threw extra posts on the threatened flank, and opened rifle and machine gun fire to enfilade the advance. The effect of Corporal Greave's conduct on his men throughout the battle cannot be overestimated, and those under his command responded gallantly to his example'

A/Cpl F. Greaves after his VC investiture.

Bill Hutchins, Fred Greaves VC, June and Edith Louise Greaves. January 1918. Award of Victoria Cross at Buckingham Palace.

On Tuesday 27th November 1917 the Derby Daily telegraph carried the headline "Twenty New V.C's:

Two for the Sherwood Foresters." The two men were Corporal Ernest Egerton and Acting Corporal Fred Greaves. Both had won their Victoria Cross fighting on the Ypres Salient. The battalion could be proud of its involvement in the Battles of Ypres 1917

Col. Scothern's notes for October through to the end of the year give the following details.

"In October the battalion entrained for Lillers, marching from there via Vaudricourt to Mazingarbe, a small village between Lens and Bethune. On the 22nd the line in the Loos sector was taken over from the 7th South Stafford's and held for seven days, Noeux-les-Mines providing billets after this. These two places Mazingarbe and Noeux-les-Mines were destined to become household words with the men of 33rd Brigade.

The next sector held was a slightly different one – the trenches in front of Cite St. Pierre, a suburb of Lens. This proved a rather lengthy stay as the line was held for 20 days, the battalion returning to billets in Les Brebis on November 25th. During this term of trench duty, a working party from the battalion erected dummy figures in front of our lines to work in conjunction with the raid carried out by the 32nd Brigade on our left.

The Brigade had at this time two battalions in the line and two out, and the general procedure was four days in the line and four out. This continued until December 22nd, when the line was taken over by the Canadians, and the battalion marched back to Fouquereuil for a rest. The stay at this village was very enjoyable. A very jolly Christmas was followed by plenty of football and games, although these were considerably interfered with by snow. This however proved a blessing in disguise, as when the time came for returning to the line, a rapid thaw set in and orders were received cancelling the move, another welcome week being added to the stay."

It is doubtful the 1/6th South Stafford's stuck in the front line were as happy.

Returning to the War Diaries for the period, the stay at Siege camp would be a short one and at 10 am on 8th the Battalion less 1st Line Transport entrained at Dirty Bucket Siding (A 30 b. ref sheet 28 NW Belgium) for Watten, arriving there at 5.30 pm. They then changed their mode of transport to omnibuses and these took them to their camp at Tournehem, arriving at 9.30pm. Tournehem was located some 10 Kilometres from Watten and just north east of St Omer.

The battalion would remain at Tournehem until 19th October 1917 before commencing its journey further south to the Hulluch/Loos sector.On the 9th and 10th the Companies were at the disposal of their O.C.s' for cleaning up, inspections etc, followed by recreational training. The 11th 12th and 13th saw training continue in preparation for the battalions new role which would be holding the front line throughout the winter. Echelon A & B and reinforcements arrived on the 11th. The 13th saw A & D Companies firing on the Lewis Gun Range. The men also attended the Baths before enjoying a battalion concert at 6 pm in 'B' Companies billet.

Sunday 14th was given over to Voluntary Services, Rest and Football matches.There followed four more days of training, which consisted of Musketry, Route marches, range practice and recreational training. On 15th Commandant of the 5th Army Musketry School gave a lecture to all Officers and Senior NCOs.

The 16th saw 2/Lt H.V. Smith report for duty with the battalion.

The billeting party proceeded to new area in order to prepare the accommodation.

On the 19th it was time to move once more and the morning was spent cleaning and packing up. Capt J Critchlow proceeded on leave prior to the battalions move.

At 12-30 pm the Battalion paraded and proceeded to Watten arriving at 3.30 pm. The battalion entrained at Watten and also changed Corps and Armies. The left XVIII Corps Fifth Army and joined I Corps, First Army. At 4 pm the train departed from Watten Station and it was at this point the official change over was recognised.At 7-30pm the battalion arrived at Lillers and proceeded to billets at Ames some 6 kilometres away, arriving at 9 pm. It would only be an overnight stop and at 9-30am the battalion proceeded to new billets in Vaudricourt (Map – sheet 36b K.4.) arriving at 3-30pm. The battalion was now close to its final destination and what would be its home for some ten months. During the morning of 21st the men packed up ready for the move. 2/Lt Gunson and 20 Other Ranks proceeded to Les Brebis on a working party detail. At 2 pm the Battalion proceeded to new billets in Mazingarbe. (Map -Sheet 36 B L. 23) arriving at 4pm.

The morning of 22nd October saw the O.C.s' Companies and Captain Harding reconnoitring the trenches in Brigade reserve and arrange for the battalion to relieve the 7th South Staffordshire Regt. At 5 pm the Battalion relieved the 7th S. Staffs in Brigade reserve in front of Loos (maps -Sheets 36 c SW & NW. Squares G36 + M6)

(France sheet 36c NW. G 36d. 6.5.) and by 8-40am the relief was complete and Companies were disposed as under –

"A" Company at the Loos Brewery.

"C" Company at the Quarry M.6 a.

"B" and "D" Companies in Mouse and Martyr Trenches.

Battalion HQ situated at G36. d. 6.5

The next seven days would be spent in the vicinity of Loos and at 6.44 pm on 23rd details received for working parties to be used on the night of 23/24th. The C.O. proceeded on leave. The following day at 7 pm 2/Lt Hudson reported his arrival. Working parties of 400 other ranks had to be found every night and they worked on Netley, Norman and Catapult trenches. On 28th a working party under 2/Lt Hill proceeded to Les Brebis on a working party detail.

The 25th at 7 pm saw the arrival of five new officers with 2/ Lieuts Archer, Schur, Cooper, White and Francis being taken on strength. At noon on 29th arrangements for the battalions relief by 8th Duke of Wellington where made. Although the relief was completed by 9.30 pm, the men continued to work until 11 pm before proceeding to Maroc (Grenay) where they embussed for Noeux Les Mines which was some 6 kilometres northwest. At 2 am on the 30th the buses eventually set off and by 3.30 am had arrived at Noeux-Les-Mines. This would seem an excessive travelling time but it was dark, the roads were not much more than tracks and an open topped double-decker bus was not the quickest form of transport.

The month finished with the men cleaning up and having inspections, followed by recreational training. A very hectic and trying month for the battalion would finish on a very quiet note.The new area would be the battalion's home for many months as the tide of the war swung away from the Allies in early 1918 before the final glorious hundred days 'Advance to Victory'.

November would be a period of training, recreation and trench occupation. The Diarist was either new or bored as he gave little detail. The battalion spent the first five days of November at Noeux-Les-Mines with two days taken up with training. Trench occupation had always caused many medical problems and the men would receive special attention from the Medical Officer. On the 1st the M.O. inoculated the men with triple Vaccine serum. This was actually a TAB jab – Typhoid plus Paratyphoid A and Paratyphoid B. The following day the M.O lectured the men of C Company on the dangers of trench feet and how to keep it at bay.

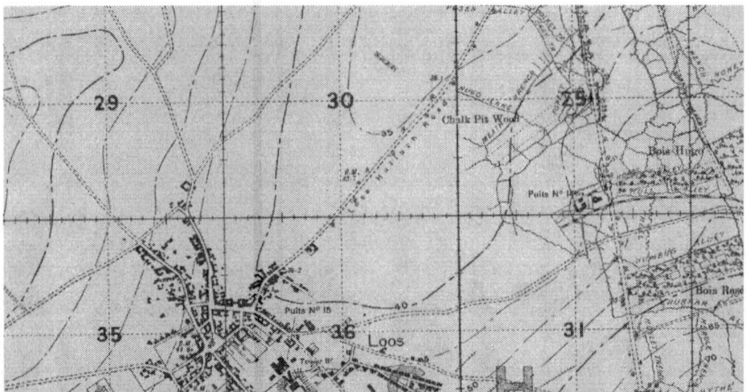

Loos.and Chalk pit

Trench foot was seen as a self-inflicted injury and frowned upon. Why only one Company received the lecture is unclear unless their men were more susceptible that is. An Army Gymnastic Instructor took the Officers and N.C.O.'s for a class in exercise techniques.

Sunday 3rd was given over to Church services and rest in preparation for the battalion stint in the front line.

The 5th would see the battalion on the move again as at 4 pm. They left to relieve the 5th Dorset's at Cite St Pierre arriving at 7.30pm. Cite St Pierre being the reserve area for the front line and the battalion would remain located here throughout the 6th November.

The 7th to 16th would be front line trench duty although this area was at the time a fairly quiet one. At 2.30 pm on 6th the Battalion moved forward to relieve the 9th Lancashire Fusiliers in the front line close to Lens. On relief 'A' and 'C' Companies were in the front line with 'B' in support and 'D' in reserve. Throughout this relief the Companies kept up continuous front line patrols whilst 'D' Company provided working parties from reserve.

From 11th to 16th the diary stated 'A quiet tour of duty in trenches. Casualties slight'The families of the three men killed may not have agreed with the statement though. All three men are buried in the Loos British Cemetery and they are -:

10 November 1917.

47915 Private Richard Dyas was 29 years of age and a native of Irby, Grimsby. He is buried in grave XX.C.24.

7065 Lance Corporal James Rowe was 38 years of age and from Ilkeston. He had previously served as T/4/088643 R.A.S.C. Grave XX.C.23.

13 November 1917.

3797 Private Frederick Foss was 20 years of age and a Leicester lad. He may have been in the Trench Mortar Battery as his unit is given as 9th Bn Sherwood Foresters attached 33rd Brigade. Buried in grave XX.C.30. Frederick died of wounds received on the 10th.

At 9 am on 10th a raid was carried out by 32nd Brigade and the battalion put in their own dummy attack in support. The battalion did everything but attack! They would have sent over mortars and raked the ground with machine guns.The men then stood to and were ready to go over the top. They would have used artillery to give the Germans the impression an attack was to come in order to confuse the enemy and stop them from reinforcing the area which the 32nd Brigade were raiding. Raids where a regular feature of trench holding – anything from a couple of men to a whole Company (250 men At 5.30 pm 'B' and 'D' Companies relieved 'A' and 'C' in the front line. 'A' Company then moved into the support line with 'C' in reserve.

The 16th would see more relief take place at 7 pm the two front line Companies (B and D) were relieved by two Companies of the 7th South Staffs and returned to Cite St. Pierre. Meanwhile 'A' and 'C' remained in the support and reserve trenches respectively. Battalion H.Q. also returned to Cite St. Pierre.

On 20th orders were received to move back to the rest billets at Noeux-Les-Mines although later this order was cancelled and the battalion would spend six more days in the front line. This decision would cost the battalion eight more men killed. The following day Battalion H.Q., 'B' and 'D' Companies moved out to relieve the front line Companies of 7th South Staffs and by 8 pm the relief had been completed.

The following three days were once again classed as quiet with only an inter Company relief taking place on 24th. The 25th would see the battalion relieved by 7th South Staffs and move back to Cite St.Pierre.

The deaths for the period of the extra front line occupation was as follows -:

Loos British Cemetery.
20/11/1917

87133 Private Percy Wilkinson a Nottingham man is buried in grave XX.B.8

21/11/1917

56412 Private James Andrews aged 21 years who was born in Manchester and living in Old Lenton, Notts.

Grave XX.B.18.

70871 Private Tom Barratt Crawford was a Leeds man who enlisted in Walsall Staffs and was formerly 26842 South Stafford's Regt. Grave XX.B.16

37434 Private Alfred George Grice aged 29 years and a member of 'A' Company. He was a West Bromwich man and related to Levi Grice who had died 30/12/1915 at Gallipoli. Grave XX. B. 13.

22/11/1917 – 56416 Private John Beeby enlisted at Nottingham. He is buried at Longuenesse (St. Omer) Souvenir Cemetery and grave IV.F.8.

25/11/1917 –
92196 Private Joseph Morris aged 31 years and

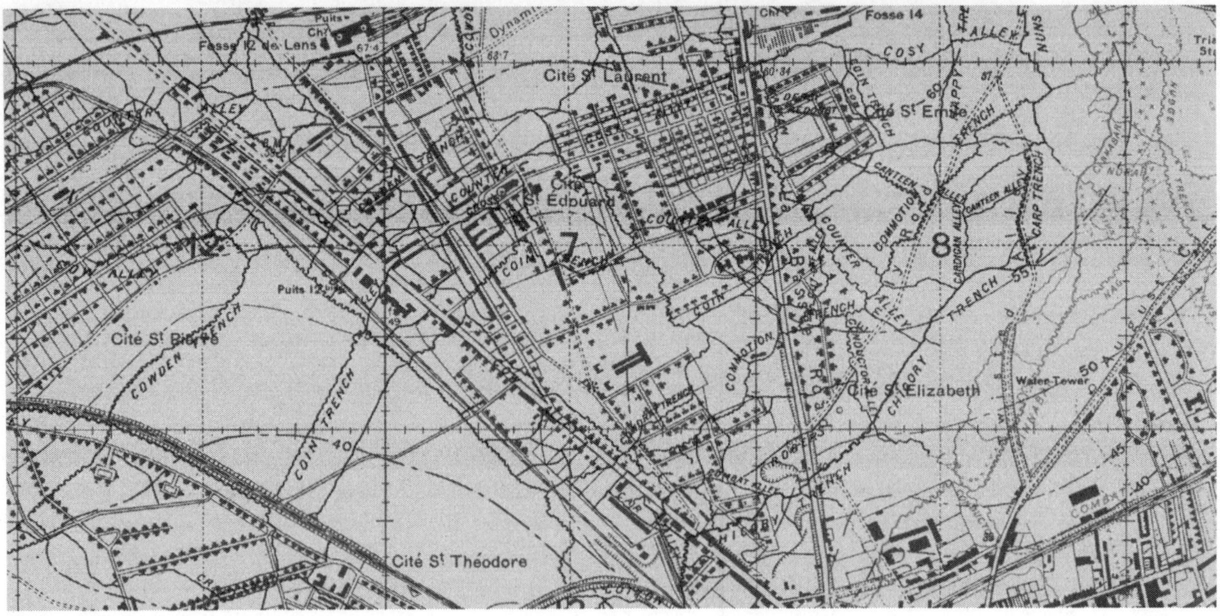

Lens – St. Laurent and Cite St. Pierre

formerly T/4/186107 R.A.S.C. He was from Stoke-on-Trent. Grave XX.B.25.

92196 Private William George Howells was aged 24 years and a native of Wales. Another R.A.S.C. man T/4/185988. Grave XX.B.24

One man would die of wounds –
26/11/1917 – 54962 Private Edward Sawyer was born at Finsbury Middlesex and is buried at Chocques Military Cemetery and grave I.N.4.

The battalion spent the day of 26th at Cite St. Pierre resting and making preparations for the move back to the rest billets at Les Brebis. The battalion moved off at 4.30 pm and all Companies were reported to be settled in at the rest billets by 11 pm. The following four days would see the usual routine of rest, cleaning up, recreation and training. The men also had the opportunity of bathing on 28th and 29th. The Medical officer also inspected the battalion although it has to be presumed this was a visual inspection as seeing nearly 1000 men separately would be impossible.

The Divisional Gas N.C.O.'s inspected the men's gas helmets. At this time gas seemed to be used more than at any other and a gas mask which was undamaged was a vital piece of kit for every man. The usual weapons and specialist training was also undertaken each morning. The highlight of the four days would be on 30th when at 9 am the G.O.C. 11th Division presented medal ribbons to the men who had gained decorations on 4th October 1917 at Poelcappelle. The list for this one battle had been impressive with the following men receiving awards:

Victoria Cross –
23715 Acting Corporal Fred Greaves.

Distinguished Conduct Medals -
6905 CSM Fred Betesta.
13016 Sgt Fred Carlile. MM.
19896 Pte George Lowe.
22726 Pte Thomas Pole.
12367 Sgt Henry Terry. MM.

Military Medal.
19774 Pte Albert Edward Buxton (killed in action 4th October 1917)
20045 Pte William Dexter Clowes.
25510 Pte Fred Doody. (Bar to MM – 4 November 1918)
3766 Pte Cecil Jepson.
13145 Cpl/Acting Lance Sgt Ernest Parkin.

The above gives an idea of the success of the battalion and the bravery of the men.

December 1st saw the men returning to the front line in the St.Laurent area

Preparations were made to move into the line and the battalion packed up all they needed and were issued with trench equipment. At 4 pm they left Les Brebis and moved of to relieve the 7th South Stafford's in the trenches at St. Laurent.

The relief was successfully completed by 8.45 pm with the Companies disposed with 'A' and 'C' in the front line whilst 'B' were in support and 'D' remained in reserve. The following day every available man worked on trench improvement although it was a quiet time in terms of action. The 3rd would see the Commanding Officer Lieut. Colonel W.B. Thornton

D.S.O. leave to take command of the 33rd Infantry Brigade during the temporary absence of the Brigadier General. This temporary move would eventually turn into a permanent one in early 1918. Major C.L. Harding, M.C., assumed command of the battalion. At 7 pm the Special Company R.E. discharged gas from the battalion lines and on this occasion the enemy did not retaliate. On the 4th every available man was employed on wiring the front, support and reserve lines as well as undertaking the normal trench duties. The 5th would see a larger gas operation and the battalion-received orders at 4 pm that the Special Company R.E. proposed a discharge of gas from N.13.c.5.9 to an area about N.14.d.15. (Lens 36.C. S.W.1. 1/10,000) this being into the area of Lens, which was still occupied by the enemy.

The battalion took special gas precautions, as the discharge would be projected over their lines. The usual plan was to put your respirator on and keep your head down for the duration of the attack, followed by immediate readiness for the enemy retaliation. The next day was quiet and orders were received that the battalion would be relieved on the night of 7/8th by the 7th South Stafford's. This duly happened the next day from 6 pm onwards and the battalion proceeded to dugouts and cellars in Cite St. Pierre some 3 kms away. The relief was completed by 9.30 pm although as the men were still only about 3 kms from the front line care had to be taken.

The period 8th to 10th gave the men time to bathe at Cite St. Pierre but they also had to put in an 8-hour day working on the support and communications trenches.

During the period 3rd to 8th the battalion had few casualties but four men are buried in the Loos British Cemetery.

03/12/1917

70037 Private Frank Robinson aged 29 years of Sibsey Lincs is buried in grave XX.B.30.

04/12/1917-

25843 Private Charles Edward Gilbert aged 26 years and a Chesterfield man is buried in grave XX.E.1.

71075 Sergeant John Potts a native of Derby is buried in grave XX.E.4

06/12/1917 –

27562 Private William Hoole aged 21 years and a Nottingham lad is buried in grave XX.E.4

One man died of wounds on 08/12/1917 and is buried at Noeux-Les-Mines Communal Cemetery Extension and grave IV.A.23

204512 Private Harry Letts was 38 years old and he lived at New Whittingham Derby's with his wife Lucy.

On 10th December the battalion returned to front line duty and relieved the 7th South Stafford's at 7.10 pm. No casualties were recorded during the relief. The following day five 2/Lts arrived as reinforcements but sadly the war diarist did not name them. Other than that the day was quiet for the Companies in the front line although not quiet enough for one man.

11/12/1917

92254 Private Thomas James Adley was a Kentish man and formerly T/4/161124 R.A.S.C. Not so for the 12th though as the enemy put down a heavy Trench Mortar barrage on the front and support lines. Only two casualties were recorded and two men were killed that day. He is buried at Loos British cemetery.

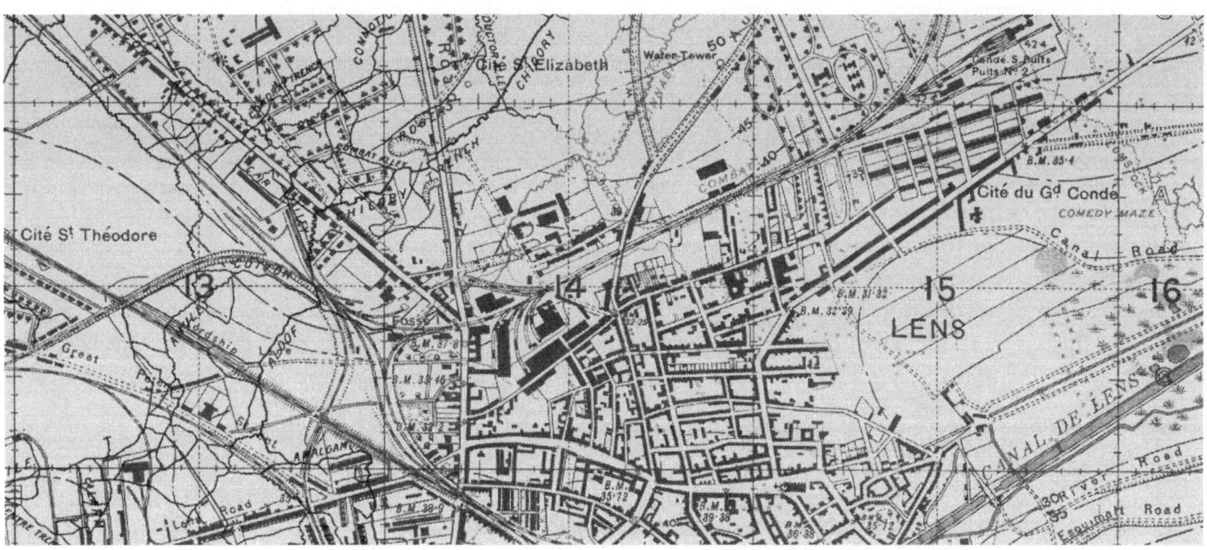

Lens

12/12/1917 –

28216 Private William Brown was born in Bedworth Warwickshire and is buried in grave XX.E.9. William is commemorated on the Bedworth War Memorial

21616 Lance Corporal Leonard Whitworth aged 34 years enlisted at Mansfield, Nott's and buried in grave XX.E.12.

At 8.30 pm on 13th November the battalion was relieved by the 6th Lincolns and returned to reserve and the positions at Cite St. Pierre. One man is listed as being killed on 13th and he is buried in grave XX.E.8 at Loos British Cemetery.

86342 Private Wilfred Simpson was aged 22 years and from Netherfield Notts.

Three other men would die during this period.

16/12/1917 –
269322 Private Cecil Linford Sheppard was 20 years of age and would be the last man from the battalion buried at Loos British Cemetery. He was living in Cheltenham prior to the war and is buried in grave XX.D.11.

12/12/1917 – 92180 Private Frederick Heal was a Yorkshire man and is buried at Nouex-Les-Mines where he died of wounds. He is buried in grave III.B.2.

The 17 December would see the final man of the battalion die in 1917.

32746 Private William Lambert aged 24 years of Keyworth Notts, died of wounds at one of the General Hospitals and is buried at Les Baraques Military Cemetery, Sangatte.

Between the 14th and 19th working and carrying parties were provided by the battalion in the immediate vicinity. The men once again had the opportunity to bathe on 14th. The 19th to 22nd would see the battalion in the front line again and they relieved the 6th Lincolns at 7.15 pm. The three days in the trenches were quiet ones and no doubt men from all nations had Christmas on their mind. No casualties were recorded for this period and on 22nd the Canadians relieved the battalion. The 116th battalion relieved 'A' and 'D' Companies whilst the 43rd battalion relieved 'C' and 'B' Companies. The Canadian Battalions were part of 9th Infantry Brigade, 3rd Canadian Division. The 43rd were also known as the Cameron Highlanders of Winnipeg and the 116th as the Ontario County.

The battalion moved into Divisional reserve at Bully Grenay (Map 36.B N.E.) On 23rd the battalion moved off from Bully and into the billets at Fouquereuil (map 36.B. N.E.) where they would spend Christmas and New Year. In fact it would be the 23rd January 1918 before the battalion would enter the front line again. The following day was taken up with the usual cleaning, inspections and re-organisation. Christmas day could be seen as a perfect day for the battalion. They were out of the line and the day was a holiday with nothing to do except enjoy the free time and it even snowed heavily during the evening. Christmas away from family and friends was never easy for a soldier though and the men would spend the day thinking of home. Those who had survived four Christmas's with the battalion would also wonder if they would see a fifth. Few men expected the war to end soon if ever and moral was not at its highest. Instances of men returning late from leave were growing as men wearied of the war and a combination of the carrot and stick was employed to keep the men in line. Recreation and entertainment was much to the fore but punishment for misdemeanours was swift and harsh.

From 26th to 31st the days followed the same pattern with training from 9 am until 12.30 pm, consisting of close and extended order drill, musketry, bayonet and specialist training. Physical Training was also undertaken and this was needed particularly for the new conscripts in the battalion's ranks. Many of these young men had had little training prior to joining the battalion and were poor specimens. Captain Warneford M.C. took a special class for musketry on 26th December. The afternoons were taken up with recreational training although with snow on the ground the usual football matches and games would be curtailed somewhat.

On 28th at 9 a.m. the C.O. and Company Commanders proceeded to reconnoitre the reserve defence line in the 46th Divisional area in case of a hostile offensive. The war was never far away even when the men were out of the line and relaxing. The 46th Division rightly or wrongly were seen as a 'trench holding' division and the Commanders had little confidence in them. They would prove everyone wrong in 1918 but at this time it was thought that they might give under an attack and rapid support would be vital.

Sunday 30th was given over to rest and Divine service and the following day would be one of training with musketry once again being the focus.

So ended another year for the 9th Battalion, their fourth of the war. The Battalion had served and fought on every sector of the France and Flanders line and also Gallipoli and Egypt. They would wonder where the Christmas of 1918 would see them but few would have expected to be at home with no war to fight.

Chapter Five

1918 – The Year of Victory

IT IS extremely unlikely that the majority of officers and men in the battalion would have believed the war would ever end, let alone before the end of 1918. The majority of 1918 saw the Battalion holding trenches in the front line and training. In the context of the year's casualty lists, the Battalion's were small. Fewer men would die in the final eleven months of the war than in some of the famous battles the Battalion had been involved in previously. The months of July and August would see no Battalion fatalities at all, although this was more by luck than anything else. The German assaults fell either side of the Battalion's front so saving them from high casualties. There would though be a final sting in the tail only one week prior to the Armistice on 11th November.

Anyone thinking that the final days would be quiet as the Armistice negotiations took place was quickly forced to alter their view. Almost half of the battalion's fatalities in 1918 would come during the final week of the Great War. Men who had heard rumours of peace began to think of home but unfortunately forty-five men would never see the guns fall silent, let alone home.

The United States troops were arriving in ever increasing numbers but they would not be battle ready for many months. A more pressing problem came from the Russian Revolution and that countries subsequent exit from the war. For a short period the German Army would have numerous troops moving from the east to the western front. The Allied generals knew that a massive assault would come sometime early in 1918 but feared the war weary troops would be unable to withstand such an attack. After over three years of an offensive spirit, new defensive plans were put into place. When the assault came on 21st March 1918, these preparations should have been ready, sadly despite the men's best efforts they were not.

January 1st dawned quietly for the battalion and the month continued in the same vein. The time would be split between training at Fouquereuil and front line trench occupation in the vicinity of Noeux-Les-Mines. This sector had seen little action since the Battle of Loos in the autumn of 1915, mainly because of the very strongly fortified defensive line protecting the coalfields of Brury and Bethune. These defences were constantly strengthened and many tunnels also led to the front line, which saved both time and casualties. The tunnels though could be somewhat confusing to the newcomer and care had to be taken otherwise men could get hopelessly lost.

The Battalion spent the period up to the 23rd January training which included musketry and rapid wiring each morning. The afternoons were given over to the more mundane but equally important tasks of cleaning and drill. On 13th an afternoon of recreational training was undertaken which would include football matches and cross-country runs. The following day would see the C.O. and O.C. Companies move off to reconnoitre the front line which was occupied at the time by the 1/6th South Staffordshire Regt, 137th Brigade, 46th Division. This was in the Hulluch Sector, left sub section. The advance party made up of the Intelligence officer, RSM and snipers also proceeded forward to reconnoitre the area and make arrangements for the relief. The remainder of the battalion continued training although they would know that their quiet period would soon end. Front line occupation in mid winter was no party and the men knew it.

The 15th saw more preparations for the move and all spare baggage was packed and moved by the regimental transport to the new Q.M. stores location at La Bourse. This as ever was undertaken during the evening when darkness would conceal movements. The relief was scheduled for the night of the 17th/18th but was then postponed under O.O. No1

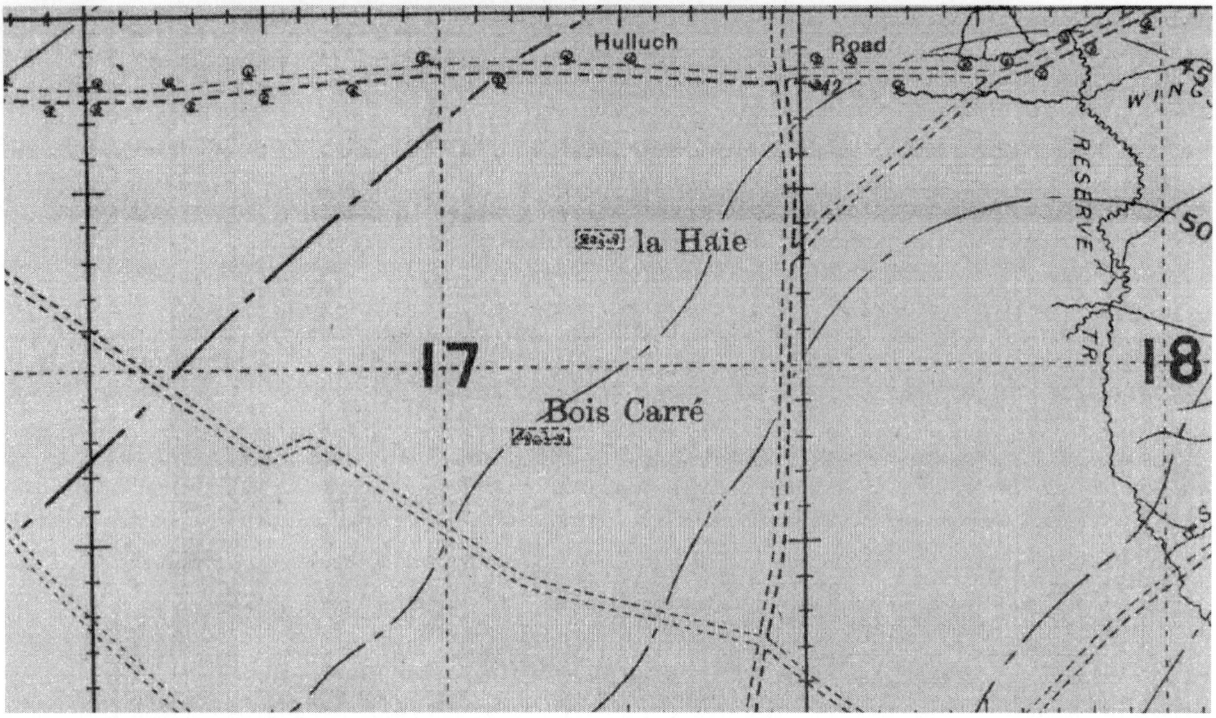

Battalion HQ – close to Hulluch Road

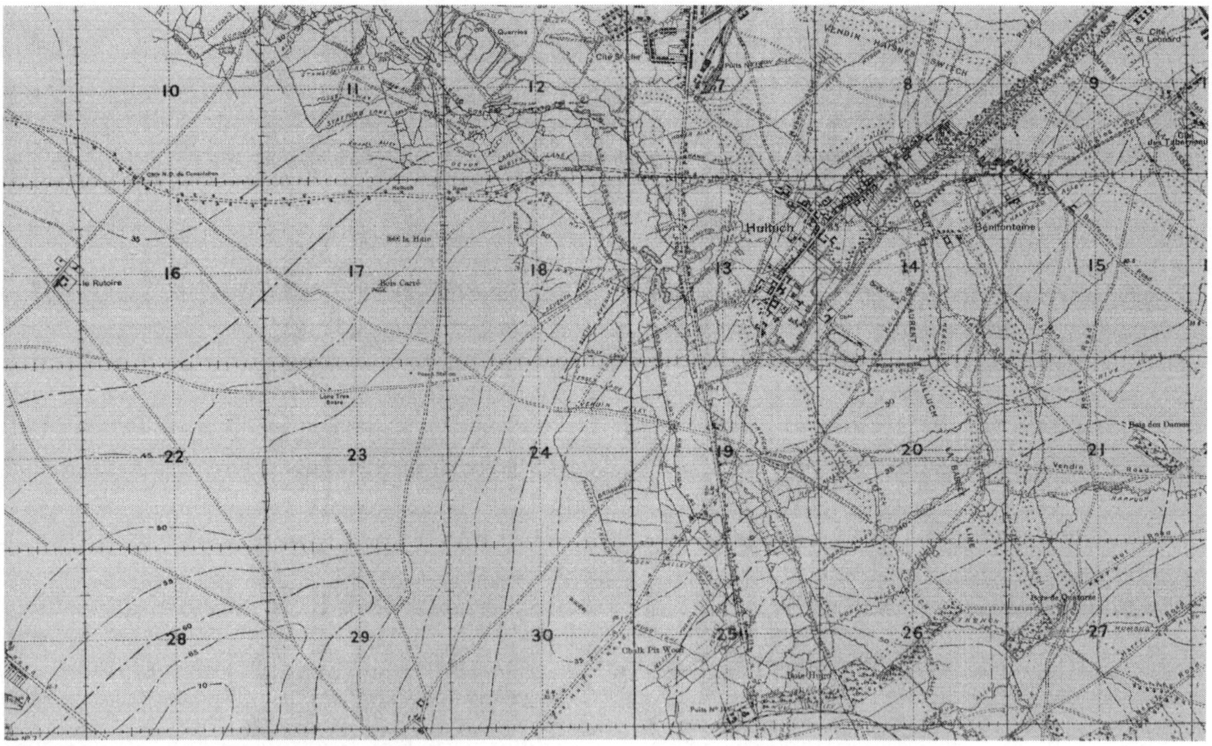

Battalion front line area G.12 to H 19.

on account of the bad weather. Training was therefore resumed on the 16th, lasting until 22nd. The advance party, which had proceeded to Nouex-Les-Mines on 14th returned to the battalion on 19th. Finally on 23rd at 11.30 am, the relief of 137 Brigade was resumed and the battalion moved to the hut camp at Nouex-Les-Mines, arriving at 1.30 pm. At 3 pm. under O.O. No 2, the advance party proceeded to take over trenches occupied by 1/6th South Stafford's Regt. At 3.15 pm which was dusk on 24th the first relief Company moved off from camp and by 9 pm, the relief had been accomplished without incident or casualty. The front line taken over was from G.12.d.75.10 to H.19.a.4.3. (Map Loos 36. C. NW edition 9a 1/10,000) under O.O. No3, with battalion H.Q., at G.17.b.88.24.

The Battalion occupied the trenches from 25th to 27th January and throughout this period the situation was very quiet. The enemy was preparing for its own Spring Offensive and were more than happy to see a 'Live and let live' situation prevail. During their tour of duty in the trenches the battalion did not have one casualty, which by WW1 standards was somewhat of a miracle.

The 28th saw the 7th South Stafford's relieving the Battalion and they would spend a few days as the reserve battalion in an area they knew well – Mazingarbe. The following day was taken up with cleaning, inspections, baths and Company training.

January had also seen a War Savings Campaign that came to an end on 31st. The amount subscribed during the month by all ranks was a healthy £ 2,150, with 250 subscribers although this was only a quarter of the battalion strength. With inflation rife at home many men had other financial pressures and saving was not high on their list of priorities.

The 1st February saw the Battalion still occupying the reserve billets at Mazingarbe (see 1917 maps). Company training was undertaken during the morning followed by preparations for a return to the front line. The battalion relieved the 7th South Stafford's during the evening in the Hulluch –Left sub sector. The move was once again without incident and the following day was a quiet one with the average trench strength of the Companies being 95 Other Ranks. Whenever possible the front line trenches were lightly held, thereby reducing the number of targets for shelling and snipers. More men could be quickly brought forward if needed to bolster the front line troops. In the Loos area the tunnels were an ideal location for troops to rest up in between spells of trench duties. Of course the enemy would know this and this was borne out by an entry on 3rd February, ' Enemy put down barrage on our Old Front Line, Vendin Alley and Reserve Lines'. The days up to the battalion relief on 9th February continued in this 'quiet' vein, with only inter Company relief on 5th, although the enemy artillery gave the British battery positions a hot time on 7th.

At 4 pm on 8th February, the battalion's numbers were increased when 4 officers and 149 Other Ranks from the 17th Battalion (Welbeck Rangers) Sherwood Foresters were transferred in. The four officers were Captain A.E. Brennan, Lieut. W.E. Barnes and 2/Lieuts. L.W. Foster and J. Turner. Officially the 17th Battalion ceased to exist on 12 February 1918 under the Army reorganization of its forces. Under the same reorganization 33rd Brigade became a three-battalion formation as the 6th Border Regiment was also disbanded. Four additional officers and 28 Other Ranks of the 17th Battalion were also transferred to the battalion and taken on strength, although this latter detail was made up of personnel on leave, courses etc. The four officers taken on strength but not yet present were Lieut. G.A. Royal (on leave), Lieut. R.F. Norland (course), 2/Lieut. H. Walker (course) and 2/Lieut. F.A. Allen (no reason given). All of the draft was accommodated at Mazingarbe until the battalion returned from its front line duties. The battalion moved out of the line on 9th February being relieved by the 6th Lincoln's and marched back to the billets at Mazingarbe. The relief was completed without incident or casualty at 10.30 pm.

The following three days were taken up preparing for their next stint in the front line. Company Commanders would supervise a clean up of the men and their equipment. The men had the opportunity of bathing and reducing the lice population for a few days. The draft of 17th battalion men were integrated into their new Companies within the 9th battalion. Training continued with particular emphasis on bayonet, musketry training, close order drill and wiring practice.

The 12th would also see another 9th battalion man succumb to his wounds and die in England.

57244 Private John William Watson was aged 36 years and a native of Lowdham in Nottinghamshire. He is buried in Lowdham (St Mary) Churchyard Extension.

The 13th saw the battalion returning to front line trench occupation and this time it would last seven days. The same day Captain W. Nason MC returned from leave in Canada. Whether he was a native of Canada was not stated. The battalion moved off at 4.30 pm to relieve the 7th South Stafford's in the right sub-sector of the Hulluch line and it was completed without incident by 10 pm. The average company strength in the line was 130 Other Ranks. It was possible that the right sector was livelier than the left, although the number of men holding the front line was always fluid. The newly transferred men would also need a turn in the trenches to learn the ways of their new battalion. The men would stay in the front line or reserve until 21st February with Inter-Company relief taking place on 17th.

Whilst the period was quiet it was not without incident and on 14th the enemy shelled his own wire during the morning opposite the left Company. The following day an enemy dog was 'captured' by the right Company carrying a dispatch and on 19th the old front and reserve lines were shelled using gas. The next day an enemy raid was expected on Vendin

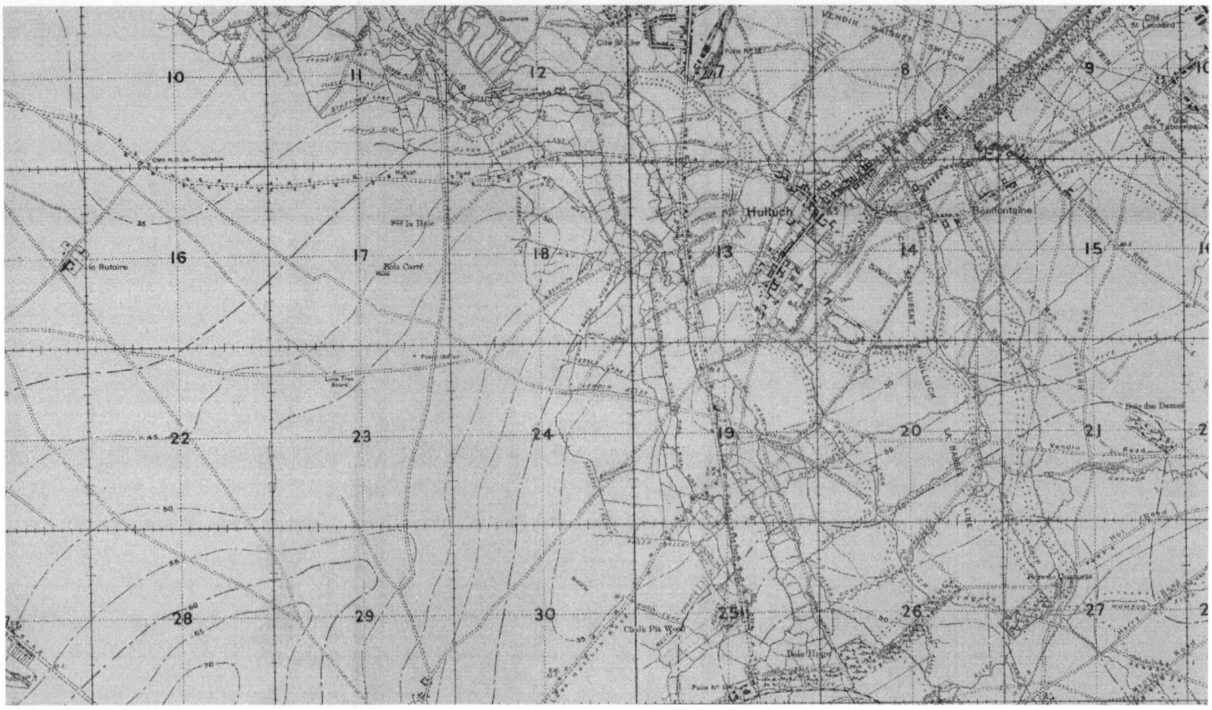

Vendin Alley leading to Vendin Post.

Post but nothing occurred. These events could be linked and it is possible that the enemy dog was carrying a dispatch, which the German's wanted to fall into the hands of the British thereby making the British think a raid was due on Vendin Post.

The Battalion were relieved by the 6th Lincoln's on 21st and returned to Mazingarbe. No doubt feeling at home amongst the coal mines and slag heaps of the area that surrounded them. Many of the men may also have longed for the boredom of working down a pit as opposed to the boredom of sitting in a trench.

The next three days were spent cleaning up and bathing followed by Company training. The 23rd saw 49 Other Ranks join the battalion from the 11th Divisional Depot. Men were no longer guaranteed a return to their old units after a wound or sickness but would end up at the Divisional Depot probably at Etaples with its infamous 'Bull Ring.' They would then be sent to whichever unit needed them. Many conscripts were also now joining front line units and young men with little training found themselves in the midst of trench life. The 24th/25th would be taken up with training and inspections – rifles and Lewis guns being checked for cleanliness. General cleaning prior to the return to the front line was also carried out.

Preparations for the move into the line and a projected raid were made on 25th. In the event the projected raid did not go ahead during the Battalions tour of duty. The Battalion relieved the 7th South Stafford's in the left Sub-sector without incident and by 8.15 pm they once again occupied the front line trenches. The 26th was an extremely quiet day but at 3 am on 27th the enemy attempted a raid on the next battalion but one on the left. A few gas shells were also sent into square G.23.C.1. – The cross roads near Posen Station.

The day was seen as quiet although a barrage was put down on Vendin Post, which resulted in three casualties, two of these were fatal.

6885 Private Edward Mortimer MM, was formerly in the 2nd battalion and born in Middlesbrough Yorkshire but living in Wellingborough, Northants prior to the war. Unusually he had the same number as another 9th Battalion man who died whilst serving with the 10th Battalion in 1916. 6885 Private Tom Alvey is commemorated on the Thiepval Memorial having been killed on the Somme 08/08/1916. Edward is buried at Philosophe British Cemetery Mazingarbe and grave III.B.28.

12500 Private Alfred James Wadsworth died of wounds the following day and is buried at Lapugnoy Military Cemetery and grave VII.B.8.

Also on 28th the enemy sent over a few gas shells into squares G.23 and 16. *(See Vendin Alley map above)*. The British batteries and trench Mortars where engaged in wire cutting in the area of the projected trench raid – H.13.a, although the raid does not seem to have taken place. It is possible that another unit undertook the raid with the Battalion in support.

So began March 1918, a month, which would see the British army pushed to breaking point with any man capable of holding a rifle being pushed into the front line. The Battalion though would be spared this onslaught and no doubt the men would be thankful that they held a quiet sector and one not being attacked by the enemy. The vast majority of men just wanted to get the job done and get home. Few if any were interested in 'death or glory'. The war had dragged remorselessly on too long for that. The make up of the army had changed out of all recognition from those heady days of 1914. The majority of the pre-war regulars had gone along with the Territorial Force. The keen volunteers had been supplemented with 'Derby men' and conscripts. This is not to say that they were not as keen but many were young and sent out to France with only barely adequate training.

From 1st to 6th the battalion continued its spell in the front line with the situation remaining quiet although not quiet enough for two men though who died during this period.

16935 Private Wilfred Witherbed was born at Long Eaton, Derbyshire. He was killed in action on 4th March and buried at Philosophe British Cemetery and grave III.B.34.

The following day 13398 Private Ernest Jackson died of wounds. He was aged 22 years and a native of Perlethorpe Nott's. He is also buried at Philosophe British Cemetery and grave III.B.39.

Trench improvements continued as the allies awaited the German offensive, which they knew had to come sooner rather than later. After years of the 'offensive' spirit holding sway a new defensive mind-set was called for. The troops all across the front line worked tirelessly in an attempt to reinforce their trench system before the inevitable happened. Trenches that had been seen as little more than jumping off points for the next offensive had to be turned into defensive positions. On 6th at 8 pm the battalion was once again relieved by the 6th Lincoln's and returned to the reserve billets and defences at Mazingarbe.

Three days out of the line followed which gave the men time to rest and recharge their batteries prior to the next tour of duty. The men bathed, cleaned their kit and had platoon inspections. The mornings of the 8th/9th were taken up with training whilst the afternoons were given over to recreational activities. The British army set high store in recreation, as it was a great team builder and engendered 'Esprit de Corps'.

92165 Private Daniel Griffin aged 25 years a Sheffield man was killed on the 8th or more likely died of wounds. He is buried at Philosophe next to his comrade Ernest Jackson in grave III.B.40.

On the 10th it was a move to the front once again and the battalion relieved the 7th South Stafford's in the Hulluch Sector South. The relief was completed by 9.30 pm and the situation was seen as quiet. As previously mentioned the term 'quiet' was a relative one and on the 10th four men of the battalion were killed. Three of the men are buried at Philosophe British Cemetery, Mazingarbe,

23127 Private Walter Parr was 33 years of age of Arnold Nott's. He is buried in grave III. B. 44.

57299 Private Samuel Redfearn aged 39 years was a native of the village of Eyam (famous for being a plague village in medieval times). He is buried in grave III. B. 46

59913 Private Donald Campbell was attached to the 33rd Brigade Light Trench Mortar Battery. Donald was born in Perthshire, living in Burton-on-Trent and enlisted at Woodstock Oxon. He is buried in grave III. B. 47.

The fourth man is buried in a battlefield cemetery and was the only person to be buried there in 1918. Haisnes Village was in German hands until the final advance but the British in the Battle of Loos took parts of the commune. The cemetery was named after a small copse southwest of the village.

92149 Private George Henry Metcalfe aged 40 years was a Yorkshireman and attached to the 33rd Brigade Light Trench Mortar Battery. Many of the graves in this Cemetery were destroyed by shellfire although George's survived and he is buried in grave H.6.

The 11th was another quiet day although every-one knew that the enemy offensive would come sooner rather than later. The 6th Lincoln's were relieved in the Hulluch Sector North but would only move back as far as the support dugouts in the Lone Trench Locality. This stiffened the defensive forces in the sector but put added pressure on the Division as every Brigade was in the front or support lines.

At 9 pm on 12th the Canadian 7th and 10th Battalions mounted a raid on the enemy trenches to the battalion right. The enemy retaliated with a barrage on the battalion front and 2/Lieut H. Cox of 'A' Company was wounded. Whilst 2/Lt Cox seemed to have survived the war the nominal roll of officers dated 31 July 1918 did not record him. It is therefore likely that he was still incapacitated by his wounds.

The period 13th to 16th remained quiet although each evening covering parties were provided for the 3rd Australian Tunnelling Company who were laying charges for blowing the anti-tank craters on the Battalions front. The 13th also saw the Company relief take place and this was successfully completed by 6 p.m. The cleaning and improvement to the trench system was also a daily task. Also on 13th 2/Lieut C.A.B. Thurburn left the battalion and proceeded to England to transfer to the Royal Flying Corps (RAF from 1st April 1918). It would seem that for some reason this transfer did not go ahead as he is mentioned on the Nominal Roll of 31 July 1918 as a Lieutenant. The War Diary gives no reason for his return although the Nominal Roll gives 24 June as the date he was taken back onto the Battalion strength.

At 10.15 pm on 16th the battalion was relieved in the front line by the 7th South Stafford's and in turn relieved the 6th Lincoln's in the Lone Trench Locality. This was completed without incident by 11.50 pm. Some of the men would be allowed back to Mazingarbe for a couple of days to clean up and bathe. At this time it was impossible to relieve a complete Battalion and the men would spend two days in fourteen out of the line. The 17th was once again quiet and the men provided a number of working parties for trench cleaning and relaying of trench boards (duckboards). Plus the usual fetching and carrying for the battalion in the front line.

2/Lieut A.A. Hill proceeded to England and a transfer to the Machine Gun Corps. He would train at Grantham which is where the battalion began its training in 1914. The following day saw more working parties and the enemy became more active with gas shells fired around square G.23.6. There were three bursts of some 100 to 150, 77 mm shells during the day but no casualties were recorded. It was a common occurrence for both sides to send over gas shells on a regular basis. Firstly it could catch the unwary and secondly the gas would lie in shell holes and trenches making life unpleasant for the men. There was a third reason, which Col. Scothern mentioned in his notes and that was of 'idiots' collecting souvenirs!

Col. Scothern's notes for March explain all.

> *"The sector was comparatively quiet until the opening of the enemy offensive on the Somme in March, when there was a good deal of gas shelling. This was rather a trying period, as an enemy attack was considered imminent.*
>
> *The Division was holding a wide front, and had three Brigades in the line. As the situation stood it was impossible to relieve a whole battalion at a time, and it was customary to allow the men to bathe and get a clean change of clothing. This meant that men were out of the line for two days in fourteen.*
>
> *Notwithstanding the trying conditions this period had its humorous side. The Officers had to keep a very careful watch on the men, who were prone to take off their gas helmets at the first opportunity. One Officer on trench duty came across a sentry standing on the fire step with tears streaming down his face and a very strong smell of gas all round. On being asked why he was not wearing his gas helmet, the sentry replied, 'They've only sent eighteen shells over here, and they were all duds'. Again one very inexperienced young officer, fresh out from England, was sent to fill in holes made by gas shells in the usual way. Unfortunately he had a taste for souvenirs, and finding a nose cap and several fragments of shells, promptly put them in his pocket, with disastrous results to his skin, and a somewhat lengthy sojourn in hospital".*

No mention is made as to whether the officer was charged with 'self inflicted' wounds. The 19th/20th saw more enemy gas shelling around G23.6, but despite this the working parties carried on as normal. Although the inconvenience of having to wear gas helmets made a difficult task almost impossible. The men did not know that the following day the massive enemy offensive would begin. One man would not see the enemy offensive begin.

204461 Private Ernest Hancock aged 30 years and from Newbold, Derbyshire, died of wounds on 20 March and is buried at Lapugnoy Military Cemetery and grave IX. A. 5.

The war diary for 21st March is fairly understated *'Enemy offensive starts South of Somme'.* The massive German offensive had begun and firstly the men on the Somme would be pushed back across the old 1916 battlefield.

Despite the massive blow they would finally stop the German thrust, although it would cost the Allies dearly in men and material. The second blow would come in Flanders and once again the British were stretched to the limit of endurance. The Loos – Hulluch area though would remain a fairly quiet sector and it would therefore be a time of trench occupation interspersed with occasional raids. It was imperative that the Army Command knew as much as possible about the enemy in front of them. Would the next blow come against this sector or could the line be held with the available troops. There was a need to know which German Regiments faced them on the Loos front. The enemy though also needed this sector to remain quiet and the continual gas attacks were used to achieve this.

The enemy launched a heavy gas attack overnight on 21st, which resulted in 2/Lieut W.G.A. Griffiths and eleven Other Ranks being admitted to hospital suffering from the effects of gas. 2/Lieut Griffiths was not shown on the Nominal Roll at the end of July and was no doubt still recovering in hospital from the effects of the gas.

The 22nd would see the battalion relieved by 7th South Stafford's and proceed to the rest billets at Mazingarbe. The day had been quiet although the battalion had been on constant alert for enemy attacks. The battalion relief was completed by 11.30 pm and by 1.30 am on 23rd the men were settled in the billets at Mazingarbe.

An ex 9th Battalion officer attached to the 4th Battalion East Lancashire Regiment would die on 23rd.

Major Henry Leslie Paddock is buried at Roisel Communal Cemetery Extension and grave I. G. 3.

The period between 23rd and 27th was taken up with the usual activities of a battalion at rest, although each day at 5 a.m. the men stood too in their billets. The situation was still tense and the Somme situation was not good as the enemy continued its rapid advance. There was still a danger of the enemy attempting a break through in the La Basee canal area and the Battalion needed to be on the alert and ready for rapid movement. Despite this the Battalion did get its baths and time to clean up in preparation for the next period of front line occupation. Training and recreation, the backbone of the British Army for hundreds of years was also carried out despite the tension. In fact the Battalion even managed a football match versus the 9th Battalion West Yorkshire Regiment (32nd Brigade) on 24th although no score was given. The following day a match versus the 6th Lincoln's was played but once again no score was given. This lack of scores could point to unfavourable results on both occasions. The matches though would have relaxed the men and taken their minds of the events of recent days.

The Battalion moved forward into the line on 27th by first relieving the 7th South Stafford's in Lone Locality with Battalion HQ, being set up at 'Howsons Post', Hulluch North Sub-sector. The following evening they moved forward to relieve the 6th Lincoln's in the Hulluch South Sub-Sector. The relief of the Lincoln's being completed by 10.25 pm with no casualties being mentioned. During this tour of duty the Battalion saw much more action with much shelling in the front line and reserve areas. The German High Command knew that breaking the British Army would in all likelihood end the war and they would throw every man they could into this enterprise.

Front line trench occupation normally saw quiet days and hectic nights. During the Battalions tour of front line duty the usual work of improvements and sentry duties were supplemented with a number of fighting patrols and trench raids. On 29th March the usual working parties carried out work on the trench system in an effort to make it impassable to the enemy. The speed of the enemy attacks on the Somme had shaken everyone and there was an urgent need to improve the defences before the blow fell on the Loos front. 2/Lieut B.J Cooper led a fighting patrol to obtain identification of the enemy troops opposite the battalion front. The patrol managed to enter the enemy trench system but as the diary stated *'Narrowly escapes capturing a Bosche'*. This seemed a fairly ambiguous entry but it would seem to mean that they nearly captured one of the enemy. The Germans held the front line with a minimum of troops at this stage in the war, preferring a rapid deployment from the reserve lines if needed. The desperate need for a prisoner was obvious as the following night a larger fighting patrol was sent out. Lieut. G.A. Royle, 2/Lieuts. W. Francis and C. Bottom and an unspecified number of Other Ranks took part. A party under Lieut, Royle reached the enemy trench but they were unsuccessful in capturing a prisoner. On the 31st arrangements were made that would see an even larger party attempt a raid on the enemies trenches in opposite the Battalion although this time it would be men of the 6th Lincoln's. Four officers and 160 Other Ranks were tasked to take part in this raid but it was later cancelled. The reason for this was that a prisoner had been taken somewhere near the Battalions front and had stated that an enemy offensive on the sector was very probable. It would be doubtful that a prisoner would know exactly where the attack would fall and it was even possible that the man had been primed to keep the British on their toes. The Lincoln's raid would eventually go ahead on 2nd April after being cancelled once again on 1st. There was some concern about an H.Q. gun firing from behind a smoke screen in the vicinity of Wingles some 6 kms away, the gap between the flash and report being 20 seconds. Although the calibre of the gun was not specified it could be assumed that it was large.

The 31st also saw Colonel Thornton DSO relinquish his role as C.O. of the Battalion, proceeding to take command of the 1st Infantry Brigade. Actually he had been away from the Battalion for some considerable time although the actual official leaving would be noted as this day. Until the arrival of Lt-Col, Scothern DSO the battalion was commanded by Major Piper. Col. Scothern had previously commanded the 6th Borders in the same brigade and he therefore had but a short distance to 'proceed'.

Colonel Thornton DSO had been the battalion's C.O. since the end of January 1916 and the men thought highly of him. Lt-Col Scothern had been with the Battalion from the early days and had fought and been wounded on Gallipoli. He had served with the Battalion throughout prior to his temporary move to the 6th Borders in August 1917. The 6th Borders being another Battalion disbanded in February 1918 and leaving 33rd Brigade as a three-battalion unit. The 9th Sherwood Foresters, 6th Lincoln's and 7th South Stafford's would see out the war in the 33rd Brigade.

At 8 am on 2nd April the fighting patrol from 6th Lincoln's moved out from the Battalion's front and completed a very successful raid on the enemy trenches bringing back one officer and 30 Other rank prisoners. The enemy put down a very heavy barrage for fifteen minutes in retaliation for the raid but no casualties were sustained. Damage was done to the trench system and wiring though and the men repaired this during the night. Men were found for fighting patrols each night from 3rd to 5th and it is probable that during one of these patrols that another man was killed. The battalion had been leading somewhat of a charmed life concerning casualties in the recent days.

22973 Private John W. Francis Illsley was from Polesworth near Tamworth Staffordshire. He is buried at Philosophe British Cemetery Mazingarbe and grave III. C. 30. Colonel Scothern saw April thus:

> *"April opened quietly, but prisoners captured on the front stated that an attack was considered likely. On April 7th the enemy commenced using gas shells in large quantities, Philosophe in particular being subjected to a very heavy fire. This shelling caused a large number of casualties in the Division, and was continued at intervals until April 17th. On the18th the enemy attacked North of the La Basse Canal, but nothing developed on the Divisional front, which continued to be fairly lively.*
>
> *Preparations had been made for a cylinder gas attack on a large scale, on the Corps Front, but although the cylinders were all in position, the operation was continually postponed. A Wiring party of 'A' Company on April 26th was passing some of these cylinders, when an enemy T.M. Shell burst nine of them and the wiring party had thirty casualties."*

The Special Company's, Royal Engineers began to install the gas cylinders on 5th April. The Battalion meanwhile continued with its front line occupation and continued work on the defences whilst still mounting fighting patrols.

The 6th saw the Battalion relieved by 7th South Stafford's and moving into Brigade support with two Companies in Lone Trench and two at Mazingarbe to provide immediate back up if needed. The companies were disposed as follows – 'B' and 'C' occupied the Lone Trench area whilst 'A' and 'D' were based at Mazingarbe. All three Brigades of the 11th Division remained on full alert with little opportunity of rest.

On the 7th working parties had to be supplied for 68th Filed Company R.E., for the whole twenty four hours as new dug-outs had to be quickly made in the front line area. At 8.45 pm the enemy commenced shelling with mustard gas and this continued until 11.45 pm. The effect was to leave a very dense gas concentration in the battalion area. The men would have to undertake working parties whilst wearing gas helmets and this would slow them considerably. The use of mustard gas would cause many casualties in the coming days. The enemy gas attack resumed at 4 am on 8th and continued for a further two hours. This caused heavy casualties and fifteen men were sent to hospital for treatment. After so much shelling by gas the residue contaminated the whole area and it was almost impossible not to be affected by it. It would linger in the bottom of trenches and shell holes causing discomfort for some and life threatening illness to others. Certainly on the 9th it achieved its main aim, which was to cause the maximum disruption and call a halt to any works, which may have been in progress. All precautions were taken and works suspended which cut the casualties to a minimum but obviously for the enemy the attacks had been a success.

Captain and Adjutant W. Nason MC received a slight hand wound during this period but remained on duty. The Battles of the Lys began on 9th with the Battle of Estaires, which included the defence of Givenchy by the 55th Division. Inter Company relief also took place during this period and on 10th the battalion would move forward once again. During the daylight hours the situation was quiet although the effects of the enemy gas attack began to take effect on the men and another thirty casualties were sent to hospital. The already hard -pressed battalion had lost forty-five of its number in two days and the gas still lay all around. Mustard gas could cause temporary blindness, respiratory problems and also burn the skin. The relief of the 6th Lincoln's took place in the evening and was completed by 10.30 pm without incident. The Battalion was based in the Hulluch Tunnel (North sector). At 11.20 pm the Battalion received details concerning some information received from enemy prisoners who had been taken during the previous days fighting between La Bassee and Givenchy. The enemy offensive was likely to be extended to the Hulluch Sector on 11th or 12th and the Battalion took the necessary precautions. It took two long days and nights for the men and even more defensive works would have to be constructed. On the 11th the Battalion took all the defensive precautions it could and waited. Defences being improved, additional fire bays made and bombing blocks positioned in disused trenches. All of the civilians were evacuated from Mazingarbe, Noyelles and La Bourse during the day. It would seem strange that an area of so much military activity and under constant shelling would still have civilians living there. The British knew that the renewed offensive would continue and the next blow could fall anywhere and at any time. The 12th remained quiet and worked continued on the defences whilst the British artillery carried out an intensive harassing barrage on the enemy trenches and communications. It was important to harass the enemy in an attempt to disrupt their preparations for any possible attack. Even if the next attack did not fall on the Divisions front at Hulluch diversionary attacks were always possible. A 'Special examination' of the prisoners captured at Givenchy confirmed that an attack on the battalions front could develop at any moment. In the event it was Hazebrouck further north that took the brunt of the next attack.

Between the 13th and 17th every available man was employed on the defences and the trenches were strengthened even more with extra wiring, fire bay improvements and putting in new dugouts. The British could not afford another disaster such as the Somme on 21st March when the new German tactics of using Storm troopers had succeeded in rolling up thousands of men and vast amounts of equipment. The 18th saw a heavy barrage on the Battalions left and an attack on Givenchy. This was officially known as the Battle of Bethune, which included the second defence of Givenchy by the 1st Division. Brigadier Thornton may have wished he had remained with the battalion and not with the 1st Brigade, which was part of 1st Division. So desperate was the situation that guns could be seen firing over open sights in Hulluch. In the event the Battalions front did not receive a direct assault but to their north as far as Ypres, allied troops were fighting a desperate battle to stop the enemy onslaught. Haig has issued his 'Backs to the wall' order, which the majority of the fighting men never heard as they had more pressing matters to worry about. The Battalion could only wait and see if their sector would be next. During the evening of 18th the Battalion was relieved by the 7th South Staffords and this was completed by 10.15 pm., with 'C' and 'D' Companies arriving at Mazingarbe by midnight. Battalion HQ along with 'A' and 'B' companies remained in Brigade support in the Lone Locality.

The men killed during April were buried at Philosophe British Cemetery, Mazingarbe and the first man was from 'A' Company killed on 18th.

8963 Private Ernest Truman aged 35 years, 'A' Company was a Carrington, Nott's man and he is buried in grave III. C. 37.

During the 19th the men continued clearing trenches and providing working parties to build new dugouts. An inter-company relief took place on 20th with 'D' and 'C' Companies relieving 'A' and 'B' respectively at Lone Locality. The two relieved Companies proceeded to Mazingarbe for a rest and baths. The left of the Battalions sector, north of the La Bassee Canal was subjected to a heavy bombardment during the day. There should have been a gas release from cylinders on the Battalion front but this was postponed. The cylinders had been installed previously in readiness but at the last minute the operation was cancelled. This could have been for a number of reasons but usually wind direction would be the major cause of cancellation. Gas shells were a much more efficient way of distribution but gas release from the front line still had its uses. The decision not to release would have horrendous results for the 'A' Company though.

The 21st was a quiet day in the Battalions sector, although between 3.30 and 4.30 pm a heavy bombardment was laid down on the right of its front and the reserve lines. At 11.30 pm, the Canadians on the battalions right flank laid down a dummy barrage on the enemy's front and support lines. The enemy would have expected an immediate trench raid and dummy barrages were used to confuse them. The Canadians carried out the raid on 22nd at 1.30am resulting in heavy artillery barrages from both sides. The evening of 22nd saw the battalion relieve the 6th Lincoln's in Hulluch South and this was completed without incident by 10.35 pm, the enemy shelled Posen Alley at about 10 pm and this lasted for fifteen minutes. The enemy had used the relief period to attempt a trench raid of their own and it would be the morning before evidence of this raid was discovered. The enemy put down three whirlwind bombardments on Posen alley in the morning and twice in the afternoon. It would be obvious that the enemy had a reason for doing this. Men from the Battalion discovered some enemy bombs (grenades) in the front line left of Posen Alley. It was thought that the enemy had entered the trench during the night and found the gas cylinders. They would do all in their power to destroy them and the British staff would know that a trench raid or barrage would destroy the cylinders. The logical step would have been to have them removed and although this would have been a difficult job, it would have saved lives.

Another man died on 23rd and is buried at Pernes British Cemetery and grave I. D. 29.

13175 Private Ernest Hood was attached to the 33rd Brigade Trench Mortar Battery and was 24 years of age. He was living in Doncaster prior to the war and died of wounds.

The officers of the 8th battalion Northumberland Fusiliers (34th brigade, 11th Division) reconnoitred the Battalion's front during the 24th. It was a misty day but a quiet one for the men. One man from 'A' Company was wounded during the day.

The morning of 25th was once again misty which made conditions ideal for enemy patrols to reconnoitre the British front line. The morning though remained quiet with no surprises for the battalion. The enemy did not leave things quiet for long though and between 3.10 pm and 7.30 pm they heavily shelled the front areas along the Loos-Hulluch road and of course Posen Alley. The British artillery did retaliate at 6 pm but only for some 30 minutes. Posen dump came in for a great deal of attention with a mixture of gas and H.E. shells, this resulted in one man receiving wounds and one killed. The gas laid down was of a particularly potent type on this occasion.

21063 Private Arthur John Spittlehouse aged 23 years enlisted at Newark, Notts and buried in grave III. C. 43, at Mazingarbe.

The following day saw more shelling with the front line and Posen Allen again receiving attention from the enemy artillery. Posen Dump and Tenth Avenue were also subjected to shelling at 8.45 pm. The 11th Divisional artillery relieved the 5th Army Field Artillery Brigade on the battalions sector.The folly of not removing the gas cylinders once the enemy knew of their location would cost the battalion dearly during the night of 26th/27th. At 2 am on 27th, 'A' Company was engaged as a wiring party in the front line, working at one of the sentry posts. The enemy shelled the area bursting nine of the cylinders resulting in 2/Lieut Harding and thirty Other Ranks becoming casualties. Fifteen of the men were killed and are buried at Philosophe British Cemetery, lying side by side in Plot III. Row D. graves 1 to 14.

14054 Corporal Frank Grimshaw aged 25 years of Didsbury Lancs.

41282 Private Edgar Buxton aged 39 years of Matlock Bath.

201136 Private Harold Archer Smedley aged 31 years of Derby.

17942 Private John Brown from Long Sutton Linc's.

71414 Private Percy Edward Keeble a Suffolk man who formerly served as 26800 Norfolk Regiment.

25210 Lance Corporal Percy Swann of Stoke-on-Trent.

81817 Private William Foster Wilson aged 20 years and from Woodville Derby's.

307707 Lance Corporal Walter Augustus Shaw aged 33 years a Derby man.

27498 Lance Corporal Patrick Churchill aged 29 years of Derby.

29638 Private Lawrence Pinkney aged 20 years and a native of Derby who had served with the 17th Battalion.

70959 Private John Tecar Wright aged 38 years was a Leicester native and formerly 24103 Leicester Regiment.

71041 Sergeant Bernard Swindell aged 25 years of Nottingham.

9253 Sergeant John Knight was born in Buxton and living in Romiley Cheshire prior to the war.

69034 Private Walter Knight whose abode was at Eggington Derby's.

The day itself was quiet except for the usual shelling of Posen Alley during the afternoon. At 11.15 pm the Canadian troops on the Battalions right mounted a trench raid and whilst not returning with any prisoners, they did ascertain the identification of the enemy troops opposite them. There was little retaliation from the enemy as a result of the raid. The final three days of April were put as quiet although the enemy artillery was as active as ever. It was amazing how everything in the Great War became 'normal' and how often the word 'usual' cropped up. The usual enemy shelling, the usual working parties and the usual patrols etc. In the fourth year of the war with no end in sight the abnormal had become normal and the unusual very much usual.

The enemy artillery continued its attempts to disrupt the front line and kept the battalion on its toes. It was imperative that British troops could not be allowed to rest or thin their line to bolster the defences further north. The 28th saw the British Field guns fairly active during the morning but otherwise it was quiet. The enemy artillery was very active in the afternoon and targeted the left reserve Company HQ using 5.9"s and 4.2"s. The 29th would see the last offensive in the Battles of the Lys with an attack at Scherpenberg and this was probably the reason for the Battalion's front being quiet. Posen Alley received its usual shelling in the afternoon although this did not stop the battalion putting out patrols and providing working parties. More work was carried out on the defences with the barbed wire being strengthened even more. The defences were now ready for any enemy attack and all the men could do was wait.

The last day of April would see the Battalion relieved by the 7th South Stafford's although only 'C' and 'D' companies returned to the billets at Mazingarbe. Battalion HQ, 'A' and 'B' Companies would be in Brigade support for two days and moved to Lone Trench (Lone Locality). The 46th month of the war began with no obvious victory in sight and in fact the Allies were hanging on by their fingertips. Although most men would not know it, the worst was now over and the German offensives had been stopped. They would attempt another attack in Champagne at the end of May and early June but once again after initial success it would peter out.

Colonel Scothern gave five lines to May 1918:
"During the early part of May, the dispositions were such only two Brigades were needed in the line at the same time, thus affording a welcome opportunity for battalions to get a rest in turn and also a change of sector. This change first affected the battalion on May 10th when the St.Elie sector was taken over. This was fairly quiet, but a good deal of work was done on the defences. The cylinder gas was discharged at 10.30 p.m. on 12th, and caused a fairly heavy artillery retaliation. About this time, gas was continually being discharged on the enemy lines."

The first day of May saw the enemy as active as ever and the British dumps received particular attention. Division had decided that the dispositions of the Brigades on the front would be changed and in line with this, the C.O. accompanied by the Second in Command and Company Commanders set off to the St Elie north sector to reconnoitre their portion of the line. The left battalion of the 32nd Brigade was holding this area and the 9th would relieve them on the 10th May. The next day the Battalion was relieved by the 11th Manchester's, 34th Brigade and this was completed by 11 pm, after which the whole of the 9th, moved to billets at Bracquemont. For the first time in almost a month the whole Battalion was together and at rest.

The German offensives had failed and the danger of an enemy victory receded. Many thousands of allied troops had become casualties or prisoners of war. Thousands of lives had been lost on the Somme (1916) and Passchendaele (1917 3rd Ypres), but by May 1918 the troops were in some areas further back than the original front line. To win the war the ground would have to be retaken and at great cost.

The 2nd also saw another man succumb to his wounds at the Casualty Clearing Station based in Pernes.

24787 Sergeant Francis Bark MM aged 26 years was the only son of John and Margaret from Curbar nr Sheffield. It is more than likely that he was wounded on 27th April when the fifteen 'A' Company men were killed. He is buried in grave II. A. 31. Pernes British Cemetery. Francis received his Military Medal for work near Beaumont Hamel on 27 November 1916.

The 3rd and 4th were yet again 'quiet' days and the Battalion made the most of them with a reasonable rest from 2 am until 7 am on the first day. The enemy shelled the area all morning and set a coalmine alight and blew up the gasometer. After the previous few weeks in the trenches and reserve five hours sleep would certainly have been seen as reasonable. The day was spent bathing, relaxing and recovering from the recent rigours of trench life. The 4th did include some light training in the morning and the afternoon was given over to football for the 'enthusiasts' of the sport. Presumably non- enthusiasts could spend the afternoon relaxing although as the C.O. Col Scothern was an ex Oxford and England footballer the men may have had little choice but to participate.

The 5th was an important day for the Battalion and two of its number in particular. The General Officer Commanding (G.O.C.) 11th Division, Major-General H. Davies inspected the battalion and also presented Medal Ribbons to Sergeant Hunt and Private Clowes who had earned Military Medals. Private Clowes would die on 4th November 1918 at Sebourg. Both men received Military Medals for work at Poelcappelle 4th October 1917.

The G.O.C. complimented the Battalion on its

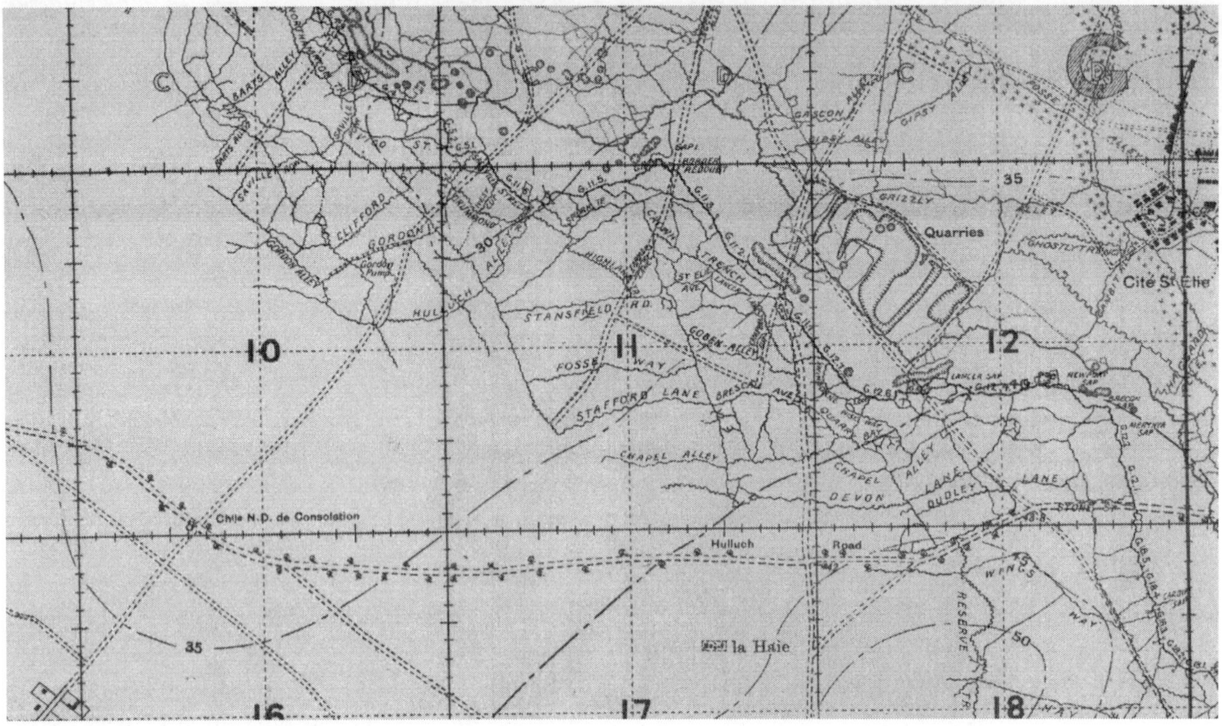

Loos NW3 G 11 and 12 showing the front lines

excellent turnout, particularly in view of the short time at their disposal for cleaning up after the recent trench duties. There followed a march past by the Battalion with the G.O.C. taking the salute and the recipients of the honours being at his side which would be a memorable moment for both men. The March past was done in excellent style with the Divisional band playing the Regimental March – The Young May Moon.

The 6th to 10th was taken up with training during the mornings and recent fighting had highlighted areas of concern, which needed working on. By this period many of the replacements were young conscripts who had seen little training prior to moving to France. The areas of concern were – Musketry and section fighting – these being addressed over the following days with a great deal of success. Every man in an infantry battalion had to be highly efficient in the use of his rifle but the high standards of the British Army had slipped during the course of the war. The basics of advancing and withdrawing as sections whilst giving mutual support through covering fire were also drummed into the men. Excellent progress was made over the four days and the training would stand the battalion in good stead for the future. Whilst the men trained the Company Officers and N.C.O's spent time in reconnoitring the routes to the new sector and of course the sector itself. This was their task for the four days and the routes were trod time and time again.

The 10th saw the battalion on the move once again with a change of scenery and sector St Elie North. This was just north of the previous sector –

They relieved the 9th Battalion West Yorkshire Regiment, 32nd Brigade, 11th Division in the left sub-sector of the St Elie North sector. The relief was completed by 6 pm and immediately the men were put to work wiring in the front of posts in Stansfield Road (Trench). The 11th was another quiet day with only a few enemy Trench Mortars sent over to keep the Battalion on its toes. The following day would probably have been the same had it not been for the Battalion discharging cylinder gas (Livens projectors) which although successful led to heavy enemy retaliation. Warning lights from the enemy trenches gave ample evidence of the confusion caused by the gas. The enemy would have expected either a raid or a full attack and sent over a fairly heavy barrage killing one man.

70861 Private Frederick Bishop was a native of Wolverhampton and formerly 26763 South Staffordshire Regiment. He is buried at Philosophe and grave IV. C. 6.

Work continued on wiring from 10.30 pm onwards and more gas was discharged on St Elie and Fosse 8 at 12.30 am. The enemy once again retaliated with heavy Trench Mortars. The days though were quiet with little activity on either side of the wire. The discharge of the gas cylinders was deemed a success as infantry and artillery observation posts reported in. The diary stated "*Boche stretcher-bearers were uncomfortably busy for 24 hours in forward areas alone"*

The 15th and 16th were once again fairly quiet except for the British heavy artillery firing on Haisnes.

The following night though was a busy one for the men with a considerable amount of movement. The 1st Division was located on the battalion's left flank and had made the Village Line their main line of resistance. It was still not known if yet another enemy offensive would be launched and on this sector. The 1st Divisions move caused problems along the 11th Divisional front and the dispositions of the front line battalions including the 9th had to be altered to comply. The change in dispositions was completed without incident or casualty.The Battalion was relieved in the left sub-sector of the Brigade front on the 18th by 7th South Stafford's and moved into brigade support at Vermelles. Three of the companies were located in the village and its immediate vicinity whilst one company was located at Le Rutoire Farm. This company was quite lucky as the Farm was seldom shelled as the enemy maps showed it as an Advanced Dressing Station.

At 7.30 am the 11th Manchester Regiment, 34th Brigade mounted a raid on the enemies third line, Hilda Trench between H.13.c.97.18 and H.13.c.99.82. The raid achieved considerable success bringing back prisoners and identifying enemy units. Considerable damage was also done to enemy dugouts and material through bombing.

The Battalion spent three days at Vermelles and nothing unusual was reported except that the weather improved and became almost tropical. The enemy kept up intermittent shelling, using Blue cross gas shells, sneezing gas and some Yellow Cross gas shells. This shelling caused no casualties but as ever with gas there was a good deal of inconvenience.

The 22nd saw the Battalion moving up to the front line and relieving the 6th Lincoln's, this being completed without incident by 5 pm. The following day the last of the Livens Projector cylinders expended their gas on to the enemy front line. At 12.30 am on the 24th a raid was carried out by the KRRC (King's Royal Rifle Corps) on the 1st Divisional front which was on the Battalions left flank. The raid netted four prisoners for interrogation. The enemy retaliated on the Battalion's front although without any real conviction. At 11 pm gas projectors (mortars) were discharged using Trench Mortars on the 1st Divisional front.

The 25th must have been an extremely quiet day, either that or 2/Lt Bull wrote the war diaries, " 2/Lt Bull, was again wounded".

The battalion's five-day stint in the front line ended on 26th with the 11th Manchester's relieving them. The 33rd Brigade going into Divisional reserve for seven days at Bracquemont and by 2 am on 27th all ranks were reported to be in billets. The men spent the 27th bathing, cleaning up and having their clothing replaced or refitted.

From 28th to 31st the Battalion would spend each morning in training, having inspections and cleaning up. The afternoons and evenings were given over to recreation. Major Harding M.C. had prepared an extensive program of sports and entertainment prior to the battalion coming out of the line. The program embraced Inter-Platoon, Inter-Company and battalion football games, a cross-country race and boxing competitions. The men also received free tickets for the cinema and performances by the 'Wunny-Wuns' at the Divisional theatre. The 'Wunny-Wuns' being the 11th Divisional Concert party (oney-ones – 11). Canteens were opened up for all of the N.C.O.'s and men with an anteroom being established for the use of officers. The cross-country race was over a course of some two and a half miles and it resulted in an easy victory for 'B' company, with 2/Lt Sutton winning in a very respectable time of 14 minutes. The last day of May saw the big football match versus the 7th South Stafford's on their ground at Boisdu Froissant. It was a very fast and exciting game with honours even at the end, the score being 1-1.

The 1st of June saw a match versus the 6th Lincoln's which the battalion lost 0 –2. The whole day was given over to rest and recreation prior to the return to front line duty. Sunday 2nd saw the battalion parading for church in the morning followed by the Inter-Platoon football tournament. The following day the Battalion left Bracquemont to relieve the 6th York and Lanc's in Hay Locality, which was the left sub-section of the Brigades right flank. The Echelon (reserves) moved to Hersin whilst 'B' company was located at Mazingarbe. The relief began at 9 pm and by 1 am it was completed. The enemy as usual knew of the relief and shelled the area heavily between 2 and 3 am resulting in four casualties in 'A' company.

The 9th Bn Royal Sussex Regiment of 73rd Brigade mounted a raid at 11.15 pm which resulted in the capture of two prisoners. The Sussex's were located on the battalions right at H.26.d.3.0. The enemy shelled the area fairly heavily between 10 and 11 pm with a mixture of H.E. and gas but otherwise the 5th June was fairly quiet. More alterations and adjustments had to be made on the Brigade front during the night of 6th/7th. The boundary between the right and left Brigades on the Divisional sector was altered, as was the boundary in the reserve line between the right and left of the right Brigade. These alterations were meant to strengthen the line as a new enemy offensive was expected at any time. The enemy had launched an offensive in Champagne on 27th May and by 6th June this was all but over. If the enemy did launch yet another offensive then the Loos/Hulluch sector would be a strong favourite for attention. The men in the front line were tasked with holding on until such time as the Allies armies were ready to go on the offensive again.

On the night of 7th/8th the Battalion less 'B' company were relieved by the 7th South Stafford's. The locations of the companies after the relief were as follows –

Battalion H.Q. – Howson's Post.

A company – Mazingarbe (northern huts)

C company – Lone Trench.

D company – Tenth Avenue.

Meanwhile 'B' company remained in reserve at Mazingarbe.

The day also saw another man die of wounds and he is buried at Pernes British cemetery.

16149 Private Alfred Bexon was aged 27 years and from Huthwaite Nott's. He was probably one of the 'A' company men wounded on 3rd June. He is buried in grave II. F. 42.

At 12.30 am on 8th at Lone Locality gas was projected from G.12.c.1.2 to 11.d.90.35. and G.11.d.45.45. on the Northumberland Fusiliers (34th brigade) front. The enemy offered little in the way of resistance. The 9th was once again quiet with 'A' company moving from Mazingarbe to relieve 'C' company in Duffers Drift (Lone Trench). At 1 am on 10th the 24th Division on the battalions right discharged a new type of gas from cylinders by projector. Once again no retaliation was reported on the Battalion front. The following day would see the battalion relieving the 6th Lincoln's in the right sub-sector of the Brigade front. The relief was completed without injury or incident by 11 pm. The following two days were without incident and the diarist wrote on both days " Nothing Unusual".

At 12.15 am on 14th a Trench Mortar gas operation took place on the Brigade front to the left of the battalion and this resulted in heavy artillery retaliation from the enemy. The barrage was concentrated on the Reserve line north of Vendin Alley which was on 'C' companies front. Relief took place on 15th with the 6th Lincoln's moving into the left sub-sector in place of 7th South Stafford's at 6 pm. The result was a heavy barrage from the enemy to welcome the new battalion. This would cause casualties in the battalion with one officer and two men being killed, whilst one man was wounded. Lieut. Philip Schur was acting O.C. of 'C' company and attended the C.O.'s conference between 6 and 8.45 pm. He had just left Battalion H.Q. when he was hit and killed by a 15cm shell near 'C' Company HQ. The reserve line and Posen alley was also heavily shelled with 15 cm shells during this period.

All three men killed are buried at Philosophe British Cemetery, Mazingarbe.

Lieut. Philip Schur was 29 years of age and attached from 2nd Battalion. He was born in Cape Town, South Africa and the son of Moses and Rachel. Philip was of the Jewish faith and his headstone carries the Star of David. He is buried in grave IV. D. 8.

19896 Private George Lowe D.C.M. was born at Duckmanton Derby's and formerly 14282 Leicestershire Regiment. He is buried in grave IV. D. 9.

72623 Private George Joshua Smith was 25 years of age and a man of Kent. He was formerly T/3/029505 R.A.S.C. and is buried in grave IV. D. 10.

During the evening of the 16th 'B' company and one officer plus 30 Other Ranks from 'C' company joined the battalion in the line from Mazingarbe and these men would take part in a raid on 18th.

At 6 pm on the 17th the 17th Infantry Brigade on the Battalion's right carried out yet another raid, which resulted in one prisoner being taken. The enemy retaliation was once again light on the battalion front.

The following morning at 7 am it was the battalions turn to mount a large raid on the enemy lines in squares H.25.b.50.69 and H.19.d.27.25

The raiding party consisted of five officers and

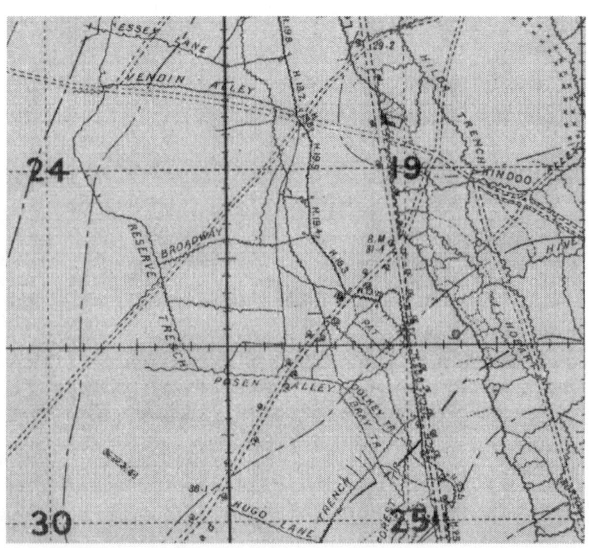

Area showing the location of the raid

160 other ranks of which four officers and 130 other ranks were from 'B' company, one officer and 30 other ranks from 'C' company. The officers who took part in the raid were as follows -:

Captain H.C.V. Warneford M.C. (O.C. Raid), 2/Lieuts. F.T. Tourt, T.R.B. Kilner, H.E. Hudson of 'C' company and 2/Lieut. F.S. Parker of 'C' company. The raid resulted in the capture of seven prisoners and one Machine Gun. It was completely successful as the gallantry awards for this action would show later. It was though a costly affair for the battalion with two officers and five other ranks being killed plus eleven men wounded. One of these men would die of wounds later at the Pernes Casualty Clearing Station. The raiding party returned to Mazingarbe during the evening. At 11.30 pm gas was projected from G.11.c.3.7 and G.11.d.4.5. This resulted in a rather heavy retaliation on the battalion's front.

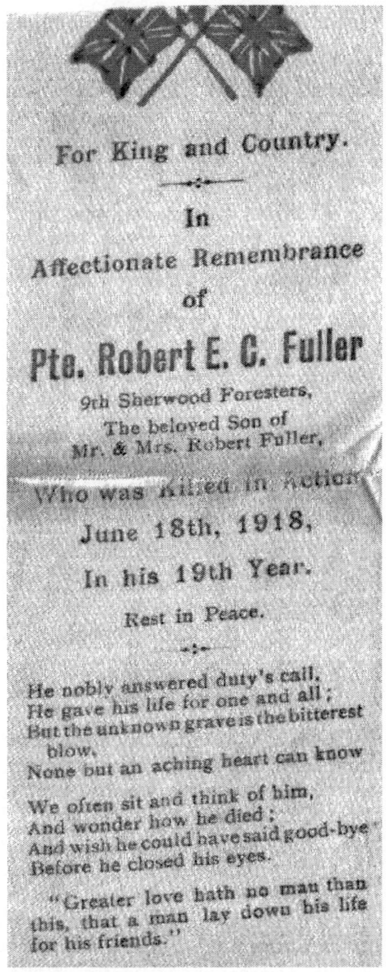

For King and Country.

In Affectionate Remembrance of

Pte. Robert E. C. Fuller

9th Sherwood Foresters,
The beloved Son of
Mr. & Mrs. Robert Fuller,
Who was Killed in Action
June 18th, 1918,
In his 19th Year.
Rest in Peace.

He nobly answered duty's call,
He gave his life for one and all;
But the unknown grave is the bitterest blow,
None but an aching heart can know

We often sit and think of him,
And wonder how he died;
And wish he could have said good-bye
Before he closed his eyes.

"Greater love hath no man than this, that a man lay down his life for his friends."

Private Fuller's memorial card in the form of a bookmark

The men killed are buried at Philosophe British Cemetery Mazingarbe. The men who have no known grave are commemorated on the Loos Memorial. 2/Lieut. Thomas Richard Burgess Kilner M.M. had risen through the ranks and had served in The Sussex and Warwickshire Regiments as a private soldier. He was a native of Sussex and had served previously as a Private – 3012 Sussex Regiment, 6092 and 241837 Royal Warwickshire Regiment. His M.M. was in the London Gazette dated 19th September 1916 and he was in the Royal Warwick's at the time. He is buried in grave III. E. 3.

102699 Private Robert Edward Charles Fuller was aged 19 years and from Lambeth London. Formerly C 3337 K.R.R.C., buried in grave III. E. 4.

His family produced a memorial 'book mark'. At least his family would eventually have a known grave to visit.

15338 Lance Corporal Robert Osborn aged 36 years and of Bourne Linc's is buried in grave III. E. 5.

30703 Private Albert Sherrard was from Hucknall, Nott's and buried in grave III. E.6.

5118 Lance Corporal George Hunt was a native of Nottingham and is commemorated on the Loos Memorial.

2/Lieut. Henry Erris Hudson was aged 19 years and would win his Military Cross during the raid. He was the son of Commander W.J.V. Hudson (RN) of Ross Herefordshire and attached from the 3rd Battalion. A brave young man who gave his life for his men and country, he is commemorated on the Loos Memorial.

18050 Private Thomas Tilley of Kirkby-in-Ashfield is also commemorated on the Loss Memorial.

71016 Private Albert Joseph Eaton aged 35 years was an Essex man formerly 5038 Leicestershire Regiment. He died of wounds and is buried at Pernes British cemetery and grave V. B. 19.

Major Scothern gave two paragraphs for the period 18th June to 19th September-:

"On June 18th a successful raid was carried out by "B" Company with one officer and 30 other ranks from "C" Company (5 officers and 160 other ranks all told) on the enemy trenches behind Posen Crater, resulting in the capture of seven prisoners and one machine gun. A considerable number of casualties were also inflicted on the enemy.

From this time until 25th August, when the Division was relieved by the 15th Division, nothing of much importance occurred. The likelihood of any enemy attack had diminished, and practically finished with the opening of the offensive in July.

After being relieved, the battalion went by rail to Chelers, and thence on to Magnicourt. The stay here was very short, as on the 30th the Brigade moved into the line East of Monchy-le-Preux at Boiry-Notre-Dame. This really commenced the period of open warfare for the Division. The battalion took over the line on September 2nd, and held the line for six days returning to Arras for four days. At the end of this period, the same sector was again taken over, and held until the 19th when the 4th Division took over, and the Division was again brought back to Magnicourt"

The 19th saw a worrying development when Major C.L. Harding M.C. was sent to hospital suffering from influenza. There was no mention as to any other ranks also succumbing but it is doubtful the Major was an isolated case. The day itself was quiet although one man listed as killed. He had actually taken part in the raid on 18th and was listed as missing believed killed then.

17564 Private Jonathan Smithurst Davey was aged 22 years and from Jacksdale, Notts. He is commemorated on the Loos Memorial.

On the night of 19th/20th the Battalion was relieved by the 11th Manchester's and moved to the rest billets at Mazingarbe. The relief was completed without incident by 3 am on 20th and the Battalion would have eight days rest before moving forward again.

Training would continue throughout the rest period although there would be time for recreation also.

During the 20th the men bathed and generally cleaned up before attending an evening of entertainment. At 6 pm, the 34th Field Ambulance Band under the direction of Captains Snelling and Lawrie, gave a concert in the Divisional Theatre.

Between 9 am and 12.30 pm the following morning the Companies attended to their own training whilst the afternoon was taken up with recreation. In the evening the men attended the Divisional Theatre, which doubled as the Cinema. The Avenue was shelled and part of the battalion HQ billets was hit, this resulted in a slight wound for Lieut. Royle, the Assistant Adjutant. The following day would see Lieut. Royle hospitalized by his wounds. Captain A. E. Brennan, 'C' Company Commanding Officer assumed the assistant 2nd in Command post. Operational Orders were issued concerning the possibility of hostile attack, which again showed that the lessons from March and April had been learned with preparations in place for any attack.

The 22nd was a repeat of the previous day although 'A' and 'C' Companies moved to the range for firing practice. Lieut. Alexander (USA) the Medical Officer, commenced leave to England and he was relieved by Captain Lawrie from 34th Field Ambulance.

Sunday 23rd saw 'D' Company take their turn on the range. Church parade services were held prior to the battalion swimming competition in the afternoon. Unfortunately no results were posted in the diary. 32nd Infantry Brigade issued order No.198 concerning the release of 3,360 cylinders of white star gas. The Battalion although at rest would have to be prepared for any retaliation by the enemy from this attack. Monday saw the battalion on a field- training day, which consisted of a tactical exercise. The training took pace near Aix Noulette (R.27 Central) and consisted of infantry and tank cooperation in attack.

Training in preparation for the allied offensive soon to come was a priority if the hoped for breakthrough was to be achieved. The 25th/26th saw morning training followed by relaxed afternoons. Each evening at 6 pm the cinema was the place to be and few men missed the opportunity of a relaxing couple of hours watching the latest films. The C.O. also carried out an inspection on 25th followed by another swimming competition. The day also saw the issue of 33rd Brigade Order no 180 concerning the forthcoming relief of the 32nd Brigade on the front line.

"The points concerning the battalion were as follows -:

The 33rd Infantry Brigade will relieve the 32nd Infantry Brigade in the St Elie Section on the 27thJune 1918. Relief to be complete by 3.0 a.m. 28th June.

The relief will be carried out as follows: -

2a. 9th Sh.Foresters will relieve 2nd Yorkshire Rgt (2nd had joined the Division in May 1918) in the right sub-section. On relief, 2nd Yorkshire Regt move to Froissart Camp. The head of 9th Sh. Foresters will pass Philosophe crossroads at 2.30 p.m. The Company of 9th Sh. Foresters for Le Rutoire will move up last of the 4 Companies.

b. Route for troops moving up – Vermelles – Clarkes Keep – Hulluch Alley.

3. All movements on roads and tracks East of Bracquemont will be by platoons at 300 yards interval. In the event of any E.A. (Enemy Artillery) flying near troops on the move, the latter must halt off the road until the E.A. is clear.

4. 9th Sh.Foresters and 7th S.Staffs.R. will each send their observers up the day before relief.

9. Units will report completion of relief by sending the code word – IOLANTHE"

10. Brigade H.Q. will close at Bracquemont at 8.30 p.m. and open at Philosophe on arrival. Command of St.Elie section will pass to B.G.C. 33rd Infantry Brigade on completion of relief.

13. Cooking utensils, held by units of 32nd Infantry Brigade as Trench Stores, will be taken over.

Battalions will take over from Battalions of 32 Infantry Brigade A.P. and tracer ammunition in Lewis Gun Drums at all recognized A.A. Lewis Gun positions. A corresponding number of L.G. Drums, filled with ordinary S.A.A., will be handed in to Quartermasters Stores of units relieved, in exchange."

An Administration order (No.9) was also issued on 25th and again the points mentioning the battalion are mentioned thus: -

2. Echelons (reserves) Captain J. Critchlow, M.C. 9th Sherwood Foresters is appointed Commandant of the Echelons of the Brigade.

5. Duties

The two Policemen at present found by 9th Sherwood Foresters for duty under the Town Major, Mazingarbe will be dismissed at 2.pm on 27th inst.

The following N.C.Os and men will report at 32nd Brigade H.Q. Philosophe, at 3 p.m. 26th inst. For duties as follows: -

Brigade main dump – Cpl. Hauxwell and 3 O R (Sherwood Fors.)

Vermelles Locality Store – 2 Other Ranks (I O.R. Sherwood Fors)

Baggage Waggons.

9th Sherwood Foresters. 10 a.m. 27th inst. Southern Huts. Mazingarbe.

(WO95/1815 226 235 National Archives)

At 2.40 pm on 27th the battalion left Mazingarbe and proceeded to the right sub-sector of the St. Elie section of line. They would relieve the 2nd Bn Yorkshire Regiment and this was successfully completed by 6 pm. Major Piper would not be with the Battalion but would instead be spending a couple of weeks leave in England.

One Other Rank died on 27th and it is possible it was from influenza as no other illness was mentioned at the time. Going by the deaths from this period it would seem that the Battalion was not too badly hit by the outbreak. The records just put 'died' for any death not on front line duty and the 9th Battalion hardly had any of these. For example there were no fatalities for two months. They were luckier than some others.

70950 Private Ernest Wheatley aged 23 years of Tamworth Staff's had formerly served as 26735 in South Staffordshire Regiment. He is buried at Mazingarbe and grave III. E.11.

Devon Lane and St Mary's Dump was 'A' Companies sector and during the afternoon of 28th it was heavily shelled with 10 and 15 cm's resulting in two men being wounded. Surprisingly on 29th a horse show was held at Q.16.b.40.00. between 10 am and 4 pm. with three officers and six other ranks proceeded from the front line to attend this event, returning the same night. The battalion won two prizes – 2nd in class IV, turn out (Individual) mounted and Corporal Wright – 2nd in class XI, Infantry Heavy Draught Horse. It would seem that the battalion did not achieve any success on the second day of the Divisional Horse show.

Reinforcements had arrived at Echelon on 27th and these men move dup into the front line on the night of 28th/29th.

2/Lieut. F.A. Allen moved out of the line and to Boulogne for a two-day course on camouflage.

July and August 1918 were kind months to the battalion with no fatalities recorded.

A number of appendices appear with the war diaries at this time and they all concern movement orders either into or out of the line.

The 1st July would see the 6th Lincoln's relieve the battalion and once this afternoon relief was completed the Companies were disposed as follows:

Battalion Headquarters at Vermelles Brewery.
A Company at Vermelles North.
B Company at Mazingarbe.
C Company at Vermelles South.
D Company at Crossway.

The battalion would be in support for three days and the enemy artillery was quiet during this period. Companies were given the opportunity to bathe at Noyelles and Vermelles during these three days. Extracts from the London Gazette were mentioned for the first time in the War Diaries –

London Gazette dated 27 June 1918 – Captain (Acting Major) C.L. Harding, M.C. to be temporary Major, July 29th 1917.

Temp/Second Lieut. S. Maishment relinquishes acting rank of Captain on ceasing to Command A Company. 24th March 1918.There seemed to be no specific reason why this mention of the LG was added to the war diary. Although a gap of eleven months for Capt. Harding M.C. announcement seemed extreme. Lt. Col. Scothern the CO may have thought that the Captain deserved a mention. Four men were awarded the Military Medal for their work during the trench raid on 18 June 1918. They were Sergeant R.Teer who was awarded a bar to his Military Medal, L/Cpl P. Griffen and Privates W. Sulley, J.A. Lee.

A telecommunications scheme was carried out between 8 am on 3rd and 8 am on the 4th to test other forms of communication. Therefore telephones and Fuller phones were not used at all during this 24-hour period.

The afternoon of 5th saw the battalion moving up to the front line once again and relieving 7th South Stafford's in the left sub-sector of the St. Elie section of line. The battalion was located in the following areas: -

The battalion boundaries were – south G.11.b.90.16 – G.11.d.35.85. – junction Stafford lane and O.B.1. – junction Chapel Alley and O.B.1. – along Chapel Alley to G.11.c.0.0., thence due west. North: G.5.c.0.1., G.10.b.1.7., G.9.b.8.4.

Dispositions:

Battalion Headquarters Chapel Alley, G.11.c.4.2.

D Company at Studio Company. Headquarters G.11.b.3.5.

1 Platoon Hairpins, I Platoon Border redoubt, 1 Platoon Better 'Ole, Studio 2 and Highland Trench, 1 Platoon Rat Creek, Slag View and tunnel entrance, G.11.1.95.25.

A Company at Gordon Company and Headquarters G.10.d.8.8.

2 Sections junction Gordon alley and Drummond trench, 1 platoon junction of Gordon Alley and O.B.1, 1 Platoon junction of Gordon alley and O.B.4, I Platoon G.10.d.8.8., 1 section G.10.b.10.60.

C Company at Manning Company and Headquarters G.11.c.30.95.

Company in Reserve Line from Stafford Lane to O.B.4. Accommodated: -

2 Sections Exeter castle, 1 section junction of O.B.2 and Fosse Way, 1 Platoon O.B.1, just north of Stansfield Road, 1 Platoon north end of O.B.2, 1 Platoon O.B.4.

Stansfield Company. Headquarters G.10.c.6.9.

Company in reserve line (Stansfield road) from O.B.4 to junction of Hulluch Alley and Dog's leg (G.9.b.9.1.)

Battalion HQ will man Limber trench and O.B.1. between Hulluch / Vermelles Road and Stafford Lane.

The St. Elie Group R.F.A. Three 18-pounder batteries, one 4.5" howitzer, covered the Brigade front.

A Brigade order was issued with reference to a Gas Beam attack, which would take place on 5th. The gas would be discharged from cylinders mounted on the light railway. Due to wind conditions the gas attack was postponed and it would be a week before it did go ahead. A further order on 6th July stated that the attack would take place at an early date.

The Battalion would not be in the danger zone but the troops occupying the Southern Hairpins would be in the Cautionary zone. This would mean that the men would be in dugouts behind drenched gas doors or gas blankets. They would also have to wear their box respirators during this period.

The Battalion settled into the trench routine once more. The allied offensive was in the planning stages and it would be 20th July before it began. After almost four years of war and the recent setbacks, few men expected the conclusion to be in 1918.

The following days would be quiet and uneventful. On 8th 2/Lieut. Ridgen, D Company proceeded on leave to England whilst 2/Lieut Percival, A Company left for the rest camp at Boulogne.

On 9th 'C' Company (Manning Company) relieved 'D' Company (Studio Company) during the afternoon. The 7th South Stafford's relieved the 6th Lincoln's in the right sub-sector of the St. Elie section at the same time. The 10th saw Captain H.C.V. Warneford, M.C. leave the Battalion on a temporary assignment to assist in training at 59th Division.

The Battalion signallers were to get some practice doing contact signalling with a contact aeroplane on the morning of 11th. Unfortunately the aeroplane developed engine trouble, which forced it to descend behind the British lines. Operational order no 56 were issued which gave details of the installation of gas projectors at G.11.c.3.7 and G.11.d.4.5. The men would remember the recent incident, which had cost 'A' Company 30 casualties and no doubt received the news with some trepidation.

Also on 11th 33rd Brigade orders detailed the relief by 34th Brigade on 13th July 1918. Major C.L. Harding, M.C. returned to the battalion on 12th after his period of convalescence. On the night of 12th/13th a Gas Beam attack took place on the Divisional front to the battalion's right. The gas was discharged from cylinders on the nine-pound track at about G.17.d.9.1. and G.24.1.2.6. The enemy retaliation was slight in the Battalion's sector with a few 15 cm shells on the Hairpin (trench) held by 'C' Company. During the afternoon of 13th the battalion was relieved by the 8th Northumberland Fusiliers of 34th Brigade and went into Divisional reserve.

The Brigade orders detailed that the Battalion would move out from the front line via Hulluch Alley, Clarke's Keep and Vermelles and would not move west of the village line until the last Company of 5th Dorset's had passed the junction of Hulluch

Alley and Crossway. They would then move to Froissart by train and the Admin orders for this move would come from the Staff Captain separately.

A signal was received later which stated –

> *"No light railway train is available. 20 motor lorries will be at Red Chateau tomorrow afternoon to convey you to Bois Du Froissart area. Further details as to times of imbussment will follow when received."*

Some 40 men per lorry would presumably make the journey fairly uncomfortable and cramped. The lorries were at Mazingarbe at 7.30 pm and conveyed the men to their new area arriving at 9.30 pm. The battalion also had to supply two anti aircraft Lewis Guns with teams to relieve the 8th Northumberland Fusiliers men at Hersin by noon on 13th.

The Brigade order also listed details of such things as –

Accommodation – with the Battalion in huts and tents at Bois Du Froissart at Q.12.c.4.0. allotted by the Town Major at Hersin.

Baths and Clean Clothing – Sherwood Foresters – Hersin 14th July from 3 – 6 pm and 15th from 9 am to noon.

Supplies – delivered daily at 12 noon.

Collection of Sick – Sick will be collected daily as follows – Sherwood Fors. By the 35th Field Ambulance.

Lewis Guns will be sent to the Divisional Ordnance Stores for overhaul as follows – Sherwood Fors. 15th inst. Half at 11 am and half at 1 pm.

A written note has 'Lewis Guns to be thoroughly overhauled by Sgts, Kirby and Greaves.

From 14th to 21st July the Battalion would be at rest at Bois Du Froissart camp near Hersin. The men would be required to undertake morning training although the afternoons and evenings would be full of sport and entertainment.

Sunday 14th saw the battalion cleaning up and bathing and attending voluntary church service at 11.30 am. The afternoon was taken up with a cricket match and the senior officers did battle with the junior officers. The juniors 'trounced' their senior's 84 runs to 48. Not a particularly high scoring match and for the junior officers, not a good way of enhancing their promotion prospects!

Captain A.E. Brennan relinquished the post of assistant second in command upon Major C. Harding M.C. re-assuming the position.

The morning of 15th was given over to company and physical training. Musketry, B.F., Gas Helmet drill, close order drill and specialized training being undertaken.

Whilst the men had a relaxing afternoon the officers were given a riding lesson under the watchful eye of Lieut. Bullen-Smith (assistant training officer). Officers were still required to ride and often did so at the head of their men on the march. At 6 pm the battalion football team played a match versus the 35th Field Ambulance Brigade and in a closely fought game went down 0-1. After this the Battalion band under the direction of Sgt. S Johnson played a programme of music.

Band Programme 15.7.18.

March.	Machine Gun Guards.	Greenwood.
Waltz.	Nights of Gladness.	Ancliffe.
Selection.	Good Time Coming.	Pether.
March.	Great Little Army.	Alford.
Waltz.	Quaker Girl.	Monckton.
Selection.	To Nights the Night.	Rubens.
Waltz.	Gold and Silver.	Schar.
March.	Colonel Bogie.	Alford.

Regimental Marches, 1st and 2nd Battalions – The Young May Moon.

It was obvious that despite failure of the German offensive to achieve a breakthrough, the General Staff still believed it to be possible. Therefore a Defence and Withdrawal scheme were issued to each battalion.

Plans for a Defence Scheme were issued to the Battalion on 15th, which included –

In case of attack whilst in the present Camp, the Battalion will move to Fosse2 de Bethune (L.28.c).

Equipment will be made up into Fighting Order each night, and water bottles will be filled.

Not more than twenty-five percent of officers or men will be absent from Camp at the same time.

The 16th saw a tactical exercise for the officers under the direction of Major Piper.

The afternoon was given over to cricket and football for the men. A draft of Eleven Other ranks also arrive during the afternoon.

The Withdrawal scheme was held on 17th and the diary mentions 'Left camp at 7.30 am and returned at 2 pm.' The scheme took place near Bouvigny-Boyeffles and the Adjutant, Captain W Nason, issued details on 16th.

> *The Battalion will be in position to commence scheme at 10 am, with "B" and "D" Coys in front position, and "A" and "C" Coys in*

Second position, not less than 500 yards behind. "D" and "C" Coys will be on the right.

Major C.L. Harding, M.C. with battalion signallers carrying flags will represent the enemy. Company flags will represent Machine guns.

At 10 a.m. "B" and "D" Coys. Will commence to retire walking – retirement to be, if possible, invisible to enemy.

Each platoon will leave a section to cover its retirement – this section will double back when platoons have passed through covering Companies.

The four platoons of a Company will not retire together.

When retirement has commenced, those covering retirement will increase rate of fire if necessary, but the need for economy of S.A.A. is always born in mind. Only one L.G. per section should be firing normally and then only at a good target.

"A" and "C" Coys. Will give covering fire, if possible, during retirement of "B" and "D" Coys. And any good positions on the flank utilized.

Fire orders are to be carefully given. Range is often omitted. An actual target on the ground should be given so that men may take careful aim; and muzzle protectors must be back during firing.

Re-organisation – Officers and N.C.Os must see that men on reaching the position, to which they have been retiring, are immediately organized into Sections.

Major S.H. Piper will reconnoitre positions in rear, and decide where the next stand is to be made. A line of Orderlies will be placed on these positions.

Companies must be prepared to counter-attack if necessary to gain time, and to form a defensive flank if flank is exposed.

A "G" sounded on the Bugle is the signal for all movement to cease, if movement is taking place, and for movement to recommence if operations have been stopped.

All Officers will make themselves acquainted with F.S. Regs, Part I, Sections 71 – 74 and Infantry Training 1914, Section 137. (Field Service Regulations)

As many Officers as possible will be mounted.

Signed W Nason Capt. & Adjt.
9th. Service Battalion The Sherwood Foresters.

The Divisional Commander, Major General Davies, C.B. was present during the scheme. The afternoon was given over to a cricket match versus the 12th Battalion Sherwood Foresters with the 9th losing 49 runs to 105. The 12th (Service) Battalion Sherwood Foresters were part of 24th Division. 2/Lieut F.S. Parker of C Company was awarded the M.C. and Company Sergeant Major S.C. Lee of B Company the D.C.M. in connection with the raid of 18th June.

On the following day was the Battalion Rifle meeting held on the range at Q.24.a, near the camp.So as to make sense of the war diary entry, which only gives the basic details, the Battalion orders for the 18th will be included.

Battalion Shooting Competition.

Other Ranks. Run 50 yards to 200 yards firing point, load on firing point. Team, which knocks down nine plates, first wins: 18 falling plates per team. Prize: Five-Franc canteen chit to each member of winning team.

Battalion H.Q won this event.

Second event – Open to one team per Coy and Headquarters of 1 Officer and 8 other ranks. The members of these teams may not shoot in first event.

Practices: Five rounds application 200 yards, second-class figure target. Fifteen rounds in one minute at 300 yards, bayonets fixed. Ditto Five rounds snap shooting at 300 yards silhouette target. Prizes for 1st and 2nd individual aggregate, also prizes for team as for first event.

"C" Company ran out the winners of this event.

Third Event – As for No. 2 Officers versus Warrant Officers and Sergeants. Teams nine.

The W.O.s and Sergeants winning this one.

Fourth Event – Individual snap shooting five rounds as 200 yards silhouette target. Entries limited to 8 per Coy and 8 for Headquarters. Not open to Officers. First prize Twenty Francs, second prize 15 Francs, third 10 Francs, fourth 5 francs (canteen chit).

1st -L/Col. W Upton C Coy.

2nd- Pte A Wagstaffe, H.Q.

3rd – L/Cpl J Shaw, band and Pte. G Beat, C Coy.

Fifth event – Pool shoot. Five rounds at 8-inch bull – 2-inch invisible ring – at 200 yards. Shots in 2 inch ring five points; bull four points, inner three, magpie 2, outer 1.

Entry 1d (penny) per clip of five rounds. Each competitor limited to a minimum of three clips. –

Prizes 1st 55%. 2nd 30%. 3rd 15% of entrance money plus 20 francs.

Only the first placed man was mentioned – Pte S.J. Smart C Company.

Sixth event – pool shoot – 200 yards at running man. Target runs 30 yards. Entrance fee 1d per run. Prize 5d for each hit.

Pte H. Mugglestone, C Company won.

Seventh event – Gas helmet shoot. Five rounds at 200 yards in gas helmets – 8 – inch bull. Gas helmets to be adjusted, rifles loaded from pouch and five rounds fire din one minute. Entries limited to eight per Coy. And 8 to Bn. Headquarters. Prizes – 1st twenty francs, 2nd fifteen francs, 3rd ten francs, 4th five francs (canteen chits).

The result was as follows –

1st -2/Lt. L.W. Foster, H.Q. and L/Cpl J Willis, C Coy.

2nd – Corpl. F. Barrett, H.Q., Pte. G.H. Lear, H.Q., Pte C Carlin, B Coy.

Company Championship – Points will be allotted on a system to decide which Coy holds the shooting championship for the Battalion.

The totals were B.H.Q. 24.5, C Coy. 20.5, B Coy – 2.

Entries with names of teams for events Nos. 1,2,4 and 7 to be sent to Major Piper by 5-pm, on July 16th.

(Signed) S.H. Piper. Major.

9th Bn. The Sherwood Foresters.

The Divisional Boxing Competition held at the Divisional Reception Camp in Coupigny commenced at 11 am on 18th and would continue for three days. The battalion had several men entered and hopes were high for good results.

2/Lieut. W. Francis of D Company proceeded on leave and his destination was Paris. Whilst leave home was infrequent the opportunity of a short break in Paris to recharge the batteries could be secured.

Lieut. J S Williams of C Company left the battalion and proceeded to the Machine Gun school at Belton near Grantham, Lincolnshire.

The 19th saw the second day of the Divisional boxing championship. The Companies spent five hours on the ranges undertaking rifle practice from 9 am 'til 2 pm. whether this was because of the state of the shooting on the previous day is not mentioned. During the afternoon the officers had another riding lesson whilst the evening was given over to athletics and the heats for the forthcoming Battalion sports.

At dawn, which was 4 am, on 19th another battalion man would die and whilst no mention of the death appeared in the diary, the whole battalion knew of it. In fact it is possible that some of the men were in attendance.

21801 Private Arthur Briggs aged 27 years of Brimington, Chesterfield is the only 9th battalion man buried at Hersin Communal cemetery Extension, grave III. E.2.

He had been tried for desertion and executed at Bracquemont. He was charged with deserting when on active service, to which he pleaded not guilty and absenting himself without leave although this charge was dropped. He was further charged with losing by neglect his arms, clothing, equipment and regimental necessaries, to which he pleaded guilty. Briggs did not realise that throwing away your arms carried a death penalty. The verdict was confirmed by Field Marshal Douglas Haig 14 July 1918.

Captain Munday a solicitor prior to the war had acted as Brigg's friend (Represented him at the Courts Martial) and a number of men gave evidence. The battalion would also have been paraded and told of the sentence and indeed this happened on the following day. Two points in a memo from the Brigadier Commanding 33rd Infantry Brigade to H.Q. 11th Division showed the problems in 1918. Firstly " The state of discipline of the 9th (Service) Bn. Sherwood Foresters is good, except for absence"; secondly "There have been several cases in this battalion of men overstaying their leave during the last 9 months". It is doubtful if any absences occurred after 19th July.

"No 21801 Private Briggs A of 9th Sherwood Foresters having been tried by F.G.C.M., and sentenced to death by shooting, the sentence will be carried out between 3 am and 4 am at Bracquemont on 19th July 1918".

The Derbyshire Times had four entries concerning the Briggs family during 1918 and Arthur's Mother certainly suffered more than most. She had though disowned Arthur long before his death.

May 4th –
Official news has reached Mrs. H Briggs of 7 Railway View, Lockoford, that her youngest son Pte. Sam Briggs, Sherwood's, has been missing since March 21st. He was aged 20 and joined up on September 7th 1916....

June 8th –
"The funeral of Mr Henry Briggs, 7 Railway View, Lockoford Lane, Brimington, who died on May 26th took place on Thursday last week at the Chesterfield cemetery" (Arthur Briggs father)

August 17th –

"The many friends of Mrs Briggs of 7 Railway View, Lockoford Lane, Brimington, will regret to hear of the death of her son Pte. Arthur Briggs who was killed in action on July 19th. Another son has been missing since March 21st last." (Arthur was obviously not killed in action)

September 21st –

"Going into action on September 1st, Pte. Fred Briggs, Trench Mortar Battery, attached to the Leicestershire Regiment, was killed after having served in France for over three years without receiving a scratch... Last year he was the recipient of a card signed by the General of his division complimenting him upon his good work"

A husband and three sons dead in less than six months, Mrs Briggs certainly did her bit for the war effort.

Battalion orders for 20th July make interesting reading.

Part 1 Orders –

Duties: Subaltern of the day to-morrow and Officer I/c Fire Picquet.

2/Lieut. Beddoe.

Routine: Reveille 6.30 a.m., breakfast 7.30 a.m., sick parade 9 am.

Divine Service: (1) Church of England – Two Officers and thirty files (Rank and file – men) per Coy will parade on the Football Field for Divine Service at 11. 30 a.m. Markers will report to R.S.M. at 11.15 a.m. Capt. A. E. Brennan will be in charge. The band will attend.

Field cashier: Sec-Lieut. Ayres will report at Orderly Room at 8.30 a.m. to proceed to draw cash for Coys.

Conference: The Commanding Officer will see Coy Commanders at 12.30 p.m. tomorrow, at Orderly Room.

Baths: Coys will bathe as follows at Hersin Baths in batches of fifty tomorrow. Clean clothing will be available.

Divisional Boxing Tournament: The Commanding Officer congratulates Sgt. Sheppard on winning the Welter-weight Championship at the Divisional Boxing Tournament. 13 points accrued by the Battalion saw them top of the Brigade.

Part 11 Orders –

Punishment and Deprivation of Pay:

No 42273 Pte. J. Farrell, awarded seven days ' F.P. No. 1 by C.O. this day for (1) Insolence to a N.C.O. (2) Using Obscene language.

No 92268 Pte. T. F. Rodgers, deprived of seven days' pay by C.O. this day for (1) Overstaying his pass from 9.30 p.m. to 10.20 p.m. 17.7.18. (2) Failing to hand in his pass as the Guard Room on his return.

No. 92261 Pte. J. M. Lannen, awarded seven days' F.P. No. 1 by C.O. this day for (1) Overstaying his pass from 9.30 p.m. to 10.20 p.m. 17.7.18. (2) Stating a falsehood to a N.C.O.

Signed W. Nason. Capt & Adjt.
9th Bn. The Sherwood Foresters.

Notices.

Sports: The following events will take place, commencing at 9.30 a.m. to-morrow: – Final 100 yards, Mile race, Final tug-o-war and Band Race.

Voluntary Services:

C.of E. Holy Communion in the Divisional Canteen at 7 a.m. and after parade service at – 12 noon.

Nonconformist service at 11 – a.m. in the Divisional Canteen.

Roman Catholic service – Mass in Hersin Church at 11 –a.m.

The above provides an interesting snapshot of battalion life when at rest. The day also saw the beginning of the Advance to Victory with the Counter-attack in Champagne.

The 20th also saw the Divisional Commander, Major General Davies C.B. accompanied by the Brigade Commander, Brigadier General Spring D.S.O. inspecting the Battalion on the Camp parade ground at 10 a.m. and afterwards presented Medal Ribbons to the following for gallantry during the raid of the 18th of June last: -

2/Lieut. L.S. Parker, M.C.

C.S.M. S.C. Lee, D.C.M.

Sergeant Tees received a bar to his Military Medal.

Lance Corporal P. Griffis, Private's J.A. Lee and W. Sulley received Military Medals.

Six gallantry awards for one action showed just how successful the raid had been and was another feather in the cap for the battalion.

2/Lieut. White proceeded to Paris on leave whilst Major C.L. Harding M.C. was attached to 6th York and Lancs, 32nd Brigade from the 20th.The battalion sports finals took place at Bois-Du-Froissart with some unusual and certainly non-Olympic events. Pole fighting being carried out throughout the sports day would have been an unusual sight.

The events were as follows –

Final 400 yards, Sack race in Gas Helmets, One mile, Drill blindfolded, Final 100 yards, Obstacle race, Final Tug-of-War, Relay Race, Beer, biscuit and Whistle race.

An enjoyable day was had by all well except for the three men on Field Punishment No 1 that is.

The 21st would see the battalion on its way to the front but firstly they would attend Sunday church parade followed by bathing at Hersin.

The Echelon moved to the Divisional Reception camp at Coupigny. Captain W. Nason who had been the Adjutant proceeded to 33rd Infantry Brigade Headquarters as understudy to the Staff Captain. Lieut. and Quartermaster W. Horsman proceeded to Paris-Plage for ten days rest.

The battalion moved out and relieved the 9th West Yorkshire Regiment in Support in the Hulluch Sector.

Sherwood Foresters	– 9th West York's
D Company relieved	C Company – Tenth Avenue.
B Company	D Company – Lone Trench (Duffers Drift)
A Company	A Company – Northern Huts Mazingarbe.
C Company	B Company – Northern Huts Mazingarbe.

A and C Companies marched to Mazingarbe whilst B and d were conveyed in Lorries.

The 22nd and 23rd passed quietly and the Companies in reserve continued with training. A cricket match was also organized versus 2nd Yorkshire Regiment on the Les Brebis football field with the battalion winning by 69 runs to 28.

The 24th was also a day of training for the reserve Companies.The battalion relieved the 7th South Stafford's in the right sub-sector of the Hulluch line on 25th. "D" Company relieved "C" 7th S.Staffs – Chalk Pit Company. "B" Company relieved "D" 7th S.Staffs – Posen Company. "C" Company relieved "A" Company 7th S.Staffs – Broadway Company. "A" Company relieved "C" Company 7th S.Staffs – Essex Company. Battalion Headquarters was located in Curzon Street and the relief was completed without incident by 11.30 p.m.

A Gas bombardment was successfully carried out at 2 a.m. on 26th. Extracts from Operational Order No. 60 dated 25 July 1918 gave an idea of the operation –

No.4 Section Special Company R.E. will carry out a Gas Trench Mortar Bombardment of the hostile trenches West of Hulluch on the night of the 25/26 .7.18. if weather conditions are favourable.

No. of Guns.	Emplacements	Targets.	Ammunition.
5		G.18.d.95.80.	Hulluch
		Trench	T.M.B.
		H.13.d.35.99	No 120
		H.13.d.13.88.	P.S. 80

All ranks of Essex Company (trench) less the minimum number of sentries will be under cover of deep dugouts by Zero plus 5 minutes.

The operation will be controlled by the following code: -

Gas will be fired tonight – Glad.

Datum being 11 p.m. Zero will be Datum plus 3 (2 a.m. 26 inst)

Operation cancelled – Gloom.

Operation successful and all clear – Glory.

Zero postponed 2 hours – Glee.

The need for the men to be in deep dugouts tells of how close the two lines were situated. Any shells falling short could easily take out a British trench and the men in it.

The 26th/27th were quiet with nothing unusual occurring, although the Gas Bombardment mentioned on 25th was successfully carried out at 2 am on 26th.

Retaliation by the enemy was slight following the Gas attack. Lieut. Bowyer proceeded on leave to England on 28th. A barrage was put down on Essex Company (G.18.d) at 6 p.m., which was "A" Companies area. The enemy barrage consisted of 15 cm shells. The British in return fired wire cutting and destructive shoots with 4.5 Howitzers and 6 inch Trench Mortars on enemy Machine Guns with good results. It was the turn of the British to keep the enemy guessing as to which area would receive the next attack. The barrage was repeated on the 29th at 11 a.m. and at 11 p.m. a thousand gas shells were fired on the enemy Headquarters (H.20.c.60.55.) Not surprisingly the next two days were quiet with nothing unusual happening.The 1st day of August saw the Battalion in the St Elie Sector and all was quiet with no unusual occurrences. Captain H.C.V. Warneford, M.C. proceeded to England for six months duty at home under the substitution scheme. This scheme had been brought in during the summer of 1917 and any Officer or W.O. who has served two years or more could return to the UK for a rest. He would be given a job in a Training or Garrison battalion. It was extended to junior ranks in early 1918 and priority was given to men who were noticeably feeling the strain or had compassionate grounds for going home. 2/Lieut Tourt proceeded to 1st Corps. H.Q. for several days.

The following day saw the battalion relieved by the 6th Lincoln's in the Right Sub Section during the afternoon. Between 2 and 7 pm the battalion proceeded as follows –

"B" and "D" Companies – Northern Huts Mazingarbe.
"A" Company – Tenth Avenue.
"C" Company – Duffer's Drift.
Battalion H.Q. – Howson's Post.

The 3rd was once again quiet with little action from either side.4th August 1918 was the fourth anniversary of Britain's entry into the War and the early fervour had long been replaced by a grim determination to get the job done. The army of 1918 had little resemblance to that of 1914. In 1914 arguably reservists and Territorial Force volunteers backed the best professional army in the world. By 1918 the majority of men were young conscripts with little training behind them. The sacrifices of so many would not be forgotten though and a commemoration service and review was held at Ranchicourt. A party of 25 Other Ranks under 2/Lieut Percival proceeded by lorry to represent the Battalion at the 1st Army commemoration service and review. Few would imagine that within four months the war would be over and the enemy defeated. The Battalion would also suffer few casualties as the German Army retreated to its homeland. Even so between September and November over fifty men would die many during the Battalions last battle.

Whilst the commemoration went ahead the war continued apace and at 11.30 pm a gas projector bombardment commenced followed at zero plus 30 and zero plus 45 by a shrapnel barrage. The barrage was directed against the enemy in the vicinity of Fosse 8 (G5.a and b). The enemy retaliation was though slight and no casualties were reported in the battalion.

The battalion was relieved on 6th and would return to the rest billets at Bracquemont for eight days. The 7th was given over to cleaning both men and equipment with the men being given the opportunity to bathe. The order of the day for 8th was field-firing practice as after months of trench occupation the men were rusty when it came to firing their weapons. It was also the day that the Advance in Picardy began with the Battle of Amiens. Few could know or even believe that the last 100 days of the war had begun or that the once invincible German army would crumble away so dramatically. Much fighting was still needed and with it many more sacrifices but the 8th August 1918 would become an auspicious date in history.

The Battalion less "A" Company proceeded to the tank ground at R34 (sheet 44b, 1/40,000) to carry out the field firing practices. The Battalion marched behind the band, leaving at 8 am – they moved off – the order of march being – Battalion Headquarters, The battalion band, "B", "C" and "D" Companies. A fine sight as the men marched and sang headed by the C.O. astride his charger. The men had a good days practice with lunch being served on the ground and they returned to billets at 5.30 pm. Meanwhile "A" Company missed all of the fun and ended up on the Gavion range from 2 – 5 pm.

The men fired the following practices –
5 rounds application fire at 200 yards.
15 rounds rapid fire at 300 yards.
10 rounds rapid fire at 200 yards.
5 rounds snap shooting at 300 yards.

Battalion orders contained the following notes –
'2/Lieut. S. Maishment takes over "B" Co., 9-7-18 vice Capt. H.C.V. Warneford, M.C. Lt. C.R.T. Wilmot takes over "C" Co, vice Capt. Charlton. 7/8/18. Lt. R.W. Bowyer 2/i/c A Co. 7/8/18. Lt. Cartledge 2/i/c C Co. 7/8/18. 2/Lt. Hetherington 2/i/c/ B Co. 7/8/18. Capt. Charlton 2/i/c D Co. 2/Lt. Cooper to be Asst. Adjt.

The surprise in these orders was Capt. Charlton losing "C" Company to become 2/i/c of "D" Company. Was it just a case of the new CO making his mark on the battalion or did Capt. Charlton need a less onerous post.

The morning of 9th was taken up with training in Companies and this comprised of Musketry, drill, specialist training, close order drill and Physical training. Recreational training in the afternoon consisted of cricket and hockey matches.

On the 10th the ranges at Bois Du Froissart were allotted to the Battalion although only "B" (9 –11 am) and "C" (11.30 am – 2 pm) Companies were sent. They fire the following practices – 5 rounds application at 200 yards, 15 rounds rapid at 200 yards and 5 rounds snap shooting at 200 yards.

Between 11 am and 12.30 pm the R.S.M. took a junior N.C.O.s class with eight men per Company attending. At 11 am three Officers per Company took part in a tactical exercise under Major Piper. "A" and "D" Companies continued with the usual training.

The afternoon was once again given over to inter battalion sports matches. The Battalion played the 6th Lincoln's in a hockey match at Bracquemont, with the 9th winning 3 –1. The soccer match held at Mazingarbe went the way of the Lincoln's with a flattering score of 4-1. Captain A.E. Brennan proceeded on leave to England. At 11pm on 10th and 2 am on 11th, enemy aircraft dropped some 60 bombs in the vicinity of Bracquemont and Noeux-les-Mines although no battalion casualties were recorded.

Sunday 11th was church parade at the Divisional theatre with the Army Corps General preaching. Between 10 am and 3 pm the enemy shelled with 4.2s and 5.9s in the vicinity of the Monument, Noeux-Les-Mines and Mazingarbe. Whilst the Battalion received no casualties during this bombardment they did lose their free concert. There should have been a free concert for the Battalion given by the 11th Division (Wunny Wuns) Concert party in the patronage at Noeux-Les-Mines but this was postponed as the Hall had been hit during the shelling. In its place a tennis tournament was arranged versus the 6th Lincoln's with the battalion once again losing. There was more enemy shelling during the night. After the allied offensive had begun on 8th the enemy would try and disrupt any possible build up of troops along the allied front line. The Battalion had used the tactics in March and April during the German offensive.

The 12th and 13th would follow the pattern of morning lectures which included lectures by Platoon Commanders and afternoon recreation. 2/Lieut. Osborne proceeded to the rest camp, firstly at Aire (near St Omer) and then Paris-Plage. The shelling of Noeux-Les-Mines continued on 13th at 5.30 pm. Despite this the battalion trials for the forthcoming sports day took place on the parade ground. The Divisional sports day would be overtaken by events though and not take place.

The enemy continued it's shelling on 14th and concentrated on the Noeux-Les-Mines area yet again. The Battalion moved into the line once more and relieved the 6th York and Lancs' in the left Sub-Sector, leaving Bracquemont at 2 pm. The relief was completed without incident or casualty by 7 pm. 2/Lieut. Sutton I/c and No 8 Platoon of "B" Company proceeded to Echelon at Coupigny. They would train under the new system of Platoon training and become a demonstration Platoon for the battalion. Major Piper proceeded to Echelon to take command of the reserves. At 11.30 pm a Gas Trench Mortar Bombardment was carried out by the 3rd Infantry Brigade (1st Division) on the battalions left.

The enemy artillery was active again on 15th, paying particular attention to Exeter Dump, Fosse Way and O.B.1, with 10.5cm and 15 cm shells sent over intermittently during the morning and night. The 16th saw 2/Lieut. F. Parker, M.C. proceeding on leave to England whilst Captain Suffolk also left for home on special leave.

Sergeant Fred Greaves V.C. began a six-day Lewis Gun course –

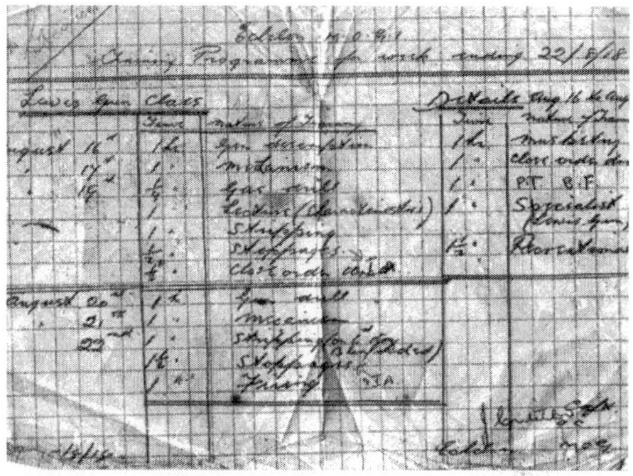

Fred's Lewis Gun course details.

At 11.30 pm Gas was projected from G.30.b.99.20. on to Hobart trench at H.19.d.55.40 to H.26.b.6.6. This being 34th Brigade's front and although the enemy sent up twin red and green lights shortly after zero opposite the Battalions front, no retaliation followed. Exeter Dump came under artillery fire once more on 17th at 4 and 11 pm. 2/Lieut. Bolton proceeded on leave to England. Between noon and 1 pm contact signalling was carried out successfully between the Battalion signallers and the contact Aeroplane. These exercises would prove vital as the period of open warfare at last began. As the speed of the advance grew aeroplanes could arrange S.A.A and food drops to the advancing troops. Situation reports could be got back to brigade and Division much more speedily. All arms cooperation would at last become a reality as the allied offensive rolled forward. . The following day Exeter Dump continued to receive unwanted attention from the enemy artillery between 11 pm and midnight, this time with 77 mm. Shells.

The 19th was a quiet day for the enemy artillery and the Battalion sent out a daylight patrol to see what was going on. The starting time was 5.30 pm and the men left from Border North. The route to be taken was G.11.b.1.9. –G.5.c.95.00 to Sap G.5.d.0.1 into the German front line trenches. The objectives were to reconnoitre the German front line and if possible obtain identification of the enemy units. A daylight raid was a risky business but the enemy tactics of thinly holding their front line trench made the enterprise worthwhile. Lieut. C.A.B. Thurburn, B Coy, 2/Lieut. F.O. Bates, and Sergeant J Burgess, both of A Company carried out the raid.

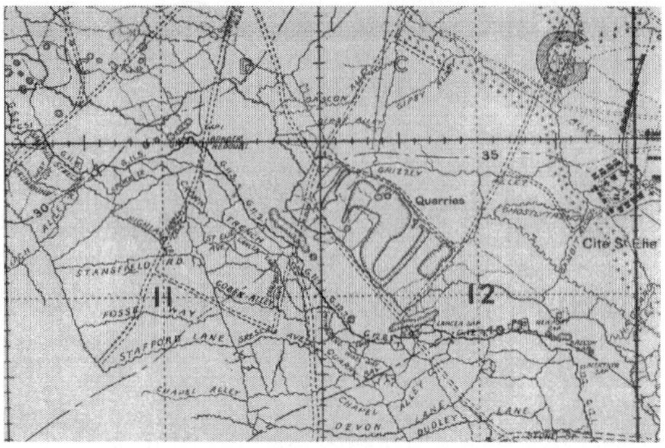

Patrol route and area for 19th August 1918

The patrol succeeded in entering the German front line and made a thorough examination of it, inspecting the entrances to dugouts and finding three stick bombs (German Grenades) inside one of them. They also saw a number of snipers plates in position (Metal protective plate with hole in for firing through). Three of the enemy were seen at 6.10 pm in a communication trench, heading towards the patrol and they lay in wait for these men. The enemy had though either changed direction or entered one of the dugouts and were not seen again. The patrol returned at 8.15 pm and they were no doubt relieved to be back. The adrenalin would have been pumping throughout the two hours of the patrol and the nerves constantly on edge.

The enemy began shelling again on 20th with the sectors held by "A", "C" and "D" Companies being hit by 77mm and 15 cm shells. The Brigadier General sent his congratulations to the patrol and stated that valuable information had been gained. Lieut. Bullen-Smith (Assistant Training officer) and 2/Lieut. Maishment proceeded on leave to England. A gas bombardment was carried out by 4.5 inch and 6 inch Howitzers on targets opposite the Brigade front. The I Corps Horse show also took place near Bruay with the Battalion sending only one entry, a Heavy Draft horse (stripped) which won 2nd prize. It would seem inconceivable that during preparations for the big push a horse show should go ahead, but it did.

The following day the 3rd and 4th Armies began the Second Battles of the Somme with the Battle of Albert. 1st Army of which the 11th Division was a part would not be called upon just yet but their time would come. The 14th Leicester's of 47th Infantry Brigade, 16th Division relieved the 3rd Infantry Brigade, 1st Division on the battalions left. This would leave the front sparsely held whilst men trained for their part in the great advance. Between 9 –11 pm Exeter Dump and battalion H.Q. were shelled intermittently by 77mm's

The night of 21st/22nd saw a follow up raid to the one of 19th with Lieut. Thorburn, 2/Lieut Bates and Sgt Burgess patrolling the same route as before. 3 Other Ranks of "A" Company with the original patrol and a second party of 6 Other Ranks from "D" Company under Sergeant Carlile would bolster the patrol this time. They left the British lines at 8.15 pm and returned at 4 am on 22nd. They found one of the dugouts inspected on 19th was actually a tunnel entrance and this was investigated further. A number of notice boards were found which were taken down and brought back for further inspection. A dynamo (electric) engine was heard working but no sign of the enemy was seen or heard in the tunnel system. A wiring party of some 40 men was seen near the enemies 2nd line and artillery fire was brought to bear on them when the party returned. The Brigadier General again sent his congratulations on a successful enterprise and the Corps Commander remarked:

> *'A good and enterprising patrol, credit is due to all ranks and I should like them to be congratulated on their work for me'.*

The following morning the men were treated to a spectacular sight at 6.30 a.m. when one of the British planes brought down two hostile balloons in flames. The enemy though continued to shell in the vicinity of the Battalion H.Q. The Battalion also received orders that it would spend an extra three days in the front line prior to the 11th Division being relieved by the 15th Division. Five N.C.O. guides from the 13th Royal Scots arrived to reconnoitre the sector prior to the relief.

Exeter Dump was shelled yet again on 23rd between 5-30 p.m. and 7-30 p.m. otherwise the day was quiet.

The following morning at 7.30 a.m. a smoke screen was placed across the front by the artillery prior to an operation by the 24th Division to the Battalions right. At 3 p.m. a British aircraft brought down yet another hostile balloon and it exploded into flames after being hit by tracer bullets.

The 13th Royal Scots relieved the Battalion on 25th although the time out of the line would be brief, as their involvement in the final phase of the war would soon begin.

Once relieved the Battalion marched to Grenay (just East of Loos) where they entrained on the light railway at 3.30 pm. and proceeded to Chelers, arriving at 7.30 pm. From Chelers they marched to billets at Magnicourt arriving at 8 pm. The Echelon under Major Piper moved from Coupigny to Magnicourt arriving at 12.30 pm after a four hour march. Captain E. Bourdas and 26 Other Ranks rejoined the battalion from the 68th Field Company Royal Engineers, where they had been providing working parties. 2/Lieut. Walker proceeded on leave to England followed the next morning by 2/Lieut. Fowler.

The next day was given over to bathing and cleaning up in readiness for the next move. The day also saw the start of The Second Battles of Arras, which would see the 11th Division take part in the Battle of the Scarpe from 26th to 30th. The whole operation would come under the name of 'The breaking of the Hindenburg Line 26th August to 12th October 1918'.

A warning order was received at 6 a.m. on 27th for all surplus kit and stores to go to the Dump and for the Battalion to be ready to move off at 2 hours notice. Lorries called for the surplus kit at 9 a.m. The movement order was extended to 12 hours later in the day. 2/Lieut. Sutton and his No 8 Platoon who had recently completed their special training now had the opportunity to put it into practice. They gave an hour's demonstration of the new Platoon tactics to the officers and men of the battalion from 10 – 11a.m. At 2 p.m. the C.O. inspected the fighting strength of the companies and Battalion H.Q.

The companies trained from 9 a.m. until 12-30 p.m. on 28th and the programme was arranged by the Platoon commanders which would include the new tactics as demonstrated by 2/Lieut. Fowler's platoon the previous day. During the morning the Divisional Commander, Major-General Davis visited the training ground to cast his eye over the men's progress. An aeroplane lecture was given at Monchy Breton at 5.30 p.m. Aircraft recognition had become much more important as the war progressed and as the final push began it was vital. Allied planes would be an important link as the troops swept forward and knowing friend from foe would be more than useful. The party attending the lecture consisted of two officers and nine other ranks from each company and one officer and three other ranks from battalion HQ. The party had the luxury of travelling by lorries to the lecture theatre at Monchy.

The following morning at 1.45 a.m. the Battalion was put under orders to move at short notice. Lorries reported to the QM stores at 9 a.m. to take the surplus baggage to the dump at Tincques. The Battalion paraded at 1.15 p.m. in preparation to move off as soon as the transport arrived. The lorries eventually arrived at 3 p.m. and it took an hour to load up the battalion. The Battalion arrived at their new location which was Ecurie just north of Arras at 7.10 p.m. and were billeted in huts for the night. The Echelon moved to the Divisional Reception camp under Major S.H. Piper and consisted of 4 officers and 110 Other Ranks, this being some 10% of the battalion strength. The remainder of the Battalion being made up of 21 officers and 630 Other Ranks would move into the trenches. Few battalions had a full compliment of men by 1918 and the 9th was some200-300 men short.

At 10 a.m. on 30th the C.O. proceeded to reconnoitre the route for the next move and to make arrangements for moving into the line, East of Monchy-Le-Preux. At 2 p.m. the battalion commenced the march to the front line, the route being via St. Laurent – Blagny – Athies – to Orange Hill about one mile south west of Feuchy. Here they halted for tea leaving at 8.15 p.m. and proceeding into the line. The transport lines being located just south of the Scarpe (river) near Feuchy. The battalion strength going into the line was 21 officers and 630 other ranks and they would be in support of the 6th Lincoln's and 7th South Stafford's who held an outpost line north east of Boiry-Notre-Dame which was some 12 kms east of Arras. This period of trench occupation would last until 7th September. The Battle of The Scarpe was over and it would be closely followed by the Battle of Drocourt-Queant, 2-3 September.

The enemy artillery was active during the 31st August, carrying out area shoots on the Brigade sector.

The 1st September was a quiet day although the battalion received operational orders detailing plans of an attack by the Canadian Corps and the 4th British Division on Drocourt. The battle began at 5 a.m. on 2nd and at the same time the battalion relieved the 7th South Stafford's on the left sector of the Brigade front. The relief was completed without incident or casualty by 11 p.m. and they would spend five days in the front line. The following day saw 2/Lieut. Jestico, Sergeant Teer, Corporal Clarke and eight men carry out a good patrol with casualties inflicted on the enemy and only Cpl. Clarke being wounded. Sergeant Teer in particular was somewhat of an expert in patrolling and a good man to have in a tight situation.

Each day was seem as quiet by the diarist although enemy aircraft brought down four British

Observation Balloons in two days between Monchy and Boiry. Two men were mentioned as killed and two wounded during this tour of the front line trenches.

Both men killed were buried in the Vis-En-Artois British Cemetery at Haucourt.

85820 Private William Wilmott Oldham was killed on 4th September 1918 and buried in grave VI. J. 18.

70920 Private Herbert Glover was a Nottingham man and previously served as 26929 South Staffordshire Regiment buried in grave VI.G. 10. He was killed on 6th September.

The 9th Battalion West Yorkshire Regiment relieved the battalion on 7th September and this was completed by midnight with the men moving to billets at Arras.

The next three days may have been spent out of the line but not out of danger as an enemy High Velocity 32cm naval gun shelled the town. The weather was inclined to be rainy but Company training went ahead with – platoon schemes – going forward in artillery formation and weaponry drill. 2/Lieut. J. Hetherington and Lieut. C.A. Koyle proceeded on leave during the rest period.

All too soon it was time to move forward and relieve the 9th West York's in the right sub-sector of the Brigade front east of Boiry and this was completed successfully despite the enemy being very active in the area. By 12.30 a.m. on 12th the Battalion was settled into the front line routine again. The day also saw the beginning of what would be termed – The Battles of the Hindenburg Line – 12th September – 9th October. The 11th Division as part of the Canadian Corps would enter the fray on 27th September in the battle of The Canal du Nord.

The 13th to 15th were quiet but hectic days for the Battalion with enemy activity almost non-existent. The battalion did though mount patrols and work on the new defences throughout the period. The fear of an enemy counter-attack was never far away and new lines had to be worked on. The enemy aircraft were active and brought down nine British balloons in the three days. One enemy plane was chased by one of the British scouts (fighters) and was forced to land behind the enemy lines. As ever the terms 'situation quiet' and 'day quiet' were somewhat misleading although they did show how normal the war had become. Daily shelling, sniper fire, living in dank trenches, wounds, death, and the smells of war had become normal. The 16th saw "C" Companies area shelled slightly but only two casualties were sustained, neither fatal. Major Piper assumed command of the Battalion as the C.O. proceeded to the transport lines prior to going on leave. The following day was yet again quiet with little enemy shelling being experienced in the front line. The C.O. of the 1st Hampshire Regiment (11th Brigade, 4th Division) came up to the Battalion's sector to reconnoitre prior to the forthcoming relief.

The 18th was not so quiet and the enemy threw just about everything it had at the Brigades artillery battery positions in the vicinity of Boiry. Enemy 8 inch, 5.9's and 77 mm shells rained down on the Brigade front. Captain H.B. Smeeton and Lieut. G.H. Kingdon joined the Battalion from base with Kingdon immediately taking command of "C" Company.

The C.O. proceeded on his leave to England on the morning of 19th although he would be recalled on 21st which would have given him one day at home at best. The battalion were relieved by 1st Hampshire's and proceeded to dugouts at Feuchy where they remained overnight whilst the Echelon moved to Tincques from St. Aubin. The lorries arrived at 10 am on 20th and conveyed the Battalion to the rest billets at Magnicourt-en-Comte near St. Pol, arriving at 2 p.m. The Echelon marched from Tincques to rejoin the battalion. The rest period would last for six days and then the battalion would be involved in the Battle of The Canal du Nord. The 21st saw the Battalion cleaning up, bathing and preparing for their next stint in the trenches. Captain E. Bourdas proceeded to the 11th Division Reception camp at Tincques to assume the duties of Assistant Commandant and Adjutant. The C.O. rejoined the battalion hopefully in time for the "C" Company Whist Drive at 6 p.m. conducted by the Padre. The 22nd/23rd were spent training in the vicinity of Nillets from 9 a.m. to 12.30 p.m. The afternoon of 23rd was given over to an attack scheme under the watchful eye of the C.O. with Major Piper and the men of the Echelon acting as the enemy.

At 4.15 a.m. on 24th orders were received for the first line transport to move to Berneville. This was undertaken at 2 p.m. according to the transport movement plan. Preparations were also made for the Battalions move into the line for active operations. The Battalion moved to Vis-en-Artois at 4 p.m. on 24th, arriving at 8 p.m. encamping about 2 miles south of the village in the open. The first line transport joined the battalion at the encampment. The area was one of rolling hills with the occasional small wood dotted around the landscape. The main obstacle to overcome would be the Canal du Nord. The following day the C.O. proceeded to Brigade HQ to receive the battalion's instructions concerning

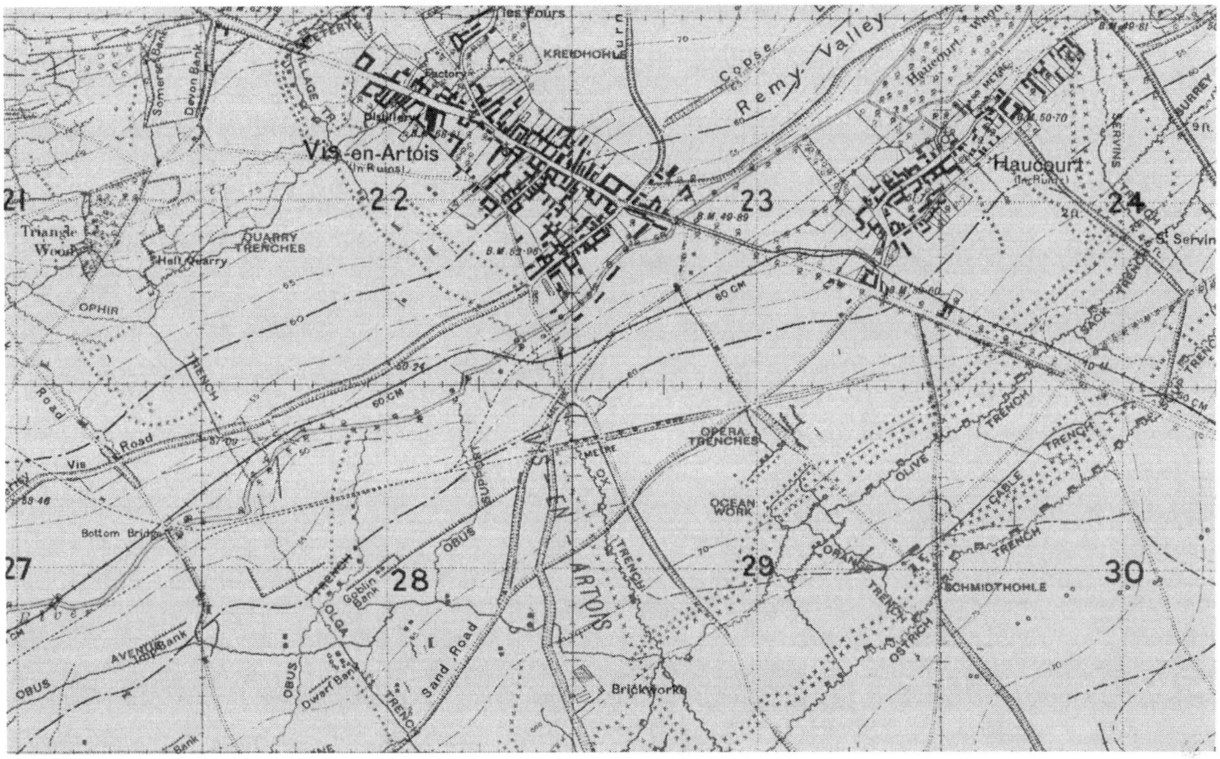

Vis-en-Artois map.

the forthcoming operations. He then made a reconnaissance of the battalion's soon to be held positions. At 7 p.m. the Battalion made its move forward to the trenches in the vicinity of the Drocourt-Queant line just east of Gagnicourt arriving at 9.30 p.m. It rained heavily during the night, which was not the best preparation for the forthcoming battle.

It is important at this stage to refer to Colonel Scothern's notes for September and October 1918.

"Period of Open Warfare. The 11th Division was now attached to the Canadian Corps, and in accordance with this the Sherwood Foresters moved up by lorries to Vis-en-Artois on September 25th in readiness for a general attack on 27th. At the commencement of these operations the 33rd Brigade was in Divisional reserve, and on the 26th took up positions in the old German Droucourt-Queant line.

The Canadians attacked the Canal-Du-Nord at 5.20 a.m. under a very heavy barrage, the 32nd and 34th Brigades of the 11th Division passing through them and capturing Epiney and Oisy-le-Vergier. To conform with this, the 33rd Brigade moved forward into the Buissey Switch.

Orders were received to move on October 1st, and the battalion crossed the Canal-Du-Nord during the night and occupied some old German trenches near Marquion, moving into the line N.W. of Sancourt in the evening. No advance was attempted here, but a very successful fighting patrol was carried out by a platoon of "D" Company on the 5th. Abancourt Station was rushed, and all the occupants killed. One machine gun was also captured.

The battalion was relieved on 6th, and went into Brigade support S.W. of Epiney, relieving the 7th South Stafford's in the line on the 8th. On the 9th orders were received to advance the line to a railway embankment N.W. of Abancourt. This was successfully carried out by "A" and "B" Coys. Meeting with some machine gun opposition during the operation. During the night the battalion was relieved by the Kensington Rifles (56th Division), and moved to a sunken road south of Abancourt, which had been evacuated by the enemy in the early morning, again acting as Brigade reserve. The area was fairly heavily shelled with H.E. and gas, but there were only two casualties. On October 11th, the line was taken over from the South Staffords between Hem Lenglet and Paillencourt, and advanced slightly during the night to the Canal De La Sensee.

The Division was relieved on the 12th, and moved into reserve, the 9th Sherwood

Foresters being allotted bivouacs behind Bourlon Wood. They stayed here for a week, the time being spent in refitting, training and salving. On the 20th a move was made to Escaudoeuvres, a suburb of Cambrai, followed the next day by one to Naves, leaving this place on 25th for Saulzior. This was quite enjoyable although there was plenty of work in the shape of training as most of the men were billeted in houses and contrived as usual to make themselves exceedingly comfortable. The Divisional Cinema also gave shows in an old barn that the Germans had used for a like purpose, and the Divisional Concert party should have performed for the battalion, but unluckily a move had to be made that day. Preparations were again made for moving into the line..."

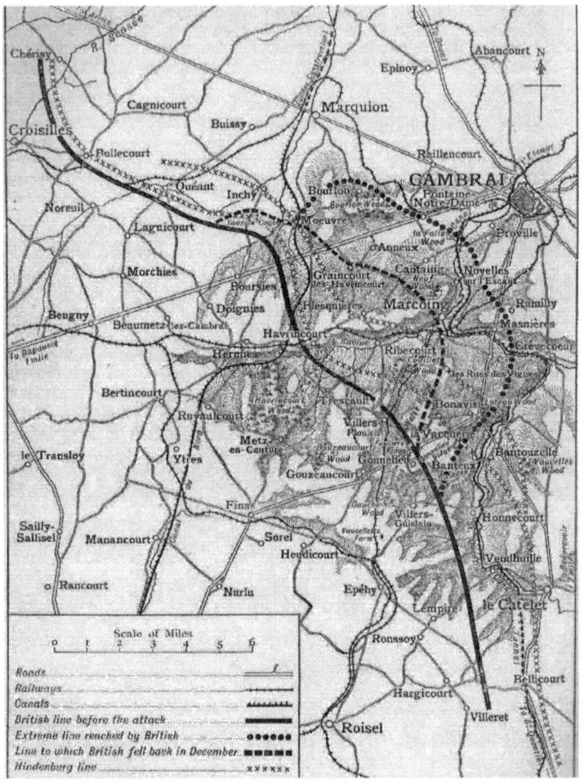

Cambrai and area.

The Canadian Corps to which the 11th Division was attached were tasked to attack the German positions east of the Canal du Nord on 27th. The Battalion would be the reserve of the 33rd Brigade who were in turn reserve for the 32nd and 34th Brigades during the attack. At zero hour, 5.20 a.m. a heavy barrage opened up on the enemy line and by zero plus 165 minutes (8.05 a.m.) the 1st phase of the attack had been successfully completed. The Battalion moved forward in support to positions in the Buissy Switch, south east of Villers-lez-Cagnicourt, arriving at 10 a.m. Reports were received during the day that the 11th Division had captured its objectives with 32nd Brigade taking Epinoy and 34th Brigade Oisy-le-Verger. The battalions sector received no hostile shelling during the operation, which was a testimony to the success of the attack. Between the hours of 5 – 8 p.m. the C.O., one officer per Company and the battalion scouts reconnoitred bridges across the Canal du Nord. The weather for the assault saw slight rain at zero but then dry and bright.

The morning of 28th saw the Battalion awaiting movement orders, the QM stores moved from Cherisy to a position some half a mile north west of the battalion and the transport lines were situated in Cagnicourt. The C.O. and platoon commanders reconnoitred the bridges across the Canal du Nord whilst the 6th Lincoln's left Buissy Switch and crossed the Canal taking up positions just south of Seuchy L'Estree. The weather had turned cold and showery and it would remain so for a few days to come. The joys of 'camping' during this period of open warfare were waning by this time.

At 6 a.m. on 29th a minor enterprise was attempted north east of Epinoy by 32nd Brigade but this failed owing to the heavy enemy machine gun fire. At 9.30 am the battalion moved forward approximately 1000 yards in a southeast direction to take up positions in the Buissy Switch vacated by 6th Lincoln's the previous evening. The diary mentioned "1st Corps of which the battalion formed a part left the First Army", although at this time the 11th Division was part of the Canadian Corps which was very much part of 1st Army and would eventually move to XXII Corps, First Army for the final week of the war. The movement of Divisions between Corps was very much an administrative procedure though. The General Officer Commanding the Canadian Corps sent his most cordial congratulations to 11th Division for their success during the attack.

The 30th was a wait and see day for the Battalion with no movement and some training undertaken.

One very interesting change was made during the night of 31 September – 1st October when after four years of war the British Army moved to 'Continental' time and after this instead of 5 a.m. the men would see 0500 hours.

The Canadian Corps attacked at 0500 in the vicinity of St. Olle, west of Cambrai with 32nd Brigade on their left. The Battalion stayed at the Buissy Switch awaiting orders to move forward whilst the Transport and QM stores moved forward to lines near Baralle west of the Canal du Nord during the morning. At 1500 the Brigade issued a warning order for the battalion to be on one and a half hours standby to move. A further order received at 2030 saw the battalion together with 6th Lincoln's and 7th South Stafford's prepare to move forward.

At 0200 on 2nd the move began and the Battalion left Buissy Switch and crossed the Canal, marching to trenches in the vicinity of Marquion, arriving at 0300. The C.O. reconnoitred the new front line positions during the morning and the battalion moved forward at 1800 to relieve the 7th Canadian Battalion in the line just north west of Sancourt arriving at 2130. The following day saw intermittent shelling of the Battalion lines and the transport lines near Barelle were also shelled. There is only a mention of seven horses being killed and four wounded at the transport lines. Surprisingly no mention is made of the two men who were killed. The locations of the cemeteries would suggest that one man died at the Transport lines and one in the front line.

41412 Private Arthur Matsell aged 35 years was living at King's Lynn prior to the war although he had enlisted at Derby. He was more than likely attached to the Transport of QM stores. He is buried at Queant Road Cemetery Buissy and grave VII. G. 11.

202064 Private Walter Edwin Herbert aged 25 years and a Leicestershire man was formerly 24877 Leicestershire Regiment. He is buried at Haynecourt British Cemetery, grave II. B. 3.

The enemy artillery was very active on 4th with heavy shelling throughout the day and night although no casualties were mentioned. The enemy bombers were also active and dropped a large number on the Battalion area.

The 5th saw Captain Munday M.C. proceed on leave to England. Summer time was also discontinued from midnight and the clocks would go back one hour.

The British artillery both Heavy and Field guns fired a successful shoot on Abancourt station (M 32 d 15.25. Map 51A S.W.). A Platoon of "D" Company sent out a fighting patrol under 2/Lieut. Osborne and they entered the Station and engaged the enemy, killing all of them and capturing a light machine gun. Identification of the enemy unit was also obtained and posts were established along the railway. The Battalions casualties were given as nil.

On 6th the 11th Manchester Regiment relieved the battalion during the night and in turn they relieved the 6th East York's in sunken roads and the old practice trenches south west of Epinoy. Battalion HQ was located at X.2.d.25.65. Map 51B S.E. The Battalion became the support for the left section of the Divisional front. Operational orders were received concerning an attack by 32nd and 33rd Brigades to be carried out at a date to be notified. This would be The Battle of Cambrai 8th –9th October 1918.Although the operational order was cancelled the following day as the enemy continued to retire therefore the battalion waited near Epinoy for new orders to advance.

Two men died on 6th.

97888 Private John Clarke was 19 years of age and from Yorkshire. He died of wounds and is buried at Bucquoy Road Cemetery, Ficheux and grave III. D. 16.

24496 Private George Hill was born in Nottingham and living in Wednesbury Staff's prior to the war. He is buried at Haynecourt British cemetery and grave II. D. 2.

On the 8th the battalion relieved the 7th South Stafford's in the line right Brigade sector north east of Epinoy during the evening although HQ remained in its previous position. An advanced H.Q. was established close to the front line and occupied by the Intelligence and Signals officers.

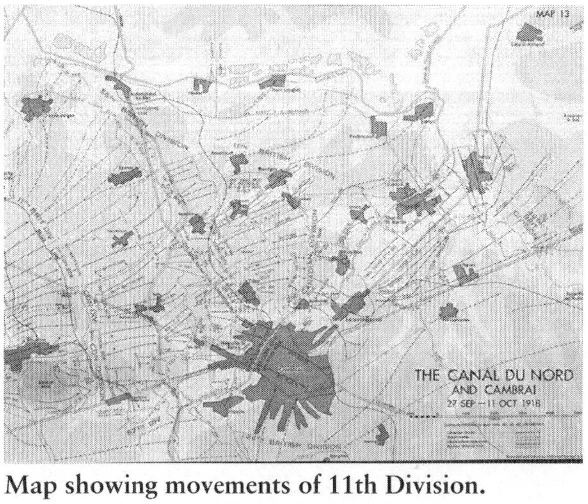

Map showing movements of 11th Division.

On the morning of 9th "A" Company sent out a daylight patrol to gain touch with the enemy who was thought to be retiring. At 1330 orders were received to advance the Battalion line at 1530 to the railway line north west of Abancourt to conform to an advance made by 34th Brigade. The C.O. took up a position at the advanced HQ and the Battalion advance went ahead successfully with A Coy on the right, B Coy on the left, and C Coy in support and D Coy in reserve. The only notable opposition except for a little shelling was machine gun fire from Fressiers, which temporarily held up 2/Lieut Bolton's platoon (No 3 platoon, A. Company). 2/Lieut Sutton was wounded by a machine gun bullet whilst on a patrol. During the night of 9th/10th the Kensington Battalion (22nd Bn The Royal Fusiliers) London Regiment had moved to the sunken road, S.3.b. south of Abancourt. The enemy had only evacuated the village at 0400 that morning.

2/Lieuts. Wightman and Pickard left the Echelon and were attached to the 2nd York's Regiment.

The following day the Battalion remained in reserve at the sunken road and the area was heavily shelled between 1800-1830 and 2200 –2230.

Two men are listed as killed and both are commemorated on the Vis-En-Artois Memorial Panel 7.

18621 Private John Robert Metheringham was a Mansfield man.

17022 Private John Williamson was a Derbyshire man from New Mills. The CO wrote to his family, 'I much regret his loss. He was killed by a chance shell and died almost immediately.

On the evening of 11th the battalion relieved the 7th South Stafford's in the right section and held the line east of Hem Lenglet with Battalion HQ situated at M.28.a (Map 51A S.W.). The battalion advanced its outpost line during the night towards the Canal De La Sensee.

One man died and is commemorated on the Vis-En-Artois Memorial Panel 7.

90792 Private Thomas William Rogers was 30 years of age and a Suffolk man. He had previously served as 013909 A.O.C. (The Royal was added later).

During the day of 12th patrols went out to gain touch with the enemy and so ended what was termed, The Pursuit to the Selle 9th –12th October 1918. The night of 12th/13th would see two companies of the 26th Canadian Regiment (2nd Canadian Division) relieve the Battalion, which then marched to Bivouacs near Bourlon Wood arriving at 0500. The 11th Division had been relieved and would not return to front line duty until the beginning of November although they would remain in reserve.

One of the Battalions number would succumb to his wounds on 13th at Etaples.

32589 Corporal John Henry Beeson aged 25 years and from Newhall Derby's left a wife Elsie Jane. He is buried at Etaples Military Cemetery and grave LXVII. J. 6.

The 13th to 19th saw the Battalion resting in preparation for what would be its final battle of the war. No doubt the rumours of the enemy seeking a peace deal would have reached the battalion and men would start to think what was unthinkable a few months previously – the war would be over soon. Despite this there would be much more heavy fighting with units engaged until the very last minute. Upwards of fifty men would not see the victory or home.

The Companies spent time in cleaning up, refitting, bathing and training. Platoon and Company attack schemes were carried out in the mornings with recreation during the afternoons. On the evening of 14th a British Aeroplane crashed in the battalion area and luckily the pilot and observer survived unscathed. They were entertained in Battalion Headquarters until the morning of 15th and could no doubt give up to date information of the enemy's retreat. On 16th a Section of Light Trench Mortars under Lieut. Roberts was attached to the battalion. The battalion band rejoined from the Echelon on 18th. At 0900 on 20th the battalion left Bourlon and marched to Escaudoeuvres just east of Cambrai arriving at 1300, taking over billets in the village vacated by 7th West Yorkshire Regiment. 2/Lieut. B.J. Cooper who had been carrying out the duties of Assistant Adjutant was officially promoted to Assistant Adjutant. At 1045 the next morning the Battalion moved off again, this time to the village of Naves arriving at 1200, taking over billets in the village vacated by the 6th Duke of Wellington Regiment. The Battalion was moving ever closer to Mons where the first shots were fired in August 1914. 2/Lieut. Radford rejoined the Battalion after completing his signalling course at Dunstable in England.

The 22nd saw the Divisional General inspect the Companies whilst they trained near Naves.

Training was continued the following day whilst the Echelon moved to Neuville St Remy on the outskirts of Cambrai. Lieut. Bennett proceeded on leave to England. Captain Brennan moved to the Echelon at Neuville and Major Piper rejoined the battalion.

From 0800 on 24th the Brigade was under two hours notice to move although the companies continued to train as normal. The following morning at 0915 they were on the move once again and marched to Saulzoir on the river Selle, arriving at 1130. The men were billeted in the village and the Brigade was put on five hours notice to move. The Battle of the Selle had raged from 17th to 25th October but was now over and the final advance in Picardy was all but over.

Saturday 26th saw the Companies continue with their training at Saulzoir. Sunday 27th was given over to Church Parade Services of which there were two with the Battalion Band in attendance. The remainder of the day was given over to relaxation although the Lewis Gunners did carry out firing practices in the morning. The Divisional cinema in the village put on two sessions for the men at 1700 and 1900. 2/Lieut. Fell proceeded on leave to England.

On 28th/29th the Battalion took part in a combined Practice attack scheme with the Machine Gun and Trench Mortar sections during the mornings. In the evenings the Divisional Cinema was open again for the men to relax.

The 30th/31st saw more Company training followed by recreation with not only the Divisional Cinema being open but a Battalion Concert was held in "D" Companies billet. This would be the last recreation before hostilities ended and for some men their last recreation ever.

The battalion strength at the end of October was given as follows –

	Officers.	Other Ranks.
Battalion strength at beginning of month	51	940
Battalion strength at end of month	48	900
No. Killed during month	0	3
No. Wounded during month	1	25
No. Evacuated during month	0	19
No. Struck off strength	2	9
Reinforcements	0	16

Colonel Scothern will be quoted once again with his thoughts on the final eleven days of World War One.

> *"... and November 1st saw the battalion at Verchain. There was always an element of novelty in these moves. One had hardly even yet become used to a war of movement, but already there was a distinct sense of fastidiousness as regards billets, and often attempts at comfort were remarkable – carpet laying and furniture removing being all in the programme. The battalion left again on 2nd, and marched to Querenang where a halt was made for tea. This was rudely interrupted by the Bosche, the area being very heavily shelled for about ten minutes, that spoiling a happy afternoon's picnic. The march was resumed and the line taken over North of Preseau. Here, owing to the guides losing their bearings, much time was lost in pulling profane men out of ditches and small brooks in which this part of the country seemed to abound. The battalion went into the line under orders to attack on 4th, but in the early morning of the 3rd it was found that the enemy had evacuated, and an immediate advance was ordered in the direction of Curghies.*

"C" and "D" Companies were in front, and met with no opposition until reaching Curghies. An enterprising Officer's patrol entered Saultain, (Which was not on the Divisional Front) returning in triumph with the Mayor. Machine Gun Fire was encountered East of the village of Curghies, but this was suitably dealt with, and the line advanced East of the Railway, where Companies dug in for the night. The advance was continued at 5.30 the next day without artillery, and Sebourg was captured, the slight opposition in the village itself being overcome. Both Sebourg and Curghies were full of inhabitants and these proved anything but a blessing to harassed platoon Commanders as their coffee, bread and even cognac had a demoralizing effect on the formation of the advance. They meant well, however, and in Sebourg especially were exceedingly kind to the wounded, dragging them into houses for safety.

On attempting to clear the high ground East of the village the leading Companies met with strong opposition from Machine Gun fire, losing all the officers except one, and suffering severe casualties. The advance was held up, and eventually "C" and "D" Companies had to fall back slightly to conform with the units on the flanks who had been meeting similar opposition. The line was taken over by "A" and "B" Companies who dug in on a sunken road East of the village. As a result of the day's operations, 30 prisoners, 3 tanks, and 10 Machine Guns were captured.

The artillery got up during the night, and the advance was continued at 5.30 a.m. the next morning under a barrage with "A" and "B" Companies leading. The high ground that had proved such an obstacle the previous day was captured, only slight opposition being encountered. The 6th Lincolns and 7th South Stafford's passed through to carry on the pursuit, and the battalion withdrew to billets in Sebourg, acting as brigade reserve.

On the 7th following a successful advance by the 6th Lincolns, the battalion moved the next day to Belle Vue farm. Considerable difficulty was by now being felt with regard to rations, and iron rations had to be eaten at the last place. The enemy in his retreat systematically destroyed all bridges and blew up mines at all cross roads hampering all transport and making it very difficult for the artillery and all kinds of wheeled traffic. Rations of bully beef and biscuits were eventually dropped by aeroplane.

On November 9th some miles were covered, billets for the night being eventually established .... (No name given but it would have been Aulnois). The advance was now being conducted in ideal conditions – beautiful weather and practically no shelling.

The battalion became the leading unit of the Brigade again on the 10th, and working in conjunction with a company of New Zealand Cyclists and cavalry reached its objective near Havay without encountering any opposition, and dug in for the night.

The next day the Hawke Battalion (63rd Division) passed through to continue pursuit, but about 9 a.m. three aeroplanes landed between "A" and "B" Companies, bringing the first news of the Armistice, the official news following shortly afterwards, where upon the battalion withdrew to billets in the Sugar Factory at Havay".

The 1st November would see the two-day battle of Valenciennes begin although the battalion would take no part in this. The 4th would see the Battle of the Sambre in which the battalion would be very much involved and finally the Passage of the Grande Honelle between 5th –7th November. By November 11th the Battalion would be at Havay some 9 kilometres from Mons.

The battalion left Saulzoir at 1400 and marched to billets at Verchain arriving at 1500. The 11th Division would be relieving the 4th Division, which had taken part in the Battle of Valenciennes. During the afternoon and evening the enemy shelled the village resulting in one N.C.O. sustaining wounds. Lieut. Roberts of the Trench Mortar Section and 2/Lieut. Ayres proceeded on leave to England.

The following day the battalion left Verchain at 1400 and marched to Querenaing where it halted an hour for tea. This break was rudely interrupted by heavy enemy shelling. Obviously the enemy still had observation posts in the area and could bring down artillery on the unwary. Two men were wounded and one would later die. The Battalion then marched into the line north of Preseau relieving as follows

"A" Company relieved the Rifle Brigade whilst "B", "C," and "D" Companies relieved The King's Own Regiment (4th Division). The relief was completed by 2200 and the battalion settled down to wait for the attack on 4th. Battalion H.Q. was established at a Chateau at Artres. The battalion area was heavily shelled during the night but no casualties were recorded. Preliminary operational orders were received for the attack on 4th.

84022 Private William Henry Kirkham aged 21 years was from Staffordshire and formerly 18411 North Staffordshire Regiment. He is buried at Valenciennes (St. Roch) Communal Cemetery and grave III. D.4.

Officer patrols were sent out from Artres on the morning of 3rd from "C" and "D" Companies and it was reported that the enemy was retiring. The town of Saultain was entered by a patrol of "C" Company at 1210 and returned with the Mayor. Saultain was just outside the Battalions area of operation. The Battalion pushed forward, with "C" and "D" Companies leading and at 1221 patrols of "C" Company entered Curgies. A party from "D" Company met with Machine Gun fire at the south end of the village, but this was soon overcome, with the crew being killed. By 1445 "C" and "D" Companies had passed through the village of Curgies without artillery support and a defence line was established east of the railway in F.29 and the Companies dug in for the night. The advance had been so swift that the artillery could not keep pace with it and this would cost the battalion the following day. The Battalion had advanced between 3000 and 4000 yards during the day, which was no mean feat.

During the day Battalion Headquarters had been situated at –

1st Stage. Chateau at Artres.
2nd Stage. K.12.b.5.9. North of Preseau
3rd Stage. Chateau at Curgies.

A 9th battalion man died at home on the 3rd November from the effects of gas.

12919 Private George Mansell MM was aged 26 years and a native of Fulbeck where his name is inscribed on the Memorial. He is buried in Fulbeck (St Nicholas) Churchyard and his grave can be found in the Southeast part of the churchyard.

The 4th would see the battalion fight its last battle after pursuing the enemy for the past few days. They would be tasked with taking the village of Sebourg, which sat, among the rolling hills of this area. There were many places in which a stubborn machine gun post could hold up and inflict many casualties on the Battalion.

At 0530 the Battalion without any artillery preparation or support continued its pursuit of the enemy and entered Sebourg and was made very welcome by the villages who plied them with food and drink. The battalion inflicted a number of casualties on the enemy and would be forgiven for

Private George Mansell MM

thinking that the job was an easy one. The problem was that beyond Sebourg the ground rises to the hills beyond and the enemy would make its stand inflicting many casualties on the Battalion. In attempting to capture the high ground east of Sebourg "C" and "D" Companies came under heavy machine gun fire and the enemy also attempted a local counter attack which resulted in the two forward companies having to fall back slightly to conform with units on the flanks. During the counter attack, which was made from the ridge at A.21 and 27, two 4.5 Howitzers which were attached to the battalion engaged the enemy over open sights and inflicted a number of casualties. The Howitzers fired from Battalion H.Q. at F.30 which was 2000 yards from the enemy positions. The result was that the two companies "C" and "D" suffered fairly heavily during these operations mainly from machine gun fire.

The following Officers were wounded: –
D Company

Capt. F.S. Suffolk, O/C, 2/Lieut. Ridgen, 2/Lieut. W. Francis. 2/Lieut. Haynes.

C Company

Lieut. C. Wilmot, O/C, 2/Lieut. J. B. Russell, 2/Lieut. F. Parker, M.C. 2/Lieut. H.M. Crowther. 2/lieut Crowther remained on duty and took command of "C" and "D" Companies.

Upward of fifty men had been killed and many more wounded during the operation and the Gallantry awards given later would be a testimony to the heroics of the men.

The advance had been 4000 yards and much of this without artillery support. Battalion H.Q. had been located at the following places during the advance –

1st Stage. F.29.d.0.6. East of Curgies.
2nd Stage. F.29.b.central (Tank).
3rd Stage. Sebourg F.30. (Ref. Sheet 51A.)

Despite the Battalions losses, the Lewis Gunners and rifle fire both in the village and on the ridge beyond had inflicted heavy casualties on the enemy. Thirty enemy were captured, three tanks recaptured and ten enemy machine guns taken during the advance.The battalion received orders during the afternoon to take the ridge with artillery support and zero would be 1700, but this was postponed to the morrow and the men dug in for the night on the eastern outskirts of Sebourg. Thirty-Five of the men killed would remain on the hillside overlooking Sebourg forever and they are buried in the small battlefield cemetery, which contains fifty-six graves in total. It is indeed a part of Nottinghamshire and Derbyshire in a foreign field.

One of the men was 20045 Private William Dexter Clowes M.M. He was 24 years of age and from Sutton in Ashfield Notts.

Private W.D. Clowes, Military Medal 4th October 1917

Sebourg British Cemetery

Barnes	Ernest	22112	Private	k in a	04/11,1918
Blunt	F J	3415	Sgt	k in a	04/11,1918
Bond	Alfred E	17955	Private	k in a	04/11,1918
Bradley	Leonard Charles	71850	Private	k in a	04/11,1918
Bradley	Robert William	306288	Private	k in a	04/11,1918
Brown	William	96117	Private	k in a	04/11,1918
Calvert	John James	71488	Private	k in a	04/11,1918
Chesham	Harry	13764	Private	k in a	04/11,1918
Clarke	Arthur	82816	Private	k in a	04/11,1918
Clowes	William Dexter	20045	Private	k in a	04/11,1918
Cornelius	Wilfred	7107	CSM	k in a	04/11,1918
Dyson	Walter	27472	Private	k in a	04/11,1918
Garton	Samuel	16895	Private	k in a	04/11,1918
Goodacre	Harry	21475	Private	k in a	04/11,1918
Green	John	86518	L/Cpl	k in a	04/11,1918
Heald	Arthur	18263	Private	k in a	04/11,1918
Henry	Frederick	94428	Private	k in a	04/11,1918
Hill	Harold Arthur	70854	Private	k in a	04/11,1918
Mackintosh	Claude.H.B.James	265578	Private	k in a	04/11,1918
Mowbray	Albert	285302	Private	k in a	04/11,1918
Nowell	John	266072	Sgt	k in a	04/11,1918
Parkin	John W	51970	Private	k in a	04/11,1918
Roadley	Harold	32065	Private	k in a	04/11,1918
Sheraton	Wallace	24144	Private	k in a	04/11,1918
Taylor	George	24784	Private	k in a	04/11,1918
Taylor	John Allen	201999	Sgt	k in a	04/11,1918
Thompson	Joseph	92209	Private	k in a	04/11,1918
Upton	William	30976	L/Cpl	k in a	04/11,1918
Venables	Ernest	93719	Private	k in a	04/11,1918
Wardle	Frederick	107632	Private	k in a	04/11,1918
Weston	William	70900	Private	k in a	04/11,1918
Wilkes	Richard Nichols	92265	Private	k in a	04/11,1918
Wilson	Albert	13041	Corporal	k in a	04/11,1918
Wootton	Leonard	26233	L/Cpl	k in a	04/11,1918
Zolowski	Ephraim. MM	73055	L/Cpl	k in a	04/11,1918

Three men would be taken back to Valenciennes and buried in the St. Roch Communal Cemetery

204439 Private Lewis George Ellis was living at Somercotes Derbyshire prior to enlisting on 24th April 1916. He had joined the 9th Battalion on 27th August 1917.He is buried in grave III. E. 1.

31385 Private George William Grainger was a Nottingham man and is buried in grave III. B. 17.

97965 Private Benjamin Rusholme was from Bridlington Yorkshire and is buried in grave III. C.3.

One man is buried at Denain and in the Communal Cemetery –

202814 Private Thomas Charles Friend was from Peckham in Surrey and in grave D. 27.

Another man died on 4th but at Rouen and it is possible that he was one of the men who contracted influenza.

11162 Private Harry Wright aged 29 years of North Collingham, Notts. He is buried at St.Sever Cemetery Extension, Rouen and grave S. II. P. 24.

A further eight men died of wounds and these were probably sustained on 4th November. 5th November 1918 – Four men are buried at Cambrai East Military Cemetery. This is an unusual cemetery as it was German. It has British, French, German and other nationalities buried within it.

12367 CSM Henry Terry DCM aged 26 years and a Nottingham man. He had been awarded the DCM for his work on 4th October 1917. He had also served with the 1/6th Battalion. Grave II. A. 9

80830 Private Belton Oldham was a North Collingham man. Grave II. A. 15.

17709 Private Robert Peel aged 22 years and from New Mills Derbyshire. Grave II. A. 31.

76384 Lance Corporal Walter Gerald Fisher, “C” Coy was aged 22 years and from Colchester. He was formerly 05449 R.A.O.C. Grave II. A. 36.

Two other men at Cambrai would die on 6th November –

70865 Private John William Butters aged 33 years a married man from Gedney Linc's and formerly 26905, South Staffordshire Regiment. Grave II. A. 30.

83624 Private Arthur Burgess was from Hawarden in Cheshire. Grave II. A. 45.

Two men received wounds on 4th November and survived the war. 263002 Private Victor C. Gelsthorpe had served in other Sherwood Forester battalions prior to joining the 9th Bn on 11 October 1917 as one of the replacements for losses on 4th October 1917. Victor was discharged from the army on 4 June 1919. 70133 Private Claude Cyril Hunt had served with the 16th Bn until he contracted influenza in February 1917. He joined the 9th Bn in late 1917 and in early 1918 received treatment for gas poisoning, returning to the battalion in August.

The night of 4th/5th had seen much planning in an attempt to take the ridge as quickly as possible. A creeping barrage had been organized and by 0530 the Battalion was ready to go forward.

The artillery opened up with a creeping barrage and "A" and "B" Companies moved forward in attack, by 0705 they had taken the ridge with little opposition and no fatalities. This shows the effect a creeping barrage could have and no doubt the other two Companies could have done with the same support the previous day. The two attacking Companies established posts on the ridge, forward of the objective in A.21/27. During the morning the supporting battalions, 6th Lincolns followed by 7th South Stafford's passed through the Battalion who withdrew to billets in Sebourg remaining in Brigade reserve. Enemy retaliation for the British barrage was put at 'feeble'. The Brigadier General Commanding sent his congratulations to the battalion for the work it had done on 3rd/4th and 5th.

The battalion remained at Sebourg in reserve during the 6th although under one hours notice to move. Even so the villages made the men most welcome and made sure they lacked neither food nor drink. At 0530 the 6th Lincoln's attacked but were held up by enemy machine gun fire. Operational orders were received for the attack to go in again on the following morning and once again it would be the Lincoln's advancing. The Battalion band rejoined in the afternoon and in the early evening the Brigade boundaries were altered. The attack by the Lincoln's on the morning of 7th was a complete success and to conform to this the battalion moved forward to Roisin were it remained for the night.

One man died of wounds on 8th and he is buried at Etaples and grave XLIX. E. 5.

330195 Private Edward Frank Hadland aged 25 years was from Tetbury Staffs and formerly 1887 North Staffordshire Regiment.

The 8th saw the advance continue with the 7th South Stafford's taking the lead and they attacked at 0820 with the battalion in close support. The battalion left Roisin at 0720 and took over the positions of the 7th South Stafford's as they vacated them.

Battalion Headquarters was located as follows during this advance –

1st Stage. B.25.d.5.5.
2nd Stage. Autreppe B.20.b.1.1.
3rd Stage. B.22.c
4th Stage. B.24.c.5.4.
5th Stage. Bellevue Farm at C.25.a.

The battalion remained at Bellevue Farm overnight after an advance of some 9000 yards and even the most sceptical man in the 9th must have realized that the war would soon be over. Owing to the enemy habit of blowing up bridges and mining roads junctions the battalions rations could not be got up and they had to resort to their iron rations of Bully Beef and Biscuits.

The following morning the 7th South Stafford's continued the pursuit of the enemy at 0730 with the battalion in support and they left Bellevue Farm at 0900. By now the Battalion had crossed into Belgium and the town of Mons came ever closer. The Battalion covered a distance of 10,000 yards during the day and at the end of it men were billeted at Aulnois and Coegnies Chause for the night.

The Battalion Headquarters for the day were as follows –

1st Stage. C.20. central.
2nd Stage. Lalouviere Farm C.29.a.
3rd Stage. Custom House. C.23.d.
4th Stage. Les Trieux. D.25.b.
5th Stage. Aulnois.

Iron rations were dropped by aeroplane during the morning in the vicinity of crossroads at C.27.d.8.9. By this time the men would be looking forward to a decent hot meal although it would be a few more days before this dream became a reality.

The 10th would see the Battalion in the van once again as they left Aulnois and moved forward to Havay working in conjunction with a company of New Zealand Cyclists and Cavalry. Companies moved off as follows – "A", "B","C","D", Battalion H.Q. – 500 yards between each company and 100 yards between each platoon. The enemy artillery was still a threat and the C.O. did not want the men bunched up and making a large target. The objective was the high ground from E.5.c.0.0. (Sheet 51) to W.28. Central. (Sheet 45). The distance between the two locations being around 100 yards and it was taken without opposition at 1135. Posts were established and the battalion dug in. Forward artillery sections were attached to the battalion and two 18 pounders came into action on high ground at E.5.c engaging the retreating enemy. Battalion H.Q. was set up at E.9.a.8.3. The Battalions rations were once again dropped by aeroplane at a road junction located at E.21.a.7.0. The 63rd (Naval) Division moved forward as an advanced guard to the Corps and the Hawke Battalion was billeted in the Battalion area for the night.

The Hawke battalion War Diary for 10th/11th November states -:

10th – 0215 – Orders were received that the Battalion would continue to march to Sars-le-Bruyere leaving at 0700 hrs. 0930 Bn arrived Sars-Le-Bruyere and stood by to move at short notice. 1430 – Bn. moved forward to take up preliminary positions. 2030 Bn. billeted in Thy together with a company of Sherwood Foresters.

11th – 0600 – Bn. moved into assembly positions and passed through Sherwoods at 0700 (zero). All objectives were taken and an outpost line established along the railway to the east of Vellervielle-Le-Sec. 1030 – Verbal orders to Cease Fire were received and to stand fast on line joined. 1100 – Armistice Commenced.

The battalion on being relieved by the Hawke Battalion withdrew to billets in the sugar factory at Havay (E.2.d. Havay). Whilst the relief was underway official notice arrived stating that an Armistice would take effect at 1100 and hostilities would cease at that time. An Aeroplane descended to convey the message to the battalions front companies, "A" and "B" who were still in the front line. A 'Special Order' from XXII Corps Commander expressing his thanks and admiration to the troops was received during the day.

On 23 July 1915 the Battalion entered the front line at Helles on Gallipoli for the first time relieving the Hawke and Hood Battalions. It was fitting that on the last day of the war the Hawke Battalion should move through the 9th Battalion and relieve them. Much had happened in the interim and both battalions had lost many men but the few in both Battalions who had survived would no doubt reflect on the first and last meeting.

Suddenly after years of constant noise, of sniper fire and shells, all was silent and many of the men just stood in a daze hardly daring to believe that the end had come. The Armistice would turn into an end of the war but that was months away and the men knew that the fighting would not reignite. They had endured the horrors of Gallipoli, the heat of Egypt, the fierce Somme fighting, the mud of Flanders and the period of open warfare. The 9th Battalion Sherwood Foresters had upheld all the traditions of the Regiment and the counties of Nottinghamshire and Derbyshire could be proud of its first Kitchener battalion.

Two men died after the Armistice –

70936 Private Robert Parish aged 21 years of Hogsthorpe Linc's and formerly 26944 South Staffordshire Regiment died on 12th November and is buried at Terlincthun British Cemetery, Wimille.

The last man from the battalion to die of wounds overseas was –

70912 Private Fred Bell aged 25 years and from Scothern Linc's died on 15 November 1918 and is buried at Cambrai East Military Cemetery, grave III. A. 39.

He was formerly 26914, South Staffordshire Regiment.

May he and all his comrades from the battalion rest in peace.

The end of the war did not mean the end of the 9th Battalion and it would continue until 30th June 1919. As with 'old soldiers' the Battalion would not die but gently fade away.The 12th was given over to cleaning up and refitting followed by training and recreation. The men were given time to reflect on their achievements and to come to terms with the wars end. They had done the job asked of them and now they wanted to go home, to forget the horrors and deprivations of the war, returning to a 'normal' life. Demobilizing hundreds of thousands of men would not be that easy though and the men would have to wait their turn before returning to 'Civvy Street'.

On 13th the C.O. Lieut-Colonel Scothern proceeded to England on leave and Major S. H. Piper assumed command of the battalion. Captain F. S. Suffolk of "D" Company rejoined from hospital. The Brigadier General Commanding 33rd Infantry Brigade addressed the Battalion telling them of his pride at their achievements. The following day saw Captain A.E. Brennan and the Echelon personnel rejoin the Battalion from Haspres. The day was spent in cleaning and Company training as the men continued to relax and recover from their exertions of the past few weeks.

The 15th was an auspicious day for the battalion when Captain Maishment of "B" Company and forty Other Ranks took part in a ceremony at Mons. This would be the official entry into Mons by the First Army, the triumphant parade and marching past the First Army Commander, General Sir Henry

Horne. The remainder of the Battalion enjoyed a Camp Fire Concert in the evening in the vicinity of the billets.

Colonel Scothern's notes tell of the period leading up to the time when the battalion would disband.

"Work was naturally relaxed after the Armistice, but some training was still carried on. Most of the time was given over to recreational training, and every effort was made to make the men as comfortable and as happy as possible. On November 15th a party of two officers and forty other ranks represented the battalion at the official entry of the 1st Army Commander into Mons, and a few days later the battalion marched there to give the men an opportunity of seeing the place.

The Education scheme for giving instruction to those men desiring it also started, the battalion up to this time not having had the opportunity of doing so before, owing to the conditions under which it had been living.

On November 26th the battalion left Havay on a three days march to Conde Sur L'Escaut, the new area allotted, being billeted in French Barracks there on arrival. A great deal of useful work was done in and about the town, cleaning up generally and salving. H.M. The King accompanied by H.R.H. The Prince of Wales visited Conde on December 5th, but there was no official parade.

Recreational training was carried on under Divisional arrangements, and the battalion did very well, winning the Football Competition for Battalion Teams and being second in the Cross-country Race. It also represented the 33rd Brigade in the Divisional Boxing Competition after winning the Brigade Contests.

Demobilisation commenced on December 12th when several miners left the battalion, followed at weekly intervals by other small parties. Christmas Day again proved enjoyable. The men's mess rooms were decorated, and a prize for the best was to "D" Company.

With the New Year demobilisation increased and the strength diminished. By the middle of February battalions had become so small that it was decided to concentrate the Division, which up to now had been scattered, over a fairly large area in Denain. A few days before this, the King's Colours were consecrated and presented to the Battalion; the G.O.C. 11th Division presented the Colours.

On leaving Conde the 33rd Brigade was presented with an address by the Mayor of Conde, worded as follows: -

'To the Brigade Commander and Colonel of the 9th Sherwood Foresters"

"The Mayor of Conde being regrettably absent at this moment, I, Deputy Mayor, and my colleagues of the Council, are very pleased to come to you in order to express, as representatives of the inhabitants of Conde, our feelings of deep esteem and the most lively demonstration of friendship at this moment of separation, we realize how short has been your stay in this place, so we wish to tell you how happy and proud we have been in receiving in our homes a part of the brave and gallant British Troops who have fought so courageously side by side with ours and those of the allies.

By their valour and sacrifice the enemy, who was believed invincible, is now obliged to accept our peace conditions. Glory to all Allied soldiers, who must be today better friends than ever.

We are glad to express at this moment how deep is our regret to see you leaving Conde: we were so happy together. I am sure that everyone feels sorrow at your parting. Your stay will be remembered in this town a long while, and we hope that it will be the same for you"

Praise indeed for the men of the 9th Battalion Sherwood Foresters.

Saturday 16th saw the Battalion take on the 6th Lincoln's at Hockey and after an entertaining and high scoring game, the Battalion eventually lost 3-5. At 1000 the following morning the Battalion attended church parade, which was followed by a lecture on the new Education Scheme given by the C.O. Major Piper. The British Army had slipped easily back into its peacetime roll with education and recreation being at the forefront.

The period from 18th to the end of November was a fairly hectic one of the Battalion, which would include a move to a new area. The C.O. (Major Piper) inspected the battalion during the morning of 18th whilst the Riding classes for officers commenced in the afternoon under Captain Munday. Three officers joined the Battalion, 2/Lieuts. B.S.F. Turner and A. Rowland from the South Notts Hussars, Major Pemberton from the Cheshire Regiment. The men also attended a Demobilization lecture given by the Divisional Education officer. On 21st the Reverend Lowndes proceeded on leave to England. The following day saw the battalion cross country competition take place with the results being;

1st – "A" Company – 120 points.
2nd – "B" Company – 145 points.
3rd – "C" Company – 203 points.

"A" Company would represent the Battalion in the Brigade and Divisional Cross country championships.

This was followed by a concert in the evening with the Brigade Officer Commanding in attendance.

Saturday 23rd saw the Battalion set off at 0915 and march to Mons returning at 1600.

The men were given the opportunity to look around the town and were no doubt nobly looked after by the locals. The positions where the first and last shots of the war had been fired being just a few paces apart.

After Church parade on Sunday 24th the men prepared for the next move which would take them out of Belgium and back into France. Prior to leaving the Brigadier General Commanding inspected the men.

The three-day march to Conde sur L'Escaut commenced on 26th November at 0915 at a leisurely pace and the Battalion arrived at their overnight stop of Dour in the afternoon. The following morning at 0900 the battalion continued on and arrived at Quarouble in the afternoon, being billeted in the village. The final days march began at 0900 with the Battalion arriving at 1300 on 28th. The Battalion would be billeted in old French barracks in the town and there would be a fair amount of cleaning up done to bring it up to British Army standards. Captain C.E. Scott and 2/Lieut Radford rejoined the Battalion whilst three 2/Lieuts. Joined – T.B. Unwin, A.W. Jones, and J.C. Boothley.

The last days of November were given over to cleaning and improving the French Barracks.

Sunday 1st December would see a Church Parade service at the 1115 in the Theatre followed by trials for the Battalion football team during the afternoon.

The 2nd was a mixture of training and recreation – "A" and "B" companies enjoying a route march through the local countryside whilst "D" Company trained in barracks. Meanwhile "B" Company had drawn the short straw and was on Fatigues in and around the barracks. Rugby trials for the Brigade team were undertaken during the afternoon.

The following gallantry awards were made in connection with operations undertaken in November 1918.

Bar to Military Cross –
Temp. Capt. J. Critchlow, M.C. "A" Coy.

Military Cross –
Temp 2/Lieut. A.W. Rigden, "D" Coy.
Lieut H. Alexander, M.O.R.C. U.S.A. Battalion Medical Officer.

Distinguished Conduct Medal –
5128 Private H. Nash.

Bar to Military Medal –
2606 Lance Corporal H. Hinkley. M.M.
16301 Sergeant H. Uttley D.C.M., M.M.
25510 Private F. Doody, M.M.

The Military Medal –
78221 Private G.A. Earle.
70306 Private G.H. Partridge.
21326 Private L. Shephard
27828 Private J. Sutton.
25298 Sergeant G. Sutton.
15537 Lance Corporal W. Thompson.
30550 Private A. Kirby.
14020 Private W. Groves.
27911 Private A. Saunders.
21775 Private W. Cresswell.
13016 Sergeant F. Carlile, D.C.M.
42182 Private E.V. Wright.
.4754 Private G. Wass.
22121 Private F. Halford.
92268 Private T.F. Rodgers.
12794 Lance Corporal A. Iliffe.
14619 Sergeant J.W. Buckley.
23034 Private J.W. Atkin.
15539 Sergeant C. Proffitt.
19207 Lance Corporal J.H. Storey.
21351 Private G. Mann.

The above tells of the gallantry of the men when taking Sebourg and attempting to take the ridge beyond without artillery cover.

Training continued throughout December although of course not with the same urgency as before. It was more a case of keeping the men busy whilst they awaited demobilization. The men also had to carry out salvage work in a designated area as the detritus of war had to be cleared. It would though take many years to remove all of the hazards and all of the men yet to receive proper burials but at least the men could make a start on the job.

The 5th December saw the King and H.R.H. Prince of Wales visit Conde were they met the Corps and Divisional Commanders at No.2 Place Rombault, which was the new Battalion Officers Mess. They Royal party left at 1400 driving slowly passed the Place D'Armes where the battalion had collected in groups to welcome them.

The important business of the day was the choosing of the President of the Mess Committee and it was decided that Captain A.E. Brennan should get the job, assisted by Lieuts. Bowyer and Hetherington.

The afternoon of 6th saw "A" and "D" Companies playing football although sadly no result is known. The C.O., Lt-Colonel. Scothern, DSO returned from leave and resumed command. The Battalions Officers Mess officially opened with a dinner at 1930 with the Battalion band in attendance. 2/lieut. Sharpe, "B" Company proceeded to 4th Army reception camp. The Cross Country Team ("A" Company) where shown around the Brigade course by the Brigade Major.

A rugby match on the afternoon of 7th saw 33rd Infantry Brigade take on 11th Division R.A.M.C., which resulted in the Medics winning 12 points to 3.At 1000 on Sunday 8th all of the Companies except "D" attended church parade in the theatre. "D" company in the meantime was on fatigues in and around the barracks. The Sergeants Mess held a meeting during the morning in the barracks. A lecture on the 'Growth of Germany' was given by Prof. Adkins (YMCA) in the Theatre from 1730 to 1900. Possibly this lecture would have been better given prior to the war and to men in much higher places.

The 9th was a busy day with training in the morning and recreation in the afternoon. All N.C.O.'s would attend at parade each day at 1400 to receive instruction. "A" Company was on fatigues in barracks, "B" Company worked under the salvage officer and the Battalion officers had to learn to ride. Captain. R. Munday, M.C. recommenced riding classes at 1430 for all officers who could not ride. Officers from "A" and "B" Coys, would have lessons on Monday and Thursdays whilst "C" and "D" had Tuesday and Fridays.

2/Lieut. Crowther proceeded on leave to England.

At 1415 "A" Company played a football match versus 33rd Brigade HQ and Light Trench Mortar Battery with honours being even at 1-1.

The Battalion Education classes commenced which would be carried out daily except for Saturdays and Sundays. The subjects were an interesting mix to say the least –

Subject	Instructor.
General (elementary) –	Lt. C. Cartledge
General (advanced) -	2/Lt. A. Rowland
Electricity and Magnetism -	Capt. J. Critchlow, M.C.
Shorthand	Private Dunn.
Book-keeping	Capt. F.S. Suffolk.

Quite what the miners of Nottinghamshire and Derbyshire made of such delights as 'shorthand' was not mentioned in the diary. The problem with the scheme was that the instructors and instructed were always liable to be demobilized at a moments notice, which disrupted the classes.

The Brigade Orchestra played at the Battalion mess during dinner and there followed a concert given by the 'Silhouettes' (33rd Field Ambulance Brigade) in the theatre.The following day "A" Company under the Medical Officer was tasked to clean out the Cavalry Barracks next to the battalions own barracks and it has to be wondered as to the state of the former. Although the term squalid was often used when describing French barracks.

The afternoon was given over to the Brigade Cross Country Championship and a team from "A" Company represented the Battalion. Presumably none of them had been employed in the mornings work at the French Barracks. The team consisted of – Capt. J. Critchlow, M.C. Cpl T. Myers, Privates R. Kierton, O. Beaumont, J. Kemp, M. Crow, H Moorley, E. Martin, A. Buxton, A. Watts, R Mellor and J. Stokes.

The course was approximately five miles in distance and the Battalion won by one point. 1st – 9th Battalion Sherwood Foresters. 140 points

2nd – 6th Lincoln's	141 points
3rd – 7th South Stafford's	207 points
4th – Brigade Headquarters	337 points

The remainder of December continued with Training and fatigues to keep the men busy followed in the afternoons with lots of sport and entertainment.

The 11th saw a football match between "B" Company and Battalion Transport with kick off at 1415. A hard fought game saw "B" Company the winners 2-1. The Battalion Boxing Tournament also took place in the theatre although with only eleven entries. 2/Lieut. Jestico proceeded to England on leave whilst 2/Lieut. A.S. Osborne heard that he had been awarded to Military Cross in connection with the capture of Abancourt Station on 5th October 1918. The Battalion Mess held a guest night with the Battalion band in attendance.

The following day saw the Brigade football

tournament begin with "C" Company representing the battalion versus "B" Company of the 6th Lincoln's. The match was held on the neutral ground of the 7th South Stafford's at Vieux Conde with kick off at 1415. The 6th Lincoln's running out very lucky winners 5-0.

2/Lieuts. F.O. Radford and S.J. Ayres were transferred to "C" Company for duty.

The most notable event of the day would see the first eight men; all miners leave the Battalion and proceed to England for Demobilization. Britain needed its miners back and men who had seen much more service than others could only sit and watch as their 'juniors' left. At the beginning of the demobilization first in last out was not a consideration. At first the demobilization would be a slow trickle but inexorably the Battalion would fade away and 12th December 1918 would be the beginning of the end.

The 'Wunny Wuns' Concert Party (11th Division) performed in the theatre on the evenings of 12th, 13th and 14th.

The Battalion running team, which consisted of the "A" Company men who had won the Brigade Competition proceeded by lorry to Raismes and were billeted at the reception camp for the night, prior to the Divisional Cross Country the following day.

The Divisional Championship was held the following afternoon and two of 33rd Brigades teams came first and second. Unfortunately 6th Lincoln's gained revenge and won with 238 points, the battalion second with 331 points. The course in the vicinity of the Foret De Raismes was one of 4 miles.

The Medical Officer Doctor (not sure why he lost his rank) H. Alexander proceeded to England on leave. Lieut. Lindow of 33rd Field Ambulance Brigade relieved the good doctor.

The Battalions teams showed their prowess at Hockey and Football on Sunday 15th. Firstly they had church parade services in the theatre at 0915. The football team played football versus the 33rd Field Ambulance Brigade winning 3-1, whilst the Hockey team beat the 7th South Stafford's 3-2.The battalion demobilization office opened its doors in the Barracks on the 16th.which would deal with the paperwork prior to the men leaving. A 30-yard Rifle range was opened up for the Companies to use on a daily basis.A football match between Battalion HQ which no doubt included the C.O. and the Transport section saw a 1-1 draw. The final of the Company football, which would decide the team to play in the Divisional finals, was played between "B" Coy 6th Lincoln's and "D" Coy 7th South Stafford's with the former winning 7-1.

Captain F.S. Suffolk proceeded to England on Demobilized draft conducting duty and was granted 14 days leave. There was no mention of any battalion men being in the party. The Night Lights Concert party from 32nd Brigade performed in the theatre on the evenings of 16th/17th and 18th.

The 17th/18th were taken up with various fatigues although the Battalion football team did find time to 'hammer' the 80th Labour Coy. 6-0. The 19th saw the Brigade Orchestra played in the barracks from 1600 to 1800 and in the Officers Mess from 1930 to 2200. A Rugby match was held between the Battalion and the Machine Gun Corps in which after a tight match the 9th men won 5-3. The Chaplain The Reverend Lowndes conducted a Whist Drive during the evening. The N.C.O.'s and men from the sniping and scouting sections rejoined their Companies.

The following day the mundane routine continued although the men still had sport and entertainment to keep them happy. The Battalion Sergeant's played a hockey match versus the 7th South Stafford's Sergeants on the latter's ground at Vieux Conde coming out convincing winners 6-1. Mr. H. Brennan also gave the men a lecture in the theatre at 1730 with the subject being Russia. The men would have to be told of the 'horrors' of Bolshevism.

The 21st saw the C.O. inspect the barracks, this after the O.C.'s Companies had already done the self same thing.The cinema at Conde was opened up for showings at 1700 and 1900 each night. On 23rd, 2/Lieut. Fletcher joined the battalion whilst five more miners were demobilized. The Brigade Boxing Championship opened at 1400 in the riding school.

Christmas Eve for the most part was much the same as any other day. The Brigade Boxing Championship was concluded and the Battalion Band was in attendance.

The final results were as follows –

Winning Team – The Battalion with 23 points.

Second – 7th South Stafford's with 22 points.

Third – 6th Lincoln's with 14 points.

Best loser on day one was Private Sanders of 9th Sherwood Foresters.

Best loser on day two was Private Corcoran of 9th Sherwood Foresters.

Lance Corporal Redgate, Sherwood Foresters won the Featherweight Competition.

The Brigade Orchestra played at the Battalion Mess from 1930.

Christmas Day in the British Army is always special although it is a day tinged with sadness. You are with your pals but away from your family and friends. Church Parade service was held at 0930 in the theatre and the men would be thankful for surviving the war but sad to have lost so many pals. The men had been hard at work decorating their Mess rooms and the Brigadier General Commanding (Brigadier General Spring) undertook the judging at 1130 to decide on the best-decorated room.

After much deliberation he awarded "D" Company the trophy of one barrel of beer. The remaining Companies, Battalion H.Q. and Transport all came a close 'second' and were each awarded one half a barrel of beer. The men then sat down to Christmas dinner at 1230 although sadly the menu was not given. The officers and sergeants acted as waiters to the men for the dinner. A football match was held at 1500 on the battalion ground between the Officers and Sergeants with the former winning 5-2.

The Officers had their own Christmas Dinner at 1830 with the Battalion Band in attendance. The Sergeants would have to wait until the following day for their Christmas Dinner but the Battalion Band would also entertain them.

The 26th saw another batch of twenty-seven miners leave the Battalion and Lieut. Royle would escort them to England and be granted 14 days leave for his trouble.

The Officers played a football match versus the Servants, which ended in an exciting 3-3 draw. It has to be remembered that the Officers had played two games in two days and were obviously tiring towards the end. The Brigade Orchestra played at a concert in the theatre during the evenings of 26th/27th with the Brigadier attending on the second evening. Major Pemberton proceeded on leave to Paris whilst Major Piper and Captain Cooper left for leave in England.

The fourth batch of men numbering twenty-one miners was demobilized on 28th.

2/Lieut. Percival proceeded to Boulogne on leave.

After church parade on 29th a football match was played between "B" company and the Vieux Conde Football team with the English beating the French 5-1.

The following day saw more men leaving the battalion as a batch of ten miners bid their farewells and the battalion band played them off. The men were entertained in the evening at the theatre by 'The Picks' (8th Corps Concert Party) and in fact the Concert Party would perform every evening for a week.

The 31st saw the Battalion playing football versus the 6th Lincoln's and losing to them once again 2-3. Lieut. Bowyer proceeded on leave to England and Lieut. Hetherington took over his duties as Discipline Officer at the Valenciennes Officers club.

The Battalion Strength was as follows –

	Officers.	Other Ranks.
Battalion Strength on 1st December	47	845
Reinforcements during month	1	31
Men demobilized during month	0	76
Strength on December 31st December	48	792

Chapter Six

1919 – Old Soldiers Never Die, They Just Fade Away

FROM JANUARY 1st 1919 until the Battalion was disbanded on 30th June 1919 there would be an endless round of Training, Fatigues, Sports and demobilization. It was very much a humdrum life as men waited for their demobilization date and officers attempted to keep them entertained and happy.
It is though right to pick out any highlights that can be gleaned from the diaries and to record them. It is important to show the winding down process of the battalion and its final demise.

On 1st January Major Piper was awarded the D.S.O. in the New Years Honours list.

The 2nd saw the Regimental censorship of letters discontinued and the men could write whatever they wished.

On 4th another batch of ten miners left the battalion with the band playing them off.The Medical Officer Doctor Alexander returned from leave and was attached to the 34th F.A.B. Captain Scott, O.C. B Company left the battalion to take over the duties of A.M.L.O., with Lieut.Gustard taking command of B Company.

Seven more miners left the battalion on 7th January and soon the trickle of men would become a flood.

Football, Rugby, Hockey and all manner of sports continued on a daily basis with the battalion playing other units in the area. One good result was that on 8th the battalion beat the 6th Lincoln's 2-1 in the semi-finals of the Brigade Competition. They played the 7th South Stafford's in the final and after a 1-1 result after 90 minutes, ten minutes of extra time saw the battalion win 3-1.The same day Major Pemberton was promoted to Lieut.Colonel (1/8/1918)

The 9th saw the first of two lectures on European history given by the Reverend Strong (attached from 7th South Stafford's). The 'Don-Acs' (11th Division Artillery Concert Party) played at the theatre during the evening.

The 19th saw all men not inoculated during the previous twelve months getting their jabs from the M.O.

The 11th was a special day for the men when permission was granted to wear the ribbon of the "1915 Star". Lieut. Brellen-Smith proceeded on leave to England.

The following day the first officer left on Demobilization – Lieut. L.W. Foster the Signalling officer left and his duties were taken over by Lieut. Radford.Entertainment for the men provided by the Wunny Wuns (11th Divisional Concert Party) on 13th January.

The 14th saw another football semi final and the battalion played the Northumberland Fusiliers of 34th brigade. The Battalion team sheet was 2/Lieut Ayres, Sgt Herbert, Pte Oakland, 2/Lieut. Unwin, Pte Nee, Pte Walker, CSM Grant, Pte Small, Pte Hughes, Pte Hart and Pte Halford. The supporters were taken by lorries to the Fusiliers ground at Denain and watched the battalion run out 2-0 winners. There followed an evening Whist Drive conducted by the Padre in the barracks.

The 15th saw Captain Critchlow leave for a ten-day course with the Royal Air Force.The 17th was the day of the Divisional Football final between the battalion and the 158th R.F.A. at Raismes with the 9th team being as on 14th. The battalion won 1-0 and became 11th Division Champions and would go forward to the Corps Competition.

The 21st saw the end of the Medical Officer fatigues, which left the men with even more time to sit around and wait for demobilization. The 2nd

Lecture on European History was given to the men. The battalion football team played the 40th R.G.A. in the Corps Competition losing 3-1. Lieut. Charlton was demobilized.

The following day the men paraded in front of the Divisional Commander who presented medal ribbons for the '1915 Star'. Captain Kingdom (Kingdon?) was demobilized. The 'Fleur de Lys' (Manchester Regiment Concert Party) entertained the men during the evening. It is quite amazing at the number of Concert Parties in the B.E.F. In fact the following evenings saw the 'Tanks' which was the 103rd M.G.C. Concert Party keeping the men happy. Lectures continued and the Reverend Strong gave one on 'Church and the National Life' on 24th January.

Demobilization continued with Lieut. Radford on 26th, 2/Lieut, Captain Critchlow, M.C. and 14 Other Ranks on 27th, Crowther and 17 Other Ranks on 28th.

The 31st January was another cold day and some members of the battalion enjoyed the first skating of the season at Vieux Conde. During the month six officers and forty-eight men had left the battalion for demobilization, leaving a total of forty-two officers and seven hundred and forty four men. The rate of demobilization increased considerably in February as men began to complain at the time it was taking. They had done the job asked of them and now wanted to go home.

On the 1st February twenty Other Ranks were demobilized followed by Lieut. Cartledge and Fifteen Other Ranks on 2nd. Lieut. Gustard along with, R.Q.M.S. Parker and twenty-two Other Ranks on 3rd. Lieut. Roberts rejoined the battalion from the 33rd Light Trench Mortar Battery and C.S.M. J. Grant was appointed Acting R.Q.M.S.

The 5th would see seventeen more Other Ranks demobilized closely followed the next day by a further twenty. The reverend Strong would treat the remainder of the men to another lecture, although the topic of the lecture was not given.

On the 7th 2/Lieuts. Fell and Wightman accompanied by thirteen Other Ranks left for demobilization. Major L.L. Ottley gave a lecture in the theatre on War Citizenship.The following day Major Harding, M.C. rejoined the battalion from the 6th York and Lanc's Regiment whilst Lieut. Roberts and thirteen Other Ranks left for demobilization.

The 9th saw the battalion parade at 1120 for a practice of the ceremonial parade for the Consecration of colours. Another nineteen Other Ranks were demobilized and would miss this important part of the Battalion history.

The Battalion practiced again on 12th February in preparation for the Consecration and presentation of the colours. Another eighteen men would leave for demobilization on 12th whilst the remainder of the battalion would be treated to the 'Wanglers' concert partying the theatre.

The 13th was in many ways a sad one for the Battalion as the four Companies became two. "A" and "B" Companies amalgamated as did "C" and "D" as by this time the Battalion consisted of 38 officers and five hundred and twenty six other ranks. Lieut. Hetherington would command A/B Company and Lieut. Bowyer C/D Company. Meanwhile Lieut. Booth and nineteen other ranks left for demobilization.

The 14th February was an auspicious day for the battalion and the 'King's Colours' were consecrated and presented to the battalion. It was though sad that so many men had already left the battalion including Fred Greaves V.C. who was demobbed on 28th January 1919. Fred was asked to stay on as an officer but this quiet man had had enough of war and wanted to return to his Derbyshire village and get on with his life. Fred would never return to France or Flanders again.

The Battalion paraded on the Barrack Square at 1115 and the ceremony of consecration was performed by the Chaplains of the Brigade, after which Major General Davies presented the colours to the Battalion. The colour party consisted of Lieut. Thurburn, C.S.M.S Cockayne and Hicks an honour they would remember for the remainder of their days. The Battalion received notification that it would shortly move to new billets in Denain at an early date. Captain F.F. Suffolk and seven other ranks left for demobilization.

The following day saw 2/Lieut. Rowland and six other ranks left for their demobilization.

Two officers left the Battalion on 16th for pastures new with Lt-Col. J. A. Pemberton assuming temporary command of the 8th Battalion Northumberland Fusiliers and 2/Lieut. Boothby would have leave in England prior to proceeding with the 2nd battalion to India.

Four more other ranks left for demobilization.

Captain S. Maishment assumed the duties of the battalion Education officer.

The 17th saw the battalion cleaning up in preparation for its move to Denain on the 19th.

The Battalion paraded at 0850 in fighting order for the march to Denain, together with the remainder of the 33rd Brigade arriving at 1600 hours. The Mayor of Conde presented an address to the Battalion on its departure expressing the councils regret at the departure of the Battalion and his appreciation of all ranks during their stay in Conde (see Col. Scothern notes above). The men spent the 20th/21st settling in to their new surroundings whilst two other ranks were demobilized on 21st.

The 22nd saw all Regimental Aid post work transferred to the 34th Field Ambulance Brigade and one man was demobilized.

After church parade services at 1015 hours on 23rd the list of officers and men for the Cadre battalion was posted. Although the officers were listed none of the other ranks were and in any event the list would be changed at a later date.

Officers of the Cadre –

C.O. –	Lieut.Col. A.E. Scothern, D.S.O.
Adjutant -	A/Captain B.J. Cooper.
Q.M. –	Lieut. W.W. Horsman.
Lewis Gun Officer	A/Capt. R.W. Bowyer.

2/Lieut. J. St J Balquy and one other rank left for demobilization.

The daily education classes continued from 1130 to 1230 hours and on 25th the men had their first lecture on 'Bolshevism', which was seen as the new threat to democracy. Six other ranks left the Battalion for demobilization.

At 1215 on 26th two men were awarded Military Medals – Private C Adlington and Private L Cooper.

The 27th saw twelve other ranks leave for demobilization and 2/lieut White would accompany them for which he was given leave in England. Lieut. Bowyer was promoted to Acting/Captain.

On 28th details were given of the number of men admitted to hospital during March, the number being thirteen other ranks. This would be mainly from influenza, which was sweeping through Europe at the time. A further twenty other ranks rejoined the battalion during the month as did one officer who had since been demobilized. Twenty-one other ranks were struck off strength for reasons other than demobilization or illness with one officer moving to the 1/4th Cheshire Regiment. The number demobilized during the month was given as One hundred and eighty three other ranks and eight officers. In total Two hundred and twenty nine men had left the battalion for all reasons and nine officers.

On 1st March 1919 Summer time began at 2300 hours and the clocks would go forward one hour.

Sunday 2nd March would see the Battalion horses being demobilized and 2/Lieut.Bolton proceeded with them to Calais. Twelve men left for demobilization.

The 3rd saw four more other ranks leave the Battalion followed on 5th by thirteen others.

On 6th 2/Lieuts. Pickard and Jones left the Battalion and were attached to the 313th and 319th Prisoner of War Companies respectively.

On the 8th Lieut. Walker, 1 N.C.O. and 9 Other Ranks from C/D Company proceeded for duty with R.T.O. at Raismes (Railway Transport Officer) relieving 2/Lieut, Fletcher and his men. The Six-a-side football tournament began on the battalion football ground at 1330. This was concluded the following day with No. 8 Platoon winning.

The 10th saw the C.O. proceeding on leave to England. The N.C.O.s and men from the Battalion Headquarters Signalling section rejoined their Companies.The following day all of the Transport personnel rejoined their Companies except for Sergeant Bailey and personnel detailed for the Cadre. Eleven other ranks left for demobilization and they were accompanied by 2/Lieut, Sharpe who was granted 14days leave in England for his trouble.

The 14th would see the men given the opportunity to bathe. 2/Lieut. Ayres proceeded on leave on 13th followed by Lieut. Turner on 16th.

On the 18th 2/Lieut. Unwin (P M C) proceeded on leave and his duties were undertaken by 2/Lieut. Percival.

Alterations were made to the list of men for the Cadre as men put in requests giving compassionate reasons for not staying on longer than they had to.

An Ambulance car was allotted to the battalion in order to convey the officers to the Hulluch sector. The officers had the opportunity to revisit the area that had been the battalion's home for so many months prior to the last 100 days. The 20th saw more officers and men leave with Lieut. Benner, 2/Lieut. Fletcher and thirteen other ranks left for demobilization.

The 21st saw all the men who would be retained on the Battalion Cadre parade at 1300. An Officer from the 63rd (Naval) Division also gave a lecture on Demobilization although this would seem to have been rather late in coming.

The 24th saw the battalion inspected by the Medical officer prior to his own demobilization a couple of day later. Seven other ranks also left for demobilization followed on 26th by nine more men. Captain R.W. Bowyer was admitted to hospital although no reason was given.

The men were allocated baths again on 27th. The day also saw the Chaplain Reverend Lowndes and the Medical Officer Lt. H. Alexander M.C. leave the battalion as they and eight other ranks left for demobilization.

Another 9th Bn. Man succumbed to his wounds at home and died on 27th March. 13281, Private William E. Beard is buried in Matlock (St. Giles) Churchyard. His brother 13277 Private Robert H. Beard also served with the battalion and survived the war.

The 28th saw the Battalion shrink to one Company as A/B and C/D/ amalgamated to become one and be known as "Z" Company. The Company would be commanded by Lt. J. Hetherington with 2/Lt. C.A.B. Thurburn as Second in Command. C.Q.M.S. Matthews took over the duties of C.S.M. and C.Q.M.S. Skoyles those of C.Q.M.S. 2/Lieut. Beddoe left the battalion and was attached to the 296th Prisoner of War Company. The 33rd Bde played 34th Bde at Hockey and the result was a 2 all draw.By the last day of March 1919 the Battalion strength was 27 officers and 271 Other Ranks.

The 1st April saw "Z" Company on a route march as part of their training.Captain B.J. Cooper, Lieut. C.C. Bolton, 2/Lieut. A.S. Osborne M.C. and 30 Other Ranks left the Battalion and were posted to No.14 P.O.W. Company at Valenciennes.

The 3rd saw the battalion depleted even more as Captain R. Munday, M.C., and Lieut. B. White, 2/Lieut. J. Percival and 80 Other Ranks left the battalion and were posted to No. 201 P.O.W. Company at Etaples.

The following day Captain R.W. Bowyer returned from hospital and took command of "Z" Company.

Captain E. Bourdas and three other ranks left for demobilization on 5th followed by on the 9th saw Captains A.E. Brennan, S. Maishment and four other ranks.

The Battalion played football versus the 11th Division Signal Company winning 5-1. Two days later the battalion beat the 34th Field Ambulance Brigade 1-0.

The 14th would see Major C.L. Harding M.C. and 2/lieut. T.B. Unwin proceed on leave prior to joining the Regular Army. The 16th saw Lieut. J Hetherington and eleven other ranks leave the battalion for demobilization. The next demobilization was that of the R.S.M. – 10927 R.S.M. A.E.M. Lawrence D.C.M. left his battalion on 21st April. The same day saw Lieut. B.P.S. Turner and twenty Other Ranks leave the battalion and they were posted to No. 277 P.O.W. Company at Mons.

Five more men left the Battalion on 28th April for demobilization and by 1st May some 569 Other Ranks and 34 Officers had been posted or demobilized and there was very little left. The Battalion was finished in all but name and the diary would contain mostly numbers of men demobilized.

On 5th May two more men were demobilized and Lieut. & Q.M. W.W. Horsman proceeded on leave to England. The 12th saw seven men leave the Battalion and the following day Lieut. C.J.W. Bullen-Smith proceeding to Raismes (R.T.O) to relieve Lieut. H. Walker who then proceeded on leave to England.

The 14th would see 2/Lieuts. S.J. Ayres, H.F. Sharp and eight Other Ranks proceed by lorry on a day trip to Lille. The 15th – one man left.

The 18th saw two men leave whilst Lieut. F.A. Allen took over the duties of Town Commandant for Denian.

On 21st Lieut. R.F. Norland who had been attached to the 11th Divisional Canteen was demobilized. Captain W. Nason M.C, and Lieut. C.A.B. Thurburn was repatriated to England although the reason for their illness was not given. 2/Lieut. H.F. Sharp proceeded to Raismes to relieve Lieut. C.J.W. Bullen-Smith who proceeded on leave to England. 2/Lieut. Sharp would be back with the battalion on 26th May.

On the 1st June Lt.Col A.E. Scothern, C.M.G., D.S.O. proceeded on 14 days leave in England. The 7th saw Captain A.E. Scott M.C. struck off the Battalions strength as he was employed as A.M.L.O. at Calais. Lieuts. C.J.W. Bullen-Smith; F.A. Allen; H. Walker; S.J. Ayres and 2/Lieuts P.W. Jestico and A.F. Sharp were posted to P.O.W. Companies and S.O.S. accordingly.

The 9th saw 12 Other Ranks proceed on a day trip to Lens by lorry and possibly get the opportunity to visit their friends buried in the area.

The 11th June saw two Other Ranks who were under suspension of sentence for crimes not mentioned leave the Battalion to join the 52nd Battalion, Sherwood Foresters, Army of the Rhine.

On 20th June the cadres of the Battalion left for dispersal; Two Officers (Lt.Col A.E. Scothern C.M.G., D.S.O. and Lieut F.T. Tourt) and twenty-three Other Ranks proceeded to England. Actually Colonel Scothern was already in England and would rejoin the Cadre there.

Finally on 30th June 1919 – two officers and twelve other ranks acting as the equipment guard left Denain and proceeded to Dunkirk with the stores.The Battalion Cadre would travel with the stores to Catterick and then the 9th Battalion The Sherwood Foresters (Notts & Derby) Regiment would cease to exist. It would pass into history as a battalion of volunteers who answered the call and fought on Gallipoli, in Egypt, France and Belgium. A farewell Dinner was held for W.O.s and N.C.O.s at the Welbeck Hotel on 11th December 1919. The following week on 19th December the Officers held a farewell dinner at the Constitutional Club Nottingham.

It is right to finish this history with the following:

"The Special Order by Lieutenant-General Sir A.J. Godley, K.C.B., K.C.M.G., Commanding XXII Corps

I desire on the conclusion of the Armistice with the enemy today, to thank all ranks of the Corps for the gallantry and devotion to duty, which they have displayed, and to express my admiration of their conduct.

The manner in which troops, after the great exertions of previous years and the desperate defensive battles of this Spring, responded to the call for a renewed offensive has no equal in history.

I am fully sensible of the strain imposed on Units often depleted in numbers, by the maintenance of the constant pressure, which has now finally worn out the enemy's power of resistance.

It was not superiority in numbers, but superiority in dogged determination and courage which, in spite of the physical obstacle of successive river lines, and in spite of the difficulties created by the enemy, and the hardships imposed by bad weather, broke down the enemy's defence.

Commanders and Staffs, R.A.F., Mounted Troops, Artillery, Engineers, Infantry, Machine Gunners, Labour Units, Transport, R.A.M.C., Ordnance Services and veterinary Services have worked loyally together towards the same end, and I congratulate them on their share in the Victory of which they may all justly be proud.

Alex. J. Godley
Headquarters 11th November 1918."

APPENDIX I

Officer's known to have served with 9th Battalion

Taken from the War Diaries, Officers Died in the Great War, CWGC, The Sherwood Foresters Museum.

Surname	Initials	Rank
Abbott	E.H.F.	2/Lieut
Ackroyd		2/Lieut
Adamson	J	"2/Lieut, MC"
Aitken	A A	Capt
Alcock	R	2/Lieut
Alexander	H	Lt/ MORC
Allen	F A	2/Lieut
Allpass	E T	2/Lieut
Andrews	J S T	Lt
Archer		2/Lieut
Askew	J	Lt
Ayres	S J	2/Lieut
Bailey	E	2/Lieut
Balguy	J St J	2/Lieut
Barber	A	"Lt, MC"
Barnes	W.E.	Lt
Barter	C E	2/Lieut
Barter	C E S	2/Lieut
Basden	E D	"Temp Lt, MC"
Bates	F O	2/Lieut
Beddoe	A H	2/Lieut
Benner	W R	Lt
Bennet		Lt
Binney	E H	Capt
Birthill	F.F.	2/Lieut
Black	T P	Capt
Blackburne	J.G.	Lt acting Major
Bolton	C	2/Lieut
Booker		Lt & QM
Booth	J C	Lt
Boothby		2/Lieut
Boothley	J.C.	2/Lieut
Bosanquet	L A	Lt-Col
Bottom	C.	2/Lieut
Bourdas	E	Capt
Bowyer	R W	Lt
Brennan	A.E.	Capt.
Briggs		2/Lieut
Brook	D G	"Temp Lt, MC"
Brown	F C	2/Lieut
Bull		2/Lieut
Bullen-Smith	C J W	Lt
Burton		2/Lieut
Buxton	W	Capt
Campion	P W S	2/Lieut
Carey	H P	Capt
Carr		Lt/ RAMC
Cartledge	G	Lt
Cave	U E	Lt
Chambers	G H	"Lt Temp Capt, MC"
Chapman	G S	2/Lieut
Charlton	R A	Capt
Clayton	A	2/Lieut

Surname	Initials	Rank
Coan	S J	Capt
Cook	C R	2/Lieut
Cookes	R V	Lt
Cooper	B J	2/Lieut
Cooper	G G	Capt
Cox	H	2/Lieut
Crawford	J	Capt
Crawford	J R	2/Lieut
Crellin	J F	2/Lieut
Critchlow	J	"Capt, MC"
Crowther	H M	2/Lieut
Crowther	W O	2/Lieut
Cudlip		2/Lieut
Cullin		2/Lieut
Darby	A	Lt/Asst QM
Davidson	C L	2/Lieut
Dean	A A	2/Lieut
Debathe	H M	Capt
Downman	B V R	2/Lieut
Egerton	B G	2/Lieut
Eley	H G	2/Lieut
Everard	C C	Lt
Ewin	"Hon, A"	Lt & QM
Farrand		2/Lieut
Fell	E	2/Lieut
Fielding	G R	Major
Fielding	S	Lt & QM
Fielding		Capt
Fletcher	J F	2/Lieut
Foster	L W	2/Lieut
Fowler	W.W.	2/Lieut
Francis	P A	2/Lieut
Francis	W	2/Lieut
Gallimore		2/Lieut
Gater	G.H.	"Major, DSO"
Goddard	C W	2/Lieut
Goldie	L.D	Capt
Gregory	R.H.	"Capt, MC"
Griffiths	W.G.A.	2/Lieut
Grimes	M J D	2/Lieut
Grimsdale	E.W.	"Capt, MC"
Gunson	E	2/Lieut
Gustard	R S	Lt
Harding	C.L	"Capt Acting Major,MC"
Harding	F J	2/Lieut
Hargreaves		2/Lieut
Harrison	J.C.	2/Lieut
Hartley	E C	Lt
Harwood		Lt
Haynes	P J	2/Lieut
Hetherington	J	2/Lieut
Hill	A.A.	2/Lieut
Hill	W F	Capt

Surname	Initials	Rank
Hind	J F M	Lt
Horsman	W W	"Lt & QM, MC"
Hudson	H E	2/Lieut
Ince	S M	2/Lieut
Ingram	T K	Lt
Jackson	M W	Lt
Jagger	G	2/Lt (MGC)
Jestico	P W	2/Lieut
Jones	A. W.	2/Lieut
Jones	O st M	Lt
Kilner	T R B	2/Lieut
King	G.E.	2/Lieut
Kingdon	G.H.	Lt
Lamb	C	2/Lieut
Lawrie		Capt.
Levene		2/Lieut
Lindow		Lt/ RAMC
Loup	L A	2/Lieut
Lowndes	J	Rev
Loyd	F.F.	Lt. & Adjutant
Maishment	S	2/Lieut
Marsh	E.H.	2/Lieut
Marshall	G G	Capt/ RAMC
Mason	L V	Lt/Adj
May		2/Lieut
Mayo	W C	Lt
McCormack	J F	Capt
Mills	H.L.B.	Capt
Morgan	G H	2/Lieut
Munday	R	"Capt, MC"
Murray	A.S.	Capt
Nason	W	"Capt & Adjutant, MC"
Nicolls	R J	Capt
Noakes	C E S	2/Lieut
Norland	R F	Lt
Odell	W.W.	"2/Lieut, MC"
Oldershaw	F W	2/Lieut
Orchard	H L	2/Lieut
Osborne	A S	"2/Lieut, MC"
Ottewell		2/Lieut
Paddock	H L	Major
Parker	F.S.	"2/Lieut, MC"
Parr	D F	2/Lieut
Parsons	R C	2/Lieut
Paull	F M	2/Lieut
Pearce	J H	Lt
Pell	J W	2/Lieut
Pemberton	J A	Major
Percival	J	2/Lieut
Phelps		2/Lieut
Pickard	A.H.	2/Lieut
Piper	S H	Major
Pomfret	W L S	2/Lieut
Prosser	A V	Lt and Acting QM
Radford	FO	2/Lieut
Randall	C D	Capt
Rees		2/Lieut
Richardson		2/Lieut
Rickett	E L	2/Lieut
Rigden	A W	"2/Lieut, MC"

Surname	Initials	Rank
Riley	H	2/Lieut
Roberts	T K	Lt
Robinson	H H	2/Lieut
Robinson	W.M.	Capt
Rogers	J A	Lt
Rogers	VGW	2/Lieut
Rowland	A	2/Lieut
Royle	G.A.	Lt
Russell	H L	2/Lieut
Russell	J B	2/Lieut
Sadler	R.A.S.	Major/Temp Lt Col
Sands	C H	Lt
Schur	P	2/Lieut
Schweder	A A	Capt
Scothern	A.E	"Lt-Col, DSO"
Scott	C.E.	"Temp Capt, MC"
Sharp	H F	2/Lieut
Sharwood		Lt
Smeeton	H.B.	Capt
Smith	H V	2/Lieut
Smith	H W	Lt
Smith	N.G.	Capt
Smith		2/Lieut
Squires	R D	Capt
Squires		Lt
Stevens	E.T	Capt
Stevenson	A	Capt
Stolworthy	H	2/Lieut
Stubbs	F W A	2/Lieut
Suffolk	F F	Lt acting Capt
Sutton	H J	2/Lieut
Sutton	R B	2/Lieut
Tarlton	C.W.	2/Lieut
Thornton	W R	Lt-Col
Thurburn	C A B	2/Lieut
Tourt	F.T.	2/Lieut
Treadgold	C E S	2/Lieut
Trenaman		2/Lieut
Trohear	T	2/Lieut
Turner	B.S.F.	2/Lieut
Turner	J	2/Lieut
Unwin	T.B.	2/Lieut
Urquhart	W T R	2/Lieut
Vann	B W	"Act Lt-Col VC,MC& bar"
Waddington	C G	Capt/ RAMC
Walker	E	QM
Walker	H	2/Lieut
Waller		Lt
Warneford	H C V	"2/Lt . Acting Captain, MC"
West	W	2/Lieut
White	B	2/Lieut
White	D B	2/Lieut
Wightman	W	2/Lieut
Wilkinson	W	2/Lieut
Williams	J S	Lt
Williams	T C O	2/Lieut
Wills	A G	Lt
Wilmot	C R T	Lt
Young	H F	2/Lieut

APPENDIX II

Nominal Roll

Taken from Medal Rolls for Victory and British War Medals held at The National Archives.
WO 329/1383-1407

Some men have also come to light through other sources such as CWGC and other Regimental Medal Rolls. Those known to have served with the 9th Battalion have been added.

Even so this list is unlikely to be every man who served in the Battalion but possibly the most comprehensive made. Men who transferred to other Regiments and Corps such as the Machine Gun Corps are normally listed on the Medal Rolls for that unit.

Number	Rank	Surname	Given name
1449	WO2	Brazil	William
2606	L/Cpl	Hinkley	Henry
2867	Pte	Brown	William C
3766	Pte	Jepson	Cecil
3834	Cpl	Whitworth	George
3861	Pte	Orchard	Hugh T
3867	C/Sgt	Shaw	Francis
3919	Pte	Daft	George
3928	Sgt	Hancock	Daniel
3948	Sgt	Hall	William Henry
3949	Sgt	Cant	George Richard
3952	Cpl	Bancroft	Frederick
3992	Sgt	Gurner	Thomas
3999	Pte	Hewitt	George
4242	Pte	Brown	Arthur William
4261	Cpl	Shelton	John Robert
4268	Pte	Green	Harold
4357	Sgt	White	George Gordon
4572	Pte	Hewitt	William
4574	Pte	Fox	Arthur
4613	Pte	Steer	Harry
4689	Pte	Farnsworth	Christopher.
4727	Pte	Mann	Ernest
4815	Pte	Brookes	Leslie
4839	Pte	Goulding	Bernard
4859	Pte	Taylor	George
4890	Pte	Parsons	Charles
5032	Pte	Francis	George
5058	L/Sgt	Hooton	John
5061	Pte	Sheldon	William
5066	Pte	Turton	Arthur
5118	L/Cpl	Hunt	George
5888	CSM	Frood	E J
6004	L/Cpl	Selby	Herbert
6005	Pte	Allsopp	William
6034	Pte	Fretwell	Harold Douglas
6045	L/Cpl	Tomlinson	William
6068	Sgt	Scott	Roland
6074	Pte	Hardwidge	Albert Henry
6078	Pte	Barfield	Daniel
6102	WOC2	Annison	Richard William
6112	Pte	Holloway	Moses
6115	L/Sgt	Gilham	John
6142	L/Cpl	Holbrook	Thomas.
6161	Pte	Blackwell	Frederick
6265	Sgt	Eldridge	Walter Joseph
6318	WOC2	Daley	Frederick
6358	Pte	Ball	Thomas
6370	Sgt	Ward	Walter.
6378	Pte	Platts	Charles
6464	Cpl	Bradbury	Edward
6592	Pte	Hinchcliffe	Thomas
6621	Pte	Smith	Robert
6627	Pte	Smith	George Henry
6885	Pte	Mortimer	Edward
6885	Pte	Alvey	Tom
6991	L/Cpl	Hillyard	James Albert
7107	WOC2	Corneilius	Wilfred
7112	Sgt	Burnett	Harry
7334	Cpl	Coffey	Joseph
7351	Pte	Fox	Herbert
7750	Pte	Parkin	Arthur
7807	Pte	Daubney	Albert
8349	CSM	Howarth	William David
8550	WOC2	Thompson	Thomas
8664	Pte	Dobbs	Handley
8988	Sgt	Piper	Reuben James
9031	WOC2	Pickford	David.
9094	WOC2	Gabbitas	Lorraine
9094	WOC2	Wheldon	Walter Edwin
9425	Pte	Twells	George
9512	Sgt	Adams	William Henry
10048	Pte	Hall	Albert
10110	WOC2	Wilson	John
10169	Pte	Topham	William
10267	Sgt	Waldron	Frederick
10295	Pte	Pyatt	John James
10313	Pte	Hinds	John Priestley
10400	Pte	Dolphin	William
10435	Pte	Longley	Ernest

Number	Rank	Surname	Given name
10488	Pte	Gee	Robert Owen
10515	Pte	Tucker	Ernest
10530	Pte	Marvill	Arthur
10536	Pte	Bond	Ernest
10578	Cpl	Hind	Frank
10610	Pte	Ward	Frederick John
10702	Sgt	Cokayne	William
10716	Cpl	Hales	Robert
10766	Cpl	Barratt	Frederick
10792	Pte	Poole	George
10805	Sgt	Adams	Henry Thomas
10851	Pte	Mason	Percy
10951	Pte	Daft	Arthur Frederick
11010	L/Cpl	Flint	Henry Ellis
11051	Cpl	Horne	Horace
11052	Sgt	Fielding	Henry Lawrence Randolph
11054	Pte	Scott	John Henry
11079	L/Cpl	Parker	Albert
11144	Pte	Staples	Robert James
11162	L/Cpl	Wright	Harry
11168	Sgt	Kirby	William
11203	Sgt	Wilkinson	John Harvey
11213	Pte	Fox	Tom
11256	Cpl	Bowler	William
11270	Pte	Painter	Horace
11286	Sgt	Greenburg	Joe
11306	Pte	Bowler	Horace James
11341	Pte	Stoakes	Fred
11497	Pte	Forrest	George
11506	Sgt	Wallace	Edward
11520	L/Cpl	Andrews	Arthur.
11539	Pte	McLean	Thomas John
11570	Pte	Mosedale	Thomas.
11600	Pte	Sheppard	Harold
11603	Pte	Pemberton	Horace
11663	Pte	Goodwin	George Henry
11675	Pte	Trelfa	Charles
11695	L/Cpl	Shakespeare	Edward Bernard
11697	Pte	Kelsall	Frederick
11699	Pte	Heath	Reginald
11700	L/Cpl	Clarke	Herbert
11707	L/Cpl	Smith	Edward.
11709	Sgt	Hinkley	Alfred Thomas
11714	Pte	Hackett	Thomas
11717	Sgt	Johnson	Alfred
11749	L/Cpl	Kennedy	Ernest Vincent
11761	L/Cpl	Rimmington	Walter George
11782	Pte	Treadwell	Charles William
11783	Pte	Barker	Thomas
11787	Pte	Flower	Thomas
11814	Sgt	Bull	Amos
11817	Pte	Machin	Harold
11844	Pte	Hall	Samuel
11851	Pte	Davidson	Frederick
11935	Pte	Brewin	William
12070	Pte	Baker	Herbert Arthur
12134	Sgt	Coleman	William
12141	Pte	Harvey	William Henry
12146	Pte	Woolley	Arthur
12147	Cpl	Littlewood	Austin
12175	Cpl	Revill	Alfred
12176	L/Cpl	Pearce	Albert William
12180	Pte	Mills	Wilfred Ernest
12185	Pte	Jenkinson	George
12251	Pte	Chapman	Arthur John William
12264	Pte	Turner	Walter
12275	Pte	Bradbury	Benjamin
12280	Cpl	Jones	Ernest
12293	L/Cpl	Upton	George Cyril
12297	Pte	Mead	George Henry
12321	Pte	Bourne	William
12341	Cpl	Hewison	Donald
12344	L/Cpl	Thornley	William
12346	Pte	Porter	Harold
12347	L/Cpl	Camm	Harry
12355	L/Cpl	Wells	Frederic Charles
12357	Pte	Castle	James
12362	Pte	Ellis	Bertram Jennings
12364	Cpl	Badger	Edward
12367	WOC2	Terry	Henry
12368	Pte	Merriman	Joseph
12369	Pte	Buxton	Ernest
12372	Pte	Buckley	William
12381	Pte	Cottingham	Thomas Walter
12383	Pte	King	Clarence Ernest
12384	L/Sgt	Dover	Percy
12393	Cpl	Voce	Thomas
12397	Pte	Worthington	William Henry
12400	Pte	Leavesley	Horace
12401	Pte	Welbourn	Samuel
12404	Pte	Riley	Percy
12407	Pte	Millington	Harold
12408	Pte	Harris	Leonard
12411	Pte	Barlow	Arthur Haslam
12412	L/Cpl	Jackson	Charles
12413	L/Sgt	Clayton	Frank
12416	Pte	Brigg	Ernest
12418	Pte	Hood	Reginald Smith
12419	Pte	Blake	Joseph
12421	Sgt	Hudson	William James
12426	Pte	Croft	Frederick
12431	Pte	Oakton	John
12434	Pte	Hutchinson	Tom
12436	Pte	Sweeney	William
12437	Pte	Green	Ernest
12438	Pte	Coles	Rupert

Number	Rank	Surname	Given name
12441	Pte	Shepherd	George
12444	Pte	Richardson	John Erskine
12445	Pte	Pell	Sidney Ambrose
12446	Pte	Pegg	Francis George
12448	Pte	Salt	Stanley
12452	Pte	Cottrell	Albert
12454	L/Sgt	Cotterell	Harry
12458	Pte	Whittaker	Walter
12460	L/Sgt	Methaven	Robert
12468	Pte	Richards.	Arthur
12472	Pte	Blakeway	Benjamin
12479	Pte	Carlin	George Frederick
12480	Sgt	Evans	Alfred
12483	Pte	Ludlam	George
12484	Pte	Ford	Laurence
12485	Pte	Shaw	Arthur
12488	Pte	Lomax	Louis
12489	L/Cpl	Holland	Frederick William
12490	Pte	Mumford	John Ernest
12492	Pte	Law	Arthur
12493	Pte	Heap	Francis William
12494	Pte	Arthurs	Henry
12495	L/Cpl	Gibbs	James
12496	Pte	Rickwood	Frederick George
12500	Pte	Wadsworth	Alfred James
12502	Pte	Ford	George Henry
12503	Pte	Thomas	Harry
12506	Pte	Pepperdine	Frank
12508	Pte	Smith	Norman Albert
12509	Pte	Turner	John William
12511	Pte	James	Frederick
12514	Pte	Inman	Henry
12515	Pte	Grice	Levi
12519	Pte	Johnson	Arthur
12521	Pte	Screeton	John
12523	Pte	Ives	James
12525	Pte	Blythe	George
12528	Pte	Jewsbury	John William Chell
12532	Pte	Burgess	Frederick
12535	L/Cpl	Chadburn	Charles Henry
12541	Pte	Ridgard	Alfred
12545	Pte	Card	Arthur Stanley
12547	Pte	Martin	Laurence
12549	Pte	Birley	John Richard
12552	Pte	Croysdill	Norman.
12554	Pte	Lowe	Frederick
12557	Pte	Brocklehurst	John
12559	Pte	Frith	John Peter
12560	Pte	Calvert	Maurice
12562	Pte	Long	John
12568	Cpl	Milner	Thomas
12569	WOC2	Grant	John
12570	Pte	Willes	Arthur

Number	Rank	Surname	Given name
12571	Pte	Chanter	Henry
12572	Pte	Rowland	John Henry
12573	Pte	Williams	Arthur
12573	Pte	Hayes	Sam
12575	L/Cpl	Fenwick	Harold
12577	Pte	Birt	Ernest
12579	Pte	Hall	Arthur
12581	Cpl	Goldsmith	Robert
12583	Pte	Mayfield	Sydney Charlesworth
12584	Pte	Taylor	Thomas
12586	Pte	Talbot	Arthur
12587	Pte	Bannister	Jim
12589	Pte	Everett	John
12590	Pte	Maskery	Francis
12592	Pte	Bardil	Albert
12595	Pte	Moody	William
12600	Sgt	Palmer	John Henry
12601	Pte	Whiten	Fred
12602	Pte	Liley	James
12603	Pte	Michie	James Halley
12604	Pte	Hunt	Ben
12606	Sgt	Hill	John Arthur
12607	Pte	Hancock	Cyril
12609	L/Cpl	Hind	Arthur
12614	Pte	Mayfield	Horace
12615	Pte	Luntley	Geoffrey
12616	Pte	Stenson	Joseph
12617	Pte	Colton	Harold
12620	Pte	Dobson	Frank
12622	Pte	Nixon	Alfred
12627	Sgt	Blurton	William
12628	Pte	Sladen	Charles
12630	Pte	Winfield	William
12640	Pte	Brown	John William
12641	Pte	Skeels	William
12644	Pte	Ainsworth	James
12645	Pte	Birch	Joseph
12647	L/Cpl	Caldwell	Walter
12648	Pte	Straw	Ernest
12650	Pte	Tatham	Oliver
12653	Pte	Christopher	Walter
12655	Pte	Spencer	George William
12656	Pte	Watkin	Herbert James
12658	Pte	Walker	Charles
12664	Pte	Longden	Frank
12665	Pte	Clewley	Tom
12666	Pte	Bennett	George William
12667	L/Sgt	Sheridan	John William
12669	Cpl	Boultbee	Joseph
12671	Pte	Hipwell	John William
12672	Pte	Featherstone	Sam
12674	Pte	Streeter	Albert William
12676	L/Cpl	Abbott	William

Number	Rank	Surname	Given name
12678	Pte	Lowe	Charles
12682	Pte	Callaghan	Charles
12685	Sgt	Denman	John Widdowson
12686	Pte	Burton	Reginald
12689	Pte	Green	Thomas
12690	Pte	Starbuck	Dan
12694	Pte	Mason	John William
12695	Pte	Woodhouse	Samuel
12701	Pte	Smith	William
12703	Pte	Lawley	Leonard
12704	Pte	Ball	George
12705	Pte	Barber	Albert
12706	Pte	Ford	Austin Thomas
12707	Pte	Brassington	George
12710	Pte	Diskin	Michael
12711	Pte	Hall	George
12712	Pte	Garrod	Ernest
12713	Pte	Green	Arthur
12714	Pte	Hancock	John
12715	Cpl	Boothroyd	Edwin
12718	Cpl	White	George
12721	Pte	Foley	Ernest Henry
12724	L/Sgt	Sheppard	Robert
12729	Pte	Watterson	Thomas
12732	L/Sgt	Bowler	W
12734	Pte	Smith	Jack
12735	Pte	Fox	John Henry
12736	Pte	Rawlins	Edward
12739	Pte	Bond	John
12740	Pte	Swords	John
12744	L/Cpl	Reeds	Joseph Arthur
12745	L/Sgt	Gregory	John
12746	Pte	Gill	Frederick William
12759	Pte	Hollyoak	Sam
12761	Pte	Ecclestone	Reginald
12762	Pte	James	Joseph
12763	Pte	Fisher	Bernard Goodby
12766	Pte	Wright	Percy
12768	Pte	Boilstone	Horace
12770	Pte	Ede	Fred
12779	Pte	Britland	Robert Charles
12780	Cpl	Brown	Herbert David
12781	Pte	Lloyd	George Edward
12781	Pte	Parker	Bertrand Francis
12790	Pte	Coster	Edward
12792	Cpl	Reilly	Charles
12793	L/Cpl	Barber	Joseph
12794	L/Cpl	Iliffe	Arthur
12796	Pte	Brindley	William
12797	Pte	Mills	Samuel
12799	Pte	Evans	William Lewis
12800	Pte	Hall	Wallace
12806	Cpl	Clarke	Edwin Wallace

Number	Rank	Surname	Given name
12810	Pte	Musson	Richard George
12811	Pte	Millott	Clifford
12812	Pte	Lintin	Thomas
12814	Pte	Story	John William
12816	Pte	Watts	Stanley
12817	L/Cpl	Webster	Samuel
12820	L/Cpl	Watkinson	Luke
12821	Sgt	Hurt	Seth
12823	Cpl	Sanderson	Frank Kennedy
12824	Pte	Brocklehurst	Herbert
12825	L/Cpl	Wood	Frederick William
12831	L/Cpl	Howell	Edward
12832	Pte	Moore	James William Charity
12833	Pte	Lilliman	Joseph
12834	Pte	Smith	James
12835	Pte	Dickman	William
12836	L/Cpl	Neep	John
12837	Pte	Mitchell	William George
12841	Pte	Harwood	Albert John
12845	Pte	Barrowcliffe	Tom
12846	Pte	Worth	Lewis
12848	Pte	Wright	Samuel
12849	Pte	Booth	Harry
12850	Pte	Dunstan	Charles
12851	Pte	Booth	Walter
12855	Pte	Turner	Alfred
12857	Pte	Burton	Edward William
12858	Cpl	Lawrie	Reginald
12861	Pte	Seston	Ernest
12862	Pte	Scott	Frederick
12863	Pte	Wynn	Albert
12864	Pte	Marsden	Frederick
12866	Pte	Watkinson	Arthur
12870	Pte	Hunt	Walter
12871	Cpl	Pearce	Charles
12872	Pte	Shepherd	Edwin
12873	Pte	Wigmore	Elijah
12875	Sgt	Shaw	Frank
12878	Pte	Poole	Charles
12879	L/Cpl	Ambridge	George William
12880	Pte	Scott	Charles
12881	Pte	Chamberlain	Alec
12883	Pte	Cocking	Albert
12884	Pte	Farrell	Thomas
12890	Pte	Verdon	William Henry
12893	Pte	Knowles	William
12896	Pte	Carroll	Michael
12897	Pte	Smith	Leonard
12898	Pte	Martin	George
12902	L/Sgt	Barber	William
12903	Pte	Mallinder	Thomas
12904	Pte	Hemming	Stanley
12905	L/Cpl	Payne	Fred

Number	Rank	Surname	Given name
12906	L/Cpl	Coates	Albert William
12907	Pte	Wakefield	James Parkes
12908	Pte	Ryan	William
12917	Pte	Gent	Horace
12919	Pte	Mansell	George
12922	Pte	Mahoney	John
12924	Cpl	Lawrence	Thomas
12927	Pte	Carter	Leonard
12932	Pte	Hampson	David
12934	Pte	Farmilo	John George Gee
12935	Pte	Worrall	Joseph Ernest
12937	Pte	Booth	Charles
12938	Pte	Hewitt	Fred
12940	Pte	Slack	Lancelot Gilbert
12942	Pte	Hudson	Charles
12943	Sgt	Dicks	Frank
12944	L/Sgt	Britland	Harry
12946	L/Cpl	Arnold	Arthur John
12947	Pte	Pidcock	Joseph
12949	Pte	Smith	James William
12950	Pte	Negus	Fred
12951	Pte	Chandler	William
12954	Pte	Hill	Tom Cash
12955	Pte	Walters	Harold
12957	Pte	Croot	Charles Thomas
12958	Pte	Edmonds	Fred
12961	Pte	Hudson	Sam P
12962	Pte	Hill	Thomas
12966	Pte	Womach	George Lewis
12968	Pte	Kennett	Frederick William
12974	Pte	Douglas	George Jesse
12976	Pte	Smith	Sidney
12978	Pte	March	Alfred Sam
12979	Pte	Goodwin	William Alfred
12981	Pte	Kirk	William
12986	Pte	Chatterton	Arthur Francis
12987	Pte	Blackwell	Robert Walker
12988	Pte	Howitt	Alfred
12989	Pte	Moakes	Douglas
12990	Pte	Carver	William George
12994	Cpl	Stubbs	Edward
12995	Pte	Bedwell	Albert James
12996	L/Cpl	Posson	Ernest Edward
12997	Pte	Grant	William
12998	WOC2	Hill	Albert
13000	Pte	Moran	Richard
13001	Pte	Poultney	James
13005	L/Cpl	Osborne	Charles Thomas
13006	Pte	Fletcher	Francis William
13010	Pte	Massey	John
13015	Sgt	Huckerby	Henry
13016	Sgt	Carlile	Fred
13017	Pte	Barnes	Harold
13019	L/Sgt	Dawson	John James
13021	Pte	Button	Noel
13023	C/Sgt	Wallace	William
13024	Pte	Chadbourne	George
13027	Pte	Moorcroft	Edgar
13028	Sgt	Kimberley	John Wilfred
13032	Pte	Lambert	Frederick William
13033	Sgt	Bigg	Albert
13035	Pte	Howard	Frank Edward
13036	Pte	Taylor	George
13041	Cpl	Wilson	Albert
13042	Pte	Chapman	Albert
13049	Pte	Bowen	Eli
13053	Pte	Kent	Robert
13054	Pte	Casborn	Edward
13055	Pte	Croft	Walter
13056	Pte	Grant	Charles Henry
13057	Pte	Johnson	Joseph
13064	L/Cpl	Heath	Arthur Charles Edward
13067	L/Cpl	Redfin	John
13069	Pte	King	James
13071	Pte	Hallam	Walter Pemberton
13072	Pte	Hibbert	Ernest Henry
13073	L/Cpl	Ward	Albert Ernest
13079	L/Sgt	Richardson	Edward
13080	Pte	Stocks	Henry
13085	Pte	Brodie	William
13086	Pte	Mottershaw	William
13087	Pte	Hanson	George Ernest
13088	Pte	Unwin	Robert
13091	Cpl	Creed	Robert Alec
13092	L/Sgt	Osborne	William Henry
13094	Pte	Keel	William Herbert
13096	Pte	Johnson	William
13102	Sgt	Gadsby	John William
13103	Pte	Edge	William
13104	Pte	Atkins	Charles Jones Orphir
13105	L/Cpl	Searle	Sidney William
13106	L/Cpl	Forbes	John
13107	Pte	Murfin	George
13108	Pte	Vick	Frank
13109	Pte	Marples	George
13111	Pte	Baker	William
13116	Cpl	Roscoe	John
13119	Pte	Neilson	James
13121	Pte	Johnson	Joseph
13122	Pte	Youson	George
13124	Sgt	Throssel	William
13130	Pte	Slack	Daniel
13135	Cpl	Gallie	Atholl Alexander
13136	Pte	Simpson	Ernest Leonard
13139	Pte	Raisin	Francis Richard Rawlings
13143	Cpl	Stapleton	Edward

Number	Rank	Surname	Given name
13144	Pte	Bennett	Alfred
13145	Sgt	Parkin	Ernest
13147	Pte	Bonser	Harry
13148	L/Cpl	Overton	Enoch
13149	Pte	Winter	Charles Edward
13150	Pte	Wilcockson	Tom
13151	Pte	Wadley	John William
13155	Pte	Stocks	Joseph Henry
13157	Pte	Foulds	Fred
13158	Pte	Robinson	Amos
13159	Pte	Fretwell	Ernest
13160	Pte	Clarke	John Percy
13161	Pte	Perrin	Charles
13163	Pte	Reddington	Thomas Edward
13164	Pte	Gill	Thomas
13165	Pte	Wigman	George Henry
13168	Pte	Otter	James
13169	Pte	Eccleshall	Thomas
13173	Pte	Harris	William Edward
13175	Pte	Hood	Ernest
13176	Pte	Greaves	Frederick
13177	Pte	Beresford	Horace
13179	Pte	Clarke	Alfred
13185	Cpl	McKechine	John
13186	L/Cpl	Hudson	Charles Sowter
13188	Pte	Manners	Albert
13189	L/Cpl	Hobster	Matthew
13190	Pte	Perkins	Francis
13191	Pte	Hempshall	George
13199	Pte	Elliott	Hiram
13207	L/Cpl	Scott	Alfred Joseph
13215	Pte	Ulyatt	Frank
13219	Pte	Powell	Thomas
13225	Pte	Scott	William
13227	L/Cpl	Snowden	Leonard
13229	Pte	Spray	James
13234	Pte	Kettleband	William
13240	Pte	Jerram	Thomas Francis
13243	Pte	Noble	Henry
13246	Pte	Lynam	John
13249	Pte	Deary	Joseph
13250	Pte	Travis	Richard
13251	Pte	Fern	Thomas
13252	L/Cpl	Bagshaw	Herbert
13255	L/Cpl	Priestly	William
13256	Pte	Poultney	Arthur
13257	Pte	Derbyshire	George
13258	Pte	Allen	Arthur
13263	Pte	Lovell	Arthur
13265	Cpl	Statham	Percy Joseph
13267	L/Cpl	Toplis	Joseph
13268	Pte	Robinson	Frank
13270	Pte	Simmons	Joseph

Number	Rank	Surname	Given name
13271	L/Cpl	Leg	Arthur
13272	Pte	Mills	Job
13273	Pte	Travis	Joseph
13275	Pte	Bunting	Owen
13276	Pte	Checkley	Herbert
13277	Pte	Beard	Robert Henry
13278	Sgt	Clarke	Reginald Harry
13279	C/Sgt	Margerrison	James
13280	L/Cpl	Holmes	Isaac
13281	Pte	Beard	William Edward
13282	Pte	Devereux	Arthur
13283	Pte	Hemming	Frank
13286	Pte	Bonser	Elijah
13287	Pte	Schmidt	Rudolph
13292	Pte	Hughes	Leonard
13300	Pte	Beard	Fred
13303	Cpl	Kirk	George Thomas
13304	Pte	Corbett	William
13306	Pte	Wilkinson	John
13312	Cpl	Hill	Horace
13313	Pte	Kirk	Samuel
13314	Cpl	Pearson	John Henry
13322	Pte	Bowler	Joseph
13326	Pte	Crutchley	John
13328	Pte	Tarr	William
13330	Pte	Cooke	Charles
13340	Pte	Thompson	Cyril
13342	Pte	Riley	James
13344	Pte	Piper	Harold
13346	Pte	Stevens	George Edward
13347	Pte	Gibson	Edwin
13352	L/Cpl	Draper	John
13353	Pte	Dixon	Matthew
13356	Pte	Scott	Richard
13357	Pte	Allen	William Henry
13359	Pte	Stead	George
13361	L/Cpl	Slattery	Edward
13365	Pte	Norman	John
13367	L/Cpl	Wilkinson	William
13368	Pte	Fagan	Bernard
13375	Pte	Hopley	Thomas
13376	Pte	Birks	Thomas
13379	Pte	Gamble	Thomas
13382	Pte	Tunnicliff	George
13385	Pte	Parker	George
13388	Pte	Cook	Edgar
13394	Pte	Rouse	Tom Arthur
13396	L/Cpl	Patterson	William Arthur
13398	Pte	Jackson	Ernest
13401	Pte	Read	John
13403	Pte	Carter	George Edward
13406	Pte	Ainsworth	William
13407	Cpl	Stopps	Sidney

Number	Rank	Surname	Given name
13412	Pte	Beardall	James Henry
13419	Pte	Brown	Sidney
13438	Pte	Woodward	John
13450	Sgt	Dayman	Thomas
13460	Sgt	Rhodes	Fred
13462	Pte	Hughes	Arthur
13465	Pte	Brunton	Harold
13472	L/Cpl	Funnell	Ernest
13484	Pte	Dutton	William
13489	Pte	Widdowson	William
13512	Pte	Hopkinson	John
13519	Pte	Hollingworth	Bruce
13520	Pte	Ferguson	James
13524	Sgt	Ward	H W
13531	Pte	Smith	Albert
13534	Pte	Bartless	Fred
13542	Pte	Langston	Samuel
13547	Pte	Hinton	Arthur Cecil
13557	Pte	Goodband	Christophe
13558	L/Cpl	Holliday	Clarence Percy
13561	Pte	Smith	Henry
13562	Pte	Robertson	George
13567	Pte	James	John Walter
13592	Pte	White	Thomas
13599	Pte	Stacey	George
13600	Cpl	Clark	John Henry
13606	2nd A.M.	Anthony	Albert Edward
13610	Pte	Page	Reginald
13614	Pte	Panther	James Thomas
13615	Pte	Lynaugh	John
13620	Pte	Thrall	Frederick
13631	Cpl	Bell	Fred
13643	Pte	Mattock	William
13657	Pte	Whittemore	George William
13665	Pte	Fidler	Edwin
13667	Pte	Davis	Joseph
13669	Pte	Carrott	Fred
13699	Pte	Riley	John William
13704	Pte	Berry	Albert
13708	Pte	Trivett	Charles Rippon
13732	Pte	Lidgett	William
13735	Pte	Bramley	Thomas
13741	Pte	Lester	Richard
13742	Cpl	Shardlow	Ernest
13746	L/Cpl	Wilson	Frederick
13751	Cpl	Pickering	John
13754	Pte	Watson	Harry
13761	Pte	Jenkins	John
13764	Pte	Chesham	Harry
13774	L/Cpl	Parke	John Henry
13776	Pte	Burton	Andrew Thoms
13790	Pte	Butterworth	James
13811	Pte	Whitehouse	Raymond
13812	Pte	Whitehouse	Fred
13829	Pte	Gillott	Harold
13840	Pte	Greensmith	Thomas
13846	Pte	Knight	George
13853	L/Sgt	Timmins	John William
13857	Pte	Lindsell	Lawrence
13858	Pte	Hart	John
13863	Pte	Fletcher	Oscar
13870	WOC2	Lee	Samuel Clements
13875	Pte	Graney	John
13876	Pte	Crane	Claude Henry
13883	L/Cpl	Humphreys	William Dann
13890	Pte	Orme	John Arthur
13903	L/Cpl	Martin	James
13904	Pte	Spencer	Arthur
13905	L/Sgt	Tebbutt	Albert
13907	Sgt	Brackner	William
13911	Pte	Anthony	Edward
13922	Pte	Walsh	Harold
13933	Pte	Mee	Arthur
13934	Pte	Turton	Albert Edward
13944	Pte	North	Frederick
13960	Sgt	Bowler	Charles
13975	Pte	Wagstaff	Reginald
13983	Pte	Carter	George
13986	Pte	Evans	Matthew
13987	Pte	Derbyshire	Joseph
14004	Pte	Steeples	Henry
14015	Pte	Walker	Ernest
14020	Pte	Groves	William
14022	Pte	Green	Frank
14032	Pte	Goodwin	Frank
14034	Pte	Nightingale	James
14040	Sgt	Marriott	George
14045	Pte	Northedge	Wilfred
14050	L/Cpl	Legge	John Maurice
14054	Cpl	Grimshaw	Frank
14066	Pte	Lowe	Albert Owen
14067	Pte	Martin	Percy
14068	L/Cpl	Harper	Hubert
14070	Pte	Spick	John
14077	Pte	Johnson	Arthur
14087	L/Cpl	Guy	John
14092	Pte	Smith	Ernest
14096	L/Cpl	Griffiths	Herbert
14105	Pte	Moore	Thomas
14106	Pte	Fines	Edward
14125	Pte	Carrington	John Thomas
14128	Cpl	Clay	James
14144	Pte	Turner	Mark Bertie
14176	Pte	Bennett	George Henry
14232	Pte	Robinson	William
14235	Pte	Green	Henry

Number	Rank	Surname	Given name
14246	Pte	Wilcoxson	John William
14277	Pte	Gretton	Frank Edwin
14318	Pte	Jones	John Willie
14405	Pte	Redfern	Harold Ernest
14440	Pte	Presbury	Thomas Archibald
14456	Pte	Brown	Joseph
14495	Pte	Sherratt	Sydney
14560	Pte	Adlington	Joseph
14721	Pte	Harris	John Thomas
14741	Pte	Woods	Harry
14857	Pte	Scott	Arthur
14866	Pte	Finch	Henry George
14879	Pte	Doxey	George Herbert
15002	Pte	Marks	William
15006	Pte	Rowan	Joseph
15034	Pte	Colton	Arthur
15040	Pte	Peachey	Walter James
15056	Pte	Gilbank	John
15068	Pte	Bradley	Peter
15084	Pte	Rigey	Thomas
15131	Cpl	Davison	Frank
15137	Pte	Cowling	Thomas Henry
15198	L/Cpl	Green	Alfred Louis
15205	Pte	Matthews	John William
15214	Pte	Robinson	Thomas Henry
15231	Pte	Jepson	George
15252	Pte	Caine	Michael
15256	Cpl	Barton	Albert
15266	Pte	Mills	John Henry
15278	Pte	Fraser	John
15291	Pte	Lee	Henry
15298	Pte	Goodall	Harry
15335	L/Cpl	Pearson	Peter
15338	L/Cpl	Osborn	Robert
15339	Sgt	Proffitt	Charles
15372	Pte	Pettit	Ernest
15402	Pte	Bradwell	Percy
15423	Pte	Phillips	Robert
15437	Pte	Holt	George
15446	Sgt	Bramley	George Walter
15453	L/Cpl	Saywell	Leonard
15493	Pte	Barber	Edward
15513	Pte	Britton	Walter Henry
15533	L/Sgt	Thompson	William
15544	Pte	Parker	Thomas
15549	Pte	Bingley	John
15558	Cpl	Turner	George Thomas
15561	Pte	McGlade	Herbert Thomas
15589	Pte	Reed	Frank
15663	Pte	Wass	Ernest
15685	Pte	Shaw	Joseph
15687	Pte	Fenton	Charles
15722	Pte	Rowan	George
15728	Pte	Cook	Charles
15741	Cpl	Whittaker	Harry
15755	Sgt	Cawthorne	John
15760	Pte	Calladine	Bickley
15762	Cpl	Nobes	Wellington
15768	Pte	Trickett	James
15772	Pte	Longdon	Herbert
15849	Pte	Eastwood	John Will
15928	Pte	Cutts	Harry
16000	Pte	Childs	Harry
16097	Cpl	Walsh	Edwin
16141	Pte	Hollingsworth	Frederick
16149	Pte	Bexon	Alfred
16171	Pte	Bexon	James Lionel
16181	L/Cpl	Owen	Edgar
16193	Pte	Whyman	George Taylor
16301	Sgt	Uttley	Herbert
16481	Pte	Marriott	Charles Albert
16542	Pte	Mayfield	Percy
16765	Pte	Barker	Hugh
16793	Sgt	Bonsar	Raymond James
16802	Cpl	Hayes	John James
16826	Pte	Ellis	William
16875	Pte	Price	Edwin
16895	Pte	Garton	Samuel
16930	Pte	Robson	Walter
16935	Pte	Witherbed	Wilfred
16952	L/Cpl	Fryer	Harry
16971	Pte	Simpson	Henry
16973	Pte	Roberts	Arthur
16983	Pte	Kirkman	John Robert
16994	L/Cpl	Glynn	Arthur
16996	Pte	Hemsley	Francis
17004	Cpl	Street	Samuel
17010	Pte	Payne	Alexander
17012	Pte	Griffiths	Stanley
17022	Pte	Williamson	John
17023	L/Cpl	Yates	Robert
17111	L/Cpl	Whitehead	Reginald Thomas
17200	Pte	Roberts	Albert
17213	Pte	Franklin	George
17247	Pte	Guy	John Henry
17323	L/Cpl	Attenborough	John
17430	Pte	Pearson	Horace
17432	Pte	Mulvey	Thomas
17437	Pte	Lee	Percy
17451	Pte	Hill	Albert Edward
17471	Sgt	Burton	Will
17496	Sgt	Ballantyne	John
17564	Pte	Davey	Jonathan Smithurst
17588	Sgt	Carter	Victor Cyril
17592	Pte	Gladish	Bernard
17596	Sgt	Winfield	Arthur

Number	Rank	Surname	Given name
17602	Cpl	Nicholls	Walter
17661	L/Cpl	Barratt	William
17674	Pte	Munks	John Henry
17690	Sgt	Mallatratt	George
17709	Pte	Peel	Robert
17758	Pte	Green	Arthur Henry
17799	Pte	Cook	William Henry
17810	Cpl	Cartlidge	Samuel
17815	Pte	Harvey	Ernest
17816	Pte	Rowley	Leonard
17817	Pte	Cameron	Hugh
17818	Cpl	Flint	Leslie
17824	Pte	Hudson	George Henry
17825	Pte	Hockin	Mark
17827	Pte	Wagstaff	Frederick
17828	Pte	Dale	Fergus O'Connor
17914	Pte	Haywood	Ernest
17917	Pte	Allsop	John George
17921	Pte	Yates	Walter
17924	Pte	Dallison	John
17928	Pte	Cooper	Richard
17933	Pte	Bostock	Matthew James
17935	Pte	Lenton	John William
17936	Pte	Morton	Edmund
17937	Pte	North	James Witham
17941	Pte	Jackson	Harold Ernest James
17942	Pte	Brown	John
17943	Pte	Hutchins	William Henry
17948	Pte	Dawn	John
17952	Pte	Ottewell	Ernest
17955	Pte	Bond	Alfred Ernest
17994	L/Cpl	Mason	George
17995	Pte	Dring	John Henry
18000	Pte	Towey	James
18007	Pte	McClure	John
18009	Sgt	Keeling	John
18010	Pte	Wright	Arthur Frederick
18013	Pte	Stevenson	Leonard
18014	Pte	Smith	Charles Henry
18015	Pte	Rushe	John
18016	Pte	Hill	John George
18017	Pte	Preston	William
18029	Pte	Brooks	Benjamin
18030	Pte	Watson	George Ernest
18031	Pte	Spink	Alfred Henry
18034	Pte	Rhodes	Harold
18036	Pte	Hales	Norman
18039	Pte	Clarke	Harold Hennings
18040	Pte	McCracken	Ernest Hollingsworth
18044	Pte	Walker	Alfred
18045	Pte	Crossland	William
18046	Pte	Hopwood	Robert
18050	Pte	Tilley	Thomas

Number	Rank	Surname	Given name
18053	Pte	Smith	William Edward
18056	Pte	Bradshaw	Robert
18064	Pte	Watson	Thomas
18069	Pte	Burton	Henry Cecil
18071	Pte	Smith	Fred
18078	Pte	Glover	John
18080	Pte	Glover	Harry
18088	Pte	Pass	William
18090	Pte	Webster	Arthur
18093	Pte	Fox	Arthur
18095	Pte	Thorpe	Arthur
18103	Pte	Hayes	William Henry
18112	Pte	Carlin	Fred
18113	Pte	Wortley	Frank
18170	Pte	Shaw	Sydney Herbert Lewin
18234	Pte	Shaw	William
18249	Pte	Boaler	William
18263	Pte	Head	Arthur
18271	Pte	Foster	William
18293	Pte	Pearson	William
18331	Pte	Sutton	Samuel
18343	Pte	Vardy	Joseph
18358	Cpl	Chatten	Richard
18365	Sgt	Riches	Frederick
18367	Pte	Fleeman	John T
18370	L/Cpl	Vickers	George Hartley
18381	Pte	Fletcher	Samuel Wright Rawdon
18397	Pte	Notman	John
18432	L/Sgt	Fisher	George
18449	Pte	Smith	Philip
18452	Pte	Allsop	Thomas
18453	L/Cpl	Bucklow	George
18454	Sgt	Newton	George
18475	Pte	Cobley	George
18512	Pte	Wass	James
18545	Pte	Taylor	John Cutlord
18546	Pte	Mullins	William Storer
18550	Pte	Berrington	Thomas
18551	Pte	Robinson	Albert
18557	Pte	Godwin	Tom
18579	L/Cpl	Shepherd	Joseph
18606	Pte	Lester	George Robert
18610	Pte	Hammersley	Thomas
18621	Pte	Metheringham	John Robert
18622	Pte	Leary	Lawrence
18644	Pte	Jackson	Herbert Bernard
18647	Pte	Wornes	Henry
18649	Pte	Eyre	Archie
18653	Pte	Webb	William
18668	Cpl	Brain	David
18675	Pte	Bingham	Richard
18702	Pte	Fowkes	George
18703	L/Cpl	Hardy	George

Number	Rank	Surname	Given name
18711	Pte	Pickin	Phillip
18712	Pte	Moss	William
18760	Pte	Eaglefield	Thomas William Horace
18771	Pte	Gamble	George
18774	Pte	Padgett	George
18809	L/Cpl	Needham	Alfred
18813	Cpl	Wilson	Edgar
18831	Sgt	Moulton	Thomas
18844	Pte	Parr	William
18875	Pte	Roome	Joseph
18880	Pte	Morris	Benjamin William
18888	Pte	Haywood	Frank
18893	Pte	Brereton	George
18897	Pte	Jennison	Frederick Ernest
18906	Pte	Hoggins	Benjamin
18907	Pte	Olsten	John William
18912	Pte	Swain	Albert Edward
18930	Pte	Tomlinson	Richard
18936	Pte	Vickers	Arthur
18938	Pte	Godfrey	Samuel
18942	Pte	Davison	Reginald
18956	Pte	Finch	George
18957	Pte	Davison	John William
18963	Pte	Watstaff	Charles
18966	Pte	Finney	John George
18968	Pte	Bower	William
18971	Pte	Rhodes	Arthur
18973	Pte	Phipps	Thomas
18980	L/Cpl	Bray	Samuel
18982	Pte	Flinders	John
18984	Pte	Senescall	Edward
18989	Pte	Watstaff	Daniel
19001	Pte	Marsden	Joseph
19002	Pte	Tansley	Gursham
19009	Pte	Caunt	Luther
19017	Pte	Sanders	Ernest
19021	Pte	Mellor	Joseph
19045	Pte	Hawson	William
19053	Pte	Causer	John James
19054	Pte	Lloyd	John
19068	Pte	Ellis	John Thomas
19074	Pte	Birks	William
19085	Pte	Haskard	William
19104	Pte	Marriott	Peter
19114	L/Sgt	Farnfield	Herbert
19132	Pte	Wheatley	William Richard
19133	Pte	Cook	Thomas
19138	Pte	Goff	Samuel
19145	Pte	Beresford	Samuel
19191	L/Sgt	Hebblethwaite	Joseph
19199	Pte	Marriott	Frank
19207	L/Cpl	Storey	Herbert
19219	Pte	Freeman	Walter

Number	Rank	Surname	Given name
19221	Pte	Careless	John Thomas
19225	Pte	Osborne	Arthur
19233	Pte	Armstrong	John Will
19240	Pte	Antcliffe	Alfred
19250	Pte	Greaves	Harold
19251	L/Cpl	Baker	Frederick
19257	Pte	Hilditch	Edwin
19258	Pte	Hill	William
19263	Pte	Williamson	George Henry
19333	Pte	Fox	Percy William
19359	Pte	Ancill	Wilfred
19388	Pte	Hill	William
19395	Pte	Birks	Alfred Henry
19418	Pte	Davenport	George
19478	Pte	Morris	Jarvis Harvey
19507	Pte	Ashton	Joseph
19511	Pte	Charlesworth	Albert
19568	Pte	Eastwood	George
19577	Pte	Rushton	James Henry
19586	Pte	Swain	Percy
19614	Pte	Bacon	Percy
19649	Pte	Hayes	Thomas
19650	Pte	Tinsley	John
19676	Pte	Mann	John
19677	Pte	Hayes	Colin Henry
19709	L/Cpl	Ibbett	Thomas
19745	Pte	Burgess	Wilfred
19756	Cpl	Bell	George William
19759	Pte	Bellamy	Joseph
19765	Pte	Brailsford	William Henry
19771	Pte	Brown	Albert
19774	Pte	Buxton	Albert Edward
19776	Pte	Bellamy	Horace
19779	Pte	Burton	Soloman
19800	Pte	Clarke	Vincent
19814	Cpl	Evans	Stanley
19817	Pte	Falconer	George
19833	Pte	Gaunt	William Leslie
19838	Pte	George	William
19840	Pte	Gibbons	Fred
19857	Pte	Hodson	Benjamin
19869	Pte	Hone	James Henry
19896	Pte	Lowe	George
19899	L/Cpl	Limb	William
19908	L/Cpl	Marsh	Ralph
19909	Pte	Morris	Thomas
19911	Sgt	Malthouse	Francis John Goodall
19912	Pte	Molloy	John
19913	Pte	Morton	Joseph
19919	Cpl	Naylor	George Robert
19947	Pte	Rushby	James
19958	Pte	Smith	Joe
19979	Pte	Tomlinson	Samuel

Number	Rank	Surname	Given name
20006	Pte	Worker	James
20012	Pte	Weaver	Charles Clifford
20018	Pte	Connor	Thomas
20035	L/Cpl	Dent	Charles
20045	Pte	Clowes	William Dexter
20077	L/Sgt	Thompson	William
20090	Pte	Adlington	Charles
20096	Pte	North	Edward
20098	Pte	Moore	Gerald
20099	Pte	Baugh	Frederick Thomas
20137	Pte	Marshall	Robert Henry
20149	Pte	Phillips	Frederick Henry
20219	L/Cpl	Potter	Frank
20220	Pte	Vickers	William Horace
20225	Pte	Weaver	John
20226	Pte	Beecroft	Thomas
20231	Pte	Elliott	Alfred
20245	Pte	Smith	George Albert
20253	Cpl	Cullen	Alfred Thomas
20262	Pte	Bent	Richard
20279	Pte	Moakes	George
20291	Pte	Cockrane	Elijah
20293	L/Sgt	Dunnicliff	Claude Nelson
20301	L/Cpl	Harrop	Harry
20303	Pte	Stanley	Sydney
20306	Pte	Winnard	Wilfred
20307	Pte	Heywood	Frank
20309	Pte	Taylor	Ephriam
20312	L/Sgt	Ward	George
20313	Pte	Frazer	Edward
20314	Pte	Arrowsmith	George Frederick
20320	Pte	Goddard	William
20321	Pte	Brooke	John Stanley
20328	Pte	Townsend	Fred
20329	Pte	Dudley	Isaac
20331	Pte	Bryan	John Stephen
20332	Pte	Hallam	Arthur
20333	Pte	South	Jesse
20338	Cpl	Taylor	Albert Edward
20340	Pte	Smith	George Henry
20343	Pte	Hallam	James Arthur
20344	Pte	Skellern	Charles Lomas
20345	Pte	Gregory	George
20347	Pte	Dexter	Thomas
20359	L/Cpl	Bainbridge	Robert
20364	Pte	Compson	Frederick Charles
20366	Pte	Causer	Thomas
20412	Sgt	Bateman	Edgar
20415	Pte	Baker	Sidney
20416	Pte	Whiten	Cyril
20417	Pte	Raynor	George
20419	Pte	Marshall	Arthur
20426	Pte	Carver	William
20450	Pte	Moule	Arthur
20496	Pte	Mille	Cecil
20509	Pte	Round	William
20529	Pte	Ward	Edward
20680	Pte	Shaw	John William
20696	Sgt	Cheshire	Alexander George
20707	Pte	Stone	Rudolph
20710	Pte	Kershaw	Edward
20712	Pte	Holmes	Percy Stuart
20738	Pte	Peach	Albert Henry
20748	Pte	Hunt	Wilfred
20759	Pte	Martin	Leonard
20788	Sgt	Summer	John
20795	Pte	Hood	Albert
20819	Pte	Simpson	Albert
20828	Pte	Shawcroft	John
20830	Pte	Chilton	William Henry
20838	Pte	Ford	Bernard
20859	Pte	Crump	Albert Edward
20863	L/Cpl	Wallace	Frank
20877	Pte	Sissons	Robert
20892	Pte	Chambers	Thomas
20895	Pte	Cole	Henry
20903	Sgt	Moore	Ernest
20909	Pte	Kent	William
20948	L/Cpl	Winterbottom	Henry
20960	L/Cpl	Britton	Willie
20962	Pte	Brown	Lawrence
20971	L/Cpl	Hodgkinson	Samuel
20972	Pte	Selby	Albert John
20981	Pte	Clifford	George Frederick
20995	Pte	Smedley	Samuel
21007	Pte	Broughton	Harry
21029	Pte	Bostock	Henry
21030	Pte	Wilkes	George Simon
21044	Pte	Wright	Walter
21063	Pte	Spittlehouse	Arthur John
21075	L/Cpl	Turner	Charles
21077	Pte	Gough	George
21087	Pte	Swift	Herbert Ernest
21090	Pte	Smedley	Henry
21092	Pte	Cook	Harry
21094	Pte	Unwin	William Henry
21095	Pte	Holmes	John William
21096	Pte	Ellis	Henry
21100	Cpl	Myers	John Thomas
21103	Sgt	Carlin	Albert
21114	Pte	Mills	John Thomas
21121	Pte	Mugglestone	Horace
21122	Pte	Woodhouse	George Wheatley
21127	Pte	Edlin	George Samuel
21129	Pte	Simmonds	Edwin
21130	Pte	Byard	Andrew

Number	Rank	Surname	Given name
21131	Pte	Peach	Joseph William
21151	Cpl	Monk	Francis Thomas
21160	Pte	Hickling	William
21164	L/Cpl	Lowe	Oscar
21170	Pte	Thompson	James
21185	Pte	Allen	William
21189	L/Sgt	Walker	John William
21195	Pte	Morley	John Joseph
21196	Pte	Fletcher	James Edward
21197	Pte	Maxey	William Edward
21198	Pte	Ashmore	Benjamin
21205	Pte	Page	John
21212	Pte	Leivers	Ernest
21249	Pte	Knight	Edward
21261	Pte	Edgson	James Herbert
21262	Pte	Wright	Frederick
21264	Pte	Clark	John James Harniess
21267	Pte	Wood	Harry
21271	L/Sgt	Chambers	Arthur Harold
21274	Pte	Leeson	Frank
21275	Pte	Dakin	George
21276	Pte	Trueman	Walker
21278	Pte	Burton	John
21279	Pte	Hodgkiss	Frederick William
21280	Pte	Parkes	Frank
21286	Pte	Robinson	Francis William
21287	Pte	Hallsworth	Bert
21288	Pte	Sanders	Harold
21289	Pte	Wintersgill	William Edward
21299	Pte	Hymas	John William
21302	Pte	Boham	James
21326	Pte	Shepherd	Leonard Wessley
21332	Sgt	Willis	John William
21336	Pte	Gilliver	Joseph
21341	Pte	Wilkinson	James Walter
21342	Pte	Cleary	Thomas
21345	Pte	Fisher	John William
21346	Pte	Webster	George
21351	Pte	Mann	George
21354	Pte	Whitehouse	Edward Ernest
21359	Pte	Cook	James
21362	Pte	Harpham	Fred
21368	Pte	Heap	George
21375	Pte	Cragg	George
21385	Pte	Fox	Edgar William
21386	Pte	Willgoose	William
21401	Pte	Bowler	Benjamin
21402	Pte	Roberts	Lewis Joseph
21422	Pte	Allsop	Harry
21428	Pte	Ashmore	David
21431	L/Sgt	Scattergood	John
21435	Pte	Skelton	George
21441	Sgt	Marshall	Henry

Number	Rank	Surname	Given name
21453	Pte	Gilliatt	Thomas
21454	Pte	Trotman	Sidney William
21456	Pte	Brown	Joseph William
21467	Pte	Tomlinson	Bernard
21475	Pte	Goodacre	Harry
21477	Pte	Allwood	Herbert
21478	Pte	Allen	Stanley George
21498	Pte	Hayes	Jim
21500	Pte	Cooling	George Herbert
21502	Pte	Marsden	George
21504	Pte	Marsh	Harold
21515	Pte	Jacques	William
21516	Pte	Tonge	Thomas
21522	Pte	Straw	Arthur
21525	Pte	Brown	Vincent
21533	L/Cpl	Braddock	John George
21540	Pte	Hartshorne	Charles
21541	Pte	Kelly	John
21543	Pte	Corcoran	Thomas
21544	Pte	Leatherland	Harold
21558	Pte	Kitchen	Edward
21560	Pte	Hewitt	Leonard
21588	Pte	Sewell	Herbert
21598	Pte	Bennett	George Edward
21599	Pte	Bunner	John Henry
21602	Pte	Byfield	Isaiah
21616	L/Cpl	Whitworth	Leonard
21617	Pte	Fox	John George
21656	Pte	Clements	Fred
21658	Pte	Mills	Herbert
21669	Pte	Clarke	Charles
21673	Cpl	Comery	Lawrence
21675	Pte	Parratt	Charles William
21680	Pte	Southwell	Ernest
21712	Pte	Smitham	Abraham
21714	Pte	DeBanke	Joseph
21716	Pte	Watson	Harold
21726	Pte	Grainger	John
21728	Pte	Allsopp	Josiah
21729	Pte	Slim	Arthur
21730	Pte	Breedon	Harry
21731	Pte	Pasey	John William
21732	Pte	Colclough	Fred
21740	Pte	Farrall	George Richard
21741	L/Cpl	Silcock	William Henry
21746	Pte	Watts	George
21753	Pte	Elliott	Benjamin
21758	Pte	Boot	George Henry
21759	Pte	Taverner	George
21766	Pte	Parkin	John Thomas
21769	Pte	Geary	Harold
21773	Cpl	Bestwick	George
21774	Pte	Goodman	Clement

Number	Rank	Surname	Given name
21775	Pte	Cresswell	William
21777	Pte	Huskinson	Frank
21778	Pte	Riley	Charles William
21789	Pte	Shirley	Charles
21827	Pte	Ryder	Leonard John
21830	Pte	Easom	William
21832	Pte	Jones	Alexander
21844	Pte	Longden	Aaron
21849	Pte	Hudson	John Joseph
21851	Pte	Nurse	John William
21891	Pte	Booth	William
21893	Pte	Hollis	Frederick
21903	Pte	Parker	Albert Leslie
21907	Pte	Pegg	Walter
21912	L/Cpl	Eades	Joseph
21917	Pte	Bee	Frederick
21922	Pte	Prime	John William
21931	Pte	Bennett	Samuel
21956	Pte	Rhodes	William
21961	Pte	Dunstan	Albert George
21984	Pte	Searson	Harold
21996	Pte	Marsh	George
22003	Pte	Kitchen	Fred
22022	Pte	Dickin	George Henry
22024	Pte	Clay	George Henry
22029	Pte	Bacon	James
22048	Pte	Jackson	Arthur William
22055	Pte	Tasker	George
22061	L/Cpl	Bray	Harry James
22065	Pte	Brown	John Thomas
22068	Pte	Radford	Thomas George
22072	Pte	Jinks	George
22073	Pte	Dyson	Norman
22074	Pte	Oldfield	John
22090	Pte	Bedford	Lamech
22095	Cpl	Riley	George
22112	Pte	Barnes	Ernest
22121	Pte	Holford	Frederick
22122	Pte	Mosley	John
22138	Pte	Walker	Walter
22142	Pte	Bacon	Arthur
22146	Pte	Thompson	Frank
22149	Pte	Oates	James
22150	Pte	Pierpoint	Albert
22151	Pte	Stainforth	John Robert
22152	Pte	Allen	John
22158	Pte	Parry	Edward Richard
22160	Pte	James	Thomas
22161	Pte	Woods	Edgar
22165	Pte	Daniels	Albert
22167	Pte	Lowe	Albert Owen
22172	Pte	Woolven	Charles Edwin
22173	Pte	Rodgers	Stephen

Number	Rank	Surname	Given name
22175	Pte	Walters	George
22177	Pte	Brown	Joseph
22178	Pte	White	Herbert
22181	Pte	Lee	James Ashley
22182	L/Cpl	Dunn	James William
22195	Pte	Smedley	John
22196	Pte	Mitson	William
22198	Pte	Barker	Joseph
22201	Pte	Knowles	Henry
22204	Pte	Rowland	George William
22205	Pte	Hardy	Edward
22206	Pte	Hardy	George
22207	Cpl	Hopewell	Harry
22210	L/Sgt	Winstanley	George
22211	Pte	Harrison	Edward Samuel
22217	Pte	Hibbert	Bernard
22223	Pte	Crooks	Frank
22224	Pte	Overton	James
22225	Pte	Blood	William Henry
22233	Pte	Howe	William Henry
22245	Pte	Bilson	John Thomas
22251	L/Sgt	Lane	John
22253	L/Cpl	Wakefield	Charles Archibald
22257	Pte	Mayes	Thomas
22265	Pte	Langford	George
22270	Pte	Perrett	Ernest Albert
22272	Pte	Lancaster	Thomas
22277	Pte	Pearson	William
22284	Pte	Southwell	Arthur
22290	Pte	Palmer	Samuel. J
22295	Pte	Leivers	John William
22314	Pte	Milner	Thomas
22332	Pte	Allen	Walter
22348	Pte	Dale	Edward
22371	Pte	Tomlinson	Francis Darwin
22373	Pte	Jones	James Arthur
22384	Pte	Tunnicliffe	John
22387	Pte	Bell	Harry
22389	Pte	Castledine	Percy
22394	Pte	Allen	George
22408	L/Cpl	Beresford	Thomas Eliot
22421	L/Cpl	Hutchinson	Louis Granville
22433	Pte	Wood	Charles Archibald
22445	Pte	Clark	William
22453	Pte	Webb	Leonard George Lewis
22455	Pte	Stanton	Benjamin
22478	Pte	Poulson	Joseph Edward
22480	Sgt	Teer	Charles Joseph Francis
22497	Pte	Durkin	Thomas
22501	Pte	Cooper	James
22502	Pte	Silcock	Ernest
22504	Pte	Taylor	George Henry
22505	Pte	Kirk	John James

Number	Rank	Surname	Given name
22508	Pte	Cartwright	Joseph
22509	Pte	Mavin	Arthur
22510	Pte	Hopkinson	William
22513	Pte	Shaw	Joseph
22514	Pte	Rudd	James
22515	Pte	Gundry	Benjamin
22517	Pte	Beresford	Christopher
22524	Pte	Chapman	Frank
22526	Pte	Simmons	John Henry
22527	L/Cpl	Davenport	Joseph Arthur
22531	Pte	Boyd	John
22536	Pte	Nurse	Thomas Ernest
22552	Cpl	Adams	Alfred
22555	Pte	Dixon	Joseph Samuel Henry
22558	Pte	Allison	Herbert
22559	Pte	Rodgers	Sydney
22561	Pte	Divine	Robert McKee
22571	Pte	Gee	Harry
22580	Pte	Dunn	Robert
22591	Pte	Butler	Thomas
22593	Pte	Carrington	William Joseph
22594	Pte	Gee	Dennis John
22605	Pte	Worness	John Edward
22607	Pte	Kniveton	Reginald William
22624	Pte	Gratton	John
22628	Pte	Buxton	Ernest
22634	Pte	Gilbody	Robert
22635	Pte	Robinson	Edward
22636	Pte	Bates	Benjamin
22638	Pte	Wilke	James
22645	Pte	England	Edwin
22646	Pte	Beardsley	Samuel
22651	Pte	Holmes	Walter
22658	Pte	Robinson	George Henry
22663	L/Cpl	Cullen	John Edward
22668	Pte	Simms	David Frankland
22670	L/Cpl	Ridgard	James Thomas
22672	Pte	Elmer	Reuben
22680	Pte	Burrows	John Thomas Lakin
22693	Cpl	White	Sydney
22695	Pte	Booker	John
22703	Pte	Busby	William
22715	Pte	Hughes	John
22726	Pte	Pole	Thomas
22728	L/Cpl	Rigby	Arthur
22738	Pte	Carter	Fred
22742	Pte	Orridge	George
22746	Pte	Lomas	Thomas
22760	Pte	Matchett	Edric William
22765	Pte	Cheetham	George
22788	Pte	Hazlewood	Joseph
22789	Pte	Ault	William
22790	L/Cpl	Beeson	George William

Number	Rank	Surname	Given name
22804	Pte	Sanders	Ernest Edward
22809	Pte	Milner	Horace
22812	Pte	Barlow	James
22817	Pte	Hipwell	James
22835	Sgt	Richard	Ernest
22845	Pte	Manderfield	Thomas
22847	Pte	Pond	Joseph Elliott
22856	Pte	Walker	William
22857	Pte	Martin	William Henry
22860	Sgt	Mellish	John
22877	Pte	Leary	Frank
22881	Pte	Fowler	John
22883	Pte	Poulton	James
22896	Pte	Edwards	William
22899	L/Sgt	Maddison	Percy
22903	Pte	Fenton	Frank
22908	Pte	Perotti	Ben
22913	Pte	Goddard	Samuel
22916	Pte	Adcock	Walter Russell
22917	Pte	Sewell	Francis Edward
22920	L/Cpl	Johnson	John Thomas
22922	Pte	Greatorex	George
22924	Cpl	Palmer	Arthur
22929	Pte	Adams	Albert Edward
22930	Pte	Barlow	William
22931	Pte	Pearson	William
22935	Pte	Silcock	James Edward
22942	Pte	Sharpe	William
22946	L/Sgt	Taylor	Thomas Joseph
22954	Pte	Smith	Wilfred George
22956	Pte	Barcock	Sydney
22961	Pte	Thorpe	Edgar Wilks
22965	Pte	Thompson	John Joseph
22968	Pte	Jarvis	John
22973	Pte	Illsley	John William Francis
22977	Pte	Hazlewood	William Charles
22979	Pte	Clemerson	Thomas Frederick
22983	Pte	Gould	Albert Henry
22985	Pte	Hasman	John James
22988	Pte	Hill	Samuel Roger
22989	Pte	Bailey	George
22991	Pte	Wedge	John William
22992	Cpl	Saville	William
22993	Pte	Wilkes	Tom
22996	Pte	Slater	Samuel
23003	Pte	Osborn	Joseph Matthew
23005	Pte	Hopkinson	George
23012	Pte	Tunnicliffe	Harold
23015	L/Cpl	Walker	William
23023	Pte	Drewry	William Henry
23025	Pte	Smith	Arthur
23031	Pte	Shirley	Thomas
23034	Pte	Atkin	Joseph Wilmot

Number	Rank	Surname	Given name
23036	Pte	Shaw	George Enos
23038	Pte	Hunt	Alfred James
23041	Pte	Walker	Ernest
23042	Pte	Stone	Walter
23045	Pte	Holmes	Charles Edwin
23046	Pte	Thompson	William
23047	Cpl	Flint	Charles Harold
23050	Pte	Flint	Francis
23057	Pte	Hopkins	Rowland Elijah
23062	Pte	Watts	Archie
23063	Pte	Lewin	Edward
23064	Pte	Hunt	William Robert
23065	Pte	Whyler	William Arthur
23067	Pte	Harrison	David
23070	Pte	Bestwick	Fred
23071	Pte	Potter	William
23072	Pte	Oldershaw	William Henry
23075	Pte	Weston	Frederick Thomas
23083	Pte	Croucher	George
23084	Pte	Mottram	Arthur Fern
23089	Pte	Colton	Percival Charles
23091	Pte	Lee	Harold
3415	Sgt	Blunt	Frederick J
17329	Pte	Harris	Edward
23092	Pte	Roe	Frank
23093	Pte	Barker	James Thomas
23096	Pte	Mellors	Charles
23097	Pte	Bateman	John
23101	Pte	Watson	Alfred
23105	Pte	Hawker	Frederick William
23108	Pte	Pickering	Edward
23109	Pte	Worthington	Arthur Harry
23111	Pte	Middleton	Clement
23121	Pte	Robinson	Ernest Henry
23123	Pte	Palmer	Edward
23126	Pte	Stenson	Garnet
23127	Pte	Parr	Walter
23128	Pte	Bingham	Walter
23133	Pte	Davis	Cornelius
23139	Pte	Ward	William
23142	Pte	Williams	George
23146	Pte	Jones	James
23149	Pte	Shipman	Allen Vessey
23151	Cpl	Adams	Thomas Wilfred
23152	Pte	Burgess	Robert Clark
23157	Pte	Chambers	William
23161	Pte	Arrowsmith	Samuel
23163	Pte	Armstrong	John Geoffrey
23168	Pte	Wright	Ronald
23181	Pte	James	Thomas Henry
23184	Pte	Brooks	William
23190	Pte	Preston	Ernest
23193	Pte	Reddish	Harold
23194	Pte	Mallinder	Walter John
23197	Pte	Terry	John Thomas
23200	Pte	Hadman	John William
23205	Pte	Smith	Joseph
23208	L/Cpl	Byard	James
23210	Pte	Brooks	Robert
23220	Pte	Pick	Harold Leonard
23223	Pte	Buxton	Thomas Henry
23226	Pte	Harwood	Charles
23227	Pte	Evans	George
23231	Pte	Baxter	Frederick
23232	Pte	Cutts	Samuel
23242	Pte	Hawley	John
23244	Pte	Clarke	Benjamin
23248	Pte	Wheeldon	George
23261	Pte	Hall	John
23262	Pte	Thompson	Frederick
23265	Pte	Taylor	George
23272	Pte	Pheasey	Sidney James
23283	Pte	Knowles	Charles
23288	Pte	Booth	Thomas
23289	Pte	Mee	George
23290	Pte	Pass	Morris Edward
23306	Pte	Fant	Ernest Albert
23314	Pte	Kemp	George Thomas
23318	Pte	Roe	John Thomas
23319	Pte	McNamara	John
23326	Pte	Webster	John
23332	Pte	Holland	Moses
23333	Pte	Foster	Samuel
23335	Pte	Burton	Walter Colin Bostock
23336	Pte	Hunt	Henry Howard
23340	Pte	Turner	Joseph
23345	Pte	Stevens	George
23346	Pte	Bramwell	Frank
23362	Pte	Hassall	Charley
23366	Pte	Hornby	Harold
23368	Pte	Hyde	Samuel Edward
23383	Pte	Wood	Henry
23384	Pte	Cowlishaw	Henry
23392	Pte	Watson	Douglas
23395	Pte	Hallam	Walter
23396	Pte	Dixon	Thomas
23398	Pte	Ward	Abraham
23401	Pte	Orwin	Herbert
23402	Pte	McGrath	Edward
23408	Pte	Boice	William
23410	Pte	Wardle	Alfred
23420	Pte	Baddeley	Henry
23438	Pte	Rodgers	Frederick
23612	Pte	Walker	Alfred
23646	Pte	Gregory	Charles
23663	Pte	Derbyshire	George

Number	Rank	Surname	Given name
23665	Pte	Harper	Wallace
23668	Pte	Bingham	Frank
23711	Pte	Farby	George Robert
23715	Sgt	Greaves	Fred
23777	Pte	Bexton	Thomas
23780	L/Cpl	Ringrose	John Willie
23785	Pte	Jones	John
23788	Pte	Marshall	James
23789	Pte	Ball	Charles
23800	Pte	Hawksley	John William
23844	Pte	Hill	Job
23851	Pte	Gascoigne	John Charles
23852	Pte	Coupe	Edward
23853	Pte	Parton	Isaiah
23874	Pte	White	Alfred
23877	Cpl	Brain	George
23878	Pte	Price	Albert William
23889	Pte	Wallhead	George
23892	Pte	Marsh	Samuel Herman
23912	Pte	Cope	John William
23915	Pte	Barrs	George Ernest
23936	Pte	Congo	George Walter
23981	Pte	Slater	William
23983	Pte	Dabell	James William
23984	Pte	Hartshorn	William John
23986	Pte	Parker	Albert Edward
23987	Pte	Parker	George Elias
23992	L/Cpl	Jeffries	Walter Machin
23993	Pte	Wormsley	George
23994	Pte	Caunt	Henry
24013	L/Sgt	Davis	Cyril
24024	Pte	Hoyes	Alfred
24029	Pte	Phillips	David
24046	Pte	Colton	Thomas Arthur
24051	Pte	Gascoyne	John William
24059	Pte	Asher	Joseph
24061	Pte	Gardner	Thomas
24064	Pte	Mycock	Albert
24094	Pte	Short	Edward
24097	Pte	Washbrook	Isaac
24144	Pte	Sheraton	Wallace
24149	Pte	Fletcher	John
24150	Pte	Lucas	Joseph George
24152	Pte	Wilkins	Harry
24169	Pte	Hampshire	William
24171	Pte	Sedgwick	Job
24174	Pte	Pierrepont	Bertram
24176	2nd A.m.	Jones	Ernest
24177	Pte	Kippin	John Walvin
24226	Sgt	Bloor	William
24235	Pte	Carratt	Charles Edward
24240	L/Cpl	Wheatley	Alfred
24263	Pte	Gower	William
24265	Pte	Bennett	Henry
24266	Pte	Siddons	James Alfred
24307	Pte	Ward	Frederick George
24314	Cpl	Thomas	Jesse Edward
24319	Pte	Prothero	George
24320	Pte	Miller	James
24322	Pte	Pollard	Robert
24332	Pte	Froggart	Alfred
24345	Sgt	Hucknall	John William
24403	Pte	Tomlinson	William
24404	Cpl	Hackford	Walter Stanley
24414	L/Cpl	Rodgers	Henry
24428	Pte	Hinton	Ebeneezer
24465	Pte	Hubball	William Henry
24469	Pte	Clarke	George Henry
24496	Pte	Hill	George
24497	Pte	Cowley	Horace Tom
24503	Pte	Potter	Percy
24514	Pte	Petford	John Henry
24527	Pte	Thorley	George
24531	Pte	Nicholls	Jeremiah
24536	L/Sgt	Fell	John
24537	Pte	Booth	George
24582	Pte	Jennings	Arthur
24585	Pte	Stewart	William Edward
24625	Pte	Oldham	Thomas
24628	Pte	Hepworth	Fred
24662	Pte	Storer	Eric
24665	Pte	Bloomfield	Walter
24669	Pte	Hopcroft	Herbert
24670	Pte	Martin	Henry
24672	Pte	Brodie	William
24704	Pte	Furness	Walter
24784	Pte	Taylor	George
24786	Pte	Parnham	William
24787	Sgt	Bark	Francis
24788	Pte	Upton	Thomas
24881	L/Cpl	Afford	Arthur
24882	Pte	Cox	Frederick
24916	Pte	Carver	George
24972	Pte	Betts	John Edward
24977	Pte	Hall	Henry
24981	Pte	Mettam	George Lawrence
24985	Pte	Middleton	Charles
24992	Pte	Needham	Henry Morris
24997	Pte	Grain	David
25003	Pte	Harris	Thomas
25008	Pte	Gibson	Robert
25009	Pte	Burton	John
25010	Pte	Fowke	William
25050	Pte	Musgrove	Edwin
25095	Pte	Terrell	Arthur
25149	Pte	Shepherd	George

Number	Rank	Surname	Given name
25206	Pte	Gregory	James William
25210	L/Cpl	Swann	Percy
25285	Pte	Webb	John
25287	Pte	Harris	Joseph
25291	Pte	Whitehead	Edwin
25295	Pte	Butler	Walter
25298	Sgt	Sutton	George
25299	Pte	Bentley	Henry
25300	Pte	Clifford	William Henry
25365	Pte	Whittaker	Matthew
25367	Pte	Bradley	William
25368	Pte	Whitehead	John
25398	Pte	Barlow	Walter
25452	Pte	Gouldin	George
25459	Pte	Goodman	Edmund James
25479	Pte	Lawson	Frank
25506	Pte	Jepson	Edgar
25510	Pte	Doody	Fred
25529	Pte	Parker	John
25531	Pte	Harrison	Ernest Arnold
25532	Pte	Mallatratt	Walter Cox
25555	Pte	Blagg	Alfred Ernest
25557	Pte	Dilkes	Arthur
25580	Pte	Hollis	Frank
25590	Pte	Wetton	James Henry
25617	L/Cpl	Moore	John Leslie
25618	Pte	Parker	Edgar
25655	Pte	Buxton	William Ernest
25659	Pte	Cutts	Matthew
25660	Pte	Harrison	George
25772	Pte	Cook	Arthur
25783	WOC2	Onion	Joel
25793	Pte	Walters	James
25843	Pte	Gilbert	Charles Edward
25908	Pte	Smedley	Samuel George
25910	Pte	Havenhead	George Francis
25944	Pte	Hunt	Thomas Alfred Girlin
25948	Pte	Bailey	James
26061	Pte	Starbuck	Thomas Isaac
26103	L/Cpl	Newton	George
26172	Pte	Marks	Maurice
26189	Pte	Bird	Herbert Arthur
26217	Pte	Crowder	William Ernest
26233	L/Cpl	Wootton	Leonard
26243	L/Cpl	Smith	John Henry
26245	Pte	Hart	Wilfred
26268	Cpl	Brown	Amos
26303	Pte	Goodyear	Harold
26358	Pte	Richardson	Bertram Alfred
26360	Pte	Wardle	Joseph Henry
26361	Pte	Illsley	Thomas
26422	Pte	Wood	Edward
26445	Cpl	Hauxwell	Arthur

Number	Rank	Surname	Given name
26454	Pte	Betts	Edward Allen
26457	Pte	Weston	Collis
26499	Pte	Clarke	Alec
26501	L/Cpl	Madin	Thomas Henry
26507	Pte	Spring	Joseph
26522	Pte	Armstrong	Frederick
26655	L/Cpl	Lowth	Issacher
26656	Pte	Allen	William
26751	Pte	Slaney	Edward
26774	Pte	Robinson	Fred
26815	Pte	Smith	Frederick Norman
26858	Pte	Greenhough	Vernon
26876	Pte	Holroyd	Thomas
26888	Pte	Trickett	Thurston
26931	Pte	Sibbring	Arthur
27036	Pte	Saunders	John
27040	Pte	Cresswell	Albert Edward
27044	Pte	Wadlington	Arthur
27056	Pte	Brien	William
27110	Pte	Birchmore	Ernest
27119	L/Sgt	Bostock	Edward
27138	Pte	Whitehead	Frederick Streeton
27154	Pte	Day	Robert
27175	Pte	Carrington	John William
27180	Pte	Hadfield	Bernard Evans
27181	Pte	Gregory	William Colin
27198	Cpl	Rushton	Arthur
27244	Pte	Croft	William
27249	Sgt	Sage	Herbert
27260	Pte	Brittain	Samuel Francis
27279	Pte	Sheppard	George Alexander
27322	Pte	Catley	Albert
27355	Pte	Bradley	Herbert
27409	Pte	Godber	Stephen
27415	Pte	Parnham	James William
27425	Pte	Wiggins	George
27448	Pte	Swann	Sylvester
27464	Pte	Martin	Fred
27472	Pte	Dyson	Walter
27486	Pte	Meakin	William
27488	Pte	Johnson	William Arthur
27498	Pte	Churchill	Patrick
27562	Pte	Hoole	William
27579	Pte	Sparham	Joseph
27645	Cpl	Kirby	Henry
27646	Pte	Oldenbittle	Stanley
27678	Pte	Brooks	Albert
27722	Pte	Bonsall	Thomas
27733	Pte	Burton	John George
27749	Pte	Atherley	John
27786	Pte	Whitehouse	William
27804	Pte	Moore	John Dawber
27828	Pte	Sutton	John William

Number	Rank	Surname	Given name
27848	Pte	Dowen	Albert Edward
27850	Pte	Baxter	John William
27852	Pte	Sentence	Charles Edward
27853	Pte	Bugg	Arthur
27854	Pte	Chambers	John
27856	Pte	Brown	George Edward
27857	Pte	Loane	Samuel
27860	Pte	Padley	Edward Cartwright
27861	Pte	Rabbitt	Harry
27862	Pte	Hickson	Edward
27863	Pte	Jackson	William
27911	Pte	Saunders	Alexander
27935	Pte	Rudge	William Francis Joseph
27965	Pte	Batty	Horace
28084	Pte	Bacon	William Henry
28104	Pte	Hutson	Ralph
28106	Pte	McKenzie	Horace
28135	Pte	West	Fred
28145	Pte	Reddish	Samuel
28152	Sgt	Fagan	William
28153	Pte	Goulding	John James
28216	Pte	Brown	William
28228	Pte	Guest	Melvin
28278	Pte	Stacey	Henry
28319	L/Cpl	Scott	Oswald
28340	Pte	Bowers	Samuel
28347	Pte	Birch	George William
28348	Pte	Ward	Cyril
28628	Pte	Turner	Jack
28645	Pte	Swift	Herbert
28646	Pte	Flint	George
28648	Pte	Smith	Samuel Henry
28815	L/Cpl	Clarke	Harry
28892	Pte	Sisson	James William
28933	Cpl	Wood	Colin Wilfred
29329	Pte	Odam	Francis Henry
29584	Pte	Wheat	William Thomas
29638	Pte	Pinkney	Lawrence
29717	Pte	Alsop	John Algie
29792	Pte	Lloyd	William Henry
30181	Cpl	Southall	Samuel
30354	Pte	Locke	Charles
30358	Pte	Bradley	George Wild
30405	Sgt	Neale	Harry
30407	Pte	Martin	Ernest
30413	Pte	Vickers	Albert Edward
30487	Cpl	Foulkes	Arthur
30535	Pte	Haynes	Oswald
30540	Pte	Simpson	Charles Dawker
30549	Pte	Burley	Ernest William
30601	Pte	Lander	William
30609	Pte	Slater	John
30614	Pte	Dudley	Jack
30664	Pte	Towle	William
30703	Pte	Sheppard	Albert
30767	Pte	Throp	Cecil Alfred
30807	Pte	Lee	William
30819	Pte	Smith	Albert Henry
30948	Pte	Osbourne	Gilbert Frank
30976	Pte	Upton	William
30993	Pte	Radford	Thomas James
31029	Pte	Swain	Arthur Richard
31031	Pte	Foster	Harold Ernest Somerfield
31063	Pte	Price	Charles William
31138	Pte	Armstrong	John Charles
31151	Pte	Sharp	George William
31253	Pte	South	Arthur James
31282	Pte	Darby	Richard
31304	Pte	Smith	William Edward
31428	Pte	Chimes	James Henry
31449	Pte	Thorpe	Henry Dexter
31471	Pte	Butters	Harold
31544	Pte	Scrimshaw	Thomas
31598	Pte	Matthews	Alfred
31615	Pte	Barnes	William Percy
31756	Pte	Dovey	Edward Isaac
31779	Pte	Slack	Samuel
31784	Pte	Rickett	James
31869	Pte	Williams	Herbert
31879	Pte	Carter	John
31911	Pte	Brough	James
31916	Pte	Potts	Henry
32007	Pte	Berresford	Frederick William
32034	Pte	Hannah	Thomas James
32160	Pte	Sleight	Alfred
32209	Pte	Cartlidge	Norman
32250	Pte	Prince	Samuel
32279	Pte	Spencer	Hubert
32323	Pte	Johnson	Wilfred
32370	Pte	Draper	Albert
32485	Pte	Davis	John Esmond
32589	Cpl	Beeson	John Henry
32636	Pte	Watts	William
32640	Pte	Bown	Samuel
32697	Pte	Smith	George
32712	L/Sgt	Stainton	William
32746	Pte	Lambert	William
32812	Pte	Johnson	Robert
32903	Pte	Thompson	Joseph
32984	Pte	Hughes	Harry
33034	Pte	Hall	Frederick
33463	Pte	Smith	William Henry
35455	Pte	Venning	Edward
35471	Pte	Scriven	Ernest
35615	Pte	Knight	Albert
35646	Pte	Bryan	John Thomas Cecil

Number	Rank	Surname	Given name
35650	Pte	Hunt	John
35652	Pte	Nix	Robert
35729	Pte	McElroy	Edward
35764	Pte	Crouch	Charles
35779	Pte	Blockley	Albert
35788	Pte	Smith	Harold Eric
35870	Pte	Wild	Arthur
35932	Pte	Crow	Moses
35937	Pte	Jenkinson	George Richard
36023	Pte	Whittaker	Charles Henry
36026	Pte	Hewitt	Harry
36066	Pte	March	Walter Henry
36070	Pte	Titley	Ernest George
36172	Pte	Frearson	Charles Henry
36212	Pte	Frow	Ernest
36338	L/Cpl	Southerill	Ernest Harold
36348	Pte	Fowers	William
36351	Pte	Gaskin	Frederick
36421	Pte	Wallace	Wilfred
36515	L/Cpl	Hinds	Frederick Herbert
37434	Pte	Grice	Alfred George
37464	Pte	Proctor	William
38034	Pte	Walker	Ernest John
38195	Pte	Stanton	Herbert
39044	Sgt	Broadhurst	Albert Edward
40376	Pte	Wall	Samuel
41219	Pte	Humberstone	Arthur
41282	Pte	Buxton	Edgar
41297	Pte	Griffin	Patrick
41412	Pte	Matsell	Arthur
41537	Pte	Twigg	Albert
41740	Pte	Booth	John Henry
41886	L/Cpl	Fisher	Arthur
41888	Pte	Powell	Samuel
41982	Pte	Yeomans	William Francis
41993	Pte	Maxwell	William Ernest
42189	Pte	Chadwick	Arthur
42190	Pte	Faulkener	Thomas
42338	Pte	Green	William Barber
42768	Pte	Gregory	Harry
42836	Pte	Clay	William
43066	Pte	Whitney	Arthur
43289	Pte	Bailey	John
43700	Pte	Miller	Bertie Edward
43701	Pte	Wallis	William Boyes
43821	Sgt	Girling	Clarence
43953	Pte	Tilbrook	Arthur George
45273	Pte	Thornhill	John
45375	L/Cpl	Brasher	Joseph Horace
45379	Pte	Hickinbottom	Walter Henry
45381	Pte	Coope	John
45387	L/Cpl	Warren	John George
45460	Pte	Hanson	Francis William

Number	Rank	Surname	Given name
45581	Pte	Brailsford	Walter
45695	Pte	Scott	John William
45704	Pte	Palmer	Alfred
45748	Pte	Jackson	George
45757	Pte	Peat	Richard
45841	Pte	Fox	Harold Kilburn
45842	Pte	Worthington	John William
45933	Pte	Sibson	George Frederick
46204	Pte	Smith	Wilfred
46210	Pte	Holmes	Arthur Henry
46244	Pte	Finney	Frank
46251	Pte	Hanson	George William
46350	Pte	Brownlee	John Thomas
46607	Pte	Harrison	Ernest Arnold
46787	Pte	Farrell	William Henry
46951	Pte	Slater	Frederick
47626	Pte	Stewart	George
47720	Pte	Spencer	Edgar
47915	Pte	Dyas	Richard
49169	Pte	Eyre	John
49178	L/Cpl	Riley	Thomas
49261	Pte	Shaw	Harry
49314	Pte	Wiggin	Thomas A
49340	Pte	Hart	Albert Ernest
49361	Pte	Robertson	Thomas George
49397	Pte	Cope	Reuben Ernest
49462	Pte	Poxon	Fred
49513	Pte	Skerritt	Henry Howard
49552	Pte	Hooson	James Frederick
49850	Pte	Picksley	Harold
50141	Pte	Parr	Benjamin
50333	Pte	James	Alma
50544	Pte	Fletcher	Walter
50568	Pte	Baines	Joshua
50576	Pte	Mills	George
50619	Pte	Dent	Harry
51314	Pte	Keene	Alexander Henry
51347	Pte	Woodward	Alfred
51438	Pte	Sprowell	Thomas Arthur
51535	Pte	Land	John William
51664	Pte	Strickson	Harry
51831	Pte	Masters	Ina
51879	Pte	Lacy	Walter
51881	Pte	Hannaford	John
51951	Pte	Gibson	George
51957	Pte	Clark	William
51967	Pte	Torn	Edward Wootton
51970	Pte	Parkin	John William
51975	Pte	Taylor	Bert
51978	Pte	Stanney	John William
52182	Pte	Parker	Ingram
52229	Pte	Bootey	Birkett Carr
52230	Pte	Slater	William Henry

Number	Rank	Surname	Given name
52247	Pte	Brown	Alexander
52251	Pte	Raymor	Frederick Anthony
52456	Pte	Henstock	Charles William
52499	Pte	King	Charles
53262	Pte	Ellerby	James
53384	Pte	Skidmore	Charles John
53498	Pte	Hill	Fred
53587	Pte	Clarke	Harry
53592	Pte	Brooks	Arthur
53660	Pte	Raynor	Harry
53708	Cpl	Humberstone	Arthur
54293	Sgt	Scott	William Ernest
54374	Pte	Stokes	William Henry
54558	Pte	Wright	Arthur Samuel
54868	Pte	Richmond	Henry Percy
54959	Pte	Pratt	Benjamin
54962	Pte	Sawyer	Edward
55465	Pte	White	Charles
55997	Pte	Haynes	Robert
56000	Pte	Inger	Frederick William
56412	Pte	Andrews	James
56416	Pte	Beeby	John
56418	Pte	Sweet	Walter
56423	Pte	Towle	Arthur
56463	Pte	Stead	Sam
56523	Cpl	Ingers	William
56717	Pte	Robinson	William Richard
56722	Pte	Foulkes	Albert
57110	Pte	Elliott	Frederick
57113	Pte	Granger	Francis Albert
57229	Pte	Harker	Eli
57234	Pte	Cox	Ernest
57244	Pte	Watson	John William
57247	Pte	Shaw	Ernest James
57272	Pte	Parkin	Wilfred Wayne
57282	Pte	Self	Charles
57283	Pte	Wright	Joseph
57284	Pte	Fells	William Ernest
57299	Pte	Redfearn	Samuel
57500	Pte	Sadler	Thomas
57836	Pte	Hudson	Charles
58088	Pte	Sketchley	Frederick Henry
58403	Pte	Gretton	Arthur
58991	Pte	Cooling	Arthur
59171	Pte	Robinson	Arthur
59455	Pte	Holland	Horace
59572	Cpl	Smith	Enoch Stanley
59731	Pte	Lomas	Thomas
59769	Pte	Thompson	Cecil
59806	Cpl	Roper	Ernest Edward
59913	Pte	Campbell	Donald
59930	Pte	Small	Charles
60010	Pte	Ward	George William
60033	Pte	Reals	Harry Brentnall
60100	Cpl	Mellar	Cecil George
60172	Pte	Walmsley	Frank
60284	Pte	Mead	Lewis Harry
60314	Cpl	Burke	Luke
60353	Pte	Bates	Victor
60402	Pte	Britton	Harold
60439	Pte	Burton	Horace
60440	Pte	Slater	John Charles
60674	Cpl	Turner	William
60738	Pte	Newton	Ernest
60747	Pte	Thornhill	Charles
60990	Pte	White	George Edward Seagrave
61005	Pte	Rowley	Arthur
61042	Pte	Slater	William
61045	Pte	Herson	Edward
61111	Pte	Walker	Alfred Henry
61176	Pte	Widdowson	Raymond
61429	Pte	Watson	Cyril Frederick
61441	Pte	Watson	Albert Edward
61482	Pte	Scragg	Joseph
61531	Pte	Widdowson	George Arthur
61537	Pte	Sherratt	John
61560	Pte	Scatterwood	Ernest Charles
61772	Pte	Dilkes	Frederick
64358	Pte	Keeton	Thomas
64534	Pte	Eyre	George
64565	Pte	Gladwin	Frank Albert
64614	Pte	Roe	Herbert
64618	Pte	Edwards	William Arthur
64688	Pte	Thorpe	Horace
64701	Pte	Glenn	Edwin James
65005	Pte	Downs	Gilbert
65007	Pte	Judson	Arthur
65013	Pte	Taylor	Fred
65014	Pte	Walter	Felix Alfred
65017	Sgt	May	Arthur
65018	Sgt	Barnes	Charles
65844	Pte	Hemsley	Thomas Reginald
67637	Pte	Waind	David Randolph
68053	Pte	Bowler	Arthur
69021	Pte	Broughton	Alfred Thomas
69029	Cpl	Glaves	Albert
69032	Cpl	Hodgkins	Edgar Hewitt
69034	Pte	Knight	Walter
69036	Pte	Marshall	Raymond
69038	Pte	Rees	John Mansell
69041	L/Cpl	Town	Frank
69046	Pte	Smith	William
69584	Pte	Gowers	Frederick William
70122	Pte	Gray	Robert Wickenden
70133	Pte	Hunt	Claude Cyril
70164	Pte	Chapman	Robert

Number	Rank	Surname	Given name
70230	Pte	Cory	John Reginald
70245	Pte	Harn	Ernest Victor
70254	Pte	Jennings	Henry Frank
70267	Pte	Oddey	Charley
70273	Pte	Raven	Arthur
70370	Cpl	Stallard	Shirley
70382	Pte	Winney	Alfred
70475	Pte	Parry	John
70506	Pte	Partridge	George Henry
70683	Pte	Prince	Leonard
70700	Sgt	Battersby	Joseph Edgar
70701	Pte	Wingfield	Harry Braithwait
70762	Pte	Williamson	Wallace
70795	Pte	Flindall	Edgar
70797	Pte	Cooper	Leonard
70799	Pte	White	Sidney
70800	Pte	Astle	George William
70801	Pte	Millward	Frederick John
70803	Pte	Bestwick	James
70804	Pte	Joel	Archie
70805	Pte	Knill	Richard
70806	Pte	Phillips	Harold
70807	Pte	Palmer	George Herbert
70808	Pte	Everitt	Walter James
70809	Sgt	Upton	Walter
70810	Pte	Burrows	Herbert
70811	Pte	Budding	Alfred
70814	Pte	Millott	Charles George
70816	Pte	Holmes	Ernest Suter
70817	Pte	Ball	John
70818	Pte	Palmer	William
70819	Pte	Copley	George William
70820	L/Cpl	Squires	Thomas
70823	Cpl	Holbery	Harold
70824	Pte	Hobson	Albert
70825	Pte	Godson	Jonathan
70826	Pte	Herring	John Joseph
70827	Pte	Parkes	Walter
70828	Pte	Pearson	Claude W
70829	Pte	Round	Robert
70830	Pte	Bellamy	Thomas Frederick
70831	Pte	Line	Sidney Albert
70834	Pte	Robinson	Leslie Blanc
70835	Pte	Thrale	Claude
70837	Pte	Hill	George
70840	Pte	Adams	George
70842	Pte	Boulger	Thomas Herbert
70843	Pte	Gwyther	Edwin Thomas
70845	Pte	Mallen	George Henry
70846	Pte	Madeley	Henry Cecil
70847	Pte	Portlock	Walter William
70848	Pte	Oseland	Arthur
70849	Pte	Sanders	Frederick Henry
70850	Pte	Wright	Victor
70851	Pte	Dodd	Fred
70853	Pte	Hill	John Timothy
70854	Pte	Hill	Harold Arthur
70855	Sgt	Bowen	Francis
70856	Pte	Swingler	Francis James
70858	Pte	Thornton	Ephraim
70859	L/Cpl	Barton	Samuel
70861	Pte	Bishop	Frederick
70862	Pte	Bailey	Samuel
70863	Pte	Butler	John William
70865	Pte	Butters	John William
70866	Pte	Butler	Horace Marshall
70868	Pte	Bowen	William Henry
70869	Pte	Brumby	Edward Jason
70870	Pte	Clark	Alfred
70871	Pte	Crawford	Tom Barrett
70872	Pte	Cutler	Arthur
70873	Pte	Carlile	Thomas
70876	Pte	Gillings	Charles Edward
70877	Pte	Hickman	Thomas Charles
70878	Pte	Heanicon	Thomas
70879	Pte	Hickling	Charles
70880	Pte	Jukes	John
70881	Pte	Kendall	Harry Braithwait
70882	Pte	Kennedy	Henry
70883	Pte	Lloyd	William James
70884	Pte	Lloyd	Arthur
70885	Pte	Lingard	Harry Firth
70886	Pte	Larder	Tom
70887	Pte	Lewis	Charles
70888	Pte	Mears	Gersham Ernest
70889	Pte	Mowbray	Bertie Wilson
70890	Pte	Mason	John Thomas
70891	Pte	Mountain	Herbert Charles
70892	Pte	Merrick	Alfred
70893	Pte	Pinson	Joseph
70895	Pte	Procter	Walter James
70896	Pte	Robinson	Henry James
70898	Pte	Truss	James William
70900	Pte	Weston	William
70901	Pte	Wardle	Herbert
70903	Pte	Willey	Daniel
70905	Pte	Whistance	William
70906	Pte	Wright	Leonard
70907	Pte	Anderson	Alfred John
70908	Pte	Armshaw	Edward John
70909	Pte	Bee	John William
70909	Cpl	Betts	Wilfred
70910	Cpl	Barrett	Charles
70911	Pte	Blakey	Harry
70912	Pte	Bell	Fred
70913	Pte	Bush	Albert

Number	Rank	Surname	Given name
70914	Pte	Bailey	William Edward
70918	Pte	Ganderton	George
70919	Pte	Gilbert	John Henry
70920	Pte	Glover	Herbert
70921	Pte	Grantham	William
70922	Pte	Goodall	John
70923	Pte	Hardy	Arthur Alfred
70924	Pte	Holden	Horace
70925	Pte	Hollins	William
70926	Pte	Hogg	Thomas William
70927	Pte	Holmes	Harry
70928	Pte	Harris	James
70931	Pte	Kirkman	Walter
70933	Pte	Mills	Benjamin
70934	Pte	Needham	Reginald
70936	Pte	Parish	Robert
70937	Pte	Post	William Frederick
70938	Pte	Price	Charles
70939	Pte	Rouse	George William
70942	Pte	Sullivan	Joseph
70943	Pte	Simpson	Victor Hugh
70944	Pte	Singleton	John Henry
70946	Pte	Taylor	Walter
70947	Pte	Tomblin	Edgar Joseph
70948	Pte	Weldon	Ernest
70949	Pte	Webster	Arthur
70950	Pte	Wheatley	Ernest
70952	Pte	Shaw	Harry
70954	Sgt	Lowbridge	William Henry
70956	Pte	Gamble	James Alfred
70957	Pte	Grace	Sidney Albert
70958	Pte	Tailby	William Henry
70959	Pte	Wright	John Teear
70960	Pte	Walker	Herbert Watson
70962	Pte	Bates	William Edward
70963	Pte	Cranwell	Newman
70964	Pte	Colkin	William
70965	Pte	Clowes	Alfred
70966	Pte	Dunkley	Albert
70967	Pte	Hubbard	Arthur Henry
70968	Pte	Spence	James
70970	Pte	Blackwell	Charles Ernest
70972	Pte	Butler	Charles Cyril
70974	Pte	Gardner	Francis Frederick William
70975	Pte	Gamble	Albert
70976	Pte	Hartshorne	Ernest
70979	Pte	Thurman	Thomas
70980	Pte	Butt	Henry James
70981	Pte	Blenkiron	George William
70982	Pte	Dixon	Frederick John
70985	Pte	Mawbey	Harry
70986	Pte	Quincey	Herbert
70987	Pte	Shilaker	Arthur

Number	Rank	Surname	Given name
70988	Pte	Shipman	John Clarence
70989	Pte	Taylor	Harold Duncan
70991	Pte	Sutton	Albert Hardy
70992	Pte	Smith	Allan
70993	Pte	Wells	Joseph
70994	Pte	Brown	Charles Henry
70995	Pte	Scotney	Arthur
70996	Cpl	Williams	William Frank Herbert
70997	Pte	Bell	Samuel
70999	Pte	Austin	Thomas Samuel
71000	Pte	Veasey	Albert
71001	Pte	Weston	Edgar
71002	Pte	Bayliss	Walter
71003	Pte	Clarke	George Harry
71004	Pte	Hilton	Arthur
71007	Pte	Glass	George
71008	Sgt	Herbert	Walter
71011	Pte	Pratt	Herbert
71012	Pte	White	Harry
71013	Pte	Hutt	Albert
71014	Pte	Kidger	Ernest
71015	Pte	Cockeril	Herbert William
71016	Pte	Eaton	Albert Joseph
71017	Pte	Freer	Gordon
71018	L/Cpl	Weston	George
71020	Pte	Bowen	Charles Albert
71021	Pte	Brown	Charley
71022	Pte	Barker	William
71023	Pte	Beecham	John
71025	Pte	Hodges	Ernest William
71028	Pte	McAusland	Robert
71029	Pte	Marshall	Edgar
71030	Pte	Marsden	Thomas
71031	Pte	Perry	Henry Joseph
71033	Pte	Smith	Fred
71035	Pte	Toplis	James
71036	Pte	Wood	John William
71037	Pte	Watts	Robert
71038	Pte	Watts	John Thomas
71040	Pte	Brown	Austin Samuel
71041	Sgt	Swindell	Bernard
71042	Pte	Nicholson	William
71043	Sgt	Burgess	James Herbert John
71045	Pte	Bradley	Walter
71046	Cpl	Clarke	Albert
71047	Pte	Baker	Joseph Claude
71049	Pte	Bishop	John
71050	Pte	Bunker	Harry Herbert
71051	Pte	Berbank	Albert Edward
71052	Pte	Coleman	Arthur George
71053	Pte	Crow	Henry Stevenson
71058	Pte	Margetts	Bertie
71059	Pte	Oakland	Nathan

Number	Rank	Surname	Given name
71060	L/Cpl	Pascoe	James
71065	Pte	Veres	Lance
71066	Pte	Summers	Walter
71067	Pte	Bamford	Frederick Henry
71068	Pte	Fisher	Jesse William
71070	Pte	Alexander	William Richard
71073	Sgt	Watts	Charles
71075	Sgt	Potts	John
71092	Pte	Powell	Albert Edward
71129	Pte	Birch	Arthur
71414	Pte	Keeble	Percy Edward
71492	Pte	Cockerill	George Nesterfield
71500	Pte	Downing	Harry
71524	Pte	Holmes	John
71549	Pte	Wennington	Alfred
71568	Pte	Gallagher	James
71574	Pte	Smyth	John Herbert
71579	Cpl	Walker	Claude
71920	Cpl	Tipping	James
71959	Pte	Eastgate	Fred
72161	Pte	Pye	George James
72164	Pte	Mendi	Joe
72165	Pte	Opie	William John
72170	Pte	Strank	Arthur
72171	Pte	Steele	Alfred
72184	Pte	Illes	James
72191	Pte	Thomson	Frederick George
72196	Pte	Smith	Charles Thomas
72295	Pte	Dunn	Vivian Gordon
72544	Pte	Jones	Herbert
72550	Pte	Smith	Herbert
72552	Pte	Bain	George
72555	Pte	Thomas	Howard William
72558	Pte	Head	George
72569	Cpl	Schofield	Charles
72581	Pte	Porter	Albert
72583	Pte	Ash	Arthur
72603	Pte	Shelley	Frederick Benjamin
72608	Cpl	Bishop	Wilfred Malcolm Evans
72616	Pte	Barnes	Frank Lawrence
72620	Pte	Gibson	George William
72623	Pte	Smith	George Joshua
72978	Pte	Ella	Thomas Andrew
73024	Pte	Gardner	William
73037	Pte	Dale	William John
73055	Pte	Zolowski	Ephraim
73064	Pte	Allcott	Joseph
73078	Pte	Cox	Edwin
73111	Pte	Jones	Thomas
73139	Pte	Micklewright	Noah
73390	Pte	Tyler	Arthur
73410	Pte	Pownall	Fred
73411	Pte	Redington	Arthur
73454	Pte	Curwood	Albert Ernest
73465	Pte	Eyre	Wilfred
73479	Pte	Kibble	Horace Percy
73485	Pte	Allum	Joseph William
73491	Pte	Blackman	William
73887	Pte	Foskett	John Thomas
73888	Pte	Gay	Edward
73889	Pte	Huband	Herbert Robert
73890	Pte	Hawkins	William Charles
73891	Pte	McLoughlin	Thomas
74311	Pte	Maris	Alfred
74368	L/Sgt	Allen	Herbert Arthur
74375	Pte	Norman	Charlie
76217	Pte	Mason	George
76222	Pte	Miller	Robert
76223	Pte	Moir	James
76224	Pte	McCraith	John
76226	Pte	Murray	Stanley William
76227	Pte	McDonald	John
76234	Pte	McCormack	Johnson
76238	Cpl	McNeill	Angus Mccoll
76261	Pte	McFarlane	Francis Binnie
76262	Cpl	Mair	William Henry Gullan
76263	Pte	McNicoll	James Waterson
76264	Pte	McDougall	Thomas Matthew
76265	Pte	McKenzie	Charles
76267	Pte	McNeill	Robert
76271	Pte	Nicoll	William Lindsay
76277	Pte	Plowman	John
76284	Pte	Rae	Charles Adam
76321	Pte	Porter	John
76329	Pte	Westwater	James Stewart
76330	Pte	Watt	Robert
76332	Pte	Weir	Alexander
76334	Pte	Watt	Alex
76335	Pte	Walker	Robert
76344	Pte	Young	Edgar
76345	Pte	Young	Peter
76347	Pte	Young	George
76384	Pte	Fisher	Walter Gerald
76396	Pte	Henley	William Frank
76398	Pte	Hampson	Thomas G
76853	Pte	Turner	Hollis William
78221	Pte	Earle	G A
78934	Pte	Kershaw	Farewell
79095	Pte	Pretty	Edwin Henry
79429	Pte	Wilson	Cyril
79657	Pte	Jones	Sydney
79673	L/Cpl	Buxton	Frederick Henry
79823	Pte	Perkins	William Henry
80247	Pte	Cooknell	Thomas
80415	Pte	Dove	Charles
80513	Pte	Wardley	Ernest

Number	Rank	Surname	Given name
80830	Pte	Oldham	Belton
80892	Pte	West	Thomas
81022	Pte	Watts	Arthur
81406	Pte	Scott	Albert Victor
81525	Pte	Ainsworth	Victor Albert
81533	Pte	Ward	Frank
81570	Pte	Taylor	Ernest
81583	Pte	Pask	Joseph William
81741	Pte	Turner	Ernest
81743	Pte	Henson	Harry
81808	Pte	Elliott	Thomas Reginald
81809	Pte	Ward	James
81817	Pte	Wilson	William Foster
81831	L/Cpl	Lilley	Arthur
81854	Pte	Eaton	Wilfred B
81856	Pte	Green	Benjamin
81983	Pte	Wainwright	James Wilton
82081	Pte	Spencer	Ernest
82104	Pte	Crossley	Fred
82114	Pte	Bartle	Jonathan Henry
82147	Pte	Smith	James
82755	Pte	Illsley	Charles Arthur
82816	Pte	Clarke	Arthur
82927	Pte	Bates	Walter Frank
83330	Pte	Hunt	Henry
83344	Pte	Binks	Charles Mortimer
83527	Pte	Davies	John
83536	Pte	Moore	George
83546	Pte	Spencer	Arthur John
83624	Pte	Burgess	Arthur
83798	Pte	Jackson	Herbert
83963	Pte	Faulks	William Arthur
84021	Pte	Gibson	Arthur North
84022	Pte	Kirkham	William Henry
84023	Pte	Shuttleworth	James Thomas
84026	Pte	Hill	John William
84027	Pte	Attenborough	William
84029	Pte	Carver	Eli
84030	Pte	Riley	Samuel
84031	Pte	Ball	Harold
85240	Pte	Turney	George
85264	Pte	Stokes	Jesse
85820	Pte	Oldham	William Wilmot
86020	Pte	Taylor	Charles William
86183	Pte	Sharpe	Alfred
86321	Pte	Howitt	John Robert
86342	Pte	Simpson	Wilfred
86391	Pte	Patrick	John Thomas
86392	Pte	Barton	Henry
86393	Pte	Brown	Thomas
86396	Pte	Watson	Harry
86401	Pte	Skerritt	Alexandra
86406	Pte	Matkin	Joseph

Number	Rank	Surname	Given name
86407	Pte	Walker	Harry
86411	Pte	Clayton	John William
86412	Pte	Widdowson	Edward
86420	Pte	Moorley	Herbert William
86426	Pte	Wood	Frank
86428	Pte	Kirk	Charles
86466	Pte	Johnson	Albert
86472	Pte	Fowkes	Samuel
86495	Pte	Walters	Donald
86518	Pte	Green	John
86535	Pte	Allport	Joseph
86546	Pte	Spencer	Sydney
86883	Pte	Walker	John
87039	Pte	Staton	Arthur
87119	Pte	Richards	Jesse
87133	Pte	Wilkinson	Percy
87711	Pte	Smith	George William
87908	Pte	Peadon	Walter Richmond
89183	Pte	Oxley	Cecil
90002	Cpl	Street	Harry
90003	Cpl	Tempess	Henry Brown
90004	Sgt	Gamble	William
90005	Cpl	Shackleton	Henry
90006	Sgt	Huddlestone	Charles
90007	Sgt	Banton	Thomas
90792	Pte	Rogers	Thomas William
91545	Pte	Jones	Samuel
91558	Pte	Tombs	William
91703	Pte	Truman	Herbert
92088	Pte	Butler	Frederick
92092	Pte	Dower	Edward James
92111	Pte	McCallum	Arthur Frederick
92125	Pte	Brunger	Charles James
92127	Pte	Cox	Sidney Francis
92130	Pte	Bannister	George William
92137	Pte	Camm	Arthur
92139	Pte	Carter	John Herbert Charlesworth
92141	Cpl	Firth	Lewis Jervis
92142	Pte	Drake	Henry
92144	Pte	Hudson	Richard
92149	Pte	Metcalfe	George Henry
92157	Pte	Ison	Smith
92165	Pte	Griffin	Daniel
92170	Pte	Hill	George Anthony
92171	Pte	O'Brien	John
92172	Pte	Preston	Arthur
92173	Pte	Rowell	Richard
92176	Pte	Allen	Henry
92178	Pte	Evans	Arthur William
92179	Pte	Fleming	Teddy
92180	Pte	Heal	Frederick
92181	Pte	Humble	Arthur Beighton
92188	Pte	Bullock	Thomas Edward

Number	Rank	Surname	Given name
92190	Pte	Cooper	Harry
92192	Pte	Coan	John
92196	Pte	Howells	Willie George
92198	Pte	Morris	Joseph
92209	Pte	Thompson	Joseph
92210	Pte	Hinton	Albert
92214	Pte	Morgan	William Alfred
92219	Pte	Parker	Fred
92223	Pte	Clarke	John Charles
92224	Pte	Clark	Joseph Osman
92225	Pte	Cape	James Willie
92226	Pte	Kellett	George
92231	Pte	Goodfellow	Ernest
92238	Pte	Birdsall	Frank
92241	Pte	Aitken	Thomas
92244	Pte	McFarlane	Robert
92248	Pte	Proud	John Edward
92250	Pte	Macrow	George Frederick
92254	Pte	Adley	Thomas James
92256	Pte	Davison	Harry
92258	Pte	Argent	Herbert Edward
92261	Pte	Lannen	John Marshall
92262	Pte	Smith	Henry
92264	Pte	Locke	Edward
92265	Pte	Wilkes	Richard Nichols
92266	Pte	Nicoll	Herbert George
92267	Pte	Smales	Lewis Henry
92268	Pte	Rodgers	Thomas Frederick
92269	Pte	Brown	Robert Oswald
92271	Pte	Berry	James
92329	Pte	Rooke	John Henry
92340	Pte	Temple	Henry
92343	Pte	Thrush	John Willie
92350	Pte	Rawding	George
92419	Sgt	Royston	Allan
92423	C/Sgt	Skoyles	Stephen William
92424	Sgt	Turner	William
92853	Pte	Cook	John
92949	Pte	Fowler	Charles Edward
93719	Pte	Venables	Ernest
93756	Pte	Thorneloe	Ernest Charles
94001	WOC2	Evans	David Williams
94006	Pte	Arnold	Cecil Sydney George
94009	Pte	Collett	Cecil James
94011	Pte	York	Lionel James Thomas
94013	Pte	Jay	Arthur Edward
94014	Pte	Lewis	Harry Penton
94428	Pte	Henry	Frederick
95439	Pte	Hunt	Walter Merrills
95468	Pte	Harris	Thomas
95548	Pte	Robinson	Harry
95610	Pte	Lennard	William
95642	Pte	Yates	Charles
95900	L/Sgt	Jordan	Frederick John
95922	Pte	Condliffe	Harry
95930	Pte	Ellerby	Arthur
95953	Pte	Rooker	Arthur
95956	Pte	Robert	Richard
96117	Pte	Brown	William
97046	Cpl	Gregory	Fred
97328	Pte	Winfield	Gilbert
97346	Pte	Townsley	Arthur Willie
97365	Pte	Whitfield	John Edward
97888	Pte	Clarke	John
97965	Pte	Rusholme	Benjamin
98594	Pte	Longley	William
99779	Pte	Watson	Walter
100001	Sgt	Johnson	Stephen
102249	Pte	Whitehead	William
102468	Pte	Boag	Alexander Albert
102503	Pte	Sortwell	Edwin Charles
102531	Pte	Novis	Charles William
102588	Pte	Woolger	Ernest
102640	Pte	Last	Bert
102669	Pte	Bartholomew	Charles
102699	Pte	Fuller	Robert Edward Charles
102755	Pte	Morrison	William Arthur
103675	Pte	Rouse	Charles William
103743	WOC2	Sales	Edward
103762	Pte	Whibley	Leslie Edward
104120	Cpl	Buckton	Thomas Newton
106056	Pte	Baker	George William
106060	L/Cpl	Cordiner	Andrew Victor
106089	Pte	Fenton	George
106113	Pte	Ainslie	Frederick Henry
106120	Pte	Abbott	John William
106901	Pte	Sillitoe	Sydney Nigel
107337	Pte	Sugden	Frederick Ellis
107343	Pte	Thomas	Simeon
107364	Pte	Wilkinson	William
108435	Cpl	Sperring	Arthur Henry
108576	Pte	Grant	Thomas Alfred
116234	Pte	Barnes	William Joseph
117336	Pte	Driver	George William
117551	L/Cpl	Belshaw	George Edwin
117932	Pte	Cooper	Isaac
118429	Pte	Blackburn	Fred
118666	Pte	Barnes	Albert Ernest Lionel
119505	Pte	Barfield	John Robert
119673	Pte	Allcock	Cyril
119816	Pte	Bosworth	Herbert Henry
119835	Pte	Cocker	Edgar
119919	Pte	Webster	William
119925	Pte	Ainsley	John George
120192	Pte	Carr	Ralph
120242	Pte	Wade	William Francis

Number	Rank	Surname	Given name
120260	Pte	Collard	Cyril
120272	Pte	Webster	Benjamin Sextile
120306	Pte	Brunt	Frederick William
120363	Pte	Boot	Harold Wilson
120365	Pte	Barker	Allan Barlow
120399	Pte	Dawson	Ewart Gladstone
120402	Pte	Allcock	John Sydney
120444	Pte	Cundy	Albert Arthur
120445	Pte	Betts	Samuel
120481	Pte	Brealey	Samuel Leslie
120489	Pte	Allen	Herbert
120490	Pte	Elliott	William Thomas
120492	Pte	Barson	William Horace
120502	Pte	Bates	George William
120509	Pte	Calladine	Joseph Alfred
120511	Pte	Cultman	John Alfred
120539	Pte	Clarke	James William
120544	Pte	Breedon	George
120547	Pte	Brooks	Lorenzo
120557	Pte	Davies	John William
120583	Pte	Daykin	Arthur
120748	Pte	Toach	James
120799	Pte	Bartelt	Charles
120869	Pte	Drury	Sam
120881	Pte	Buxton	John James
120901	Pte	Clark	William
121343	Pte	Emerton	John
121977	Pte	Taylor	Thomas
122112	Cpl	Walters	James
122138	Pte	Taylor	William
122178	Pte	Barnett	Ernest
122193	Pte	Attenborough	John James
122238	Pte	Ramsdale	Fred
122302	Pte	Kemp	John
122335	Pte	Stanley	Luke
122337	Pte	Marsh	James
122357	Pte	Lamb	James
122358	Pte	Hart	John
122358	Pte	Cook	William Edward
122388	Pte	Bird	Jesse
123435	Cpl	Davison	Armine
123869	Pte	Metcalfe	James Henry
123878	Pte	Jackson	Percy
124592	Pte	McColgan	Thomas
124633	L/Sgt	Webb	Samuel John
124639	Pte	Willis	George
124828	Pte	Chambers	John
124847	Cpl	Middleton	Jack
124853	Cpl	Pell	Albert Edward
124857	Cpl	Booth	Matthew Sheriff
124860	Pte	Taggart	Arthur
124921	Pte	Smith	George
124928	Pte	West	Sydney Ernest

Number	Rank	Surname	Given name
124930	Pte	Lang	George Leonard
124931	Pte	Burton	John Bernard
124933	Pte	Miller	William
124939	Pte	Twigg	Frederick William
124940	Pte	Annable	Thomas
124943	Pte	Kidd	William
124944	Pte	Sadler	James
124947	Pte	Murray	John William
124952	L/Sgt	Pickstone	Charles Richard
124970	Pte	Baker	Albert Edward
124975	Pte	Bellamy	Herbert
124977	L./Cpl	Cotes	Charles
125020	Pte	Blatherwick	John
125094	Pte	Beat	George
125095	Pte	Barrett	John Wilson
125096	Pte	Binns	Frank
125117	L/Sgt	White	Walter Richard
125139	WOC2	Lawrence	Albert Edward
125140	Sgt	Conduit	Arthur Whitt
125141	C/Sgt	Hunt	William
125142	Cpl	Woodward	Henry
125144	Sgt	Bailey	Abraham
125149	Pte	Staples	Albert
125157	Pte	Coulbeck	John
125173	Pte	Dawson	John Edward
125183	Sgt	Matthews	Charles
125244	Pte	Hutson	George
125250	Pte	Ward	William
125301	Pte	Allsopp	Wallace
125325	Pte	Riley	William
125355	Pte	Ranford	Albert
126125	Cpl	Fretwell	Allan
126146	Pte	Hall	Sidney Arthur
126186	Pte	O'Brien	Walter
127010	Pte	Turner	Thomas
127018	Pte	Buck	John
127087	2nd A.m.	Twigg	Henry
127126	Pte	Flint	John
127175	Pte	Perry	Richard
198577	Pte	Smurthwaite	Arnold
200199	Pte	Rockley	Arthur
200349	Pte	Hall	Hedley
200946	Pte	Staley	Thomas
201045	Pte	Bird	Alfred
201058	Pte	Wren	Thomas
201081	Pte	Bellamy	George
201099	L/Cpl	Jackson	Joseph
201136	Pte	Smedley	Harold Archer
201173	Cpl	Gaskin	Lawrence Cecil
201208	Pte	Powell	Jacob
201863	Pte	Harrison	Edward
201984	Pte	Wilson	Alfred
201999	Sgt	Taylor	John Allen

Number	Rank	Surname	Given name
202027	Pte	Warden	Richard Samuel
202064	Pte	Herbert	Walter
202240	Pte	Jack	Thomas Stirling
202351	Pte	Parish	Fred
202400	Pte	Midgley	Walter
202466	Sgt	Reader	Thomas
202596	Cpl	Luke	Joseph
202597	Pte	Rice	Joseph
202619	Pte	Hollenshead	Oliver
202666	L/Cpl	Brown	Arthur
202683	Pte	Fells	Reuben Alfred
202814	Pte	Friend	Thomas Charles
203036	Cpl	Fox	Alan Harold
203133	Pte	Kierton	Reginald
203206	Pte	Parsons	Frederick William
203334	Pte	Beaumont	John Oswald
203463	Pte	Toder	Sydney
203485	Cpl	Ashmore	Frederick
203490	Pte	Dalby	William
203494	Sgt	Holmes	George Henry
203500	Sgt	Pope	James
203543	Pte	Wyatt	Walter Freeman
203725	Pte	Dolphin	William
203832	Pte	Bradley	Arthur Cecil
204145	Pte	Rowland	Stanley
204172	L/Cpl	Mayfield	John
204358	Pte	Holmes	Percy
204396	Pte	Presland	William
204403	Pte	Shaw	Joseph
204404	Pte	Slater	Robert
204406	Pte	Hackney	Thomas
204413	Pte	Hartley	Thomas
204419	Pte	Bullin	Bernard
204422	Pte	Vickers	Charles
204423	Pte	Woodward	John
204424	Pte	Ashland	Arthur Simpson
204426	Pte	Harrison	Charles Henry
204429	Pte	Bugg	William
204430	Pte	Priestley	William Jolly
204431	Pte	Scott	Anthony
204432	Pte	Smart	Sidney John
204433	Pte	Ash	Frank Arthur
204434	Pte	Mason	Frank
204436	Pte	Reader	Albert Edward
204439	Pte	Ellis	Lewis George
204440	Pte	Clark	Harry
204441	Pte	Houseley	Bernard
204442	Pte	Williamson	John Henry
204443	Pte	Jones	Charles
204445	Pte	Case	Harry
204446	Pte	Pymm	Claude Alfred
204447	Pte	Cowley	Joseph
204449	Pte	Glossop	Frank
204453	Pte	Smith	Charles Archibald
204454	Pte	Brighouse	Leonard Arthur
204455	Pte	Jalland	Thomas
204456	Pte	Dicken	Tom
204457	Pte	Weston	Henry James
204458	Pte	Swinscoe	Thomas William
204460	Pte	Webster	Fred
204461	Pte	Hancock	Ernest
204462	Pte	Poskett	Tom
204489	Pte	Smith	Charles Daniel
204512	Pte	Letts	Harry
204578	Pte	Burnett	John William
204702	Cpl	Teasdale	William
204870	Pte	Williams	William George
235072	Pte	Earnshaw	Harry
235183	Pte	Stendall	Albert
240013	Sgt	Wilde	Thomas Henry
240574	Pte	Flint	Cyril
240654	Pte	Lomas	Cyril
240791	Pte	Jacques	Frank Leighton
241211	Pte	Breeze	George
241561	Pte	Brown	Bert William
241842	Pte	Jackson	Arthur
241942	Pte	Shaw	Harry
242225	Pte	Bland	Stanley Harold
242536	Pte	Hallam	Joseph Edward
242601	Pte	Josh	Frank Frederick
242633	Pte	Searson	George Herbert
263002	Pte	Gelsthorpe	Victor Charles
265287	Pte	Redgate	Albert
265418	Pte	Paling	John
265428	C/Sgt	Hind	George
265509	Sgt	French	John Edmund
265578	Pte	Mackintosh	Claude Henry Bertram James
265892	L/Cpl	Stokes	George
266054	Pte	Ward	William Patrick
266072	Sgt	Nowell	John
266189	L/Cpl	Lovitt	Vernon
266218	Pte	Harrison	Herbert
266716	Pte	Spencer	Edwin
267004	Pte	Pinkett	Arthur Henry
267029	Pte	Jessey	Robert Clifford
267540	Pte	Scott	George William
267556	Pte	Smith	Samuel
268047	Pte	Copping	Anthony
268247	Pte	Turner	Joseph
268412	Pte	Lomax	Thomas Leslie
268551	Pte	Warren	Samuel George
268856	Pte	Sulley	William
268985	Pte	Dickinson	George
269303	Pte	Ivins	Alfred Vincent
269332	Pte	Sheppard	Cecil Lindford
269814	Pte	Hammond	Frank Reginald

Number	Rank	Surname	Given name
269874	Pte	Athey	Harold
305030	Pte	Foster	Henry
305301	Pte	Kirkby	Alfred
305502	Pte	Smith	Arthur Ernest
305619	Pte	Chester	Graham
305667	Pte	Carlin	Cecil
305728	Pte	Glenn	John
305811	Pte	Dean	Frank
305852	Pte	Lambert	Charles William
305963	Pte	Merrin	Arthur
305968	Pte	Johnson	Albert
306105	Pte	Gibson	William
306123	Pte	Storey	George
306190	Pte	Hunt	John Henry
306288	Pte	Bradley	Robert William
306295	Pte	Baker	Arthur
306371	Pte	Herrod	Edwin
306500	Pte	Lacy	Edgar
306686	Pte	Goulding	Norman
306901	Pte	Knowles	Sydney Leslie
306992	Pte	Hepworth	James
306996	Pte	Johnson	Sydney
307044	Cpl	Wright	Harry
307064	Pte	Partridge	Joseph Henry
307079	Pte	Moon	John
307080	Pte	Peach	Samuel
307436	Pte	Morton	Ted
307614	Pte	Jones	John
325048	Pte	Thornton	Osman
330056	Pte	Hargreaves	Sidney
330195	Pte	Hadland	Edward Frank
330418	Pte	Mundell	Albert
330945	Sgt	Worrall	John
330965	WOC2	Marshall	Luke
333145	Pte	West	George
333159	Cpl	Kirkland	Joseph
333567	Pte	Sawdy	Charles Henry
333634	Pte	Shipley	Arthur
333650	Pte	Bailey	Harry
333658	Cpl	Mullins	Terence
333680	Pte	Tyers	Harold
333727	Pte	Spencer	John James
333784	Pte	Mottershead	Lawrence
333808	Pte	Kirk	John William
333816	Pte	Regan	Martin
333842	Pte	Wallis	William
333862	L/Cpl	Barker	Thomas
333915	Sgt	Truman	John George
333951	Sgt	Whelan	Frederick
333981	Pte	Lakin	William
333990	Sgt	Sage	Alfred
334037	Pte	Walker	Thomas Holmes
334041	Cpl	Smith	Harry
334075	Cpl	Lacey	Henry Thomas Smedley
334363	Pte	Gibson	Walter
334553	Pte	Kirk	Edwin
334557	Pte	Millington	Leonard
334559	Pte	White	John William
334594	Pte	Fox	Henry
334612	Pte	Barker	John
334640	Pte	Burgess	John Henry
334645	Pte	Sellers	John Samuel
334687	Pte	Smith	Frank Henry
334749	Pte	Feetham	Arthur
334809	L/Sgt	Newstead	Reginald Charles
334816	Pte	Beckett	Albert
334835	Pte	Hurst	Bertram
334852	Pte	Hayes	Edward
334853	L/Sgt	Cosgrove	Walter Charles
334913	Pte	Curtis	Isaac
334924	Pte	Pearson	Ernest
334956	Pte	Pounder	Horace Albert Victor
334965	Pte	Trout	Raymond
334973	Pte	Raynor	Thomas
335046	Pte	Watson	John Thomas
335050	Cpl	Legard	Ernest
335053	Pte	Toon	Mark
335064	Pte	Morley	Frederick
335097	Pte	Wardle	Frederick
335107	Pte	Allsopp	Herbert
335128	Cpl	Nash	Henry
335148	Cpl	Asman	Alfred
335155	L/Cpl	Baines	Albert George
335157	Sgt	Smith	Arthur Ernest
335187	Pte	Riley	Ernest Walter
335815	Sgt	Miller	Thomas
336018	WOC2	Padley	John Louis
336029	Pte	Turpie	Arthur John
336030	Sgt	Harris	James
336032	WOC2	Patrick	John
336060	Pte	Walters	Thomas
336088	C/Sgt	Murphy	Thomas James
336093	Sgt	Daley	Isaac Newton
336104	Pte	Oakes	James
336107	Pte	Malkin	Walter
336146	WOC1	Frow	John Cooke
336165	Pte	Allen	George
336203	Sgt	Burke	Thomas
336268	Sgt	Bucklow	Albert Roe
336271	Pte	Fell	Benjamin
336289	Sgt	Treece	George
336353	Sgt	Cusack	William
336402	Pte	Hewitt	George
336480	Pte	Black	Robert
336517	Pte	Ratford	Thomas
336522	Pte	Mycroft	John

Number	Rank	Surname	Given name
336584	Pte	Watson	Frederick Mark
336607	Pte	Jones	William Arthur
336730	Pte	Marriott	Frederick
336744	Sgt	Renyard	George
336774	Pte	Innis	William
336793	Pte	Johnson	John
337018	Pte	Richardson	Robert
337022	L/Cpl	Bray	William
337046	Pte	Lowe	George Henry
337095	Pte	Hill	Frank Clayton
337299	Pte	Jodrell	David Harris
337329	Pte	Kingston	Edward
337665	Pte	Thompson	John
337675	Pte	Perkins	Walter
337822	Pte	More	Albert Edward
338421	Cpl	Mitchell	Joseph
339452	Pte	Newton	Fred
339645	WOC2	Whitworth	John
339871	L/Cpl	Flowers	Frederick
6/50737	Pte	Brown	Herbert
6/54248	Pte	Bloxham	Joseph
6596	Pte	Jones	W H
42182	Pte	Wright	E V

Men moved to Labour Corps

Number	Rank	Surname
13949	Pte	York
22170	Pte	Hibbert
18900	Pte	Taylor
19018	Pte	Underhill
24328	Pte	Herring
13910	Pte	Hazzledine
18497	Pte	Shaw
12929	Pte	Morrell
20507	Pte	Fulwood
6148	Pte	Smith

A number of men have recently been proved to have served with the 9th Battalion –

Number	Rank	Surname	Given name
3981	Pte	Lakin	W
4913	Pte	Curtis	J
9966	L/Cpl	Morton.	Fred
22800	Pte	Crofts	Edward
22801	Pte	Crofts	Thomas

25007 Pte John Batchelor was with the Battalion between 13 September and 17 December 1915.

120442 Pte Joseph Ernest Bramham, 'C' Company aged 19 years died on 28.December 1918 and is listed by the CWGC as being with the 9th Battalion.

12932 Private D Hampson 9th , 1st and 17th Bns.

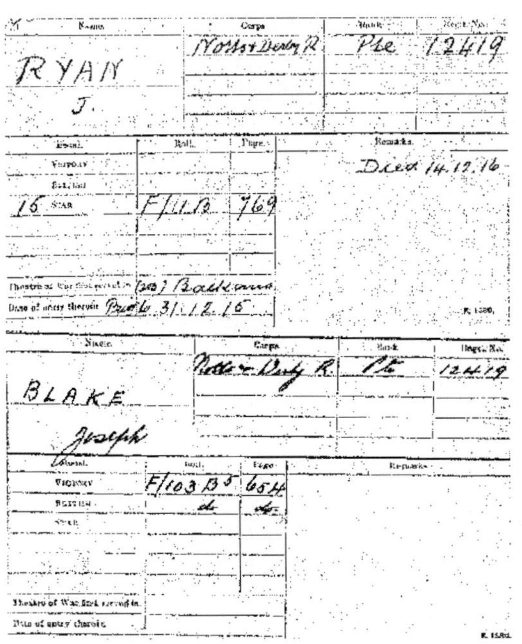
RYAN J. Notts & Derby R. Pte 12419
Died 14.12.16
15 Star F/1/B 769
(2a) Balkans
31.12.15
BLAKE Joseph Notts & Derby R. Pte 12419
Victory F/103 B3 654
British do. do.

12419 Joseph Blake –

It is possible that Joseph Blake and 12419 John Ryan are in fact the same person although research at the moment is ongoing. The Medal index cards below seem to be that of one man.

12419 J Ryan is mentioned in The Derbyshire Mercury 8th October 1915 as being wounded in Gallipoli.

Both men are listed as dying on 14 December 1916 whilst with 1st Battalion. Blake Died of Wounds and buried, Ryan as died and commemorated on the Thiepval Memorial.

Only J Blake shows as being in the 9th Battalion on the Medal Rolls.

Appendix 3

Men of the Battalion Killed in Action, Died of wounds and died August 1914 until November 1918.

Surname	Given name	Number	Rank	Date	Buried/Commemerated
Sweet	Walter	56418	Private	09/02,1917	Abbeville Comm Cem Ext
Bacon	Percy	19614	Private	26/09,1916	AIF Burial ground Flers
Calton	Edward	22511	Private	14/06,1915	Aldershot Military Cem
Buxton	Ernest	22628	Private	04/10,1915	Alexandria (Chatby) mil
Chatterton	Arthur Francis	12986	Private	25/09,1915	Alexandria (Chatby) mil
Deary	Joseph	13249	Private	27/11,1915	Alexandria (Chatby) mil
Dessaur	Myer	2902	Private	05/02,1916	Alexandria (Chatby) mil
Ford	George Henry	12502	Private	25/08,1915	Alexandria (Chatby) mil
Mills	Job	13272	Private	14/09,1915	Alexandria (Chatby) mil
Taylor	George	13066	Private	12/08,1915	Alexandria (Chatby) mil
Webster	Arthur	18090	Private	29/08,1915	Alexandria (Chatby) mil
Smedley	John	22195	Private	13/05,1916	Alexandria (Hadra) Cem
Chapman	Charles	40741	Private	08/08,1916	Arras Memorial
Clarke	Vincent	19800	Private	09/08,1916	Arras Memorial
Coulam	Herbert	40776	Private	08/08,1916	Arras Memorial
Davenport	George	19418	Private	09/08,1916	Arras Memorial
Denman	John Widdowson	12685	Sgt	03/05,1917	Arras Memorial
Finch	George	18956	Private	09/08,1916	Arras Memorial
Hayes	Colen	19677	Private	09/08,1916	Arras Memorial
Langston	Samuel	13543	Private	09/08,1916	Arras Memorial
Manderfield	Thomas	22845	Private	06/08,1916	Arras Memorial
Wheatley	William Richard	19132	Private	08/08,1916	Arras Memorial
Widdowson	George Arthur	61531	Private	03/05,1917	Arras Memorial
Wragg	William	5009	Private	09/08/1916	Arras Memorial
Wright	John Tecar	70959	Private	27/04,1918	Arras Memorial
Byfield	Isaiah	21602	Private	17/08,1917	Artillery Wood Cem
Eades	Joseph	21912	L/Cpl	16/08,1917	Artillery Wood Cem
Allen	William	22656	Private	23/09,1916	Aveluy Com Cem Ext
Smith	Norman Albert	12508	Private	31/07,1916	Avesnes-Le-Comte Comm
Bowler	Joseph	13322	Private	06/09,1915	Azmak Cemetery Suvla
Goddard	William	20320	Private	05/10,1915	Azmak Cemetery Suvla
Griffiths	Stanley	17012	Private	16/12,1915	Azmak Cemetery Suvla
Heywood	Frank	20307	Private	29/11,1915	Azmak Cemetery Suvla
Hodgkiss	Frederick William	21279	Private	06/09,1915	Azmak Cemetery Suvla
Hopkinson	John Thomas	13512	Private	17/11,1915	Azmak Cemetery Suvla
Jarvis	John	22968	Private	13/11,1915	Azmak Cemetery Suvla
Kitchen	Fred	22003	Private	14/11,1915	Azmak Cemetery Suvla
Lowe	Charles	12678	Private	29/08,1915	Azmak Cemetery Suvla
Palmer	Samuel J	22290	Private	27/11,1915	Azmak Cemetery Suvla
Sheldon	William	5061	Private	19/11,1915	Azmak Cemetery Suvla
Stocks	Joseph Henry	13155	Private	13/11,1915	Azmak Cemetery Suvla
Street	Samuel	17004	A/Cpl	29/11,1915	Azmak Cemetery Suvla
Paull	Frederick Major		2/Lieut	27/11,1915	Azmak Military Cemetery
Bayliss	Walter	71002	Private	11/06,1917	Bailleul Comm Cem Ext
Holmes	Harry	70927	Private	11/06,1917	Bailleul Comm Cem Ext
Matthews	Alphonso	31598	Private	12/06,1917	Bailleul Comm Cem Ext
McFarlane	Francis B	76261	Private	11/07,1916	Bailleul Comm Cem Ext

Surname	Given name	Number	Rank	Date	Buried/Commemerated
Phipps	Thomas	18973	Private	17/08,1917	Bard Cottage Cemetery
Crawford	John Russell		2/Lieut	27/09,1916	Blighty Valley Cemetery
Metcalfe	George Henry	92149	Private	10/03,1918	Bois-Carre Mil Cem Haisnes
Abbott	William	12676	L/Cpl	20/10,1916	Bolsover St Mary
Cowley	Horace Tom	24497	Private	30/09,1916	Bolsover St Mary
Cutts	Harry	15928	Private	02/10,1916	Bolsover St Mary
Evans	George	23227	Private	02/10,1916	Boulogne Eastern
Guy	John	14087	Corporal	14/10,1917	Boulogne Eastern
Hyde	Samuel Edward	23368	Private	03/10,1916	Boulogne Eastern
James	John Walter	13567	Private	12/04,1917	Boulogne Eastern
Trickett	James	15768	Private	03/10,1916	Boulogne Eastern
Watson	Douglas Duncan C	23392	Private	05/10,1916	Boulogne Eastern
Downman	Bernard Vincent Ridout		2/Lieut	21/09,1916	Bouzincourt Comm Cem Ext
Egerton	Bertram Gustavus		2/Lieut	08/09,1916	Bouzincourt Comm Cem Ext
Everard	Clement Charlie		Lieut	07/09,1916	Bouzincourt Comm Cem Ext
Hudson	Charles Thomas	12942	Private	06/09,1916	Bouzincourt Comm Cem Ext
Jerram	Thomas Francis	13240	Private	08/09,1916	Bouzincourt Comm Cem Ext
Stevenson	Alan		Captain	26/09,1916	Bouzincourt Comm Cem Ext
Dolphin	William	10400	Private	20/08,1917	Brandhoek New Mil No 3
Clarke	John	97889	Private	06/10,1918	Bucqouy Rd Cem Ficheux
Fox	Herbert	7351	Private	03/09,1917	Calais Southern Cem
Bell	Fred	70912	Private	15/11,1918	Cambrai East Mil Cem
Burgess	Arthur	83624	Private	06/11,1918	Cambrai East Mil Cem
Butters	John William	70865	Private	06/11,1918	Cambrai East Mil Cem
Fisher	Walter Gerald	76384	L/Cpl	05/11,1918	Cambrai East Mil Cem
Oldham	Belton	80830	Private	05/11,1918	Cambrai East Mil Cem
Peel	Robert	17709	Private	05/11,1918	Cambrai East Mil Cem
Terry	Henry, DCM	12367	CSM	05/11,1918	Cambrai East Mil Cem
Hodges	Ernest William	71025	Private	20/07,1917	Canada Farm Cemetery
Birley	John Richard	12549	L/Cpl	05/10,1917	Cement House Cemetery
Meads	John Arthur M.C.		Captain	10/10,1917	Cement House Cemetery
Nicholls	Jerimiah	24531	Private	04/10,1917	Cement House Cemetery
Scott	John George	45695	Private	04/10,1917	Cement House Cemetery
Widdowsom	Edward	86412	Private	04/10,1917	Cement House Cemetery
Ibbett	Joseph Thomas	19709	L/Cpl	26/09,1916	Cerisy-Gailly Mil Cem
Sawyer	Edward	54962	Private	26/11,1917	Chocques Mil Cemetery
Bell	George W	19756	A/Sgt	26/09,1916	Connaught Cem Thiepval
Robinson	Fred	26774	Private	22/11,1916	Connaught Cem Thiepval
Wass	Ernest	15663	Private	26/09,1916	Connaught Cem Thiepval
Weaver	Charles Clifford	20012	Private	26/09,1916	Connaught Cem Thiepval
Bainbridge	Robert	20359	A/Cpl	26/09,1916	Contay British Cem
Calladine	Bickley	15760	Private	27/09,1916	Contay British Cem
Clarke	Benjamin	23244	Private	01/10,1916	Contay British Cem
Connor	Thomas	20118	Private	27/09,1916	Contay British Cem
Rushton	James Henry, MM	19677	Private	02/12,1916	Contay British Cem
Smith	Wilfrid	46204	Private	04/12,1916	Contay British Cem
Walters	James	25793	Private	09/08,1916	Delville Wood Cem
Friend	Thomas Charles	202814	Private	04/11,1918	Denain Comm Cemetery
Wardle	Herbert	70901	Private	28/01,1917	Doullens Comm Cem Ext 1
Bates	Victor	60353	Private	24/07,1917	Dozinghem
Burke	Luke	60314	Corporal	09/10,1917	Dozinghem
Burton	Soloman, MM	19779	L/Cpl	24/07,1917	Dozinghem
Buxton	Frederick Henry	79673	L/Cpl	06/10,1917	Dozinghem

Surname	Given name	Number	Rank	Date	Buried/Commemerated
Cox	Edwin	73078	Private	07/10,1917	Dozinghem
Daubney	Albert	7807	Private	05/10,1917	Dozinghem
Ellmer	Reuben	22672	Private	05/10,1917	Dozinghem
Fisher	George	18432	L/Sgt	06/10,1917	Dozinghem
Hart	Albert Ernest	49340	Private	15/10,1917	Dozinghem
Hinkley	Alfred Thomas	11709	Sgt	05/10,1917	Dozinghem
Pettit	Edward	15372	Private	17/07,1917	Dozinghem
Roe	John Thomas	23318	Private	05/10,1917	Dozinghem
Slater	William Henry	52230	Private	07/10,1917	Dozinghem
Smith	John Henry	26243	L/Cpl	06/10,1917	Dozinghem
Wornes	John Edward	22605	Private	17/07,1917	Dozinghem
Barber	William	12902	L/Sgt	14/05,1917	Duckmanton Church Cem
Black	Robert	6480	Private	16/10,1915	East Mudros Mil Cem
Dickin	George Henry	22022	Private	04/12,1915	East Mudros Mil Cem
Patterson	William Arthur	13396	Private	09/10,1915	East Mudros Mil Cem
Rowland	John Henry	12572	Private	22/08,1915	East Mudros Mil Cem
Towey	James	18000	Private	14/08,1915	East Mudros Mil Cem
Hollingworth	Edmund Bruce	13519	Private	27/10,1916	Eckington Burial Ground
Darby	Richard	31282	Private	16/07,1917	Essex Farm Cemetery
Foster	William	18271	Private	17/07,1917	Essex Farm Cemetery
Hill	George	70837	Private	20/07,1917	Essex Farm Cemetery
Hughes	Harry	32984	Private	22/07,1917	Essex Farm Cemetery
Rodgers	Henry	24414	L/Cpl	17/07,1917	Essex Farm Cemetery
Taylor	Ernest	81570	Private	17/07,1917	Essex Farm Cemetery
Bannister	George William	92130	Private	12/10,1917	Etaples Military Cem
Beeson	John Henry	32589	Cpl	13/10,1918	Etaples Military Cem
Buckley	William	12372	Private	25/12,1916	Etaples Military Cem
Hadland	Edward Frank	330195	Private	08/11,1918	Etaples Military Cem
Hutchinson	Tom	12434	Private	26/09,1916	Etaples Military Cem
Lawley	Leonard	12703	Private	14/10,1916	Etaples Military Cem
Richardson	Edward	13079	A/Sgt	02/10,1916	Etaples Military Cem
Hancock	John	12714	Private	06/10,1916	Etretat Churchyard
Young	Harold Farquhar		2/Lieut	20/08,1917	Flying Services Mem, Arras
Mansell	George	12919	Private	03/11/1918	Fulbeck St Nicholas, Lincs
Blackburne	John George		Major	22/08,1915	Green Hill Cemetery
Malkin	Walter	6107	Drummer	09/08,1915	Green Hill Cemetery
Mitchell	Joseph	8421	Corporal	09/08,1915	Green Hill Cemetery
Thorpe	Edgar Wilkes	22961	Private	15/10,1915	Green Hill Cemetery
West	William		2/Lieut	07/08,1915	Green Hill Cemetery
Wortley	Frank	18113	Private	09/08,1915	Green Hill Cemetery
Bailey	George	22989	Private	11/05,1917	Grevillers British Cem
Milward	Frederick John	70801	Private	11/05,1917	Grevillers British Cem
Taylor	Walter	70946	Private	04/05,1917	Grevillers British Cem
Alexander	William Richard	71070	Private	24/11,1916	Hamel Mil Cemetery
Barton	Samuel	70959	L/Cpl	24/11,1916	Hamel Mil Cemetery
Bell	Samuel	70997	Private	24/11,1916	Hamel Mil Cemetery
Bradley	William	25367	Private	24/11,1916	Hamel Mil Cemetery
Goddard	Samuel	22913	Private	24/11,1916	Hamel Mil Cemetery
Shillaker	Arthur	70987	Private	18/01,1917	Hamel Mil Cemetery
Robinson	Edward	22635	Private	20/12,1916	Hamel Military Cem
Smith	Allan	70992	Private	24/11,1916	Hamel Military Cem
Taylor	Harold Duncan	70989	Private	12/11,1916	Hamel Military Cem
Taylor	Bert	51975	Private	24/11,1916	Hamel Military Cem

Surname	Given name	Number	Rank	Date	Buried/Commemerated
Crowther	William Osborne		2/Lieut	24/11,1916	Hamel Militray Cem
Herbert	Walter	202064	Private	03/10,1918	Haynecourt Brit Cem
Hill	George	24496	Private	06/10,1918	Haynecourt Brit Cem
Ainsworth	William	13406	Private	09/08,1915	Helles Memorial
Allpass	Esmond Theodore		2/Lieut	21/08,1915	Helles Memorial
Ambridge	George William	12879	L/Cpl	09/08,1915	Helles Memorial
Annison	Richard William	6102	CSM	09/08,1915	Helles Memorial
Arthurs	Henry	12494	Private	09/08,1915	Helles Memorial
Bacon	James	22029	Private	05/12,1915	Helles Memorial
Bancroft	Frederick	3952	Cpl	09/08,1915	Helles Memorial
Barber	Joseph	12793	L/Cpl	09/08,1915	Helles Memorial
Barlow	Arthur H	12411	Private	21/08,1915	Helles Memorial
Beard	Fred	13300	Private	09/08,1915	Helles Memorial
Birks	Thomas	13376	Private	09/08,1915	Helles Memorial
Black	Thomas Porteous		Captain	09/08,1915	Helles Memorial
Blythe	George	12525	Private	09/08,1915	Helles Memorial
Boilstone	Horace	12768	Private	14/10,1915	Helles Memorial
Bosanquet	Lionel Arthur		Lt-Col	22/08,1915	Helles Memorial
Bradbury	Edward	6464	Corporal	09/08,1915	Helles Memorial
Bratton	Charles	29249	Private	01/12,1915	Helles Memorial
Brooke	John Stanley	20321	Private	21/08,1915	Helles Memorial
Brown	Frederick Charles		2/Lieut	07/08,1915	Helles Memorial
Bugg	Arthur James	27853	Private	09/08,1915	Helles Memorial
Burgess	Robert Clark	23152	L/Cpl	02/10,1915	Helles Memorial
Burgess	Fred	12532	Private	09/08,1915	Helles Memorial
Burton	Henry Cecil	18069	Private	09/08,1915	Helles Memorial
Calvert	Maurice	12560	Private	09/08,1915	Helles Memorial
Camm	Harry	12347	L/Cpl	09/08,1915	Helles Memorial
Card	Arthur Stanley	12545	L/Cpl	09/08,1915	Helles Memorial
Carey	Henry Pattison		Lieut	7-11/08,1915	Helles Memorial
Cartwright	Joseph	22508	Private	10/08,1915	Helles Memorial
Carver	Walter CS	17011	Private	10/08,1915	Helles Memorial
Casburn	Edward	13054	A/Sgt	27/08,1915	Helles Memorial
Checkley	Herbert	13276	Private	09/08,1915	Helles Memorial
Clark	John Harnless	21264	Private	09/08,1915	Helles Memorial
Clarke	John Percy	13160	Private	09/08,1915	Helles Memorial
Cooper	Richard	17928	Private	03/12.1915	Helles Memorial
Cottrell	Albert	12452	Corporal	09/08,1915	Helles Memorial
Cottrell	Henry (Harry)	12454	L/Cpl	09/08,1915	Helles Memorial
Croysdill	Norman	12552	Private	09/08,1915	Helles Memorial
Daft	George	3919	Private	09/08,1915	Helles Memorial
Dakin	George	21275	Private	21/08,1915	Helles Memorial
Dallison	John William	17924	Private	09/08,1915	Helles Memorial
Dawn	John	17948	L/Cpl	09/08,1915	Helles Memorial
Dawson	John James	13019	L/Sgt	09/08,1915	Helles Memorial
Elliott	Hiram	13199	Private	09/08,1915	Helles Memorial
Evans	William L	12799	Private	09/08,1915	Helles Memorial
Everett	John	12588	Private	09/08,1915	Helles Memorial
Ewin	Arthur, Hon		Lt & QM	7-11/08,1915	Helles Memorial
Farrell	Thomas	12884	Private	09/09,1915	Helles Memorial
Fell	Alfred.	9758	L/Sgt	09/08,1915	Helles Memorial
Fern	Thomas	13251	Private	10/08,1915	Helles Memorial
Fletcher	Francis William	13006	Private	09/08,1915	Helles Memorial

Surname	Given name	Number	Rank	Date	Buried/Commemerated
Ford	Austin Thomas	12706	Private	09/08,1915	Helles Memorial
Frith	John Peter	12559	Private	09/08,1915	Helles Memorial
Gamble	Thomas	13379	Private	09/08,1915	Helles Memorial
Gibbons	Fred	19840	Private	15/10,1915	Helles Memorial
Gilham	John	6115	A/Sgt	09/08,1915	Helles Memorial
Glover	Harry	18080	Private	09/08,1915	Helles Memorial
Goodband	Christopher	13557	Private	28/09,1915	Helles Memorial
Grant	Charles Henry	13056	Private	27/11,1915	Helles Memorial
Gundry	Benjamin	22515	Private	09/08,1915	Helles Memorial
Hall	Arthur	12579	Private	09/08,1915	Helles Memorial
Hall	George	12711	Private	25/08,1915	Helles Memorial
Hallam	James Arthur	20343	Private	09/08,1915	Helles Memorial
Hallam	Walter Pemberton	13071	Private	09/08,1915	Helles Memorial
Hancock	Cyril	12607	Private	09/08,1915	Helles Memorial
Harris	Leonard	12408	L/Cpl	09/08,1915	Helles Memorial
Heap	Francis William	12493	L/Cpl	25/08,1915	Helles Memorial
Hemming	Frank	13283	Private	09/08,1915	Helles Memorial
Hempshall	George	13191	Private	09/08,1915	Helles Memorial
Hemsley	Francis	16996	Private	11/08,1915	Helles Memorial
Hewitt	George	3999	Private	09/08,1915	Helles Memorial
Hill	John George	18016	Private	09/08,1915	Helles Memorial
Holliday	Clarence Percy	13558	L/Cpl	06/10,1915	Helles Memorial
Hood	Reginald Smith	12418	Private	09/08,1915	Helles Memorial
Hopkinson	William	22510	Private	25/10,1915	Helles Memorial
Hopwood	Robert	18046	Private	09/08,1915	Helles Memorial
Howard	Frank Edward	13035	Private	19/08,1915	Helles Memorial
Hudson	Charles Sowter	13186	L/Cpl	09/08,1915	Helles Memorial
Hudson	George Henry	17824	Private	22/09,1915	Helles Memorial
Humphreys	William Dann	13883	L/Cpl	09/08,1915	Helles Memorial
Hunt	Alfred James	23038	Private	15/10,1915	Helles Memorial
Ives	James	12523	Private	09/08,1915	Helles Memorial
Jackson	William	27863	Private	09/08,1915	Helles Memorial
Johnson	William	13096	A/Sgt	09/08,1915	Helles Memorial
Kennett	Frederick William	12968	Private	09/08,1915	Helles Memorial
Kirk	John James	22505	Private	09/08,1915	Helles Memorial
Knowles	William	12893	Private	09/08,1915	Helles Memorial
Lakin	William	3981	Private	09/08,1915	Helles Memorial
Leeson	Frank	21274	Private	09/08,1915	Helles Memorial
Legge	John Maurice	14050	L/Cpl	09/08,1915	Helles Memorial
Lenton	John William	17935	Private	09/08,1915	Helles Memorial
Lilliman	Joseph	12833	Private	09/08,1915	Helles Memorial
Loane	Samuel	27857	Private	09/08,1915	Helles Memorial
Lomax	Louis	12488	Private	09/08,1915	Helles Memorial
Lovell	Arthur	13263	Private	21/08,1915	Helles Memorial
Ludlam	Geo	12483	Private	09/08,1915	Helles Memorial
Luntley	Geoffrey	12615	Private	09/08,1915	Helles Memorial
Mahoney	John	12922	Private	04/10,1915	Helles Memorial
Mallinder	Thomas	12903	Private	04/09,1915	Helles Memorial
Martin	James	13903	L/Cpl	09/08,1915	Helles Memorial
Maskrey	Francis	12590	A/Cpl	09/08,1915	Helles Memorial
Mayfield	Horace	12614	Private	09/08,1915	Helles Memorial
Mayo	William Charles		Lieut	7-11/08,1915	Helles Memorial
Michie	James Halley	12605	L/Cpl	09/08,1915	Helles Memorial

Surname	Given name	Number	Rank	Date	Buried/Commemerated
Mills	Samuel	12796	Private	09/08,1915	Helles Memorial
Milward	Walter	6090	CSM	29/08,1915	Helles Memorial
Moorcroft	Edgar	13027	Private	02/09,1915	Helles Memorial
Noble	Henry	13243	Private	09/08,1915	Helles Memorial
Oates	James	22149	Private	04/10,1915	Helles Memorial
Pass	Morris Edward	23290	Private	09/08,1915	Helles Memorial
Pass	William	18068	Private	19/08,1915	Helles Memorial
Pell	Sydney Ambrose	12445	Private	02/10,1915	Helles Memorial
Pepperdine	Frank	12506	Private	21/08,1915	Helles Memorial
Perrin	Charles	13161	Private	01/09,1915	Helles Memorial
Poultney	Arthur	13256	Private	21/08,1915	Helles Memorial
Rabbitt	Harry	27861	Private	21/08,1915	Helles Memorial
Randall	Charles Deschamps		Captain	7-11/08,1915	Helles Memorial
Rawlins	Edward	12736	Private	09/08,1915	Helles Memorial
Rhodes	Harold	18034	Private	09/08,1915	Helles Memorial
Richards	Arthur	12468	L/Cpl	10/08,1915	Helles Memorial
Riley	James	13342	Private	09/08,1915	Helles Memorial
Robinson	Frank	13268	Private	09/08,1915	Helles Memorial
Rouse	Tom Arthur	13394	Private	21/08,1915	Helles Memorial
Rudd	James	22514	Private	09/08,1915	Helles Memorial
Rushe	John	18015	Private	10/08,1915	Helles Memorial
Ryan	William	12908	Private	09/08,1915	Helles Memorial
Scott	Fred	12862	Private	09/08,1915	Helles Memorial
Searle	Sidney William	13105	L/Cpl	09/09,1915	Helles Memorial
Shaw	William	18234	Private	09/08,1915	Helles Memorial
Shaw	Joseph	22513	Private	15/08,1915	Helles Memorial
Simmons	Joseph Price	13270	L/Cpl	09/08,1915	Helles Memorial
Simpson	Henry	16971	Private	19/08,1915	Helles Memorial
Smith	Sidney	12976	Private	09/08,1915	Helles Memorial
Smith	William	12701	Private	09/08,1915	Helles Memorial
Smith	Leonard	12897	Private	13/10,1915	Helles Memorial
Smith	George Henry	20340	Private	19/08,1915	Helles Memorial
Smith	James	12834	Private	21/08,1915	Helles Memorial
Smith	James William	12949	Private	21/08,1915	Helles Memorial
Spink	Alfred Henry	18031	Private	09/08,1915	Helles Memorial
Spray	James	13229	Private	09/08,1915	Helles Memorial
Squires	Roger Dewer		Captain	07/08,1915	Helles Memorial
Stacey	George	13599	Corporal	09/08,1915	Helles Memorial
Stead	George	13359	Private	09/08,1915	Helles Memorial
Stevens	George Edward	13346	Private	09/08,1915	Helles Memorial
Sutton	Horace Josiah		2/Lieut	24/11,1915	Helles Memorial
Sweeney	William	12436	Private	09/08,1915	Helles Memorial
Thomas	Harry	12503	L/Cpl	21/08,1915	Helles Memorial
Turpie	Arthur John	6029	A/Cpl	21/08,1915	Helles Memorial
Turton	Albert Edward	13934	Private	09/08,1915	Helles Memorial
Turton	Arthur	5066	Private	14/10,1915	Helles Memorial
Vick	Frank	13108	Private	09/08,1915	Helles Memorial
Wallace	Francis George	20863	Private	13/11,1915	Helles Memorial
Ward	Albert Ernest	13073	A/Cpl	03/10,1915	Helles Memorial
Watkins	Herbert E	12656	Private	21/08,1915	Helles Memorial
Watson	Frederick Mark	6584	Sgt	09/08,1915	Helles Memorial
Welbourn	Samuel	12401	Private	09/08,1915	Helles Memorial
Wells	Frederic Charles	12355	L/Cpl	09/08,1915	Helles Memorial

Surname	Given name	Number	Rank	Date	Buried/Commemerated
Whittaker	Walter	12458	Private	04/10,1915	Helles Memorial
Whittemore	George William	13657	Private	15/10,1915	Helles Memorial
Wigmore	Elijah	12873	Private	09/08,1915	Helles Memorial
Wilcockson	Tom	13150	Private	09/08,1915	Helles Memorial
Williams	Arthur	12573	A/Cpl	09/08,1915	Helles Memorial
Wills	Arthur George		Lieut	07/08,1915	Helles Memorial
Winchcomb	William T	17805	Private	09/08,1915	Helles Memorial
Winnard	Wilfred	20306	Private	09/08,1915	Helles Memorial
Womack	George Lewis	12966	Private	21/08,1915	Helles Memorial
Worth	Lewis	12846	Private	09/08,1915	Helles Memorial
Shaw	Harry	70952	Private	10/05,1917	Hermies Brit Cem
Briggs	Arthur	21801	Private	19/07,1918	Hersin Comm Cem Ext
Brackner	George	13908	Private	25/10,1915	Hill 10 Cem Suvla
Button	Noel	13021	Private	01/11,1915	Hill 10 Cem Suvla
Hazelwood	William Charles	22977	Private	23/11,1915	Hill 10 Cem Suvla
Johnson	Joseph	13057	Private	14/11,1915	Hill 10 Cem Suvla
Mycock	Albert Harold	24064	Private	01/08/1918	Home
Bond	Ernest	10536	Private	16/06,1917	Irish House Cemetery
Clayton	Frank	12413	A/Sgt	16/06,1917	Irish House Cemetery
Sibbring	Arthur	26931	Private	10/06,1917	Irish House Cemetery
Strickson	Harry	51664	Private	16/06,1917	Irish House Cemetery
Booth	Thomas	23288	Private	22/04,1916	Ismailia War Mem Cem
Larder	Tom.	70886	Private	01/06,1917	Kemmel Chateau Mil Cem
Padgett	George	18774	Private	03/09,1916	Knightsbridge Cm mesnil
Banton	Thomas	90007	Sgt	21/07,1917	La Belle Alliance
Barnes	William Percy	31615	Private	24/07,1917	La Belle Alliance
Brooks	Arthur	53592	Private	23/07,1917	La Belle Alliance
Buxton	Thomas Henry	23223	Private	23/07,1917	La Belle Alliance
Funnell	Ernest	13472	Private	21/07,1917	La Belle Alliance
Margetts	Bertie	71058	Private	21/07,1917	La Belle Alliance
Marsh	Harold	21504	Private	23/07,1917	La Belle Alliance
McAusland	Robert Hamilton R	71028	Private	09/06,1917	La Belle Alliance
Millott	Charles G	70814	A/Cpl	22/07,1917	La Belle Alliance
Petford	John Henry	24514	Private	23/07,1917	La Belle Alliance
Street	Harry	90002	Corporal	24/07,1917	La Belle Alliance
Veres	Lance	71065	Private	28/07,1917	La Belle Alliance
Webster	Arthur	70949	Private	24/07,1917	La Belle Alliance
Foley	Ernest Henry	12721	Private	23/08,1915	Lala Baba Cem
Bunting	Owen	13275	Private	11/08,1915	Lancashire Landing
Parkin	Arthur	7750	Private	19/01,1916	Lancashire Landing
Trotman	Sidney William	21454	Private	21/01.1916	Lancashire Landing
Hancock	Ernest	204461	Private	20/03,1918	Lapugnoy Mil Cem
Wadsworth	Alfred James	12500	L/Cpl	28/02,1918	Lapugnoy Mil Cem
Pickford	David . DCM	9031	CSM	23/10,1916	Leek Cemetery
Lambert	William	32746	Private	17/12,1917	Les Baraques Sangatte
Carrington	John Thomas	14125	Private	13/06,1917	Lijssenthoek Mil Cem
Jackson	Harold E James	17941	A/Cpl	28/07,1917	Lijssenthoek Mil Cem
Keeton	Thomas	64358	Private	25/07,1917	Lijssenthoek Mil Cem
Lloyd	George Edward	12781	Private	24/07,1917	Lijssenthoek Mil Cem
Stead	Sam	56463	Private	22/08,1917	Lijssenthoek Mil Cem
Towle	Arthur	56423	Private	24/07,1917	Lijssenthoek Mil Cem
Beeby	John	56416	Private	22/11,1917	Longuenesse (St Omer)
Vickers	William Horace	20223	Private	27/09,1916	Lonsdale Cem, Authuile

Surname	Given name	Number	Rank	Date	Buried/Commemerated
Adley	Thomas James	92254	Private	11/12,1917	Loos British Cemetery
Andrews	James	56412	Private	21/11,1917	Loos British Cemetery
Brown	William	28216	Private	12/12,1917	Loos British Cemetery
Crawford	Tom Barratt	70871	Private	21/11,1917	Loos British Cemetery
Dyas	Richard	47915	Private	10/11,1917	Loos British Cemetery
Foss	Frederick	3797	Private	13/11,1917	Loos British Cemetery
Gilbert	Charles Edward	25843	Private	04/12,1917	Loos British Cemetery
Grice	Alfred George	37434	Private	21/11,1917	Loos British Cemetery
Hoole	William	27562	Private	06/12,1917	Loos British Cemetery
Howells	William G	92196	Private	25/11,1917	Loos British Cemetery
Morris	Joseph	92198	Private	25/11,1917	Loos British Cemetery
Potts	John	71075	Sgt	14/12,1917	Loos British Cemetery
Robinson	Frank	70037	Private	03/12,1917	Loos British Cemetery
Rowe	James	7065	L/Cpl	10/11,1917	Loos British Cemetery
Sheppard	Cecil Lindford	269322	Private	16/12,1917	Loos British Cemetery
Simpson	Wilfred	86342	Private	13/12,1917	Loos British Cemetery
Whitworth	Leonard	21616	L/Cpl	12/12,1917	Loos British Cemetery
Wilkinson	Percy	87133	Private	20/11,1917	Loos British Cemetery
Davey	Jonathan Smithurst	17564	Private	18/06,1918	Loos Memorial
Hudson	Henry Erris		2/Lieut	18/06,1918	Loos Memorial
Hunt	George	5118	L/Cpl	18/06,1918	Loos Memorial
Tilley	Thomas	18050	Private	18/06,1918	Loos Memorial
Watson	John William	57244	Private	12/02,1918	Lowdham St Mary Churchy
Mason	Percy.	10851	Private	12/01,1916	Manchester Southern Cem
Wheatley	Ernest	70963	Private	27/06,1918	Mazingarbe Comm Cem
Betts	John Edward	24972	Private	07/10,1917	Mendinghem
Green	Alfred Louis	15198	L/Cpl	05/10,1917	Mendinghem
Throssell	William. MM	13124	Sgt	09/10,1917	Mendinghem
Barker	William	71022	Private	07/06,1917	Menin Gate, Ypres
Cook	Cyril Ramsay		2/Lieut	09/06,1917	Menin Gate, Ypres
Cox	Ernest	57234	Private	20/07,1917	Menin Gate, Ypres
Curtis	Isaac	4913	Private	07/06,1917	Menin Gate, Ypres
Elliott	Frederick	57110	Private	09/06,1917	Menin Gate, Ypres
Fox	Arthur	4574	Private	09/06,1917	Menin Gate, Ypres
Frood	Edward James	5888	CSM	09/06,1917	Menin Gate, Ypres
Harris	John Thomas	14721	Private	09/06,1917	Menin Gate, Ypres
Hebblethwaite	Joseph	19191	L/Sgt	19/07,1917	Menin Gate, Ypres
Marshall	Arthur	20419	A/Cpl	08/06,1917	Menin Gate, Ypres
McCraith	John	76224	Private	09/06,1917	Menin Gate, Ypres
McNeill	Robert	76267	Private	07/06,1917	Menin Gate, Ypres
Parr	Henry T	56012	Private	09/06,1917	Menin Gate, Ypres
Pratt	Herbert	71011	Private	07/06,1917	Menin Gate, Ypres
Price	Charles	70938	Private	09/06,1917	Menin Gate, Ypres
Roberts	Frank	70052	Private	31/07,1917	Menin Gate, Ypres
Sheppard	George Alexander	27279	Private	24/07,1917	Menin Gate, Ypres
Smith	Samuel Henry	28648	Private	10/06,1917	Menin Gate, Ypres
Sutton	Albert Hardy	70991	Private	10/06,1917	Menin Gate, Ypres
Westwater	James S	76329	Private	09/06,1917	Menin Gate, Ypres
Whyler	William A.	23065	Private	07/06,1917	Menin Gate, Ypres
Whyman	George Taylor	16193	Private	24/07,1917	Menin Gate, Ypres
Prosser	Albert Victor, DCM		Lieut	26/11,1916	Mesnil Comm Cem Ext
Heal	Frederick	92180	Private	12/12,1917	Noeux -Les-Mines Com Cem
Letts	Harry	204512	Private	08/12,1917	Noeux -Les-Mines Com Cem

Surname	Given name	Number	Rank	Date	Buried/Commemerated
Hillyard	James Arthur	6991	L/Cpl	26/09,1916	Norfolk Cem Becordel-Be
Fielding	S		Lt & QM	12/11,1914	Normanton Cemetery
Willies	Arthur	12570	Private	24/09,1915	Norton Cuckney Notts
Scattergood	Ernest Charles	61560	Private	17/04,1917	Nottingham General Cem
Adcock	Walter Russell	22916	Private	07/09,1916	Ovillers Mil Cemetery
Baker	Sidney.	20415	Private	13/09,1916	Ovillers Mil Cemetery
Barker	Thomas	11783	Private	11/09,1916	Ovillers Mil Cemetery
Burton	Reginald	12686	Private	17/09,1916	Ovillers Mil Cemetery
Colclough	Fred	21732	Private	15/09,1916	Ovillers Mil Cemetery
Crump	Albert Edward	20859	Private	11/09,1916	Ovillers Mil Cemetery
Fines	Edward	14106	Private	19/09,1916	Ovillers Mil Cemetery
Hardy	George	18703	Private	19/09,1916	Ovillers Mil Cemetery
Hopcroft	Herbert	24669	Private	10/09,1916	Ovillers Mil Cemetery
Kitchen	Edward	21558	Private	08/09,1916	Ovillers Mil Cemetery
Marriott	Peter	19104	Private	20/09,1916	Ovillers Mil Cemetery
Marsh	Ralph	19908	L/Cpl	09/09,1916	Ovillers Mil Cemetery
Sanders	Ernest	19017	Private	22/09,1916	Ovillers Mil Cemetery
Sellers	John Samuel	4645	Private	23/09,1916	Ovillers Mil Cemetery
Sharpe	William	22943	Private	08/09,1916	Ovillers Mil Cemetery
Walker	Harold	10521	Private	26/09,1916	Ovillers Mil Cemetery
Winstanley	George	22210	L/Sgt	21/09,1916	Ovillers Mil Cemetery
Nicolls	Richard Jeffreys		Captain	01/10,1916	Peake Wood, Fricourt
Bark	Francis, MM	24787	Sgt	02/05,1918	Pernes British Cem
Bexon	Alfred	16149	Private	07/06,1918	Pernes British Cem
Eaton	Albert Joseph	71016	Private	18/06,1918	Pernes British Cem
Hood	Ernest	13175	Private	23/04,1918	Pernes British Cem
Scott	John Henry	11054	Private	06/08,1916	Perone Rd Cem Maricourt
Bishop	Frederick	70861	Private	12/05,1918	Philosophe Mazingarbe
Brown	John	17942	Private	27/04,1918	Philosophe Mazingarbe
Campbell	Donald	59913	Private	10/03,1918	Philosophe Mazingarbe
Churchill	Patrick	27498	L/Cpl	27/04,1918	Philosophe Mazingarbe
Fuller	Robert Charles	102699	Private	18/06,1918	Philosophe Mazingarbe
Griffin	Daniel	92165	Private	08/03,1918	Philosophe Mazingarbe
Grimshaw	Frank	14054	Corporal	27/04,1918	Philosophe Mazingarbe
Illsley	John W Francis	22973	Private	03/04,1918	Philosophe Mazingarbe
Jackson	Ernest	13398	Private	05/03,1918	Philosophe Mazingarbe
Keeble	Percy Edward	71414	Private	27/04,1918	Philosophe Mazingarbe
Kilner	Thomas Richard Burgess		2/Lieut	18/06,1918	Philosophe Mazingarbe
Knight	John	9253	Sgt	27/04,1918	Philosophe Mazingarbe
Knight	Walter	69034	Private	27/04,1918	Philosophe Mazingarbe
Lowe	George. DCM	19896	Private	15/06,1918	Philosophe Mazingarbe
Mortimer	Edward. MM	6885	Drummer	27/02,1918	Philosophe Mazingarbe
Osborn	Robert	15338	L/Cpl	18/06,1918	Philosophe Mazingarbe
Parr	Walter	23127	Private	10/03,1918	Philosophe Mazingarbe
Pinkney	Lawrence	29638	Private	27/04,1918	Philosophe Mazingarbe
Redfearn	Samuel	57299	Private	10/03,1918	Philosophe Mazingarbe
Schur	Philip		Lieut	15/06,1918	Philosophe Mazingarbe
Shaw	Walter Augustus	307707	L/Cpl	27/04,1918	Philosophe Mazingarbe
Sherrard	Albert	30703	Private	18/06,1918	Philosophe Mazingarbe
Smedley	Harold Arthur	201136	Private	27/04,1918	Philosophe Mazingarbe
Smith	George Joshua	72623	Private	15/06,1918	Philosophe Mazingarbe
Spittlehouse	Arthur John	21063	Private	25/04,1918	Philosophe Mazingarbe
Swan	Percy	25210	L/Cpl	27/04,1918	Philosophe Mazingarbe

Surname	Given name	Number	Rank	Date	Buried/Commemerated
Swindell	Bernard	71041	Sgt	27/04,1918	Philosophe Mazingarbe
Truman	Ernest	8963	Private	18/04,1918	Philosophe Mazingarbe
Wilson	William Foster	81817	Private	27/04,1918	Philosophe Mazingarbe
Witherbed	Wilfred	16935	Private	04/03,1918	Philosophe Mazingarbe
Wright	John T	70959	Private	27/04,1918	Philosophe Mazingarbe
Ball	George	12704	Private	10/09,1915	Pieta Military Cem
Britland	Robert Charles	12779	Private	16/09,1915	Pieta Military Cem
Chambers	William	23157	Private	06/12,1916	Pieta Military Cem
Chanter	Henry	12571	Private	01/09,1915	Pieta Military Cem
Colton	Harold	12617	Private	26/11,1915	Pieta Military Cem
Dilkes	Arthur	25557	Private	19/01,1916	Pieta Military Cem
Edgson	James Herbert	21261	Private	13/09,1915	Pieta Military Cem
Grice	Levi	12515	Private	30/12,1915	Pieta Military Cem
Howitt	Alfred	12988	Private	16/09,1915	Pieta Military Cem
Hughes	John	22715	Private	04/10,1915	Pieta Military Cem
Clayton	John William	86411	Private	04/10,1917	Poelcappelle Mil cem
Derbyshire	George	23662	Private	18/10,1915	Portianos Mil Cem Lemnos
Burrows	John Thomas Larkin	22680	Private	26/09,1916	Pozieres Brit Cem
Buxton	Ernest	12369	Private	26/09,1916	Pozieres Brit Cem
Farby	George Robert	23711	Private	26/09,1916	Pozieres Brit Cem
Jacques	William	21515	Private	26/09,1916	Pozieres Brit Cem
Keel	William Herbert	13094	Private	26/09,1916	Pozieres Brit Cem
Moore	Thomas	14105	L/Cpl	21/09,1916	Pozieres Brit Cem
Trelfa	Charles	11675	Private	29/09,1916	Pozieres Brit Cem
Youson	George	13122	Private	26/09,1916	Pozieres Brit Cem
Armstrong	John William	19233	Private	28/09,1916	Puchevillers Br Cem
Boice	William	23408	Private	14/09,1916	Puchevillers Br Cem
Brown	William Charles	2867	Private	28/09,1916	Puchevillers Br Cem
Cresswell	Albert Edward	27040	Private	18/02,1917	Puchevillers Br Cem
Fowke	William	25010	Private	27/09,1916	Puchevillers Br Cem
Marriott	Frederick	6730	Private	03/10,1916	Puchevillers Br Cem
Morley	Frederick	5064	Private	27/09,1916	Puchevillers Br Cem
Pearson	William R.	22931	Private	28/09,1916	Puchevillers Br Cem
Truss	James William	70898	Private	03/12,1916	Puchevillers Br Cem
Walker	John William	21189	A/Sgt	29/06,1916	Puchevillers Br Cem
Matsell	Arthur	41412	Private	03/10,1918	Queant Road Cem Buissy
Barfield	Daniel	6076	Private	24/07,1915	Redoubt Cem, Helles
Carter	George E.	13403	Private	28/07,1915	Redoubt Cem, Helles
Antcliffe	Alfred	19240	Private	26/09,1916	Regina Trench Cem
Chambers	Thomas	20992	Private	26/09,1916	Regina Trench Cem
Colton	Percival Charles	23089	Private	26/09,1916	Regina Trench Cem
Hammersley	Thomas	18610	Private	26/09,1916	Regina Trench Cem
Jones	Alexander	21832	Private	26/09,1916	Regina Trench Cem
Mears	George	9192	Private	26/09,1916	Regina Trench Cem
Tarr	William	13328	Private	26/09,1916	Regina Trench Cem
Paddock	Henry Leslie		Major	22/03,1918	Roisel Comm Cem Ext
Barnes	Ernest	22112	Private	04/11,1918	Sebourg British Cem
Blunt	Frederick J	3415	Sgt	04/11,1918	Sebourg British Cem
Bond	Alfred Ernest	17955	Private	04/11,1918	Sebourg British Cem
Bradley	Leonard Charles	71850	Private	04/11,1918	Sebourg British Cem
Bradley	Robert William	306288	Private	04/11,1918	Sebourg British Cem
Brown	William	96117	Private	04/11,1918	Sebourg British Cem
Calvert	John James	71488	Private	04/11,1918	Sebourg British Cem

Surname	Given name	Number	Rank	Date	Buried/Commemerated
Chesham	Harry	13764	Private	04/11,1918	Sebourg British Cem
Clarke	Arthur	82816	Private	04/11,1918	Sebourg British Cem
Clowes	William Dexter	20045	Private	04/11,1918	Sebourg British Cem
Cornelius	Wilfred	7107	CSM	04/11,1918	Sebourg British Cem
Dyson	Walter	27472	Private	04/11,1918	Sebourg British Cem
Garton	Samuel	16895	Private	04/11,1918	Sebourg British Cem
Goodacre	Harry	21475	Private	04/11,1918	Sebourg British Cem
Green	John	86518	L/Cpl	04/11,1918	Sebourg British Cem
Heald	Arthur	18263	Private	04/11,1918	Sebourg British Cem
Henry	Frederick	94428	Private	04/11,1918	Sebourg British Cem
Hill	Harold Arthur	70854	Private	04/11,1918	Sebourg British Cem
Mackintosh	Claude.H.B.James	265578	Private	04/11,1918	Sebourg British Cem
Mowbray	Albert	285302	Private	04/11,1918	Sebourg British Cem
Nowell	John	266072	Sgt	04/11,1918	Sebourg British Cem
Parkin	John W	51970	Private	04/11,1918	Sebourg British Cem
Roadley	Harold	32065	Private	04/11,1918	Sebourg British Cem
Sheraton	Wallace	24144	Private	04/11,1918	Sebourg British Cem
Taylor	George	24784	Private	04/11,1918	Sebourg British Cem
Taylor	John Allen	201999	Sgt	04/11,1918	Sebourg British Cem
Thompson	Joseph	92209	Private	04/11,1918	Sebourg British Cem
Upton	William	30976	L/Cpl	04/11,1918	Sebourg British Cem
Venables	Ernest	93719	Private	04/11,1918	Sebourg British Cem
Wardle	Frederick	107632	Private	04/11,1918	Sebourg British Cem
Weston	William	70900	Private	04/11,1918	Sebourg British Cem
Wilkes	Richard Nichols	92265	Private	04/11,1918	Sebourg British Cem
Wilson	Albert	13041	Corporal	04/11,1918	Sebourg British Cem
Wootton	Leonard	26233	L/Cpl	04/11,1918	Sebourg British Cem
Zolowski	Ephraim. MM	73055	L/Cpl	04/11,1918	Sebourg British Cem
Sibson	George Frederick	45933	Private	29/11.1916	Serre Road Cem No 2
Easom	William	21830	Private	25/09,1916	Shirebrook Cemetery
Fielding	George Rudolf		Major	24/07, 1915	Skew Bridge Cemetery
Payne	Alexander	17010	Private	20/07,1916	Southampton Hollybrook
Wadley	John William	13151	Private	21/09,1916	St Pierre Cem Amiens
Dale	William John	73037	Private	10/10,1917	St Sever, Rouen
Gilman	Charles	9015	Private	06/12,1916	St Sever, Rouen
Hopkinson	George	23005	Private	04/12,1916	St Sever, Rouen
Perry	Henry Joseph	71031	Private	11/10,1917	St Sever, Rouen
Wright	Harry	11162	L/Cpl	04/11,1918	St Sever, Rouen
Parish	Robert	70963	Private	12/11,1918	Terlincthun Br Wimille
Allsop	Thomas	18452	Private	26/09,1916	Thiepval Memorial
Armstrong	John G	23163	Private	26/09,1916	Thiepval Memorial
Ault	William	22789	Private	26/09,1916	Thiepval Memorial
Bailey	Richard	8576	CSM	24/11,1916	Thiepval Memorial
Baker	Frederick	19251	L/Cpl	26/09,1916	Thiepval Memorial
Baker	Willie	13111	Private	26/09,1916	Thiepval Memorial
Baker	Joseph Claud	71047	Private	29/11,1916	Thiepval Memorial
Barlow	Walter	25398	Private	26/09,1916	Thiepval Memorial
Barratt	William	17861	L/Cpl	27/11,1916	Thiepval Memorial
Bennett	Henry	24265	Private	26/09,1916	Thiepval Memorial
Bentley	Henry	25299	Private	29/11,1916	Thiepval Memorial
Berry	Albert	13704	Private	26/09,1916	Thiepval Memorial
Blakeway	Benjamin	12472	Private	26/09,1916	Thiepval Memorial
Briggs	Ernest	12416	Private	26/09,1916	Thiepval Memorial

Surname	Given name	Number	Rank	Date	Buried/Commemerated
Brown	Sydney	13419	Private	26/09,1916	Thiepval Memorial
Burrows	Herbert	70810	Private	24/11,1916	Thiepval Memorial
Carter	Fred	22738	Private	07/09,1916	Thiepval Memorial
Carter	Charles	17796	Private	26/09,1916	Thiepval Memorial
Causer	Thomas	20366	Private	26/09,1916	Thiepval Memorial
Clarke	Joseph William	12594	Private	11/09,1916	Thiepval Memorial
Cockayne	Walter	20698	Private	26/09,1916	Thiepval Memorial
Cooper	William	12962	Private	26/09,1916	Thiepval Memorial
Cowling	Thomas Henry	15137	Private	23/09,1916	Thiepval Memorial
Croucher	George	23083	Private	26/09,1916	Thiepval Memorial
Daft	Arthur Frederick	10951	Private	26/09,1916	Thiepval Memorial
Dawson	Walter	34773	Private	16/09,1916	Thiepval Memorial
De Banke	Joseph	21714	Private	29/11,1916	Thiepval Memorial
Dent	Harry	50619	Private	24/11,1916	Thiepval Memorial
Ede	Fred	12770	A/Sgt	26/09,1916	Thiepval Memorial
Ellis	William	16826	Private	26/09,1916	Thiepval Memorial
England	Edwin	22645	Private	26/09,1916	Thiepval Memorial
Flint	Henry Ellis	11010	L/Cpl	29/09,1916	Thiepval Memorial
Forbes	John	13106	L/Cpl	26/09,1916	Thiepval Memorial
Freeman	Walter	19219	Private	26/09,1916	Thiepval Memorial
Fretwell	Ernest	13159	Private	26/09,1916	Thiepval Memorial
Furness	Walter	24704	Private	26/09,1916	Thiepval Memorial
George	William Henry	14367	Private	26/09,1916	Thiepval Memorial
Glover	Fred	3686	Private	26/09,1916	Thiepval Memorial
Gregory	James William	25206	Private	26/09,1916	Thiepval Memorial
Hadman	John William	23200	Private	26/09,1916	Thiepval Memorial
Hartshorn	Charles	21540	L/Cpl	26/09,1916	Thiepval Memorial
Hind	Jesse Francis Montague		Lieut	27/09,1916	Thiepval Memorial
Hodson	Benjamin	19857	Private	26/09,1916	Thiepval Memorial
Hollis	Frank	25580	Private	11/09,1916	Thiepval Memorial
Holloway	Moses	6112	A/Sgt	09/10,1916	Thiepval Memorial
Hollyoak	Sam	12759	Private	07/09,1916	Thiepval Memorial
Holmes	Charles Edward	23045	Private	26/09,1916	Thiepval Memorial
Hone	James Henry	14311	Private	26/09,1916	Thiepval Memorial
Horlock	Henry	6924	L/Cpl	26/09,1916	Thiepval Memorial
Hudson	John Joseph	21849	Private	08/08,1916	Thiepval Memorial
Jinks	George Irvine	22072	Private	17/10,1916	Thiepval Memorial
Jones	William H	6596	Private	26/09,1916	Thiepval Memorial
Kirkham	Harry	24023	Private	26/09,1916	Thiepval Memorial
Knight	George	13846	Private	26/09,1916	Thiepval Memorial
Leavesley	Horace	12400	Private	26/09,1916	Thiepval Memorial
Leivars	John William	22298	Private	26/11,1916	Thiepval Memorial
Liley	James	12602	Private	26/09,1916	Thiepval Memorial
Lloyd	John	19054	Private	26/09,1916	Thiepval Memorial
Lloyd	William John	70883	Private	26/11,1916	Thiepval Memorial
Longdon	Herbert	15772	Private	26/09,1916	Thiepval Memorial
Lowe	George Henry	7046	Private	26/09,1916	Thiepval Memorial
Marks	William	15002	Private	26/09,1916	Thiepval Memorial
Marsden	George	21502	Private	26/09,1916	Thiepval Memorial
Martin	Leonard	20759	Private	22/09,1916	Thiepval Memorial
Page	Reginald	13610	Private	23/09,1916	Thiepval Memorial
Page	John	21205	Private	26/09,1916	Thiepval Memorial
Parker	George Elias	23987	Private	09/08,1916	Thiepval Memorial

Surname	Given name	Number	Rank	Date	Buried/Commemerated
Parry	Edward Richard	22158	Private	26/09,1916	Thiepval Memorial
Pearson	Peter	15335	L/Cpl	26/09,1916	Thiepval Memorial
Perotti	Ben.	22908	Private	26/09,1916	Thiepval Memorial
Pierrepont	Bertram	24174	Private	26/09,1916	Thiepval Memorial
Richardson	Robert	7018	Private	26/09,1916	Thiepval Memorial
Riley	Percy	12404	Private	26/09,1916	Thiepval Memorial
Rimmington	Walter George	11761	A/Cpl	26/09,1916	Thiepval Memorial
Sansom	Albert	4409	Private	26/09,1916	Thiepval Memorial
Schweder	Archibald Alan. M.C.		Captain	26/09,1916	Thiepval Memorial
Sewell	Herbert	21588	Private	26/09,1916	Thiepval Memorial
Shaw	Arthur	12485		26/09,1916	Thiepval Memorial
Shawcroft	John	20828	Private	26/09,1916	Thiepval Memorial
Shepherd	Joseph	18579	L/Cpl	26/09,1916	Thiepval Memorial
Shirley	Charles	21789	Private	26/09,1916	Thiepval Memorial
Simpson	Victor Hugh	70943	Private	29/11,1916	Thiepval Memorial
Smedley	Samuel George	25908	Private	29/09,1916	Thiepval Memorial
Smith	Frank Henry	4687	Private	21/09,1916	Thiepval Memorial
Spencer	Herbert	32279	Private	27/11,1916	Thiepval Memorial
Staniforth	John Robert	22151	Private	11/09,1916	Thiepval Memorial
Stenson	Garnet	23126	Private	26/09,1916	Thiepval Memorial
Straw	Ernest	12648	Private	26/09,1916	Thiepval Memorial
Swift	Herbert Ernest	21087	Private	22/09,1916	Thiepval Memorial
Thompson	William	23046	Private	26/09,1916	Thiepval Memorial
Turner	Joseph	23340	Private	26/09,1916	Thiepval Memorial
Undy	William Henry	9719	Private	26/09,1916	Thiepval Memorial
Vickers	George Hartley	18370	L/Cpl	27/09,1916	Thiepval Memorial
Wakefield	James Parks	12907	Private	26/09,1916	Thiepval Memorial
Waplington	Arthur	27044	Private	26/09,1916	Thiepval Memorial
Ward	Abraham	23398	Private	09/08,1916	Thiepval Memorial
Ward	Joseph	19549	Private	26/09,1916	Thiepval Memorial
Whitehouse	William	27786	Private	26/09,1916	Thiepval Memorial
Wilkinson	John	13306	Sgt	26/09,1916	Thiepval Memorial
Wilkinson	William	13367	L/Cpl	26/09,1916	Thiepval Memorial
Worker	James	20006	Private	26/09,1916	Thiepval Memorial
Burton	John George	27733	Private	19/08,1917	Tyne Cot Cemetery
Caunt	Luther	19009	Private	19/08,1917	Tyne Cot Cemetery
Coan	John	92192	Private	04/10,1917	Tyne Cot Cemetery
Locke	Charles	30354	Private	19/08,1917	Tyne Cot Cemetery
Taylor	John Clifford	18545	Private	19/08,1917	Tyne Cot Cemetery
Allen	Henry	92176	Private	04/10,1917	Tyne Cot Memorial
Allwood	Herbert	21477	Private	04/10,1917	Tyne Cot Memorial
Ash	Frank Arthur	204433	Private	04/10,1917	Tyne Cot Memorial
Austin	Thomas Samuel	70999	Private	04/10,1917	Tyne Cot Memorial
Bartle	Jonathon Henry	82114	Private	04/10,1917	Tyne Cot Memorial
Bird	Herbert Arthur	26189	Private	21/08,1917	Tyne Cot Memorial
Birdsall	Frank	92238	Private	04/10,1917	Tyne Cot Memorial
Bowler	Arthur	68053	Private	04/10,1917	Tyne Cot Memorial
Bradley	George Wild	30358	Private	04/10,1917	Tyne Cot Memorial
Bullock	Thomas Edward	92188	Private	04/10,1917	Tyne Cot Memorial
Buxton,MM	Albert Edward	19774	Private	04/10,1917	Tyne Cot Memorial
Careless	John Thomas	19221	Private	04/10,1917	Tyne Cot Memorial
Cope	Harry	31822	Private	04/10,1917	Tyne Cot Memorial
Cory	John Reginald	70230	Private	03/10,1917	Tyne Cot Memorial

Surname	Given name	Number	Rank	Date	Buried/Commemerated
Cowlishaw	Henry	23384	Private	04/10,1917	Tyne Cot Memorial
Crossley	Fred.	92104	Private	04/10,1917	Tyne Cot Memorial
Devine	Robert Mckee	22561	L/Cpl	04/10,1917	Tyne Cot Memorial
Fleming	Teddy	92179	Private	04/10,1917	Tyne Cot Memorial
Fletcher	John	24149	Private	04/10,1917	Tyne Cot Memorial
Glass	George	71007	Private	04/10,1917	Tyne Cot Memorial
Goulding	Bernard	4839	Private	04/10,1917	Tyne Cot Memorial
Grace	Sidney Albert	70957	Private	04/10,1917	Tyne Cot Memorial
Greenhough	Vernon	26858	Private	04/10,1917	Tyne Cot Memorial
Heath	Reginald	11699	Private	26/08,1917	Tyne Cot Memorial
Hickinbotham	Walter Henry	45379	Private	04/10,1917	Tyne Cot Memorial
Hill	Tom Cash	12954	Private	04/10,1917	Tyne Cot Memorial
Hinton	Albert	92210	Private	04/10,1917	Tyne Cot Memorial
Hunt	Thomas A Girlin	25944	Private	04/10,1917	Tyne Cot Memorial
Hutson	Ralph	28104	L/Cpl	26/08,1917	Tyne Cot Memorial
Jackson	Herbert	83798	Private	04/10,1917	Tyne Cot Memorial
Jones	Oliver Saint Michael		Lieut	04/10,1917	Tyne Cot Memorial
Keene	Alexander Henry	51314	Private	04/10,1917	Tyne Cot Memorial
Martin	George	12898	Private	04/10,1917	Tyne Cot Memorial
Mason	John Thomas	70890	Private	04/10,1917	Tyne Cot Memorial
Maxwell	William Ernest	41993	Private	04/10,1917	Tyne Cot Memorial
McCormack	Joseph Francis		Captain	04/10,1917	Tyne Cot Memorial
Mead	George Henry	12297	Private	04/10,1917	Tyne Cot Memorial
Mills	George	50576	Private	04/10,1917	Tyne Cot Memorial
Nash	Frank	24257	Private	19/08,1917	Tyne Cot Memorial
Oddey	Charles	70267	Private	04/10,1917	Tyne Cot Memorial
Odell	William Ward, M.C.		2/Lieut	04/10,1917	Tyne Cot Memorial
Oldenbittle	Stanley	27646	Private	04/10,1917	Tyne Cot Memorial
Painter	Horace	11270	Private	04/10,1917	Tyne Cot Memorial
Poskett	Tom	204462	Private	04/10,1917	Tyne Cot Memorial
Pymm	Claude Alfred	204446	Private	04/10,1917	Tyne Cot Memorial
Reed	Frank	15589	Private	04/10,1917	Tyne Cot Memorial
Riley	Thomas	41978	A/Cpl	04/10,1917	Tyne Cot Memorial
Robertson	George	13565	Private	04/10,1917	Tyne Cot Memorial
Robinson	William	14232	L/Cpl	04/10,1917	Tyne Cot Memorial
Rowell	Richard	92173	Private	04/10,1917	Tyne Cot Memorial
Scragg	Joseph	61482	Private	05/10,1917	Tyne Cot Memorial
Simmonds	Edwin	21129	A/Cpl	04/10,1917	Tyne Cot Memorial
Simpson	Charles Dawkes	30540	Private	04/10,1917	Tyne Cot Memorial
Sprowell	Thomas A.	51438	L/Cpl	04/10,1917	Tyne Cot Memorial
Tebbutt	Albert	13905	L/Sgt	20/08,1917	Tyne Cot Memorial
Thompson	Frank	22146	Private	04/10,1917	Tyne Cot Memorial
Toon	Mark	5053	Private	26/08,1917	Tyne Cot Memorial
Turner	William	92424	Sgt	04/10,1917	Tyne Cot Memorial
Waind	David Randolf	67637	Private	21/08,1917	Tyne Cot Memorial
West	Fred	28135	L/Cpl	04/10,1917	Tyne Cot Memorial
West	George	3145	Private	04/10,1917	Tyne Cot Memorial
White	Harry	71012	L/Cpl	04/10,1917	Tyne Cot Memorial
Williams	Arthur	29778	Private	04/10,1917	Tyne Cot Memorial
Woodward	John	13438	Private	26/08,1917	Tyne Cot Memorial
Young	Edgar	76344	Private	04/10,1917	Tyne Cot Memorial
Ellis	Lewis George	204439	Private	04/11,1918	Valenciennes Comm Cem
Grainger	George William	31385	Private	04/11,1918	Valenciennes Comm Cem

Surname	Given name	Number	Rank	Date	Buried/Commemerated
Kirkham	William Henry	84022	Private	02/11,1918	Valenciennes Comm Cem
Rusholme	Benjamin	97965	Private	04/11, 1918	Valenciennes Comm Cem
Basham	Arthur Claude C	8516	A/CSM	08/09,1916	Varennes Mil Cemetery
Bates	William Edward	70962	Private	25/12,1916	Varennes Mil Cemetery
Tyers	Harold Leslie	3684	Private	20/01,1917	Varennes Mil Cemetery
Orchard	Hugh Thomas		2/Lieut	20/08,1917	Villers-Faucon Comm Cem
Glover	Herbert	70920	Private	06/09,1918	Vis-En-Artois Haucourt
Oldham	William Wilmott	85820	Private	04/09,1918	Vis-En-Artois Haucourt
Metheringham	John Robert	18621	Private	10/10,1918	Vis-en-Artois memorial
Rogers	Thomas William	90792	Private	11/10,1918	Vis-en-Artois memorial
Williamson	John	17022	Private	10/10,1918	Vis-en-Artois memorial
Nurse	John William	21851	Private	25/07,1917	Vlamertinghe New Mi Cem
Lewis	Charles	70887	Private	24/02,1917	Warlincourt Halte Br Cem
Harrop	Harry	20301	Private	23/09,1916	Warloy-Baillon
Kelly	John	21541	Private	17/09,1916	Warloy-Baillon
Kennedy	Ernest Vincent	11749	L/Cpl	08/09,1916	Warloy-Baillon
Price	Albert William	23878	Private	27/09,1916	Warloy-Baillon
Winfield	William	12630	Private	21/09,1916	Warloy-Baillon
Maxey	William Edward	21197	Private	02/10,1916	Wimereux Comm Cem
Wheatley	Alfred	24240	L/Cpl	01/10,1916	Wimereux Comm Cem
Watkinson	Arthur	12866	Private	09/10,1916	Worksop
Binney	Edward Hibbert		Captain	11/10,1917	Wybunbury Churchyard
Dunkley	Albert	70966	L/Cpl	10/06,1917	Wytschaete Mil Cem
Green	Harry	14235	Private	07/06,1917	Wytschaete Mil Cem
Morton	Fred	9966	L/Cpl	04/10/1917	Tyne Cot Memorial
Lakin	W	3981	Private	09/08/1915	Helles Memorial
Bramham,	Joseph Ernest,	120442	Private	28/12/1918	Etaples Mil Cemetery

APPENDIX IV

9th Battalion Sherwood Foresters Gallantry Awards.

Victoria Cross

GREAVES, Fred: Acting Corporal 23715 (later Sergeant): 9th Battalion The Sherwood Foresters: London Gazette - 26.11.1917: For most conspicuous bravery initiative and leadership on 4th October 1917, at Poelcapelle, East of Ypres, Belgium, when his platoon was temporarily held up by machine-gun fire from a concrete stronghold. Seeing that his platoon commander and sergeant were casualties, and realizing that unless this post was taken quickly his men would lose the barrage, Corporal Greaves, followed by another non-commissioned officer, rushed forward, regardless of his personal safety, reached the rear of the building and bombed the occupants, killing or capturing the garrison, and taking four enemy machine-guns. It was solely due to the personal pluck, dash and initiative of this non-commissioned officer that the assaulting line at this point was not held up, and that our troops escaped serious casualties. Later in the afternoon at a most critical period of the battle, when the troops of a flank brigade had given way temporarily under a heavy counter-attack, and when all the officers in his company were casualties, this gallant non-commissioned officer quickly grasped the situation. He collected his men, threw out extra posts on the threatened flank, and opened up rifle and machine-gun fire to enfilade the advance. The effect of Corporal Greaves's conduct on his men throughout the battle cannot be over-estimated, and those under his command responded gallantly to his example: (Brother of H. Greaves, DSO, MC and two Bars)

Distinguished Service Order

Major George Henry Gater –
3rd June 1916
Bar to D.S.O (Temp Lieut-Col) 17 September 1917(C.O.- 6th Lincolnshire Regiment)
Ended the war as a Brigadier.

Temp Major, Acting Lieut-Col Albert Edward Scothern –
1 January 1918.

Military Cross

2nd Lieut. Joseph Adamson –
26 September 1917 (3rd Ypres)

Lieut. Arthur Barber –
16 August 1917. (Whilst attached to York and Lancs Regiment)

Temp Lieut. Edward Duncan Basden –
15 March 1916 (Gallipoli)

Temp Lieut. Donald George Brook –
18 October 1917
(Poelcappelle 4 October 1917)

Lieut. Temp Captain. George Harold Chambers –
2 February 1916 (Services when in Gallipoli. Indian Army attached to 9th.)

Temp. Captain John Critchlow –
26 September 1917 (For raid 24/25th July 1917 Ypres)
Bar – 2 April 1919 – (4 November 1918 Sebourg)

Lieut Temp. Captain Ernest Webster Grimsdale –
17 December 1917 (Poelcappelle 4 October 1917)

Temp Capt. Charles Leslie Harding –
17 September 1917 (3rd Ypres)

Lieut & QM William Wake Horsman –
3 June 1919.

2/Lieut Henry Erris Hudson 2 December 1918
(raid on Posen & Chalkpit Locality 18 June 1918. Killed in this action)

Captain Ralph Munday –
3 June 1918.

Temp Captain & Adjutant William Nason-
17 September 1917
(August shelling of Battalion Headquarters)

2/Lieut William Ward Odell –
17 September 1917
(Patrol July or August)
(Killed 4 October 1917)

Temp. Captain Reuben Henry Gregory –
14 November 1916 (26 September 1916, Somme)
Killed 9 June 1917 – Messines

2/Lt Alfred Stanley Osborne –
2 April 1919
(Capture of Abancourt Station 5/6th October 1918)

Lieut. Frank Southcombe Parker-
21 October 1918
(Raid on Posen & Chalkpit Locality)

2/Lieut. Alec William Rigden –
2 April 1919
(4 November 1918 Sebourg)

10023 CSM Vernus Frederic Bernard Sanders –
1 January 1917
(New Year Honours)

Temp Captain Charles Edward Scott –
17 December 1917
(Poelcappelle 4 October 1917)

2/Lieut. Acting Capt. Harry Charles Vere Warneford –
17 December 1917
(Poelcappelle 4 October 1917)

Distinguished Conduct Medal

6905 CSM Frederick Betesta-
4 March 1918
(Poelcappelle 4 October 1917)

12627 Corporal/ Acting Sergeant William Blurton –
10 January 1917
(Beaumont Hamel 27 November 1916)

71043 Sergeant James Herbert John Burgess –
1 January 1919
(Patrol 21 August 1918)

13016 Sergeant Fred Carlile –
4 March 1918
(Poelcappelle 4 October 1917)

12770 Acting Sergeant Fred Ede –
15.March 1916
(Suvla Bay 28 November 1915)

18966 Lance Corporal John George Finney –
4 March 1918
(Poelcappelle 4 October 1917)

12569 CSM John Grant –
3 June 1919
(Blecourt 9 October 1918)

8349 CSM W.D. Howarth –
22 October 1917

12821 Lance Corporal Seth Hurt M.M. –
14 January 1916
(Suvla Bay 20 August 1915)
Military Medal serving with 16th Bn (Chatsworth Rifles)
(Killed 3 October 1918 with 1/8th Bn at Ramicourt)

19896 Private George Lowe -
4 March 1918
(Poelcappelle 4 October 1917)
Formerly 14282 Leicestershire Regiment.
Killed 15 June 1918

5128 Corporal Henry Nash –
18 February 1919
(Sebourg 4 November 1918)

9031 Acting CSM David Pickford –
3 June 1916
(Gallipoli)
Died of wounds 23 October 1916.

22726 Private Thomas Pole –
4 March 1918
(Poelcappelle 4 October 1917)

9685 Sergeant Robert Teer M.M. & Bar –
15 November 1918

12367 Sergeant Henry Terry –
4 March 1918
(Poelcappelle 4 October 1917)
Died of wounds 5 November 1918.

9645 CSM John Whitworth –
14 January 1916
(Suvla Bay 7 to 10 August 1915)

Military Medal

20090 Private Charles Adlington
28 August 1919

23034 Private James Wilmot Atkin –
19 February 1917
(Sebourg 2 November 1918)

24787 Lance Corporal Francis Bark –
19 February 1917
(Beaumont Hamel 27 November 1917)
Died of wounds 2 May 1918.

31911 Lance Corporal James Brough –
28 January 1918
(Poelcappelle 4 October 1917)

46530 Private John Thomas Brownlee –
28 August 1917

14619 Sergeant J H Buckley –
23 July 1919
(Sebourg 4 November 1918)

19779 Lance Corporal Soloman Burton –
16 August 1917
Died of wounds 24 July 1917

19774 Private Albert Edward Buxton –
2 November 1917
Killed in action 4 October 1917
Formerly 14348 Leicestershire Regiment

13016 Sergeant Fred Carlile D.C.M. –
23 July 1919
(Sebourg 4 November 1918)

16000 Private Harry Childs –
23 January 1918
(also 11th Battalion)

71046 Corporal Albert Clarke –
24 January 1919
(Sebourg 4 November 1918)

20045 Private William Dexter Clowes –
28 January 1918
(Poelcappelle 4 October 1917)

70797 Private Leonard Cooper –
20 August 1919
(Sebourg 4 November 1918)

21775 Private William Cresswell –
23 July 1919
(Sebourg 4 November 1918)

6353 (336353) Sergeant William Cusack –
28 January 1918
(Poelcappelle 4 October 1917)

25510 Private Fred Doody –
2 November 1917
(Poelcappelle 4 October 1917)
Bar to MM
23 July 1919
(Sebourg 4 November 1918)

78221 Private George Arthur Earle –
23 July 1919
(Sebourg 4 November 1918)

22571 Private Harry Gee –
28 January 1918

41297 Lance Corporal Patrick Griffin –
21 October 1918
(Posen Raid 18 June 1918)

14020 Private William Groves –
23 July 1919
(Sebourg 4 November 1918)

22121 Private Frederick Halford –
23 July 1919
(Sebourg 4 November 1918)

24169 Lance Corporal William Hampshire –
28 September 1917

70976 Private Ernest Hartshorne –
28 January 1918
(Formerly 30766 Leicestershire Regiment)

2606 Corporal Henry Hinkley –
28 January 1918
Bar to MM
23 July 1919
(Sebourg 4 November 1918)

15437 Private George Holt –
28 January 1918

11373 Sergeant William Hunt –
28 January 1918

12794 Lance Corporal Arthur Illiffe –
23 July 1919
(Sebourg 4 November 1918)

3766 Private Cecil Jepson –
2 November 1917

13121 Private Joseph Johnson –
9th December 1916
Bar to MM
23 July 1919
(Sebourg 4 November 1918)
French Croix de Guerre for rescuing a wounded soldier

71014 Lance Corporal Ernest Kidger –
28 January 1918
(Formerly 27305 Leicestershire Regiment)

305301 Private Alfred Kirkby –
23 July 1919
(Sebourg 4 November 1918)

22181 Private James Ashley Lee –
21.October.1918.
(Posen Raid 18 June 1918).

22181 Private George Mann –
23 July 1919
(Sebourg 4 November 1918)

12919 Private George Mansell –
9 December 1916
Died at home on 3rd November 1918 as a result of being gassed.

76238 Lance Corporal Angus McColl McNeil –
28 January 1918

20903 Sergeant Ernest Moore –
14 January 1918

9966 Lance Corporal Fred Morton –
28 September 1917
(Killed in action 4th October 1917

70506 Private George Henry Partridge –
23 July 1919
(Sebourg 4 November 1918)

15339 Sergeant Charles Proffitt –
23 July 1919
(Sebourg 4 November 1918)

5101 Private Fred Ramsdale –
28 January 1918

53660 Private Harry Raynor –
28 January 1918

22095 Sergeant George Riley –
9 December 1916

92268 Private Thomas Frederick Rodgers –
23 July 1919
(Sebourg 4 November 1918)

27911 Private Alexander Saunders –
23 July 1919
(Sebourg 4 November 1918)

18170 Private Sidney Herbert Lewin Shaw –
28 January 1918

21236 Private Leonard Wessley Shepherd-
23 July 1919
(Sebourg 4 November 1918)
92423 Colour Sergeant Stephen William Skoyles-
28 January 1918

31253 Lance Corporal Arthur James South-
14 January 1918

13265 Corporal Percy Joseph Statham-
17 June 1919
(Sebourg 4 November 1918)

19207 Lance Corporal J. Herbert Storey-
23 July 1919
(Sebourg 4 November 1918)

268856 Private William Sulley-
21 October 1918
(Posen Raid 18 June 1918)

25298 Sergeant George Sutton-
23 July 1919
(Sebourg 4 November 1918)

27298 Sergeant John William Sutton-
23 July 1919
(Sebourg 4 November 1918)

9685 Sergeant Robert Teer D.C.M.-
14 January 1918 with 17th Bn Welbeck Rangers.
Bar to MM
21 October 1918
(Posen Raid 18 June 1918)

15533 Lance Corporal William Thompson-
23 July 1919
(Sebourg 4 November 1918)

72191 Private Frederick George Thomson-
23 July 1919
(Sebourg 4 November 1918)

24527 Private George Thorley-
28 January 1918

13124 Lance Sergeant William Throssell-
16 August 1917
(Died of wounds 9 October 1917)

21467 Private Bernard Tomlinson-
28 January 1918

16301 Sergeant Herbert Uttley D.C.M.-
28 January 1918
Bar to MM
23 July 1919
(Sebourg 4 November 1918)

4754 Private George Wass-
23 July 1919
(Sebourg 4 November 1918)
42182 Private E. V. Wright-
23 July 1919
(Sebourg 4 November 1918)

73055 Private Ephraim Zolowski-
17 June 1919
(Sebourg 4 November 1918)
(Killed in Action 4 November 1918)

Cliff Housley has compiled the list for all the Sherwood Foresters awards and all of the citations can be found in his book:
British Gallantry Awards 45th & 95th Foot, The Sherwood Foresters, 1854-1970.
Extra information added by J.S. Morse (2007)

APPENDIX V

Selected Bibliography and sources

A Record of the Battles and engagements of the British Armies in France and Flanders, 1914-1918 – Captain E.A. James (reprint 1990)

Blindfold and Alone – Cathryn Corns and John Hughes-Wilson (2002)

British Regiments, 1914-1918 – Brig. E.A. James, O.B.E., T.D. (4th Edition 1993)

Boy Soldiers of the Great War – Richard Van Emden (2005)

Gallipoli – Nigel Steel (1991)

Gallipoli 1915 – Joseph Murray (2004)

Gallipoli 1915 – Tim Travers (2000)

Messines Ridge – Peter Oldham (Battleground Europe 1998)

No Man's Land The Story of 1918 – John Toland (1980)

Passchendaele – The Hollow Victory – Martin Matrix Evans (2005)

Passchendaele 1917 – Stephen Snelling (1998)

Pillars of Fire, The Battle of Messines Ridge June 1917 – Ian Passingham (2004)

The Germans at Thiepval – Jack Sheldon (2006)

The Great World War – Frank A. Mumby (1920)

The Somme – Malcolm Brown (1997)

The Somme Battlefields – Martin and Mary Middlebrook (1991)

The Somme, The day-by-day account – Chris McCarthy (1993)

Thiepval Somme – Michael Stedman (1995)

Tommy – Richard Holmes (2004)

The Unknown Soldier – Neil Hanson (2005)

With A Poppy and a Prayer – Keith Parry

Derby Daily Telegraph

Mansfield and North Notts Advertised

De Ruvignys Roll of Honour

London Gazette

Appendix VI

Acknowledgements

Whilst writing this history I have been overwhelmed by the generosity of many people and organisation. Many children of the men who served have contacted me and helped with information and photographs, as have other relatives.

Hazel Greaves the daughter of Fred Greaves VC shared her recollections of her father and gave me access to many family mementos and photographs. We have also been in constant telephone contact and Hazel has inspired me when I was buried under mountains of paperwork and wondering – 'why'.

My sincere thanks also go to Major Hackett, Mr I G (Eddie) Edwards BEM, the Archivist, Cliff Housley and all the staff at the WFR HQ. They have freely given their time and help and attempted to answer my questions. The War Diaries, Year Books and Colonel Scothern's notes have been the basis for the history.

I would like to thank all of the people who have supplied documents and photographs of men who served in the Battalion during the Great War, as without their help the History would have not have been so 'personal' in nature. I do hope that I have not missed anyone from the following list but if I have please accept my sincere apoligise and contact me so that I can rectify the error: -

John Armstrong, Mrs Maureen Baker, Dr Mike Briggs, Jeff Bugg, Michael Cross, Paul Ellis, Barry Fines, John Gregory, John Hallam, John Harris, Andrew Hesketh, Hilary Hillier and Jack Bagshaw Milward, David Millott, John Newbold, John M Parr, Mrs Esme Stone, Rod Thompson, Karen Walker, Mick Webster, Margery Whitham. My sincere thanks also go to Lyn Pring for helping me with my research.

My thanks also go to the Derby Record Office, Nottingham Record Office, National Archives, Kew, Imperial War Museum and Commonwealth War Graves Commission (www.cwgc.org) for their help and permission to use the documentary material. The CWGC in particular have had numerous queries from me and have always acted in a friendly and efficient manner.

To my wife Barbara and family a special thank you. They have put up with my obsession and supported me throughout. Barbara has visited numerous Military Cemeteries with me and acted as navigator as we drove around the Belgian and French countryside. She has also put up with my burning the midnight oil and asking her to 'read this' and 'what do you think'.

My final thanks go to the thousands of men who have inspired me to write this history and in whos memory I dedicate it

The Officers and Other Ranks of 9th (Service) Battalion The Sherwood Foresters (Nott's and Derby Regiment).

Pictures and maps were supplied by many people.

Frontispiece	Fred Greaves and friends and at Buckingham Palace: courtesy of Hazel Greaves
Page 8	Reg Ecclestone: courtesy of Mr and Mrs W F Thompson
Page 8	Major George Henry Gator: courtesy of S Broomfield
Page 9	The three photographs are taken from M Company, Staff College are courtesy of Stuart Wilson
Page 12	Drummer Parker: courtesy of Margery Whitham
Page 21	A facsimile of a contemporary map of Suvla bay: courtesy of The Imperial War Museum London.
Page 23	"Troops relaxing on the beach" is a photo from The Great World War Volume IV page 151
Page 29	Lieutenant-Colonel Bosanquet: both pictures are courtesy of Peter Garwood
Page 32	Private John Newbold: courtesy of John Newbold, son of John.

Page 38	Bertrand Parker and Friend continue on their road to recovery: courtesy of Margery Whitham
Pages 46 and 47	Reg Ecclestone: photo and Poem courtesy of Mr & Mrs W F Thompson
Page 55	James Walters: photos courtesy of Jeff Bugg
Page 61	Private Edward Fines: courtesy of Pat Fines
Page 69	Private Samuel George Smedley: courtesy of Deborah Reville
Page 106	Private Harry Green: courtesy of Susan Shooter his Great Niece
Page 108	Captain Gregory MC: courtesy of WFR, HQ at Beeston, Notts
Page 143	Lt. Oliver Saint Michael Jones: image courtesy of the WFR, HQ, Beeston, Notts
Page 145	Fred Greaves with his family and at Buckingham Palace: courtesy of Hazel Greaves
Page 175	Fred's Lewis Gun course details: courtesy of Hazel Greaves
Page 181	Map of movements of 11th Division: courtesy of Robert Bridgman

There are many maps in this book, those on pages 26, 33, 50, 67, 80, 81, 85, 86, 101, 109, 112, 118,120, 129, 133,146, 148, 149, 152, 154, 162, 164, 176 and 179 are all from the National Archive in London

May their memory
never die.